D1161551

ONCE
A
PATRICIA

Vanwell Publishing Limited
ST. CATHARINES, ONTARIO

ONCE
A
PATRICIA

*(Memoirs of a Junior Infantry Officer
in World War II)*

Colonel C. Sydney Frost, CD, QC, LLD.

Vanwell Publishing Limited
ST. CATHARINES, ONTARIO

Canadian Cataloguing in Publication Data
Frost, C. S. (Charles Sydney)
  Once a Patricia

Includes bibliographical references and index.
ISBN 0-920277-19-5

1. Frost, C. S. (Charles Sydney), 2. World War, 1939 - 1945 — Personal
narratives, Canadian. 3. World War, 1939 - 1945 — Campaigns — Italy.
4. World War, 1939 - 1945 — Regimental histories — Canada. 5. Canada.
Canadian Army — Officers — Biography. 6. Canada. Canadian Army.
Princess Patricia's Canadian Light Infantry. I. Title.

D811.F76 1988   940.54'81'71   C88-093931-1

IN MEMORY OF MY FATHER
MAJOR CHARLES SYDNEY FROST, MC, LLD, DCL
late The Royal Newfoundland Regiment
and
The Royal Regiment of Canada
and
The Saint John Fusiliers (MG)

TABLE OF CONTENTS

DEDICATION

FOREWORD

AUTHOR'S PREFACE

CHAPTERS

TABLE OF CONTENTS

LIST OF MAPS

Maps 1, 2 and 4 were drawn by Peter Brown. The remaining maps were adapted from Volume Three of the history of Princess Patricia's Canadian Light Infantry by GR Stevens, OBE.

FOREWORD

"Once a Patricia — always a Patricia" is a saying among the members of the Princess Patricia's Canadian Light Infantry, the Regiment of which I have had the great privilege of being Colonel-in-Chief for the past 14 years. I know well the strength of this feeling and the depth of the pride and affection my Patricias feel for their Regiment because I share these feelings myself. If they are felt strongly in peacetime it is not surprising to find, as we do in this remarkable biography, what a very vital part Regimental loyalty and pride play in the agonies of war and the struggle to keep going and give of one's best, far beyond the ordinary limits of endurance.

This book is so remarkable because it is written from the standpoint of a very young and junior officer who can really tell us what it feels like to be totally involved in the day to day business of war, the excitement and fear, the exhaustion and suffering, the frustration and boredom, the horrors of seeing your friends killed around you. But it also tells us of the amazing endurance of the human body and spirit and the will to survive, when the motives are really strong.

I am of the same generation as the author and served in the war in the Women's Royal Naval Service, and my husband, aged 19, fought his way from Normandy to Germany with the Coldstream Guards and was also wounded, so it is easy for us to relive these vivid memories. But, mercifully, for many younger readers it may be the first time they have been able to understand what the war was really like at grass roots level and the complete physical, emotional and intellectual challenges it presented. That these challenges were met so successfully was due not only to rigorous peacetime training and discipline but also to the deep sense of loyalty and support within the

Regiment, without which such success would not have been possible.

If Colonel Frost's straightforward yet moving story of surviving a world war, told in these very different times, can, as I believe, give a better understanding to us today of the values that are really important in life, he will have done us all a great service.

Mountbatten of Burma

AUTHOR'S PREFACE

"As I get older I find my memory gets better. Events that I only faintly remembered in early life I now recall with great clarity; events that never happened I remember best of all."

Not my words, but those of an old comrade, said partly in jest, when I asked him to describe an action mentioned in this book.

In the hope that I will not be accused of similar powers of recollection, let me state at the outset that the events I have described are based on two primary sources — my personal war diary and letters I wrote to my parents, without which the book could not have been written.

In contravention of strict army regulations I kept a diary throughout the war, written down in dozens of notebooks of all sizes and descriptions. Incredibly, all the notebooks survived; some went missing after I was wounded in October, 1943, but were eventually delivered to my home in September, 1946. My notes are necessarily brief and to the point, such as an entry describing a day-long patrol into enemy territory: "I'm sent away to find another route to the river — no such."

If the diary forms the bare bones of the action, the real meat of my story is found in my letters home, in which I had ample opportunity to fill in the details omitted from the diary, subject only to the scrutiny of the censors. This restriction, however, was not too serious, as officers were themselves censors and were supposed to exercise a little discretion in their personal letters. I do not believe I ever compromised this trust, but I skirted the borderline quite frequently.

Three further sources are *The Canadians in Italy* by LCol G W L Nicholson, Volume III of the *Official History of the PPCLI* by G R Stevens, and the

War Diary of the Regiment. One would expect these sources substantially to agree on the basic facts — and they do. What is surprising, however, is that they generally agree with the events as recorded in my notes and letters, if not with my interpretation of those events.

In my reflections and comments on the actions described in this book, I have tried to capture the impressions of a young man rather than merely record the jaded opinion of old age. To this end, I have quoted from my letters at length. They tell the story 'like it was' — unrevised, uncensored and unrepented.

Other works I have consulted are the RMC Reviews. The quotations from speeches by the Earl of Athlone, Gen Crerar and MGen Hertzberg have been included because they gave relevance to my training at RMC. In any event, they influenced my general military education and, together with the words of Winston Churchill, vividly describe the desperate war situation of 1940 and 1941, as I personally experienced it.

To understand this book one has to appreciate how the Hitler terror and the Jap peril affected me and my generation. To us, it was a personal threat to the life and liberty of ourselves and our families and not just a far away challenge to our sovereignty. Only when one appreciates this fact is it possible to understand why young men cast aside all other pursuits, took up arms and eagerly went off to war, determined to strike the enemy a mortal blow, no matter what the cost. That these young men were ultimately successful in their quest has been described as the miracle of the century. Be that as it may, but let us never forget that it was their fortitude and sacrifice that stemmed the evil tide and gave the supernatural powers a chance. How a handful of these kind of men played their part in overthrowing the Nazi tyranny that so nearly enslaved the world is what my story is all about.

While the fighting record of the Princess Patricia's Canadian Light Infantry is the central theme of the book, my reader must not expect to find blood and gore on every page. War is simply not like that. Only a very small part of a soldier's life is spent on the battlefield. By far the majority of his time is involved in training for action, special courses, leave, being conveyed to the war theatre (including long sea voyages for the troops going to Italy), being transferred from one battlefield to another, recuperating from wounds, malaria, jaundice and a hundred other maladies, and just plain waiting while the generals and staff officers make up their minds what to do next.

Thus, my reader will learn about the long years I spent in training at The Royal Military College and at various camps in Canada and in England; my ocean voyages across the Atlantic and the Mediterranean, including one aboard the hospital ship *Lady Nelson;* my long periods in hospitals in Sicily, Italy, Africa and England; the thrill of being quartered in some of the Stately Homes of England; the excitement of London, Rome, Marseilles and Algiers in wartime; the frustrations and inefficiencies of the base depots and reinforcement groups; the importance of the troops who are not actually killing the enemy — the padres, the despatch riders, the postal corps, the truck drivers, the cooks, the surgeons, the nurses and, for a platoon commander the most important person of all, his batman. Indeed, I gave serious thought to dedicating this book to the honourable company of batmen but decided that my father, who "had forgotten more about war than I would ever know", and to whom I owe so much, came first.

To MGen C B Ware DSO, CD, for his invaluable criticisms and suggestions on the Sicilian Campaign; to LCol Donald J Goodspeed, CD, and to LCol M H McMurray, CD, PPCLI, for reading the manuscript and giving me much helpful advice and encouragement; to Col D W Strong, CD, Executive Director of the Royal Military College Club of Canada, for his ready attention to my many enquiries; to Maj P A Ronksley, CD, director of the PPCLI Museum, for the provision of essential documents and photographs; to Aileen Howes (Corkett) for her impressions of Basingstoke Hospital as a Red Cross Volunteer; to Dr H H Campbell and Dr R D Appleford for reading the chapter on Basingstoke Hospital and supplying important photographs; to my wife, Margaret, for deciphering and typing the original drafts and sustaining me when the work began to falter — to all of them my heartfelt thanks.

It only remains to add that if, despite my efforts to ensure accuracy, my memory has strayed into the field of my imaginative comrade, any errors, omissions or embellishments are mine alone.

Throughout the book, two expressions appear which probably require a word of explanation.

The first is 'Field Marshal F F Fate'. My reader will search in vain for any reference to such an officer in the official histories of World War II, the reason being that Field Marshal F F Fate did not, in fact, exist. His full name is Field Marshal Fickle Finger (of) Fate, and he is strictly an invention used to personify the element of luck.

Many a soldier will attest that it was all a matter of luck whether he lived or died, whether he was wounded or came home unscathed, whether he was promoted or fated to serve in obscurity. The examples are endless. Furthermore, Field Marshal Fate's influence was ever present in the overall conduct of the War — Hitler's insane decision to invade Russia, instead of England; Japan's suicidal sneak attack on Pearl Harbour that brought the United States into the War. A person with a religious bent might attribute these acts to Providence or to the invervention of the Almighty. Whatever one calls such a miraculous power, I have no doubt it exists and governs the affairs of men, from the lowest to the highest rank.

The second expression is 'D-Day Dodgers'. The words have nothing to do with baseball. They have everything to do with the soldiers who fought with the Canadian Corps in Italy — we were called the D-Day Dodgers.

After the Invasion of Normandy, in the eyes of many of the strategic planners, Italy became an irrelevant sideshow, tying up men, material and supplies that should have been thrown into the cauldron in France. Division after division were taken away and fresh reinforcements and equipment denied to the 8th Army fighting up the long, rugged Italian peninsula against some of the toughest formations in the German Army.

Then came the insults — snide references about the idle troops in the 8th Army. We were said to be basking in the sun while the armies of Eisenhower were forging prodigious feats of valour on their way to Berlin. We were a scruffy, undisciplined, drunken bunch, filled with venereal disease. We were, indeed, D-Day Dodgers, deliberately avoiding the Second Front in France where the real war was. We sloughed off all these ridiculous charges and responded to the D-Day Dodgers canard by composing a song that describ-ed what a fine holiday we were really having in sunny Italy — always on the vino, always on a spree, free beer, German bands to cheer us on, bathing in the Po River. Many of these verses will be found throughout the book.

Some of the slanderous remarks, particularly the one about the D-Day Dodgers, we attributed to Lady Astor — an American who became a British peeress and the first woman Member of Parliament.

Lady Astor always denied she had made any of these charges. In her biography, John Grigg explains how the name D-Day Dodgers came about:

> *In December 1944, she received a letter from a Private in the Buffs Regiment, serving in Italy, which was signed 'D-Day Dodgers'. She, assuming this was a humorous nickname like 'Desert Rats', began her reply 'Dear D-Day Dodgers', only to find that it was soon being put around she had cast an odious slur on the army in Italy.*[1]

This belittling of the Italian Campaign persists to the present day. Each year many veterans celebrate D-Day in Normandy, but deliberately ignore another D-Day which has a special significance that can never be claimed for the Normandy invasion. That 'other D-Day' was July 10, 1943 when the 1st Canadian Division, as part of the famous 8th Army, and the Americans assaulted the beaches of Sicily. It was significant because it meant the Allies had finally landed in Europe, and it marked the beginning of the end of Hitler's Festung Europa (facts that most people, except the soldiers of the 1st Division, attribute to Normandy).

Why has there always been such a deafening silence in Canada about the 1st Canadian Corps and the Italian Campaign — no memorial observances, no recognition? The irony of the matter is that there is still one group who will never forget the Canadians — their prime antagonists, the German paratroop and panzer divisions.

C Sydney Frost

Toronto
January 1, 1988

Chapter I

THE ROYAL MILITARY COLLEGE

Basic Training

September 1939 to December 1940

Who was the man who said – "Parade stand at ease.
Carry on with the inspection gentlemen please.
See that their buttons are shiny and bright.
For that is the way that we teach them to fight."

When World War II broke out in September 1939, I was just entering Grade 12 in Saint John, New Brunswick. Everyone my age was caught up in the excitement of the war; most of us wanted to enlist right away. Heated debates ensued as to the merits of the Navy, Army and Air Force, with the Navy winning most of the points.

Saint John, after all, was a seaport town. From the windows of our school, perched on a hillside, we could easily see the busy harbour below, crowded with ships from all over the world, except of course the German Navy, but even they were expected any day. My favourite was the *Lady Nelson*, one of the sleek, white Lady Boats of the CN Line, bringing rum and molasses from the Caribbean. Sometimes, at recess, I would nip down to the docks where the *Lady* was berthed and try to fill a bottle or two with rum as it leaked from large wooden casks on the wharf (I can't remember trying to salvage any molasses). Being under the legal drinking age, I naturally refrained from touching the stuff and dutifully brought the rum home to mother to be used for cooking.

If rum was not at that time in my blood, salt water and the lure of the sea were. Both my father and mother came from seafaring people. Grand-

15

mother Frost was a Baker, from Yarmouth, whose father and uncles had been masters of famous clipper sailing-ships that roamed the Seven Seas before the advent of steam. On my mother's side, Grandfather Hains had been captain of the *S S Prince George*, sailing between Yarmouth and Boston.

My uncle, Capt Jud Hains, also had his masters papers and was instructing at a marine school in Halifax. Like my father, he had started out as a banker, but he was a sailor at heart and soon went off to sea. From exotic ports-of-call around the world he would send me stamps, coins and presents — heavily lacquered boxes from Yokohama; sea-shells from Honolulu; brass from Madras; leather wallets from Genoa; cameras from Hamburg; toy soldiers from Edinburgh.

With such a seafaring background it was only natural I would daydream in class about running away to sea, as my forebears had done; but my dreams were 40 years too late. Nobody ran away to sea any more, especially not the son of a well-known banker, who ran his household along the lines of a battalion orderly room in The Royal Newfoundland Regiment.

My only alternative was to take a summer job, so I cruised the docks hoping to ship aboard one of the White Ladies for a couple of months. I soon found the CN Line was not signing up any ordinary seamen for such a short spell, much less a sub-ordinary type such as myself.

My last port-of-call was the office of the Eastern Canada Coastal Steam Ships which operated a small fleet of steamers and motorships plying the eastern coast and the Saint John River. Putting on as rough an appearance as I could muster, I inquired of the Manager if he was taking on any deck hands for the summer, and gave him my name.

"Sydney Frost?", he queried. "Are you the son of our bank manager?"

I could see my chances of a naval career sinking even faster than the *Titanic*.

"Yes," I gulped, "My father thought this would be excellent training before I entered the Navy next year."

My father had no such ideas whatsoever; nor did he know I was prowling around the docks looking for a job.

"Well, young fellow, you're just the man we need. There's an opening for an Assistant Purser on one of our river boats, the *D J Purdy*. With your background you must be pretty good at figures. You can start tomorrow. Would you accept $50 a month?"

"Would I accept? . . . Of course I would. I'd be delighted."

I rolled away from the office like a veteran Petty Officer, highly satisfied with my performance — until I confronted my father with my fait accompli.

"Don't you know that that company is in financial difficulties?" he roared, "I was about to call their loan. Look at the position you have placed me in."

The only 'position' I could see was that he might have to pay my wages if the bank appointed a Receiver. I stuck to my guns, ill-manned though they were, and father finally accepted the fact I had compromised his relations with a hard-pressed customer; I could even detect a hint of amusement in his generally stern demeanour.

I spent a very pleasant summer as Assistant Purser (there was no chief) on the motorship *D J Purdy*, cruising up and down the river from Saint John to Fredericton. The grand old days of romantic boat trips on the river were coming to a close, so I made the most of it, knowing it was to be my one and only attempt at impersonating a sailor.

Despite all the attractions of a life at sea I had realized I wanted to follow in my father's footsteps. Father was a military man who had served with the Royal Newfoundland Regiment in World War I and won the Military Cross. Subsequently he enjoyed a distinguished career as a banker, but he never forgot the principles of discipline and leadership acquired during his army service. The official history of the bank describes him in these words:

> *. . . A tall man, with more than a hint of military bearing, he was disciplined and efficient. To some he seemed perhaps a little cool — one of his associates felt he had never really left the army.*[1]

Our family library contained a pictorial history of the Great War, as it was then called, which ran to many volumes. From early childhood I had been fascinated with the heroic battle scenes shown in the books, and occasionally I persuaded my brother to play war games based on these pictures. He always represented the enemy — the brutal Hun — and he always got thoroughly beaten, sometimes physically if he out manoeuvred me tactically.

Father had brought us up on tales of the great battles of his regiment ('The Fighting Newfoundlanders' as they were known throughout the army) — Gallipoli, Beaumont Hamel, Somme, Ypres. Yet the terrible slaughter of these engagements did not deter me, as I was convinced that getting killed was something that happened to other people, particularly the enemy; a wound or two was quite acceptable — as long as one didn't lose any vital part.

Father was delighted, of course, that I was so enthusiastic about military affairs, but he wanted me to get at least some university education before I enlisted. One evening in the spring of 1940, as we were discussing the war, he dropped a bombshell: "What would you think of applying to the Royal Military College? Along with the discipline, you'll get some education, and perhaps learn to get up at a decent hour in the morning. I'll pay all the fees."

It was an offer I couldn't refuse. At that time only two candidates for RMC were allotted for the whole of New Brunswick and my chances seemed pretty slim. While I had good marks in school, I hadn't the foggiest notion what real soldiering was all about. Nevertheless, I sent in my application and waited.

Finally, on August 22nd, 1940, I received the following telegram from Ottawa:

> *Charles Sydney Frost, Jr selected for Royal Military College. Should report Commandant, Royal Military College, Kingston, two pm, Eastern Standard August thirty-first. Wire Department of National Defence immediately whether he will report.*
>
> *Adjutant General*

Thus began a military career with the infantry which lasted 40 years.

In the fall of 1940 the war was going very badly for the Allies. France had collapsed in the face of the powerful German Panzers and Luftwaffe. The gallant British Expeditionary Force had been extricated from the continent in the miracle of Dunkirk; over 300,000 Allied troops had been saved, but nearly all their equipment had been destroyed. Britain was alone — but Britain would never surrender. Churchill, almost single-handedly, had rallied the nation with his bulldog determination, and defied the Nazis with his masterful prose.

The Luftwaffe pounded London and other British centres with a savagery only Hitler was capable of unleashing. The fate of the free world now rested in the willing hands of the Royal Air Force. With superb courage, skill and endurance they bested the Luftwaffe and won the Battle of Britain, one of the decisive battles of the world. Churchill summed up the great debt owed to these gallant airmen in his memorable House of Commons speech:

> *Never in the field of human conflict was so much owed by so many to so few.*

For anyone who lived through those dark days of 1940, their memory is still a nightmare. We believed that Churchill and the British Commonwealth would somehow survive, but we knew, deep down, that only another miracle could save us. In Canada, it was abundantly clear that the Army would require thousands of reinforcement officers if it were to honour its commitment of raising five or six divisions. At one point it had been recommended that RMC be closed as a Cadet College in 1940 and the facilities used for training senior officers and staff officers.[2]

The government finally decided to keep the College open for two more years. My class of 100 cadets (instead of the usual 50) would enter in August 1940 and receive a condensed two-year course, with a longer academic year and covering practically all the military work which ordinarily would have taken four years. The cadets would be divided into two groups according to their scholastic standing, the higher group to cover work equivalent to two years' engineering at the universities, and the lower group to do work equivalent to senior matriculation and first year university.

Arrangements were made with the leading Canadian universities so that graduates of the higher group would be allowed credit for two years, and graduates of the lower group credit for one year, at these universities after the war.[3] We would graduate in June 1942 when RMC would be closed as a Cadet College and used solely for advanced officer training. The whole plan was, however, specifically stated to be subject to change without notice according to the progress of the war.

August 31st, 1940 will always remain seared in my memory. As the CPR train bearing new RMC recruits pulled into the station at Kingston, I nervously scanned the platform for any sign of a welcome committee from RMC, otherwise known as members of our Senior Class. Several ramrod figures in blue uniforms and pill boxes, carrying thin sticks, patrolled the area, glaring at the passengers as they tumbled off the train. These gentlemen in blue were obviously our Seniors preparing to descend from a great height upon a hundred green recruits. Expecting to be overwhelmed by a hoard of these monsters, I was happy to see only a handful, which our class outnumbered by at least ten to one. My fears subsided and I relaxed — thus committing my first mental lapse at RMC.

"All recruits for RMC fall in, on the markers, in threes, at the double — move, move."

I knew what double meant, but 'fall in on the markers' sounded strange and I allowed myself a small smile.

"That man — wipe that smirk off your face and get moving."

It was the last time I grinned for many a month. My false sense of security in numbers had evaporated. With awesome authority our Seniors lined us up and put us in buses that soon deposited us on the College Square, shaken, intimidated and bowed.

Further words of command in rapid succession came from every quarter. I tried to take refuge in the middle of something called a platoon but was ferreted out by a Senior who had known me in Saint John. He bellowed at me to run around the Square to atone for at least ten offences I had committed since arriving at the College only ten minutes earlier; after which I was to report to him for further punishment. This mercifully turned out to be a relaxed session in the quiet of his room where he gave me a little pep talk to restore my damaged ego, and ended with, "For God's sake don't lose your sense of humour." It was excellent advice that I never forgot.

No one was immune from the wrath of our Seniors who seemed to know everything about us — where we came from, the name of our high school, whether we were good at sports, bad at academics, the whole lot. There was no escape.

I was allotted to A Company under one CSM P A Hertzberg, whose very name gave me the quakes — it was the same as our Commandant, MGen H F H Hertzberg, CMG, DSO, MC (it turned out my company commander was a nephew, not a son, but that was close enough). To add to my worries my room was exactly opposite CSM Hertzberg, again much too close for comfort. Our indoctrination continued far into that first night but most of the horrors have happily faded from memory.

My immediate problem was to understand a whole new military language as well as the idiom of RMC. Some of the military terms were familiar to me through father's brand of military discipline — 'as you were', 'carry on', 'steady', 'form fours' (only now we apparently 'threemed threes'). But RMC language was something else. Words like 'uphole', 'downhole', 'suckhole', 'surly', 'coon roar', 'lids off', 'ear pound', 'dome', 'froust', 'slime' — bewildering but descriptive. Then came the RMC College motto, 'Truth, Duty, Valour', and the unofficial mottoes added over the years, such as 'For God's sake use your dome'.

Next, a host of historical facts about the College, its buildings and its environs — the sacred Arch bearing the names of 156 cadets who had laid down their lives, and the following inscriptions on its walls:

> On the inside: *The immortal words of Rupert Brooke,*
> *Blow out you bugles over the rich Dead!*
> *There's none of these so lonely and so poor of old,*
> *But, dying, has made us rarer gifts than gold.*
> On the lakeside:
> *Je me souviens.*
>
> On the outside — front:
> *To the glorious memory of the Ex-cadets of*
> *The Royal Military College of Canada who*
> *gave their lives for the Empire.*

All these inscriptions were neatly recorded in a large black notebook (known as an S Book), quickly memorized, and instantly recited to any Senior who roared "Shoot the names on the Arch" or "Shoot the inscription on the inside of the Arch." I don't believe anyone ever memorized all 156 names, but you could sometimes satisfy your Senior by giving the first name on the Arch, Maj Agnew, followed by a rush of unintelligible words, and ending with the last name, Lt Wright. If you could throw in half a dozen of the actual names on the Arch, so much the better.

I eventually got pretty good at playing these games and could rhyme off a stream of names that sounded quite authentic. Yet I was no match for the ingenuity of my Senior, who, after having me 'shoot' everything on the Inside, Lakeside and Outside of the Arch, stopped me cold with two further demands:

"What's on top of the Arch? What's under the Arch?"

These facts were not in my black book and I was speechless. For my sins I was instantly dispatched to the Arch, at the double, to use my skills of observation and my powers of imagination to find the answers. Find the answers I did and promptly entered the information in my S Book under the heading 'Don't lose your sense of humour'. Reporting back to my Senior the result of my expedition to the Arch, I was given, so I thought, an easy task as a reward for my good work.

"What's your motto?"

"Truth, Duty, Valour," shot back the instant reply.

"Wrong. I said *your* motto. You haven't been sworn in yet, you're not a cadet and probably never will be. What's your motto?"

"Same as the College," I tried in desperation.

"Don't be nervy. I'll see you in my room at 1900 hours. In the meantime, memorize this:

> *Suckhole when they're looking*
> *Slime when they're not looking*
> *And at all times pass the buck.*

Shoot that to me whenever I ask for your motto."

I was shattered and could only whisper, "Yes Sir."

"Don't call me Sir, I'm not an officer."

"No S . . . "

Another item high on the hit list of our Seniors was the list of the last ten Battalion Sergeants Major of the College. A demand for this vital information came at us in the form of "Shoot the last ten BSMs." This seemed like a reasonable request, and I would have been happy to include the incumbent BSM, if someone would only give me a gun.

Still a further list of names, ranking even higher on the totem pole, was the Old Eighteen, the first cadets to enter the College in 1876. Five of these hardy gentlemen were still living. Facts, and more facts, were hurled at us and hastily put down in our S Book:

Formation of RMC:

> *The Royal Military College had its inception in 1875 when the government under the Honourable Alexander Mackenzie decreed by Act of Parliament that there be established in some one of the garrison towns of Upper Canada 'an institution for the purpose of imparting a complete education in all branches of military tactics, fortification, engineering, and a general scientific knowledge in subjects connected with and necessary to a thorough knowledge of the military profession, and for qualifying officers*

for command and for staff appointments.'

The government selected Point Frederick as the location for this military college. The site chosen was a small peninsula formed by the confluence of the Cataraqui River and Lake Ontario immediately east of Kingston. The College was opened in June 1876.

Point Frederick:
In 1789 the British Admiralty established a naval depot at Point Frederick to serve as a base for warships operating on Lake Ontario. During the War of 1812, as part of the defences along the shores of Lake Ontario in that region, a rough stockade fort was erected at the tip of the peninsula. Some years after the war the stockade was replaced by the present Fort Frederick, which still survives in an excellent state of preservation within the grounds of the Royal Military College.

The Stone Frigate:
Principal among the dockyard buildings was the naval barracks now known as 'The Stone Frigate'. This name is derived from the fact that the floors were left open and hung with hammocks after the fashion of the men-of-war of that period. It was in this building that the new military college was opened in June 1876, with a class of 18 gentlemen cadets under the command of the late LGen (then Col) E O Hewitt, CMG, Royal Engineers. With suitable modifications 'The Stone Frigate' is still in use as a dormitory.

Martello Towers:
There are several of these fortifications in the Kingston area: one at Fort Frederick, two at Fort Henry, and several in Kingston harbour. One of the stone masons who worked on these towers was Alexander Mackenzie.

West Point Hockey Game:
RMC has won all the games except one, and tied one.

Somehow I survived that first day and night at RMC — only another 630 to go. Regular classes would not commence until the following week, but the indoctrination proceeded at a frantic pace.

A classmate, Robert Cannon, who was killed near the end of the War while serving with the RCE, has given a vivid description of these first days:

That first week — revolting to say the least. PT as a refresher in the morning — then a quick dash of Infantry — then PT again so we wouldn't get stale, then perhaps Weapon Training followed by 'Quickly into PT clothes, Nip.' After that perhaps a swim, perhaps more Infantry but always followed by the inevitable PT.

About this time we were given a number to be proud of, but at the time just something more to tax our memories. With our number came long sieges of QM Stores.

Still more seniors arrived to upset our already upside down world.

Looking back, it does seem silly — the sight of rook and senior at a maximum of two inches apart, roaring at each other. To tell the truth the rook wasn't saying much — just 'Yes,' 'No', or 'No excuse,' with the occasional 'Didn't hear' thrown in. This last remark, though nonsensical under the circumstances, gave the rook time to ponder on the rather baffling question that has just been hurled at him.[4]

My letters home gave a somewhat different version of our activities:

September 1, 1940
This is just a note to say that I have arrived and am getting along fine.

Discipline is firm but just. There is a place for everything and everything must *be kept in its place.*

Meals are excellent, with milk, beef, bacon and eggs, and good substantial things, as well as fruits, cakes and cookies.

In general I am having a great time. As a matter of fact I never felt better in my life.

There are 97 other recruits of all sizes and descriptions who are just as green as I.

How I managed to write such a cheerful letter in the heat of battle, I don't know. It almost sounds as if my Senior dictated it, but I think not; he may, however, have censored it.

A few days later I wrote another mild note to my father:

Life at RMC is more removed from civilian life than I had expected but that's what is the fun.

To date our time has been taken up with drill and getting outfitted with uniforms, kit, rifles, etc. Everything is supplied by the College except cleaning material. I would appreciate your sending me the following:

one pair of old leather gloves, or just one glove (to be used for rubbing in polish on boots)

one sewing kit, needle, thread, etc

rags for dusting (wish I had brought along a duster)

old toothbrush for cleaning rifle, etc

rags for polishing (rags are at a premium around here)

> *I guess that's about all. I have already bought broom, whisk,*
> *silvo, brasso, blanco, etc at our canteen.*

My obsession with securing large quantities of cleaning material may sound exaggerated but cleanliness was not only next to Godliness — it was the sine qua non of a good soldier. Without shiny buttons, a clean uniform and tidy room you simply couldn't go off to war. My classmate, Cannon, was also impressed with the need to keep a room tidy and clean:

> *And pointers about keeping a room tidy — we're experts now*
> *without exception. Drawer inspections, rifle inspections,*
> *accoutrement inspections, kit inspections, extra room*
> *inspections, bayonet beds — we've survived them all. As for*
> *dusting — we've long since mastered that science — even to daily*
> *dusting the moulding at the ceiling.*

By mid-September I had acquired enough knowledge about military affairs to talk to my father man to man:

> *I can appreciate your fondness for the army. No man is a man*
> *until he has gone through a period of military training and*
> *learned the meaning of true discipline.*
>
> *The timetable for recruits is always on the double and it is*
> *doing us good. I think I can understand many of your words*
> *of command now and perhaps carry out my duties as your*
> *batman.*
>
> *I am looking forward to the day when we can get together,*
> *and under your generalship, win the war in short order.*
>
> *I like it all, and although it is difficult at first, one soon gets*
> *into the swing of things.*

Pressing uniforms, both for ourselves and for our Seniors, presented a special problem. I believe the flat iron had been invented but no recruit was allowed to have one, probably because it might be used as a defensive weapon against our tormentors. We soon found the answer to this new predicament — sleep on your trousers. If properly placed on the mattress, they would have a knife edge crease the next morning. This worked fine except when your Senior's trousers were laid beside your own, and you thrashed and turned during the night. The result could be most horrid — both for the trousers and you.

One winter morning, after a particularly rough night, I reported to my Senior with his trousers neatly folded over one arm of my naked, shivering, wet body. He felt my arm to check that I had taken a cold shower and then examined the trousers.

"What's that on your arm?"

"Your trousers."

"You . . ., you've railroaded them. Give yourself five Defaulter Drills and bring me my other pair."

What had happened was that his pants had slipped in my bed during the night and instead of one crease they now had two — like a railroad.

Another indignity sometimes committed to Seniors' trousers was obliterating the crease completely. This took special talent and was only for a journeyman presser. One recruit did such a fine job that his Senior's screams were heard throughout the dormitory: "You oaf, you've ruined my trousers again. Why can't you learn to sleep on them properly?" The recruit came right back with an answer that endeared him to all recruits for many months, but received the wrath of the whole Senior class "Please," he loudly declared, "I'm a light sleeper."

When we got bored with the senior class indoctrinating us with their version of military discipline, our drill instructors were standing by to break the monotony. The College Regimental Sergeant Major was CSMI (Company Sergeant Major Instructor) G E Miller of the PPCLI. A trim, youngish man, he impressed me immediately with his military bearing, presence on parade, knowledge of weapons, ability to teach and his quiet but firm authority.

Our officer in charge of drill was quite another type — Temporary Lt J Wyatt, MBE, DCM of the RCR. He had just been promoted from RSM and was said to have been the Senior RSM in the Canadian Army. If there was ever a typical RSM it was Jake Wyatt. Big, blustering and bullying, he blasted the recruits with a voice that could be heard clean across the bay to Kingston. His repertoire of admonitions and rebukes for sloppy drill were varied and endless. He was never at a loss for words, despite the challenges offered by our slackness.

Some of his exhortations are still being copied by budding RSMs: "And when you hit that rifle make the sparks fly" and "When I say 'tention' I want to see a flash of lightning and a cloud of dust, and when it all clears away, a row of livin' statues."

His favourite pastime was to single out some unfortunate recruit and bellow, "What's your name?"

"Armour, Sir."

"Well that's a good name for you m'boy. You look like an armoured tank when you try to march. Swing them arms."

Then another recruit would draw Jake Wyatt's fire.

"What's your name?"

"Cannon, Sir."

"Cannon? Well I'm not surprised. You move like a cannon. Get the lead out of your backside."

One morning my movements, or lack thereof, caught his attention.

"What's your name?"

"Frost, Sir."

"Ah, yes, and you're rightly named. You're frozen to the Square. Get moving. Leftright, leftright, leftright, left."

I took off across the parade ground, arms and legs chopping the air, and didn't touch ground until I reached the other side. From that moment my performance had earned me a nickname that stuck for life — 'Chop Chop'. When I became a CSM the following year in charge of C company, I was known as CSM Chop Chop, head of the Coolie Company, from Chinatown.

Jake Wyatt was not just a blustering RSM; he was a master showman with a heart of gold. His talents on the parade square were soon recognized by higher authorities and he was taken from us to instruct at the Brockville Officer Training Centre, where he rose rapidly in rank and finished the war as a lieutenant colonel — probably the only officer in the British Commonwealth to obtain such a rank mainly on the strength of his magnificent parade ground voice and manner. He had no use for staff officers and military studies. The study of tactics he dismissed as being some kind of childish game — 'tic tacs', he called them.

After he got us straightened out on the parade ground he relaxed a bit and became more kindly disposed to our efforts to please him. Toward the end of the year we had a dinner and invited Jake as our special guest. His stamina at the bar equalled his prowess on the parade ground; he regaled us all evening with perfect recitations of 'Dangerous Dan McGrew' and other ditties. His rough exterior was only camouflage and gave us hope that our Seniors would soon follow his example.

Such a hope wasn't only wishful thinking — it was downright dangerous. The impossible demands and orders of our Seniors continued unabated, and probably for good reason as most of us were still committing terrible sins. On September 23rd my name was posted in orders after an inspection of my room revealed the following deficiencies: untidy cupboard, bottles to be removed, sweaters and underwear to be placed in bottom drawer, watch hanging on belt hook, dirty towel on rack, dust on dispatch box, etc, etc, etc. Despite such a shocking inspection report, for which I was quite rightly punished, I was still able to write happy letters home:

October 1st

We have a compulsory exercise period between 4 and 6 o'clock every afternoon, and after supper we can go to either of the two gyms and play basketball, etc. But the time is limited as we are still recruits.

I hope everyone is feeling as good as I am; if not, the formula is — bed 10:30 pm; rise 5:30 am; lots of exercise; lots of food; play sports.

This ability I had acquired to write 'uphole' letters home, regardless of the circumstances, proved most helpful later on when I encountered real trouble in action.

At a subsequent inspection my room was much improved, but some of my friends drew heavy punishments for rather interesting breaches of regulations. One recruit had the following posted in orders after his name: '*Why are all the rifles in this room?*' Another cadet had the following after his name: '*Cartridges under the bed — why?*' Both recruits got well and truly soaked for such conduct, but surprisingly neither our Seniors nor the staff ever found out 'the reason why', despite the wildest rumours. Luckily for all concerned, whatever the two cadets had in mind, their alleged plans were scotched before they were able to bring rifles and cartridges together.

Apart from these aberrations, we were actually making considerable progress in becoming cadets, officers and gentlemen. Jake Wyatt, however, was still not impressed. "Gentlemen, perhaps, but cadets only by Act of Parliament."

We were now issued with battle dress uniform, neatly tailored, brown boots for dress, black ammunition boots for drill, puttees, belt, gloves, swagger stick and pill box; also, recreation clothes consisting of a red jacket, white flannel pants, white shirt and RMC tie. Later on we received khaki service dress, again neatly tailored, great coat, trench coat, fur hat and seal-skin mitts with a trigger finger for firing in the winter. Our Lee-Enfield rifles, which we had carefully cleaned and cared for, were soon withdrawn for use by the Army, so desperately short of weapons, and replaced by American Winchester rifles from World War I. Whether they were any good for firing I never found out as we completed our range work with Ross rifles.

October 15th marked another plateau in our gradual ascent from nothing to nothing plus one — the obstacle race. Despite dire warnings from our Seniors, and prayers from our parents, the course was not as tough physically as we had feared, and certainly nothing like the obstacle courses we encountered later on in the Army. But if it was not tough, it was dirty. My Senior friend from Saint John had tipped me off that the race would be a battle against mud and slime, and he was right. Nonetheless, I took the course in stride and was even able to dash off another cheerful note to my parents:

> *Our obstacle race was held today. You remember what my Senior from Saint John said about the oil, mud, etc. Well it was quite an experience. All the recruits were lined up and started off by a pistol shot. The obstacles were no cinch for anyone; it took me about twenty minutes of hard grinding to complete the course — over walls, under logs, into waterholes, through bogs. Of the ninety-odd competitors, I finished in the top twenty which wasn't*

too bad, especially as we had a track meet in the morning.
After the obstacle race (what fun) we cleaned up for a dance
that evening. We wore our new recreation clothes and went into
town to get our girls. I have never spent a better twenty-four hours
and you can imagine that I flopped into bed late that night
thinking what a swell place RMC is, and what a lucky fellow
I am to have a place in its body of gentlemen cadets.

Track meet, obstacle race and dance, all in one day? It was true; we were becoming hardened, if not seasoned, cadets. But activities such as a track meet and an obstacle race were only a fraction of the demands made upon us by our Seniors and the Staff. A full programme of inter-company sports was also in full swing — football, soccer, harriers, basketball, hockey, boxing, skiing, tennis, squash. Furthermore, all cadets were required to participate in aquatic sports in the cold waters of Navy Bay — swimming, diving, sailing, canoeing (including an inter-company war canoe race). For anyone who claimed he couldn't play team sports, the Seniors thoughtfully devised a special physical education programme.

Besides this heavy schedule of inter-company sports, the College also played football, soccer, hockey and basketball against teams from Queen's University, University of Toronto, Western University, the Army, Trinity College School and Kingston High Schools. Our inter-collegiate teams were, however, greatly hampered by the small numbers of cadets then attending RMC. At no time were there more than 150 cadets at the College, and in our final year only 80 — quite insufficient to field a balanced team against universities with a male student body many times our numbers.

Nevertheless, we battled all comers and what we lacked in finesse we made up by our superior physical condition. Our Commandant, MGen Hertzberg, in his graduation address, referred to our gruelling game against Queen's:

I do propose, however, to refer to one great tradition of this
College and one you have indeed most loyally upheld. I mean
the way the 'Red Team' fights in the last period.
You remember the game with Queen's last autumn; when the
score was 40 something against you. Well, we know what
happened in the second half! You did not win but you did tackle
and you fought from the kick-off until the last whistle blew.
They did not make many points in that last half and you got
a touchdown — and that, you may again have gathered, was
a matter of intense satisfaction to the Commandant. I am
prepared to admit now that, after that game, your Commissions
were 'in the bag'. You need never have opened another book
— too bad you didn't know![5]

28

There was no lack of recruits trying out for the College football team. If you were successful two very important, almost lifegiving, 'perks' came your way: you were excused fagging for the Seniors for 60 days, and you ate at a special training table, which meant steaks every day and second helpings. This last 'perk' was eventually cancelled, presumably because the recruits on the team had consumed the Army's reserve of beef for the fighting troops overseas.

Boxing was a very big part of our athletic programme, particularly recruit boxing, where every recruit was required to put on a pair of gloves and get in the ring for three rounds. No one was excused except two or three who, according to the Seniors, were malingering in hospital. I was one of them. Despite the fact I had an infected foot and could not walk, I knew very well I would forever be considered a 'slimer' if I missed recruit boxing, no matter what the reason. Consequently, I had no choice but to enter the open championships a few weeks later when my foot had healed.

My opponent was a Senior who had a few years' boxing experience under his belt and some championships to his credit. The result of the match was a foregone conclusion even before the bell rang. A letter to my father tells the sad tale:

> *I am now fully recovered from my bad foot. Actually I had a combination of 'foot' and 'flu disease' which kept me in the hospital a couple of days.*
>
> *Having missed the recruit boxing, I was determined to get in it somehow, so I entered the 'Open'. This was only for the best boxers of the College — Well, I boxed against last year's Champ, and of course lost, but I stayed in the full three rounds and got in a few good ones at him. I consider myself lucky that I wasn't knocked out, as most of the fellows thought I would be, boxing against such opposition. Of course I netted a few slight bruises here and there, which have even now almost disappeared. I have some pictures I'll send you next week — no doubt, Dad, you've heard a great deal about this boxing, so I won't need to say much, except that our class put on the best fights seen here in years, lots of knock-outs, etc, but nothing serious. Just good fun!*

Physical fitness wasn't the only thing at RMC, but it was second to none. The superb athletic programme at the College undoubtedly stood us in good stead, not only during our wartime service, but, for many of us, for a lifetime. I am absolutely convinced that without this athletic training I would not have survived the war.

MGen Hertzberg was a firm believer in physical fitness. In a speech to the Kiwanis Club of Montreal on October 15th, 1941, he explained why organized sports were so important:

> *I have talked at some length about moral and physical training because we place great importance on it at RMC. One means to the end in moral training is the responsibility placed on Cadets in controlling and leading their fellows to which I have referred, and another means is teaching him to play games — organized sport.*
>
> *All sports are carefully supervised and every Cadet, generally speaking, plays all games, not only the first or second teams, but everyone plays either for the College or for his Company or Platoon. Everyone plays football or hockey, everyone runs, everyone swims, and above all, everyone boxes in his recruit year, where he learns self-control, to keep his temper, to take punishment and to fight fair. He is learning all the time the value of 'character building' — in those two words you have the slogan of the RMC.* [6]

Two Sergeant Majors were largely responsible for inculcating us with a respect, if not a fondness, for physical fitness — RSM T O'Riordan and RSM J E Coggins. Both sergeant majors had spent most of their Army career instructing physical training. They were excellent gymnasts and staggered us with their feats on the high bar, parallel bars, boxes and mats. Timmy O'Riordan, like most RSMs, loved to put on spectacular displays on the Square — intricate gymnastic tableaux, unarmed combat, Indian club swinging, sword swinging — everything timed to a split second. Timmy soon got his commission and took over from Wyatt when he left RMC for Brockville near the end of our first year. Timmy was eventually made a captain in which rank he travelled across the country teaching thousands of soldiers how to perform giant swings, back flips and long arm drops. Coggie received his commission on the day we graduated, and continued to instruct PT and drill at Army Training Centres. After the war he returned to the College, reverted to his former rank and for many years was the College RSM. On his retirement he was made an Honorary Member of the Ex-Cadet Club, much loved and respected by all.

With physical fitness taking such a large part of our programme, one might well ask how there was time for military and academic training. The answer was 18 hour days and a College year of 11 months, with a further month at an Army camp. The military training alone covered some 15 subjects, each with numerous sub-divisions. For example: leadership and discipline; map reading, photo reading and field sketching; organization and administration; military law; tactics; artillery; military engineering; signal training; surveying; military history; international affairs; infantry training; weapon training. The weapon training included rifle, bayonet, Lewis gun, Bren gun,

Thompson submachine gun, Vickers medium machine gun, pistol and grenade. Academic subjects were similar to those required for the first two years of an engineering degree at most universities.

In my letters home I kept my father posted on my military training, which he now read with some respect as he had just joined the Reserves in Saint John, New Brunswick, and found he was a little rusty.

> *A few words about the military subjects. I have pamphlets on every conceivable phase of army training. Our Military Organization subjects require about 30 books, most of which are in pamphlet form. A favourite subject is Tactics for which we have many sand tables and models.*
>
> *We have studied in detail the Infantry Battalion, Machine Gun Battalion, Field Artillery Regiment and the various types of Divisions. It is all most interesting as we have every battalion laid out on a sand table, man for man and vehicle for vehicle. This gives one a very good idea how a battalion is operated and organized. As you know, an infantry battalion has 773 men, over 100 vehicles and 10 carriers; so it requires a great many models to show a battalion on a sand table.*
>
> *In our tactics we are appreciating various situations. The problems are complicated and quite difficult but with practice I am learning how to handle many tactical situations. I will leave grand strategy to the politicians.*
>
> *I am receiving the best military instruction in the world.*
>
> *In academics I'm taking the B Course (the senior group) which means that when (if?) I graduate in 1942, I will have two years' engineering to my credit, or possibly three years on a BA.*
>
> *Many of our subjects are new. I find I am behind in some, ahead in others. Every subject is most practical, especially our French. When I come back this Christmas (happy day!) I will be an Anglo-French Gentleman Cadet.*

RMC was well ahead of its time in bilingualism, and remains so today. The Christmas break was now in sight, but so were exams and the Seniors, who also never lost sight of us. Knowing that they had only a few more weeks to 'bend' us before we became classmen, they kept up the pressure, forcing some of us into foolish misdemeanours we would not ordinarily have committed. On November 22nd my name appeared in Orders:

> *No 2761 G C Frost, CS — Improperly dressed for 0830 hours Infantry Drill Parade, in that he was present on parade without gloves. Awarded five days' R L and forfeits 10 marks.*

A bitterly cold day, with snow on the ground, and I forgot to wear gloves!

31

"Take his name," bellowed Jake Wyatt "his brain, if he has one, is as numb as his hands." It was a well deserved rebuke but I believe it was my last 'soak' at the College. At least I ended my long list of sins with a dandy.

Finally, the last exam was written — our recruit term was finished. We looked at each other with weary but supremely satisfied grins — we had made it. The incredible rigours, ordeals and challenges of the past four months had changed our lives forever, making us aware, for the first time, of the outer limits of our endurance; and binding us together as a tight-knit class that had overcome every hardship.

Our Commandant explained the reason behind all this training in a speech given on October 15th, 1941, to the Kiwanis Club of Montreal, referred to earlier:

> *Cadets of the Senior Class are placed in command of the Battalion, Companies, Platoons, Sections, etc, each Senior being held responsible for the efficiency of his sub-unit, through the proper channels, to the Commandant. It is this responsibility that teaches the Cadet to handle men, the necessity for strict discipline in so doing, entailing immediate obedience to an order from his superiors. All of which he must know before he can be fit to command men in action.*
> *'He who will not accept orders has no right to give them;*
> *He who will not serve has no right to command;*
> *He who cannot keep silent has no right to speak.'*

All that remained was to catch a train home. Father had put me in funds for a berth on the CPR which cut through the States and was much faster than the CN running through Canada. However, like some of the Cadets, I had blown my budget on the Christmas dance and had only enough left for a coach fare on the CN. I explained this change in plan to my father by saying I wanted to avoid the trouble of having to change into civies at Montreal, as I was not allowed to trespass the territory of a neutral United States in uniform. (This, of course, was true enough, but it didn't tell the whole story.)

Leaving Kingston at 1300 hours Friday, December 20th, I changed trains at Montreal for the Ocean Limited (notorious for its delays), changed again at Moncton, and finally arrived in Saint John late Saturday evening.

Chapter II

THE ROYAL MILITARY COLLEGE
Advanced Infantry Training
January 1941 to June 1942

We are the Gentlemen Cadets of RMC
We have sworn to love and serve His Majesty,
And we'll defend this land of liberty,
And strive to keep our Empire's unity.

Classes resumed early in the New Year, but with a great change in our status — at last we were classmen. I wrote my mother:

Back to another life again, but full of activities of every sort. No more recruiting as we are now classmen and have a few privileges.

I enjoyed every minute of my glorious holiday at home even if I did sleep a great deal. Strangely enough it is no effort to get up at 6:30 am. I still take a shower although I don't have to, and it's a cold one at that. I really like a cold shower in the morning, especially now that it isn't compulsory.

Obviously, I had been brain-washed, or I was overtrained, or Jake Wyatt was right when he said my brain was so numb my body couldn't feel the cold. In a letter home the following week I continued in the same vein:

I have never before so thoroughly enjoyed my work at RMC than during the past week. Not only the work but life in general seems so much more enjoyable now that we are classmen.

> *Quite a thrill to be allowed to walk the Square. However we are still kept smart and snappy and we don't slouch around the place like those dull university freshmen.*
>
> *Saturday evening, for the first time, I went into Kingston with a couple of cadets and really had a big time — saw a show and went to a restaurant. From now on we are allowed passes from 7:00 to 11:00 pm on Wednesday, Saturday and Sundays and occasionally a special pass from 2:00 to 11:00 pm. on these days.*

On March 15th, 1941 MGen HDG Crerar, DSO, Chief of the General Staff*, visited the College and gave a memorable address at a Mess Dinner that evening. In vivid language he told the story of the arrival of the 1st Canadian Division in England in December 1939 and went on to describe a visit to France in May 1940:

> *During my period at our Headquarters in London I was lucky enough to visit the British and French fronts on three occasions — the last of these ending on the 4th day of May just before the great German offensive broke loose. The main impression that each visit gave to me was that the last war had never really ended and that we were just carrying on, after a gap in time, with the same old struggle. Here we were with the same ruthless enemy, the same French countryside we had previously known, with the same little villages, or towns, populated only by old men or by women and children. It really seemed to both of us that we had only been away from the 'front' on a somewhat extended leave of absence and had simply returned to the job once more. Well, what we failed to finish in 1918 it is to be hoped that you of the younger generation will successfully accomplish.[1]*

We of the younger generation did indeed help to fulfill his hope, but at what cost.

Later in his speech Gen Crerar referred to the drastic, but inevitable decision to close the College, which was such a sad blow for us and for every Ex-Cadet:

> *I know that this seems a drastic step to take and is hard to accept by those whose lives have been associated with the College. All I can say is that no one, with the exception of MGen Constantine, can claim his life has been more associated with the College than my own and in spite of that I accept this temporary 'changeover'*

---

*The late Gen H D G Crerar, CH, CB, DSO, General Officer Commanding First Canadian Army.

in function as in the interests of the State, and indeed, of the College itself. When a nation and an Empire are fighting for their lives, sentiment and traditional conceptions cannot be the deciding factors.

I refuse to admit that the Royal Military College Battalion of Gentlemen Cadets, which will be reborn after this war is over, will not typify in the future all of the best of the College traditions we have known in the past. So long as any Ex-Cadets remain to form the Officers of that Cadet Battalion, that renaissance is assured. And, should there be no Ex-Cadets alive, it will only be because Canada is no longer Canada.

Spring arrived at the College, turning other young men's fancies to various pursuits, but ours to preparing for a host of ceremonial parades. Point Frederick is a delightful setting for the College and in spring the grounds are especially beautiful, yet few cadets have ever had time to enjoy these pleasant surroundings until they returned as Ex-Cadets. Our first ceremonial parade was on April 19th when Ex-Cadets from far and wide gathered in annual reunion. I described this reunion in my weekly letter home:

Another thing which gave me a feeling of pride was the Parade of the Ex-Cadets to the Memorial Arch, where they took part in their annual Memorial Service. In this parade were officers from Major-Generals to Lieutenants, side by side, everyone an Ex-Cadet, and each with the same smartness and style. Of course, owing to the war, a great many were unable to attend this Ex-Cadet gathering, 14 having already given their lives for the Empire in World War II, and many others being stationed overseas in England, India, Egypt, etc.

Our next parade, on May 2nd, was for the Honourable Albert Matthews, Lieutenant-Governor of Ontario. I reported to my father:

On the conclusion of the Ceremonial, the Lieutenant-Governor called for the BSM and four CSMs and complimented them and the Battalion for its fine performance. Then he addressed the Battalion:
> *'I can't tell you how much I have appreciated this sterling performance of the Cadets.*
> *I have inspected the First Division of the US Army recently, and most of the Ontario units, but none can compare with RMC.'*

We knew we were better than any other unit in Ontario. But the whole US 1st Division? No one had ever heard of them; they weren't even at war.

I didn't fully appreciate the compliment of the Lieutenant-Governor until some two years later when I met the US 1st Division in Sicily. It had previously fought in North Africa and was known as 'Big Red One', one of the best divisions of the US Army.

Our final ceremonial parade was the biggest — the graduation of our senior class, when His Excellency MGen The Earl of Athlone, KG, Governor General of Canada, accompanied by Her Royal Highness, The Princess Alice, GBE, made his first visit to the College as Governor General. On the evening of May 22nd, His Excellency dined in the College Mess and gave a short address. In the course of his remarks to the cadets he referred to the fact that he himself had graduated from RMC Sandhurst and gave his unbiased opinion on RMC Kingston:

> *I am indeed happy to have been given this opportunity of paying you a visit because, in the first place, I was myself a Cadet at the RMC Sandhurst, in England, and, secondly, because I have a vivid recollection of the last time I was at the RMC Kingston, when I accompanied King George V, at that time Duke of Cornwall and York, on an inspection of the College 40 years ago.*
>
> *In 1901 the Cadets here numbered only 87, but quality, not quantity was then evidently the aim, for I remember that I was greatly impressed by the smartness of the Cadets and the precision of their drill. In spite, however, of the increase in numbers since then, the Cadets do not appear to have lost anything of their smartness, for on the occasions of my visits, since my arrival in Canada, to various units of the three Services, whenever there has been a notable smartness in the drill, in most cases the Officer responsible has been trained at the RMC.[2]*

And then, some helpful advice on how to maintain discipline among the men we would soon be leading into action, and how to handle the old soldier.

> *And now one word, before I conclude, about discipline in the Army, which may be a guide to you young fellows who are about to join the Forces.*
>
> *The first duty of a young Officer is to gain the confidence, the respect and affection of his men. Once this has been accomplished, the handling of the men becomes quite an easy matter, and they will follow him anywhere. In order to attain this object there are two cardinal principles to be observed. First of all, you must know your work from A to Z, so that you need never ask a man to do something you cannot do yourself. Secondly, in all your dealings with the men be strict but scrupulously fair. No man objects to being punished as long as he knows that he has deserved it. It is, therefore, important, when*

a man is brought up before you, to sift the evidence carefully, and not to accept blindly any statements by a witness, for these are often found to be biased against the accused.

Then I must warn you against the man who tries to play 'the old soldier' on a young Officer, which is no rare occurrence. My advice to you is this; just think quickly and turn the joke against the man. You will find the other men will appreciate your adroitness and you will be saved from any further inconvenience on this score.

On May 23rd, His Excellency took the Royal Salute and inspected the Battalion of Gentlemen Cadets. As our Seniors slow marched off the Square for the last time, the new BSM from our class, NB Corbett, gave the command, "To the Colours and Graduating Class, Present Arms." We were on our own — we were Seniors.

In the afternoon His Excellency and Her Royal Highness attended track and field sports and Her Royal Highness presented the prizes. Jake Wyatt's urgings to me to "get moving" had made their impression and I received medals for placing second in the 220 and 440 yard dashes.

That evening we attended the May Ball, not quite up to the elegance of the pre-war June Balls, but still a highly sought-after affair for Kingston belles and young ladies from Havergal College, Branksome Hall and Bishop Strachan School. The Ball ended at 0400 hours, the girls were escorted back to their homes or heavily chaperoned hotel rooms, and we returned to the College at 0500 hours to clean up the mess and stow away the decorations for next year.

Promptly at 1100 hours on May 24th, the Orderly Officer appeared and found the cadets present and the premises correct. He made no finding as to the correctness or otherwise of the cadets.

That day had also marked a milestone in my budding military career. Along with three other members of my class I was made a Corporal and acting CSM in charge of C Company — soon to be known as the 'Coolie Company'. Norm Corbett was made a sergeant and acting BSM. There was no time to relax, except for sleep, and precious little of that. My responsibilities as a CSM soon increased, final exams loomed on the horizon, and preparations for summer camp had to be made.

We were Seniors all right — but senior to whom? No recruits would appear in August to receive the benefit of all the discipline and training we had learned from our seniors. It was very depressing. A more serious matter was how to control our class without having the safety valve of sloppy recruits on whom to vent our steam. Corbett and his four acting CSMs spent many an evening mulling over the right approach to take. To his credit, he adopted and maintained the iron fist in the velvet glove approach, liberally laced with humour, and was very successful in maintaining discipline throughout our

37

last year.

Exams came and went, the usual way of all exams — bringing relief to some and disappointment to others. Then we were hit with a body blow. We would have to move from our modern quarters in Fort Frederick Dormitory to the old Stone Frigate, which had been used as a dormitory before the war, but could trace its origins back to 1823. What annoyed us most of all was that our dormitory was to be taken over by officers taking various courses at the College. These officers even infiltrated our Mess Hall and talked and smoked while announcements that undoubtedly might affect the course of the war were being made by our BSM.

Even the Commandant sympathized with our feelings. In his address to the Annual Dinner of the RMC Club in Ottawa on June 25th, 1943 he put it this way:

> *As there was no dinner last year following the Graduation of the last War Class of 1942, I thought I might say something about that Class.*
>
> *I am quite certain that no Class in the history of the RMC faced the difficulties in maintaining College traditions and customs that they did and let me assure you, Gentlemen, they were successful. You know the conditions — the war; they had only two years at the College; they had no recruits; there were many annoying things that seemed unjust and that almost broke their enthusiastic young hearts. Such things as officers on courses who, because they had never learned to run the Square, now lounged across it with cigarettes drooping from their lips, officers who were slack in returning their salutes. The Class, by example, taught those officers a lot and the officers realized it and appreciated it.*[3]

If we had to face total war with the senior officers, the sooner we could get started the better. The move across the Square to the Stone Frigate was made without incident, except one major, who was strolling across the Square smoking a cigarette, got a bedpost in the eye — *"Excuse me, Sir."*

Now followed a week of intense practical training in the field before setting off on a two-week tour of the main Canadian Army training establishments in Ontario, under the guidance of LCol A H C 'Archie' Campbell, our Chief Instructor and Second-in-Command of the College. LCol Campbell was a big man, with a commanding military bearing and presence, on and off parade — a sort of sophisticated version of Jake Wyatt, but unlike Wyatt, he loved 'tic-tacs' and conducted his classes with panache and wit. Sometimes his background scenarios for our tactical schemes had little to do with the problem in hand, yet he kept us awake and eager for his next class — more than could be said for some of our academic professors.

The truth was that the academic side of our training was becoming a heavy burden as it seemed so irrelevant in time of war and we were all so keen to 'cross the pond' and deal the Hun a mighty blow.

Archie Campbell and his relaxed, practical approach to our military training had a lot to do with keeping us 'down on the farm' and not straying away to greener pastures in the regular army. During our week's preparation for the grand tour of army camps in Ontario, he conducted company and platoon schemes in the attack, withdrawal, defence and advance to contact, and gave every cadet an opportunity to practise being a company commander, platoon commander and section commander — pretty heady stuff for 18-year-olds. In the evening or on the weekend we received special treats — inspecting a newly launched corvette in Kingston; witnessing a dive bombing display by the RCAF at Trenton; visiting a signal centre at the RCCS (Royal Canadian Corps of Signals) at Vimy. To compensate us for taking away the horses at the start of the war, motorcycle instruction was commenced, and as a natural concomitant, first aid appeared on our syllabus.

After a final smartening up parade on the Square and a PT refresher, we were ready to see what the regular army was like and let them have a look at us.[4]

We left RMC at 0800 hours on Monday, July 7th, in chartered buses and arrived at the Small Arms Anti-aircraft Training Camp at Point Petre, where we were given a 'crash' course on how to shoot down enemy aircraft with small arms. At the conclusion of the demonstration by the professionals, we were driven down a winding road, at about 20 mph, in an open 15 cwt truck, mounted with a Bren gun, and invited to shoot down a balloon tethered to the ground by a long cord. I thought this a rather dangerous activity — dangerous for any light aircraft flying in the vicinity. However, neither balloon nor aircraft were harmed or even threatened by our barrage.

Our next stop was at Long Branch, the home of the Canadian Small Arms Training Centre (Eastern Canada), on the outskirts of Toronto, where we received advanced training in rifles and LMGs, and spent hours stripping and assembling Bren guns until we could do it blindfolded. We were also shown a 2 inch mortar, purportedly the only one in the whole of Canada. The weapon seemed to impress our instructors more than it did us.

Nearby was a small arms factory turning out Bren guns and Lee-Enfield rifles for the Allied Armies. We toured the factory and saw how these weapons were manufactured from scratch and assembled by many hundreds of skilled workers, mainly women. Here, as everywhere, we were treated with the greatest hospitality and shown everything that might be of interest or value to us. No visiting Inspector General could have received more attention.

Then followed five days of demonstrations and training at Camp Borden, where we were quartered at the A11 Infantry (Advanced) Training Centre. Our first thrill was a trip to the training ground in the new universal carrier, or Bren carrier. The drivers were delighted to demonstrate the cross-country performance of these tracked vehicles and gave us the works.

At the ranges we were introduced to a new anti-tank weapon, the Boys .55 anti-tank rifle, which, with two magazines of ammunition, weighed about 50 pounds. It had a long, wicked-looking barrel that reminded us of the old-fashioned elephant guns we had seen in the movies. We were glad we didn't have to carry the brute.

Only a few shells were available, as ammunition was expensive and in short supply. In view of my seniority in the cadets I was detailed to fire one round. Taking careful aim at an old tank, I pressed the trigger and nearly lost my shoulder from the recoil. I staggered to my feet and found that by the sheerest chance I had scored a direct hit. My marksmanship was, however, on behalf of a lost cause, as the anti-tank-rifle was soon found to be quite useless against German tanks and was withdrawn for other uses — presumably for shooting elephants, armadillos and other lightly armoured targets. I also fired the Tommy gun, which hitherto had been a favourite weapon of gangsters in the United States. At this point the Canadian Army had no submachine guns and was forced to adopt the Tommy gun until the Sten gun came into production.

On our final day at the Infantry Training Centre we fired 3 inch mortars and the rifle grenade and were given lectures and demonstrations on the tactical handling of all infantry weapons. Our training concluded with a pleasant hour or two of trap shooting for what purpose I couldn't fathom, unless the German army were still using carrier pigeons.

We then moved on to the RCAC (Royal Canadian Armoured Corps) Training Centre. There was very little to see in the way of armoured vehicles. The Sherman tanks we would later take into action in Italy and northwestern Europe were just coming off the drawing boards and into production. However, the Armoured Corps people were an aggressive bunch and if modern tanks were not available, they would train on old World War I tanks borrowed from the Americans.

At Camp Borden we also visited the RCAF Station and inspected some training aircraft on the ground. Despite our pleas, the Commanding Officer refused to allow a hundred cadets to take to the air, claiming it would disrupt, and probably finish, the entire Empire Air Training Plan.

Hoping to placate our disappointment with the Air Force, our officers took us to the RCASC (Royal Canadian Army Service Corps) School of Cookery to sample its wares. Such bribery didn't work. No cadet of our class would be caught dead in the Service Corps — we were fighters, not bakers. Nevertheless, we dutifully devoured all the pies, cakes and cookies we could lay our hands on, to satisfy our senior officers who had gone to so much trouble to arrange the demonstration.

As a grand finale, we were taken to the School of Chemical Warfare, given gas masks and shoved into the gas chamber. After a few minutes to get used to the respirator, the sergeant in charge yelled: "Now, gentlemen, off with them masks." Not a man moved, gentleman or not. The sergeant then tried coaxing "Now lookee here, it's only a little bit of chlorine gas." I knew enough about the First World War to realize he had to be joking — even a little bit of chlorine gas is too much. Finally he came clean, took off his own mask and confessed it was only a touch of tear gas.

It was now our turn to show our stuff, and we put on a demonstration of drill for the entire camp.

On July 15th we left our hosts at Borden and travelled to Connaught Ranges, near Ottawa, to fire our annual range courses on rifle and LMG. Generations of sharp shooters from Canada had qualified on these ranges (said to be one of the finest in North America) for the famous Bisley Teams which competed in England each year against the best shots in the British Empire. We were assuredly not in that league, though we tried our best with the rifle now issued to us — the infamous Ross rifle, condemned in the First World War for seizing up when it came in contact with the mud and filth of the trenches. Actually, this old shooting iron was fine for range work on a clear, dry day, once you had learned how to sight the weapon — at a blade of grass about ten feet off the target. When not firing on the range we were kept busy working in the butts or taking first aid lectures behind the firing point from our MO.

For a change of pace we took part in a night scheme designed to test our ability to defend our camp area against all things alien. Despite smoke, thunder flashes and Verey lights we held our perimeter and even made prisoner the Camp Commandant who was on a tour of inspection.

Next morning our MO, who had been teaching us first aid, almost became a casualty himself when, conscientiously supervising the burning of refuse, he aroused a slumbering thunder flash left over from the night before.

The last military camp on our tour was at Petawawa where we were guests of the A5 RCE (Royal Canadian Engineers) Training Centre. The Sappers took a fiendish delight in showing off their expertise in demolitions by blowing up houses, old vehicles and anything else that was war surplus. They also assembled a pre-fabricated bridge, erected a pontoon bridge, and let us play with the newest assault boats. It was a good sales pitch and I am sure many cadets decided that day to become Sappers.

Next day the artillery had their turn and they, too, put on a fine show. A battery of eight guns demonstrated the range and power of the new 25 pounder field guns, while we observed the whole procedure, from the time the GPO (Gun Position Officer) received his orders until, only a few moments later, the guns opened up. Then we were allowed to join the gun crews and fire a couple of rounds. A few lucky cadets got practice in playing FOO, (Forward Observation Officer) directing the guns onto their targets.

Fortunately it was a large area and no rounds fell on any adjoining villages.

On our last day of training, Brig M H S Penhale, the Camp Commandant, asked us to put on an abbreviated ceremonial "to be attended by just a few spectators". Word soon spread throughout the camp and when the time arrived to fall in we realized that the camp had been paraded en masse to watch our demonstration. Parading before thousands of civilians was one thing, but these spectators were all veterans who knew their drill pamphlet, and we had not practised ceremonial parades for weeks. Our BSM, Norm Corbett, took the bit in his teeth and went through the full ceremonial — slow march, march past in column and advance in review order. The loud applause at the conclusion of the parade indicated we had shown the old soldiers something about drill. When the brigadier complimented us and asked if we would mind doing it again, we knew we had made an impression on our Sapper and Gunner friends.

Thus concluded our 17 day tour of the main Army Training Centres in Ontario, if not in the whole of Canada. We had gathered knowledge and practical experience of the various arms that would ordinarily have taken months or years to acquire. Of particular value was the first-hand knowledge gained of weapons and vehicles hitherto known only through verbal description or diagram. Not only had we profited from the instruction and experience of the regular soldiers, we had impressed them with our skills and eagerness to learn. From every point of view it had been a tour de force.

We returned to the College on July 23rd, and in rapid succession held a final parade and inspection for Brig F L Armstrong, OBE, District Officer Commanding, MD3; attended prize-giving and closing exercises; held a dance; packed our kit; closed down the College for the summer break; and left for home on July 25th — all in two days.

Arriving in Saint John on July 26th (this time via CPR with a much needed berth), I just had time to get outfitted in khaki drill and organize myself for a month's attachment to a training centre at Aldershot, Nova Scotia, as a temporary second Lieutenant. Apart from the benefit of this practical training with troops, I would receive the magnificent sum of $3.00 per day, plus travelling expenses. Best of all I would be wearing my first highly polished pip, just a few weeks after my nineteenth birthday. In only two months I had gone from Gentleman Cadet, to corporal, to Acting CSM, to Temp 2 Lt. If I could only keep up the pace I would soon be a general. What I had not realized was that there is nothing lower, absolutely nothing lower, than a Temp 2 Lt — a 'one pip wonder'. I would have to reach up to touch bottom.

On August 4th I donned my new khaki drill, adjusted my pill box to just the right angle, and set off for the docks to catch the Digby Ferry, swinging my swagger stick ever so parallel to the ground. As I marched past the wharf where my White Lady, the *Lady Nelson,* had docked before the war, I

42

wondered what had become of her. It would be two years before I found out.

The ferry docked quite near my old friend, Eastern Canada Coastal Steamship Company, which I was pleased to see was still in business despite my father's dire warnings of insolvency and my amateur efforts as a purser two years before. I resisted the temptation to drop in on the General Manager and ask if he had any openings for Temp 2 Lts.

As soon as I boarded the ferry, I fell in with a group of officers from my father's reserve unit, the Saint John Fusiliers. One officer, a kindly old major from the last war, took me aside and gave me a short lecture on officer deportment: "First of all, relax — then throw away your swagger stick — take off that silly pill box and put on your blue field service cap if you haven't any better head gear. And please join us below for a 'touch of the whip' as soon as we push off."

It was the first time I had heard that expression, and for a moment I had serious doubts as to the intentions of my brother officers. My fears were soon put to rest and I learned to cope with and enjoy 'a touch of the whip', right out of the bottle if needs be.

A14 ITC (Infantry Training Centre) at Aldershot was an army camp about 1 1/2 miles from Kentville, NS where new soldiers (trainees) received their initial training. It also served as a summer camp for the Reserves and as a staging area for troops on their way to various destinations throughout the Empire. When I arrived a large draft of English officers and men were encamped waiting for the next ship to take them to some unknown war theatre — probably North Africa.

Like all good soldiers arriving at a new station, I immediately reported to the Adjutant for posting and duty. Looking back, I wonder how many times I repeated this exercise over the years and how many times I was happy with the result — probably about half the time. On this occasion I got exactly what I wanted — a platoon of 30 men to train. I picked up my kit and headed for the barracks at the double, almost knocking over another figure dressed in a pill box on his way to see the Adjutant — my classmate Bob Huestis from Chatham, New Brunswick.

For the next two weeks Huestis and I became instant instructors on the weapons we had fired, seen fired or inspected during our visits to Long Branch, Borden and Connaught Ranges; also we taught our men drill, map reading, field craft, section tactics, hygiene and all the other skills required of a good soldier.

For some reason the Training Centre was very short of officers and before long I found myself in charge of a full company of a hundred men. This brought new duties, such as holding Company Orders and handing out punishments for all manner of crimes I had studied in military law but never dreamt I would have to deal with — drunkenness, AWL, insubordination, more drunkenness.

My first Company Orders were a disaster. The accused, it was alleged, had been drunk, AWL and insubordinate. Being unable to resist the temptation to look at his conduct sheet giving details of past misdemeanours, I took a peek and found he had been drunk on several other occasions, but never AWL or insubordinate. My action was, of course, contrary to Kings Regulations and Orders, which provided that an officer could only consult an accused's conduct sheet after the man had been found guilty, thus ensuring that his past record would not prejudice a fair hearing of his case.

Before I had a chance to think about how to proceed with this obvious drunkard, the CSM banged on the door, threw it open, and bawled out, "Sir, first case. Escort, accused and witness, quick march. Leftright, leftright, leftright, left. Mark time, halt, left turn. Sir, No 0000 Pte Snooks, SRD."

I was trapped. A federal case loomed before me and I hadn't the slightest idea how to proceed or what punishment to hand out. I looked for divine guidance from the Highest Court of Appeal — no words came down from above. I looked for a hint or two from the CSM — nothing but a surly stare.

I glanced at the witness and a flow of evidence issued forth that would have convinced the Judge Advocate General himself of the culpability of the prisoner. He was clearly a bad actor and should be put away for the duration. I ought to throw the book at him. A quick look at the accused confirmed the evidence. He was standing there, without hat or belt, shifting from foot to foot and avoiding any eyeball contact.

"Guilty." I banged the table. "Twenty-eight days' detention and fined ten days' pay."

"Sir," stammered the CSM, "You haven't asked the accused if he wants to make a statement. He has the right to elect trial by court martial."

Something twigged in my mind about the rights of an accused, "Of course, Sergeant Major. Case remanded to the Commanding Officer. March him out," I uttered, as if I had been holding orders for years and was having a little fun at the expense of the accused.

When my company commander returned from leave he was not amused with my attempt to take over the powers of the Commanding Officer of the Training Centre. That night in the Mess he told me quite bluntly that a Temp 2 Lt had no power to punish anybody for anything, and he explained the legal intricacies of sentencing soldiers for every sort of offence, particularly drunkenness, on which subject he was obviously an expert. In fact, he had just been sent back from England for incurring excessive bar bills in his mess. After I carried him home that evening no more was said of my attempted coup d' état of the Training Centre.

If only I had remembered the wise words the Earl of Athlone had given our senior class: "In all your dealings with the men be strict but scrupulously fair."

On my next Company Orders I went out of my way to sift the evidence carefully, hear the accused, give him the benefit of the doubt and never convict on his past record. I also took care to consult KR&O (Kings Regulations and Orders) to ascertain my powers of punishment.

Nevertheless, in defence of my irregular orderly room procedure and illegal punishments, it should be recorded that during the remainder of my stay at Aldershot Camp no one in my company was ever drunk, AWL or insubordinate.

Shortly after this sensational case, my trainees finished their course and were pronounced trained soldiers. What to do with a young cadet who was getting to be known as "28 days Frost"? The answer was to put him on a course. I reported this development to my father:

> *August 21, 1941*
> *I am now attached for these last two weeks to an officers' training course, as all our trainees have gone and there was nothing for us to do. This course is for qualifying First Lieutenant, and I only wish that I had started out with it when I first came here and taken the whole course.*
>
> *I find that I am well up with the other officers and could easily qualify for a first lieutenant. If I were another year older I would get my two pips right away, but I guess it's best to go back to the College and graduate when I am 20 and then be eligible for service overseas.*
>
> *I will be seeing you in Toronto some time around the 2nd or 3rd of September.*

Some months earlier father had informed me that he was being transferred to Toronto toward the end of August, but because of the confidential nature of his appointment I could not breathe a word to anyone until the move had taken place. The bank, it seemed, was more security prone than the Army. Consequently, I could only get travelling allowance back to Saint John, my recorded home address. The family left for Toronto on August 23rd while I was still finishing my lieutenant qualifying course at Aldershot.

On August 31st my temporary commission of 2 Lt expired and I was a Gentleman Cadet again, despite having qualified as a first lieutenant or, at least, having taken a course leading to such a qualification. I caught the ferry at Digby, crossed the Bay of Fundy to Saint John, and took the CPR to Toronto, where I barely had time to see my parents in their new home before retracing my steps to Kingston.

It had been an exhausting two months; in July preparations for camp and the conducted tour; in August, the attachment at Aldershot. I had not had a holiday since the war started and none was forthcoming, as classes at RMC began within the week. Indeed, no real holiday was forthcoming for the rest of the war, except convalescence leave and a few days here and there when the exigencies of the service permitted.

On September 7th, 1941 I returned to RMC to complete the two-year course, only to find that 19 of my classmates had left the College during the summer. Five had accepted naval cadetships with the RCN, one had accepted a commission in the Fleet Air Arm of the Royal Navy, and 13 others had taken their commissions with the Canadian Army or the RCAF.

I have often wondered whether I should have left the College in the fall of 1941, thus gaining a whole year's seniority in rank. Very likely I would have gone overseas, joined my Regiment, taken part in the assault landing in Sicily and been involved in the heavy fighting there. As it turned out, I landed as a reinforcement officer in Sicily on D + 3 (three days after the assault) and took part in only the final stages of the Sicilian campaign.

The loss of a year in seniority is a critical factor when vacancies for promotion become available. There are, however, even more important factors that one cannot control — you have to be alive and well, and in the right place at the right time. On balance I doubt if my career would have been advanced by my leaving the College in 1941 instead of 1942. The chances are that one of the other factors would have intervened, perhaps with a terminal result. The casualties suffered by the 19 cadets who left in 1941 give some support to this statement — six were killed.

Banishing to the rear all thoughts of leaving the College, at least for the time being, I reported to Maj C H Walker, Staff Adjutant, for the usual posting and duty.

"Frost, you're improperly dressed. Don't you read orders?"

"Sorry Sir. I've just arrived."

"No excuse. You've been promoted to CSM in charge of C Company, on the top flat of the Stone Frigate. Better report to the tailor right away to put up your four bars."

With a broad smile he extended his hand. "Congratulations and good luck to you and the Coolies."

Nothing could have made me happier. I flew across the Square and rushed up the stairs of the Stone Frigate to the third floor. Straight ahead was a door with a name plate — No 2761 CSM Frost, CS. I threw open the door and was confronted with several happy classmates sprawled on my bed, wearing huge grins and two or three spanking new gold bars — my corporals and sergeants. Clearly this was no time to 'pull rank' and throw the beggars out; so I relaxed and gave myself, and them, a 'lids off' while we exchanged mutual congratulations on our new promotions.

Any thoughts of leaving the College and joining the Army were now firmly put aside. I would have plenty of opportunities in the year ahead to improve my leadership abilities and management skills as CSM of these high-spirited members of Coolie Company. Moreover, now that our recruit year was finished, our professors demanded that we devote all our energies to studying (and hopefully passing) our academic subjects — the equivalent of the second year in a four-year engineering degree.

Our Chief Instructor, LCol 'Archie' Campbell, had different ideas on how we should spend our time. Now that we had mastered basic training — drill, weapon training, field craft — we should get on with studying higher tactics, appreciations, orders, staff duties, military history and strategy.

Lt Timmy O'Riordan and RSM Coggins were also standing by, ready to serve us large helpings of advanced gymnastics, boxing, wrestling and unarmed combat. Woe betide any cadet who, now that he was a corporal, thought he had mastered a particular exercise, such as unarmed combat.

"Come here m'boy," purred Coggie, "and stick a knife in my ribs." The cocky cadet never knew what hit him. "Sorry buddy," smiled Coggie, half killing the cadet with a judo chop.

Under the heading 'voluntary-compulsory PT', our spare moments were occupied with inter-company sports, inter-collegiate sports, aquatic programmes, field and track meets. The training table for the football team, cancelled in our recruit year, was happily reconstituted. Apparently, the Army's stock of western beef had been replenished.

Such a full programme of academics, military training and athletics left little time for idle pleasures, yet it was inevitable that a crack would develop somewhere in this high-pressure boiler. Each floor of the Stone Frigate had one or two fire reels, with tempting lengths of hose, which would easily reach the next floor. On the pretext of practising fire drill, one company would invade the other with hoses well charged, only to be met by the other company, equally armed and ready for the fray. When the battle finally subsided, there was enough water in the halls and basement to float HMCS Stone Frigate and send it off to sea.

Another caper with hoses almost caused a casualty. One cadet from the west had an aversion to water, rather a strange affliction after the terrible drought on the prairies. One evening some of his classmates resolved to cure his peculiar paranoia. While he was in Kingston on a pass, they securely nailed down his window from the outside and caulked the window frame until it was quite water tight. Later that night, the cadet returned to his room completely worn out from his extra-curricular activities, threw himself on the bed and promptly fell asleep. His classmates quickly and quietly went into action, locked the door and caulked the door frame. Then they inserted the nozzle of the fire hose into the transom, turned on the water, slowly at first, then opened the valve until a good flow started to rush forth and fill the room.

At what point the cadet awoke and found his bed sinking beneath the waves will never be known. All that is certain is that he did awake, screaming in terror, as the water rose to the top of the door. His classmates had done a thorough job of battening down the hatches and not a drop of water escaped. Just as the screams of the cadet turned into gurgles, someone remembered the poor fellow couldn't swim. Now panic seized the marines. How to save the screaming seaman aboard his sinking prairie schooner? There was no way the door, which swung inwards, could be opened.

"Quick," someone shouted. "Send a boarding party through the window!" They were just in time.

Our classmate survived to enjoy a distinguished academic career and actually became an avid lover of boats and the sea. He also developed into a tough boxer and repaid some of his tormentors with solid body blows they probably remember to this day.

Such daring combined operations were not commonplace — we simply didn't have the time to make the necessary military appreciations and draw up orders for their proper execution. Individual feats of derring-do were more frequent and more difficult to control — such as an episode involving a motorcycle.

We were now becoming quite proficient with our Indian motorbikes and were practising intricate formations on the Square in preparation for some display or other. One cadet felt he needed more practice than he was receiving at the College. In the course of an evening pass into town he spied a motorbike idling at the curb of a local restaurant. No harm in a quick spin around the block. As the bike and cadet disappeared around the corner, a stunned policeman rushed out of the restaurant in hot pursuit. The cadet found he rather liked the feel of the machine, so much easier to control than the heavy army types, and decided to do a couple of laps around City Hall before returning the bike to its owner. His good intentions were unhappily frustrated by several gendarmes who calmly pulled him over and cautioned him as to his rights.

A further unauthorized feat, that turned into an act of valour, occurred when two cadets, in contravention of standing orders, took out a dinghy onto Lake Ontario, after hours. A storm came up and the boat capsized. The cadets would have drowned but for the courageous action of one of them.

These and other wild pursuits were always punished, but not as severely as they might have been, under a Commandant not having the understanding, wit and good sense of MGen Hertzberg. He was not an ex-cadet, but he understood the spirit, tradition, customs and training of RMC as fully as any ex-cadet. As recounted earlier, he realized the special difficulties and frustrations we laboured under — the war; only two years at the College; no recruits; slack officers abusing our Square. He acknowledged and even encouraged our high spirits, and when they got out of control he disciplined us with a firm but reasonable hand, often alleviated by a fine touch of dry humour. We thought so much of him, that on our graduation we made him an Honorary Class Member; later the RMC Club bestowed on him the rare distinction of Honorary Membership in the Ex-Cadet Club, with the No

48

H.2727, the first number of our class.

We also asked him to command our last parade to Kingston for the Laying Up of the RMC Colours in the Cathedral Church of Saint George. He hadn't marched in a parade for years and probably hadn't done any sword drill since the First World War. Nevertheless, he accepted our invitation and submitted to taking drill instruction from Timmy O'Riordan.

In the following excerpt from his graduation address he pokes fun at his efforts to learn how to march again and then slyly, but effectively, chastises us for some of our foolish escapades:

Of an evening lately Capt O'Riordan proceeds to my quarters and marches me smartly up and down my driveway. He enjoyed it, I think, much more than I did; in fact I do not think Capt O'Riordan has enjoyed himself quite so much since he became part of the RMC. Some of you may have seen us one night on your way back from town — where you do those things which you ought not to do, of which the Commandant knows nothing — perhaps, after one of your motorcycle practices around the City Hall! The point I can never understand about that jaunt is why you picked a motorcycle belonging to a military policeman!

You do so many stupid things! I am going to refer to another. Just a week ago tonight, two Cadets broke RMC Standing Orders. They took out a dinghy after hours, and without having passed their sailing tests — for that they have been punished. They struck a storm and were capsized. They hung on to the dinghy for six or seven hours. The water was cold and, presumably, they became so chilled and numb that they realized they could not hang on much longer. So one of them swam ashore — a mere mile! He managed to make it in a very exhausted condition, secured help and eventually picked up his comrade who was still hanging on to the upturned dinghy and by this time, I should judge, pretty far gone.

It was a stupid thing to take out the dinghy — it was a rather fine thing to swim that mile of cold water. There are those who wear a blue riband on their right breast for less. I thought I should mention the affair to give the Class an opportunity of indicating to that lad that The College is proud of him. He is No 2793, LCpl F W Parsons. I hope his parents are here.

Perhaps Parsons wondered why, after just finishing an unpleasant punishment, he should receive promotion. I hope he knows now.

He was punished for disobeying orders. He was promoted for behaving, in a critical situation, in the best traditions of the RMC.[5]

As mentioned earlier, our pranks and peccadillos occurred infrequently and were generally recognized as a simple venting of excess steam brought on by the frustration of being a wartime class. Heading the list of our annoyances were the senior officers on course who continued to encroach on our territory.

Two entries in Part I Orders kept the kettle boiling:

Bounds   *Fort Frederick Dormitory and the Mess Building, with the exception of the mess hall, RMC Institute, sports and decoration storage rooms, are out of bounds to all Gentlemen Cadets until further Orders*

Tennis Courts *Effective this date and until further orders, No 2 & 3 Courts are reserved for the use of the Senior Staff, attached officers, and their families*

Generations of cadets had passed through Fort Frederick's dormitory and now it was out of bounds. The tennis courts were not so serious an issue as few of the officers had time to use them; for that matter, neither did we. The Commandant, always on our side, mollified us somewhat by declaring that even if we lost the odd skirmish or two, we were still teaching the officers a lot about discipline and the ideals and spirit of RMC.

To help break down the cold war between the cadets and officers, an instructor on the Company Commander's Course gave a lecture to the cadets: subject — Iceland; instructor — Maj G S N Gostling of The Royal Regiment of Canada. Speaking from experience gained during the Canadian occupation of the island, Maj Gostling touched on the strategic importance of the place to the Royal Navy and to the US Navy in keeping open the North Atlantic trade route. It was a good lecture and we began to realize that perhaps some of our senior officers had a few parts.

The next time I saw Maj Gostling he was a brigadier in charge of a large officer reinforcement camp in England, of which I was one of the inmates. Like all good goslings he was known as the 'Goose', and his coat of arms, so it was alleged, was a large goose flying at great height, dropping 'bombs' on the reinforcement officers.

After the war we became good friends and I often kidded him that his rapid rise to such great heights, both as a goose and as a general, was due solely to his association with the cadets of RMC. He took my ribbing good naturedly, and when I took command of his regiment, gave me his sword, dress uniform and bearskin.

A further olive branch from the senior officers was offered by the Canadian Junior War Staff Course, when they asked us to participate in a night attack, in the form of a trench raid to capture prisoners and destroy enemy weapons.

We were somewhat surprised that the officers were still studying trench warfare from the First World War, but accepted the invitation in the interest of maintaining peace and harmony in the family. Anyway, we were due for a little excitement.

Our enthusiasm soon evaporated when, the day before the exercise, we were taken to the field and told to gather up every rock and stone in sight and lay them in neat lines to represent German trenches. Then we were issued with large buckets of white-wash and ordered to paint the stones. We were mortified. Even the prisoners at the Kingston Penitentiary would not be subjected to such an indignity. It was worse than asking us to paint the Last Post.

What stratagem the Commandant employed to appease us has passed from memory. Perhaps he encouraged one or two senior officers to join us in our painting bee. Anyway, the job was done and we actually did take part in the night attack, acting as CSMs, platoon sergeants and members of sections.

Like all exercises planned by the Staff, the scheme was, of course, a smashing success. The final summation said so:

> *The attack was successful; the enemy, though elusive, were all captured, and while the ground was very muddy and wet owing to recent heavy rains, the exercise was enjoyed by all. The brilliancy of the flares and signal lights was a new experience to many, and, added to the lessons brought out by the difficulty of controlling even small formations by night across strange country, helped to make the exercise a success.*

As far as we were concerned, we hadn't learned a damn thing!

We did, however, meet some of the officers on the course and found they were quite good types. One was Capt R S Malone, a former PPCLI Officer*. In his book *A Portrait of War,* Brig Malone gives his impression of this great exercise, which coincides exactly with our appreciation of the matter:

> *Next, to my amazement, came our first big field exercise, on a divisional level, complete with supporting engineers and artillery, conferences, umpires, appreciations, O Groups, operation orders down to battalion levels and so forth. It was a two-day exercise or TEWT (tactical exercise without troops) — a trench raid based on World War I experience. Having recently been briefed in*

---

* The late Brig R S Malone, OBE, former publisher and editor of the *Globe* and *Mail,* who took part in every D-Day invasion of the Canadian Army (Sicily, Italy and Normandy), was wounded in Sicily, and represented Canada at the Japanese surrender on the USS *Missouri.*

England about mechanized warfare and the advent of armour and blitzkrieg tactics, I felt we might just as well have gone back to cavalry charges and siege warfare. However, the Directing Staff was mad keen on the project, so we all got lost in the dark out on Barriefield Common one night and learned how to clear enemy trenches.[6]

After the war I met Brig Malone on many occasions and had the pleasure of accompanying him to England where, in our capacities as Honorary Colonels of our Regiments, we attended the wedding of Prince Charles and Lady Diana.

Another officer on the course, whom I liked and later got to know quite well, was Maj H F Cotton, also of the PPCLI. He was an ex-cadet, had been a renowned athlete at the College and in the Army, and went on to command an infantry battalion before serving in the Far East.

Still another course debouched officers onto our Square — the Senior Officers Course. Two members of the Directing Staff whose paths crossed mine during the war were Maj R H Mitchell, PPCLI, who subsequently commanded a Training Centre I was posted to, and Maj W K P Gilbride, whom I tried in vain to locate on the beaches of Sicily in July 1943.

Christmas exams were now approaching. We put aside our petty feuds with the senior officers and tried to concentrate on our studies, which we found were becoming more difficult as the war progressed. Hitler's invasion of Russia in June 1941 had drastically changed the course of the war. The Russian armies, caught by surprise, had been overwhelmed by the German juggernaut and were fighting for their lives, deep in their homeland. Churchill had bravely declared that despite all ideological differences, Britain would form a common front with Russia against the evil Nazis. How could any self-respecting cadet go on studying such subjects as descriptive geometry and integral calculus when his rightful place was in the front line with other ex-cadets?

More devastating news was in the offing: news that would almost paralyse our will to continue with such irrelevant studies. On December 7th Japan attacked Pearl Harbour. I immediately wrote my father:

December 7, 1941
What an evening! Japan has at last come out of her shell and done what we have been expecting she would do. As a matter of fact this was predicted by our Colonel in Charge of Tactics, at our last class.

I'm pretty 'downhole', as are most of us around here. No fooling, these exams are not so easy coming at a time like this when the most important thing is the latest developments in the War. It is really an effort to get down to studying all these

academic subjects — it seems so futile and useless when we should
be putting every hour, every minute, into the great struggle.
However, I won't fail if I'm lucky, but I'll certainly come down
a few notches; it can't be helped.

When the results of our exams were published in the New Year, it was
clear we had all suffered from 'Jap fever' and our marks were, indeed, down
a few notches.

Again, our Commandant stepped in and saved us from defeat at the hands
of the professors. He wouldn't allow us to falter, even if it meant that
practically the whole class would have to write some of the exams all over
again.

We got over our 'downhole', surly mood and went back once more into
the breech. After the initial shock of Pearl Harbour had subsided we began
to realize that with Russia and the United States now drawn into the battle,
the Allied Armies could not lose the war. Their combined force was at least
twice, and maybe three times that of Germany, Italy, Japan and their
satellites. How the war would be won was something we couldn't foresee,
but neither could the members in the highest Allied Councils.

On March 16th, 1942, the College was honoured by a visit from LGen
A G L McNaughton, CB, CMG, DSO, the Canadian Corps Commander.
It was the only time I would see this distinguished soldier-scientist, who
became known as the 'Father of the Canadian Army'.

Slowly, inexorably, the happiest and yet saddest day of our young lives
drew upon us — graduation and the closing of our College. Yet there was
still much to be done before that day arrived.

On a lovely day in May we held our final track and field meet. The cinder
track was firm, I was in the best physical condition of my life and the
'moving' words of Jake Wyatt were still in my ears. The result was that I
placed first in the 100, 220 and 440 yard dashes and established a record
in the 220 yard dash. This record was never broken, due mainly to the fact
that some time after the war all distances were changed to metres.

One of the nicest traditions of the College was that the senior class gave
photographs of themselves to their friends, and to recruits who had given
faithful service. We had no recruits, but very close ties had developed between
almost every member of our class. Giving pictures to everyone would be a
very expensive matter, so a certain amount of discretion had to be exercised.
Who should we retain to capture our fine faces for posterity, for a reasonable
fee? After much debate we decided to go with an up-and-coming
photographer by the name Karsh. We claim no credit for starting him on
his way to pre-eminence in his profession, but I would like to think that
our clean-cut features gave him some inspiration.

Soon exams were written and the decks cleared away for practising our closing exercises which again would be held in the presence of His Excellency The Earl of Athlone, Governor General and Her Royal Highness, Princess Alice.

Finally the most sorrowful and crowded day in the history of the College arrived — June 20th, 1942. More than 40 years later the poignancy of that day remains:

Morning's Exercises

Arriving precisely at ten, His Excellency and Her Royal Highness were received by the Battalion in line under command of BSM Corbett. Following the Royal Salute His Excellency inspected the Battalion accompanied by the Commandant and MGen H F Letson, MC, ED, Adjutant-General, who represented National Defence Headquarters for the occasion.

Immediately following the inspection, the Battalion marched past, first in column of platoons, then in column of route and, having reformed on the inspection line, advanced in review order, again giving a Royal Salute. Following the old custom, the Graduating Class — in this case the whole Battalion — marched off the Square in slow time behind the Colours, while the band played Auld Lang Syne.

In past years when this ceremony was carried out by the Graduating Class the remainder of the Cadets stood fast, presenting arms to the Colours and their Seniors as they moved off the Square. Perhaps the full significance of the day was evident for the first time when the last file moved out of sight through the doors of the Education Building, leaving the Square forsaken by Cadets.

Afternoon's Exercises

The next event was one in keeping with the times. A motorcycle display by 12 Cadets held the interest of the spectators by going through complicated figures for some ten minutes. Then a quick change into PT kit and at 1445 hrs the arrival of His Excellency and Her Royal Highness was the signal for the commencement of the Physical Training and Gymnastic Display. Under the direction of Lt Coggins, who had been promoted from Sergeant Major the same day, this went off with the usual precision and finish.

Laying Up of the Old Colours

Twenty minutes from the conclusion of the PT display again saw the Battalion on parade with its Colours, this time to lay up the Colours which had been in service since their presentation by HRH The Prince of Wales in October, 1919.

At 1600 hours the parade was handed over to the Commandant, who with the Staff Adjutant as second in command, marched it to the Cathedral Church of St George for the service. On arrival at the entrance to the Cathedral, the Commandant advanced to the closed doors and, knocking three times with the hilt of his sword, asked permission for the Battalion to enter for the purpose of laying up the Colours. On arrival of His Excellency and Her Royal Highness the service commenced with the processional hymn, after which the Colour Party moved up the centre aisle to the foot of the chancel steps in slow time to Elgar's 'Land of Hope and Glory' played by the Signals Band. At the chancel steps the Battalion Sergeant Major took the Colours from the Cadet Officers of the Colour Party [CSM Frost and CQMS Elliot], handing them to the Commandant, who in turn advanced and handed them to the Archdeacon. Thus the Old Colours passed from the possession of the College. The service concluded with the National Anthem. For this service the third verse of our National Anthem, long since discarded, was reintroduced; for at no time has there been more need of Divine assistance to confound the politics and frustrate the knavish tricks of the King's enemies.

Forming up on King St under LCol A H C Campbell, Chief Instructor and Second in Command of the College, with Lt T O'Riordan as second in command of the parade, the Battalion marched back to the College. A dramatic note was sounded on the return march as the Battalion swung through applauding crowds with the Colour Party in the usual position but with empty colour belts. Halting on the Square , the Battalion was handed over to the BSM.[7]

Let the Commandant, MGen Hertzberg, describe the final act in this day-long drama:

Although many of you were present at that graduation, few, if any, saw the Battalion dismissed for the last time — that was a very private affair, every foot on the Square belonged to a Cadet — because the Commandant moved off the Square to the side-line and turned over to the BSM. The Commandant had had his full innings in marching the Battalion to St George's Cathedral to lay up the Colours, which was the greatest honour ever done him. This dismissal was the BSM's show. We broke the RMC 'House' Flag on the short mast at the Saluting Base and the last command given by the BSM before 'Dismiss' was 'Gentlemen Cadets — to the Royal Military College — Present Arms.' The saluting base was empty — but for the RMC Flag. The salute was not acknowledged. There was no one there qualified to take it![8]

Seventy-seven cadets passed off the Square that afternoon and were commissioned as temporary lieutenants the following day, June 21st — my twentieth birthday. We were the largest class to have ever graduated, at one time, in the history of the College.

Our class had started 102-strong in September 1940. One was killed in an accident shortly after joining the College, and two were withdrawn, leaving 99 cadets in our class. Of this number, 19 left the College at the end of the first year, a further three during the last year, and all 22 took commissions in the Navy, Army and Air Force. The remaining 77 who graduated on June 20th, 1942, joined their units and went off to war. Eleven never returned. A further six cadets, who had left the College before graduation, were also killed.

Of those who returned from the war, many had been wounded in action, some more than once; others had been injured in training accidents. Four members received the Military Cross, one the Distinguished Flying Cross, and several were mentioned in despatches. Two further members of our class received the Military Cross in Korea.

LGen Crerar, in his speech to our class on March 15th, 1941, had charged us, of the younger generation, with accomplishing the task that his generation had failed to finish in 1918. Our record speaks for itself. Our College Hymn is our valedictory:

Fight the good fight with all thy might
Christ is thy strength and Christ thy right
Lay hold on life, and it shall be
Thy joy and crown eternally.

Chapter III

CANADA
Infantry Officer
July, 1942 to March 31, 1943

You're alright in the ASC
Drunk every night in the cavalry
But, when you're in the Infantry
It's sans fait ri, sans fait rien.

On his appointment as an officer in the Canadian Army, every cadet received a Commission granted by King George VI, and a Scroll signed by the Deputy Minister of National Defence and endorsed by His Excellency The Earl of Athlone, Governor General, under the Great Seal of Canada.

When I examined the document I was pleased to see it was dated June 21st, 1942, my 20th birthday, but I was shocked to find the word 'Temporary' had been stamped just above the words 'George The Sixth' and opposite the signature of the Earl of Athlone. Whether 'Temporary' referred to His Majesty or the Governor General was not clear, but in either case the document was manifestly libelous, if not seditious. The Deputy Minister needed a new draftsman or, possibly, the Government needed a new Deputy Minister.

After further study, I finally concluded that the word 'Temporary' probably applied to my name tucked away in the body of the document. This seemed like a terrible hoax to play on someone who had spent two long years qualifying for His Majesty's Commission.

I was an expert in the organization of corps, divisions, brigades and

57

battalions; I could write appreciations and operation orders for a divisional attack; I had qualified on, and in most cases fired, all manner of weapons from the last war as well as those just coming off the assembly lines — Vickers medium machine gun, Lewis machine gun, Bren light machine gun, Thompson submachine gun, Ross rifle, Lee-Enfield rifle (Mark II), .55 inch Boys anti-tank rifle, 2 inch mortar, 3 inch mortar, 36 Mills hand grenade, Smith & Wesson revolver and a shotgun. On my cadet uniform was a badge showing I was a qualified layer on the 18 pounder field gun from the First World War. I had even survived a gas attack.

I had studied some military engineering, become quite proficient sending messages by morse code and acquired various other military skills. I was, indeed, the very model of a modern, keen young subaltern — so I was led to believe.

The thought that I might have to take further training to clear my record of the awful stigma 'Temporary' was almost too much to endure. However, my father was not at all upset and thought a littler further training would probably do me a lot of good — at least it might do something to get rid of my cocky attitude. I responded by saying I was a fully trained officer and hinted I really didn't need his outdated advice any longer. His reaction was typical: "Fully trained," he snorted, "Why, I've forgotten more than you'll ever know." To my credit I refrained from making the obvious rejoinder that the real problem was that he had, indeed, forgotten.

But father had a point. What did I know about leading a platoon of infantry? Fortunately, I had been a CSM at the College in charge of some 30 cadets and had enjoyed some success handling them on the parade ground, in the classroom and in barracks. That was fine, but what about leading 30 men in the field, in an attack or even in a defensive position?

While I was short on practical training I had learned very well some basic lessons about the army and the infantry which stood me in good stead for the rest of my life. The RMC College motto formed a solid base: 'Truth, Duty, Valour.' The unofficial mottoes were also engrafted on my mind: 'But for God's sake use your dome' and 'Don't lose your sense of humour.' These principles, plus a deep sense of discipline, loyalty and respect of superiors, made up my creed and helped me over the rough spots ahead.

There was, of course, no question that I would join the Infantry. The only problem was to choose a unit. A lot of peer pressure came from my class to join the glamour boys — the armoured corps — and ride into action in an armoured car or tank. At least 20 per cent of my class joined the Recce, but most of them ended up marching and climbing over the mountains in Italy *sans* armoured cars.

I didn't succumb to these pressures but still my problem remained — which infantry regiment? Having been born in Newfoundland, I might well have followed my father and joined the Royal Newfoundlanders. But after the awful casualties of World War I, the Newfoundland Government decided not to raise an infantry regiment in World War II and formed artillery units instead.

My family were now living in Toronto. Both my father and brother were serving in the reserve battalion of a famous Toronto militia unit, The Royal Regiment of Canada; again I received some pressure to become a member of this unit or some other Toronto regiment. I was so sure, however, I would be a professional soldier, that I dismissed the thought of joining any of the fine militia units as I believed, in my ignorance, they simply were not in the same league as a permanent force regiment. It is rather amusing to record that a mere six years later, I joined my father's Toronto militia unit, rose to command, and served as its Honorary Lieutenant Colonel and Honorary Colonel for some 15 years.

There were three permanent force infantry regiments to choose from — The Royal 22nd Regiment, the RCR (Royal Canadian Regiment) and the PPCLI. The Royal 22nd Regiment was not in the running, as far as I was concerned. It was basically a French Canadian outfit and my French was not equal to giving commands to troops, particularly under the strain of battle. The RCR were known to be a very formal, stiff and proper bunch, who went mainly by the book. They were also very keen on many of the customs of the British Army including, so I was told, the tradition of officers carrying a handkerchief up the left sleeve. In fact, the RCR were reputed to go one better by having a handkerchief up each sleeve.

On the other hand the PPCLI, stationed in western Canada, with companies at Winnipeg and Victoria, were known as a friendly, outgoing Regiment, with a great family spirit. Whether this was due to the influence of the west, or the dashing reputation they had acquired in World War I, I had no idea, but I knew their war record was second to none.

My first contact with the PPCLI (the Patricias — never the 'Pats') was during the 1930s when father was a bank manager in Saskatoon. Practically all his closest friends had served in the Great War, which was still fresh in their minds. Every November 11th, sharp at 0800 hours, father and his friends would gather at the local armoury and toast their 'fallen comrades' in neat rum. After the ceremony, the glasses were solemnly thrown into the fireplace. When I asked my father how he could afford such waste in the depths of the depression, he became quite emotional and said that it would be a dishonour to the memory of the dead ever to drink out of the same glass again. It was a noble sentiment that appealed to me then and still does.

One of my father's friends was Col Arthur Potts*, who had served with the Patricias in the Great War. Through Col Potts and other military friends,

---

*The late MGen Arthur E Potts, CBE, ED, who commanded The Saskatoon Light

father often met serving PPCLI officers who visited Saskatoon in the course of their duties. One was Capt H F Cotton, already mentioned in connection with the staff courses at RMC. They sometimes came to the house on quite unofficial business and I would get a glimpse of their fancy mess kits from my dug-out in the kitchen. They always seemed to enjoy father's parties.

While the Patricias were highly regarded in Saskatoon they had no presence in the city during the 1930s except for a few officers and NCOs who instructed the local militia units including the SLI (The Saskatoon Light Infantry). One of the up-and-coming officers in that unit was Scott Dudley, the accountant at father's branch of the bank. Dudley seemed to spend a lot of time training with the SLI, firing on the ranges and attending various camps and courses. I was very impressed with Dudley's military activities and am certain I would have joined the SLI as a militiaman had my father not been transferred to Saint John NB in the fall of 1938.

I would not see Scott Dudley again until July 1943 aboard a ship in a convoy bound for Sicily, when he was LCol Dudley, Commanding Officer of the SLI. His Second-in-Command was Alan Embury whose father, BGen J F L Embury, CB, CMG, had been a friend of my father.

Saskatoon was also represented in the Sicily landings by another famous son, Farley Mowat, sailing in an assault convoy. His father was a war veteran who had been a librarian in Saskatoon and was also a friend of my father. I had never met Farley; he was too involved with an amazing animal called Mutt — the famous *Dog Who Wouldn't Be*.

My ties to Saskatoon and the SLI were thus very strong, but I really had no doubt at all that I would become a Patricia, almost from the day I entered RMC. My decision was strongly influenced by two members of my senior class, Bob (Sam) Potts (eldest son of MGen Potts) and Willie Mulherin. They were outstanding athletes and to me were the typical, keen, tough, infantry officer. Subsequently, they served in the PPCLI with distinction, and stayed in the permanent army after the war. Sam Potts won the DSO in Italy and became a full colonel before his tragic death in 1968. Willie Mulherin won the George Medal in Italy and a mention in despatches in Sicily and became a lieutenant colonel before he, too, died prematurely in 1966.

Further encouragement to join the PPCLI had come from LCol K C Burness, MC, a Patricia officer who was the Chief Instructor on a staff course at RMC. Tragically, he was lost at sea when the ship taking him to England for other duties was torpedoed.

Two other Patricia officers on a staff course at RMC had added their influence: Maj R L Mitchell, already referred to, who later commanded A15

Infantry at the outbreak of World War II and went on to enjoy a distinquished military career in that conflict. At his death, age 93, he was the senior Patricia officer, much admired and respected by all ranks.

Canadian Infantry Training Centre at Camp Shilo, Manitoba, and Maj David Rosser who commanded the Regiment in action for a short time until he was wounded.

As mentioned earlier, my commission as a Temporary Lieutenant dated from June 21st, 1942, the day following my graduation from RMC. However, before I could actually join the Army there was a lot of work to be done to close the College for the duration of the war, and to conclude, or consummate, outstanding affairs (including the marriage of one member of our class to a Kingston girl). Finally, all our duties were finished and I received orders to proceed to Toronto, No 2 District Depot, to complete my attestation papers and become a Provisional Reinforcement Officer for the PPCLI. I was then to report to Shilo, Manitoba for further training and duty.

At Toronto, I reported to Stanley Barracks, an ancient officers' quarters by Lake Ontario, and was duly attested, swearing to be faithful and bear true allegiance to His Majesty. I scarcely had time to catch my breath before the Orderly Room Sergeant shoved a will form in front of me and said, "Fill in your mother's name and sign."

I felt it was a little premature to be thinking about my decease when I had only joined the army two minutes before. Anyway, I signed the document, which as far as I know was never required throughout my service; nor for that matter, to the present day.

The last item of business before proceeding out west was to complete my kit. I can still remember the thrill of purchasing my first uniform, as a full lieutenant, bearing the bugles of the PPCLI. A friend came along to help me choose the appropriate cloth for both winter and summer service dress and select such important accoutrements as Sam Browne Belt, gloves and swagger stick. I had no trouble until it came to deciding whether the fly on the pants should have buttons or a zipper. My helpful friend said he once knew a person who had a zipper on his golf jacket and it sliced off the end of his tie! Heedless of such a fate, I opted for the fancy zipper and neither my golf jacket nor my pants ever gave me any trouble of that nature.

After a few days at home, I left for the A15 CITC at Camp Shilo, some 120 miles west of Winnipeg, as a reinforcement officer for the PPCLI, knowing, however, I had little chance of joining my Regiment for many months, as reinforcements were not yet required overseas.

Shilo, like most army camps, was a pretty desolate place, encompassing a large tract of bald, rolling prairie, interspersed with alkaline sloughs, occasional poplar bluffs and small hills. Part of the area was almost a desert, never having recovered from the terrible drought of the 1930s. In summer, the hot winds whipped up the sands and tumble-weeds, searing the skin and blinding the eyes; in winter one simply froze. The whole terrain was quite useless, except as a habitat for coyotes, gophers and jack rabbits — and infantry soldiers.

Before the war Shilo had been a summer camp for the Manitoba militia. The accommodation consisted of a few wooden huts serving as messes and quarters for the senior officers, while the junior officers and men lived in tents. When I arrived, there was considerable panic to erect permanent accommodation for everyone before the winter set in. Until these new quarters became available we junior officers had to perform our ablutions outside, rain or shine.

I reported to LCol R L Mitchell who had now assumed command of the Training Centre. He made it very clear what he expected of his PPCLI officers — in short, we were to set the example for the rest of the camp. I was not reluctant to assume such a responsibility, but in order to perform my duties adequately I thought something should be done about my temporary rank. LCol Mitchell seemed somewhat surprised about my status and consulted my dossier. "Well," he said, "there *is* something wrong here; you're not a temporary lieutenant — you're a provisional lieutenant."

I didn't know if this was a step forwards or backwards. "I assume, Sir, that means I will not have to take any more qualifying courses. When can I be a . . . an unconditional lieutenant?"

"That's a good question. Suppose we put you on the Advanced Officers Qualifying Course, under Mr Potts and Mr Mulherin, and see how you make out."

"My God," I thought, "I'm scuppered. Sam Potts and Willie Mulherin will still think I'm a recruit at RMC and give it to me all over again."

My fears were entirely unfounded. After three days of being a student with 'one pip wonders' from the Gordan Head Basic Officers School, I was called in by the Chief Instructor and told it was obvious someone had made a mistake. How to rectify it? No problem — make me an instant instructor on the course I was taking as a student and confirm my promotion to a qualified lieutenant on the completion of the course. Simplicity itself — and what a relief!

As promised, at the end of the course I was issued with an imposing certificate of military qualification:

CERTIFICATE OF MILITARY QUALIFICATION
CANADIAN ARMY
NATURE OF QUALIFICATION
Infantry (Rifle)
THIS IS TO CERTIFY THAT
P/Lieut Charles Sydney Frost Corps Princess Patricia's Canadian Light Infantry has attended the required Course of Instruction held at Shilo Camp, Manitoba from 11 July 1942 to 14 August 1942 and has qualified as Lieutenant — Infantry (Rifle) Canadian Army (AF).

NOTE — This Certificate is registered at National Defence Head-quarters Ottawa, Ontario, Canada.

	'R L Mitchell' Lt Col
for Adjutant-General	*(R L Mitchell) Commandant,*
	A-15 Canadian Infantry
	Training Centre, MD 10

It is probably safe, now, to disclose that the certificate is fraudulent. It states that I attended a course from July 11th to August 14th, 1942. In fact, I did not report to the camp until July 15th and left on July 29th for another course at Nanaimo, BC. Moreover I was a student on the course for only three days.

I immediately went to work as an instructor on the Advanced Officers Qualifying Course, teaching tactics, organization, military law and map reading to my former fellow students. In short order I found that even with my limited practical experience I knew as much as anyone in the camp, except my two seniors from RMC, Sam Potts and Willie Mulherin. They were really a tower of strength, giving me excellent notes on the various courses I was supposed to instruct. This was a lucky break. I had no real experience in teaching and all the students were much older than I.

Soon I acquired some expertise in the subject of military law, which served me well throughout the course of the war and helped me out of the various scrapes and legal difficulties I encountered. After the war I put this knowledge to good use in my second career.

My first class of student officers included a Rhodes scholar and a Member of Parliament. I was amazed to find that I could debate the fine points of the law and hold my own against such tough opposition. The Rhodes scholar subsequently became an eminent lawyer and is now a judge of the Court of Appeal. I would like to believe he profited from my instruction!

As time went by all the instructors became quite proficient in their fields; at least our students seemed to think so. One of the fine instructors was Johnny Koensgen, who later won the Military Cross in Italy and became Second-in-Command of a PPCLI battalion before his untimely death from cancer; another was Andy Mills, who had joined the PPCLI before the war. He subsequently served in action as Adjutant of the Regiment.

We were all very proud that we were Patricias and, following LCol Mitchell's lead, we just assumed it was our right and duty to set high standards for all the other regiments. This did not sit too well with some of the older officers from the Militia, who had served many years and had a fair knowledge of the army, even though they were certainly not up to date on the latest military doctrine, such as battle drill.

Other PPCLI officers I met and admired were LCol Ken McCullouch,

LCol A H Hunt and LCol A C (Spike) Delaney, who were stationed at Shilo or at the PPCLI depot in Winnipeg, and inspected our courses from time to time. The apparent reason for their inspections was to check on training and administrative matters, but I suspect they also wanted to see how their PPCLI officers were performing.

It must have been obvious to them that, not only in training and administration but also in the mess, the Patricia officers led the way. After a long day in the field, on the ranges or in the lecture room, we Patricias gathered in the mess and, under the leadership of Sam Potts gave lusty renditions of the favourite Patricia songs — *The Ric-a-dam-doo, Clear the Way, The Shiny Two Brigade, Who was the Man Who Invented the War, Stand By Your Glasses Steady* and a host of others. From our days at RMC, Sam knew that I could bang out a tune on the piano — if I was in the right mood — and he knew how to get me that way. On my second night in the mess he led me to the piano. "Frost, play *The Ric-a-dam-doo*." (Sam loved to give orders and sometimes forgot I was not still a recruit at RMC). I tried, but it sounded awful.

"Sam, I don't know the damn thing!"

Our performance must have sounded like a scene from the movie *Casablanca*: "Well, play it again," exploded Sam. In short order I picked out the chords as Sam led us through *The Ric-a-dam-doo* and all the other songs. He had a remarkable memory, and knew the words to every army ditty as far back as the Boer War.

Besides giving me this excellent training in Regimental traditions, Sam ordered me to read the Regimental History of the PPCLI. The fact that not one copy was available in the mess was, of course, irrelevant; but this didn't faze me. The senior Patricia officers were only too happy to help me out. From them I learned how the PPCLI was formed in August 1914 by Hamilton Gault, who personally equipped the Regiment. HRH Princess Patricia of Connaught consented to give her name to the battalion, composed largely of ex-servicemen and commanded by LCol F D Farquhar, DSO, who was then serving as Military Secretary to HRH, the Duke of Connaught, Governor General of Canada.[1]

I also learned the story of the Regiment in the First World War — the dreadful casualties and the valour of its members, who won 369 decorations, including three Victoria Crosses.[2] I was proud to be a Patricia.

LCol Mitchell seemed to take a special interest in this young fellow from RMC who could be a student one day and an instructor the next. He called me in, and after saying how pleased he was with my efforts, told me that an opening had just become available to attend an excellent PT course at Nanaimo, BC. With my condition I obviously wouldn't have any trouble with the course and when I returned I would be appointed Camp Athletic and Sports Officer as well as continue to instruct on the Advanced Officers

Course.

I am very quick at accepting postings that have several side benefits not realized by the authorities: "Yes Sir," I said smartly, "When do I leave?" "Tomorrow, and good luck."

What LCol Mitchell did not know was that my grandmother Frost, my uncle and all my aunts on my father's side lived in Vancouver. Moreover, by judicious use of train schedules I could stop over in Saskatoon as well as in Prince Albert where a young lady I had become interested in resided. A further consideration was that I was getting a little tired of ablutions out in the bald prairie and felt I needed a change of scenery and some good mountain air.

My train trip through the Rockies was most enjoyable, travelling first class, of course, with a chair in the observation car at the rear of the train. The ferry trip across to Vancouver Island provided a nice diversion and I reported to the PT school at Nanaimo in a fine frame of mind.

This school, like all Army establishments, had a long name designed to intimidate the candidates as soon as they arrived — Canadian Small Arms Training Centre (Western Canada) Physical Training Wing — which, even when abbreviated sounded impressive, PT Wing CSATC (Western Canada). If these words failed to daunt a new student, a Latin phrase emblazoned on an arch over the entrance undoubtedly would: *Mens sana in corpore sano.*

After the usual issue of kit and run around the camp, we were allowed to sit down in the centre of the sports field while we awaited the arrival of the Chief Instructor who would, no doubt, give us the usual introductory lecture. The Chief Instructor soon appeared, sprinting down the track, and leaped onto a small dais. He was clearly not the usual PT instructor. An older man, probably in his late 40s, he had a lean frame and an exaggerated erectness almost to the point of leaning over backwards. We later learned that he had suffered terrible injuries in a car accident, including a broken back. By dint of perseverance and hard work he had 'lifted himself up with his own boot straps' and regained most of his former athletic ability; though we could tell he often suffered considerable pain as he led us through the exercises.

His introduction was also not the usual harangue given to new students. He told us his name and then asked why it was necessary to have PT. After hearing a few stumbling answers from the students, he answered his own question with words that are as true today as they were then:

Under modern conditions, with the increase of all forms of motor transport, the increase of mechanical forms of manufacturing, things have been made very easy for us and the average individual tends to use his muscles less and less. At the same time, the hustle and bustle, the speed of movement, the noise of machinery and vehicles increases the nervous strain and tends to unbalance that harmony of body and mind which is so essential to human well-being.

The average person gets along more or less satisfactorily while pursuing his normal life but along comes a war and millions of men and women are called upon to lead a vastly different life from that to which they have been accustomed and find themselves partially unfit for active service under modern war conditions.

The reason for PT then is obvious: many men, originally fit, have been earning a living in occupations which have rendered them unfit for soldiering.

The Chief Instructor then gave us a short history on the development of PT through the ages. I found the subject so interesting that I made extensive notes:

(a) Prussia — *after their several defeats (notably Jena) at the hands of the French under Napoleon, they incorporated PT into their school system. The war of 1870 and the present conflict tell how successful were their efforts at building up a physically fit people.*

(b) British Army
  (1) *The Army Physical Training Staff (APTS) was formed in 1919-20. Headed by a group of competent officers, including eminent medical officers, this Staff formed the School at Aldershot and made great strides in modern physical training.*
  (2) *Since that time, the APTS has been constantly working on the Army system. Selected men were sent to many of the recognized centres of PT learning throughout the world where they took courses of instruction and reported back to Aldershot. Niels Bukh came over from Denmark and the Army adopted his system of changes. The medical experts studied these hundreds of exercises and their effect on the human body and after years of research and testing produced the modern PT Tables (1937) Without Apparatus.*
     These tables will be found to contain exercises taken from Ling's Swedish, Bukh's Danish, Bloch's German, Atlas of USA, the Czech's Sokols and many others. It will be apparent, therefore, that these Tables are not the result of any haphazard guessing but the result of years of painstaking research and study.

Such a reasonable, sensible approach to PT made all of us instant believers, even those who obviously had been banished to this course as punishment or for general smartening up. After RMC I didn't have to be convinced of the value of PT, but here was a new approach for the ordinary soldier. Whereas at RMC the emphasis had been on developing gymnasts on the high bar, parallel bars, high box and mats, the purpose of this course was to teach us how to exercise our men and keep them physically fit. We were taught that every officer and man in the field should be able to march 25 miles and be in good fighting condition at the end of it. Every Unit should have its own obstacle course and every officer and man should go over it, first in PT kit and then in full battle order, at least once a week. All ranks should take part in a cross-country run, majors and higher ranks over 40 to walk, the rest to run.

The whole programme was based on a progressive series of exercises in six Tables that gradually called for the use of a greater amount of muscular energy and strength as the man progressed from Table to Table. The purpose was not so much to produce a muscular soldier as to develop character, mental alertness, co-ordination, bodily fitness and endurance. In accomplishing these objects the playing of organized sport was an important part.

This idea of a scientific, progressive approach to PT gained wide acceptance and after the War was copied by many other plans with fancy names.

Not only were we taught how to play games but, even more important, how to supervise, coach and referee organized sports. Heading the list were boxing, unarmed combat and army wrestling, followed by team sports such as soccer, speed ball, volley ball and tug of war; also a thorough grounding in anatomy and physiology.

While the course put considerable emphasis on theory and methods of instruction, it was tough physically, and I silently thanked my PT instructors at RMC, Timmy O'Riordan and Coggie (and even my seniors), for getting me into shape, even if their system was sometimes at variance with the methods advocated by the Course. For example, we were told:

(a) *Avoid loud shouting, noisy, impatient, discouraging and bullying methods of handling the class. A quiet encouraging manner, free from hesitation and indecision produces the best results.*

(b) *Coaches must be more than drill sergeants. Keep away from parade ground procedure as much as possible — in this way PT will be given more of a recreational aspect with greater appeal to the men, who will doubtless put forth more energy and get more good from it, instead of regarding it as a chore and necessary evil.*

I am not saying that Timmy and Coggie didn't understand, or seldom used these principles of instruction; after all, they had received their training at the British School of Physical Training. In fact Coggie had a natural way of getting the most out of us by quiet example and encouragement. But he could also be very tough. Our seniors were in a class by themselves.

The final phase of the course was boxing. I had a distinct advantage over most of the other students on the course as all recruits at RMC were required to box, and I had received quite a bit of instruction in this manly art. In the last match I was paired with a huge NCO of the PPCLI. Despite my finesse I could not dodge all his blows and the contest really turned into a survival course for me. When the final bell sounded I staggered to my corner, thankful to have escaped with my life.

I passed the course with a 'distinguished' qualification, which was quite rare. In a burst of shameful immodesty I wrote my mother after I returned to Shilo:

> *I just read in orders today that Lt C S Frost received a 'D' (Distinction) in PT. I am told it is the first 'D' they have ever had around here in PT and have been congratulated by the CO and all the senior officers. Strangely enough, Sam Potts went out to Nanaimo about a year ago and got a 'D' in a Gas Course, the first one to do so in that line.*
>
> *I have also been informed that my 'D' was not only the first one for PT in Shilo, but the first in the last eight hundred graduates from the Nanaimo school.*

My training at RMC was beginning to reap big dividends.

As soon as the course finished I left in haste to carry out the secret plan I had made when the course was offered to me by LCol Mitchell. At Vancouver I stopped over and spent an enjoyable evening with grandmother Frost and relatives I had not seen in years. Then on to Saskatoon, where I had grown up during the depression, but had to leave in 1938, much to my sorrow, because father was transferred to Saint John, NB.

I found most of my friends had joined the Forces and were overseas, or on the way. Only one remained a civilian — a conscientious objector. I felt very sad for my friend as, with his ethnic background and the pacifist views of his parents, he really had no choice in the matter. A highly intelligent person, he was forced to spend the war as a farm labourer. One potential benefit of all my pals being away was the availability of girlfriends — theirs and mine. Unfortunately, I could not really take advantage of the situation, as I had formed a new interest in Prince Albert, whither I promptly proceeded, making train connections that were not thought possible in the official timetables.

Returning to Shilo toward the end of August I assumed once more my duties as an instructor on the Advanced Officers Course. With my new distinction in PT, I was also the camp sports and athletic officer, qualifying me to give PT to all officers from the Colonel down to the junior lieutenants. The Colonel excused himself, but directed all other officers to turn out at 0630 hours for half-an-hour of PT every morning before breakfast. I enjoyed this immensely, taking great delight in 'bending' the senior officers. The fact that I would now be on their 'hit list' never occurred to me, or, if it did, I shrugged it off as I hoped I would soon be on my way to join my Regiment overseas.

My hopes were encouraged by the departure of Sam Potts and Willie Mulherin as reinforcement officers for the PPCLI. But when I approached LCol Mitchell on the possibility of my joining them, he reminded me they had waited over a year to get overseas and further reinforcements were not required by the Regiment. He also pointed out that he had gone to some pains to get me on the PT Course and he now expected some dividends — like my whipping his officers into shape (himself excluded). Besides these duties, I would take over from Sam Potts, and teach all the subjects he had instructed, on the Officers' and Senior NCO courses. If I wanted any more tasks to keep me from getting bored, LCol Mitchell would be glad to oblige. In fact, he had a special duty for me that he was certain I would enjoy — drilling the CWACs.

I thanked the good Colonel for going to such lengths to keep me occupied and out of mischief while I waited to go overseas. The drilling of CWACs was not quite in my line, but I was not unduly upset. The saltpetre I had been given at RMC, in such large doses, was now beginning to take effect. It was also proof against a queer Chinese disease that had recently invaded the camp, called 'Laka Nookee'.

The next 4-1/2 months at Camp Shilo were the busiest and probably most rewarding of my career. All the study and training at RMC, Borden, Petawawa, Aldershot and Nanaimo were at last put to use as I instructed officers and senior NCOs on practically every subject in the book — and a few not found in any army manual. I thought nothing of teaching five hours a day and a further two hours in the evening, six days a week; then taking my class on a five-day scheme the following week. The only difficult part was to find time to prepare the lectures and organize the exercises.

In my letters home I told my father what real soldiering was all about (as opposed to the Reserves), trying hard not to sound too patronizing, as he took his reserve training very seriously.

Another interesting thing we have here is what is called the Battle Practice Range. On this we fire live ammunition of all sorts — rifles, TSMG, LMG, anti-tank and mortar — and carry out attacks under fire. Every scheme is first rehearsed with blank ammunition and then with live, so that no chances are taken of running into one's own fire. It's really great sport, just like in actual warfare, with no butts or anything to stop the bullets. They just carry right on into the blue. On the last scheme my section gave covering fire until my assaulting section was only within five or six feet from the 'path of lead' from the covering section — good experience!!

In another letter I gave my father a few pointers on how to conduct classes in my favourite subject — military law:

Among my many subjects I find military law the most interesting. I was rather amused with one young officer who thought he hadn't the time to do all the work I had given him. How surprised he was when I told him that if he had time to sleep and eat he . . . well had time to work. Poor chap, I hope he doesn't starve!!

When my class in military law isn't getting on with its work I tell them to look up KR Can, Section 777 — well, it states that candidates for promotion must obtain 50% in each subject.

The technicalities of military law intrigued me. The main body of law was contained in two volumes known collectively as the Bible, and comprising, naturally, the Old Testament and the New Testament. The Old Testament was the *Manual of Military Law* (Manual) issued by the British Army Council. The New Testament was the *King's Regulations and Orders for the Canadian Militia* (KR&O or KR Can) issued by the Governor General in Council (the Canadian Government).

The Manual, comprising some one thousand pages, was first published in 1884 and had been revised from time to time, the last Manual having been issued in 1929. Included in the Manual was the British Army Act, listing all the military crimes and maximum punishments, from death to confined to barracks.

When war broke out in 1939, the Manual, like most matters connected with National Defence, was 20 years out of date. With millions of new soldiers requiring discipline and only a handful of tattered old copies of the manual available to guide officers in punishing their troops, the British government simply reprinted the 1929 edition. In typical legal jargon, and with a touch of British understatement, the editors of this out of date monster noted on their 1939 reprint that 'Owing to heavy demands for the Manual, it became necessary to reprint it on short notice. The incorporation of the various amendments, which have been made since 1929, would have involved re-paging and re-indexing, which was not possible in the time available.

Translated into ordinary English, what the editors meant was: 'Because of the blasted war, which caught us flatfooted, we haven't the time or money to spend on revising this book. We have more important things to do — like shooting down the German aircraft that are bombing our plant.'

Canada, on the other hand, seems to have had more than its usual amount of foresight in matters of National Defence and published KR&O on April 1st, 1939, just before the war started. It was an excellent compendium of all the rules and regulations pertaining to the Canadian Army — the Militia Act, enlistment, promotion, discipline, duties, training, education, movement of horses and ceremonial drill. The book had, however, one glaring deficiency — Canada did not have the equivalent of the British Army Act setting forth the military crimes and punishments. This was not an oversight; the government had just not got round to passing such an Act. Instead, the government adopted the British Army Act with all its amendments throughout the years, holus-bolus, except where inconsistent with the Canadian Militia Act. Paragraph 69 of the Canadian Militia Act provided as follows:

> 69.   *The Army Act for the time being in force in Great Britain, the King's regulations, and all other laws applicable to His Majesty's troops in Canada and not inconsistent with this Act or the regulations made hereunder, shall have force and effect as if they had been enacted by the Parliament of Canada for the government of the Militia.*

It was a neat way of saving the Canadian Government and its Judge Advocate General the trouble and expense of drawing up our own Army Act. Surprisingly, the system worked, in a rough and ready sort of way, until after the war, when national pride finally goaded the government into producing our own act — The National Defence Act.

It isn't difficult to imagine the 'field day' a lawyer could have applying the British Army Act to Canadian soldiers, 'except where inconsistent with Canadian military laws.' Depending on whether the lawyer was representing the King (the prosecutor) or the accused, he could skillfully nail the offender with the appropriate references to both British and Canadian laws, or he could create confusion among the untrained members of a court martial as to some supposed 'inconsistency' in the British and Canadian laws.

Another loophole in applying the British Army Act to Canadian troops went to the very basis of British justice. This Act, of itself, had no force because it had to be brought into operation annually by another Act of the British Parliament. The idea behind this was to ensure that the constitutional principle of the control of Parliament over the Army was maintained. Thus, if the Army Act were not renewed in any particular year, it had no force, and accordingly thousands of soldiers could, technically, commit misdemeanours without fear of punishment. At least it was a good constitutional argument sometimes raised by a desperate lawyer on behalf of an accused, in an attempt to stay proceedings while the court checked to ensure that the Army Act was still in force.

But in reality these sophisticated legal arguments carried little weight with a Commanding Officer who was trying to keep discipline in his unit. All he wanted to hear was a clear, snappy statement from the witness, abject silence, acquiescence or mumbles from the accused, and a quick reference from the Adjutant to the appropriate section in the Army Act or KR&O. Yet, even in the simplest of cases, the paths of justice sometimes did not run smoothly. Many men, and most of the NCOs, soon became very knowledgeable about the loopholes in the Army Act and KR&O, and gained prominence, or notoriety (depending on your point of view), as 'barrack room lawyers'.

Section 15 of the Army Act — AWL (absent without leave) — was probably the most common offence in the army, yet many offenders avoided punishment on some technicality or other. For example, if the charge sheet read 'absent from quarters from *on or about* 15 Sept 42 to *on or about* 18 Sept 42', this could be thrown out because the exact date, and even hour, in some cases, should have been given.

Again, if the charge sheet failed to show the exact time and place for a parade, from which the soldier was absent, this would invalidate the charge. Further, the evidence had to prove that the accused had notice of the time and place appointed for the parade. If not, the accused went scot-free, but he might find himself caught by a section of KR&O which provided that ignorance of published orders was no excuse.

Another well used section of the Army Act was Section 19 — drunkenness. Here again, the well-read soldier could throw up many roadblocks. Sometimes a zealous NCO would charge a man with drunkenness based on the fact that the accused could not walk a straight line (which line could be as straight or as crooked as the NCO). On other occasions a soldier might be brought up before the Commanding Officer while still under the influence and sentenced. All these sort of cases could be thrown out under the appropriate paragraph of KR&O.

Perhaps the most popular section of the Army Act (popular with Commanding Officers) was the 'last resort', or 'catch all' section — Section 40, conduct, disorder or neglect to the prejudice of good order and military discipline. All sorts of loopholes existed here for the crafty soldier; the Section could only be used if no other section applied; the 'conduct' had to be proven to be to the prejudice of *both* good order *and* of military discipline; the neglect had to be wilful and not just the result of forgetfulness or error of judgment.

The above digression into military law will, I hope, give the reader a feeling for my fascination with the intricacies of this subject. The general principles were easy enough to understand; it was the exceptions that caused the difficulty. Or, as I later learned to express the matter, 'the exceptions ate up the rule'.

The study and teaching of military law was only a small part of my duties at Camp Shilo in the fall of 1942. Every morning I continued to follow the directive of LCol Mitchell and put the officers through the PT Tables I had learned at Nanaimo.

Winter comes early on the prairies. One morning, toward the end of September, I awoke to find snow on the ground and a deputation outside my tent imploring me to postpone the morning PT exercises. I thought of citing paragraph 7 of the Army Act, making a combination of two or more persons resisting any lawful authority a mutiny, which in certain cases was punishable by death.

Common sense, if not common law, however, prevailed and I agreed to the earnest pleas of the deputation, without prejudice and without creating a precedent.

Occasionally, my routine of lectures and schemes was broken by a welcome trip to nearby Brandon and other centres, to referee boxing and wrestling matches. It was nice to be on the outside of the ring looking in for a change.

Another break from my regular training that I enjoyed was an occasional weekend assignment to Winnipeg on boards of officers to examine Reserve NCOs at the Minto Armouries. In a letter home, I could not resist getting in a dig at my father who was still soldiering in the Reserves, as well as my brother, Bob, who was now an NCO in his unit:

> For my little scheme I had a sandtable with a given tactical exercise, and I asked the NCO's, 'You are fired on from some point by LMG. What is your immediate action as Section Commander?' Then you might ask an NCO to give a fire order, after showing him where the fire was coming from, or ask him to send back a field message — some simple question. It can't be too hard for these Reserve chaps. (No hard feelings, please!)

For these services in Winnipeg, beyond the normal call of duty, I received an extra $18 for two days, almost double my standard rate of pay.

The authorities now decided that Canada should have a parachute regiment with a base at Camp Shilo. A jump tower was erected and a call for recruits went out across the land. There were no lack of volunteers. This seemed like a very exciting way to fight the Germans and, incidentally, save countless miles of shoe leather and effort in marching to the battle field.

One member of my class at RMC, Hugh MacDonald, a reinforcement officer for the Patricias at Shilo, was enticed into the paratroops and soon started jumping off towers and out of airplanes. He managed to survive the

73

war intact.

Two other members of my class who were also PPCLI reinforcement officers at Shilo were Bob Huestis and Vaughan Allan. Like me, they were attached to the Instructional Cadre and performed other duties at the Camp until they proceeded overseas. Huestis, barely 19 when he graduated from RMC, had to wait many months before he could join a draft, as the minimum age for overseas service was 20. He eventually joined the Regiment in northern Italy and served with distinction until the end of the war. Vaughan Allan was killed in Italy leading an attack on a house.

As winter approached, our outdoor living became less and less attractive and we wondered whether the new barracks would be completed before the bitter prairie winter set in. There was no way I was going to stand out in the snow trying to shave and perform other ablutions; moreover the teaching game was beginning to pall. I determined to move on and somehow join my Regiment overseas, without any further alarums or excursions.

Accordingly, I paraded before Colonel Mitchell and demanded to be placed on a draft, immediately, for the United Kingdom. He said, "Frost, you are an excellent instructor. Your place is here at the Training Centre and not overseas where they have more officers than they can handle." Looking back I suppose he was right, but that certainly didn't suit my plan of action.

That evening in the Mess, after a few drinks, I joined in a little horseplay with some brother officers and ended up punching a hole clean through the wall of the old mess building. This was not as great a feat as it sounds, as the wall was about to collapse of its own accord. I was promptly paraded before Colonel Mitchell who was absolutely livid that I would cause such wanton damage to his mess. After a proper dressing down in his high pitched voice, he dismissed me "If you want to fight I have just the place for you. You are posted (he may have said 'banished') to the next battle drill course in the wilderness of British Columbia." And he may have added, "May God have mercy on your soul."

While hardly a posting overseas, it was quite an acceptable punishment. I had been trying for months to get on this course as it was said to offer the finest training in Canada for an infantry officer.

On December 18th, 1942, I reported to A31 Canadian Battle Drill Training Centre at Vernon, BC to take the eighth course. Looking over the list of instructors I spotted the name Hertzberg. "Pray God," I murmured, "Not my senior from RMC." A second glance revealed that it was not in fact my senior, but one Lt P H A Hertzberg, the son of the Commandant of RMC, and an expert in explosives. He was not an Ex-Cadet and fortunately had no interest in 'bending' me. The fact that his father was a major general he considered to be more of a handicap than an asset, as he wanted to make his own way in the army. I met him next in Italy, shortly before he was killed in action.

Battle Drill. What was this 'sacred cow' of modern warfare that was upsetting all the old tactical doctrines and many of the high brass? According to the latest manuals, Battle Drill was "The shifting of tactics into high gear through the rapid execution of terse orders, based on drills which are designed to cope with any tactical problem." A fine, concise definition, but it did not tell the whole story.

After the fall of France in the spring of 1940 and the subsequent evacuation at Dunkirk, a few hard-thinking generals, notably Gen Alexander (later, His Excellency Field Marshal Lord Alexander of Tunis, a Governor General of Canada) realized that in many cases our troops had been out-fought and demoralized by the German technique of fighting — the German battle drill. This became apparent to Gen Alexander when he saw groups of men collected in shell holes, willing but ignorant, and psychologically out-done by the German dive bombers and screaming shells.

It has been stated that we are indebted to Gen Alexander for the idea of battle drill. In a preface to his first notes on the subject, written soon after the Dunkirk evacuation, he wrote:

The technique of field craft is not taught by rules of conduct but by principles, because it is commonly supposed that anything more definite than principles tends to destroy initiative. Is this really true? Surely a soldier on the battle field, beset by fear and doubt, is in far more need of a guide to motion than any games player at Madison Square or Maple Leaf Gardens. Better to know instinctively some orthodox line of conduct than to be paralysed by the uncertainty of what to do.

Let us therefore study and draw up lines of conduct — simple guides for the simple soldier, so that we may ensure that our soldiers when faced with problems on the battlefield will have an answer to them.

A great debate ensued as to whether it was possible to teach tactics as a drill. "It would kill initiative. Impossible to lay down anything definite about tactics," said the diehards. "The superior power of the British soldier to be able to think and act for himself was more than a match for German automation."

Advocates of the new drill said this was all nonsense. "The man who has got initiative will use it whatever you teach him; if he hasn't got initiative, he will dither and meander unless you teach him exactly what to do and when to do it. Practical experience has shown that Battle Drill encourages initiative."

The new school then set about creating a drill for every movement and operation of war, in ideal conditions. Once a soldier had learned these basic drills he was taught a number of variations to adapt them to the various circumstances he would meet on an actual battle field. If he had imagination he would quickly work out a suitable plan. More often than not, the drills he had been taught would fit. If he had no imagination he would just carry out the drill woodenly — and he still wouldn't do too badly.

Vernon was an ideal location to conduct this rugged new training. An entire ranch of 11,000 acres was made into a manoeuvre area by an Order in Council of the Canadian Government. A log village was then constructed for village fighting, and an obstacle course consisting largely of natural obstacles was laid out. A bayonet assault course was built and a trench was blasted from solid rock on the side of a hill, where sections experienced overhead fire from all platoon weapons. A dam was built on Coldstream Creek to provide for river crossing drills. Finally, a Pill Box with necessary wire and slit trenches was constructed. The background of the hills made possible the firing of all platoon weapons at selected spots.

The Commandant of the school, LCol J F Scott, ED, a Queen's Counsel from Calgary, had recently returned from overseas. Despite his kind, almost fatherly mien, he firmly believed in battle drill and that it should be made as tough and as brutal as possible. In an interview given by LCol Scott to A W O'Brien and reported in the *Montreal Standard* of August 22nd, 1942, the Commandant gave a frank answer to the critics of battle drill:

> *There can be no glamorizing to the awful business of war. Killing is brutal and harsh on the soul, and war can never be a refining influence for the future. But the fact remains that until our men are taught the battle urge — to kill joyfully — they are no match for the brutality of the Nazi or the savagery of the Jap. The Canadian soldier deserves at least an equal break in pitched battle and he won't get it without the killing mentality our enemies have used with such success to date. What all this will do to them for peace days to follow I don't know, but Battle Drill will at least fit them to live through the interim of hell before peace does come.*

My three-week course began on December 19th and it was just as rigorous and punishing as LCol Mitchell of Shilo had predicted and as LCol Scott could make it. Once again, my athletic training at RMC and my PT course at Nanaimo helped me through the roughest spots. A further article in the *Montreal Standard* of September 5th, 1942, describes some of the special features on the course:

> *Considerable comment was raised by the exclusive feature published by this newspaper in a recent issue. It showed just what a staff writer saw during his recent visit to Battle School. The story was that of men crawling elbow deep in stale animal*

intestines, getting doused with pig's blood, running 12 miles a day carrying a 40 pound pack, missing meals during all-day tests, working with live ammunition in an atmosphere of constantly bursting thunderflashes, whining Bren bullets and snarling instructors.

Another innovative feature dreamt up by the fiendish instructors was to put us in slit trenches while Bren carriers roared over our heads firing live ammunition. Then we were made to jump 14 feet into a smoke-filled pit whose only exit was a narrow tunnel. The catch was that you couldn't squeeze through the tunnel unless you took off your pack and dragged it behind you. I got well and truly stuck, eventually was hauled out, gasping for air, and finished the course on one lung.

Mercifully, I had short breaks at Christmas and New Year, giving me a chance to recover somewhat from smoke inhalation in the bear pit. Following my usual custom, in my letters home, I tried to paint an 'uphole' picture of my activities on the course:

December 26, 1942
I am spending Christmas in the hotel in Vernon along with several other chums, among whom are two ex-cadets of my class — Densmore and Cockburn.
I was invited out for Christmas Dinner to a lovely home and really had lots to eat. Other than that I have been sleeping and enjoying the comforts of the hotel. As you know, out at camp we are under canvas with oil lamps, outdoor plumbing, etc. Actually I don't mind it, but boy it was nice to have a bath here, Xmas eve.

I also spent New Year at the local hotel, cleaning up and writing letters:

January 2, 1943
I'm doing quite OK due again to valuable experience of RMC. Instructors' 'hazing' just runs off my back. As a matter of fact I could show many of them how to shout. We have been having a great deal of snow. About eight inches I believe. For New Year amusement there was a dance in the Vernon Armouries. Lots of fun. LCol Cotton was there and I had quite a nice chat with him. At last I was able to find out that he remembers Dad well as he used to play bridge with him in Saskatoon. I guess Cotton was a lieutenant then. Now he is Lieutentant Colonel and a good one. He took this battle drill course a few months ago.

By January 10th I knew I had the course licked and I could now tell my family some of the minor irritations I had suffered:

Actually the course has not been as tough as I had expected. About the only bad feature was the constant wetness and the occasional chilly weather. The heavy fall of snow made it difficult to run but was better than mud. We only ran into mud 'up to our ears' on the obstacle course which we went through last Thursday. What a field day! Out of the whole school, I was the first man to go through — in other words the 'trail breaker'. The idea is to get your section through all together. I did, and made quite good time. I'll tell you about it 'à la maison'.

Yesterday, Saturday, I carried the anti-tank rifle (wt 40 lbs) about a mile and a half — at the double. Perhaps Dad will appreciate that! When we arrived at our destination, I was given the job of Pl comd and had to put in an attack against a pill box. It is one of the most difficult tasks there is.

Really I'm having the time of my life, and am looking forward to a great discussion with Dad when I get home. By the way, I am buying a battle drill book for Dad, as I imagine he wants to know some of the very latest changes in the Drill.

It will be noted that once again I could not help giving my father thinly veiled hints that our roles had vastly changed. Now I was the teacher.

I was looking forward to the end of the course, not only because it meant the cessation of hostilities with our instructors, but also I was due for annual leave; and I felt I had earned it after 2-1/2 years of continuous study and training. But it was not in the cards. On the last day of the course I was told I had passed out at the top of my platoon with a Q1 standing and I was asked by the Commandant to stay on as an instructor. When a lieutenant colonel makes a request it is as good as an order. I promptly accepted but reminded LCol Scott I was a reinforcement officer for the PPCLI and I would not want my chances of going overseas to be prejudiced by staying on as an instructor. He agreed.

That evening in the Mess, by the sheerest stroke of good luck, I met one of the most distinguished officers of the PPCLI, Brig W G Colquhoun, CBE, MC, who had commanded the PPCLI at the start of the war and was then commanding one of the brigades in the 6th Canadian Division on the west coast. An impressive man, with a fine military bearing, he must have been at least 6 ft 6 in tall — so naturally he was known as 'Shortie'. He was delighted that one of his Patricia officers had done well on the course. I told him I had agreed to stay on as an instructor, but was afraid it might affect my chances of joining PPCLI. I pleaded with him to get me on the first draft overseas. He said he would see what he could do.

The course finished on January 13, 1943, and I became an instructor on the Ninth Course which commenced on January 18th. I joined Lt Hertzberg, as well as a classmate, Lt G H Sellar, who went on to a distinguished career in the Regular Army after the war and attained the rank of brigadier. Another classmate who instructed on the course was Lt E E Cockburn. He was later killed in action.

I spent an enjoyable three weeks making other poor devils go through the battle drill and obstacles that I had endured, yelling my lungs out with such slogans as 'down, crawl, observe, fire'; 'kill the enemy'; 'sweat saves blood'; 'brains saves blood and sweat'. There was a battle drill for every movement and operation of war: field craft, camouflage, observation, appreciation, attack, defence, village clearing, attack on a pill box, patrols, river crossing, wood clearing.

The last three drills — patrols, river crossing and wood clearing — turned out to be of immense value in my forthcoming service in the Regiment: as a Scout and Sniper Officer in southern Italy; crossing the endless rivers in northern Italy; in the final operation of the war in Holland when the Regiment crossed the Ijssel River.

Toward the end of the course I was called to the Orderly Room for an important message. True to his word, Brig Colquhoun had got me on the next draft for overseas. I left for Shilo on February 5th.

Following my 'personal battle drill' that I had developed for making the most out of my trips out west, I squeezed in stop-overs at Saskatoon and Prince Albert before reporting to LCol Mitchell at Camp Shilo. He congratulated me on my efforts at Vernon and confirmed I would be leaving for overseas in three weeks. In the meantime, he would put me on a 'quickee course' to learn how to operate every vehicle in the Army — carriers, jeeps, 15 cwt trucks, 3 ton lorries, gin palaces (command vehicles) and motorcycles. Word had come back from England that officers were having an inordinate number of accidents involving vehicles because they had not learned how to drive properly. For the next week I had great fun barrelling down the straight frozen prairie roads in all manner of vehicles; but it seemed to me that practice in heavy traffic, in city streets, on the *left*-hand side of the road, would have been more to the point, or at least more exciting.

I spent my final week at Shilo buying kit and stacking up on luxury items I would need for bartering overseas — silk stockings, cigarettes, chocolate bars. Most of my civies, summer uniform and kit not required overseas were dispatched home including, fortunately, all my précis, pamphlets and materials which have been so helpful in writing this book. There was no chance for any leave to say goodbye to my parents in Toronto. Security precautions would not even allow me to write or phone to say I was leaving for overseas.

We left Shilo on March 7th during a very cold and stormy night. The train travelled through northern Ontario and then, to my surprise, cut down into the United States. I had assumed that we would sail from Halifax and I had formed some tentative plans to meet my family there secretly.

In the vicinity of Taunton, Massachusetts, the train suddenly lurched to a stop. The officers jumped out on the tracks to make an 'appreciation' of the situation. Rumours flew around that the engine had been sabotaged by some enemy agent to delay the sailing of our convoy. This seemed pretty silly — a convoy of perhaps a dozen ships and protective destroyers would hardly care about a draft of 300 men from Shilo, even if most of us were Patricias. The fact remained, however, that, from whatever cause, the engine had indeed broken down and despite the urgings and advice of the officers, the beast refused to move. After further delays the troops were detrained and taken to Camp Myles Standish near Taunton, Mass.

We subsequently learned that we had missed the pleasure of a cruise in northern waters on the *Queen Elizabeth*, sailing from New York.

Camp Myles Standish was a huge camp for American GIs with all the amenities, including a well stocked PX, sports facilities, theatres and enormous meals. But I was still disturbed I had not had a proper chance to say goodbye to my father and mother and I now took a calculated risk with security. We were absolutely forbidden to write or telephone anyone about our train mishap or the fact that we were in Taunton. Nevertheless, I sent a postcard to my parents with a very harmless message, and of course did not give my address or make any reference to the fact that I was a Canadian soldier, or even their son. I allowed a couple of days for the postcard to reach home and then called from a telephone outside camp. I had to be very careful what I said, but father, being an old soldier, understood exactly what I was trying to do.

"Syd here," I said, "Has Gertrude [my mother] received my postcard?"

"Oh yes, it is a very interesting card."

"Please tell her I'd like to meet her in the local Inn, if she can make it."

"Would Friday be OK?"

"Sure. I'll phone her shortly after she arrives."

Father had, of course, noticed that my card was postmarked Taunton. He immediately made arrangements through his banking connections in New York for mother to travel to Taunton. I phoned the 'local Inn' (there was only one Inn) on Friday, two days after my telephone call to father, and to my great joy found she had just registered. It was a little tricky to get a pass out of camp and keep the whole matter quiet, but fortunately, the draft conducting officer was Maj Henry E Ford, an old military friend of my father from Saskatoon days. When I quietly put him in the picture he gave me every consideration.

Mother and I spent a very happy time together for a couple of days. She brought me up to date on the news of the family while I described my experiences since leaving RMC and my hopes and plans for the future. Mother had not been at all well and this visit, I am sure, gave her quite a lift. Many times after the war she told me that our meeting did much to ease the strain of the next two years while I was overseas.

I thought my little indiscretion with security regulations had been justified. Indeed, it turned out to be a minor peccadillo compared to the wholesale breaches of security which followed shortly after mother left Taunton. First, all ranks were allowed leave to visit Boston and other centres — which we promptly did. We soon returned, much the worse for wear, after encountering an American secret weapon called bourbon. Then the local dignitaries insisted that these wild Canadian soldiers put on a parade for the good citizens of Taunton. Our Commanding Officer was glad to oblige and had one of our officers, Lt D A Smith, parade in kilts to further confound the populace. Whether these actions also confused the enemy I do not know; but the whole business certainly dumbfounded me after going to so much trouble to circumvent security regulations.

The crowning touch to the whole farce occurred on March 18th, when I opened the local newspaper, the *Taunton Daily Gazette*, and saw a photograph on the front page of Maj Ford, Lt Smith, me and 297 well seasoned Canadian troops marching down the main street of Taunton. An accompanying article brazenly gave the world, including the Hun, full particulars of our draft, which hitherto had been clothed in such secrecy. The following is an excerpt from the article:

CANADIAN TROOPS HONOR AMERICAN
SOLDIER DEAD

A contingent of six hundred Canadian and American troops marched five miles in the rain to historic Taunton Green Wednesday afternoon as Maj Henry E Ford, Commanding officer of the Canadian unit, decorated the Soldiers' and Sailors' monument in tribute to American dead of all wars.

The three hundred well-trained and seasoned Canadian soldiers, accompanied by 300 American troops, stood at attention on the north side of Taunton Green while a wreath, containing green carnations and a red, white and blue ribbon bearing the inscription 'Canada, CA(A)SF', was placed at the foot of the monument by Lt D A Smith, aide to Maj Ford.

Drums rolled and the American Flag snapped and cracked in the breeze high above the historic plot as Lt Smith, attired in his colorful regimental kilt, stepped forward to place the wreath at the foot of the monument.

The gesture was witnessed by hundreds of men and women, augmented by students from Taunton high school. It was preceded by a short prayer, offered by Maj Guy H Madara,

> *United States Army Chaplain, and was followed by the sounding
> of 'Taps' and playing of* The Star Spangled Banner *and* God
> Save the King *by an army band.*[3]

Apparently the censors had lost all interest in our draft of 300 seasoned soldiers bound for England's shores. We hoped the Germans felt likewise. At this stage, I, too, had lost my concern about security, and in a mood of 'damn the torpedoes', fired off a copy of the *Taunton Daily Gazette* to mother.

On March 21st we left Camp Myles Standish, arrived in New York and boarded the *Empress of Scotland*, formerly the *Empress of Japan* until the treachery of Pearl Harbour. Five thousand officers and troops were crammed into every available space; meals were served in shifts; washing and sanitary facilities became overcrowded — soon they could not keep up with the demand and many broke down or overflowed. In the lower decks the toilets were Japanese-style without seats. You simply inserted your feet in slots, squatted, and hoped your aim was on target. The smell of the toilets, mixed with the smell of food, permeated the whole ship and was quite indescribable.

Ocean voyages on the Atlantic in March are usually rough, and this trip was no exception. Everyone was sick, but still the officers were obliged to turn out and take submarine watch on a poop-deck overhanging the stern of the ship. Whether anyone ever spotted a submarine I very much doubt, as it was a struggle just to grasp the rail and keep from being hurled into the boiling sea. We hardly needed to be reminded before every shift that the ship did not stop for 'man overboard'. I found a new respect for my naval friends and thanked God I had chosen the infantry where I could fight my battles on firm ground — the firmer the better. As one very ill soldier expressed the matter: "Take me back to terra firma — the more firma, the less terra."

The rough weather was actually a blessing in disguise. Unknown to us at the time, the U-Boats under Grand Admiral Doenitz had reached the peak of their effectiveness. He now had 400 submarines to launch into the shipping lanes of the world in a last-ditch effort to cut Britain's lifelines and end the war.

That he failed to intercept the *Empress of Scotland* was due to a number of factors, not least of which were the heavy seas that kept the U-Boats and their periscopes well under the surface. Furthermore, the *Empress* was a fast ship and could outrun any German submarines; she therefore ran the Atlantic gauntlet on her own, without a destroyer escort. Any U-Boat lurking in our path was outwitted by the ship changing its course every few minutes. For a while these abrupt turns seemed quite exciting and kept us guessing when the next one would come. But soon they only added to our miseries caused by the Atlantic gales.

We swung around northern Ireland in bitterly cold weather and finally arrived at Liverpool on March 31st. The voyage had taken only nine days despite the rough seas and our zigzag course through the submarine-infested waters.

The other officers on the PPCLI draft were Bud Auger, Cecil Shea and Vaughan Allan. Auger seemed very old — I suppose he was 29 or 30 — and acted as Godfather to Allan and myself, who were only 20. Shea was the same vintage as Auger. He had served as an Other Rank in the permanent army before the war; had already been to England with the Regiment; had then returned to take his commission at Shilo where he was a student in one of my courses. He was subsequently killed in Italy in the Hitler Line. Vaughan Allan, as already noted, was also killed in Italy. Bud Auger died before the war's end.

One of the few bright spots of the voyage was the presence of a draft of 'girl soldiers' — CWACs including one Charmian Sansom, the daughter of LGen Sansom, at that time the commander of the Canadian Corps. She suffered the rigours of the passage along with the rest of the troops. I couldn't understand why she hadn't obtained a commission in Canada so she could enjoy some of the perks of being an officer on board ship. But she wanted to prove a point and gamely went overseas as a private.

Charmian did in fact prove her point and later gained her commission overseas. I had the pleasure of escorting her from time to time during my short visits to London.

Chapter IV

ENGLAND - SCOTLAND
The Regiment
April 1 to June 26, 1943

The Princess Pat's Battalion
They sailed across the Herring Pond
They sailed across the Channel too
And landed there with the Ric-a-dam-doo, dam-doo, dam-doo

What a relief when the ship finally docked at Liverpool and the heaving and rolling ceased! After the snows of Shilo and the bitterly cold voyage we could scarcely believe the mild English climate at this time of year. 'Oh, to be in England now that spring is here'. We were in England, spring was here and it was great to be alive.

Everything seemed in miniature: the fields were small; the houses were small; the trains were small; the cars were small; even the people *looked* small, but only in the physical sense — we soon found they were the toughest, most friendly, generous people on earth.

We boarded one of these funny little trains, whose old-fashioned coaches reminded us of something out of Dickens, and arrived at Aldershot at midnight. Our final impression of Day One in England was the way the people coped so well with the fog and blackout. While we stumbled about, they moved around with the greatest ease and confidence, like so many ghosts.

We were posted to 1 CIRU (Canadian Infantry Reinforcement Unit) and assigned quarters in Barrosa Barracks, built well before the turn of the century and named after a battle in the Peninsular War. The only heating was supplied by huge fireplaces that consumed enormous quantities of wood and coal. When supplies ran out the prior occupants had tossed in any old sticks of furniture lying about, and by the time my draft arrived there was scarcely a piece of furniture in the place. We simply undid our bedrolls and slept on the floor. The euphoria of the English springtime quickly vanished as we faced the hardships endured by military and civilians alike.

Before leaving Shilo I had filled a trunk, kit bag and suitcase with all sorts of canned food, cigarettes, chocolate bars and other such goodies I knew were in short supply in England. Intelligence of this secret cache soon spread throughout the barracks. The temptation proving too much for some needy soldiers, in very short order my supply pretty well vanished. About all that was left was a can of Spam so I invited a fellow officer up to my room to enjoy this remnant. He brought along a bottle of whiskey, and between us we finished off both items with a predictable result. I was so desperately sick that to this day I cannot look a can of Spam in the face. (For some strange reason I haven't the same trouble with a bottle of whiskey!)

After a week of Ts OET (Tests of Elementary Training) during the daytime and forays into the local pubs at night, our draft (Auger, Shea, Allan and me) was posted to the PPCLI as Special Increment Officers, to give us practical training in handling a platoon in the field. On April 10th I joined 17 Platoon, No 3 Company under Capt Ronnie Waterman, billeted at Eastbourne, on the south coast near Brighton.

Capt Waterman, a strict disciplinarian of the old school, had been a permanent force NCO and was known as 'Ronnie the Rat'. I am sure he did not mind this at all, although rumour had it he preferred 'Ronald the Rodent' on formal occasions. He had previously instructed at Camp Shilo where he had left a reputation as a very tough customer, particularly on junior officers. Everyone was scared of him, including some of the senior officers, not only because of his abrupt and intimidating manner but because he knew his stuff and was a highly professional soldier.* My period under his command was mercifully short and I managed to survive without any battle scars.

I was home at last — but what a long and frustrating journey it had been. Starting at RMC in 1940, my progress had taken me to Borden, Petawawa, Connaught and Aldershot, Nova Scotia, in 1941; to Camp Shilo with a side trip to Nanaimo and back again to Shilo in 1942; then to Vernon, British Columbia, in early 1943. In the wilderness of British Columbia the call finally came to join my Regiment, some 7,000 miles away. My journey had continued from Vernon to Shilo, to Taunton, to New York; then across the ocean to Liverpool; a brief stint at Aldershot and finally, home.

LCol Bob Lindsay, the Commanding Officer, briefly welcomed me to the Regiment and wished me luck. I have to confess I was more than a little

---

* He later rose to command the West Nova Scotia Regiment in Italy where he won the DSO.

let down with my reception into the Regiment after all my effort and troubles to get there, but then I cannot readily say what sort of greeting I expected - certainly not a brass band and red carpet. Quickly I realized I was only a small cog in a very active Regiment, just off a gruelling exercise. Everyone was busy with his own duties and had no time to nurse a newly joined subaltern, particularly one just arrived from Canada. I would have to stand on my own two legs and prove myself, regardless of my prior training and qualifications.

Most of the officers and men had been soldiering in England since 1940 and were a highly skilled team. All the young NCOs and men had been brought up during the Depression; many had been unemployed. When the call went out for recruits in September 1939, they were the first to join. They could take care of themselves in any situation and were tremendous fighters in action.

The men in my platoon were a tough bunch. They knew all the tricks of the professional soldier and were not at all impressed with my two pips and neatly pressed service dress. Luckily, my platoon sergeant understood my problem and came to my rescue with helpful hints on how to deal with this bunch of desperados. He told me, quite frankly, that the men were over-trained and would not brook any nonsense from a young officer just out of the Officer Training School; they would take their time to assess me and until they were satisfied I knew what I was doing, I would have a pretty rough time. He suggested I avoid talking about how great things were in Canada, and the tremendous war effort the folks were making back home. On the subject of discipline, I was to interpret very liberally, and in the men's favour, any regulations and rules restraining their extra-regimental activites, particularly during the evening hours. This was all very good advice, but obviously not what I had been taught and practised since RMC.

Once again my physical condition partly made up for my other deficiencies. I was confident I could out-march, out-run and if necessary out-fight any man in the platoon. Looking back, I'm glad I didn't have to prove myself immediately, in combat, with them or against an enemy. I subsequently learned that some of the men had 'records' of which they were very proud and could dispatch friend or foe in ways that were not laid down in any army manual.

My platoon sergeant was Sgt R Carter, my batman Pte D Anderson and my three section commanders (No 7 Section) Lance Sgt F Stevens, (No 8 Section) Cpl W S Sansom and (No 9 Section) Cpl L J Hamilton. The four NCOs had joined the Regiment in 1939; they and my batman would all see action in Sicily and Italy.*

---

* Sgt Carter was killed by shellfire on October 17th, 1943; Lance Sgt Stevens became

My immediate problem as a green young lieutenant, was how to take command of such fine, seasoned soldiers. I took Sgt Carter's advice and kept a very low profile. At first I let the men think that he was pretty well running the show and gave most of my orders through him.

My first experience with the men was a long march, in full marching order, to Seaford, through hilly country and in the pouring rain. As I had hoped, the marching was no problem. I walked up and down the line giving encouragement to my troops and tried to make them understand I was concerned with their welfare.

My relationship with the other officers was also difficult at first. No one knew me personally and I knew them only by reputation: names such as Majors Cammie Ware and Slug Clark; Captains Rowan Coleman and Bucko Watson. I saw little of Capt Waterman as he was usually at Brigade Headquarters telling them how to run the brigade. These officers, and others of course, formed the backbone of the Regiment and are mentioned again and again in the Regimental History.

I had then, and continued to have, a special affection for Maj 'Pokey Joe' Paquet. He loved to talk but his mother tongue was French and he never really understood the idiomatic English language. This led him to utter quite remarkable statements which, over the years, came to be known as 'Pokey Joeisms'. Some of them he actually said, but a great number are apocryphal.

> *How did you cut your finger? Burn it?*
> *Get some boots for them shoelace.*
> *You think I know fuck nothing. Well I know fuck all.*
> *Knife on the gun put (for fix bayonets)*

My first chance to meet some of the junior officers was during a TEWT (Tactical Exercise Without Troops), a new experience which I found interesting and stimulating although I could see it was very old stuff to them.

Sometimes I led my platoon on beach patrols. This could be a risky matter as there was barbed wire everywhere, some of it booby trapped, and the area was liberally sprinkled with mines which in theory had been recorded on some master plot. I placed my entire faith in the hands of my platoon

---

a CQMS and was one of the first to die in Sicily on July 12th, 1943; Cpl Sansom became a sergeant, was twice wounded in northern Italy, the second time so seriously that he never rejoined the Regiment; Pte Anderson gained two stripes before he, too, was wounded twice, first in the Hitler Line in May, 1944, and again, seriously, in the Gothic Line in September 1944, when he was SOS the Regiment, never to return. Only Cpl Hamilton escaped death or injury and continued to serve the Regiment until the end of the war.

sergeant who knew all the routes by heart and had no use for the recorded information.

Among the various exercises the Regiment carried out was an assault river crossing, at Plashett Wood, north of Seaford, complete with assault boats and river crossing equipment. I was quite excited about this exercise, my first as a platoon commander with the Regiment, and wanted to put on a really good show. Everything was going fine and I felt completely in control until that inevitable phenomenon of war descended — 'the fog of battle'. I had difficulty finding the FUP (forming up place), was late for the start line and overloaded an assault boat, which promptly swamped. It was a snafu. I fully expected to receive rockets from everyone up to the brigade commander. To my surprise nothing whatsoever happened; apparently the confusion wasn't limited to my platoon.

I was impressed with the calm and professional way in which everybody accepted the mistakes of officers and men alike. Indeed these shortcomings seemed to make the umpires very happy and were called 'lessons', presumably on how not to win the war, but what was more important to me was how my platoon sergeant and men assessed my conduct during the exercise. Again there was nothing but silence, except from Sgt Carter who indicated my performance was about par for the course.

I would like to think that the 'lessons' I learned were of great assistance to me in the forthcoming river crossings in northern Italy but I cannot honestly say they were, although I did eventually learn to cope with 'the fog of battle' — that great leveller of generals and privates.

With hardly time to dry our clothes and get re-organized we were off again on a field firing exercise. This time I did much better. My platoon was mainly involved in firing various weapons which I had previously fired and even instructed on. At last I could see a small glimmer in the eyes of my men that I might succeed as a platoon commander — but not quite yet.

The exercise was not without its mishaps, however, as my classmate Vaughan Allan and two of his men were seriously wounded by a 3 inch mortar bomb.

It was now time for a further re-organization of the infantry battalions. The authorities had been playing around with an organization of three companies numbered 1, 2 and 3 instead of the usual four companies lettered A, B, C and D. Apparently the experiment did not work as we now reverted to four companies, with much disorganization, repainting of signs and cross-posting of personnel. I was happily transferred to C Company, under Capt Rowan Coleman, and we moved to Denton where the company was quartered in some very filthy barracks on top of a wind-swept hill. The situation was so bad we had to mess with another company until the kitchen and adjoining quarters were cleaned up. My job was to go through the entire company area and note down all the barrack damages and deficiencies in the huts and quarters. After working several hours, I presented an interim report to Capt Coleman: "I'm sorry, Sir, the list is by no means complete. It will take the rest of the evening to finish it off."

Capt Coleman gave me a friendly wink, "If that's the case I think we should complete it in the pub down the street."

I was beginning to feel more at home and even believed I was well on the way to being accepted by the Regimental family. It was therefore a great disappointment when I received orders that all Special Increment Officers were to return to the reinforcement unit and all experienced officers were to report back to the Regiment. We were told that the Regiment was moving north to take part in some very important exercises (which we junior officers were obviously not fit to undertake). We could not argue, even though it meant returning to a very monotonous existence at the reinforcement unit. The truth of the matter was, however, that 1st Canadian Division was being brought together for a landing on Sicily, scheduled for July 10th. We had no hint of this whatsoever.

On April 30th, Auger, Shea and I returned to 1 CIRU at Aldershot; Vaughan Allan was still in hospital recovering from his mortar wounds. Our future careers looked very bleak indeed. We had come so far only to be banished to the back waters of a reinforcement unit where paper work took precedence over training. We decided to make the best of it and for the next little while we partied it up in London, as if this was our last spree — sadly for many of us it was.

My favourite watering hole was the Park Lane Hotel, a happy hunting ground for Canadian officers. On one occasion I really splurged and took a room at the Hotel Mayfair where the bill came to £5. It was definitely not worth it. Five pounds sterling was the equivalent of about $25.00 Canadian, and represented five days' pay for a full lieutenant. Translated into today's values (a lieutenant now earns about $70.00 a day), $350 for one night is pretty extravagant, even for a general.

To a young, impressionable soldier, London was an exciting place in wartime. The trains, the underground, the hotels, the streets were crowded with sailors, soldiers and airmen wearing the uniforms, so it seemed, of every nation on earth, except the Axis Powers and their satellites. Even they could probably have passed unnoticed in the throng, if they behaved themselves.

During the day, business seemed to go on as usual, as though a truce had been declared: London Bobbies calmly directed hordes of traffic; double decker buses teetered along the Strand; strange little hacks hustled about for business; bank clerks presented their drafts; barristers in wigs and silk gowns argued their cases before the Lord Chancellor; doormen in ornate uniforms welcomed guests to the many posh hotels; and teatime was religiously observed.

At night the war occasionally broke out again in the skies overhead as the Luftwaffe tried to penetrate London's defences and were firmly repulsed by anti-aircraft fire, night fighters, radar and searchlights. Reichsmarschall Goering's vaunted airmen had been severely punished in the great air battles of 1940 and 1941; their attacks were half-hearted and caused little damage.

I was still not accustomed to the total blackout which, combined with the London fog, somewhat hindered my evening progress. Nevertheless, my system soon acquired a kind of radar system that guided me to my objectives without harm. I have never heard of anyone being killed due solely to the blackout, but all sorts of minor mishaps and interesting liaisons must have occurred. One such occasion was the night I joined the Cocoanut Grove Club.

Groping along the street trying to find my hotel or any port in a storm, I bumped into a bulky form which later turned out to be a naval captain, also somewhat at sea. I apologized, but he seemed delighted to have met another ship adrift and offered to introduce me to his club, the Cocoanut Grove in Regent Street. This was one of London's well known and expensive bottle clubs, where food and drink were available at all hours, or until the money ran out or the place was bombed. (Other than these bottle clubs, everything closed up tight at 10:00 pm every night.) A few very charming hostesses were always in evidence, but were strictly for intelligent conversation over a bottle or two of the best champagne. 'Drink up, but please don't handle the merchandise.'

I became a full-fledged member of the club and made liberal use of its amenities whenever I came to London. Among my papers is a legal document I was required to sign to comply with, or really to circumvent, the laws enforcing the curfew and prohibiting the sale of liquor in a public place after 10:00 pm:

> *We the undersigned hereby declare that we have been invited to the Private Party given at the Cocoanut Grove on May 26, 1944, and that we have contributed ..... pounds each towards the costs of the party. We hereby undertake that we will not attempt to purchase any intoxicating liquor on the Company's premises, save that we may take delivery of liquor ordered from wine merchants.*
> *Lt C S Frost*
> *Miss Sansom*

My naval friend also introduced me to the English £5 note which he produced in payment of another bottle of champagne (the equivalent of $25.00 in 1943). It was about the size of a business letter, exquisitely printed on the finest white paper. I thought it was a phony but it turned out to be legal tender as the Maitre D' happily accepted it, but politely asked my friend to endorse the bill with his signature and home address, ensuring that he personally guaranteed payment. I later heard that the Germans forged these bills and eventually they were withdrawn from circulation.

Meanwhile, things were at last beginning to happen in the reinforcement unit. I was transferred from 1 CIRU to a depot with a more impressive name — 4 Battalion, 1 CBRD (Canadian Base Reinforcement Depot). It was the same weasel with a different colour. We were given endless inspections and tests and the officers' kit was cut down to the basic essentials known as G1098. I packed my service dress, civilian clothes and all non-military equipment and sent off the lot to Pickford's Depository in Aldershot, wondering if I would ever see them again. Obviously something pretty big was in the air but still we had no idea where or when we were going.

It seemed only prudent to have one or two last bashes in London even though we were at this time supposed to be confined to barracks. Our company commander at the reinforcement unit was a dithery type who, for the sake of anonymity, shall bear the name Capt Snafu. His way of doing things, or rather, undoing things, suited this cognomen very well — with the result that there were endless snafus with training and paper work. We junior officers were quick to take advantage of the confusion in the Orderly Room and helped ourselves to 'French leave' (AWL) whenever we felt like it, knowing our buddies in camp would cover up for us.

During one memorable AWL party I bumped into Capt Snafu in London. In his rather peculiar way he inquired, "Mr Frost, what are you doing here?" I could only offer a feeble, "The same as you are, Sir." My budding legal talent acquired from those courses in Camp Shilo had shifted the onus to the other side. It was a Mexican stand-off. Neither of us should have been in London and he knew it. Once again, I had escaped the wrath of higher authority.

Our London leaves were not always pleasure bent. We took advantage of them to get to know the history of London and its environs. I attended a service in Westminster Abbey and toured the Tower of London. Our itinerary always included Grosvenor House, where Vincent Massey presided with various matrons and hosted tea dances and other such proper affairs. At one of these soirées I met my CWAC friend from the *Empress of Scotland,* Charmian Sansom, who was still soldiering as a private. The next time we met she had gained her commission and had become a very popular announcer on the Allied Expeditionary Forces Radio Program.

Orders were now received to pack up and proceed to Scotland. We left camp near Aldershot at 1530 hours on May 30th and travelled by lorry to Woking; from there by train to London and Barrhead, Scotland, arriving 0630 hours, May 31st. We were quartered in excellent barracks: a former calico printing mill, recently occupied by the Royal Army Service Corps who were known for always having the finest accommodation.

Excitement mounted as we received tropical kit, cut down our belongings to the bare essentials and sent away, to heaven knows where, our bedroll and other gear in kit bags bearing strange numbers such as 'Herrick II - Casket EE5/68/B-189/E1'. The numbers meant nothing but the word 'casket' gave me something to think about.*

Still no solid evidence was forthcoming as to our ultimate destination. We all knew we were first-line reinforcements for some large formation, probably a division. By observing the various cap badges of the officers it was not difficult to conclude we were reinforcements for 1st Division, which obviously must be going into action. The question was where? The issue of tropical kit narrowed the area of operations to a warmer climate. But the cynics were willing to bet it was all a gigantic cover plan to disguise our real objective — Northwest Europe, possibly Norway.

Other clairvoyants wagered on our landing on some Mediterranean shore such as Greece, Sardinia, Corsica or even Albania. I cannot remember anyone who put his money on the target — Sicily — although many would later claim they had. Still others, myself included, took the more pragmatic view that no matter where we were going, we had been granted another last chance to live it up and we had better take advantage of it. Incredible as it may seem, for the next three weeks we had no responsibilities or duties of any kind except muster parades, kit inspections and orderly officer. Training was a joke, consisting mainly of route marching up the hill to the nearest pub and rolling home again. I remembered my old college motto — 'For God's sake don't lose your sense of humour!'

Barrhead, a mere eight miles from Glasgow, was close enough for an evening pass if we couldn't wrangle a pass for the entire day. I was particularly keen to visit Edinburgh where my father had been stationed as a private soldier with the Royal Newfoundlanders in the First War. This was just the sort of project I knew would appeal to Capt Snafu. I obtained a pass and, accompanied by my pal Bud Auger, spent a weekend touring Edinburgh Castle and nearby points of interest.

Arriving at the castle, we crossed the Esplanade, passed over the moat and through the gate where the sentry threw up a smart butt salute, which I casually acknowledged. I could imagine my father 28 years earlier, saluting some other cheeky young officer of his Regiment in the Other War. From my many talks with father I knew quite a bit about the castle and tried to impress Auger with my knowledge of history. I pointed to a small plot of land surrounded by a fence, and said that long ago the King of England had declared that this plot was a part of Nova Scotia to enable the Baronets of Nova Scotia to take title to their new estates. Before the King could grant

---

* My bedroll and other gear actually did turn up some three years later! They were delivered to my home in Saint John in September 1946, all in good order and containing some of the diaries and materials used in this book.

the estates, the Baronets actually had to stand on Nova Scotia soil. Naturally, neither the King nor the Baronets were inclined to travel to the New World so they devised a scheme whereby the Baronets got legal title without having to leave England's shores. Nova Scotia, or at least a part thereof, came to them.

We spent the afternoon cruising about the castle. We inspected the six gun battery of ancient artillery pieces and the famous 'Mons Meg', a huge gun dating back to the 15th century which, it was alleged, could project an iron ball almost a mile. This was one weapon I had not yet fired and had no intention of doing so. We also paid our respects at the Scottish National War Memorial, an impressive edifice erected after the First World War.

As we were leaving the castle, I spotted the shoulder badges of a soldier in the Royal Newfoundland Regiment, a heavy artillery unit then stationed in Edinburgh. When I told him my father had served in the First War, he immediately recognized the name and said that his father, Pte Harvey T No 1768, had served under my father in C Company. We spent an hour talking about Newfoundland and exchanging stories of the Other War, learned so well at our fathers' knees, including how Pte Ricketts, a member of my father's company, had won the Victoria Cross. So ended a rather emotional tour of one of father's old stamping grounds.

On returning to Barrhead we found the camp in a great dither because of the impending arrival of some more brass from CMHQ in London. We were ordered to lay our kit on the floor — there were no beds — and to stand rigidly to attention, just like a private soldier, while a coterie of senior officers checked our meagre belongings. They severely took us to task if any items of our G1098 kit were damaged or temporarily missing, but their main concern seemed to be whether any unauthorized items had been smuggled into the barracks. This ridiculous performance was repeated several times for the benefit of different groups of senior officers who, like us, apparently had nothing better to do.

One of my more pleasant memories is the friendship I made with the McArthur family who lived in a village near our barracks. The mother and father had been born in Scotland, emigrated to Canada but returned just before the war with their son and two daughters. Their son had joined the Canadian Forces and been taken prisoner at Dieppe. Both the daughters were very attractive young ladies but it was the older one, Betty, I was most interested in. They treated me just like a son, shared their meagre rations with me, entertained me at the local pub and generally provided me with a home away from home. On my 21st birthday they gave me a great party, showered me with presents and, I am sure, used up a week's ration coupons. It was impossible to repay such hospitality at the time but I later arranged with my parents to send them parcels while I was away fighting in Italy.

It was at this time that I made a very wise investment. The pay of a

93

lieutenant was $150.00 a month. Taking into account that I would surely soon be on active service, where I assumed money would be superfluous, I was satisfied that $100.00 would be more than ample to satisfy my needs. Furthermore, I was confident I could augment my finances from poker and other similar games of skill. So I assigned home $50 a month to be accumulated in a savings account. This little nest egg, increased by further assignments from time to time, grew to a substantial sum which, after the war, helped me to start a new career.

On June 26th we at last received a Warning Order: "4Bn - 1 CBRD will move tomorrow." There was just time for quick goodbyes to the McArthurs and my many other friends in the area. Mrs McArthur gave me a three pence coin and a sprig of heather which she insisted I carry at all times to bring me good fortune and ensure my safe return. I was soon to need all the luck I could muster.

Chapter V

CONVOY TO SICILY
The Atlantic — Mussolini's Lake
June 27 to July 12, 1943

Who was the man who invented the war
Why did he do it and what was it for
Ships on the ocean and ships in the air
The silly old blighter he ought t' been there

Leaving Barrhead on June 27th at 0400 hours (a terrible hour but presumably for security reasons), we arrived at Glasgow and embarked on the *Arundel Castle,* one of the ships of the famous Union Castle Line. She was a fair size — 20,000 tons — and had been in the East Africa service before the war. Rumours quickly spread that we too were bound for that area and action against Japan.

Even though 3,000 troops were aboard, there was not the same crowding and disorganization of my last voyage on the *Empress of Scotland.* It was almost like a peacetime cruise. It was unreal. Waiters in starched white uniforms served our meals in the first class dining room at tables set with shining silver flatwear and the finest bone china. The printed menu offered a superb choice of food — our only problem was how much we should tip the waiters when the ship docked.

Our illusions were soon shattered by the ship's adjutant who vividly described the previous voyage of the *Arundel Castle* from South Africa, when it was attacked by dive bombers and submarines and nearly sunk.

Our battalion included four other officers destined as first line reinforcements for the PPCLI: Herb Barclay, Bud Auger, Cecil Shea and

R D Browne-Cleighton. 'Brownie', like Cecil Shea, had been a private soldier with the Patricias before being commissioned. He too was a fine officer and served the Regiment well until he was severely wounded in the Hitler Line in May 1944, when Cecil Shea was killed. Brownie was taken prisoner but escaped and was invalided home to Canada.

Capt Snafu was still our company commander, but he was not a sailor. He retired to his cabin where he remained for the entire voyage, giving us a new lease on life. Another welcome change was that each of us now had a platoon of men to look after during the voyage.

Slowly the harbour filled with transport ships and warships gathering for the convoy — ten transport ships (including the *Empress of Russia, Dunotter Castle* and the *Caledonian*), seven destroyers and one cruiser.

Finally on July 1st, at 2137 hours, we began to move out of the Clyde. At last we were on the way to high adventure. That night I stayed on deck until quite late, thinking about my experiences since leaving RMC a year earlier, and wondering what lay ahead. My only regret was that after all my efforts to join my Regiment for their first big show, I would not be with them.

Next day, we were well out to sea, heading for Northern Ireland. A flying boat circled overhead to give us air cover.

Much to our astonishment we were now paid in notes, known as BMA (British Military Authority), issued by the British Government for temporary use in occupied countries. The bills gave us no clue as to our destination, as the currency was all in pounds, shillings and pence. Some of the troops claimed it was only play money and used it for that purpose in various card games all over the ship.

Very soon the weather became warmer, and by July 4th it was rumoured we were about 500 miles off the Bay of Biscay. In the morning, the Canadian hospital ship *Lady Nelson*, still sleek and white, with three large red crosses painted on her side, appeared on our starboard bow, about two miles away. I was happy to see my old friend from Saint John days. Little did I know I would be returning on her a mere four months later, in quite different circumstances.

We had been told that the convoy would probably be attacked by submarines. The warning was hardly necessary. It was apparent to all that a convoy the size of ours had little chance of escaping detection by the hungry U-Boat wolf packs. While we had great faith in our destroyer escort, we still made sure our Mae Wests were always close at hand; and no one objected to the constant boat drills. We accepted these minor irritants with good humour and made up rude jokes about having to sleep with Mae West.

The first submarine attack came about noon. I was orderly officer supervising the dumping of garbage from the galley through a large opening in the ship's side, just above the water line.

"Pay attention. Take cover. Take cover. All troops return to your quarters. Crew take up your battle stations."

Immediately, our destroyers took off at high speed and began to circle the convoy, their klaxons yelping like a pack of hounds in full chase. From my post in the galley I could see depth charges rolling off the stern of a nearby destroyer. I waited for the underwater explosion. Would it mean the death of the sub or that its torpedo had pierced our own ship? Here I was, in the galley, amid a pile of garbage, almost at the water line. What a rotten way to go!

The depth charges exploded. I scanned the destroyer's wake for tell-tale signs of success — oil slick, bits of wreckage, perhaps even a mangled German sailor, but nothing appeared. The depth charges had missed their quarry. Then a Liberator bomber appeared and joined in the hunt. Soon the all-clear sounded but was immediately followed by another emergency alarm. This time the depth charges hit the mark — the U-Boat blew up.

Shortly after this exciting prelude the officers were called together and given our objective — Sicily. We were first line reinforcements for 1st Division and would land on the beaches of southeast Sicily on July 13th, three days after the assault troops. The invasion would be made by 11 Allied Divisions from the famous 8th Army under Gen Montgomery and from the American 7th Army under Gen Patton.

I was then detailed to give all ranks a full briefing of the operation and told to report to the swimming pool which throughout the voyage had been out of bounds. In the bottom of the empty pool was a cloth model of the Sicilian beaches showing in fantastic detail every house, road and field, as well as the enemy's emplacements and positions.

Briefly, orders for 'Operation Husky' ran as follows:

Own Troops:
1st Canadian Division is part of 30th Corps of the 8th Army under Gen Montgomery
51th British Division is on our right and a commando unit is on our left
2nd United States Corps, part of the US 7th Army under Gen Patton, is on our far left

Intention of 1st Division:
Secure the beach, capture the airfield at Pachino and push northwest through the island
Contact 51st Division on our right and the commando troops on our left

Intention of our Battalion:
4 Battalion CBRD will land D + 3, proceed to assembly area just north of the beaches and report to LCol P Gilbride

Strength of Enemy on the Island:
Italian army 229,000
German army 18,000
Italian air force 10,000
German air force 24,000
Total aircraft 452

Here was an operation on the grand scale. Never before had so many men, ships and aircraft made such an assault on an enemy-held coast. The number of ships alone exceeded 3,000. I confess I found a new respect for the staff which hitherto I considered as paper soldiers — under-employed, overpaid and over us. Working day and night for months in great secrecy, the staff had developed this grandiose scheme and put it all down on paper so that every man, in every platoon, in every company, in every battalion, in every brigade, knew exactly what was expected of him and his fellow soldiers in the division. All the machinery of war — men, rations, equipment and replacements — had been brought together from England, America, Egypt, Malta and North Africa, and landed at the correct time and place. Just the problems of loading and unloading a ship were enormous. Every piece of equipment had to be loaded in reverse order so that when the ship arrived on the beach the assault elements came out first. In other words, last in, first out, or 'LIFO' — an expression my chartered accounting friends later claimed they had invented.

The briefing continued with an Intelligence Report giving information on every conceivable aspect of the operation. My original notes for this briefing somehow survived the war and are before me as I write, 40 years after the event. The examples here give an idea of the research done by the staff.

1. Political:
   Sicily is governed by fascists appointed by the Duce (Mussolini)
   Prefects of the 9 Provinces appointed by the Duce
   Mayors also appointed by Mussolini
   Murder rate high — knives
2. Characteristics of people:
   Tempermental, inconsistent, poor, proud
   40% cannot read or write
   Girls closely supervised — code of honour
3. Water:
   May be contaminated
   June to August are worst months
   Each man will receive one gallon per day for all purposes
4. Diseases in Sicily:
   Malaria — 626 deaths in Sicily in 1932 but gradually

decreasing — take Mepacrine pills
Dysentery — fields are fertilized with human excreta
Yellow Fever — few cases
Sand fly fever — lasts only three weeks, contracted around
bombed buildings
Relapsing fever — from lice
Dog tick
Rat fever
Undulant fever — from goats and milk
Typhoid fever — 33,000 cases

While I appreciated having all this information on what afflictions we might suffer through disease or at the hands of irate fathers, it seemed that we might well be rendered *hors de combat* before the Italian or German soldiers even got a crack at us.

After the briefing we were issued a helpful pamphlet on Italy and its soldiers. The pictures were clear enough but the text was all in French. For a moment I lost my new respect for the staff but quickly the correct carton of pamphlets was located. Some of the notes on the Italian soldier make amusing reading:

Fighting Value
The Italian has not distinguished himself in desert warfare, but in close conditions (East Africa and Tunisia) he has proved a much more serious opponent and he may fight very energetically and gallantly in defence of his homeland. The Italian is excitable temperamentally, and his morale is likely to show very rapid fluctuations.

Identification
The unit is entered on the pay-book and sometimes on the identity disc, but these are nearly always out of date and should not be accepted without a check.
The surest way to make certain of an identification is to look in the prisoner's pocket-book and find an envelope recently addressed to him.

Food
Italians normally eat large quantities of rice, macaroni and similar foods, cooked in olive oil. Food of British type, where meat predominates, is not likely to be readily available in Italian camps, nor is it readily acceptable to the Italian soldier.

Characteristics
The Italian is emotional, excitable and proud. He responds best to gentle treatment. UNLIKE THE GERMAN, THE BEST RESULTS ARE GOT FROM AN ITALIAN BY KINDNESS.

On paper the operation looked like a piece of cake, as long as the Germans would allow the Italians to do all the fighting. Unfortunately, after the beaches were taken, the Germans devoured our cake and fought tenaciously to hold the island.

It was now July 6th (or D - 4) on board *Arundel Castle*. Our peacetime cruise was over and we readied for battle. The first thing we thought of was naturally our loved ones at home. I sat down to compose a letter to my family, as did most of the other soldiers. What I wrote was not a masterpiece of the English language — just the sincere and honest feeling of a typical young soldier trying to ease the strain of his parents and unconsciously making a final testament if his luck ran out. By today's standards the words sound trite, even maudlin; yet after all these years they still move me, as I am sure they did my parents.

> *When you receive this letter everything will be clear to both of us, but right now I find it rather difficult to know what I should say. In a short time I'll be having a spot of excitement and thank goodness — my uneventful life of the last couple of weeks is making me fat and lazy; actually fat!*
>
> *In my previous note, which was an air letter, I told you to wait patiently until you heard from me again, and now I'm going to ask the same thing once more. What I am about to go into will be flashed to the world long before this letter reaches you, but whatever happens you all know that my thoughts are constantly with you. There will be times when you will wonder just where I am, what I am doing, and how I am feeling. It is then you cheerfully await my letter with the same feeling of confidence Mother had 28 years ago [when father went off to war].*
>
> *I believe that what I am doing is right, just as the many other sons of good families believe in the cause they are fighting for, and it is that common feeling which will help us along the road and make it easier for the folks at home. It is a grand thing. So do I believe, so will I succeed.*
>
> *Now 'bye for now, God bless you all.*

Preparations aboard the *Arundel Castle* for the landing on Sicily now swung into high gear. Our heavy battle dress was withdrawn and all ranks went into tropical kit — shorts, puttees and bush shirt. Mosquito ointment and Mepacrine tablets were issued. Weapons were checked. All over the ship small groups of men gathered to take crash courses in Italian given by the few lucky soldiers who could *parlare italiano.*

We now had constant air support but not a hostile plane appeared to challenge our aircraft. The submarine threat was quite another matter. One U-Boat had already tried to penetrate our escorting destroyers and been sunk.

A second attack the next day had been driven off with depth charges. The fates seemed well disposed toward our enterprise. On July 6th, at 1600 hours, another good omen favoured our mission. Venus appeared in the heavens close to, and behind, the new moon — a very rare occasion.

Word now spread throughout the ship that we were approaching Gibraltar and would enter the Mediterranean during the evening of July 7th. The 'Rock' had considerable significance for me. Father had taken part in the bloody landings at Gallipoli in the First War. He was invalided home with enteric fever aboard a filthy Italian ship serving as a hospital ship. Due to mechanical and other problems the ship stopped off at Gibraltar and stayed there for weeks, while father nearly died of the fever.

During the evening of July 7th I remained on deck. At 0200 hours we entered the Strait and a massive shape dimly appeared on our port bow. The total blackout on the 'Rock' gave me some comfort because our ship would not be silhouetted against the horizon and provide an easy target for a U-Boat commander.

But as we slipped into Mussolini's Lake, I was shocked and angered. The lights of the Spanish town of Algeciras were blazing away as if the German high command had placed a beacon in every window. No matter that Spain was supposedly a neutral country. This was an open act of co-belligerency that placed all Allied ships in jeopardy. How the Royal Navy kept the U-Boats away from this critical area I do not know, but I was thankful when *Arundel Castle* finally melted into the darkness again.

"Land in Sight." At 1730 hours, July 9th, *Arundel Castle* entered the harbour of Algiers: a modern looking city with many beautiful buildings spread along the North African coast. (I would have a very different opinion of the city some four months later.) The convoy regrouped, picked up the battleship HMS *Anhowe*, and sailed out of the harbour: destination — Sicily.

"The Allies have landed on the southeast beaches of Sicily." This is the first message we received on July 10th from a German radio station. Then the Allies announced that the attack was in the western part of Sicily. In fact the Allies were wrong and the Germans were right — the attack was actually in the southeast corner of Sicily. This was the first time, to my knowledge, that the Germans told the truth about anything. It was not long, however, before they spoiled their record.

On *Arundel Castle* we thought of our friends who were assaulting the beaches of Sicily and wished them luck, tinged, perhaps, with a shade of envy, and certainly with regret that we were not with them. Soon good news started to come in: all the landings had been successful; everything was going according to plan; casualties were light and Italian soldiers were surrendering in droves. The official pamphlets had been right — the Italians were fed up with the war. If only the Germans would now go home . . . .

Preparations for landing our reinforcement battalion proceeded according

101

to plans made so many months before. Boat drills were rehearsed; weapons and ammunitions were given a final check; rations were issued — a tin of hard biscuit, a tin of bully beef, a tin of pudding, a set of water tablets, a box of matches, 12 sheets of toilet paper (each sheet marked 'Government Property'), a tin of mixed tea, sugar and milk, a tin of canned heat and a tin of sandwich spread.

Where to carry these unexpected supplies presented a small problem. The prudent soldier soon found a way even though he was already encumbered with a rifle and bayonet, ammunition, steel helmet, small pack, blanket, gas cape, water bottle, entrenching tool, web equipment and other impedimenta, weighing some 50 pounds. In action he would also carry extra ammunition for the Bren guns, grenades and mortar bombs, adding another 20 pounds. Little wonder so many of us ended the war with flat feet, sore backs and crushed discs.

Finally, all preparations were complete, and to celebrate the successful landing of the Allies and relieve some of the tensions of the past few days, all ranks gathered on deck for a sing-song. Eager voices filled the air with all the war songs — *We're Going to Hang Out Our Washing on the Siegfried Line, White Cliffs of Dover, Roll Me Over in the Clover, Waltzing Matilda, A Nightingale Sang in Berkley Square,* and the haunting melody we had 'captured' from the Germans — *Lili Marlene.* It seemed as though this huge chorus was broadcasting to every enemy ship in the Mediterranean and even to Rome and the Quirinal Palace itself — we hoped so.

So ended July 10th, 1943, on *Arundel Castle.*

Meanwhile, the convoy had been hugging the North African coast to avoid air detection. We passed Tunis and Bizerta during the night of July 11th. At times we were so close to shore that the arid heat from the desert sands crept out and penetrated every nook and cranny of the ship and reduced our movements to slow motion.

Every ship in the convoy now had a large balloon trailing in its wake, attached to the stern by a long thick cable. The purpose of this was to fend off any daredevil enemy pilot who tried to press home a low flying attack — his aircraft would end up 'sans' wings. The ship's anti-aircraft Oërlikon guns were constantly at the ready and the crews occasionally fired off a burst or two to keep the guns in shape, and, I suspect, to keep up morale — theirs and ours.

Submarines remained a threat. I confess that the thought of being blown up by them worried me more than anything else — it seemed like such a lousy way to die. Thus, with great satisfaction and relief I heard the news that one of our accompanying destroyers had sunk another U-Boat which had been shadowing us for some time.

To ease the suspense a bit, we listened to enemy propaganda on the radio. The Germans boasted that the Allied offensive had been stopped cold on the beaches; many soldiers had been thrown back into the sea and perished; all reinforcement convoys (including ours, of course) were being heavily bombed and the Luftwaffe and U-Boats were in complete control.

Our comedy hour from Germany was suddenly interrupted by orders from the officer commanding our reinforcement battalion "Get packed and be ready to land tomorrow at 0700 hours." Even though we were in a war zone, and subject to destruction at any minute from the air or by sea, we still observed the niceties of the peacetime cruise we had originally booked. My last act on the evening of July 12th was to pay our mess waiter (still wearing his spotless white uniform) his well earned tip — 3 pounds, 6 shillings (about $18.00 in Canadian funds).

SOUTHERN ITALY

Route of The P.P.C.L.I.
July 10, 1943 - March 13, 1945

Map #1

NORTHERN ITALY

Route of The P.P.C.L.I.
July 10, 1943 - March 13, 1945

0 _____ 100
Miles

N

VENETIA

Trieste

Milan

Verona

LOMBARDY

Venice
Gulf of Venice

Genoa

Ferrara

Bologna   Bagnacavallo
Faenza   Ravenna
        Forli   Cervia

ADRIATIC
SEA

Gulf of Genoa

Spezia

TUSCANY

Pisa   Florence   Pontassieve
Leghorn

Siena

Rimini
San Fortunato   Pesaro
San Marino
Urbino

MARCHES

Ancona
Jesi

TO MARSEILLE

ELBA

Perugia   Foligno

Orvieto   Spoleto

San
Benedetto

CORSICA

LATIUM

Pescara
Ortona

TYRRHENIAN SEA

Rome

Map #2

LANDING IN SICILY

July 13 to July 16, 1943

And then we came to Sicily
We leapt ashore with vim and glee
The Colonel said the Wops are through
Let's chase the Hun with the Ric-a-dam-doo, dam-doo, dam-doo

July 13th. "Prepare to disembark."

These orders came over the PA system as *Arundel Castle* dropped anchor at 0700 hours. We quickly clambered down scrambling nets hanging over the ship's side and jumped into landing craft for a fast run to the beach. I was lucky to land in a new type of amphibious craft known as a DUKW — a combination of boat and truck. The letters DUKW were simply an identification code allotted by the American manufacturer, nevertheless the floating truck was called a 'Duck' from the day it was born. No word could describe its performance better. It swam like a duck and walked like a duck, except it had a propeller for locomotion in the water and wheels for operation on land. It was, in fact, an army truck that could swim.

Conveyed by this incredible vehicle I arrived with most of my platoon on the shores of Europe in fine style. As the DUKW touched the sandy beach, its wheels dug in and we were whisked off the beach and deposited on dry land. Unlike Gen MacArthur, I didn't even get my feet wet. The cheer of my men drowned out the jeers of the other troops who landed from the usual type of landing craft, and in the accepted way — up to their waists in water.

According to orders, my reinforcement battalion was to assemble in an area north of the beach and report to one LCol P Gilbride.* I personally never saw Col Gilbride until some five years later, in Toronto. It was a tall order for anyone to find him. 4 Battalion, comprising some 1,500 all ranks, was being landed piece-meal along a wide stretch of beach crowded with personnel, ammunition, rations and stores, not only for 1st Canadian Division but also for 51st Highland Division and other formations. In the makeshift harbour, some 75 ships lay at anchor as flocks of DUKWs, landing craft and even life boats ferried personnel and supplies to the beach. Hanging over the whole operation was a feeling of extreme urgency which I could not understand. That evening, when the German bombers appeared, I understood.

In the midst of all this frantic activity 4 Battalion struggled to reorganize and locate LCol Gilbride. Happily, as a junior officer, it was not my responsibility so I left the matter to the senior officers who were trained to solve such problems and paid accordingly. To their credit we eventually found our assembly area and dug in.

The whole operation reminded me of the 'fog of war' during my first exercise in England, only now it was called 'an administrative snafu'. If this was typical of what went on behind the lines, what would real war be like?

Our assembly area was about 500 yards from the beach, in the fields of a poor Sicilian peasant who, dazed by the assault, bombardment and other events of the past three days, resolutely refused to leave his miserable limestone hovel. I thought of appropriating his *casa* for a headquarters but the filth and smell were too much. Despite it all, the poor fellow welcomed us with a bottle of vino that the forward troops had somehow overlooked. I responded with a hesitant *"mille grazie — tu siete un bon'uomo — come state,"* which I had practised onboard ship so many times. He seemed to understand and replied with a long harangue about the shortcomings of Mussolini, his fascists and his forebearers. When I tried to tell him *"non capisco"*, he only talked louder and faster. I had learned my first lesson in speaking Italian to Sicilians — don't, until you know how to tell them to shut up.

In view of the dire warnings of air raids given us by the veterans on the beach, my platoon lost no time in digging slit trenches. It was tough going as the fields were mainly sand and rocks interspersed with tiny patches of poor soil. A few vines, a small olive grove and a few stalks of wheat were

---

* Assistant Adjutant and Quartermaster General of First Canadian Division and later BGen P Gilbride, OBE, DSO of Toronto.

the only vegetation. How that peasant eked out a living from the 'soil' remains a mystery to me. His only asset of any military value was a dry-wall stone fence which we 're-arranged' to give extra protection for our slit trenches.

As evening approached my company commander showed up to check on the disposition of my platoon. He warned that the previous evening four soldiers had been killed in this area by a roving enemy patrol. I could scarcely believe this as the only enemy I had seen were droves of Italian prisoners on their way to the beach. Anyway, I organized my platoon in all-round defence, posted sentries and reminded every man of the password for the evening: 'Desert Rats — kill Italians'. It seemed a little hard on our retreating enemy who wanted only to surrender.

As mentioned earlier, the Patricias had landed on July 10th, quickly secured all their beaches and pushed northwest toward the town of Ispica, capturing hundreds of Italian soldiers and considerable guns and equipment. By July 13th (D-Day for 4 Battalion), the PPCLI had passed through Modica and occupied positions overlooking Ragusa, only 30 miles from my present position. This was the closest I had been to the Patricias for many months. Surely they had suffered enough casualties that they would now be glad to have my services. I contemplated leaving 4 Battalion and setting out alone for the front lines, but soon realized I would be promptly charged with desertion, probably in the face of the enemy. I had no desire to be shot by my own men.

Setting aside these wild thoughts, I concentrated on the job at hand — making sure my platoon on the beach was well dug in and ready for the air attacks that the 'beach boys' had warned us were coming that night. They were not joking! At 2300 hours the first bombers appeared. Flak guns went into action, filling the sky with lead; search lights pierced the darkness seeking out the intruders hiding in the thick clouds.

Anxiously, I cowered in my slit trench. The drone of the bombers' engines grew louder. My muscles tightened as I waited for the first deadly stick of bombs to explode on the beach.

"Dammit," yelled a voice in the slit next to mine. "Why don't the AcAc gunners knock down those bloody Heinkels?"

"Don't be such a silly bugger," came back another voice. "The gunners can't hit what they can't see."

Then one of our search lights caught a plane in its beam and lit up the dreaded swastika emblem on its tail. I was fascinated by the sight, but fearful of the outcome — that SOB overhead was a German bomber, filled with German bombs that were about to be dropped on me and there was nothing, absolutely nothing, I could do about it. I tried to claw deeper into the stony ground and cursed not having dug a better trench.

Then just as quickly as my 'first night' jitters appeared, they were overcome by a calm determination not to be cowed by this bomber with its ugly Nazi cross. I looked up at the aircraft and saw that two more search lights had locked upon it. A loud cheer went up from the troops on the beach.

"Give it to him, AcAc," shouted a relieved man in my platoon. Instantly our gunners obliged. Shells tore into the fuselage and blew away the tail. The doomed aircraft rolled crazily over on its back and went into a fiery dive; its crew consigned forever to the deep waters of the Mediterranean.

But the Luftwaffe were not deterred by the loss of one bomber. Hundreds of flares suddenly appeared and hung in the air like chandeliers, casting an eerie light over the crowded harbour and beach. Then came the bombs, screaming toward their prime targets — the ships at anchor. Luckily none received a direct hit.

More bombs exploded on the beaches, so crowded with stores that it was impossible not to cause some damage. An ammunition dump went up with a roar, throwing debris all over my platoon. Then an oil bomb landed 100 yards from my position, setting fire to a supply dump and scaring the hell out of my men — their first time under fire. Chunks of exploded flak flew about and fell in our slit trenches. Not for the last time was I obliged to make a decision where to place my tin hat — on my head or over some other more vital part!

By 2400 hours the attack petered out. Little damage had been done and casualties were light. Exhausted, we fell asleep where we lay, except the officers and hopefully the sentries. Our first day in Sicily was over.

After only a few hours' sleep we received orders to return to the beach and help unload ammunition and stores from the ships, still riding peacefully at anchor, untouched by the air attack of the previous night. Our efforts were rewarded with a swim in the clear, warm waters of the Mediterranean and some extra rations from the crews on the ships. One skipper suggested I return in the evening, "Well before the aerial display, old chap" and wet my mess tin with something to ward off the evening cold. I promptly accepted his invitation.

That evening I returned to the beach, found my skipper, downed two or three gins as nonchalantly as I could, and scampered back to the safety of my slit trench in my platoon area. Just in time. The 'aerial display' was earlier this evening and with the same results as the night before. We were almost beginning to enjoy these fiery, nocturnal visits of the Luftwaffe.

After three days on the beaches, our rations issued on the ship were gone. No further rations were forthcoming from 4 Battalion, even though we had manhandled tons and tons of food from the ships to the depots on shore. The situation was 'desperate but not serious'.

I have never heard of a Canadian soldier starving to death. He is a past master in the art of 'scrounge and liberate'. From my friendly skipper I scrounged tinned stuff — lamb stew, bully beef and biscuits. From the surrounding countryside we liberated tomatoes, cucumbers, onions, garlic,

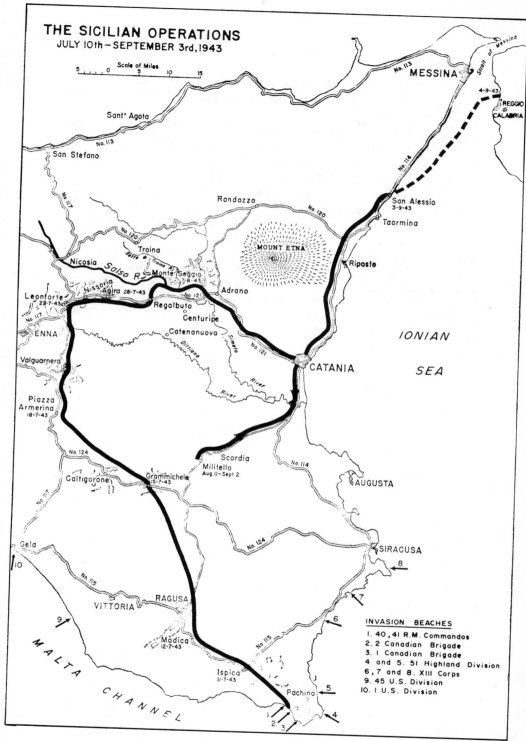

THE SICILIAN OPERATIONS
JULY 10th – SEPTEMBER 3rd, 1943

Scale of Miles
5   0   5   10   15

MESSINA

REGGIO
di
CALABRIA
4-9-43

No. 113

Sant' Agata

San Stefano
No. 113

San Alessio
3-9-43

Taormina

Randazzo   No. 120

MOUNT ETNA

Riposto

No. 117

Troina
No. 120

Serra di Troina R.

Nicosia   Salso R.

Monte Seggio
7-8-43

Nissoria

Agira 28-7-43

Leonforte
22-7-43

Regalbuto

Adrano

No. 121

Centuripe

ENNA

Catenanuova

Dittaino

Simeto

No. 121

CATANIA

IONIAN

SEA

Valguarnera

River

River

Piazza
Armerina
18-7-43

No. 124

Scordia
Militello
Aug. 11 – Sept. 2

No. 114

AUGUSTA

Caltigorone

Grammichele
15-7-43

No. 117

Gela
10

No. 115

No. 124

SIRACUSA

8

RAGUSA

7

VITTORIA

6

9

Modica
12-7-43

No. 115

MALTA

Ispica
11-7-43

Pachino   5

CHANNEL

1
2 3   4

INVASION BEACHES
1. 40, 41 R.M. Commandos
2. 2 Canadian Brigade
3. 1 Canadian Brigade
4 and 5. 51 Highland Division
6, 7 and 8. XIII Corps
9. 45 U.S. Division
10. 1 U.S. Division

Map #3

111

peppers and a few eggs. The whole lot went into a large kettle borrowed from our landlord — the Sicilian peasant. The resulting mixture was a stew worthy of the finest chef.

Early the next morning (0400 hours July 16th) our pleasant holiday on the beaches ended abruptly. Orders came to move immediately and occupy the town of Ispica, some 15 miles to the northwest, which the Patricias had passed through on July 11th on their way north.

We quickly formed up and headed toward our objective, laden down with as much fruit and vegetables as we could carry. It was a tough march in the boiling sun over roads pulverized into a fine limestone dust by the tanks and vehicles of the forward troops. My platoon, choked with dust and exhausted from the heat, started to lag behind. I pulled them well off the road and hoped a vehicle would come along and give us a lift. Eventually a slow convoy appeared. I waved down the leading vehicle and persuaded the NCO in charge to halt while my men attached themselves like leeches to the already overloaded vehicles. In this way we entered the hairpin bends in the road leading to Ispica.

ISPICA
Town Major
July 16 to August 3, 1943

Has anyone seen the Major? I know where he is
He's down in the deep dug-out
How do you know?
I saw him, down in the deep dug-out

Ispica, a typical Sicilian town perched on a steep cliff overlooking the country to the southeast as far as the beaches, was a natural defensive position; manned by a determined enemy, it could have offered a stout defence, but it had been occupied by Italian troops. After a heavy shelling from HMS *Delhi* on July 11th and a heavy aerial bombardment, the town had surrendered without a fight.

As I entered Ispica with my platoon on July 16th I wondered how the Sicilians would greet my tiny occupying force — friend or foe? We found the place almost deserted. The shelling and bombing on July 11th had killed and wounded a number of civilians and driven the people into caves and nearby fields. Subsequent bombings of the beaches and roads leading to Ispica by the Luftwaffe had prevented the terrified civilians from returning.

The first person to appear was a very nervous *podesta* (mayor) accompanied by an equally scared chief of police. Behind them, a retinue of lackeys carried vino and fruit. Again I made the mistake of trying out a few words from my Italian phrase book; again I was overwhelmed by a burst of rhyming words. (Much later I learned that the Sicilians have their own *dialetto*, with much waving of hands, which is not even understood by the mainland Italians.) With an upraised hand I gave them a short burst of my own:

"Niente parlare italiano, solo parlare inglese." A stunned silence greeted my command. I had won the first round.

A chastened *podesta* then offered, *"Peut-être, vous parlez français?"* Now I was on more familiar ground — my high school French was more than a match for his. In a few words I told him that my troops came as friends to help restore order to his beautiful town as quickly as possible. Until a civil affairs officer from AMGOT (Allied Military Government of Occupied Territories) appeared, I was the officer commanding the town and he and his police chief would be under my authority. With beaming faces and many *"mille grazie"* the *podesta* and his retinue ushered us into his office and we all toasted the liberation of Ispica.

At the ripe old age of 21, I had taken over the administration of a town of more than 13,000 inhabitants, without any real authority from my superior officer or from anyone else. During the next two weeks I ran the town with hardly any outside help, not even from the headquarters of my own 4 Battalion, still 15 miles away in Pachino, near the beaches. But I thoroughly enjoyed every minute and concluded that perhaps a benevolent dictatorship was not, after all, a bad thing!

The first priority was to establish a command post or headquarters and find billets for my troops. The *podesta* showed me a monastery recently occupied by Italian soldiers. The place was filthy, littered with the offal of an army in hasty retreat. A stern, disapproving look from me soon produced a fine command post and barracks. I took over the former fascist head-quarters *(Casa del Fascio)*, while my men occupied their former billets.

Soon the people started to return from their caves in the cliffs. First to appear were the ones who had been wounded from our bombardment or from handling grenades left behind by their own soldiers. One person had both hands blown off; another an arm; another a foot. We did what we could with our inadequate medical supplies. From early morning until late at night (even though I had imposed a curfew) a constant stream of Sicilians begged our help.

I wrote my father from my headquarters at the *Casa del Fascio*:

> *At last I was on my own. I had my lads billeted in the former quarters of the big shots of the* Fascisti *and had my HQ in their former HQ. Both places were quite elaborate, and we found many souvenirs. I wish I could have taken them along with me, but I have enough to carry as it is.*
>
> *After a day or so, the people began returning to the town and my worries started. Many of them had been living in caves, some under the trees, and all were starving and filthy. For three years they had been drained of their resources which had been exported to Italy and Germany.*

In most hovels the animals are kept in the same building as the family. Once, when I visited a dying old woman, I had to go through a room full of donkeys, pigs and chickens, before getting to her sick room. The smell was terrific, not only in the houses but also in the small, uneven streets. Refuse is piled outside the door, and plumbing runs into open gutters along the streets. It is easy to understand why the people welcomed us with open arms, went down on their knees, and implored our help.

The Italian soldiers were no better. Day after day they drifted in completely fed up with Mussolini and the war, and begging us to take them prisoner.

Within a week we had the people with us almost 100%. They gave us what little food they had, and each day the Mayor and Chief of Police brought me bottles of wine, vermouth and quantities of fruit. Quickly I discovered there was sufficient food for the people, the problem being to find the hoarders. We opened up the flour mill and kept it running day and night, and so the people at least existed on bread, wine and fruit, which was of course plentiful. How Mother would enjoy the melons, grapes, oranges, lemons, pears, etc, I have had in this country.

The people of Ispica were not the only ones to benefit from the friendly relationships that developed. Before I realized it, I was conversing in Italian, both verbally and manually — at least the townspeople were responding to my questions and I was understanding theirs. From an old man I received the supreme complement: *"Voi parlate italiano con accento siciliano."* And I still do!

A further letter home explains how I accomplished this linguistic feat:

Every afternoon when the sun was hottest and the people were having their siesta, *I would go down to the inn and take lessons in Italian over a few glasses of wine. The innkeeper spoke excellent French, so we would converse in French, and from our common understanding of French he would teach me Italian. I improved my high school French greatly and got so I could make myself understood in Italian. Also there were several retired professors living in the town who had me out to their villas and helped me with the language in return for some small bit of advice I gave them. Then, too, there was a priest who had spent a year or two in London and spoke fair English. I think he will always remember me, as the first day I arrived I gave him permission to reopen his Church. He is the best Italian I have met.*

115

My new fluency in Italian opened many doors. I became a regular guest of the Baron of Modica, one of the large land owners in Sicily. On one occasion he invited me to look over his lands and suggested we do a little rabbit shooting. I was surprised he had a gun as I had given strict orders that all fire arms were to be registered at my headquarters. Nevertheless, I accepted his invitation, but brought along two soldiers, supposedly as gun bearers and to retrieve any wounded hares.

This little manoeuvre didn't fool the Baron. In his flowing Italian he asked, "Why does the Lieutenant bring armed soldiers? Does he not trust me?"

"Of course I do, but why hasn't the Baron reported his fire arms?"

He was happy to let the matter drop.

Another friend of mine was Dr Lentini, the only doctor in town. He worked long hours tending not only his own people but also the men of my platoon who were now beginning to suffer from the filthy conditions all around us — malaria, dysentery, jaundice. From our conversations I got a vivid impression of the excesses and degeneracy of the Fascist regime. Mussolini had done some good things in the early days — built roads, hospitals, sports arenas and many fine public buildings. He had tried to impose some organization and discipline into the Sicilian way of life. He had even got the trains running on time. But he had gone too far and now his name was an object of scorn and hatred. He had become a puppet in the hands of Hitler who had drained Sicily and Italy of all their resources. There were even Italian Divisions fighting with the Germans in Russia. What was left of the Italian Army in Sicily and Italy was a joke and would continue to disintegrate.

Dr Lentini predicted that Mussolini and his Fascists would collapse in a matter of weeks, perhaps only days. During one of our talks I asked him, "What about Mussolini's brave boasts we see plastered on signs all over your town? *Millione baionette. Credere, obbedire combattere.*"

"Idle dreams, castles in the air. That's all they are," he replied.

His anti-Fascist views were shared by a school teacher, Signorina Franzo, who hated Mussolini with a vengeance because her brother was in the Italian Army on the Russian front and hadn't been heard from for months. Her personal vendetta against the Duce was further fuelled by her obvious leanings towards communism, which she was not afraid to express at any hour of the day or night to anyone who would listen to her. At times she taxed my patience but I put up with her rantings because she helped Dr Lentini treat the sick and wounded, and she tipped me off as to who was hoarding grain. She knew everybody and seemed to have quite a following in the town. Why she hadn't been put away by the Fascists I could not understand.

Another young lady, of quite a different mould, was Signorina Anna Fratele. Her father was a retired professor who had a fine home in town and a large farm in the country. He too was an anti-Fascist, but was not against the King, thinking Italy would best be served by a strengthened monarchy. It was not politics, however, that brought me to his home. He loved music, was an accomplished violinist and, accompanied by his daughter, sang operatic and popular airs. When he learned that I played the piano he was delighted and invited me to consider his home as my home. It was a tempting offer, not only because of the piano, but one I could not accept.

Despite the kindess of the townspeople, our rations were getting low and the supply lines from battalion headquarters were still not functioning properly. I took the mayor's car, filled it with vino and fruit and headed for Pachino and the beaches on a scrounging mission. Service corps types were still unloading rations and stores from ships in the bay. As soon as they saw my car laden with produce they rushed forward to make a deal — one can of tea for one melon; one tin of cigarettes for a small bottle of vino. I drove a hard bargain — I was learning to think like a Sicilian.

On the way back to Ispica I passed a sign indicating that a paymaster had actually landed on the beach and had set up shop. My driver could not believe it "What the hell's the Army coming to — Paymasters landing with the fighting troops!"

As a lark, I decided to visit this financial warrior and try out my bartering technique on him. He firmly rejected my offers of fruit and vino for cash but added, "The King, whom I represent, would be pleased to receive some gifts. It might then be possible to give you an advance of pay." The deal was quickly made and I departed with £60 in my pocket, charged to my officers' field pay book.

As a courtesy, I also stopped at our battalion headquarters in Pachino to see how Capt Snafu was getting along.

"Hello, Sir. How's the battle going? Any chance to draw a few rations?".

"Certainly not. Your platoon has had more than its share."

"Well, how about paying my men a few bob so they can buy some stuff from the Ities?"

"Impossible. No one has been paid in the whole division, not even me."

That evening in Ispica my platoon dined in style thanks to the success of my expedition to the beaches. Each man also received one pound, or 400 lire, more than enough to keep him happy for the remainder of his stay in Ispica.

While I had been away scrounging, my command had been augmented by three Australian soldiers, three lambs, a very irate Baron Modica and his chief overseer, Signor Salvatore. When I arrived, the Aussies and Sicilians were shouting at each other while my sergeant tried to avoid bloodshed. The Baron claimed that the Aussies had stolen three lambs from Signor Salvatore and insisted the animals be returned forthwith. He didn't want money or goods in exchange; he just wanted his lambs back.

The Aussies just laughed and gave me a conspiratorial wink. They were only exercising their right to scrounge whatever they wanted.

Here was a fine point. There is scrounging Type I and scrounging Type II. The first type is where the troops (scroungor) clearly require the scrounged article and the Italians (scroungee) will not be seriously deprived. This type is usually permitted, particularly if the scroungee receives payment or goods in exchange. Type II is scrounging for the hell of it, where the article is required by the scroungee, the troops really don't need it, and the Italians are going to suffer. This type is usually not allowed.

The evidence in the case was that the Aussies were off on a frolic of their own. Fortified by vino, they had thought it a great caper to bring back three live sheep to their lines for the amusement of their buddies. On the other hand, the Sicilians were almost starving and needed these lambs badly. Furthermore, the animals belonged to the Baron who had helped me to solve the food shortage by threshing his grain and opening his flour mill.

It was a clear case of Type II — *proibito assolumente*. Signor Salvatore got his lambs and the Aussies got the boot.

The Luftwaffe visited the beaches again. As usual, most of their bombs fell inland, some quite near Ispica; the inhabitants panicked and headed for the caves, screaming *"apparecchi tedeschi"*. The best efforts of my men could not stem the tide and in a few moments the town was once more deserted.

On the evening of July 25th our wireless picked up an incredible radio announcement from Rome: "His Majesty the King and Emperor has accepted the resignation of the head of the government, the Chancellor and State Secretary, tendered by His Excellency Cavalier Benito Mussolini." Dr Lentini had been right. Mussolini and his Fascists were finished — finito Benito.

The townsfolk went wild. Shouting and singing, they converged on my headquarters in the piazza, and overwhelmed us with their embraces. Signorina Fratele pushed her way through the crowd and appeared before me with a bottle of marsala she had been hoarding for years, just for this occasion. She begged me to join her family for a late dinner and continue the celebration around the piano at her home. It was, of course, impossible.

Other friends dropped in to toast the occasion — the mayor, the police chief and Dr Lentini. Signorina Franzo, the school teacher, insisted that I write an appropriate message in her autograph book which she would read to her students every year in honour of this occasion and the heroic Canadians. I was in no state to compose such a message for posterity on behalf of Canada, and I tried to think what Churchill might have said in similar circumstances. According to my diary the best I could do was this gem: "May the lights come on again all over the world and all people live in freedom, justice and equality." At least it appealed to her republican views.

The day following Mussolini's dramatic resignation I received an American visitor, Capt Guthrie, a Civil Affairs Administrative Officer. He told me he would take over my duties as soon as I left for the front, and that some American brass from the US 7th Army would inspect Ispica the next morning. I spruced up my platoon and sent a warning order to the *podesta*, the chief of police, interpreter and other local officials.

We all lined up early next morning in the piazza waiting for the generals. None appeared. By noon, still no generals. I had better things to do than stand around in the sun all day, but I deferred to Capt Guthrie, not wanting to create a breach in Allied relations, "Captain, what do you think? We stay here or we go for a swim with a couple of signorinas at Pozzallo?" (This little seaside resort was well removed from the American forces.)

His answer was immediate, "Lootenant, lead the way!"

Reports now began to filter back from the front of the stiff resistance the Allied troops had been encountering from four German divisions (the Hermann Goering, the 15th and 29th Panzer Grenadier and the 1st Parachute Division). The Patricias' first serious battle with these tough professionals had been at Leonforte on July 22nd, when the Regiment had driven the Germans from the town and won its first battle honour and decorations for bravery; but the cost had been high — 21 killed and 40 wounded.

On July 26th at Nissoria Ridge, and again on July 28th at Agira, the Regiment had routed Hitler's best troops, gaining further honours. The battle for Agira had been the division's biggest of the Sicilian campaign and had cost the division 438 casualties.

While the Patricias had been fighting these battles and suffering casualties, I had been cooling my heels in Ispica, waiting for the call to join my Regiment. My little problems seemed trivial indeed compared to the hardships and sacrifices being suffered by the troops in action. Surely I would soon be given a chance.

The call finally came on August 3rd. I lost no time in handing over my duties as Town Major to Capt Guthrie. I was relieved to be on my way at last and excited about the prospect of action, but I left my first real command with a tinge of sadness. As Town Major of Ispica, I had received a unique education that was not printed in any army manual and that very few young officers would ever experience. None of my prior training had prepared me for such a test.

In only a few weeks I had seen the people of Ispica shake off the terrible yoke of Fascism and make a fresh start on the road to democracy. They had worked hard to rebuild their town and their Sicilian way of life; they had found new confidence and hope for the future.

At the *Casa del Fascio* I held my last parade to say goodbye to the people I had come to understand and respect — the mayor, the police chief, the Baron of Modica, Dr Lentini, Father Pietro (the priest), Signor Salvatore, Signorina Franzo, Signor Fratele and his daughter. As I turned to leave, Signorina Fratele pressed into my hand a good luck charm; with tears in her eyes she said, *"Noi amoriamo voi. Per favore ritornate presto."* I jumped into my vehicle and drove away.

I did in fact return to my beloved Ispica 13 years later, but that is another story.

Chapter VIII

THE REGIMENT
Monte Seggio
Scouts and Snipers
August 4 to August 22, 1943

So clear the way for the men of the PPCLI
We're stalwart men, stout-hearted men
And we know we can't go wrong
We fear no foe as on we go
In the fight for liberty
We're all for one and one for all
Marching along to victory

The Patricias were now moving forward to attack their next objective in Sicily — Monte Seggio, a formidable peak rising to the west of Mount Etna and lying about four miles northwest of the town of Adrano. I didn't know it then, but this was my last chance to see action in Sicily.

My route to the Regiment was a circuitous one. The retreating Germans had blown the bridges and mined the roads, forcing our troops to take secondary roads and and even trails until our engineers had repaired the destruction. The few direct routes to the front were clogged with traffic.

My vehicle got as far as Syracusa on the east coast of Sicily, where a train of sorts, recently 'liberated' from the Germans, delivered me to the end of the line north of Augusta. The next station was still in German hands. From there I was taken by truck over trails that even a mule would have the intelligence not to attempt. The final mile was special torture — a bumpy ride over the ties of a railway bridge at the Salso River. The Germans had cleverly left this bridge intact knowing that we would use it and ruin our vehicles as well as our backs.

We stopped at divisional headquarters to give both vehicles and men a rest. Here I involuntarily committed another breach of regulations when I carelessly lost my dog tags. Every soldier is issued two identity discs made of permanent material on which are stamped his name and number. Both tags must be worn around the neck at all times. If a soldier is killed, one of the tags is removed and sent to the authorities; the other remains with the body. During our break we found a well and caught up on our ablutions. For some reason I removed my dog tags and placed them nearby. When I returned, they were gone. I am not a superstitious person, but it seemed like a bad omen on the eve of battle. I had visions of becoming just another fallen soldier whose whereabouts are unknown.

There was no possibility of getting new dog tags at this stage — that would doubtless require forms in triplicate and possibly a charge of 'conduct to the prejudice of good order and military discipline'. I looked in my pack and found the goodluck tokens I had received from my Ispica friends. One token was a small, metal plaque suspended from a chain with a message engraved on the front; the reverse side was blank. I etched in my name and number and furtively placed the charm around my neck. It remained there during the rest of my service and fulfilled its main purpose of bringing me through the war more or less intact. Its secondary purpose of identification was fortunately never needed, but I often wondered what would have happened if one of my original dog tags had found its way into the hands of the War Graves Commission.

At divisional headquarters the time was now 0930 hours, August 5th, and I prepared to move forward. A vehicle eventually arrived and drove me and 11 men the last few miles to the rear echelon of the battalion. There we were met by the Regimental ration truck, and delivered to the forward companies, arriving at 2000 hours. I was told to report immediately to A Company, which was just then moving off to attack Monte Seggio.

Silent forms began to glide past in the darkness, broken only by flashes from the guns and fires in the valley ahead and on the surrounding hills. I had not the slightest idea where I was, much less where our troops, the enemy or the objective were. I thought for an instant of the 'fog of battle' I had experienced so often on exercises. This was going to be a peasouper.

As the troops filed by, I thought I recognized an officer. "I've just arrived at the battalion and been posted to A Company. Any idea what platoon I'm supposed to join?"

"Take the first one that goes by without an officer," a voice from the dark commanded.

I took over 8 Platoon, temporarily commanded by one Sgt Inverarity. Let the Regimental History take up the story of the attack that night:

The night was very dark but along the hills on both sides were large fires — burning straw stacks and houses and in one spot an ammunition dump which flared up every now and then.

At 2300 hours we contacted a sentry by the side of the road who led us down a long track to a farmhouse where we met LCol Hoffmeister at Battalion Headquarters of the Seaforths.

We were given the story of the hard fight the Seaforths had had in gaining their ground that afternoon. They also told us about Monte Seggio. To the best of their knowledge the hill still was held in some strength, although no mortaring or shelling of their (the Seaforths') area had occurred since nightfall. In our experience of the Germans, this had little significance.

Our plan was discussed with Col Hoffmeister before we pushed off. On reaching the road again we encountered a squadron of tanks on their way forward to relieve another squadron which had expended its ammunition and petrol. We accepted the offer of a lift and loaded two companies on the tanks. Unfortunately a wrong turning was made and we finally offloaded on the edge of an irrigation ditch which the tanks could not cross.

Then began our search for the forward companies of the Seaforths We moved forward once more and at 0230 hours we were inside the Seaforth area.

It was decided to rest the men for a few hours and to attack Monte Seggio at first light.[1]

At 1100 hours the next day, A and B companies went into the attack supported by artillery as well as by the heavy mortars and medium machine guns of The Saskatoon Light Infantry.

Under cover of this massive bombardment, we struggled up the rugged slopes of Monte Seggio and assaulted our first objective, a suspected German strong point. Luck was with us. The enemy had decamped in haste, leaving behind a damaged heavy machine gun, tools, 'potato mashers' (grenades), ammunition belts and a dead officer — a paratroop lieutenant.

It was my first view of a dead German soldier. He had been caught in our barrage and his lower body was a horrible mess of bone, flesh, guts and torn uniform. I reached inside his camouflaged jacket and pulled out a wallet. Papers, postcards and pictures fell to the ground. I picked up a blood-stained postcard he had apparently written home but never posted. On the front was a picture of his idol — Adolph Hitler.

"The poor misguided bastard," I mumbled to myself. "Thousands of miles from home, his shattered body lies abandoned by his comrades on a barren Sicilian mountainside. Soon the peasants will steal his boots; the follow-up troops will take his watch and iron cross."

I was tempted to take them myself, but I had to move off quickly to keep up with the timing of the barrage now falling on the next objective. I slipped the postcard into a pocket of my bush jacket, wondering if fate would be so unkind to me. The paratrooper was such a young, blond, good-looking....

"Come on platoon," I heard myself shout. "He's just another dead Kraut. Let's get moving."

In the course of the War I would see many, many more German dead, but only one remains etched in my memory — a paratroop lieutenant whose blood-stained postcard rests among my souvenirs.

We gained our final objective without difficulty and dug in on the slopes of Monte Seggio in all-round defence. The Germans had fled northward towards the Strait of Messina and the Italian mainland. Our only enemy was the intense heat — a searing 110 degrees.

We soon received a small consolation prize for our efforts, when three German paratroopers wandered into our A Company area. They were promptly 'arrested' for loitering in a place reserved for our battalion and sent down the line for interrogation. At divisional headquarters they gave some useful information:

> *In the Canadian Sector a hint of the disorganized nature of the general German withdrawal came from three German paratroopers captured on August 6th, who declared that the enemy had broken up into groups of two or three, with instructions to make their way back as best they could to rejoin the main body of troops.*[2]

Considering the helter skelter way I had joined the attack at Monte Seggio I could count myself lucky that my first action had not been a bloody affair. But the two follow-up companies, C and D, were not so fortunate. They were heavily shelled as they marched to join us and an officer, Lt J d'A Horn, was killed when a shell landed in the middle of his platoon.

Then an incident occurred which shocked me, as a newly joined subaltern, and saddened many officers and men of the Regiment. Our Commanding Officer, LCol Bob Lindsay, was removed from command and sent back to England.

At first there was no explanation for this drastic action and rumours abounded, but gradually the facts emerged. LCol Lindsay had been given orders to attack and capture Monte Seggio on the evening of August 5th — the very night I joined the Regiment. However, due to the delay caused when the tanks carrying A and B companies lost their way that night, the attack was postponed to morning, when the troops would have the benefit of supporting artillery fire. The brigade commander would not accept any explanation for the failure to assault Monte Seggio on the night of August 5th. In his opinion, if the Patricias had attacked with all four companies that night they might have greatly disrupted the enemy's withdrawal.

Whether this opinion was right or wrong can never proved, but it seemed to me then, and it seems to me now, that it did not warrant removing our gallant commander in such a harsh manner. His Regiment had performed magnificently throughout the campaign and was on the eve of completing its part in the stunning victory of the Allies over the Axis Forces in Sicily.

If the brigade and divisional commanders wished to replace him they could have accomplished their purpose in a much fairer way by waiting until the division was withdrawn from action. Then he could have been transferred to another command and given a second chance. There were innumerable examples of such transfers throughout the war and, as often as not, the officer concerned proved himself to the complete satisfaction of his new commander. LCol Lindsay got a raw deal.

Fortunately the Patricias had an officer who knew the Regiment intimately and exemplified its great spirit — Cammie Ware, who had joined the Regiment in 1935. In short order he put an end to the rumours and uncertainties that LCol Lindsay's removal had caused, and imprinted his own personality on the Regiment.

From our perch on the heights of Monte Seggio, my platoon had a commanding view of the surrounding countryside. To the northeast rose the mass of Mount Etna whose volcanic crater was only five or six miles from our position as the crow flies. Between the two peaks lay the fertile Simeto Valley watered by a river of the same name. In sharp contrast to this scene was the view to the southwest — the wild rugged terrain of the Salso Valley and the dry bed of its river, from which we had launched our assault on Monte Seggio.

The Germans were now shelling the Salso Valley and we could clearly see the shells bursting on C and D companies as they moved to join us, but we could not detect where the fire was coming from.

We had more success, however, in locating enemy guns in the Simeto Valley, to the east of our position, where the Germans were retreating to the north. On the evening of August 7th my platoon spotted two six-barrelled enemy mortars (Nebelwefers, or Moaning Minnies as they were called by the 8th Army) mortaring the troops of the British 78th Division as they pushed the Germans up the valley. We spotted the flashes of the mortars, took compass bearings and sent them to battalion headquarters. C Company had also seen the flashes and reported the bearings. From this information the artillery from both our division and the British 78th Division were able to engage the target and soon silenced the mortars.

The next day, fully recuperated from our strenuous climb up the slopes of Monte Seggio, some of my boys asked permission to descend to the Simeto Valley and make a reconnaissance of the area that had been plastered by our artillery the night before. What they really wanted to do was to go swimming in the river and perhaps liberate a chicken or two, some eggs and some tomatoes from the farms we could see in the valley. While a few enemy rear guard soldiers might still be in the area it was worth the risk, as our rations were running low. Supplies could only reach us by mules, not known for their attention to duties.

The expedition to the valley was a success. I had to remain with my platoon headquarters on the mountain so I followed the progress of the 'scroungers' with my binoculars until the troops disappeared into the orchards. Suddenly a rifle shot and then another echoed down the valley. Were they fired in anger or in sport? I never did find out.

When my platoon returned, well laden with *galline, uove and pomodori*, they denied all responsibility for the shots. "Probably the Limeys taking pot shots at us!" Sgt Inverarity suggested.

These fresh supplies, mixed with the remainder of our rations, made a fine meal which we washed down with an EFI issue we had just received via mule train — one bottle of whiskey to be shared by Sgt Inverarity and me; one half-bottle of beer per man. Mindful of a prior experience with whiskey and spam, I gave away a shot of whiskey to any man who needed it, regardless of standing orders prohibiting such fraternization with the troops.

At a Commanding Officers' conference at 1700 hours on August 10th we were warned that the battalion would move from our mountain top at 0200 hours next morning to a rest area south of Catania. I foolishly let my men sleep until 2400 hours, when I roused my platoon cook, Pte O'Brien, and got him to start breakfast. We had hard luck trying to light a fire (too bad we hadn't saved a little alcohol) with the result that my platoon was 20 minutes late moving off. I could have left on time by cutting out the men's breakfast, but I gambled that the vehicles sent to pick us up would also be late. They were — four hours to be exact.

Quite rightly I got ticked off by my company commander for not allowing extra time to deal with such emergencies as fires that would not start. As he put it: "When the Commanding Officer tells me to move off at 0200 hours, I am ready at 0130 hours and you should be ready at 0100 hours. It doesn't matter whether its only a bath parade or an attack. One late platoon could screw up the entire battalion."

Perhaps the fiasco of the delayed attack on Monte Seggio was still in his mind, but he had a point. Never again was I late moving off, due solely to poor planning on my part.

The battalion was loaded into 15 TCVs (Troop Carrying Vehicles), 30 men to a vehicle, and set off along the rough and twisting roads we were now so familiar with. We arrived at our destination, outside Militello, at 1300 hours, having taken seven hours to go 73 miles; still, it was better than marching.

My platoon took up a position in a vineyard on the side of a hill. We unloaded our kit, found a place to lie down and curled up in our blankets. This was to be our home for the next three weeks.

Following the appointment of LCol Ware as Commanding Officer of the battalion, a number of switches were made in the officer personnel. Some were promoted, others transferred to brigade headquarters to assume more responsible duties; a few were sent to the holding unit.

A Company now had the following officers: Company commander - Capt Bucko Watson, Second-in-Command - Capt John Brophy (transferred from Brigade Headquarters), 7 Platoon - Lt Rex Carey MC, 8 Platoon - Lt C S Frost and 9 Platoon - Lt Herb Barclay. I had last seen John Brophy during the assault river crossing in England, near Seaford, when I had been a platoon commander in No 3 Company under Capt Waterman and John had been Second-in-Command of the company.*

Our divisional commander, MGen Guy Simonds, in a rare moment of compassion, expressed the wish that everyone should be as comfortable as possible during this rest period. We took him at his word and lost no time scrounging the countryside for physical comforts such as tables, chairs and dishes. Capt Brophy demonstrated he had acquired at brigade headquarters a taste for some of the finer things of life. From one expedition he brought back a beautiful mahogany table, silverware, crystal and bone china to set up our Officer's Mess amid the vineyards; also bread, cheese, fruit, vegetables and six different kinds of liqueur.

Perhaps the most welcome amenity of all was a visit to the Mobile Bath Unit. All ranks stripped off their worn and dirty uniforms and enjoyed a hot shower: for many, the first since the landing. They emerged from the shower several shades lighter in colour and received a fresh uniform and underclothes.

Now we looked like soldiers again, but it was a mixed blessing. The higher authorities could not resist the temptation to give such fine-looking troops a little drill to smarten them up further and the piazza in nearby Militello provided a perfect parade ground. Each day a formal changing of the guard took place among the three units in the brigade (PPCLI, The Loyal Edmonton Regiment and The Seaforth Highlanders of Canada) and the townspeople greeted our efforts with loud applause and shouts of *"bravo, fortissimo; soldati canadese"*. I was given the honour of commanding the PPCLI guard and tried my best to outdo the guards from the other units, while movie cameras recorded the event for posterity. My former company commander, Maj Coleman, now Second-in-Command of the battalion, seemed to think we had not lost our parade ground ability and complimented

---

*He was subsequently killed in June 1944 in a vehicle accident near Rome.

us on our efforts.

We tried to do some training, but the heat was so intense we were only required to work from 0500 to 1100 hours each morning. These hours were later changed as we found it was too dark to commence training at 0500 hours, so it started at 0600 hours and finished at 1030 hours — rather good working hours for non-union employees.

The usual round of inspections began with a visit from our brigade commander, Brig Chris Vokes. He was a gruff, tough commander who had driven his brigade relentlessly from the landing and was not about to let it get soft now. If it was too hot to train we could play sports, perform guard duties and listen to lectures on artillery and other supporting arms. In a letter home I described our upcoming field meet:

> *Now we are out of the fight and enjoying a rest for a while and it is hard to imagine ourselves in a theatre of operations. For instance we are planning a sports meet. I intend to run in the 100, 220 and 440, just as I used to in Canada. Little did I ever think in those days that I would be running races in Sicily. Actually we are running two races, ie the Germans and Italians.*

Brig Vokes' great ability as a fighting commander was recognized by both his superiors and his men. My sergeant declared that the brigadier was afraid of nothing — "man, beast nor fighting reptile". The brigadier's aggressive leadership was soon to be rewarded, for he was promoted to major general in charge of our division. Many stories circulated about the colourful brigadier. His order of the day for the landing in Sicily was typical: "Actions speak louder than words. Go in and get the bastards!"

Another story related to the prohibition against eating the local fruits and vegetables because they were fertilized by human excreta, but no one paid much attention to this regulation. During an inspection the brigadier spotted a soldier leaning against a tree, enjoying a large watermelon. The brigadier glared at the man and he jumped to attention.

"You know the regulations against eating these fruits," growled the brigadier. "They've been fertilized by shit!"

For probably the first time in his career the brigadier got his come-uppance. "Sorry Sir," grinned the soldier, "but it doesn't smell like it, look like it, or taste like it."

Brig Vokes' inspection was followed by visits from all the high brass — MGen Simonds, Gen Montgomery and Gen McNaughton. All spoke in glowing terms of the magnificent contribution made by the Patricias to the Sicilian campaign. Gen Montgomery was particularly complimentary: he gathered the troops around his jeep and delivered a typical Monty speech in which he managed to use the word 'magnificent' four times in two sentences. There is no doubt he impressed the men with his 'blood and guts' speeches, but some of the officers were not taken in. I heard one officer, who had seen more than his share of fighting quietly observe: "Yeah, his guts and our blood!"

Our spirits soared. We were proud of our Regiment. It was an exciting time to be a Patricia. My duties as guard commander in Militello were not onerous and afforded me good opportunity to get to know "my boys".

To my surprise my platoon was not upset by the return to parade ground soldiering in Militello and general smartening up. It turned out there were certain perks attached to the job — living in houses, sleeping in a bed, having indoor ablutions and the like. Fresh bread from the town baker was available for the ridiculous price of two cents a loaf. Life was most pleasant and I was looking forward to leading my platoon in the forthcoming landing on the toe of Italy.

Once again the 'fickle finger of fate' intervened to disrupt my plans and hopes. Fresh from my spit and polish duties in Militello I was posted to the most informal bunch of irregular soldiers in the battalion, if not the army — the horse-mounted Scout and Sniper Platoon. Worse still, the platoon existed only on paper, having just been dreamt up by higher authority — quite possibly by our head-hunting Brig Vokes who loved to keep the action rolling.

The War Diary describes its formation.

A Scouts and Snipers platoon is in the process of being formed, to consist of 30 all ranks, and to be horseborne. 10 horses were requisitioned today, through the authorities in Militello, and training commenced. One of the horses, a stallion, gave the Pl a lot of trouble, and eventually became so wild that it broke away and has been AWL ever since. Horse lines were established, and there remained only the problem of providing 'rations', which proved a difficult one. However, a vehicle was despatched and successfully picked up enough fodder for a few days for the new recruits.[3]

and later, its progress:

The Scout and Sniper platoon have now procured 18 horses and extensive training has been carried out with them. Unfortunately no saddles were available and the men have had to ride bareback, causing many blisters on that portion of the body most exposed to riding. However, this new type of training has been taken up with great interest by all the men and some have considered it better to have blisters where they now have them than the continued monotony of having them on the feet.[4]

To remedy the deficiency of saddles, the adjutant sent me on a mission to purchase saddlery wherever I could find it. A letter home explains my procedure:

> *Armed with the necessary authority I went to the Italian Town Marshal and requisitioned horses. Of course he tried to hold out by bringing in all the old plow horses, mules, donkeys. It was really quite funny. I sat at the entrance to the town hall and accepted or rejected the beasts, yelling out "vada via" (take it away) when a particularly horrible specimen came before me. At last I bawled out: "Nienti chevali — nienti Maresciallo", which means "No horses — no Marshal". He nearly passed out and in a jiffy I had all the horses I could handle.*

For each beast I acquired, I solemnly wrote out a requisition, a receipt and a IOU which I handed to the Marshal. What these documents said I cannot remember; in any event they probably should remain military secrets forever. I do remember, however, seeing receipts and IOUs, prepared by officers from other Regiments, purporting to be signed by all sorts of military authorities — Mickey Mouse, Guy Lombardo, Carol Lombard, Mackenzie King. Perhaps some of these documents are still floating around the country, having been negotiated as paper money or used to pay off half the national debt of Italy.

The best account of the birth of the Scout and Sniper Platoon appeared in the *Winnipeg Free Press*:

> With the Canadian in Sicily, Sept 9 — *Establishment of the Double PP ranch, first Canadian riding academy in Sicily and undoubtedly the forerunner of a great era in the reborn, though quite unofficial Canadian horsed cavalry, is announced by* Aicirtap, *daily newspaper of the Princess Patricias Canadian Light Infantry.*
>
> *Already 30 Sicilian horses have been branded with the PP and Lt Syd Frost has taken on the assignment of foreman of the outfit. Frost frankly admits he is no ex-cowboy, but has received much sympathetic understanding on all sides. His big problem is to find proper feed for his equines. They look good, sound, upstanding animals but they haven't the staying power that comes from good grain.*
>
> *Patricias have been scouring hills and plains for good oats and barley, even a little macaroni, but the Eyeties don't seem to have much of it, and it's quite a chore building up the stable. There is no end of straw, plenty of cactus and prickly pears, and even a sufficiency of army biscuits, but Rowan Coleman, Stu Graham, Wally Dewar and the other officers will not be satisfied*

130

*until they've got a corral filled with spirited saddle horses with
real staying power.*

*There's so much of the spirit of the old west in this regiment
that one stretcher bearer was seen wearing a 10-gallon hat during
one of the most important engagements.*[5]

My transition from a proper parade ground soldier at RMC and Camp
Shilo a year before, to the command of a most irregular mounted infantry
unit, was now complete. My platoon had no status in any army organization and I therefore had to find my men from the companies who themselves
were under strength. This led to difficulties with the company commanders.
They were loathe to part with any man except a 'trouble maker' — a soldier
who was great in action but had a definite aversion to discipline. Some of
these men had been sergeants in action but once out of the line had committed
some indiscretion and been demoted. I was not at all daunted by these tough
customers. They were just the kind of men I wanted for the forthcoming
operations — determined men with initiative who could operate on their own.

Sicily was now fully occupied by the Allied Forces and plans were well
advanced for the immediate invasion of Italy; our division would be among
the first to land on the mainland of Europe. Having missed one invasion
I was particularly keen to be part of this one.

But once again fate gave me her fickle finger — malaria.

Chapter IX

MALARIA

August 23 to September 14, 1943

When you hear the Minnies moaning loud and clear
Shaking up your insides and landing mighty near
That is the time I have no fear
As I drink up your NAAFI beer
When I am LOB, when I am LOB*

S hortly after joining the Scouts and Snipers I started having headaches but put them down to the frustrations of forming this novel platoon and tried to carry on with training. The headaches became more severe; my muscles ached and I started to run a fever of 104°. Despite my objections, the MO put me to bed in the RAP for observation. After 24 hours I felt better and tried to return to my duties, but it was hopeless. Severe chills racked my body, alternating with a fever of 105°. It was obvious to everyone, except to me, that I had to be evacuated. I refused to go and the medical officer called in the CO, LCol Ware, to give me a direct order.

By now the fever had taken hold and I was not making any sense. I vaguely remember LCol Ware persuading me that, for my own good and for the good of the Regiment, I had to go to hospital immediately. He assured me I would be back with the Regiment in a few weeks when my

---

* LOB — Left out of Battle, a term applied only to those men held back in reserve when the Regiment went into action — usually about 10% of the unit.

132

job with the Scouts and Snipers would be waiting for me.

I shall always be grateful to LCol Ware for having me evacuated without delay. I am sure he didn't give me any order. He didn't have to; it wasn't his way. During the time I served as his scout officer I had such respect for him that I always carried out his wishes without hesitation.

I was taken to an ADS at Francofonte where the MO made me a stretcher case and took my revolver. I tried to keep my weapon (for what purpose I can only imagine) but was too weak to offer any resistance.

After a hot and bumpy ride in an ambulance I arrived at 5 Canadian General Hospital situated on a high hill overlooking Catania; it had formerly been a modern Italian TB Sanatorium. My last recollection of that day is a montage of high, airy rooms; sheets, pillowcases and nursing sisters — lots of nursing sisters. A letter to my mother, written after I recovered, describes my condition:

> *Malaria is something I hope I never get again. Hot and cold all the time, with severe headaches and aching muscles. The MO here says I am over the worst part of it now, so there's no need to worry. The hospital has been taken over by us completely, with nursing sisters by the dozen and all modern conveniences. Cool in the daytime, too.*
>
> *When I came here at night I was running quite a fever and mumbling a lot of nonsense, like most people do. The Sisters told me later that when I heard a Canadian girl's voice, I straightened right out, mumbled something about a girl, and didn't say another thing until next morning!*

Needless to say, I was not the only soldier afflicted with malaria, despite the precautions:

> *During these two weeks the number of cases of malaria in the division rose to epidemic proportions... for the whole period July 10th to August 31st there were approximately 1,200 Canadian cases.*[1]

Ever since our briefing on board ship I had tried to take mepacrine tablets regularly, even in action, but the 'exigencies' of the service often made it impossible. Furthermore, the last stages of the campaign had been fought in a highly malarial area. The fact there were another 1,199 cases besides me was little consolation for being rendered *hors de combat* by this insidious fever. However, other Patricia patients came round to cheer me up, including Capt Colin McDougall. We all agreed that the treatment was almost as bad as the disease — three doses of quinine daily. It was effective, but it was foul-tasting stuff.

A remedy to neutralize the taste of quinine now appeared, like magic, in the form of parcels from home. One morning the postal clerk deposited five parcels on my bed and declared "manna from heaven". To which I could only add "Amen".

My parcels had travelled, I suppose, at least 10,000 miles: from Toronto to England, to Sicily, to the Regiment and back to hospital. If Hitler had realized how much these parcels boosted morale, he would have intensified his efforts to intercept them, or at the very least sink them. During the war my parents and relatives sent me more than 70 parcels of foodstuffs, 30 boxes of Laura Secord chocolates and tens of thousands of cigarettes; 80 per cent survived all attacks by enemy aircraft and U-Boats and arrived in excellent condition. Some parcels kept chasing me as I moved about from England to Sicily, to Italy, to North Africa, to England again, then back to Italy and on to Northwest Europe and England once more. In the end most of them caught up with me.

That evening our ward, Colin McDougall and the nursing sisters had a real feed which soon developed into a party; from a secret cache, bottles of vino and cognac appeared; from the kitchen a scrounging party delivered bread, pies and cakes. One sister played the guitar while another sang and we all joined in the chorus. The healing effect of this non-medical treatment was marvellous to behold — no one complained of pain that evening. Next morning was quite a different story.

These sisters were another secret morale builder that Hitler missed. Not enough can be said about these angels of mercy. Many a soldier survived the war due to their care and devotion, above and beyond the call of duty.

The harbour at Catania, clearly visible from our hospital ward, was crowded with ships and landing craft of all sorts. Every evening, just before dark, German planes whizzed by the hospital so close you could see the pilots' faces, and bombed the ships in the harbour. We didn't worry too much about these cheeky intrusions as, in our naiveté, we believed our hospital immune from danger because of a large red cross painted on the roof.

About 1600 hours on September 2nd, after our party, 12 nursing sisters were having tea on the roof, not expecting any German planes so early in the evening. Suddenly three enemy aircraft zoomed past, heading for the harbour. Our anti-aircraft guns opened up; one shell burst prematurely and wounded all 12 nursing sisters, two seriously. Sister Forest was wounded in both legs and evacuated.

It was a terrible shock to the ward and we did what we could to help. Nurses now became patients and patients became nursing orderlies. We filled their ward with flowers and shared the contents of our parcels with them. We felt the loss of our 'angels' deeply.

Early next morning the Allies landed on the Italian mainland: our division at Reggio, across the Strait of Messina with orders to advance up the centre of the Calabrian Peninsula; the British 5th Division on the left, to proceed along the west coast road.

Rumours of these landings had gone round the hospital several days before, even the exact hour of the attack. It would not have been difficult for any of the Italian cleaners or orderlies at the hospital to learn of the impending assault and pass the information to the Germans. It is a fact that the air attacks on Catania harbour increased on September 2nd, when the nurses were wounded. I have often wondered how much the Germans knew about the Allied plans.

Gen McNaughton, Commander of the Canadian Army Overseas, made a brief visit to the hospital during his tour of the island. The last time I had seen him was at RMC when he had inspected the battalion and addressed the cadets. I had missed his earlier visit to the Regiment due to absence on other duties. As it turned out, this was my last chance to meet him before he resigned and returned to Canada. However, some new exigency, which I don't recall (probably I was knocked out with fever), again intervened and I never did meet our famous general who had formed the Canadian Army in World War II.

Other visitors came to our ward: one was a military friend of my father from Saskatoon, Dr Duncan Croll, who had served with The Saskatoon Light Infantry and was in charge of surgery at the hospital. I wrote my father a note:

> Today I was having a little chat with one of the nursing sisters in bed (only I was in bed!). Just as I was asking the sister if a certain Maj Croll was in this hospital, he dropped in to the ward. That's the way these things always happen — I mentioned you, and immediately Croll bounded over to shake my hand and sit down for a half hour's chat. He promises to write you a line as soon as he can get the time.

One thing I didn't mention in my letter was that Dr Croll left me an issue of Esquire, which helped no end to restore my morale, if not my morals.

With all this medical and extra-medical attention I couldn't help but feel better. The quinine treatment was also doing its job but I was still weak, especially in the legs — a typical symptom. I tried to walk around the ward, collapsed, was ordered back to bed, and given further medicine — pamoquin.

After two weeks of enforced confinement I was finally allowed up, got dressed and made the rounds of the hospital visiting friends. Colin McDougall was also pretty well recovered so we made plans to visit Catania. Two other Patricia officers who had been sick with the fever — Lt Willie Mulherin (my RMC senior) and Lt Norman Cousens — joined our expedition. We requisitioned a horse and buggy and with me cracking the whip like a latter-day Ben Hur, raced into Catania in fine style. To our chagrin, most of the interesting places were out of bounds; the city teemed with military police. Eventually, we managed to find a *ristorante* where we had a wonderful meal of spaghetti, vino and *coni gelati*. There were probably regulations against eating ice-cream but, as the soldier devouring the watermelon had observed to Brig Vokes, 'it sure didn't taste like it!''

My study of the Italian language in hospital continued to pay big dividends; I was now an expert haggler in the market-place and knew how to get directions to any spot in town. If I got in trouble with some fast-talking Italian, I had learned to raise my hand and say, *"sole parlare inglese"*. As often as not the reply would be, "OK boss — you knowa *mio fratello* in Taranto. Itsa nicea *Italiano citta* in Canada." (He assumed Toronto was named after Taranto in Italy.)

On rare occasions, when all efforts failed to establish communication, I had an ace up my sleeve that I played for all it was worth. During a visit to Catania I found I had inadvertently strayed into an Out of Bounds area, for what purpose I can't remember. One of the Carabinieri spotted me and was about to yell *"Proibito, Proibito"*, when he saw my red shoulder flash bearing the letters PPCLI. He hesitated and then pointed to the flash — *"Polizie?"* I immediately understood his question and replied, with considerable relief, that of course I was a policeman. He saluted and went his way. When I returned to hospital I told one of the Italian orderlies I had been mistaken for a policeman. With a large smile and many *"Bravos"* he explained, in halting English, that the letters PPCLI, when pronounced in Italian, sounded very similar to *Polizie;* further, the two words looked alike.

Several more expeditions to Catania soon restored my strength and I felt ready for the field again. In my eagerness to get forward I left the hospital on September 6th, skipped the usual week's convalescence after a malaria attack, and went straight to my old friend 4 Battalion, CBRD where I was again posted to Capt Snafu's company. It was indeed situation normal, all fouled up. The battalion was camped on the beach south of Catania, in a filthy area formerly occupied by German troops. Signs of heavy air attack were everywhere — craters, bombed out buildings, smashed German equipment. The battalion, in the process of moving to Italy, could not cope with the unexpected arrival of Colin McDougall and me, so we were left behind as rear party.

I soon found I was not ready to lie down on a rocky beach without even a blanket. I tried to sleep on a German mattress and paid the penalty — it was occupied by other creatures. In the morning I located an RAP and received the usual treatment for lice; my body hair was shaved off — chest, arm pits and the rest — and blue ointment applied. It was a treatment I never forgot and I avoided all single mattresses, German or other, for the rest of the campaign.

On September 8th at 1730 hours we received electrifying news — Italy had surrendered. The jubilant Italians rushed out of their homes and down to the beach, letting off fire crackers and firing old Italian weapons hidden away for such an occasion. At last the hated Germans would be driven from their country and the war would soon be over — perhaps by Christmas. But the Italians under-estimated the resourceful Germans who had long before made plans to take over the country if the Italian army surrendered. They now proceeded to occupy Rome and all the key centres. It was going to be a long war.

On September 9th we received news of a further British and American assault at Salerno on the west coast of Italy, followed by Airborne landings at Taranto. The paratroopers were virtually unopposed. The fighting at Salerno, however, turned out to be a bloody affair, and the troops barely escaped being thrown back into the sea.

Again I had been caught napping in a reinforcement unit while great events were unfolding at the front, and I cursed my luck. In desperation, Colin McDougall and I commandeered a vehicle and headed north along the coastal road for Messina, past Taormina, a charming hillside resort on the eastern approaches to Mount Etna. This was now the headquarters of Gen Montgomery who had recently kicked out the prior tenant, Gen Rommel, former commander of the defunct Afrika Corps. Before the war, Taormina had been a favourite holiday haunt of Col Gault, the Founder of the Regiment. I made a mental note of the name and determined to return after the war — I did, 13 years later, and fell in love with the place.

At Messina we had no trouble hitching a lift with one of the many landing craft ferrying troops and supplies across the Strait, less than four miles wide at that point. We touched down on a beach near Reggio (where the Patricias had landed on September 4th without any opposition) and reported to Capt Snafu at 4 Battalion. He greeted us with the good news that we would be on a draft to the Regiment next day. His information, as usual, was slightly exaggerated — a week went by before we left for the front. In the meantime, it was a matter of playing the old army game of wait and see. Willie Mulherin and Norm Cousens were also bogged down at 4 Battalion trying to find ways and means of getting forward to the Patricias. A contest developed as to who would escape first.

The situation at 4 Battalion had now become even more chaotic than usual. The battalion was crammed together with a British reinforcement depot; 3,000 Canadian and British troops were milling about in a small area, waiting to go forward, competing for accommodation and rations. Rumours flew around the camp that the other ranks would stage a mutiny if the mess was not straightened out. For once the trouble could not be laid entirely at the door of Capt Snafu. The problem arose from two factors beyond his control — casualties had been light, so reinforcements were not required at the front;

the advance of the forward troops had been delayed by the mountainous terrain and the demolitions of the Germans, causing endless traffic jams in the roads ahead — only the most urgent convoys could get through.

Since landing at Reggio, the Patricias had been clawing their way north through the centre of the Calabrian Peninsula, along secondary roads in the Aspromonte Range, whose peaks rose 6,400 ft above sea level. Numerous streams, known as *fiumare,* cut through this mountain mass confining communications to the roads, whose gradients were stiffer and turnings more frequent than in any part of Italy, except the Alps.[2]

The Germans were quick to take advantage of this difficult topography. They mined the roads and demolished the bridges, forcing interminable delays on our troops until sappers repaired the damage. As soon as our division resumed its advance, the Germans rapidly withdrew to the next obstacle. As a result, the Patricias suffered few casualties and 4 Battalion was not asked to send forward reinforcements.

This information from the front trickled down the line to 4 Battalion where McDougall, Mulherin, Cousens and I were becoming very impatient with Capt Snafu and his fafu crowd. Determined at least to satisfy the inner man, we hitched a ride back to Reggio, where we had landed a few days before, and went looking for a *ristorante.* We soon found one that purported to offer steak, rice and vino for only a few lire. Half way through the meal I spotted something alien in the rice that wriggled for cover when I touched it with a fork — worms! We decamped, leaving the meal to the enemy forces.

Years later I was again visiting Reggio and looking about for a *ristorante.* My earlier experience was long forgotten. I found what seemed to be a good restaurant and went inside. The special of the day was steak, spaghetti and vino, which I ordered. The meal arrived, I started to roll the spaghetti on my fork when suddenly — déjà vu. "My God, not again!", I bellowed at the waiter. I can't say it was the same *ristorante,* but it certainly had the same species of lower life in the spaghetti.

A stubborn streak in my nature surfaced and I determined to complete my meal. I called over the head waiter and shoved the disgusting mess at him. With many *"Dispiace, signor",* he apologized and suggested other choices on the menu. I decided that a boiled egg was the only safe item; at least the inside of the egg would not be contaminated by the filth in the kitchen. The egg arrived, I broke it open and found more fowl than egg. Reggio is not on my list of gourmet restaurants.

Chapter X

ITALY
Off into the Blue
Reggio to Potenza
September 15 to September 25, 1943

Off we go into the wild blue yonder — crash*

On September 15th we finally received orders to move forward. The Patricia officers, McDougall, Mulherin, Cousens and I, and a draft of men, would travel in a convoy to join the Regiment, somewhere north of us. In fact, the Regiment was resting near the town of Catanzaro on the east coast of the toe of Italy, about 150 miles north of our 4 Battalion at Reggio. We set off along the coastal road at 1000 hours.

At 1530 hours, some 5 km south of Monasterace Marina, another vehicle coming south side-swiped my truck and drove us into the ditch. I made a note of the number, name and unit of the driver**, intending to have him court martialled as soon as I reported to the Regiment. Happily for him more serious events intervened and he got off scot-free.

No one was hurt, but the truck was damaged beyond local repair. The other vehicles in our convoy went on ahead with a message to send back another truck, while I and my 22 men camped on the side of the road near

---

* Parody on the song of the United States Army Air Corps.

** No 2115874, Pte Herberts of No 11th Mechanical Engineering Section, Royal Engineers.

139

the beach. That old fickle finger was putting it to me again. The Patricias would be in Rome while I was still messing about in the mountains of Calabria.

Still, the situation could be a lot worse. We had rations for an evening meal and the cool waters of the Mediterranean beckoned only a few feet away. After a swim and dinner we curled up in our blankets on the beach. Now it was the turn of the ants and sandflies to attack — the lice and worms had already had their turn at Catania and Reggio. We spent the rest of the night in the truck, on the side of the road, as convoy after convoy of tanks and equipment roared by on their way to the front. All next day we waited for a vehicle — none came.

Remembering my earlier success of commandeering vehicles in Sicily, I tried to stop one of the convoys and nearly got run over. This piece of road along the coast was a flat stretch which the Germans had not touched, and the drivers were barrelling their trucks along, trying to make up for lost time.

Rations ran out as they eventually do even in the best of circles. "Not to worry," I told my men, "S and L (scrounge and liberate) will provide."

Almost immediately help arrived from an unexpected quarter. Out of the north, in a cloud of dust, roared an American jeep. I snatched a bottle of vino we had been keeping for just such an emergency and waved it at the driver as he flashed by. Screech — the jeep skidded, turned about, practically in mid-air, and came back to our position. It was an American sergeant going south to Messina on some top secret mission. That didn't impress me. It was the large attractive box of American compo rations in his jeep I had my eye on.

The American sergeant was definitely interested in my vino. Exchanges were made and we cooked up a meal on the side of the road with the sergeant as our guest of honour. More bottles of vino were produced. Toasts were drunk to the President of the United States, Churchill and the King of Italy (for having the good sense to surrender). Finally the sergeant jumped in his jeep and careened off into the dark. We bedded down in our truck for the second night.

Next morning, September 17th, a TCV arrived from the Regiment. My message, sent forward two days earlier, had incredibly got through. The vehicle was a new Italian army truck, fresh from the Fiat assembly lines, which the forward troops had liberated from the defeated Italians. One thing the Italian Army had was an excellent TCV. It was almost twice as large as our vehicle, with a luxurious cab for the driver, with padded leather seats, and benches for the troops.

We gaped at this fine vehicle until the driver opened the door, jumped to the ground and gave me a half-ass salute.

"Oh no!" I muttered to my sergeant, "Not an Itie!"

"O yes!" growled the sergeant, "And worse — he's our only driver. We have to leave Pte Harrison with his truck here at this God-forsaken place. Anyway, who the hell could drive one of those monsters around the hairpin bends in the mountains up ahead?"

I had a tentative solution. "Sergeant, I'll ride in the cab with the Itie and be ready to grab the wheel if he gets into trouble." The look on the sergeant's face told me he was not impressed, but he didn't volunteer to take my place in the cab: "Well, Sir, good luck. I'll ride with the boys in the back and yell at them when to jump clear. I hope you make it."

We left our campsite on the beach near Monasterace Marina at 0930 hours that day and joined the congested traffic heading north along the coastal road — destination the Patricias, wherever they might be. We had no way of knowing their location as they, too, were on the move. Much later I learned that on that very day, in a remarkable dash by vehicle, the Patricias had travelled from Catanzaro along the coastal road to Cassano, a distance of 145 miles. Monasterace Marina, where I was camped, was only 40 miles from the Patricias at Catanzaro. If I had known this I suppose we could have reached the Regiment by a forced march.

What followed was a fresh series of mishaps, compounded by misinformation and plain bad luck. Whenever I thought I was getting close to the Regiment someone fumbled. It was like playing catch-up football.

All day September 17th we drove slowly north along the coastal road, in very heavy traffic, sometimes at a snail's pace. There was nothing I could do as, after all, I was not carrying a special pass from Gen Montgomery. At least I had an opportunity to size up my Italian driver whom we now affectionately called Joe.

At 2300 hours the truck started to shake, the engine coughed and went dead — out of gas. For the past two or three hours I had been trying to make Joe understand that we must be getting low on gas and should stop and scrounge some from passing vehicles. Now the traffic had thinned out and we were umpteen miles from nowhere.

Joe was not disturbed. "Impossible," he protested in Italian. "The gauge shows the tanks are half full." So much for the Fiat automobile works in Milano!

After trying for hours without any luck to wave down passing vehicles, I finally stopped one that had a few Jerry cans to spare. We filled up, Joe jumped into the cab, turned on the motor and we lurched forward into the night.

No lights were allowed, of course. I started to worry about Joe who didn't seem to like night driving any more than I. We had been driving, albeit slowly and intermittently, for the past 15 hours and I thought of pulling off the road. Field Marshal F F Fate made the decision for me. At 0030 hours the truck gave up and stopped. I looked at Joe who shrugged and said "Impossible..."

"Silenzio," I roared, *"Carro non buono, cativo, finito."* We pushed the truck off the road, climbed into the back and fell asleep.

In the morning Joe diagnosed the trouble as something wrong with the differential. I told him he had two hours to fix it up or I would have his differential for breakfast. That reminded me that my men hadn't eaten since the previous noon and we had no rations. I went round to the back of the truck and found someone had already solved the problem by acquiring another box of American compo rations. How or from where I didn't ask.

I debated whether I should send a man forward on one of the passing vehicles to find the Regiment and get another TCV. I hesitated to do this as there was a good chance he might get lost or even disappear for days or weeks; I would be held responsible, charged with incompetence and sent back to the reinforcement battalion. Even if the messenger found the Regiment, what chance did he have of convincing the adjutant I needed another truck?

On the other hand, if I just waited at the side of the road for Joe to fix the differential, the war might well be over before I reached the Regiment and I would be court martialled for desertion!

I decided I would rather be dismissed with disgrace than shot and sent my best man, Pte Duncan, ahead to notify the Regiment of our troubles and send down another vehicle. It turned out I should have waited one more hour as Joe somehow fixed the differential and we were on our way by noon. Whatever became of Pte Duncan I have no idea.

We didn't get very far along the coastal road. Near a small place called Squillace, a bridge had been blown by the Germans, forcing us around a 20 mile diversion. A monumental traffic jam developed as this secondary road through the mountains soon petered out into trails, and it took six hours to go 20 miles. We camped that night at a base repair shop near Catanzaro where Joe had the truck checked over and repaired by the expert mechanics of the 1st Infantry Repair Shop.

That evening, September 18th, I made an appreciation of the situation worthy of any staff officer. According to information I had received from rear headquarters of 1st Canadian Division, the PPCLI were moving next day from Cassano, on the east coast, to an area south of Potenza, in the heart of the Basilican highlands, a distance of 150 miles. The eastern coastal road which the Regiment was taking was a circuitous route, following the instep of the Italian boot, and was said to be jammed with traffic. The last 100 miles would be through mountainous country where doubtless the Germans had blown the bridges and mined the roads. As nearly as I could estimate, the distance by road from my position to the Patricias at Potenza, following their route, was at least 250 miles, probably a lot more.

On the other hand, a quick glance at the map showed an attractive alternative route. The 5th British Division had been rolling north along the west coast of Italy and by September 17th had made contact with American troops, who had fought such a stiff battle at Salerno. This coastal road ran in a direct line almost due north to Sapri. I estimated that the distance from my position to the Patricias, following this road, was 150 miles, of which only the last 50 would be through the mountains.

It was true I had to traverse a mountain range from my position to the west coastal road, but this was the narrowest point in the whole Calabrian Peninsula and the coastal plain lay only 15 or 20 miles due west. Nobody seemed to know anything about this short stretch of road; apparently it had been by-passed by the Allied troops.

If I were the corps commander and had to send 22 men from Catanzaro to Potenza, which route would I use? The road along the west coast, to be sure. I discussed my plan with some officers at rear divisional headquarters and they thought it brilliant. I had visions of becoming the next corps commander.

In a rejuvenated vehicle and in a new frame of mind we set off from the repair shop at 1400 hours on September 19th. Passing through Catanzaro, we easily climbed the mountain range, heavily forested with magnificent chestnut, beechwood and pines. By night-fall we had reached a picturesque forest retreat near Soveria on the crest of the Sila Mountains, where we camped. Local inhabitants greeted us warmly, giving us chickens, eggs, potatoes and tomatoes. It was obvious we were the first Allied troops through the area. We were not concerned, as tomorrow we would quickly descend the other side of the mountain to the coastal plain and be on our way north to join the Regiment.

Next morning, September 20th, we started off in high spirits and were barrelling down the road when suddenly Joe yelled, *"Madona, ponte bomba!"* and slammed on the brakes. Somehow we had wandered onto the wrong road and the bridge ahead was blown. Now I understood why the villagers had been waving their arms as we rolled along, shouting *"Proibito!"* Joe had saved our lives.

We retraced our steps, tried another road and promptly delivered ourselves into the hands of an artillery regiment of the 212th Italian Coastal Division with headquarters in Soveria. A road block, guarded by grim-looking Italian soldiers, fully armed, barred our way. My sergeant murmured to me through the window of the cab, "Holy cow! Look at all those fucking Italians!"

This was no time to imitate Gen Custer's last stand. I only hoped that the CO of the artillery regiment knew about the Italian surrender, and more important, agreed with its terms. I was escorted into the presence of an Italian capitano, wearing his full dress uniform and highly polished jack boots. He couldn't have been more pleasant. In perfect English he introduced himself and said what an honour it was to have some 'English' guests call on his regiment. His CO was away but could we stay for lunch and perhaps dinner?

He took me on a tour of his regimental area, showing me with great pride his artillery pieces, which I agreed looked pretty impressive, especially now that they would be shooting Germans. He didn't say yes and he didn't say no, so I dropped the subject.

The forest was alive with Italian soldiers, gathered in small groups, excitedly jabbering away and pointing at me and my men. I remembered the advice I had received months before on board ship — 'Treat the Italians kindly.' Giving them a broad smile, I raised my hand in a victory salute. They seemed to understand and smiled back. When I said *"Viva Italia"*, I knew I had won a bloodless victory.

One battery was cooking up what smelled like minestrone soup, in an enormous cauldron over a wood fire. The troops, gathered round with mess tins full of vino, were making rude remarks at the cooks — just like any other army. The captain renewed his offer to stay for lunch but I demurred, explaining I had to get up front and fight *tedeschi*. With this he heartily approved.

Before leaving Soveria, I sat down with the captain, and for the sake of protocol, shared a bottle of marsala with him, while my boys were likewise entertained. As a final gesture of goodwill, he gave me a detailed map of the countryside, indicating where the bridges and roads had been blown and showing the shortest route to the coast.

We set off amid lusty Italian cheers, passed through Nicastro and rapidly descended from this mountain redoubt to the coastal plain below. While we were negotiating the hairpin bends I was thinking of other matters and not keeping a sharp eye on Joe. As we came out of a turn, going much too fast, I vaguely saw a donkey and cart, laden with wares, in the middle of the road. There were really only two courses of action — hit the donkey fair and square, or take off into the valley below. Joe desperately attempted a third course. He tried to avoid the donkey by swinging his wheel to the right and then, at the last second, back to the left. It was no use. The truck mowed down the guard rails and several telephone poles and stopped with its right front wheel on the thin edge of nothing. The donkey, cart and contents went ass over tea kettle, literally, spewing chunks of the aforementioned all over the road. Only the driver of the cart escaped.

My boys were shaken up a bit, but not injured. After being side-swiped, having differential problems, running out of gas and encountering blown bridges they were ready for anything. Their attitude, no doubt, was fortified by the hospitality of the 212th Italian Division.

I apologized profusely to the driver, Signor G Montoni, and explained how we were hurrying to drive the hated *tedeschi* from his country, supported by my brave Italian driver (who incidently had done the damage) and indeed by the entire 212th Division. I had no doubt he would be compensated in due course by the proper authorities. In the meantime, would he accept 2,000 lire as a token? Of course he would. (2,000 lire was worth about $20.00 Canadian.) I got a receipt from him, as I intended to make a claim against the government for reimbursement as soon as I returned to the Regiment, but 'exigencies of the service', as always, put this and many other matters in the shade. Perhaps a grateful government will one day make me an *ex gratia* payment — I am not holding my breath. In a way, I suppose I was only paying off some of the IOUs I had issued in Sicily.

A quick inspection of our truck revealed we had suffered damage only to the bumper, fenders and the side of the cab (where I had been sitting). The vehicle was made of sterner stuff than I had imagined. A good crow bar soon pulled off the bumper and fenders and we started down the mountain again, with a new driver at the helm — me.

Soon we reached the coast and turned north, joining the convoys of the British 5th Division. It was easy going compared to our trek through the mountains; while the traffic was heavy, it was not nearly as congested as on the eastern coastal road. That night we camped at Campora San Giovanni, about 30 km south of Paola.

Next day, Joe seemed to have recovered from his confrontation with the donkey, so I gave him a turn at the wheel. We passed through Belvedere at noon and arrived at rear headquarters of 13th Corps, about 25 miles south of Sapri, at 1630 hours. I found the signal master, one Lt Moffat, and asked him to locate the PPCLI. After trying three hours he reported that the Regiment had just reached Potenza and gave me a trace showing the route.

While waiting for news from Lt Moffat, I sniffed around the rear headquarters of 13th Corps in search of any useful supplies for my men. Never before had I even seen a corps headquarters, much less infiltrated one, though I had heard it was a great place to scrounge attractive items seldom received at the front. My information was correct. The place was a Mecca for a penniless, hungry, infantry soldier. The first item on my shopping list was pay. My finances were a little short from making restitution, on behalf of the King, for a war-damaged cart and mule; my men were also down to their last lira. I spotted a field cashier and arranged with him to pay the men £12 each (£12 was the equivalent of 4,800 lire, or $48.00 Canadian).

Next on my list were rations. A helpful Service Corps officer supplied all we needed, throwing in for good measure cigarettes and extra chocolate bars. I considered asking him for a rum ration but decided not to press my luck.

That night my boys sat down to dinner at tables, in a manner befitting important visitors at corps headquarters. I was afforded similar treatment in the Signals Mess where I spent a very pleasant evening. It was to be my last dinner in an Officers' Mess for many, many months.

At 0715 hours next morning, September 22nd, we left corps headquarters and made good time along the coastal road. At Sapri we turned inland, following the route laid out by the signal master, and passed through the towns of Rivello, Lagonegro and Corleto, where we halted at dusk. As I had suspected, our route through the Apennines was much easier than any we had encountered in the south.

The Regiment was now a mere 25 miles north of us, digging defensive positions near Potenza. At last I had them in my grasp. The only question was whether to push on in the dark and try to locate the PPCLI headquarters, probably a three hour drive through country only recently cleared of the enemy, or camp for the night and leave early next morning. In Sicily I had already had one experience of joining the Regiment at night, which I was not keen to repeat. I decided to camp at Corleto.

I then got in touch with rear divisional headquarters and received a briefing on recent operations, enemy dispositions and the location of our own troops. In the evening I had a moment to reflect on the events of the past eight days and my incredible unguided tour of southernmost Italy, from Reggio in the very tip of the toe, to Potenza in the middle of the ankle. We had driven at least 500 miles, on all manner of roads, trails, diversions and donkey tracks; over mountains, through valleys and across chasms bridged by the most doubtful structures; we had survived encounters with other vehicles, a donkey, telephone poles, blown out bridges and the Italian Army, to name but a few of the obstacles. We had scrounged, liberated and bartered rations the whole time at no cost to His Majesty's Government in Right of Canada (but at considerable cost to other governments and people). I had lost only one man, Pte Duncan, who had been sent ahead to find the Regiment, and even he might turn up some day.

My troops were in fine fettle, ready to come to grips with the Hun. As one of my boys put it — after the dinner party at corps headquarters — "We're fighting fit, and fit to fight, just fighting fools." It had been another new test from which I had learned much and gained valuable experience. And it had been fun.

In this buoyant mood I arrived at headquarters PPCLI at 1100 hours, September 23rd, and reported to the adjutant, with my 22 men less one. He gave me the worst dressing down I had ever experienced. In his view I had been AWL for eight days on a frolic of my own in southern Italy; I should be court martialled but there were more pressing matters to be considered — like winning the war. For my sins I would be posted to D Company, 17 Platoon, the forward platoon of the forward company of the forward battalion. I was home again, but it was not too sweet.

Fortunately my platoon sergeant was Sgt Green whom I had known in England. He was happy to see me and quickly gave me the picture. My sections were ably commanded by Cpl Turcott and Cpl Dick. The company commander and second-in-command were also old friends, Capt Foo Hunter and Capt Colin McDougall.

The battalion was in the process of moving forward to seize a position six miles north of Potenza. My 17 Platoon was ordered to proceed along a mined road and make a diversion where a bridge had been blown by retreating Germans. Working with a bulldozer, picks and shovels, we hacked out a road of sorts from the southern approach to the bridge, down to the river bed and up the other side to join the road. It was not a professional job but it was good enough to let a field battery and anti-tank platoon get through.

We now received news of casualties being suffered by the platoons patrolling the road ahead. The Scouts and Snipers under Lt D E Jones had just had an exciting encounter with seven German armoured cars while approaching Atella, some 18 miles north of our position. The platoon had been fired on and Lt Jones and four men had been wounded; three men were missing. A further patrol had then been dispatched to Atella under Lt Don Munro. It, too, had been fired on; three men had been wounded and the platoon sergeant was missing.

I must confess, I was not too unhappy about Lt Jones (who was only slightly wounded) being sent down the line, as it meant there was an opening for me to return to the Scouts and Snipers. Perhaps old Field Marshal F F Fate had at last posted me to the Regiment at just the right time.

In any event, I still had my hands full commanding 17 Platoon at the blown bridge, where we were completing the diversion and stopping vehicles from hurtling over the gap where the bridge once stood. We had been warned that enemy patrols were still very active in the area and that they might try to infiltrate our lines and destroy us and our diversion. I placed two sections, under my command, at the north end of the bridge where an enemy attack was most likely to come; the other section at the south end of the bridge, closest to our own troops.

During the day there were no problems stopping traffic but at night it was difficult to tell whether the approaching vehicle was friend or foe. Obviously if we detected an enemy vehicle in time, we would welcome it and let it go through the barricade and into the river.

The first night we had a couple of near misses, including a patrol from the famous Popski's Private Army. During the North African Campaign, Maj Vladimir Peniakoff (later LCol Vladimir Peniakoff, DSO, MC) had formed an elite group of bold adventurers to make deep patrols in the desert behind enemy lines, usually hundreds of miles from home base. Once inside enemy territory, they wreaked havoc upon the enemy supply depots and troops, and obtained valuable information for the 8th Army. At first they received no official recognition, like the Scout and Sniper Platoon, but gradually, owing to their spectacular successes, they were accredited official status (unlike the Scouts and Snipers); they even designed and wore their own cap badge.

The entire group never exceeded more than 80 all ranks, officially at least, organized into four or more patrols. What they lacked in numbers, however, they made up in fire power. Each patrol had several jeeps heavily armed with 50 inch Browning machine guns, mortars, grenades, mines and small arms of all sorts. The fire power of one patrol must have equalled that of a regular company of infantry.

No one could pronounce Maj Peniakoff's name so they simply called him Popski and his group became known as Popski's Private Army, or the PPA.

Gen Montgomery, normally a stickler for proper form, surprisingly liked this irregular body and took them with him to Sicily and Italy. There, they continued to run amok behind enemy lines, spreading fear and despondency among the confused Germans.

Standing at my barricade across the road, I suddenly heard the roar of jeeps coming south at high speed toward the non-existent bridge. All day I had been stopping vehicles. Now it was dark and no lights were permitted except a small lantern I kept for an emergency. Swinging the lamp and shouting at the top of my voice, I somehow caught the attention of the lead driver. At the last second he skillfully swerved off the road, careening down the rough diversion into the river bed. It was Popski and his crew heading south after shooting up more Germans. Tragically a few nights later, another Popski patrol went over a blown bridge ahead of us, and all were killed.

Like Horatio of Old, I continued to guard the bridge against all comers or, really, to guard them from the bridge. My next customer was a vehicle from the Regiment bearing great news for me — I had been posted to command the Scouts and Snipers! I lost no time bidding goodbye to my boys, whom I had known only four days, and took off in a jeep heading south towards BHQ. My driver seemed to know the route back as it twisted and turned, bypassing bridges and gaps. I tried to act as his co-pilot.

I saw the barricade at the last second. Thankfully so did my driver. He braked the vehicle and we slid down the embankment without causing any damage. I silently apologized to Popski for calling him a damn fool an hour earlier.

I reported to the adjutant, who now seemed to have forgiven my little frolic in southern Italy and confirmed I was to proceed at once to command the Scouts and Snipers at Castello di Logopesole, some ten miles north of our position.

I was ready!

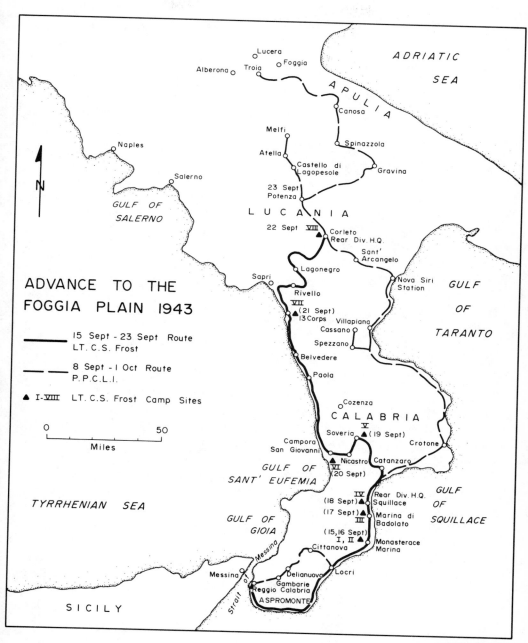

ADVANCE TO THE
FOGGIA PLAIN 1943

———— 15 Sept - 23 Sept Route
LT. C.S. Frost

- - - - 8 Sept - 1 Oct Route
P.P.C.L.I.

▲ I-VIII LT. C.S. Frost Camp Sites

0 _____ 50
Miles

Map #4

149

Chapter XI

SCOUTS AND SNIPERS

September 26 to October 12, 1943

The Princess Pats' Battalion Scouts
They never know their whereabouts
If there's a pub within a mile or two
You'll find them there with the
*   Ric-a-dam-doo, dam-doo, dam-doo*

On September 26th I drove north once again, past my diversion and many others, this time taking great care to follow the detours. At Castello di Lagopesole*, an immense thirteenth century castle overlooking the surrounding countryside, I reported to Maj D Brain who was in command of a large patrol force (known as Force X) consisting of C Company, 18 Platoon of D Company (which had just lost four men) and the Scout and Sniper Platoon; also, a battery of artillery, seven anti-tank guns, and detachments of mortars and medium machine guns from The Saskatoon Light Infantry. This Force, packing more fire power than the whole PPA, had been briskly and effectively ousting the Germans from towns in the area, including Atella, Rionero and Melfi.

Force X had pretty well completed its tasks when I arrived on the scene, and was now beseiged by a gaggle of war correspondents, including Greg Clark who immediately impressed us with his knowledge of the ground, the enemy and our own troops. He referred to our weapons and those of

---

*The castle was built by a German, Frederick II, in 1242. The present owner was an Italian Prince, Doria Pamphyli, who had been interned.

151

the Germans by their correct names and knew exactly how Force X was organized. Had I known his army background, perhaps I would not have been so amazed at his expertise.*

In a letter home I reported on my transfer back to the Scouts and Snipers:

> *Once again I am back at my old job at BHQ as OC of the Scout and Sniper Platoon.*
>
> *I have the greatest bunch of lads in the Bn. As a matter of fact, I always seem to hit a good bunch, but these boys have been picked for their scouting and initiative, and they are real soldiers. This platoon is a little different from the other rifle platoons. That is, we are all on our own and away from the normal Battalion bull! Day and night we are off into the blue, poking around, and having the odd bit of fun.*
>
> *As you know from the news, we are always on the move and right now I am writing this from a dirty little shack where my patrol H.Q. is. Tomorrow we are away again, and I shall send this letter back on the ration truck — if it gets here! (Damn this Wop ink, I must get some Jerry stuff.)*
>
> *Just a few days ago I was lucky to receive your letter of July 16. It contained a lot of good advice — so good that I read out part of it to my men. You can bet your life that I'm looking after the lives of my boys and myself. The old College motto 'Truth, Duty, Valour' is all very well, but every ex-cadet always adds to the end 'And for God's sake use your head!'*
>
> *The people in Italy are so much better off than those in Sicily. They also have a better understanding of the war and the grievous mistakes of their government. Consequently, we are welcomed in a more hospitable way, and up to date have been given most useful information on Jerry. What has turned these people so deathly against the Germans is the way they have treated the Italians since the Armistice. By now you will have read the report from Gregory Clark of the Toronto 'Star', of the killing of 17 civilians for no good reason by the Jerries in a town not so far from here (Rionero). I got quite a kick out of chatting and comparing notes with Canada's famous War Correspondent. He's a good egg!*

The Scout and Sniper Platoon had been on the go for some time, patrolling the countryside day and night, usually behind enemy lines, and had suffered casualities. They now needed time for rest and re-organization. With the CO's permission I gathered them together and withdrew to a rest area near

---

*Later on I learned he had fought with distinction in World War I and won the Military Cross.

battalion headquarters. The platoon still had no official status or formal organization; no vehicles, wireless sets or equipment of its own. The men were still on strength of the companies from which they were drawn, causing needless confusion in procuring rations, clothing and pay. In fact, the platoon was at the mercy of the company quartermaster sergeants who drew rations and allocated them to the platoon by some mysterious formula.

Even I had no official status as commander of the Scout and Sniper Platoon, being nominally on strength of some company as a platoon commander. I fought like a tiger (paper tiger, my friends said) to have the platoon recognized on paper as a legal entity. It was futile. If only I had the status of a Popski . . . . .

However, by shamefully wheedling the quartermaster, gently goading the paymaster, and pulling rank on the Signals NCO, I got rations, pay, vehicles and wireless sets for my men; also writing paper and even identity discs (I still kept my Italian dog tags for good luck). The padre donated sweaters; my parents unwittingly contributed cigarettes for the entire platoon (another batch of parcels had caught up with me).

Next I turned my attention to promoting deserving soldiers and again ran foul of the company commanders whose men they legally were. Much against their advice I promoted one Pte J Slimkowitch to lance corporal. 'Slim' was a born scout and had performed well on recent patrols. He was well known throughout the battalion as a rather carefree soldier of fortune, which indeed he was, having fought in the Spanish Civil War with the Papineau Brigade. He knew more about real fighting than he cared to admit; but peacetime soldiering and training in rear areas made him restless and he soon forfeited any stripes he had won in action. I never regretted my decision to promote Slim. Both in and out of action he served me loyally and helped me out of a difficult situation on my last patrol. Under my successor he continued his good record until he himself was badly wounded and returned to Canada in 1944. There, he got in touch with my parents and gave them much hope and comfort when news of my condition was sporadic and often inaccurate. After the war he joined a Toronto Militia Unit and rose to staff sergeant; later he transferred to the Cadets and became an officer in the Cadet Services of Canada — a remarkable soldier.

Another man I promoted to lance corporal was Pte E G Brautigan, also a loyal soldier and splendid fighter. During my last action he gave me vital support without which I would not have made it back to my own lines. He was wounded later, but survived the war.

A mobile bath for all ranks completed the new look of the Scout and Sniper Platoon. Whether it was a legal entity or not could not have mattered less to the men.

We were now ready for the arduous patrols we knew lay ahead, always well in advance of the battalion, or on its flanks. Our task was clear — to be the eyes and ears of the CO. The next four weeks were to be the most exciting and exacting of my entire military career.

The battalion resumed its advance through the Apennines, in the general direction of Campobasso, 90 miles to the north at the foot of the great Matese Mountains. It would be the same kind of mountainous terrain we had traversed before; the same deep ravines and rivers; the same twisting roads and trails. But now it might be possible to move across country by foot and mule instead of being confined to the roads. This terrain was made to order for the German defenders who would continue to mine every road and blow every bridge, forcing us to fight for every feature.

On September 30th, at 0700 hours, the battalion moved off in TCVs. Mindful of my solemn promise to myself in Sicily never to be late for a move, I awoke my Scouts and Snipers in good time so they would be ready to cross the start line at 0630 hours, a half-hour before the time appointed. As a guide to future moves, I noted in my diary that the cooks required one hour to prepare breakfast, the men one-half hour to eat, and a further 15 minutes to pack.

The route lay south to Potenza, then east to Gravina and northwest to Spinazzola where we arrived at 1345 hours, some 2-1/4 hours ahead of schedule. To my knowledge this was the first and only time a convoy in Italy arrived at its destination with so much time to spare. Furthermore the convoy had travelled 90 miles in 6-3/4 hours, another notable achievement on the circuitous mountain roads. We were rolling!

It could not last. Late that evening we received orders to be ready to move at 0515 hours next morning; at 2200 hours the start time was put back to 1045 hours — a more civil hour, I thought, to commence operations against the enemy. The truth of the matter was, however, that our division and the 78th British Division were competing for the same road north and the 78th Division had won out. Finally at 1130 hours we crawled a mere seven miles and then had to pull off the road and wait in the fields for the mighty 78th Division to pass through. I wasn't sure whether this was fog of war or an administrative snafu. It didn't really matter — someone had fumbled the ball. Yet the staff would not easily admit defeat by the enemy, by their own troops or by circumstances. They tried to confound the enemy and direct our attention from the mess they had created by churning out a mass of paper including a new pass word, 'Jack Hobbs-Surrey and England'. I was certainly impressed with such sang-froid.

At 2315 hours we set off again, travelled all night, and arrived outside Troia at 0530 hours on October 2nd. While the companies consolidated their positions I reported to the IO, Capt Walter Dewar, who gave me orders to send out a patrol immediately to a small village, Casteluccio, some seven miles to the west, to see if it was occupied by the enemy. Reports had trickled in from escaped POWs that the Germans had withdrawn from the town.

That didn't mean a thing. One of the Germans' favourite tricks was to pretend to leave a town and then sneak back, ready to give our unsuspecting patrols a warm reception.

Seven miles is not much of a distance unless you have to do it on foot, without any sleep the night before. A carrier was not the answer as the road might well be mined. Furthermore, there seemed no point in taking seven or eight men when one officer could probably do the job. I sniffed around the BHQ area looking for a motor bike. A despatch rider, propped up against his bike, catching a few winks of sleep, seemed a likely prospect. "Let's go get ourselves a Jerry prisoner," I suggested. This seemed a more attractive way to put it than giving the DR a command to take me along a road, possibly mined, towards a village probably held by Germans.

The DR grinned. A prisoner was just what he wanted for breakfast. He cranked up the pedal, the motor spurted and we took off, with me riding pillion on an improvised seat — my own. The DR was now fully awake and beginning to think more clearly. "What do we do, Sir, if there are Jerries in that town who don't want to surrender, and start shooting at us?"

"Gun the bike into the ditch, on the right — but watch for mines," I yelled back.

We made our way along the road, weaving from side to side, the DR keeping a sharp eye for evidence of mines, while I watched for any movement in the village, now only a few hundred yards away. Suddenly I spotted an Italian flag, then another. Then a few people ventured out into the street waving and shouting at us. As we got closer I could make out their words: *"Tedeschi scarpe via"* (The Germans have left).

Greatly relieved, we drove into the village and were swamped by the townsfolk offering the usual vino, fruit and bread. I asked for the head man and found I was talking to him, so he claimed. This was vehemently disputed by half a dozen others. I was not about to get embroiled in local politics and used my old crutch *"Sole parle inglese"*, whereupon several old men pushed forward with cries of "You knowa *mio fratello* in New York?"

My mission was to check whether the village was occupied by the enemy. Time was of the essence. I could almost feel the hot breath of LCol Ware blowing down my neck. I gave a nod to my DR, we jumped on the bike and roared off down the narrow streets looking for Germans and avoiding Italians. The place seemed 'clean' except for the Italians, and we were about to head back when our way was barred by three or four old ladies in black. We slid to a stop. I started to bulldoze my way through these determined *signore* when one cackled *"Tedesco Malato"* (a sick German). She led me to her hovel, past the chickens and into her bedroom, where she pointed to a form lying on a cot — a German paratrooper. In a few moments I established he was a very sick member of the 3rd Parachute Regiment whom the Germans, in their hasty retreat, had left behind. After being assured he would not be shot, he was willing to give us any information he had about his own troops. He knew the game was up. Too many nations were aligned against the Germans. He only wanted to get to a hospital.

This talkative paratrooper was a bonus I had not expected. It satisfied my DR who got the prisoner he had come for; the IO would have a field day grilling him.

All that remained was to transport our catch seven miles to battalion head-quarters. Three on a bike was clearly a crowd. I told the DR to return to BHQ at the high port and get a vehicle while I frisked my paratrooper and kept a close watch over him. His belt, badges, insignia and other items of equipment are still among my collection of war trophies.

Back in my platoon area, I received welcome news that the battalion would not be moving for at least 24 hours, giving me a chance to rest, clean up and get a decent meal. For some time the troops had been living on compo rations (canned bully beef, spam, lamb stew, meat and vegetable stew, pork and beans) served buffet style — cold. Now we switched to bulk rations: fresh meat, fresh vegetables and bread — wonderful bread instead of hard tack. We augmented these rations with local produce, as before, only now it was considered bad form not to pay the farmers a fair price.

During my absence on patrol, the platoon cook, Pte MacKay, had bought a pig for $20.00, and Pte Atkinson had built an oven. That night we had a fine 'pig out' despite a heavy rainfall that threatened to spoil our dinner party. Just as things were getting dull we heard the great news that Naples had, at last, fallen to the Allies. Soon the men started to talk about being home for Christmas. The observation in my diary is short and to the point — 'Ballocks'!

The troops were still going sick from malaria, yellow jaundice and other maladies; at least ten men reported to the battalion RAP every day. Since taking command of the Scouts and Snipers I had lost five men, or 20% of my understrength platoon, making it difficult to perform our patrolling tasks.

According to the *Official History*, one unit medical officer

> *attributed much of sickness to the unsuitability of the normal bulk rations to an enterprise of this nature. The inconvenience and danger of preparing and serving food in such adverse conditions emphasized the superiority of the 'compo', box-type ration, which Canadian troops had received in Sicily. But provisions were only occasionally issued in this form during the campaign in Italy.*[1]

In my view, however, the real culprit was the cold weather and heavy rain we were now enduring in the mountains. Our tropical kit, bush jacket, shorts and puttees — issued so long ago aboard ship — gave us no protection.

Through yet another snafu, our winter dress had not come forward, except in dribs and drabs, leaving us no alternative but to liberate clothing from Germans or Italians.

Our heavy battle dress did not arrive until about mid-October, by which time most of us were thoroughly chilled and soaked to the bone. Yet even in our misery we could find something to laugh about. Along with the battle dress came an item we had requested way back in Sicily: a special type of margarine that would not melt in hot weather. We soon found it would not melt in cold weather either. You could cut it with a saw, pulverize it with a sledge hammer, but it would not melt or spread.

A letter to my mother describes our running battle with elements, Jerries and Ities.

> *Today, is the first bit of a rest we have had for some time now. It is too wet and muddy to sleep, so I am in an office truck while it pours rain outside. Every day in October has been wet and miserable, but a soldier seems to get used to it.*
>
> *I would like to have a picture of myself now. Besides a good bit of mustache, I've got a good week's beard. My uniform consists of whatever I can get to keep warm, and it is extra chilly this morning. I have an old pair of German pants, a summer drill shirt, home-knit sweater, German shirt, battle dress blouse, and a pair of Australian boots! Fine looking officer, eh wot! I've got maps, binoculars, compass, etc, hung about me, and although I haven't got one now, I usually carry a German pistol or my issue revolver. My head-dress is anything I happen to have at hand: a beret, skull cap, field service cap, or nothing at all. All in all, I am a peculiar looking specimen.*
>
> *Well, I'm waiting patiently for our next move. I suppose I'll have a patrol or two to send out tonight. This is an 'uphole' job, this Scout work. I know all the moves of the enemy at all times, what his strength is, etc, and also the same with our own troops. So in this job I can see a more complete picture of what is going on, what is likely to go on, and what has gone on! Still my Italian improves, and is a constant help in getting around the country.*

One thing gave me more trouble than anything else — lack of sleep. Long ago, at RMC, I had developed a certain tolerance toward lack of sleep. Much to the annoyance of my professors I had learned to sleep in class, sitting bolt upright, at attention, looking straight ahead, with eyelids not quite closed. (In this condition I absorbed about 50% of the instruction — not much different from when I was fully awake!) But this wasn't the same as learning to do without proper sleep for long periods, sometimes days, during patrols behind enemy lines. The toughest part was returning to home base over mountain tracks, across swollen rivers, through fields of mud, in drenching rain, thick fog and pitch-black darkness.

First the legs begin to go, then the stomach tightens and starts to ache. Breathing becomes difficult and comes in short angry gasps; the weakness spreads to the whole body. The mind fights to keep going, but deep down you know you are not going to win. Still you fight on and suddenly — relief — the legs recover some strength and the pain in your stomach subsides; you find your second or your third or your fourth wind. But then the aches, tension and weakness return — worse than before. You have to have five minutes' sleep . . . you have to . . . you wake up and you are still on your feet, staggering, muttering, like a boxer on his last legs — it's the end! You collapse on the side of the trail.

Such are the recuperative powers of a young man that after 40 minutes' sleep he can be aroused and, almost automatically, go at it again, and again, and again — until finally the body quits and nothing can persuade it to move until it is ready.

On October 4th, at 0900 hours, the Regiment set off for Montefalcone, by motor transport, in heavy rain, following the route Popski had taken two days earlier when, accompanied by a squadron of armoured cars of the PLDG, he had driven the Germans from Alberona. In typical Popski fashion, the combined force of jeeps and armoured cars had worked its way behind Alberona, forcing the startled Germans to flee for the hills and leave 15 dead comrades behind. It was the first of many instances of active co-operation between PPA and Canadian troops.[2]

As the Patricias passed through Biccari and entered Alberona on October 4th, I hoped to catch a glimpse of the ubiquitous Maj Popski, but he had left the previous day on a fresh mission behind enemy lines. We envied his free-wheeling patrols and saluted his courage.

Our route continued through Castelfranco to our final destination north of Montefalcone, where we arrived at 1400 hours, having covered 30 miles in five hours — not much faster than marching! The companies immediately moved into positions covering the cross-roads south of San Bartolommeo, in a wide valley surrounded by mountains from which the Germans had perfect observation of our movements. The area had just been shelled and no time was lost digging in. Fortunately the Germans were now concentrating their fire on a high bridge that crossed the valley about a mile north of our position.

While the battalion completed its defensive positions I sent out two patrols: one under LCpl Slimkowitch to Baselice, six miles to the northwest, to contact the Edmontons (The Loyal Edmonton Regiment); the other patrol under LCpl Lewis to Roseto to contact the Seaforths (The Seaforth Highlanders of Canada). LCpl Slimkowitch's patrol had great difficulty locating the Edmontons, finding once again that distances on a map often bear no relation to the ground; but he accomplished his mission and returned to BHQ. LCpl

Lewis, after a determined effort, could not establish contact with the Seaforths.

Later that night information trickled in that the Edmontons and Seaforths had bumped the enemy at Baselice and Foiano. It was no wonder that LCpl Slimkowitch and LCpl Lewis had run into trouble trying to get through to these battalions.

The enemy shelled our area intermittently all night, but the men were well dug in and no casualties were suffered. Sickness, however, continued to take its toll, as I had to evacuate two more men with yellow jaundice; also the IO, Capt Dewar, took sick, but remained with the battalion, while I assumed his duties. (This was not new to me as I was supposed to be understudying his job.)

In the morning (October 5th) our field artillery and anti-tank guns moved into our BHQ area and took up positions about five yards from my platoon. If I had been the CO I would have told them to move on, but not LCol Ware – if they required our area for gun positions, by all means be our guests.

At 1400 hours the artillery opened up on an enemy concentration of troops about three miles away, giving them a solid pounding with three minutes' intense fire. It was the closest I had ever been to guns firing in action. I had never heard or seen anything quite like it. When the gun position officer gave the command "fire", the guns exploded with a shattering blast that shook the ground and filled the air with acrid fumes and smoke. The gun numbers jumped to their tasks with a will, throwing open the gun breeches, ejecting the casings, shoving in another round, packing the charge, slamming home the breech and letting go another salvo.

Little wonder some of my artillery friends often appeared a little stand-offish. I had always assumed they adopted this attitude because they considered the artillery second only to God. Now I realized they were stone deaf and half-stunned from the blasts of their own artillery pieces.

The gunners, obviously enjoying their work, continued to put on quite a show for the benefit of us infantry types. I shared their enthusiasm, visualizing their shells exploding in the midst of a company of German infantry, sending them all to their version of Valhalla. My fantasy was soon shattered as the Germans promptly returned our fire, giving us an opportunity to join their departed comrades, which we gratefully declined.

In the afternoon the brigadier came round to observe the show; the Germans spotted his flaming red tabs and entourage and promptly started to mortar the area. Enemy weapons have no respect for man, beast or brigadier. When a bomb fell a little too close to our guest, I offered to have my Scouts and Snipers dig him a slit trench. He demurred, as required by the customs of the service, but I insisted and the job was completed — just in time before the brigadier, I and others went to our own Valhalla.

Later that day I received a warning order to stand by to take up ammunition and rations to A Company who had been supporting an attack by the Edmontons on Baselice. As I was about to set off in a carrier, information was received that a patrol from A Company had bumped into a roving tank; a sergeant had been wounded and taken prisoner along with another man from his platoon. I was not too disappointed when the CO cancelled my orders to proceed until he received further information.

Next morning (October 6th), A Company reported the area clear of enemy tanks so I went forward in my carrier over a road that had not yet been travelled by our vehicles or swept for mines — an experience I didn't particularly enjoy.

Meanwhile the Seaforths, attacking Mt San Marco on our left flank, had run into some real trouble. Their C Company met a storm of fire "such as had never before been experienced by this battalion"; but C Company persevered and took the hill at a cost of some 30 casualties.[3]

The day following this gallant action by the Seaforths, I received orders to take a patrol to their position on Mt San Marco and from there recce forward toward Point 750, the next feature on our line of advance. Despite their ordeal the day before, the Seaforths were in fine fettle and gave me valuable information. I was told that following the assault by C Company on Mt San Marco, their D Company had run into German armour on the road ahead and suffered more casualties; the company commander and one sergeant had been killed. Armed with this helpful but disquieting information, my patrol set off on foot in the rain, across muddy fields toward Point 750, taking care to avoid the road where the German tanks had been reported. After a long and slippery climb we reached the top of the feature and found it unoccupied. Tired and soaked to the skin, we now had to report to BHQ some 15 miles in the rear, using a different route in case the enemy had seen our patrol going out and was waiting to ambush us on the way back.

We pushed on past the Seaforth outposts, halting a moment to report Point 750 clear. We set off again hoping the Seaforths could relay this information by wireless set to our headquarters, but knowing the set had little range in this mountainous terrain and it would probably take hours to get through.

It was now nearly midnight and we had been plodding along in the wet and cold for over 12 hours. That insidious enemy now assailed us — lack of sleep — and our bodies cried out to stop this terrible punishment. Just as we were about to quit we stumbled into the arms of a detachment of the RCAMC at Foiano, about half way to our BHQ. They led us into their ADS where their OC, Capt W L C (Bill) McGill, took one look at our bedraggled band and gave us permission (albeit without authority) to collapse on the floor. Later I asked one of my men how he managed to keep going. "Well," he explained, "I guess my feet just kept going from memory."

After an hour's sleep we were roused by our good samaritan, Capt McGill, with a steaming hot mug of tea and sent on our way with cans of bully beef and lamb stew to devour enroute. Not long after this incident Bill McGill became our MO and continued his good works among our troops for many months.

On arriving at BHQ I found that our information had miraculously been received by the CO and he was now preparing to move the battalion forward to occupy Point 750 and Point 960. I reported to LCol Ware who thanked me and asked if I would mind returning to Point 750 (this time by carrier) to check that the enemy had not returned, as was their custom. At the same time I might as well check Point 960 and possibly have a look at Decorata crossroads which the battalion had been ordered to capture.

I immediately set off in my carrier along the road I had trudged early that morning. At the Seaforths' headquarters I was informed by their CO that the road ahead was not yet cleared of mines and he advised me to leave the carrier and go on by foot. My legs did not respond too well to this fresh endurance test but I am glad I took his advice. Later that evening, as our battalion moved forward over the road ahead, a carrier from the mortar platoon struck a mine, wounding the commander, Lt A G C Richards, his driver, Pte C A Calder, and one other man. Calder died that night in the ADS where I had spent part of the previous evening with Capt Bill McGill. Lt Richards returned to duty but was again wounded on December 7th, this time seriously, and was evacuated.

We slipped and clawed our way up the slopes, through the rain and mud, arriving at Point 750 at 1530 hours. This time I abandoned all caution and took the most direct route, not caring whether the place was occupied by Germans, Italians or the Holy Ghost. The rain persisted but the fog and mist had now cleared enough for us to see the Decorata crossroads, and they too appeared to be free of enemy.

Once more it was a matter of urgency to return to BHQ with this important information, and again it was a struggle of mind over matter to get there. If we were exhausted the day before, no words could describe our present condition. Somehow we made it back to the Seaforth headquarters by 1730 hours, mostly by sliding and slipping through the muck, to find that the Patricias had moved up in preparation for their assault on the Decorata crossroads. I reported to the CO that I believed the crossroads were not occupied by the Germans.

This was welcome news indeed, as careful plans were just being made for the Patricias, supported by tanks and artillery, to make an attack next morning. The CO suggested I might now like to get back into my carrier and proceed directly to Decorata to confirm my belief the place was free of enemy, thereby saving numerous officers and men the trouble of having to mount a full scale attack.

I left by carrier at 1900 hours down the old familiar road, determined to push right through to Decorata, mud, mines and the Hun bedamned. We slewed past the rifle companies at a good clip and ran into a wall of fog blanketing the road and fields on each side. Visibility was zero but we churned slowly forward until suddenly the driver slammed down the brake pedals and we slid into the rear end of an armoured car. The driver and the rest of the patrol dived for the ditch, bringing their personal weapons to the ready. I shouted at them to hold their fire. We had run into not one, but four disabled armoured cars of the PLDG that the Germans had knocked out two days before. I had known about these vehicles from my various briefings with the CO of the Seaforths and had carelessly neglected to inform my driver and the rest of the patrol.

Our carrier was not damaged but our nerves were somewhat frayed; it didn't take much persuasion from my corporal to convince me to leave the carrier and proceed by foot. Unbeknown to me we had used up another ration of our luck, as we had gone over the very mine which blew up Lt Richards' carrier later that evening. This was not an uncommon stroke of luck as the Germans often set mines to go off after a certain number of vehicles had passed over them. Our number had simply not come up.

We pushed on by foot along the mountain road through the fog, wind, sleet and rain, clad only in our tropical kit and such other bits of clothing as we had acquired from the Italians and Germans. With less than a mile to go I figured we could make it to Decorata, but I didn't see how we could get back in time to call off the pending attack. I was pretty sure that if the Germans were still in the area we would have bumped into them by now, so I sent back LCpl Lewis to report our progress to LCol Ware and tell him I was pushing on to Decorata, less than a mile away, which I was confident we would reach in half an hour, maybe less; but we had had no rest for over 24 hours and would have to grab a few winks before returning to BHQ.

Sooner than expected I saw the faint outline of one building, then another. Summoning our last reserves of strength, we quietly eased off the road and into the fields surrounding the hamlet. Taking our time, we advanced upon the first building in open order, dropping back two men to provide covering fire. A haystack loomed out of the fog. Knowing this was a favourite outpost for Jerry, we quickly closed on it with weapons at the ready. Something moved in the straw; I gave a poor imitation of a German corporal — *"Raus, raus"*; a figure emerged from the haystack with his hands up — a very frightened Italian farmer. I quickly told him in Italian who we were and asked the vital question, *"Dove tedeschi?"* The farmer embraced me and my men, yelling at the top of his voice *"Canadese soldati sono qui!"* I could have knifed him!

Decorata was not occupied by the Germans. They had left earlier that evening after ransacking every dwelling, smashing furniture and paintings, and taking away personal belongings of any value. We cursed the Hun but thanked the gods of war he had departed, and collapsed on the mud floor

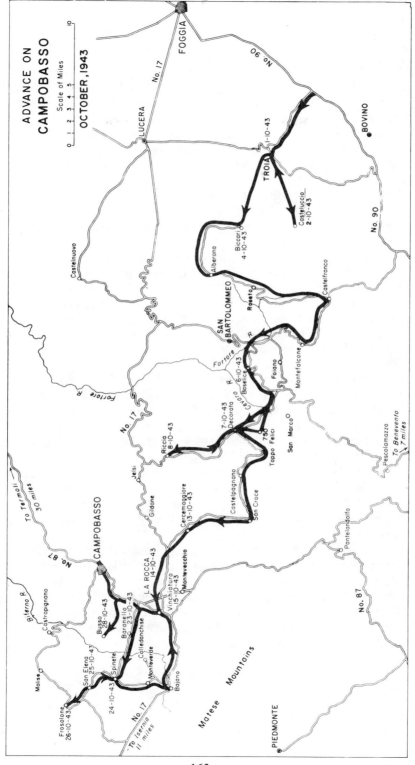

ADVANCE ON
CAMPOBASSO
OCTOBER, 1943

Scale of Miles
0 1 2 3 4 5   10

Map #5

of the farmer's house. Why he had been sleeping in the haystack I could not understand, nor care less. Probably the Germans had kicked him out and he was afraid to return.

We rested an hour and set out for home. My feet went by memory but I have no memory of the journey. We arrived at BHQ and I reported to the CO at 0400 hours: "Sir, no enemy in Decorata." I had earned my $5.00 that day!

At first light on October 9th the battalion advanced along the road which my Scout and Sniper Platoon now considered its private right-of-way, to occupy positions around Decorata crossroads which the platoon had recced the night before.

We caught a few hours' sleep and started to follow the battalion in a carrier, when suddenly a loud blast on the road ahead told us another mine had exploded. This time, a vehicle belonging to the 4.2 inch Mortar Platoon of The Saskatoon Light Infantry had hit a mine at the same place where the Patricia vehicle had been blow up the night before. Three men from our D Company, who had been filling in the hole created by the first mine, were wounded. My good luck charm was working overtime to preserve me once more from a similar fate.

For the next few days the battalion remained at Decorata while the Seaforths and Edmontons continued the advance. Rain, cold and wind continued to permeate our tropical clothing; the roads became quagmires. The quartermaster and his staff performed miracles getting the bulk rations up to the troops, and the troops showed their resourcefulness by setting up scores of improvised kitchens in the open. My diary of October 12th records it had rained every single day that month. As the elements worsened, my platoon cooks, Pte Hill and Pte McDonald, seemed to improve and prepared some of the best meals we had ever eaten — greatly assisted by the rum ration we now received. And we gleefully hacked away at the no-melt, no-spread margarine.

On October 12th, the battalion, having been ordered to seize Cercemajore some nine miles northwest of Decorata, left by vehicle at 0900 hours in the pouring rain. Slithering along the mountain roads in a sea of mud, we encountered a series of difficult diversions and had to stop while the sappers tried to clear the way. After five hours of churning about we pulled off the road one kilometre east of San Croce, about half way to our objective. It had taken five hours to go ten miles.

THE LAST PATROL

October 12 to October 26, 1943

Has anyone seen the Subaltern?
I know where he is. He's out on a night patrol
How do you know? I saw him, out on a night patrol

My Scout Platoon left immediately on patrol for Cercemajore, over — or rather through — the mud we had now learned to navigate like a cross-country skier. After six hours of this healthy outdoor activity we slid into Cercemajore and found it unoccupied. This time we had lugged along an 18 wireless set. After much difficulty getting through, we reported our information to BHQ. Later that night the battalion rolled through the town and took up positions without meeting any opposition.

Next day, October 13th, we came under heavy enemy artillery fire; a shell landed in B Company, killing one man and wounding ten others, two of whom died later that day. I was therefore quite happy to receive orders to take out a patrol to recce La Rocca (Point 1000). We left smartly at 1000 hours.

Nearly all orders for patrols were given verbally by the CO, the adjutant or the IO, as there was seldom time to commit anything to writing and if I were captured, the orders might be very useful to enemy intelligence. In any case the paper would soon disintegrate in the rain and mud. On this particular patrol, for some reason I cannot remember, I received written orders; incredibly, they have survived.

> *1. Recce route for Bn around flank to 1000 m feature.*
> *2. See if 1000 m is held by enemy. If so what strength approx.*
> *3. Any guns behind it?*
> *4. Are reverse slopes suitable for Bn position?*
> *5. Try and send one or two men to x rds 520212 to verify heavy*
> *guns there and pinpoint position.*
> *Route rd Junc 578203.*
> *Thru wooded feature around right.*
> *Investigate 700 m feature (5423) and 880 m feature (5323) as*
> *springboards for attack (i.e. cover for forming up place and*
> *covered approach to them) and open ground between these two*
> *features and objective.*
> *Platoon can then act as guides.*

La Rocca, a commanding feature 3,000 ft high and about six miles to the northwest of our position at Cercemajore, overlooked a road junction some two miles southwest of La Rocca. According to our maps, this junction was named Monteverde.* The Patricias had received orders to move off next morning at 0800 hours and occupy La Rocca as a necessary preliminary to seizing the road junction.[1]

As I set off I realized that time, again, was of the essence. Could we reach the objective and report back before the attack was launched? While the summit of the feature was only six miles away I knew it was going to be a long, difficult climb. Unfortunately we could not fly there, nor could we take a direct route as the approaches and the mountain itself were in enemy territory and reported to be occupied. All we could do was take advantage of what little cover the sparsely wooded ground offered and climb steadily toward our objective, keeping a constant eye on the summit where we were certain the Germans had an OP.

About half way up the slopes a stone cottage aroused our suspicions. We shook out into attack formation; one section advanced while the other two remained behind to give supporting fire. We burst into the cottage and found an old farmer and his family cringing in the corner. A German patrol had been there an hour earlier.

We continued our ascent, the sections spread out rather than in single file, ready to take cover and support each other if we encountered German patrols or outposts. About 50 yards from the summit, LCpl Slimkowitch's section, which had been leading the way, suddenly opened fire on a house perched

---

* Our maps were wrong. Monteverde was the name of another road junction some 8 miles due west of La Rocca.

166

on the very peak. I quickly brought up a section to help and met Slim coming out of the house with his pugnacious lantern jaw protruding more than usual.

"What's up, Slim?"

"Those yellow SOBs wouldn't even stay for a fight. The three of them beat it down the hill and left their dinner on the table. I may have wounded one of them."

As the sections took up all-round defence on the summit, Slimkowitch and I moved down the enemy side of the slope to see what the Germans had in covert. In the failing light we spotted two tanks about 500 yards down the slope and two mortar positions; also two more tanks further down.[2] We were tempted to descend further and try for a German prisoner or two but it was getting dark and we had a long way back to base.

We returned to the summit, checked the OP for any notes or maps the Germans might have left behind and headed for home, some six miles away. To save time I tried to take the most direct route, lost my bearings in the darkness, and stumbled on to a farmer's cottage. Fortunately it was occupied by an Italian who gave us excellent directions back to our lines and guided us most of the way. We arrived at A Company at 2000 hours, dead beat, and reported to the IO over a field telephone. Some time later a carrier arrived and took us back to BHQ at Cercemajore where I gave the CO a detailed report on our mission.

The stage was now set for the battalion to seize La Rocca. At 0830 hours, October 14th, after an impressive bombardment by two field artillery regiments[3], A Company moved off to occupy the top of the feature, followed by the other companies along the routes the Scouts and Snipers had recced the day before. LCpl Slimkowitch was happy at last. "I hope the bastards we chased off the mountain are getting their arses full of lead."

The Scouts and Snipers, still all in and limping along, guided the companies as they scaled the heights under heavy shellfire and occupied their positions without any opposition. After scouring the mountainside, I finally located all my platoon, gathered them together in the farmer's house we had passed on patrol, and accepted his earlier offer to give us a meal of spaghetti, eggs, cheese and sausage. We barely had time to finish before orders arrived to send out two more patrols: one to the crossroads which the battalion was to attack at 0200 hours next morning; the other, under Cpl Konyk, to investigate Vinchiatura. Meanwhile, the rest of the Scouts moved forward with the battalion.

The heavy shellfire continued all night as the Germans, having retreated, tried to 'defend' the area with artillery fire. My friend of Shilo days, Lt Cecil Shea, was wounded in the advance. Sgt R Carter, who had been my first platoon sergeant when I joined the Regiment in England, was killed two days later during intense shelling. He had been a good soldier and his death saddened me. The veterans of 1939 were again starting to fall.

167

The Patricias had now completed their tasks for this phase of the operation and had earned a brief rest, while the Seaforths and Edmontons threw the Germans out of Vinchiatura and Baranello. The shelling never ceased, but the troops were well dug in, and accepted this enemy activity as a minor irritant of war. Of more concern was the continual cold and rain.

Finally the sun broke through, presaging a host of amenities for the troops. First, the Scouts and Snipers acquired a trained RCASC cook, Pte Fletcher; rations which hitherto had arrived by mule now came up regularly by vehicle; the NAAFI issued one bottle of beer per man and chocolate bars; another 2,000 cigarettes arrived from my parents which I distributed among the platoon; each scout received one sweater and an extra blanket (guaranteed free of fleas and crabs); and all ranks enjoyed a mobile bath — the first in weeks.

The rest period also gave me a chance to re-organize the Scouts and Snipers. I recruited two excellent men from the companies: Pte Zastre and Pte Menaar (the latter helped me out of a bad situation a few days later). The CO agreed to my platoon having a carrier, under Pte Hare, on permanent loan from the carrier platoon. Once again, we were fighting fit and fit to fight and eagerly looking forward to the next operation.

During this rest period we had ringside seats of bombing attacks by the Desert Air Force. Kitty-Hawks, Douglas Bostons and Glen Martin Marylands made devastating attacks on enemy positions in Boiano, Colle d'Anchise and Baranello, a few miles ahead of our position, creating great damage to those towns and giving us a big boost in morale.

On October 21st the Patricias received preliminary orders to capture Spinete, some ten miles away, on October 23rd. Following the pattern now established, the Scouts and Snipers were ordered to recce a route for the battalion and supporting mules, tanks and vehicles, from Baranello, across the Biferno River to Spinete. We set off at 1600 hours in great spirits, the weather having at last cleared. At Baranello I checked with the Seaforths who had captured the town on October 18th and obtained valuable information about the difficult terrain ahead. From Baranello the ground fell away sharply to the Biferno River about 1 1/2 miles west.

It was now quite dark and I would have to rely on my compass to guide us to the point on the river where the Patricias were supposed to cross. For once we had a chance to prepare the patrol properly: faces were blackened; equipment was made snug so it would not rattle; luminous watches were turned inwards or removed.

We passed through the Seaforths' lines, making sure we both agreed on the current password, and headed down into the deep valley in single file. Over rocks and across gullies we went, hoping my compass and our innate sense of direction would keep us on course. After an hour of rough going the man behind me touched my arm and whispered. "Sir, I think a German patrol is following right behind us.''

This was not as silly as it sounds. There were cases on record where, on a very dark night, a German patrol would attach itself to the end of one of our patrols and after quietly taking out the last man would fall in step with the remaining men. As soon as our patrol was well within German lines, the enemy would pounce on the remainder, easily killing them or taking them prisoner.

A subtle variant of this enemy tactic was for the German patrol to let us pass and then attach itself to the end of our patrol as we returned. Chances were that we were so tired we would not detect the Germans and would guide them right through our lines.

Being well aware of these little games, I took my man seriously, halted the platoon and checked back to the last man whom I was happy to recognize as one of our own. We set off again, aided now by a weak moon. After climbing a wooded knoll, we saw through the trees a broad silver streak 200 yards ahead — the Biferno River. We had arrived at the exact spot where the Patricias were to cross.

We had found a route for troops and mules, difficult though it was in the dark, but it was certainly not a passage for tanks or heavy vehicles. From our vantage point on the knoll we saw a small wooden bridge which the troops could use if it wasn't blown up before they arrived. So far we had not encountered any enemy, but who knew what lay ahead.

I decided to move right down to the bridge with one section, leaving the second section behind under LCpl Slimkowitch to give us support or, at the very worst, to escape if we were ambushed. We crept forward until, 50 yards from the bridge, we saw the dark outline of a house hidden in a gully. Quietly we surrounded it and entered. In the pitch black I called out softly first in German and then in Italian, "Anyone here?" No response. A flicker of light showed underneath the door leading to the basement. My corporal pushed it in and almost fell onto a family of terrified Italians, sobbing and praying for mercy.

I sent back for LCpl Slimkowitch to join us, and as quietly as I could, tried to tell the Italians we were *canadese soldati,* and asked where the Germans were. We were surrounded by the enemy — so the Italian farmer claimed. German sections had been posted in the building all day and had just withdrawn to the other side of the river. Other German sections were dug in on this side of the river on hills overlooking the house, but whether they, too, had withdrawn the Italian could not say. Sentries patrolled the bridge and sometimes entered the house to get warm and eat.

Our grips tightened on our rifles as we anticipated having two or three German prisoners fall into our hands. The thought flashed through my mind that killing or capturing the sentries might compromise my orders to locate enemy positions and get an estimate of their numbers. Nevertheless I decided to have a try at taking the sentries as they might well 'talk' and give us the the information we were seeking.

LCpl Slimkowitch arrived. With one section I crept forward to the bridge, while the other section remained near the house in support. When only 50 feet from the river we found our way barred by a small creek, not shown on the map. A quick recce revealed no crossing over this new obstacle. I resolved to wade across the creek with my section and wait on the far side for the sentries. Passing this information to the section, I started to ease gently into the ice cold water when I heard the unmistakable tramp of German jack boots on the bridge. In a moment the sentries appeared only yards away.

I froze. "Oh my God!" I breathed. "If they spot us here our goose is cooked!"

The other members of the section had the same helpless feeling. It was too much for one man, a new member of the platoon, who promptly cocked his rifle, raised it to fire and slipped, hitting the water with a crash. The Germans shouted to their comrades and hightailed it back across the bridge. My carefully laid plans were in ruins and I was very angry.

Expecting Jerry to light up the area immediately with parachute flares and drill us with tracer bullets, we dashed through the creek and took cover on the far side. The Germans, however, were too cute: no flares or bullets pierced the darkness. Either they hadn't seen us and thought the noise was some bumbling Italian, or they were waiting for us to show our hand and reveal the strength and position of our troops. We lay doggo.

Our chances of nabbing a prisoner had evaporated, but there was still work to do — locate enemy positions and estimate their numbers. Any further advance to the river's edge or attempt to cross the wooden bridge was clearly foolhardy. On the other hand, a recce of the hills on our side of the river, supposedly occupied by Germans, might yield useful information, particularly if we waited for daylight when we could see what we were doing.

Silently we slipped into the water again, recrossed the creek and headed back to join LCpl Slimkowitch and his section at the farmhouse. It was now 0300 hours on October 22nd and I knew that LCol Ware was waiting patiently to hear from us before giving out his orders. Better, I thought, to give the CO half the information he needed now than wait until daylight to complete the recce, when our report would be too late. I briefly reviewed with Slimkowitch the information we had so far: a route for the battalion and mules, but not for heavy vehicles; the location of the farmhouse we now occupied; the wooden bridge; the creek not shown on the map; the sentries. With any luck, we would know more about the enemy as soon as day broke.

Armed with this information LCpl Slimkowitch set off in the dark to find BHQ, 1 1/2 miles in the rear of our position, and report to the CO; the remainder of the patrol re-organized in and around the house waiting for daylight. As the first streaks of dawn appeared we started to climb one of the hills the farmer had said were occupied by the Germans. Compared to our stumbling efforts in the dark, our movements in daylight were quick and purposeful. Soon we gained the top of the hill and found the enemy had withdrawn. The area had been a platoon position with slit trenches dug in all-around defence, perfectly sited to cover every approach. Bits of worn clothing and equipment, German papers and empty cans revealed the enemy had only recently departed.

From our vantage point we had an excellent view of the farmhouse and bridge. As I scanned the terrain on the other side of the river I could hardly believe my eyes. About 250 yards away, in a fold in the ground, surrounded by trees, I could make out 30 or 40 Germans gathered around an officer or NCO who was giving orders. Obviously they were not concerned about the nocturnal noises at the bridge the night before.

What a splendid target! Even at this range the combined fire power of two sections could wipe out a good many enemy, bunched so tightly together. But after our fiasco in the creek I wasn't about to have my plans compromised again. I gave strict orders to the patrol not to fire, to remain in deep cover and observe, observe, observe.

Soon the enemy 'O' Group broke up and disappeared into the trees. I turned my attention to the bridge where all seemed quiet and peaceful, until I spotted a glint of sun reflecting from a metal object in a haystack, about 25 yards from the bridge, on the enemy side. I raised my binoculars a fraction and saw two figures enter a barn behind the haystack — a German position covering the bridge? We had to investigate.

Making good use of cover we crawled down the hill toward the bridge and took up positions where we could observe the haystack and the barn in rear. Nothing moved. We waited half an hour — still nothing moved. If there was a machine gun in the haystack or the barn, surely Jerry would go for breakfast or something. Still nothing happened.

As the battalion would likely cross the river at this point, it was vital that we pinpoint the enemy positions and weapons. Time, as always, was running out. I couldn't wait any longer for our unseen enemy to show himself. Someone had to do something to draw his fire and in this situation there are only two choices: either you call for a volunteer or you do the job yourself. In making this decision you take into account that you, an officer of His Majesty, are being paid $5.00 per diem to lead troops and take certain risks, whereas a private soldier receives only $1.50 per diem to be led by you. Furthermore, only a very determined and experienced officer would send someone else when every man in the platoon expected him to go.

I took the easy way out. Indicating to my platoon to give me covering fire, I spurted along the river bank in full view of the enemy, breaking all records for the 50 yard dash, and dove behind a solid oak tree. Not a burst from any enemy weapon rewarded my efforts. Then I repeated the exercise, this time not trying for a world record. The enemy could no longer resist a chance to take a crack at this crazy officer. An MG 42 opened up from the haystack, another from the barn; bullets cracked about as I accelerated to take cover behind some rocks. I made it with only two nicks from bullets that grazed my arm and leg. I was thoroughly scared but it had been an exciting race.

The rest of the platoon, who were supposed to be giving me covering fire, had been observing my one-man track meet with considerable amusement. I had been too fleet of foot for them to bring their weapons into action, but they had pinpointed enemy positions, identified weapons and confirmed my brief glance at the river that it appeared shallow and easily fordable.

We turned for home, exhilarated by this encounter with the Hun. The ravines and ridges that had given us so much trouble the night before presented no obstacle in daylight, and we reported to BHQ.

Early next morning (October 23rd), as the CO prepared his orders for the attack, the Scouts and Snipers were again despatched to see if they could locate, in daylight, an easier route to the river that would take heavy vehicles. Time, however, was too short to scour the area for such a route and we returned empty handed. My diary, in a fine burst of brevity, describes the results of this patrol more succinctly than even the Regimental History might have done: "I'm sent away to find another route to the river — no such."

At 1200 hours the battalion moved off from its concentration area to cross the Biferno River and attack Spinete. As we approached the river, squadrons of Boston bombers from the South African Air Force passed overhead on their way to bomb enemy positions in and around Spinete.[4] The crash of bombs and strafing of enemy positions were welcome sounds, even if we couldn't see the results from our position in a gully leading to the Biferno River.

At exactly Zero hour (1400 hours) artillery and mortars opened up and laid down an intense concentration of fire and smoke on our objectives, while we stormed across the river. Seldom had I seen such a display of fire power by combined air force and artillery and I hoped those gunmen in field grey uniforms were getting their just desserts for taking pot shots at me.

The attack went precisely according to plan and by 1800 hours all objectives had been occupied.[5] It had been another bloodless victory for our side, except for two mules who had neglected to keep their heads down.

I was beginning to think that my presence in an attack pretty well guaranteed there would be no heavy fighting. The truth of the matter was, however, that our attack had coincided exactly with the German withdrawal.[6] The enemy 'O' Group that my patrol had seen in the trees on the far side of the river was probably in preparation for this move. In fact, I had speculated about such a possibility in my patrol report, especially as the German troops were wearing their long greatcoats and packs; not having a transcript of their orders in my pocket I left it to others to draw any necessary inferences from my observations.

Early next morning (October 24th), LCol Ware sent me back to the Biferno River to contact an engineer recce party in the vicinity of the river crossing to try to find a route for transport to bring much needed ammunition and rations. The engineers soon confirmed my earlier recces — there was no route or even a trail in this sparsely populated area that would carry heavy traffic. The road-builders of ancient Rome had sensibly avoided these remote highlands.

My sapper friends were not deterred. If there was no road they would build one — and build one they did. With bulldozers and manual labour they forged a route across the river and up into the hills in less than two days, allowing our ammunition and rations to come forward. In recognition of their determined efforts the Patricias named the route Burma Road.[7] Until the arrival of vehicles, the battalion was supplied by mules that had learned to keep their heads down, thus managing to get through without any casualties.

Early next day (October 25th), the Scouts and Snipers were ordered to send out two patrols: one to Sant'Elena and Point 799, some three miles to the northwest; the other to Casalciprano, about four miles to the northeast. I set out with one section for Sant'Elena at 0830 hours while Cpl Konyk took another section toward Casalciprano.

My section, travelling quickly cross-country over the rolling uplands, got into Sant'Elena without difficulty. As soon as the citizens realized we were *canadese soldati* they flocked into the narrow streets, waving Italian flags and offering us the usual gifts we now expected as our rightful reward. I received a special present from a former Italian major: a beautiful Beretta pistol and a supply of ammunition. The weapon was quite small and could easily be carried in my pocket as an emergency weapon for close quarter action.

Large flags were now unfurled from some of the taller buildings, and church bells started to ring, supposedly in our honour. Immediately German artillery began to shell the town with some pretty heavy stuff, sending the people inside their sturdy dwellings. I was not at all convinced that the flags and bells had been for our benefit. Despite the outward showing of enthusiasm our troops received from the Italians, occasionally fascist sympathizers lingered behind in the towns evacuated by the enemy and sent information back to the Germans by waving flags and ringing bells.

Keeping a careful lookout for Germans and fellow travellers, we completed our patrol of the town and found no enemy, at least none dressed in German uniforms. We passed this information back to BHQ by wireless and scouted the area ahead, in the direction of Frosolone, again without encountering the enemy.

Once more we were hampered by time. It was getting late and we had orders to return to BHQ no later that 1800 hours. We turned about and headed for home, taking a different route to gain more information and avoid any enemy lying in wait. We found no Germans but picked up a few escaped POWs who had been hiding for months in the high mountains to the west, waiting for a chance to slip through enemy lines.

We reported in at BHQ at 1800 hours. Cpl Konyk, who had been given a much tougher assignment to Casalciprano, had made faster time and reported at 1700 hours that the town was clear.

October 26th dawned a cool, cloudy day with fair visibility. For the first time in many days the Scouts rested and caught up on personal matters — shaving, repairing clothes and equipment, writing letters. Three huge parcels from my parents arrived to add to our enjoyment.

Just as we were about to dig into the contents of these precious bundles, orders arrived to send out a strong fighting patrol to Frosolone some five miles in a direct line from our headquarters at Spinete, but probably eight miles by foot. The route lay through Sant'Elena which we had scouted the day before without any trouble; from there the terrain opened into a wide, treeless valley surrounded by mountains, with no cover except to the west of Frosolone where the ground began to rise into the high Matese Mountains. During the previous night a small patrol from one of the companies had run into enemy outposts along this route and had to withdraw.

On our right flank the RCR, the 48th Highlanders and The Hastings and Prince Edward Regiment had encountered some stiff opposition as they moved toward Molise and Torella, small hamlets northeast of Frosolone.

The map indicated that as soon as my patrol left Sant'Elena the enemy would have excellent observation of our movements, not only from Frosolone but also from the hills on each side of the valley.

And it was high noon.

I didn't like the situation at all and for once I told the adjutant. He agreed the ground was less than ideal but he had received orders from brigade HQ to "tidy up our front", as our division was being relieved by the 5th British Division.

I asked for and received written orders:

1. *Take a strong fighting patrol to Frosolone.*
2. *Is it held by the enemy?*
3. *If so, what strength and weapons?*
4. *Are the roads mined?*
5. *Are the bridges blown? — possible diversons.*
6. *Route out — direct route cross country to Sant'Elena and Frosolone.*

7. Route back — follow the road checking for mines and bridge diversions.

The mission would clearly require all the strength we could muster so I took the entire platoon — 25 all ranks organized into one section of ten men under LCpl Slimkowitch; another section of ten men under LCpl E G Brautigan; and the third under-strength section of five men under my direct command. It would be the last patrol in our long drive up the Italian peninsula — from Reggio in the southern tip to our present position near Campobasso, where the division was to be concentrated for a long period of R&R (rest and recreation).

We left at 1330 hours knowing we had to make good time. The platoon advanced in single file to Sant'Elena, then spread out into open formation as the cover thinned out in the treeless valley. It was soon apparent we would have to check the roads for mines and blown bridges on our way out as it would be dark when we returned. I therefore took my section near the road while the others continued cross country. We found two blown bridges that would not cause any trouble to by-pass but we could find no traces of recent minelaying.

We were now less than half a mile from Frosolone. I halted and scanned the ground ahead and on the flanks. No movement in the village; no apparent enemy positions there or on the surrounding hills — only an eerie silence. LCpl Slimkowitch came up. "Sir, I don't like it. Not like the Germans not to mortar such a good target. I smell Jerries all around but I can't see them."

We pressed on until I found a wooded knoll just south of the road leading into Frosolone, from which I could size up the situation and give orders. Our task was simple enough to state — "Is Frosolone occupied and, if so, enemy strength and weapons?" How to carry it out was another matter. From our OP on the hill we studied the approaches to the village, searching for cover. Very little was available. The left or west flank seemed the most promising, where folds in the hills might offer some protection; the right or east flank was entirely open except for a small creek cutting across our line of advance; the south or centre was the shortest route into town and the creek gave some cover, except for the last 50 yards.

As we examined these approaches we kept a close eye for any movement in the town or fields ahead. LCpl Brautigan thought he spotted two Italians in the doorway of a cottage on the outskirts of town, not far from the creek running across our front. Still not a sound from the village or surrounding hills.

We couldn't wait any longer. If the place was occupied, the Germans were showing remarkable restraint in not clobbering us long ago. For the past hour we had been advancing in full view of the village and the hills; even now the enemy would have no trouble bringing down heavy artillery and

175

mortar fire on our OP and the gully behind us, where the platoon was waiting for orders to advance.

I turned to Slimkowitch "Jerry isn't going to give us our information without a fight."

"That's right, Sir. And he's picked the right platoon to give it to him."

After all, we were a fighting patrol and if the Germans wanted us to fight for our information we would be happy to oblige. I issued my final orders:

1. *On the left, LCpl Brautigan and his section will enter the town using the west or left flank approaches.*
2. *On the right my section will advance straight ahead to the creek and from there rush for the outlying houses.*
3. *In the centre LCpl Slimkowitch and his section will advance in between my section and LCpl Brautigan and give us supporting fire.*
4. *If the town is unoccupied all sections will RV at the church in the centre of town (easily identified from our OP).*
5. *If the town is occupied, engage the enemy, pinpoint his fire, locate his positions and capture prisoners if possible (a pretty tall order).*
6. *If the town is held by more than platoon strength, the sections will withdraw to our present location (RV2) giving each other mutual support.*
7. *LCpl Brautigan and LCpl Slimkowitch move off to the left flank now and take up positions to attack the town. I estimate it will take you 20 minutes to get there.*
8. *My section has the shortest distance to go and will leave in ten minutes.*
9. *Zero hour is 30 minutes from now — 1700 hours.*

Off we went in high spirits, as we had done so many times before. My section, in open order, moved down the knoll to the road below and crossed to the far side where we were glad to find a solid bank about two feet high.

Leaving three men along the bank to give us covering fire, I took Pte Menaar and Pte Knox with me down the steep slope into the creek. The two houses on the outskirts of town were only 50 yards away. We waited a few minutes for Zero hour and then, with Menaar and Knox on each side and the rest of the section ready to fire from the road above and behind us, I stood up to rush the houses.

Chapter XIII

WOUNDED

October 26 to November 2, 1943

Take me back to dear old Blighty
Put me on the train for London Town
Take me over there, drop me anywhere
Liverpool, Leeds, or Lancaster, for I don't care
I would like to see my best girl
Cuddling up together soon we'd be
So hi tiddly iti, carry me back to Blighty
Blighty is the place for me

CRACK.

I'm on my back in the creek. "What the hell am I doing here?"
CRACK — CRACK — CRACK over my head. Three thuds in the bank
behind. "What the . . . Christ I've been hit!"

Like a boxer rallying after a near knockout blow, I rolled over on my
side and got up on one knee. Menaar motioned frantically to keep my head
down. I did, and found my chest covered in blood. I felt around to locate
the wound — nothing wrong with my chest.

"Why am I coughing blood? Where am I hit? Eyes OK, thank God!"

My hands went up to my face and I realized something was badly amiss.
Then Menaar rolled over with a field dressing. I tried to ask him where
I was hit but to my utter astonishment no words came out — only gurgles
and blood.

Menaar wrapped the field dressing under my chin and around my head and yelled that I had been shot in the jaw. Then I felt pain for the first time — not an ordinary pain but a deep pervasive pain that I knew was going to get much worse. Yet I was not afraid.

While I am not by any means the calmest of men, something in me had been triggered that brought forth a cool, detached strength and determination I had never experienced before, and never experienced again with the same intensity. I wasn't going to die in this miserable, dirty creek beside some remote Italian village. My platoon and I were going to get out of this mess in one piece and return to BHQ together. If I had any concern it was that I might be taken prisoner, which in my state could mean the end.

The fight was now on in earnest. Four or five German MG42s and many rifles from covered positions were sending torrents of lead at my platoon, who were returning the fire; but it was clearly an unequal match. The Germans outnumbered us two or three to one and had superior fire power. It was time to withdraw.

Our mission had been fulfilled except for the last task — reporting back to BHQ. From our position in the creek, with a steady stream of machine gun bullets hissing over our heads, it was difficult to see how we could extricate ourselves and join the rest of the section on the road.

There was one chance. It was now 1800 hours and would soon be dark. If the rest of my section and the other sections kept up their covering fire until dusk and kept the Jerries away from us, we just might be able to climb back to the road and head for the RV.

Night started to fall and the German fire subsided. Would they send a patrol to try and pick us up, or worse? We were almost out of ammunition and had to move now or not at all.

I confess I made a silly show of gallantry toward my two faithful men, Menaar and Knox, who had stayed with me and fought off the enemy. I waved at them to get out now and leave me in the creek so I wouldn't hinder their climb back to the road. I would join them later. It was true I was pretty weak, having lost some blood, and I couldn't climb with my hands — they were holding my jaw together. Yet, honestly, I didn't want to be left behind.

Menaar and Knox, soldiers to the core, ignored my gestures, pulled me to my feet and half-carried, half-pushed me up the incline to the road, where we picked up the rest of the section and headed for the RV on the knoll.

The relief of having escaped from such a difficult situation now surfaced. I knew I could march the eight miles back to home base. My second wind had taken over, although waves of pain had started to flood in.

We arrived at the RV and to my intense joy all my platoon were present and in good health. After a short rest, we set off down the road, clambering around the blown bridges, and finally reached BHQ at 2130 hours — mission completed. We had fulfilled our tasks and, best of all, we had returned together as a platoon. Had anyone in the platoon not followed orders precisely, not fought with determination, and above all not worked together as a team, the story would have had a much different ending. Not enough can be said of the devotion of my men, particularly LCpl Slimkowitch, LCpl Brautigan, Pte Menaar and Pte Knox.

All this is not to suggest that similar and indeed far more difficult and dangerous patrols seldom took place; they did, frequently. The account of our little action is only one example of the many, many patrols made before and after Frosolone that performed far greater deeds with far less recognition.

The War Diary records the following:

> *The patrol commanded by Lt C S Frost returned at 2130 hours. The patrol had reached the outskirts of Frosolone shortly before 1700 hours. Lt Frost decided to converge on the town from three directions. One section commanded by LCpl Brautigan to go in from the west, one section commanded by Lt Frost to go in from the south and the remaining section commanded by LCpl Slimkowitch to go in from the southwest. All sections came under heavy MG and rifle fire at approximately 1700 hours. LCpl Slimkowitch's section knocked out one MG position, killing two enemy and a further one when assaulting a second MG post. LCpl Brautigan's section killed one enemy and these two sections claimed a possible three more enemy killed and an unestimated number wounded.*
>
> *Lt Frost's section which came under very heavy fire, were pinned down and had difficulty in getting out. In so doing Lt Frost was wounded by a bullet through the jaw. However in such a condition he succeeded in regrouping his patrol and returning to 'D' Company with himself as the only casualty. The patrol estimated Frosolone held by one company of enemy with at least 5 MGs.[1]*

The Regimental History has the following account of the action:

> *The relief of 1st Canadian Division by 5th British Division now was imminent. It only remained to tidy the territory in preparation for the hand-over. To this end Lt C S Frost on the afternoon of October 26th went out with his scouts and snipers to see how matters stood at Frosolone, a village on a track which led northward from Sant' Elena into the mountains. On approaching the hamlet the officer split up his men into small parties. When fire opened from machine gun posts and rifle pits on the edge of the village an attack went in from three sides. LCpl J W Slimkowitch's section destroyed one machine gun post and silenced a second; LCpl E G Brautigan's men shot down a number of the enemy in the open. Only Lt Frost and the*

179

remainder of the platoon were out of luck. They were pinned down and their commander received a bullet in the jaw — the only casualty of the encounter. The Frosolone garrison was estimated to be about 60 strong.[2]

There was one other casualty of the encounter — my fancy Beretta pistol given me the day before by the Italian major was missing. Otherwise both versions of the action are substantially correct.

While LCpl Slimkowitch and LCpl Brautigan gave LCol Ware a full report, the Regimental MO, Capt Bill McGill (my good Samaritan on an earlier patrol) and Cpl Bob Middleton, MM skillfully tended my wounds and sent me back in a jeep ambulance of 9 Canadian Field Ambulance to 15 Canadian CCS at Campobasso. The town had been made into a leave centre, which I had hoped to visit after the patrol. I got my wish, but in slightly different circumstances.

The route back to Campobasso was over the rough trail the sappers had just carved out of the mountain; then across the Biferno River where I had run races for the benefit of German machine gunners a few days earlier. The river was now swollen from heavy rains that had started during the evening and the jeep ambulance got bogged down in the stream. The last I remember of that journey is the intense cold, the fight to keep breathing and the pain.

I was unconscious by the time I arrived at 15 CCS. I was resuscitated and the wound dressed, then I was evacuated by 132 Canadian Field Ambulance to 7 CCS at Foggia, where my face and jaw were operated on by a Maxillo Facial Unit (No 1 Maxillo Facial Team) composed of surgeons and dentists specializing in wounds to the face. Some of the shattered teeth and bits of bone were removed and the remaining teeth wired together to keep the jaw in place. Only a local anaesthetic was used as I had now developed pleurisy in one lung.

After the operation I was given a thorough examination and the doctors found I had also received two slight flesh wounds in the shoulder. Whether this was from the bullet that passed through my jaw or another bullet I couldn't say and didn't care.

A more serious matter was a laceration on my left hip that had become infected. I couldn't account for it unless it was from the nick I had received from the German machine guns at the Biferno River, or perhaps I had received another scratch at Frosolone. The doctors thought the wound might have been aggravated by a hot water bottle during my evacuation. Whatever the cause it was an aggravation I didn't need. A letter to my father written some months after the event describes my evacuation:

No need to tell you, Dad, how I felt, as I no doubt felt just the same as you did when you were hit last war! I can honestly say there wasn't a great deal of pain at first as my face naturally went numb. A bit of blood, yes. A shell dressing tied around my jaw and over the head held the fracture in place. Worst part was not being able to speak, but I managed by sign talk, and I had a smart bunch of lads.

After dusk when we got out it was a bit tricky keeping the jaw together as I stumbled over the rocks. It was during this latter phase that the worst damage was done to the jaw, as it gradually worked into my air passage, along with teeth, etc. But by using both hands I was able to get in enough air to breathe. Well, I arrived at the RAP about 2100 hours. The MO was right on the job and had me rushed straight to the CCS after having applied 'sulfa' to the wound. There wasn't much he could do.

Then a rough ride to the CCS — at one place the jeep had to plough through a stream. Which reminds me that I was soaking wet from being about 1-1/2 hours in the creek. I arrived at the CCS (didn't bother with FDS) and was on the operating table by midnight. So by 0100 hours, 27th October, 1943, my teeth were wired together and stayed that way for five months, except during further operations. It was at the CCS that I received the bad hot water bottle burn to my hip. This caused me more trouble than the jaw, as it of course caught infection.

Now from here I don't remember a great deal until I ended up at the 98th Gen in Bari. From looking at my medical cards I find that I was started on my journey to the 98th Gen (British Hosp) but my chest got worse so I was kept at 54th Gen until I improved. I arrived at 98th Gen about a week after being wounded.

Thus ended my brief service with the Regiment — or so I believed at the time. All the training, sacrifices and hardships of the past three years had been erased in a split-second by an enemy bullet.

HOSPITAL
98th British General Hospital
Bari, Italy
November 2 to November 19, 1943

As through the mud you drag your weary feet
Underneath your tunic your heart has ceased to beat
No matter what becomes of thee
I'll always laugh, and sing with glee
That I am LOB, that I am LOB

Italy — 2nd Echelon Records
November 2, 1943

A clerk in the Records Section of 1st Canadian Division sits at his desk, in a warm office, well removed from the fighting up front. Before him are a number of garbled messages from Field Ambulance Sections, Casualty Clearing Stations and hospitals, reporting on casualties, one of which is especially ambiguous. It lists the names of two officers who have been wounded, Lt Charles Sydney Frost, PPCLI and Lt M Delues, and reports that both were removed from the Dangerously Ill list and placed on the Seriously Ill list on November 2nd. The message gives brief particulars of their wounds:

> *Gunshot wounds upper neck and chin*
> *Gunshot wound, rifle, upper neck and chin with severe fracture*
> *mandible*

It is not clear from the message whether there are two separate diagnoses,

182

one for each officer or whether the second line is a more detailed description of the same wound suffered by both officers. If there are two diagnoses, which one applies to which officer? For that matter, how many wounds are there?

The clerk ponders the problem and notes that the message does not give any indication when the officers were wounded or what hospital they are in. He decides to wait a day or two before passing on the information to London. Perhaps some more details will come down from the front now that 1st Division is out of action. In the meantime he will check his records to see what other information he has on the two officers.

November 5

No further reports have arrived at 2nd Echelon, but the clerk has confirmed that Lt Frost is a member of the PPCLI. The files at 2nd Echelon contain no particulars on a Lt Delues.

The clerk decides he had better get off some kind of cable to London and let them figure out the mess. He'll report on Lt Frost first as he, at least, appears to have been a member in good standing with the PPCLI. He is still confused how he should describe the wound or wounds but decides to keep it simple and not worry the next of kin by mentioning a fracture or the fact that the officer has progressed from the dangerous to the serious list.

London — Canadian Military Headquarters
November 5, 1943

A cable arrives at CMHQ from 2nd Echelon of 1st Canadian Division in Italy giving particulars of recent battle casualties, including Lt Charles Sydney Frost:

Serious gunshot wounds upper neck and chin.

The clerk who takes the message at CMHQ loses no time checking the particulars of the next of kin and transmits the information to the Director of Records, Ottawa. The cable is dispatched at 2015 hours and arrives on the desk of the Director of Records at 2227 hours on November 5th.

Toronto
November 6, 1943 — 1430 hours

A young messenger boy from the Canadian National Telegraph office, his uniform tightly buttoned up against the cold, wearily pedals his bike along a Toronto street. He has spent the morning delivering telegrams from Col Laurin, Director of Records, Ottawa, to the mothers and wives of soldiers who have been killed or wounded in the fighting in Italy. After leaving each message he respectfully tips his hat and tries to get away before the woman tears open the envelope and reads the shattering news. Today he has been an unwilling witness to the grief of six mothers and one wife. All the sons had been wounded, two dangerously, and the mothers have taken the news pretty well. The wife had trouble opening the envelope, glanced at the message and collapsed — she was a widow.

"Well, one killed out of seven is not too bad", the messenger mutters to himself. But it is a sad and dreary job and he is thankful he has only one more delivery. He parks his bike against the curb and knocks on the door of 80 Glengrove Avenue West. "Pray God", he murmurs, "this will be an easy one for Mrs Frost".

Minutes before the messenger arrives at my home, father has alighted from a streetcar on Yonge Street and is slowly making his way along the snow-covered sidewalk. He is glad it is Saturday afternoon after a strenuous week at the bank and two evenings down at the armoury, training with The Royal Regiment of Canada. Like everyone else, he goes to the office every Saturday morning, and often doesn't arrive home until four or five o'clock. Today he has been lucky and got away in good time. He glances at his watch — it is only two-thirty. In a few moments he'll be home.

Then he sees the messenger. He calls out to wait and breaks into a dead run to intercept the fateful message. He is too late. Mother has ripped open the envelope and reads:

CANADIAN NATIONAL
TELEGRAPHS
CASUALTY (Report Delivery)   Ottawa 6th November 1943

To MRS GERTRUDE REBECCA FROST
*   80 GLENGROVE AVENUE WEST*
*   TORONTO ONTARIO*
*   SINCERELY REGRET INFORM YOU LIEUTENANT CHARLES SYDNEY FROST OFFICIALLY REPORTED SERIOUSLY ILL AS RESULT OF WOUNDS RECEIVED IN ACTION STOP DATE NOT YET AVAILABLE STOP WOUNDS DESCRIBED AS GUNSHOT WOUNDS UPPER NECK AND CHIN STOP FURTHER INFORMATION FOLLOWS WHEN RECEIVED.*
*   DIRECTOR OF RECORDS*

Bari, Italy 98 British General Hospital
November 6, 1943

Far away, in a British hospital in Bari on the east coast of Italy, doctors and nursing sisters are tending a new batch of wounded soldiers in a cold, dark ward. Outside, German aircraft are pounding the harbour and military installations in the town. Some of the bombs stray from their intended targets and explode very near the hospital, shaking the building and shattering glass in the heavily taped and blanketed windows. For some patients who have endured more than their share of enemy action, this unfair punishment by the Luftwaffe is almost too much.

The doctors and nurses, oblivious of the danger, continue changing dressings, administering morphine and comforting dying soldiers through their last agony. Finally, the all clear sounds and blankets are removed from some of the windows to let out the smell of the wounds and the stench of the excrement of men unable to control themselves. Soon it will be daylight; the surgeons will return to their operating tables and the nurses and orderlies will strive to clean up the wards before matron makes her morning inspection.

How long is it since I was wounded? How long have I been in this hospital? Why am I in a British hospital? Surely there are lots of Canadian hospitals in Italy.

I toss on my hospital bed and try to reconstruct the events of the past ten days. The lower part of my face, mouth and neck are covered with bandages. My mouth won't open. I can't speak. The slightest movement of my head produces an exquisite pain. Chest is very sore and breathing difficult. I would like to cough up whatever is in my chest, or be sick, or do both; but how will the stuff get out through my mouth?

A nurse comes to my bed and tries to ease the pain. She tells me it is Sunday, November 7th. I arrived here November 3rd from 54 British General Hospital. I am in this hospital because it is the only one in Italy that has the doctors, dentists and facilities to look after my wounds. The unit is the Main Section of No 1 Maxillo-Facial Team.

Nurse says not to worry. The doctors are going to operate today to relieve some of the pain by removing infected teeth and bone, and put the remaining teeth in silver casts or splints. A small metal bar will replace the missing teeth. Then the splints and the metal bar will be wired together and will hold my fractured lower jaw in place until the infection has cleared up. Later on they will do a bone graft and fix me up like new. The only catch is that the whole procedure will take several months.

This sounds fine except I wonder how I am going to eat in the meantime. So far I have managed to suck in some liquids through a small hole in my teeth but most of the food leaks out into my bandages. Unable to speak, I growl at the nurse and make signs to bring me a pad and pencil. In very large letters I print — 'EAT?' — 'HOW?' She gets the message and assures me that a small hole will be left in the splints so that I can continue to suck in some liquid nourishment; after the operation the wound will soon close over and the liquid will end up in my stomach instead of in the bandages.

Nurse also tells me that they were not able to operate any sooner as I had pleurisy and couldn't handle a general anaesthetic; also I have an infection in my hip wound they have been trying to get under control before involving me in a big operation.

185

Apart from these problems I'm not in bad shape and will probably recover to lead a normal life.

I wonder how my parents are taking the news. Have I sent them a letter or a cable? I write down on my pad, 'Have parents been notified?' Nurse assures me that I asked them to send a cable when I arrived and it was done immediately. Anyway, the Records Office will have sent an official cable. I should get some sleep now before the operation.

Later that day I am 'prepped', given a sedative, and wheeled into the OR .... "Breathe deeply and count - One ... Two .... T-H-R...E...E...."

Toronto
November 7, 1943
Mother took the shock of the telegram bravely. At least I was alive and there was hope of my recovery. However, there was no indication when I had been wounded or what hospital I was in. My parents were greatly disturbed by the words describing my wounds as being in 'upper neck and chin'. Not familiar with the word 'gunshot' they assumed I had been hit by a shell from a heavy gun or blown up on a patrol while crawling through a mine field. In their despair they consulted a leading doctor in Toronto to interpret the telegram and were told I had probably been wounded by a shell, both in the back of the neck and in the chin. The truth of the matter was, however, that I had been wounded by a rifle in only one place — in the chin, which was fractured. If only that clerk in Italy had included the word 'rifle' in his message and referred to only one wound. The nicks in the shoulder and hip were of no consequence at that time and properly were not mentioned.

Father went into action. He immediately wired Col Laurin, Director of Records, for further information — when was I wounded and where was I hospitalized? On November 9th Col Laurin replied that I had been wounded on October 27th (actually it was October 26th) but he had no idea where I was.

This information, or lack of it, was simply not acceptable to father and he fired off cables, wires and letters to his friends at NDHQ in Ottawa and overseas, including Maj Duncan Croll, in whose hospital I had sojourned when I had malaria in Sicily. Father also kept up a steady barrage with Col Laurin and his Records Office throughout November without receiving any further word of my condition from him. Actually, there was very little that Col Laurin could do. He continued sending cables to London and reported regularly to mother by way of a standard letter:

> *Please be advised that this office has no further information*
> *concerning your son. However, a cable has been despatched to*
> *Canadian Military Headquarters, Overseas, requesting a report*
> *on your son's present condition. Rest assured that immediately*
> *on receipt of a reply you will be informed.*

This kind of letter did not impress father, who perhaps did not realize the problems involved in getting information from a war zone 7,000 miles distant, over cables jammed with messages for thousands of other parents and next of kin. He was probably still thinking of the First World War, when the front lines were static and lines of communication well established. But if he didn't understand the logistics, he still knew how to lay down a barrage, learned so well in the First War. He kept up the pressure on Col Laurin and despatched further letters to his old Militia friends from Saskatoon and elsewhere, who now held quite high rank in Ottawa.

Despite the best efforts of father's friends, not one of them could find a clue as to my whereabouts. Apparently I had established a new category for casualties, 'wounded but disappeared' — an expression that has its modern equivalent in the phrase used to describe a missing person in Argentina as 'the disappeared one'.

While the embattled Col Laurin and his red tape colleagues were churning out messages, a glimmer of hope appeared out of the blue. On November 23rd a letter arrived from Matron C Kelly of 54 British General Hospital, through whose hands I had briefly passed on the night of November 2nd/3rd on my way to 98 British General Hospital.

I write to tell you that your husband Lt C S Frost came in this hospital yesterday and we have today sent him on to a larger hospital nearby, where they have a special department for dealing with facial injuries. Except for his injuries he is really not too ill, considering the wounds he has, and I am told he has made daily improvement each day. His face is wired up so he can't talk much, writes for what he wants, and tells sister he feels better. I hope this will be a comfort to you and that in the very near future you will hear he is well on the road to recovery.

It is not hard to imagine the joy and relief this thoughtful act of kindness brought my parents — the first news they had received about my condition since the telegram of November 6th. The fact that I was a little confused who my next of kin was (apparently I had written down 'wife' instead of 'mother') didn't matter. As of November 3rd I was alive and receiving special care. Mother immediately sent the good Matron the largest box of Laura Secord chocolates she could find.

One thing Matron Kelly had not said, and couldn't say, was the name and location of the larger hospital I had been sent to. Father speculated that I had been sent to North Africa, out of the war zone, but he had no address and could only hope for more news from Col Laurin.

Finally, on November 30th, five weeks after I had been wounded, mother received this letter from Col Laurin:

Further to my letter of the 24th instant, I am directed to inform you that official information now received from Overseas in reply to a cable despatched from this Office is to the effect that when your son, Lieutenant Charles Sydney Frost, was wounded in action on the 27th of October, 1943, he suffered a gunshot wound in the upper neck and chin. The report further states that he is still seriously ill in No 45 General Hospital.

The relief of having found me at last overshadowed everything, even a report in the *Toronto Daily Star* on the same day, that I was reported 'dangerously' wounded in the latest army casualty list. Father immediately despatched a cable to 45 General Hospital, while mother sent a telegram to Col Laurin asking for a correct mailing address. My father's cable was, he realized, a shot in the dark. It turned out he might just as well have sent it to the Moon; there was no 45 General Hospital in Italy or North Africa, unless it was behind German lines. The cable ended up, six weeks later, in Malta where there was a 45(UK) General Hospital. The Matron checked in vain to find my name in the hospital records, finally handed the cable to a Welfare Officer, and it was never seen again.

Apparently what had happened was that the same negligent clerk at 2nd Echelon in Italy, or at CMHQ in London, had transposed the figures of 54 British General Hospital. In any event, even if Col Laurin's letter of November 29th had referred to 54 General Hospital and not 45 General Hospital, it would not have made any difference. I had only stopped briefly at 54 General Hospital on the night of November 2nd/3rd. By November 29th, the date of Col Laurin's letter, I was in North Africa and had been there ten days.

Another shot in the dark from father produced a similar result. The cable sent on November 6th to his friend Maj Croll at 5 Canadian Hospital in Sicily did not arrive until December 4th, having gone first to Egypt. He immediately put through signals to every Canadian Hospital in Sicily and Italy, as well as to Canadian 2nd Echelon. None had any word of my being a casualty, except for malaria many months before.

The long battle with Col Laurin and his cohorts was soon to be resolved, but not before he received a few more blasts from father and some supporting fire from quite unexpected sources.

When my name appeared in the *Toronto Daily Star* as having been reported 'dangerously' wounded in the latest casualty list, a few (I would like to say dozens) interested young ladies wrote to Col Laurin for particulars of my wounds, and my address. They received the same standard letters my mother had been getting. One girl from Kingston was not at all satisfied and put the matter quite bluntly:

Dear Sir:

A Lt C S Frost has been reported wounded in Italy. Rumour has it he has been killed.
Could you inform me which of these is true?
Yours sincerely
F B

She was probably the only one to get a straight answer.

A letter from another lady must have given Col Laurin a jolt. She wrote that she had known me in Public School in Toronto years before and asked after my health, signing her name 'A Hooker'.

Joyful news was about to be received by my parents, but one mystery would remain unsolved for several weeks. What had become of Lt Delues? The answer was finally cabled by CMHQ London to Col Laurin on December 24th.

Ottawa

London, England
24/12/43

Important
Re: Lt N Delues
Second Echelon now advises identification as Lt Charles Sydney Frost.

Thankfully, this mix-up was never communicated to my parents and only came to light when my dossier was released under The Canadian Human Rights Act of 1977.

To complete the story of Col Laurin, one last fact remains to be recorded. My file shows that on November 11th, 1943, when Col Laurin was getting considerable flak from father and others about my condition and whereabouts (as well as countless queries from other concerned next of kin), he found the time and energy to inform the Commissioner of Income Tax and the Department of Labour that I had been wounded in action on October 27th, 1943 — a fact my parents didn't know until November 14th.

Bari, Italy — 98 British General Hospital
November 7 to November 18, 1943

I have just received orders from the Commanding Officer of the PPCLI to return to Frosolone to see if the Germans are still holding the town after our attack yesterday. I try to give orders to my men, but they are not paying any attention. I try to shout and a terrible pain wrenches my body. I am going to be sick . . . .

I open my eyes and dimly see a figure in white leaning over me, supporting my head and neck and softly speaking my name: "Mr Frost, Mr Frost, you have just had an operation. Try not to be sick — you'll feel better soon."

189

Vague memories surface and fade away. "Where am I? Am I still in the creek? My God, I've been hit again."

"No, no, Mr Frost, you're in hospital, you'll be alright. You mustn't be sick again. Your teeth are wired together. Rinse out your mouth with a sip of water."

I lapse into a fitful sleep and the terrible retching goes away. Once more I am back with my scouts.

Next day I fully regained consciousness and shook off the crazy nightmares for awhile. The events of the past week were still hazy but I realized I had not written to my parents. Nurse gave me an airmail letter form and I scribbled a note to father.

Well, I'm following right in your footsteps. First I had malaria, and now I've been silly enough to get myself wounded. Nothing serious at all, but just enough to put me out of action for a couple of months. Right now I am in a Gen Hospital in Italy, and as most of the painful operations on my wound are over, I am just sitting up enjoying a rest.

I suppose you want to know how all this happened. Well, a bullet went through my mouth and out my left cheek. Sort of a freak, eh wot?

I am in the hands of a famous facial expert, and he's really good. He fixed up all my teeth and is now working on my face, and by the time he gets finished he says I'll be better looking than I ever was!!

In the meantime, I am passing the time by reading, practising Italian (always), and feeding like a king. As I have to drink through a feeder, I get a special diet, the main part of which is fruit juices! Pretty soft, eh? In two weeks I shall be able to eat ordinary foods again, and I have two of your lovely parcels waiting to be eaten!

The operation of November 7th had greatly relieved the pain and discomfort in my face and mouth; my jaw, minus the missing bone, was now held firmly in place. I could turn my head slowly and even bend my neck a bit without being nauseated with pain. My lungs were still sore but now I was able gently to cough up some of the phlegm that seemed to have been there for weeks. The problem of getting it out of the mouth was solved by simply swallowing the stuff and letting nature dispose of it in other ways.

Feeding, I admit, remained a problem, despite my 'uphole' letter home. As the nurse had promised, the doctor left a small opening in the silver splints covering the space where my front teeth had been. Through this opening I sucked in all the fluids the nurses could provide — fruit juices, tea (no coffee in a British hospital, dear chap), cocoa, Ovaltine. Hot soup was pure ambrosia — to this day it is my favourite food. Gradually I discovered I could avoid losing half the liquid through the wound by drinking on my right side.

When I told my parents I would be eating ordinary foods in two weeks, I was actually reporting what the doctor had told me before the operation and what I earnestly hoped would be the case. But the doctor, like old Capt Snafu, was prone to exaggeration (probably for my own morale, quite unlike Capt Snafu). Two weeks stretched to two months, then to five months, before my splints were removed and I could finally eat again.

In the meantime, it was a matter of taking things day by day and trying to find something to laugh about, silently. Not being able to speak was more of a novelty than a handicap. Probably for the first time in my life I learned to be a good listener.

Our ward was a mixed bag of army, air force and even a few navy officers — all British. I was the only Canadian. Most of the patients had awful facial wounds or burns and suffered terribly. One night two airmen arrived who had crash-landed in the nearby Foggia airfield. It was obvious there was little that could be done for them and their moans filled the ward for two days and nights until they were taken away.

Another patient from another ward provided a little comic relief. Apparently he had been wounded in both buttocks by a bullet that had passed clean through both cheeks, and severed the anus. After a painful operation to sew up the torn orifice he naturally suffered a monumental case of constipation.

Each morning he would visit our ward and graphically describe his efforts to obtain relief. Finally, success; the log jam broke and filled the bed pan. He described it as being not unlike passing the *Queen Mary* — sideways. However some cad in his ward 'stole his stool' before the nurses could inspect his handiwork. They refused to believe his story since he could not produce any evidence and continued to fill him up with milk of magnesia. Whether the 'stool' culprit was ever caught or confessed I do not know as the patient left the next day for another hospital — presumably one with a 'stool pigeon'.

The days passed pleasantly enough, with sisters to soothe the aches and pills to ease the pain. Nightfall ushered in a completely different world. There was no heat or light, of course; the cold and damp crept into every bed despite piles of blankets. The pitch-black darkness of the ward, broken only by the sisters' candles, seemed to intensify the pain and fears of the patients. Each of us had our favourite nightmare. Mine was always the same, night after night. I was out scouting again and had run into a German ambush. I drew my service revolver, fired a few shots and ran out of ammunition; I pulled out my Beretta pistol and found it, too, had no bullets. After a few nights of this it was like seeing a bad horror movie, and instead of being scared I would get mad and try to shout in my sleep. This always gave me a shocking pain in the jaw and I awoke with a jolt. Finding that I was safely in bed, in hospital, between sheets, was a great relief, and almost made up for these sweaty nightmares.

To this day I sometimes dream about the war, as most veterans do, and the dream is still the same. The fear has long since departed; only the anger of not having any ammunition remains.

Just as I was beginning to feel comfortable, during the daytime at least, my hip started to flare up. Whatever the cause, the doctors felt the wound had been aggravated by a hot water bottle during my evacuation. Due to the seriousness of the facial wound, pleurisy and the recent operation, the hip had more or less been forgotten. Now it was badly infected. The bandages were removed, taking with them a fair amount of skin and flesh, and I passed out. Of all the pains one has to endure from being wounded, I would venture to guess that changing bandages, that have stuck to open wounds, ranks as one of the finest tortures invented by man. There are two methods to remove such bandages: tear the bloody thing off and pass out, or gradually lift it off inch by tortured inch, with great gentleness and care, applying some soothing cream as the agony progresses. Neither method is satisfactory but it is helpful to alternate the procedure each time, giving the patient a little surprise and the nurse a little practice.

Thanks to liberal doses of sulpha, frequent changes of dressings and TLC from the nurses, the infection in the hip was brought under control and life began to look interesting again. On November 18th, the doctors gave me a thorough check-up and pronounced me ready to move to the next hospital — Algiers.

ALGIERS
94th British General Hospital

November 19, 1943 to February 1, 1944

When the bugle sounds the order
For the sick to toe the line
All the officers get brandy
All the privates Number Nine*

The Douglas DC-3 lumbers along the uneven runway, its twin engines straining to lift the aircraft into the early morning mists. Finally, the tail wheel comes up, the plane quickly gathers speed, lifts itself off and steadily climbs above the Adriatic Sea. Straight ahead, 150 miles distant, are the rocky coasts of Yugoslavia and Albania, still in the hands of the Germans. The pilot has no intention of continuing any farther on this easterly course. He gently banks the plane in a circle to the right and heads south through a gap in the Italian mountains toward Taranto.

The aircraft is crowded with patients from 98 British General Hospital, securely strapped into stretchers that are stacked in racks, with barely 18 inches between the rows. They have been told it will be a long, cold flight to Algiers. While the aircraft has large red crosses painted on both sides of the fuselage and on the wings, there is no guarantee that the Luftwaffe will grant safe passage. The plane is the same type as those used for trans-

---

* First War ballad. Number 9 was a 'cure-all' pill, like 222s in World War II.

porting VIPs and supplies for the Allied Armies. Who would blame an eager German flyer if he mistook it for one loaded with generals? To be sure, the patients would complain, but it wouldn't do them much good.

In the hope of avoiding any such contact with enemy aircraft, the DC-3 will fly only a few feet above the Mediterranean Sea and along the coasts of Italy, Sicily and North Africa. The flight will take five or six hours.

This is my first 'ride' in an airplane and my reactions are mixed — concern that we will never make it; relief that I have at last left the cold, dank wards of 98 General Hospital and the threat of enemy air raids for the sunny shores of Africa, far removed from the sounds of battle.

Prior to the flight, the surgeons had loosened the wires binding my jaws together, in case I was air sick. After three weeks of having my mouth shut, this was somewhat of a relief, but it made my face and teeth ache so much that I soon clamped my jaws together again and prayed my stomach would have the good sense to keep calm.

The DC-3 droned on. Nursing orderlies came by every few minutes checking bandages and plasma bottles of the very ill patients and reassuring everyone we would soon land in Algiers, where waiting ambulances would whisk us off to our hospital and a warm bed.

Finally, at 1330 hours, the DC-3 lowered its wheels with a shudder that scared some of the novice flyers, and the aircraft touched down smoothly on the runway, in pouring rain. The journey had taken exactly five and a half hours. The waiting ambulances were nowhere to be seen and did not show up until two hours later, while we shivered in the cold. Had I remembered some of my high school geography I would have known that the coasts of North Africa in November are just as cold, and the rains just as persistent, as in sunny Italy at this time of year! Finally, the vehicles arrived and took us to 94 British General Hospital on the outskirts of Algiers. By this time some of the more seriously wounded were in bad shape and wondered if their journey was really worth it. Time would tell.

94 British General Hospital had taken over the former quarters of a French Foreign Legion Unit, located on high ground overlooking Algiers and surrounded by a garden of orange groves and vineyards. To the south loomed the Atlas mountains, thrusting forward their rugged slopes, where tribesmen grazed their goats, sheep and camels. Beyond the mountains lay an Africa very different from our cold, rain-soaked garden — the endless, hot, arid sands of the Sahara. All of us would happily have exchanged two weeks in the desert for a weekend in our present abode.

It was hard to realize that a scant four months earlier I had entered Algiers harbour aboard the troopship *Arundel Castle,* dressed in tropical kit because of the oppressive heat and bound for the beaches of Sicily, eager to come to grips with the armies of the detested Mussolini and Hitler. Now Mussolini was gone, Italy had surrendered and our armies had pushed the Germans out of Sicily and up the long toe of Italy. Yet, momentous as these victories were, the Hun had shown himself to be a tough, brave foe, who had every intention of contesting every foot of the Italian peninsula.

It had been three long weeks since my little patrol to Frosolone and I wondered what the Regiment was doing. Had it returned to action? Who had taken over my Scout and Sniper Platooon? Had they suffered more casualties? Had any of my friends been hit? I was not to get answers for many weeks as I was out of the normal evacuation stream for Canadian casualties and was in fact still 'wounded but disappeared' as far as the Canadian authorities were concerned. Much later, I learned that right after I was wounded, the Patricias were withdrawn to a little town called Busso, not far from the Divisional Leave Centre at Campobasso. There they were to remain at ease for the next month, resting, cleaning up and preparing for the bloody battles of Villa Rogatti and the Moro River.

While the Patricias were enjoying their well earned rest at Busso, I was likewise at ease, but as a guest of a British hospital, courtesy of the French Foreign Legion. In the course of many years of listening to my father's stories of French hospitals in the First World War, I had developed a certain hostility to such asylums, which soon surfaced when I looked over my new quarters. The buildings were little more than shells built of stone, with rusted tin roofs through which the rain dripped into strategically placed buckets. Openings for windows had been provided, but there was no glass and the wind and rain blew in at will.

Through these same openings came other forces to torment us — dirty, brown arms and sticky fingers of local Arabs (called Wogs and worse names by the British soldiers) who purloined our meagre personal belongings and small caches of food.

The patients in my ward were not just plastic cases, such as myself, but suffered from every kind of wound, sickness and illness — a combined medical, surgical ward. Cases of palsy, meningitis, appendicitis and pneumonia were mixed in with patients who had abdominal wounds, or who had lost legs, arms, genitals. Some of the patients had been there since the fighting in Tunisia the previous April and May. As in the British hospital in Bari, Italy, I was the only Canadian — 'The Lone Ranger'.

The surgeons and doctors were a very talented and dedicated group, particularly the Maxillo-Facial team of surgeons and dentists who performed surgery and took care of me. Many had practised on London's famous Harley Street before the war — my surgeon had trained under a brilliant English surgeon, Sir Howard Gilles.

Yet, despite all their talents and dedication, they could not overcome the filth and disease that permeated the old barracks, cook houses, hospital compound and adjoining areas. While we patients had, at least, a roof over our heads, and walls and stone floors, many of the doctors, and most of the nurses, had to live in tents and marquees, surrounded by a sea of mud. Everywhere the Wogs infiltrated the loosely guarded hospital compound and pestered the staff and patients with their wares, in most cases articles they had stolen at least once from their prospective purchasers. They even had the audacity to appear draped in sheets and blankets taken from the hospital and marked with a large WD (War Department). The combination of continued rain and cold, the lack of proper sanitation, the inability to control infection and disease, the depredations of the Arabs, all seemed to have an effect on the morale of the doctors and nurses, which naturally rubbed off on the patients. My hip wound, which at first had seemed so secondary to my face, now caught further infection and spread to such a wide area that a skin graft was attempted and failed.

Other patients had similar problems due to infection spreading out of control. The poor fellow with meningitis got worse and worse; his screams filled the ward night after night; mercifully, he finally died. We buried him on the side of a hill in a nearby cemetery.

It is my sad duty to relate a most distressing tale of incompetence and uncaring, even hostility of some of the sisters in our ward. Their attitude was so contrary to the tender care and attention I received before and after this hospital, that it deserves comment — my remarks apply only to two or three of the nurses however, not by any means to the whole staff. The rough, indifferent treatment I myself received was also experienced by most, if not all, of the other patients on the ward and they tended to indict the entire staff, and indeed the whole nursing service. I admit that at times I too cursed the entire organization for their inefficiency, but that was unfair.

Queen Alexandra, the consort of Edward VII, gave her name to a body of nurses known as Queen Alexandra's Imperial Military Nursing Service Reserve QAIMNSR of which many of the nurses in this hospital were members, including the very few who gave us so much trouble. Things came to such a pass that, for the first time, in one of my letters home, I described the problems as they really were.

> *I do nothing but argue with these nurses. They know all the tricks of the trade, and I swear are absolutely sexless. They manhandled me like a sack, a few weeks ago, when I got bathed by them. A person can't remain sick with them around. Either you die or recover, tout de suite!*

Some of the remarks I confided to my diary.

> November 20. *Finally had dressing changed. Sisters only fair. I can see that to get well I shall have to push them. Very little care being given to my jaw.*

November 30. *Operation — skin graft on hip. Swore at the sisters. They and the orderlies are particularly useless.*
December 2. *Disgusted by inefficiency of nursing sisters. Get little help from them.*
December 4. *Got told off by Major C for row with sisters. Most unreasonable as sisters are definitely not good.*
December 25. *Sister Cleghorn is an old cow! Gave out my cigarettes so sisters wouldn't steal them.*
December 26. *Great row between Sister Cleghorn and the other sisters!*

The foregoing are only a few samples of the vituperation described in my diary. However, in fairness to the large majority of sisters who tended their patients with care, efficiency and understanding, I offer these further extracts.

December 31. *Was kissed by the new luscious night nurse.*
January 7. *Went to concert, 'Tin Hats'. After show sat around with night sister (lovely gal) and had a few drinks of wine. Pleasant evening.*
January 8. *Had a nice chat with Night Sister and got rid of a corporal who was hounding her.*

When Sister Cleghorn was not annoying me she was taking out her vicious nature on some other patient who couldn't defend himself. One chap in the tanks had just come in, minus a leg, and was moaning piteously. Sister Cleghorn roughed him up a bit and yelled, "Stop that silly crying. Don't you know there's a war on!"

The captain who had palsy was getting worse and was a special target for Sister Cleghorn because he couldn't talk. One night she made him so mad that he sat down and wrote out a verse damning her and (most unfairly) all other members of QAIMNSR, right back to the good Queen herself.

Oh Alexandra, did you mean
When you were England's gracious Queen
That every nurse should be a hag
However young, and nag and nag?

Did you intend them all to wear
A frown of hate, a look of fear?
As if poor crippled men in bed
Would violate their maidenhead

Was it your pleasure women then
Should bait and browbeat wounded men
Who oft have made no worse mistake
Than risk their lives for England's sake

And did you plan that wenches sour
Called up in Britain's greatest hour
Should don the trousers and the pips
Of those who suffer from their quips

Oh! QAIMNSR
We sadly ask, for sad we are
"Is it some sin to be polite?
And are you nurses always right?"

Three days after arriving at the hospital, my jaw and chest were x-rayed, and although I still had a cold, the surgeon decided he had to operate right away on both the jaw and hip to try to control the infection and remove diseased teeth, bone and tissue. On November 23rd, I had my third major operation which, like the others, left me pretty weak and nauseated, but thankful that the doctors were doing all they could for me.

At this time the main drug used for controlling infection was sulpha and it was applied in as large doses as the patient could safely take. To ensure that an overdose was not given, samples of blood were taken every few hours by a syringe that I am sure had been used in the Battle of Paardeberg — probably in the hands of Sister Cleghorn herself, who was still wielding it like a lance. The mere sight of this weapon was enough to reduce to tears soldiers who had fought the best of Hitler's paratroopers.

The advent of penicillin later in the campaign, besides saving thousands of patients, saved countless more from the jabs of Sister Cleghorn. The importance of this wonder drug during the later phase of the war was considerable.

Experience in reconstructive surgery in the final stages of war and in the post-war period strengthened the surgeons' faith in the efficacy of penicillin, for with its aid results were obtained which had hitherto been regarded as impossible, and which, even if taken alone, would have earned for it a place along with the large-scale use of blood and plasma transfusions as one of the advances seen in the treatment of wounds in the Second World War.[1]

Another development in medical science that made life easier for patients about to undergo operations was sodium pentothol. This wonderful anaesthetic was injected in the arm and quickly put the patient to sleep without putting him through the ordeal of having to breathe the revolting ether gas through a mask clamped securely over his face. Best of all, the post-operation nausea was greatly reduced. Whether the nature of my wounds precluded the use of pentothol, or whether it was in short supply at 94 General Hospital, I do not know, but it was never given to me, at least never to put me to sleep.

A few days after my operation, the hospital staff were put in a fine dither by the impending visit of the Director of all Medical Services in the British Army — LGen Sir Arthur Hood. What a splendid chance, we thought, to complain about our slip-shod treatment at the hands of Sister Cleghorn! We resolved to give the general an earfull.

When the great day arrived, we were brought to attention like soldiers on parade. Those who could stand, including the 'one leggers', stood at attention beside their beds; those in wheelchairs sat upright, with chairs parallel to the beds; those in bed, including me, lay at attention, hands stiffly down the sides. The general and his entourage appeared at the door, paused a moment, as if waiting for a band to play a general salute, then quickly marched down one side of the ward and back the other. If the general showed any intention of speaking to a patient, his aides were quick to steer him away, though he managed to break through the cordon and say some kindly words to one or two of the more seriously wounded. The whole thing was over before I or anyone else had a chance to voice our complaints. Too bad I hadn't the nerve of the 'Anti-Authority' groups that started parading with large placards after the war. I would have held up a large sign over my bed: 'This place stinks'.

On the very day I was undergoing this rather novel inspection (novel to me then, but oft-repeated during my months in hospital), my father's Militia Regiment was being inspected in far-away Toronto by the new District Officer Commanding, MGen Arthur Potts. The fact that the general and father had been great friends in Saskatoon was of course irrelevant to the general and awkward for father, who was only a major. A letter from father told all about the inspection and gave me something to chuckle about.

> Gen Potts gave us quite a thorough going over. Two men from my company fainted and one other had to get down on his knees. However we were well turned out — in battle order — and the DOC praised us for our steadiness. He found quite a bit of fault, though, with the Syllabus. Unfortunately we had Coy drill for one period and that came in for a lot of criticism. Curiously enough I had mentioned only the previous Monday at Coy Comdr meeting that I didn't think we should be doing Coy drill when the DOC came. I have all along been stressing cutting out some of the ceremonial of which we have too much, and getting down to business.

Well, I thought, even if the old man is 50 years old, he's trying hard to be a fighting soldier. Perhaps he has been studying some of the precis on battle drill I sent him from Vernon so long ago. "Long ago?" I asked myself. "What am I talking about? That was only a year ago." It seemed like ten.

On November 30th, the doctors took another look at my hip and found the infection was still spreading. By now, an area as large as a saucer was an open, festering wound from which the skin and much of the flesh had disappeared down to the bone. "Is it sore?" enquired the doctor.

My answer does not appear in my diary. The doctor, however, got the message. He decided that the wound would never close on its own and that the only thing left was to do a skin graft. He even suggested that I was very lucky.

"Lucky?" I mumbled through my teeth, "How do you figure that?"

"Well, you're lucky you're here, in this hospital. It's the only one attempting skin grafts in the whole area".

I was not all that thrilled with my great stroke of luck, and I didn't like his using the word 'attempting'. All the same, his last operation on my face had gone pretty well. My jaws and teeth were now firmly locked together, giving the bone a chance to heal and greatly easing the pain. The wound had almost closed over so that I could quite easily suck in liquids without losing half of them. I could even mumble a few words through the bandages and clenched teeth and I was getting more vocal every day.

The skin graft operation proceeded and I awoke to find both hips tightly strapped together; my left hip, inside thigh, back and kidneys were hurting like blazes. What in the name of heaven have they done now, I wondered, but no explanations or help came from the sisters on duty. After a few days the straps on the hips were removed and the terrible pressure on my back and kidneys eased. I looked down at my left leg and found I now had a new wound on the inside of my thigh, which was covered with a bandage larger than the one on my hip. This new wound was aching worse than the original one and had an itch that was driving me crazy.

The nurse finally explained what had happened. Skin from the inside of my thigh had been peeled off in patches and placed over the wound on the hip, which was now pretty well covered. I had nothing to worry about the 'donor' area. Though it was quite extensive, enough skin had been left that new skin would soon fill in the empty patches. My thigh resembled a patchwork quilt of skin and raw flesh. The only worry was whether the transferred skin would 'take' on the old wound and not become infected. Nothing was said about whether I should be concerned about the new wound also getting infected, so I let the doctors worry about that one. At least the problems with the skin graft took my mind off the wound in the face, and I had high hopes I would soon be on my feet and out of bed for good.

The blow came on December 7th. The bandages were 'taken down' and it was found I had streptococcus in both the hip wound and the donor area — the skin graft had been a failure.

The doctors were very apologetic but explained that because of the septic, unsanitary conditions throughout the hospital, there was really very little chance that a skin graft operation would succeed. The same thing applied to the bone graft they were waiting to do on my jaw. Their considered prognosis was that it would take five to seven more months to do all the operations, skin grafts, bone grafts and dental work, and further time for convalescence. There was no point in trying anything further in the unsanitary conditions of North Africa. They would recommend that I be sent to England and then to Canada for further treatment and convalescence.

The only fly in the ointment (a particularly apt phrase for the conditions in the hospital) was that it might take weeks before they could find transport for me to England. I would, of course, understand, that as I was a Canadian in a British hospital, my priority for leaving on a British ship was low — so low, in fact, that really my only chance was if a Canadian hospital ship visited Algiers. "When", I asked, "is the next Canadian ship due?"

The doctor had no idea, but he pointed out that if one didn't arrive in, say, six weeks, he would have to do some work on my lower lip which was gradually turning inside out and being pulled down into the wound in the jaw.

Six weeks! It was now December 8th. My boat had to arrive no later than, say, January 21st or I would be on that filthy chopping block again. One last problem remained. I had been confined to bed for the past six weeks, and I had had enough. No matter that the two wounds in my left leg were infected and would take weeks to heal, if at all, in this unhealthy place. Using all the powers of advocacy I could summon, liberally sprinkled with a good assortment of medical and non-medical terms, I persuaded the doctor to let me get up and start walking around the ward, aided by crutches if necessary. To hell with the wounds — let them take care of themselves. Everything else had failed; maybe this novel treatment would work.

At least it worked wonders with my morale:

December 8. *Allowed up. Got fully dressed in battle dress and PPCLI flashes. Oh boy! Feeling fairly good. Only sore spot is where they have taken off the skin!*
December 9. *Still up and dressed. Feeling 100% now except for slight limp.*

I could hardly wait to write to my mother:

Here's some big news for you. Yesterday I was informed that I'm going to England after Xmas! Isn't that swell?
In England I shall be some 5-7 months taking treatments, skin and bone grafts, etc. Then I'll be due a nice fat leave and should get special consideration from point of view of my time in hospital. In other words, I have high hopes of getting a spot of leave home, just as Dad did last war. Now, dear Mom, I don't want you getting unduly excited, but I feel that looking ahead to next summer I'll be showing you how well they patched me

up. Pretty uphole! eh wot?

In such a happy state of mind I soon cast aside the crutches and hopped about on my good leg visiting other wards. To my great joy I found two other Canadians who had just arrived from Italy — one from the Royal 22nd Regiment (The famous 'van-Doos'); the other from the 5th Division. From them I learned that the 5th Armoured Division had just arrived in Naples from England and would soon be going into action with 1st Canadian Division, as a corps, under Gen Crerar. Rumour had it that this Canadian Corps would be landed in Yugoslavia.

This rumour, like all really good rumours, had been manufactured in some staff officer's latrine, and served the useful purpose of confusing friend and foe alike — but more often the former. Best of all, such rumours, known as 'latrineograms', gave the troops something to talk about and lay bets on.

An officer in my ward I soon got to know was Lt Marcus Mander of the Coldstream Guards who, like me, had been wounded in the face and needed plastic surgery. He too was waiting around for transportation to England because the doctors would not attempt such an operation in North Africa. We became good friends, even though we were supposed to be competing for passage on the next boat or plane to England. In reality there was no competition. Being a Canadian I was out of the race, even though my wounds were more serious than his — a fact he was gentleman enough to acknowledge; he even volunteered to give up his place.

It was a gallant gesture but the authorities would not hear of such interference with their well established procedures and red tape. Marcus left for England, by air, on Boxing Day. I remained behind with a king-sized headache from drinking Algerian wine smuggled into the ward by some friendly Arabs.

Shortly after he arrived home, Marcus thoughtfully wrote a letter to my mother enclosing some snaps of me he had taken before leaving.

Kilsall Hall, Shifnal
Shropshire, UK
Sunday, February 6th, 1944

Dear Mrs Frost

I was in hospital with your son Sydney at Algiers, for some weeks. He should be coming home to you any time now, but it always takes a long time for the machinery of hospitals to turn out a case for evacuation. He was improving a great deal when they sent me away by air on Boxing Day, and I know he was cheered up by getting a bunch of mail on Christmas Eve from all his family, which he read feverishly in the sister's room after lights were out.

We had interesting discussions on Canadian education

compared with our own, and on the differences between RMC
where Sydney was commissioned and ours at Sandhurst. It was
rather pathetic that he was only able to eat such a little of the
contents of parcels sent from home, but contrived to grind up
into pastes the most amazing selections — including lobster or
chocolate bars melted in hot custard.

Apart from my letters home, this note from Marcus, and his pictures, did more to comfort mother than anything else she received during my service overseas. I shall always be grateful to him.

A sequel to this chance encounter with a fine English gentleman in a hospital in Algiers occurred 12 years after the events just described. In 1956 my wife and I were visiting England and passed by the town of Shifnal. I immediately remembered my good friend whom I had corresponded with for a brief period after the war, but whom I had not heard from for years. In enquired at the local pub for directions to Kilsall Hall. When I appeared at the door I was informed that, on the death of his father, my friend had moved to another residence. Finally I tracked down my quarry and was somewhat stunned to find he was now Sir Charles Mander.

We spent a wonderful time together, reminiscing on our 'Algerian connection' which even then, only 12 years after the event, seemed unreal. We compared the results of our numerous plastic surgery operations and agreed, with the encouragement of our wives, that our appearance had been markedly improved by the surgeons.

Returning to my compulsory holiday in North Africa, my self-prescribed treatment for a hip that wouldn't heal was miraculously beginning to work. The infection had almost cleared up and the open wound had shrunk to the size of an English penny. Contrary to established medical learning that wounds were best treated by keeping immobile and getting lots of rest, I was thriving on my 'ward hopping' and regular PT exercises that I now went through every morning. All this activity also helped to ward off the terrible cold that kept us shivering day and night. Two subjects appear daily in my diary of those bleak days — cold and food. Typical of my entries on the weather are these: "Bloody cold and rainy. Not sleeping at night because of the cold. Still cold. Damn the cold, I can hardly write."

It is not surprising that everyone in the ward suffered from chronic colds which hampered medical treatment of wounds, especially during and after operations, when breathing became very difficult.

The subject of food was constantly on my mind, even to the exclusion of that other subject soldiers are supposed to be continually thinking about. Not that the food was bad or inadequate for those who could eat. They had no complaints. It was the jaw cases (who could not open their mouths) who dreamt about gorging themselves on mountains of roast beef and apple pie.

As Marcus Mander had written my mother, I became very adept at mashing almost everything into a paste, mixing it with soup or other liquids, and sucking the concoction down.

My issue rations were daily supplemented with oranges purchased from the Arabs, who conveniently brought their wares right to the open windows of the ward and did business 'over the counter'. Pure juice from a dozen oranges made a nice breakfast drink, particularly when the entire cost was only 15 francs (about 30 cents). Of course, one had to be quick to squeeze the oranges before the Arabs grabbed them back and resold the fruit to another customer.

Another source of 'buckshee' rations was the night orderly, one Pte Outrum. Unlike Capt Snafu of Sicily days, Outrum's name did not suit him at all. He was never 'out of rum', at least while on duty. He always kept me well supplied with hot drinks — tea, cocoa and Ovaltine — as well as items in very short supply, such as sugar, canned milk and coffee. Good old Outrum! Sometimes he was so drunk he couldn't eat (or see) his meal and I would mash it up and poke it down my tiny life line.

On December 19th, I received the first parcel from home since being wounded eight weeks earlier. That date marked a watershed in my quest for nourishment. From then on my food supply was assured and I had the sisters and some of the doctors literally eating out of my hand. First to be bribed was the doctor who had threatened to do more operations if my ship didn't arrive. He got a can of lobster, with a hint that more might be forthcoming if he found me passage on a British boat.

Next on my list to be coerced were, naturally, the sisters. They received Laura Secord chocolates, an almost unbelievable treat at that time. Pte Outrum got his reward for not living up to his name and being so generous in his hand-outs — a small bottle of rye father had secreted in a cake. Other members of the ward received items I could not mash up, and I kept a tactical reserve hidden in a locker in Outrum's kitchen, safe from the sticky fingers of the Arabs and the prying noses of the nursing sisters.

While I appreciated receiving these parcels, I don't think I fully realized how difficult it was for my parents to obtain some of the foods, especially tinned delicacies such as lobster, chicken and ham. Mother and father would often spend days snooping around neighbourhood grocery stores to find some treat that they knew I would enjoy. Later mother wrote to me about one expedition.

> *I found two tins of lobster on my tour yesterday. Quite a treat. I go out early to do battle for eats now. Tomato juice came on the market yesterday (2 to a customer) so I was there at 9am and have them stored away in your cupboard. Dad discovered (hold your breath) a can of steak and mushrooms in a little fruit*

store. This will go in your parcel next week. Dad has been sending
300 cigarettes per week, sometimes 1000, also Laura Secords, but
we can only buy one pound boxes for Overseas. There must be
a lot of them somewhere between Laura Secord Candy Shops
and you!

Just as important as the parcels, if not more so, were the letters that at last started to arrive. On December 20th I received the first letter from my parents since I had been wounded, telling me they knew of my injury. The letter was dated November 16th, at which time they had received only the telegram and one letter from Col Laurin advising the date of the wound. They did not hear from me until December 7th when my letter of November 15th from Bari, Italy, arrived, having taken only three weeks in transit. This was remarkably speedy service considering the fact I was in a British hospital and the mail had to go via the United Kingdom. Mail from home took longer, as it first went to the PPCLI, and was re-routed back to Algiers. Still I received every letter in less than a month.

I feel quite strongly that the postal corps never received the recognition they deserved for getting mail through so quickly and with so few losses. Their record puts to shame the dismal performance of our present-day, so-called postal service.

Most letters, both to and from home, were sent by airmail. One type was a blue, armed forces, airmail letter form, on one sheet of paper that folded into an envelope. All mail was supposedly censored, yet very few letters ever received the censor's scissors or black pen. Being an officer I 'censored' my own mail and signed my name to that effect on the outside of the letter. Whether this expedited the mail I have no idea.

A number of my parent's letters arrived with a jagged patch missing. Curiously, the piece cut out was nearly always the area where a large 10¢ stamp, depicting the Parliament Buildings, had been affixed. I have no reason to blame the censors or the postal corps for this philatelic philandering, but I do suspect that some orderly at the hospital may have done a little extra-curricular surgery on my letters.

Another type of airmail letter was the 'Airgraph' form, purchased from the postal service. This form, on a standard, letter-sized sheet of white paper, would take writing on only one side. The form was then photographed and reduced to about one-quarter of its original size and mailed in an envelope marked postage paid, thus removing the temptation for any stamp collector to augment his collection illegally. These Airgraph letters were supposed to be quicker than ordinary mail, but I never found there was much difference between the two; both were speedy forms of communication, given the circumstances of those days.

Perhaps one of the greatest feats of the postal service, both in terms of speed and timing, occured on Christmas Eve, when 30 letters were delivered to me at 94 General Hospital in Algiers. Prior to the descent of this avalanche of mail I had received only one letter since October 26th. As Marcus Mander mentioned in his letter, I stayed up all night, reading and re-reading my mail by candlelight, drinking hot tea and sipping Algerian wine to ward off the cold, in the room of the night sister whom I had compromised with another box of chocolates.

As I read all the thousands of words, in a cold, damp hospital in Algiers, only one paragraph from one of mother's letters upset me.

> *Dad and I have been gathering up clothing for the Russians and you'd be* surprised *at the pile. I won't have many things to air and pack away after this onslaught on trunks and closets. Even your winter underwear has helped to heighten the pile!*

I wasn't surprised. I was horrified! Here was I, freezing to death in weather that would castrate two brass monkeys, and my own mother was giving away my lovely, warm, winter underwear to the bloody Russians! The more I thought about it the madder I got. Forty years later it almost gives me a coronary.

New Year's Eve gave the patients an excuse for fraternizing with the sisters, aided by a few bottles of fine French wine someone had procured from the Arabs. By midnight, those who had not been anaesthetised joined in a round of Auld Lang Syne, and collapsed. The sight of badly wounded men, some without a leg or an arm, weaving and hopping around in the candlelight, singing songs and trying to make a play for some tough old sister, started me on a laughing jag that caused havoc with my jaw next day. Outside, the local Wogs stood in the rain, peering in at this mad ritual and casting their dark eyes covetously about for the loot that would soon be theirs.

New Year's Day was business as usual. I was called in and told I was at the top of the list for evacuation by hospital ship, or perhaps by plane. I had heard that story before and I had now been languishing in this hospital for six weeks. "What about a troopship?" I asked the doctor. "I can mash up just about everything now and my hip is not bothering me."

I could see from the doctor's face that this procedure was not in the manual for evacuation of jaw cases. He had another look at my wound. "You can't go on a trooper unless you can masticate."

I didn't quite catch the last word and thought he was trying to be funny. "I don't care a damn about that. I'll get by alright."

"But the colonel will have to convene a medical board."

"OK, OK, convene the bloody thing." I was not going to be intimidated by a mere colonel in the RAMC (Royal Army Medical Corps).

I knew what the doctor was going to say next before he even opened his mouth. "It will take some time to convene a - - - - - - - - -." I walked out of the room before he could finish.

There was no question that I had been in hospital longer than any other officer, except for Sandy, an English Captain in the engineers. His was a pitiful case. He had been blown up on a mine in the desert campaign and by some terrible quirk of fate had lost his genitals — testicles, penis, the lot. His legs, though wounded, had long since healed and he insisted he was ready for action again. Perhaps he was, physically, but emotionally he was a sick man. He absolutely refused to be sent home. He had married just before leaving England.

Sandy tried hard not to show his inner turmoil and kidded his fellow officers and the nurses about his disability. I admired his fortitude but he did not fool me or anyone else. After a while we became good friends and he suggested we visit Algiers together. "With that ugly face of yours, you need a good-looking young sapper like me to seduce some of those French ladies in the Red Cross who come round the ward with their little gifts."

That seemed like a splendid idea because I knew what his next line was going to be. "After I get them in the mood you can step in and finish the job."

With great guffaws and winks at the sisters, he marched me out of the ward and into a waiting bus, bound for town. This was my first expedition to the outside world and I was a little nervous about the whole undertaking. I didn't even have a pass, but my friend had apparently taken care of all the red tape, and no one stopped us on our suicidal mission.

As the bus careened along the narrow streets I tried to recall what I had read about this exotic city in the hospital library:

> *Algiers - Melting Pot of Humanity — Moslem, French, Spanish, Italian, Maltese, Turk. Each race has ruled in Algiers or left its mark. The city is a blend of East and West, of Africa and Europe, where tall modern buildings contrast with narrow, winding streets in the mysterious Casbah.*

The bus continued to weave in and out of the teeming throng of American GIs, British soldiers, Frenchmen, Arabs, men in their burnooses, women in their veils. I had fantasies of ending up in an Arab harem in the Casbah. Suddenly I felt a little faint and sheepishly grabbed my stalwart friend's strong arm. "Steady, steady, we'll soon be there. You're just a little out of practice."

I put my head between my knees and held on until the bus made a violent turn and screeched to a stop. I looked up a saw a fine looking modern building, set back from a wide street lined with palm trees. Two British sentries stood guard on steps leading up to an impressive door. Above the entrance a sign declared 'Officers Club'.

I pulled myself together, mounted the steps, entered a magnificent hallway and headed for a sign saying 'Messieurs'. Finally the nausea passed and I was led to a quiet corner in a large salon, where uniformed waiters brought us drinks. I had lost all interest in visiting the Casbah.

On the way home my friend apologized for talking me into this little escapade before I was quite ready for it. "You obviously need a tough course before we tackle the Casbah." I had no idea what course he had in mind. I only wanted to get back to my bed, in that nice, quiet hospital.

It didn't take me too long to recover from this venture into the outer world and I was soon eager for another try. This time I decided I would confine my operation to a more realistic objective. Not far from our hospital was another British hospital, 95 General, which, I was told, had recently admitted several Canadian casualties. Leaving my friend Sandy behind, I spruced myself up, obtained a pass and set off in the bus again.

At 95 General I was overjoyed to find a Patricia officer, Maj Patty Crofton, who had been wounded in the bloody fighting at Vino Ridge during December. Patty had joined the Regiment in August, 1940, was a very popular officer, and had been kind to me during my brief service. It was a great tonic to see one of the Regimental family after these long weeks in a British hospital, which had seemed, at times, more like an enemy bastion.

Patty Crofton told me of the hard fighting the Regiment had just been through in Villa Rogatti, The Moro River and Vino Ridge, south of Ortona on the Adriatic Coast. Maj Brain had been killed, Maj Watson wounded, and Lt 'Knobby' Clark had received a bullet in the throat which would severely affect his speech. Despite the fighting and casualties, the great Patricia spirit was high as ever and Patty hoped he would soon be back in the fray again.*

After bringing me up to date on Regimental news, Patty looked me over with a paternal gaze and declared that my tattered old uniform hardly measured up to the high standards of the Patricias. Fortunately there was an officer's kit shop in Algiers that should be able to outfit me in a manner befitting an officer in the PPCLI.

No transport was available at the hospital, so we hitch-hiked a ride into town. There we boarded an ancient tram car, jamp-packed with civilians of all types and smells, who could be anybody, but probably were Frenchmen and Arabs. Only the brute strength of Patty kept them at bay until we arrived at our destination.

---

* He was to return and see many more months of action, including two further wounds. He survived to take command of the Regiment after the war and bring it home to Canada. For a short time during that period I acted as his Second-in-Command.

The shop was well supplied with every kind of officer's kit. I couldn't resist the display and spluged 20 days' pay (£20) on completely outfitting myself with new battledress, beret, shoes, socks, shirts and a trenchcoat. Eventually I was reimbursed by the Army as I was only replacing kit that had been lost. Later still my old kit turned up and I had to reimburse the government. It was a sound purchase just the same — I still wear the trenchcoat in a heavy rain.

While it was wonderful to see Patty Crofton and get news of my friends, it was also sad to realize that I would probably never serve with the Regiment again. Had my luck not run out so quickly I would now have been in line for promotion. In this unhappy mood I wrote home.

Looking back on my adventure of the last five months I realize that I've spent too much time in hospital and not enough with the Regiment. I was getting to be a senior Lieutenant, too, when I got hit, but that's luck. However, I believe I can say I've left my mark on the Bn as the original organizer of the Scout and Sniper Platoon. I think there's a great future ahead for it, and I wouldn't be surprised to find it being made permanent. I'll certainly be able to give them a lot of dope on it. I think I shall write a book some day. Say, that's a dandy idea. Scouting and Sniping *by Lt C S Frost!!*

I will confess that this thought has remained with me all these years and I am, at last, doing something about it.

Despite all the frustrations and uncertainties I was able to finish off with a light touch.

What's this about my picture appearing in Toronto Star? *Whatever did they put in it about me? Please send me a copy, I'm sure I'd get a big kick out of it! I'll tell you why — last week, among various letters, I received one from a girl by the name of Hooker of Toronto. What a letter!! This is the first fan mail I have ever received, so I got quite a bang out of it. And so help me, she enclosed a picture of her honourable self. Evidently we had been in the same class at Runnymede School when I was a 'young fella'. Well, it was nice to hear from a friend of Public School days!*

Next day I was informed that my medical board, to determine whether I was fit to travel by a troop transport, would be convened that afternoon. I got all decked out in my new kit and marched before the board, feeling the very model of a fit, smart, infantry officer.

The colonel untied wires holding together the silver splints over my teeth, and one splint fell out on the floor. It had apparently been loose for some time, perhaps from my laughing jag on New Year's, and the cement had worn away. The result was that the fractured jaw had not been kept immobile and had not joined together; I couldn't attempt to chew anything as the pain of moving the jaw was too severe. I would therefore not be allowed to return to England on a troopship.

By now I was becoming accustomed to these set-backs, though they were never very pleasant. In this case, a further complication that influenced the opinion of the Board was my hip which had started to flare up again. The bandages were taken down and more infection found.

So it was back to bed with more sulpha and needles while the surgeons recemented the loose splint again and locked the jaw together.

It was now January 13th and I had been languishing in this hospital eight weeks. My only hope was a Canadian hospital ship but no one had any idea when, or even if, it might arrive. I remembered the injunction I had received from my doctor four weeks earlier — if a boat hadn't arrived by January 21st, he would have to do some preventive surgery on my lip before it became too disfigured to repair. Clearly I was in a time squeeze.

Unbeknown to me, on or about this date, a Canadian hospital ship was leaving Halifax bound for the United Kingdom via North Africa. The name of the ship was the *Lady Nelson*. She had been taken over by the government, refitted as a hospital ship and put into service in early 1943 — the first to be commissioned as a Canadian hospital ship.

When the Sicilian Campaign began the British suggested that the *Lady Nelson* be placed on the run between North Africa and the United Kingdom. The Canadian authorities at first completely rejected this idea on the grounds that she had to be kept on the North Atlantic run. They pointed out there were three British hospital ships operating between North Africa and the United Kingdom. However, the Canadians finally agreed that the *Lady Nelson,* on her eastbound trip, would call at North Africa and evacuate both British and Canadian casualties to England.[2]

I shall be forever grateful that the Canadian Government agreed to having the *Lady Nelson* call at North African ports, particularly Algiers, otherwise I might still be there — probably in the Casbah.

On January 26th another British Hospital ship arrived and took away all the remaining serious cases, while I cursed my luck and made very rude entries in my diary about the English in general, and their evacuation procedures in particular:

> *Bloody English Hospitals. Looks like I'll be here for the rest of the war. Damn these rotten Limeys. Situation looks hopeless.*

Apart from the pure frustration of being left behind time and time again, there was the more important matter of the steady deterioration of my jaw and face which were now aching constantly. It was also past the January 21st deadline for an operation on my lip. Furthermore I suspected that my lower splint had now become loose but I didn't dare tell the doctors for fear they would insist on another operation and I would leave the hospital feet first.

The only hope seemed to be the padre. He was a very decent chap who had thoughtfully given me a cigarette holder to help me continue with this filthy habit. The least I could do was to attend his next church service, which I did the following Sunday. The next day my ship arrived.

Thirty-six years later a brown parcel from National Defence Headquarters Ottawa arrived at my door. I broke open the seal and found a very tarnished medal and ribbon with a scribbled hand-written note: "Enclosed is your Africa Star. Sorry it is so late."

ENGLAND AGAIN
Lady Nelson Hospital Ship
10 Canadian General Hospital
February 1 to February 15, 1944

A hospital ship is just leaving Algiers
Bound for Old Blighty's shore
Heavily laden with wounded men
Bound for the land they adore
There's many a soldier has lost a good limb
One blighter is missing them all
So Pray God Almighty, take me back to old Blighty
And cheer up my lads bless 'em all.

The ambulance rolls onto the busy docks at Algiers and stops at the check point. MPs, in their immaculate battle dress, white belts and scarlet hat bands, throw open the doors, take a cursory look at the patients inside and tell the driver to move along quickly, as No 1 Canadian Hospital Ship is about to depart. The patients howl out to the driver to step on it, but he hardly needs their encouragement; he knows he is a dead man if he misses this ship — one patient with a wound in the face has already made that quite clear. The ambulance races along the dock and slides to a stop a few paces from the gangway.

"How many patients, driver?" demands a voice on the dock.

"Only four, Sir."

"Four? I thought only two from 94 General were well enough to travel. The ship is bulging at the seams."

The ambulance doors fling open and a medical officer confronts four

212

very determined men. The SOP (Senior Officer Present), a major with one leg missing, wastes no words stating that all four patients are fit and ready to travel, if necessary in the bilge of the ship, bulging or not. No 1 Canadian Hospital Ship leaves shortly after with 510 wounded soldiers, including four patients from 94 General safely aboard.

To say this was the happiest day of my life may be an exaggeration — suffice it to say that my joy at that point in my life was second to none. The moment I stepped on board my worries, aches and pains vanished. Here were my friends and comrades from the Regiment, Shilo and RMC; also Canadian nursing sisters in blue uniforms, white veils and starched cuffs, instead of baggy battledress, abounding with TLC. Sister Lindy Carr, whom I had last met in Shilo, was one of the first to greet me; then Sister Meisner and Sister Bateman, also friends from earlier days.

Two badly wounded Patricia officers were also aboard: Lt AGC Richards and Lt GA Garbutt. Both had joined the PPCLI in Sicily shortly after I had arrived, and both had served the Regiment bravely. Lt Richards, after his encounter with the mine, had returned to action and was then severely wounded in the heavy fighting at Villa Rogatti in December. Lt Garbutt had also been wounded at Villa Rogatti but had remained on duty. A few days later he was severely wounded at Vino Ridge, where the Regiment had suffered so grievously.

It saddened me to see so many friends being struck down and sent home with terrible wounds, without recognition or remembrance. It was becoming a dirty war. The glamour was beginning to fade. But the desire to get back and avenge the suffering of these and so many other brave men was stronger than ever.

For the moment, at least, such depressing thoughts were completely overshadowed by the intense happiness of being with friends again, bound for home, in a clean, warm cabin, with plenty of good nourishment supplied by beautiful nursing sisters. On the second day at sea I wrote my mother:

> *My dream boat came yesterday and so, today, I am once more on the Mediterranean Sea, en route to England.*
>
> *The programme seems to be that I have a couple of minor operations in England, then go to Canada for convalescence — and then, I must return as soon as I am fit and get back into the fight.*
>
> *Looking out the porthole I can see the Spanish Coast quite distinctly. The sea still has its delightful bluish tinge — no, it's stronger than a tinge — it's definitely a full colour. So rich looking that I feel like hopping out and bathing myself in its depths. The sun is just pleasantly warm, so that this afternoon I must away to the boat deck for a sun bathe.*

There's a piano somewhere below decks which I shall get on to shortly. Perhaps might organize a sing-song tonight. This ship is a grand little *palace. When it used to come into Saint John several years ago I never dreamt of my being invalided back to England on her. That's just one of the many coincidences of my time abroad.*

Many Patricias are aboard, who tell me of the Regiment and its doings. I am proud to be numbered amongst its officers. The terrific struggles it has had to go through since I left it make me feel so much like a malingerer. Many of my best friends have gone and some fortune spared me. Why? Time will produce. There must be a better test ahead for me, and I look forward to it eagerly.

That night we passed Gibraltar and headed out into the Atlantic Ocean with all the ship's lights blazing away, as if in retaliation for similar illumination from the houses of Algeciras, which had so upset me the previous July. Now, it seemed to me, we were flaunting our presumed immunity from the hungry U-Boat commanders, so desperate for a kill. Nevertheless, each night the hospital ship was lit up like a floating casino, as required, so I was told, by the Articles of War. Any German U-Boat commander was entitled to stop the ship and come aboard to check if she was carrying war stores. Once or twice, when the ship slowed down, I felt certain we would be boarded at any moment by a band of bearded sailors from a German U-Boat, brandishing Schmeissers and Lugers, but none appeared. No one seemed to be worried about such a possibility or by the thought that some crazy Nazi submarine commander might blow us all up now that the War was going badly for his equally deranged Führer.

It would not have been the first time the *Lady* was torpedoed by a U-Boat. In 1942, while lying at the dock at Port Castries, St Lucia, she had been severely damaged by a German 'tin-fish' and was for a time abandoned. Later the ship was towed to Mobile, Alabama where she was rebuilt and outfitted with the most modern medical and surgical equipment available. She was put into service in April 1943, just in time to accompany the convoy that had taken me to Sicily.[1]

Perhaps one reason the *Lady Nelson* was never attacked was that she sometimes carried wounded prisoners of war. One German POW who was repatriated by the *Lady* composed a poem in honour of the matron and nurses of the ship.

No flower on earth can fuller bloom,
No glittering star can brighter loom
Than a sister's love on the hospital ship
Across the Atlantic on my homeward trip.

I couldn't have expressed my gratitude for these 'angels of mercy' any better. There were, after all, some decent Germans.

Whether the *Lady Nelson,* which bravely made 37 voyages across the Atlantic, with lights ablaze, or her sister ship the *Letitia,* which was put into service in November 1944, were ever stopped or boarded by German submarine commanders, I do not know. No doubt it would have been a thrilling adventure.

However, no one was about to let these wild thoughts ruin such a pleasant cruise, passage paid in advance, courtesy of His Majesty. Though we were now feeling the rough seas of the Atlantic, few patients passed up the fine meals the chef provided throughout the voyage.

Food, as every good general knows, even those who fought before Napoleon issued his famous dictum, is as necessary for morale as it is for the belly. The Captain of the good ship *Lady Nelson* was a firm believer in this maxim. Best of all, I was now allowed to sit down at a table with others and politely slurp up my delicacies.

By February 7th we were sailing close to the southeast coast of Ireland; next day we docked at Bristol at 0900 hours. The voyage had taken less than eight days.

While I was happy to be back in England once again, the excitement of my first arrival, ten months earlier, was missing. Then I had been a green, fit, impressionable young officer setting foot for the first time on a beleaguered outpost of the Allied cause. Now all this was changed. No longer could anyone say I was green or impressionable and I could hardly claim to be fit. Whether I was still 'young' was a matter of semantics. Young at heart? Young in spirit? Young in age? Only the last question could be answered in the affirmative.

On the battlefronts of the world the Allied fortunes had vastly improved over the past ten months. Everywhere the enemy had been repulsed and thrown back. North Africa had been cleared; Sicily and southern Italy occupied; Mussolini had abdicated and Italy had surrendered. On the eastern front, the Germans were being driven back by the fearsome Russian hordes. In the Far East, the Japanese Empire was on the defensive. On the sea, the U-Boat threat had been mastered. In the air, the Luftwaffe was impotent against the growing air superiority of the Allies. In short, Germany was isolated and surrounded.

Momentous as these events were, there was one further development that had more significance for the Canadian Army in the UK because it would be directly involved — the massive Second Front.

Intensive preparations for this assault across the English Channel were now in full swing, consuming all the energies of the British, American and Canadian forces stationed in the United Kingdom and elsewhere. Gen Eisenhower had been appointed Supreme Commander of the whole operation code-named 'Overlord'.

As the hospital train, carrying the patients from the *Lady Nelson,* sped through the peaceful English countryside, I ruminated on these developments in the war and wondered what part, if any, I could play as events unfolded. According to the doctors in North Africa I had many months of operations and convalescence ahead of me before I could even consider getting back into action. By that time the Second Front would have been launched and perhaps the Germans would collapse. But from what I had seen of them in Sicily and in Italy, the Hun was still a formidable foe.

Yet, the enemy would then be fighting on three fronts — France, Italy and Russia. Somewhere, the line had to crumble. To my way of thinking, not having the benefit of the studies and appreciation of the Allied planners, the Italian front would be broken first and the 8th Army would quickly advance up the peninsula to the Alps where they would finish out their war in a holding position, while the Second Front rolled on to Berlin. If events turned out this way, there would be little need for reinforcements to be sent to the far off Italian theatre and they would be reduced to a trickle. All available resources would be thrown into the Second Front.

Given this amateur appreciation of the situation, my only hope of action seemed to be as a reinforcement officer for some unit fighting on the Second Front. For a Patricia, it was a depressing thought.

The hospital train pulled into the station at Watford, just northwest of London, at 1930 hours, some ten hours after our arrival in Bristol, and we were taken by ambulance to 10 Canadian General Hospital. How many hospitals had I passed through these past four months? It didn't really matter as long as someone started pretty soon to repair my jaw and face and get me fit for action again. Actually I wasn't in bad shape. The food on the *Lady Nelson* had restored several of the pounds I had lost and my private exercise programme had greatly strengthened my legs.

I soon found that the purpose of 10 General Hospital was to determine the extent of my wounds and decide which operations had to be performed before sending me to the hospital that would actually do the work. In the meantime, I was instructed to eat as much as I could. The thought passed through my mind about a lamb that was fattened for the slaughter. Well, it was better than dying of starvation. I gorged myself on the wonderful food, served to me in a private ward. In no time I was putting on weight and was judged by the doctor to be fit enough, and thirsty enough, to attend the local pub for further nourishment. After passing this crucial test with flying colours, I was granted an unbelievable privilege — a pass to nearby London! I kept my family informed of my good fortune.

> *For breakfast this am I had two scrambled eggs and about four cups of coffee!! Being on a special diet, I can get a glass of milk*

whenever I want, besides Ovaltine, malted milk, etc. What with heated wards, breakfast in bed, shows, lots of reading material, officer's mess, I am really in the lap of luxury. Now that I am so close to home, the mail service should be much improved.

This place is 'grandiferous', 100% Canadians, and lovely Sisters. I'm in heaven, or as close to it as I'll ever get! There are many ex-cadets here and chaps from Saint John.

One ex-cadet was my senior 'Ace' Savard. Another chum is Jim Harding, from Saint John. We went into London yesterday. Grand time. The quality of English 'mild and bitters' is as good as ever. London seems alive and happy, and there's plenty to eat. At this point I am very adept with my eating. Although teeth are still together, I can now manage to get down just about everything.

London — dear old London-town — the focal point of all my week-end passes and 'French leaves' whenever I was within striking distance. In the eight months I had been away the city had become so glutted with soldiers and their machines that it seemed a miracle it had not disappeared into the North Sea.

My first pass from the hospital was, fortunately, only for a day, as it would have been quite impossible for me to have survived the rigours of an overnight pass, assuming I could have found lodging, which was most unlikely. A further stroke of luck was that I was in the company of my friend from Saint John, Jim Harding, who took me with him to meet his cousin Jane Carton. Both she and her husband, Ronald Carton, were journalists who wrote for *The Times*. Like everyone else his age (he had fought in Salonika in the First War), he was a member of the Home Guard where he spent most of his evenings when he was not working at the War Office on some top secret project. What impressed me most of all, however, was that he also made up crossword puzzles for *The Times*.

The Cartons took us to lunch at the Café Royal and then started to show us a bit of London. But the crowds were too dense, and we were too tired to make much headway in the throng, so they took us home to tea where Ronald chatted about the sights we had missed. His knowledge of the city was so intimate, and his descriptions so vivid, that I soon realized he was a gifted writer with a special fondness for his native city. Thus began my education of London, its history and its architecture, which was broadened on every occasion I had the privilege of being with the Cartons.

Shortly after the War he published a book, *This Our London*, which he thoughtfully sent to me. His employer, *The Times*, commented on his work:

He has almost a muscular compulsion over vigorous words to make them do his bidding. To have written a whole work with

217

signposts for the things of the spirit as well as the eye, is a feat and should endure.

The book has endured and has been a valuable 'map' for me whenever I have visited Ronald Carton's City.

1. The Right Honourable Countess Mountbatten of Burma, CD, JP, DL.
Colonel-in-Chief.
Princess Patricia's Canadian Light Infantry.

2. *Graduation parade of our senior class, the Earl of Athlone taking the salute, May, 1941. Note the senior class are in full dress scarlet, our class in service dress. In the background, Fort Frederick Dormitory.*

3. *'Under logs, through bogs.' Recruit obstacle race, RMC, 1940.*

4. The author, as Honorary Colonel of the Royal Regiment of Canada, returns to the Arch, flanked by his aide and the senior cadets at RMC.

5. The author as President of the RMC club inspects the cadets at Royal Roads Military College.

6. *Three members of the author's class attained general rank. In the uniform of the Colonel of the Regiment, PPCLI, is MGen George Brown.*

7. *BGen Bill Turner, Commandant of RMC, 1973 - 1977.*

8. *BGen Gordon Sellar.*

9. *Capt Bob Huestis, PPCLI, newly appointed ADC to the Corps Commander, LGen Foulkes, May, 1945.*

10. *George Brown as a lieutenant in the Loyal Edmonton Regiment, as seen through the eyes of an Italian photographer.*

11. *LCpl George Brown (later MGen) commanding Sunday meal parade, Bill Turner (later BGen) on extreme left of front rank.*

12. *Herb Pragnell outside his platoon HQ in northern Italy, winter 1944. Herb transferred from the engineers to the PPCLI and became pioneer officer.*

13. *The author's father as a 2nd Lt, The Royal Newfoundland Regiment World War I.*

14. *Maj C S Frost of the Royal Regiment of Canada and his son Lt C S Frost, newly commissioned into the PPCLI, Niagara Falls, June, 1942.*

15. *The author's father and brother Bob (a sergeant in The Royal Regiment of Canada), Summer 1943.*

16. *C S M Frost, Graduation picture by Yousuf Karsh, May, 1942.*

17. *Lt Charmian Sansom, daughter of LGen Sansom, went overseas as a private in the CWAC and became a very popular announcer on the Allied Forces Radio Program, BBC.*

18. *Military identity card of the author, April 9, 1943.*

19. Lts' Qualifying Course Camp Shilo, Man, Oct, 1942. Front row, Lt Bill Stinchcombe 5th from left. Second row sitting, the PPCLI Instructors: Capt John Koensgen, the author, LCol Mitchell, Lt Willie Mulherin and Lt Vaughan Allan are 1st, 2nd, 4th, 6th and 7th from left. Rear row, Lt Cecil Shea is 2nd from right.

20. Lady Patricia with Brig Hamilton Gault and LCol Bob Lindsay. England, 1942.

21. MGen Simonds and his ADC Lt Stu Graham with Brig Vokes (in steel helmet). England, 1942.

22. PPCLI wounded by a mortar bomb Sicily. In the foreground Pte Ches Helgason attended to by Cpl Bob Middleton on the right. Capt Fairfield, MO, rushes up to assist stretcher bearers.

23. *LCol CB Ware receives the DSO from LGen Sir Oliver Leese, commander of the 8th Army.*

24. *A group of Canadian nurses on the hospital ship Lady Nelson evacuate Canadian wounded from Italy (including the author). From left to right: Lts (N/S) R MacLennan, J Goodstow, R Moffat, E Covey, D E McTier, E Bateman, Y Carr and J Jackson, Capt (Matron) C I Nixon, Lts (N/S) M McLeod, R. Hughes, H J Battram, E K Sutherland, and M B Meisner.*

25. *Lady Nelson in port in Naples, January, 1944. Note the number 46 and three red crosses and a wide band painted along her hull, and red cross on her funnel. These identification marks are required by the Articles of War.*

26. *Lt Marcus Mander, Coldstream Guards, and the author at 94 British General Hospital, Algiers, December, 1943.*

27. *Capt George (Corky) Corkett with Dorothy Blanche wife of Brig A Hamilton Gault, at their home, Hatch Court, near Taunton, Somerset. Corky was killed in Italy, 1944.*

28. Former Fascist HQ in Ispica when the author set up his own HQ in July 1943.

29. PPCLI guard, commanded by the author, awaits arrival of the old guard. Note one of Mussolini's slogans inscribed on the building — 'Attention! This olive tree springs from an immense forest. A forest of 8 million bayonets!'

30. *Scouts and Snipers report back to Brig Vokes, near Potenza. From left to right: Pte Alex Kushnieryk, Pte J W Slimkovich, Lt D E Jones (bending over map), Brig Vokes, LCol Ware.*

31. *LCol Lindsay and Lt Colin McDougall before the capture of Agira, Sicily.*

32. *Gen McNaughton chats with LCol Ware and Maj Coleman just before the invasion of Italy, September, 1943.*

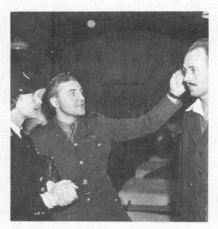

33. Dr Hoyle Campbell, a surgeon at Basingstoke, explains to Lady Mountbatten an operation he has performed.

34. Aileen, wife of Capt Corkett, who was a Red Cross Volunteer worker at Basingstoke Hospital.

35. Photo of the hospital huts erected on the grounds of Hackwood House during the war, taken from a Spitfire, May, 1945.

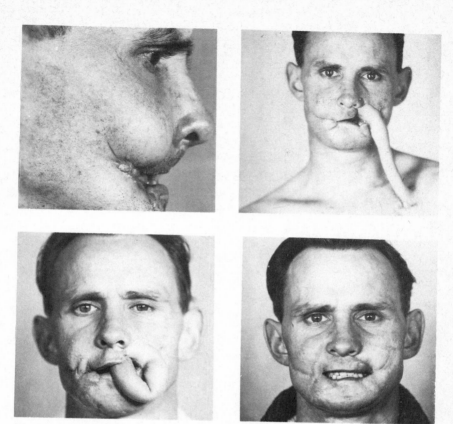

36. *An example of the miracles performed at Basingstoke and the difficult and painful operations willingly endured by the patients.*

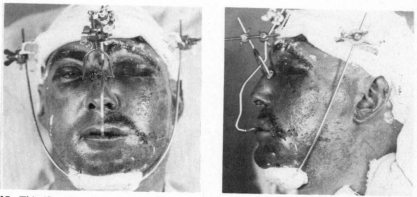

37. *This 'Star Wars' headgear is similar to the one fashioned for the author.*

38. *Membership card of a woman in the Fascist Party, Ispica, Sicily.*

39. *The issue cigarette of the 8th Army. Guaranteed free of cancer and tobacco.*

40. *Typical Italian propaganda postcard showing Bersaglieri soldiers fighting to the death. 'All Bersaglieri are soldiers, but not all soldiers are Bersaglieri' — Mussolini.*

41. *The author's company commander at San Fortunato, Capt Sam Potts, enjoying a tub after the battle.*

42. *Maj 'Bucko' Watson, DSO, MC served the Regiment continuously in Sicily and Italy except for 3 periods in hospital due to wounds.*

43. *LCol 'Slug' Clark (and friend) and Capt John Koensgen at ease in the Romagna.*

44. *Maj 'Patty' Crofton joined the Regiment in 1940, served throughout the Sicilian, Italian and Holland campaigns, was wounded 3 times and brought the Regiment home.*

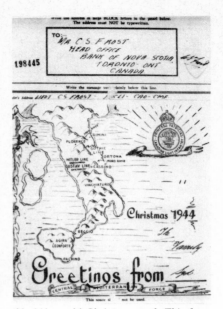

45. *The author, August, 1944, fully recovered and ready to rejoin the fray.*

46. *'Airgraph' Christmas card. This form was cheaper than the standard airmail letter, saved a lot of writing and was popular with the troops.*

47. *Defence Minister J L Ralston speaks to the PPCLI in a fish factory in Cattolica, September, 1944 and asks for questions about the reinforcement problems. He gets an earful.*

48. *Final inspection of the Regiment by MGen H W Foster, Commander 1st Division, August, 1945, Holland. MGen Foster, followed by the author and Maj Crofton, inspects the author's company.*

49. *Lt Allan McKinnon's Buffalo touches the enemy bank of the Ijssel River, Holland and his men quickly pile out and head for their first objective. That's Allan McKinnon in mid-air carrying a case of mortar bombs. On his right with Sten gun, is LSgt T Hanberry who, minutes later, will win a military medal for knocking out a German tank.*

50. *Officers of D Company at a transit camp near Pisa, Italy, enroute to Northwest Europe, March, 1945. Standing from left to right: Lt Corky Pyne, Lt Harvey Beardmore, the author, Maj Snuffy Smith, Lt Larry Harrington. Kneeling, from left to right: Lt Bert Bolton and Lt Allan McKinnon.*

52. *Capt R J Frost, PPCLI, 1957. The author's brother followed him into the Patricias and served in Korea.*

51. *Maj R W Potts receives his DSO from the Governor General, Lord Alexander. Sam Potts landed in Sicily and served continuously with the Regiment until December, 1944 when he was seriously wounded. He was the author's senior at RMC and was largely responsible for him joining the Patricias.*

53. *Lt Doug Armstrong exhibits Nazi flag captured in Holland. In the background are the Regiment's billets in Bilthoven, July, 1945.*

54. *Lady Patricia, flanked by LCol C B Ware DSO and Maj P D Crofton, immediately prior to the last Review in Britain — Esher, September 19th, 1945.*

55. *Lady Patricia's last inspection of the 1st Battalion of her Regiment — August 10th, 1964. This historic photo shows Lady Patricia presenting a Laurel wreath to be attached to the Regimental Colour. MGen C B Ware, DSO, CD, Colonel of the Regiment, stands to the right of Lady Patricia. LCol George Brown, CD, CO of the 1st Battalion, with sword, observes the ceremony. Lt M McMurray holds the Colour.*

57. *PPCLI veterans visit the Cassino cemetery during 1975 1st Canadian Corps Pilgrimage. Left to right: John Klassen, the author, Timlick, Howard Weldon, George Upton MM, Alvin Reilly.*

56. *Hotel Sydney beside the Hotel Progresso that made the author wonder what had really happened after the mess dinner.*

58. *PPCLI veterans at reception for the members of the 1st Canadian Corps Pilgrimage, Park Hotel, Ravenna, May, 1975. From left to right: Alvin Reilly, George Upton MM, Wilfred Reilly MM, John Klassen, MGen Chris Vokes, the author, Howard Weldon.*

59. *PPCLI veterans visit Dr J H J van Blommestein, Mayor of Voorst. Left to right: the author, John Moore, Dr. Blommestein, Bert Bolton, LCol Ritse R. Reitsma (Chief Engineer), Mr J. van de Visch (Chief of Protocol) - 1985.*

60. *Veterans parade through the streets of Apeldoorn lined with 140,000 inhabitants — 'buried in tulips we pressed through the throng in single file, in twos and threes, some, like the author all by themselves' - 1985.*

61. *Happy group of Patricia veterans at Keukenhof Gardens, Holland - 1980. Left to right:* **Rear Row** *- Buzz Mainprize, John Moore, Bert Bolton, the author, Treeske Blase (member of Amsterdam Committee), Brighton Fraser, John Klassen, George Howe.* **Front Row** *- Smokey Green, Walter Kuzyk, Larry Harrington, Don MacCulloch.* **Missing** *- Lloyd Rains.*

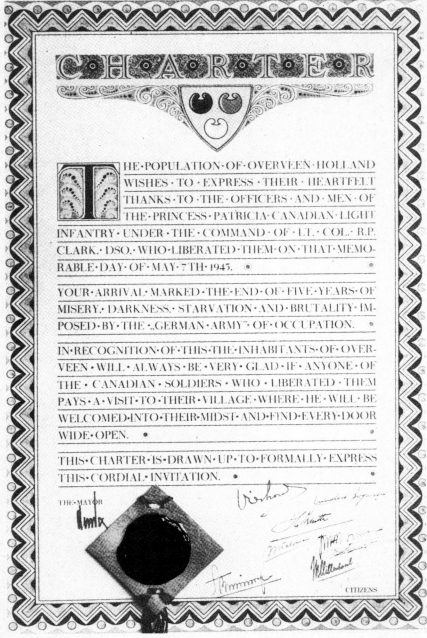

CHARTER

THE·POPULATION·OF·OVERVEEN·HOLLAND
WISHES·TO·EXPRESS·THEIR·HEARTFELT
THANKS·TO·THE·OFFICERS·AND·MEN·OF
THE·PRINCESS·PATRICIA·CANADIAN·LIGHT
INFANTRY·UNDER·THE·COMMAND·OF·LT.·COL.·R.P.
CLARK,·DSO.,·WHO·LIBERATED·THEM·ON·THAT·MEMO-
RABLE·DAY·OF·MAY·7TH·1945.

YOUR·ARRIVAL·MARKED·THE·END·OF·FIVE·YEARS·OF
MISERY,·DARKNESS,·STARVATION·AND·BRUTALITY·IM-
POSED·BY·THE·„GERMAN·ARMY"·OF·OCCUPATION.

IN·RECOGNITION·OF·THIS·THE·INHABITANTS·OF·OVER-
VEEN·WILL·ALWAYS·BE·VERY·GLAD·IF·ANYONE·OF
THE·CANADIAN·SOLDIERS·WHO·LIBERATED·THEM
PAYS·A·VISIT·TO·THEIR·VILLAGE·WHERE·HE·WILL·BE
WELCOMED·INTO·THEIR·MIDST·AND·FIND·EVERY·DOOR
WIDE·OPEN.

THIS·CHARTER·IS·DRAWN·UP·TO·FORMALLY·EXPRESS
THIS·CORDIAL·INVITATION.

THE·MAYOR

CITIZENS

62. Charter presented to the Regiment by the citizens of Overveen, May 7, 1945.

PLASTIC SURGERY
Basingstoke Neurological and Plastic Surgery Hospital
February 16 to April 18, 1944

Good night nurse
Tell the doctor I'm no better
Write my wife a nice long letter
Hold my hand a little longer
Your touch helps to make me
stronger

Chorus:
Call me in the morning
Or I'll get worse
Kiss your little patient
Good night nurse*

When I returned to hospital I was informed that my pleasant interlude in English pubs and posh London restaurants was over and I would now have to face the music — proceed forthwith to Basingstoke Neurological and Plastic Surgery Hospital for my fifth major operation. The next morning I said goodbye to 10 Canadian General, which had really been a luxury hotel masquerading as a hospital, and set off in a staff car for Basingstoke about 60 miles southwest of London. Again I was reminded of that lamb — now he was being led in style to the slaughter. Two hours later I arrived at the gates of Hackwood House on the beautiful estate of Lord Camrose, proprietor of the *Daily Telegraph*. This would be my home for the next two months.

Very early in the War, Canadian medical authorities had organized a neurological hospital at Basingstoke to provide treatment for brain and

---

* Sung by patients in the 3rd London General Hospital in World War I.

219

spinal injuries; closely involved with this innovative development had been the eminent Montreal neurosurgeon Dr Wilder Penfield. In May 1943, a plastic surgery unit specializing in surgery of the face and head, and treatment of serious burns, joined the hospital, which then became known as the Basingstoke Neurological and Plastic Surgery Hospital. The original 200 beds expanded to 750 beds as Hackwood House spread to huts erected on the estate.[1]

To my great delight, the first person I met was our family doctor from Saskatoon, Dr Croll. When I was wounded, father had sent Dr Croll a cable asking his help in locating me. The cable went to Egypt and finally reached him in Sicily. Despite his best efforts he could not find any trace of my whereabouts and was apparently still looking for me. He seemed a little surprised.

"Where the devil have you been, young man, these past four months? I've spent weeks trying to find you and now you have the cheek to blow in here as if you'd been away on a holiday." He pretended to glare at me, but couldn't suppress a chuckle. Not willing to give him an inch, I returned his camaraderie by making a sign with two fingers. He was good-natured enough to accept it as a 'V' for Victory.

No sooner was I nicely ensconsed in a warm, friendly ward than two charming ladies appeared at my bedside bearing news of the PPCLI: Mrs Aileen Corkett of the Red Cross and Sister Finlayson.

Aileen Corkett was the wife of Maj George 'Corky' Corkett, whom I had not yet met, but knew by reputation as an outstanding officer. He had graduated from RMC before the War and was with the Regiment when War broke out. He had been one of the selected few who had been sent to North Africa to gain battle experience; had been seriously wounded in March 1943 while attached to the British Army and was now back in England trying to return to the Regiment in Italy. Corky was a gallant officer and taught me much before he was killed, not far from me, in the plains of Northern Italy.

Sister Finlayson was a sister of Maj Jack Leach* also a graduate of RMC, who was then serving with the Regiment in Italy.

News of the Regiment, Corky Corkett and Jack Leach was a great tonic and more was on its way. A day or two later I received a letter from Johnny Koensgen, my great pal and mentor from Shilo days. He had reverted to lieutenant from captain in order to go to Italy. How Johnny had found me at Basingstoke I couldn't understand, but I knew there was a very strong,

---

* After the War he remained in the Army where he attained the rank of lieutenant colonel before becoming ill and dying prematurely. We had been good friends both during and after the War and his death after surviving the fighting in Italy was a deep shock.

far-flung Patricia network that was even more efficient than the Postal Corps.

I immediately got in touch with Johnny and he insisted I sneak away from the hospital and visit him in Aldershot, only 25 miles distant. I demurred, saying I was supposed to be resting up for a big operation in a day or two.

"To hell with your operation. That's no excuse. There was a time you'd run 25 miles in full pack to have a drink with some old friends."

"Who are these friends who want to kill me, or at least get me thrown out of hospital?"

"You'll see when you get here."

There was no use arguing any further with Koensgen. I somehow managed an 'impromptu' leave, otherwise known as AWL, and caught a bus for Aldershot at 1700 hours. Three hours later (only 25 miles!) and slightly weary from all this unaccustomed activity, I arrived at 1 CIRU (Canadian Infantry Reinforcement Unit) and checked in at Barrosa Barracks where I had been quartered almost a year earlier when I first arrived in England.

As I entered the Officers' Mess, a host of Patricias greeted me: LCol Bob Lindsay, whom I had last seen on the slopes of Mount Seggio in Sicily; Maj 'Pokey' Joe Paquet who had been wounded in Sicily and whom I have already mentioned as occupying a special place in the hearts of all Patricia officers; Maj Early who had left the Regiment before I joined, but was one of the originals; and Capt Steve Lynch who was one of the first to be wounded on the beaches of Sicily.

What ensued was a typical Patricia party with Bob Lindsay at the piano and me substituting from time to time to give the good colonel a break. We parted on the understanding that one and all would re-assemble on March 17th to celebrate the birthday of Lady Patricia, our Colonel-in-Chief.

Returning to Basingstoke late the following night, I had more luck with buses and it only took two hours, but I had to walk the last couple of miles. I was obviously getting back into shape. Though I was exhausted it had been worth it. Even the night nurse, Dee Simpson (whom I had known in Shilo), could see that the trip had done me some good and let me sneak quietly into bed.

Next morning the surgeon read me the riot act and made it quite clear that it was time to get down to business — no more alarums or excursions would be permitted. I had the distinct feeling that he couldn't wait to get his hands on me as my case had aroused considerable curiosity among his colleagues in the Maxillo-Facial Unit.

In preparation for the operation, the dentist, Capt McDonald, now spent long hours pounding my teeth with hammer and chisel, chipping off the old cement which had held the splints in place. Then he fashioned a weird-looking steel brace that would keep my jaws firmly locked together after surgery. It consisted of a steel band around the forehead, supported by cross bars over the top of the head, with side plates that connected to a steel chin strap.

Across the front of the face a steel bar, secured to the side plates, supported a post that entered the mouth and was screwed into splints covering the front teeth. The whole contraption looked like a modern-day football helmet complete with face guard, or possibly like the headgear used in *Star Wars*. I wish I had had the foresight to have the thing patented. The dentist was so proud of his handiwork he called in his associates for a peek and pictures were duly taken for the record. I was terrified.

Then LCol Gordon came around to explain the bone graft operation he was going to perform. The dead part of my lower jaw bone (mandible) would be replaced by taking bone from the right hip (not the left hip which had already had its share of wounds and grafts). Then the old scar tissue would be cut out and the face 'moulded' together. With any luck I would be up in a couple of weeks with a new jaw and face to match. It all sounded so easy I wondered why someone hadn't done it months earlier. On reflection, I remembered the filth of North Africa and how fortunate I was to be in such capable hands now. It helped me forget the dread of my fifth major operation in almost as many months. Actually I was not too disturbed about the bone graft — it sounded quite exciting and almost too incredible to be true. I asked LCol Gordon, "How big a hunk will you take out of my hip?"

His reply was honest but it shook me a bit. "We won't be taking a large 'hunk', as you describe it, out of your hip. What we do is chip quite a few small pieces from the pelvis and introduce them into the bone fracture. As these are 'live' pieces of bone they should knit with the jaw bone fairly quickly and form a union that is just as strong as the original bone."

Once again I thanked my good luck tokens that this intricate operation was not going to be done in North Africa. There was one further matter, however, that did concern me greatly and that was whether I would be put to sleep with that horrible ether gas, with all its sickening effects after the operation.

"Don't worry about that," assured the doctor. "We'll knock you out with a pentothol injection."

I had waited a long time for this operation and had travelled some six or seven thousand miles to have it done. It was time to get on with the job. Let my diary describe the events before and after.

1944	
Feb 21	*Being fitted for a new splint. Dentist's chair gives me the creeps now. Can't stand him pounding on my loose jaw.*
Feb 22	*Feeling OK but another trip to the dentist's gave me the works!*
Feb 23	*Watkins got his operation and not looking too good after it. God help me when I have my big*

one this Friday.

Feb 24　*More dentist work. God, what a piece of apparatus he has made for my jaw! Started on Sulphathiazole pills and put to bed after dinner.*

Feb 25　*On the table at 0900. Finished at 1230. No feeling from anaesthetic but hip bone and neck very painful. Quite sick from blood having been swallowed and unable to spit it up. Coughing causes terrific pain. But sisters are very good and try to make me comfortable and give me a hypodermic. Sick a bit that night. Have a special bed.*

Feb 26　*Feeling better. Bandage all around my head. Tight steel plate on outside not very comfortable but have not the headache and sore throat of previous operations. A sgt took my blood test and had to stick me about six times before he got the vein.*

Feb 27　*Steve Lynch and Maj Rusty Gordon came round to see me. Not able to talk very much. Sisters giving me excellent care and already I feel 100% better.*

Feb 28　*Hip not painful now, but still a terrific pressure on face.*

Feb 29　*1100 hrs my metal plate taken off and bandages removed. Well I don't know how I look. There is a large scar down to my neck where a flap has been cut into place. My lip is swollen but both lips meet. Half the stitches (32) were taken out. This was rather painful. Bandage is still a bit tight.*

Mar 1　*Lips are almost normal, however one slightly swollen at corner but it closes OK and looks like a lip! I am getting damn hungry. Aileen Corkett called around to have a chat. Had dressing changed and 32 more stitches removed making 64 stitches in all. Sister Wannop is taking excellent care of me and gives me all sorts of drinks. Very conscientious.*

Mar 2　*Up in a wheelchair to bathroom. Second rear I've had in one week. Plug taken out so that I can now suck in more food.*

Mar 3　*Had eight stitches taken out of hip. It feels almost OK now.*

Mar 4　*Eight stitches out of hip making 16 altogether.*

Mar 5　*Up and dressed. Feeling just a bit unsteady. Face is rather sore and swollen. Hot saline compresses are still being applied.*

Mar 6　*This evening I 'dressed up' in blazer and flannels and played ping pong and won at the Red Cross Party. Pretty good effort after being in bed a week!*

Mar 7　*Back to bed with sulpha tablets and saline com-*

*presses because of swollen face. Really browned off
this time and I made no bones about it to the sisters.
God, how I hate these pills and the 'blood sucker'
in the veins.*

The next day, March 8th, I wrote to my mother my usual cheerful letter,
but it was becoming more difficult each time to paint a glowing picture of
my condition and immediate prospects. Indeed, my parents were not always
taken in by my efforts to gloss over my troubles. One of the first things
mother said when I returned home after the War was, "Sydney, you really
told me some awful fibs, now, didn't you?" Anyway, this is my letter of
March 8th.

*I'm writing from bed, propped up with countless soft pillows in
a well lighted, warm ward, with the pleasing notes of the radio
just at my elbow. I had my operation about ten days ago. The
great improvement in my appearance is remarkable, even after
just this one operation. There is now no missing link in my face.
From a distance I am told that I appear quite normal. And by
having a look-see at my humble self in the mirror, I would say
that I look OK. Thus, what further operations that remain to
be done will be of a minor nature. Time is the big factor. Well
I think that's all I can give you on my 'operational role'.*

There was one further 'operation' in the offing that I had not mentioned
to mother, which gave me some concern — the celebration of Lady Patricia's
birthday on March 17th. I was still confined to bed taking those damn sulpha
pills and getting jabbed in the arm by the blood suckers. Well, it just had
to stop. It was unthinkable that I would miss a March 17th birthday party.
A short appreciation of the situation was in order.

The aim, factors which would affect the attainment of the aim, and courses
open were all quite clear.

Aim. *Attend Colonel-in-Chief's birthday party.*
Factors which affect the Aim. *Mainly LCol Gordon, but I have
no decent uniform (can't appear in a Limey battledress purchased
in Algiers).*
Courses Open. *Really only one — frontal assault on LCol
Gordon.*
Plan. *Have nurses arrange to get my trunk and suitcases out of
storage at Pickford's Depository. Get fully dressed in serge
uniform, Sam Browne Belt, dress hat, swagger stick and all.
Confront LCol Gordon.*

It need hardly be reported that such a well laid plan was completely successful and LCol Gordon surrendered, but on one condition. If I were fool enough to upset any of the careful surgery he had done on my jaw, he would perform other surgery on my private parts that would be irreversible!

I had every reason to believe him then, and even more so two years later, when I was again having plastic surgery operations in Christie Street Hospital, Toronto. LCol Gordon was a skillful plastic surgeon but he did not suffer fools gladly. One officer at Christie Street had lost part of his penis and undergone a number of delicate operations to have the member restored to good working order. After some weeks in hospital, spent in total abstinence, the officer pleaded with LCol Gordon to be allowed home to see his wife. The colonel at first refused, but then relented on condition that there would be absolutely no intercourse or anything remotely connected therewith.

It was like trying to stop the breach in the Mohne River Dam in Germany. The inevitable happened and the officer returned to the hospital with his member in the same plight and condition of three months earlier. The shouts of LCol Gordon could be heard clear across Christie Pits playing field. "You numbskull, you've ruined months of work. I'm not going to waste any more time on you. Get out."

I left the hospital shortly after this disaster and I have no idea what became of the officer who couldn't control himself. Probably LCol Gordon once more relented and the damaged member regained, and hopefully increased, its former estate.

Such antics by patients were quite unheard of at Basingstoke and indeed would have been thought unpatriotic. I readily accepted LCol Gordon's injunction and prepared for the March 17th party. One contingency, however, had been overlooked in my appreciation of the situation. My service dress, hastily stored away when I left for Sicily, had not been cleaned and it was full of moth holes. My carefully laid plans were literally in tatters, but help was at hand. Aileen Corkett came to my aid and skillfully repaired all the damage. I left Basingstoke by bus at 1400 hours and arrived at the Officers' Mess in Aldershot two hours later, eager to meet my brother officers, many of whom I had not seen for nearly a year.

Forty-two Patricia officers and their guests sat down to dinner that night, including the following:

Brig A Hamilton Gault, DSO	Maj A T (AT) Smith
LCol R A (Bob) Lindsay	Maj George R (Corky)
Maj R M (Rusty) Gordon	Corkett
Maj A E T (Pokey Joe)	Capt Howard Smith
Paquet	Capt J L (Foo) Hunter
Maj R P (Slug) Clark	Capt Norman M Cousens

> Capt H G (Hec) Munro   Lt J W MacNeill
> Capt G S (Steve) Lynch   Lt J W D Lewis
> Capt W H J (Bill) Stutt   Lt H R (Herb) Barclay
> Capt R G M (Bob) Gammell   Lt W L (Smudger) Smith
> Capt T H Knight   Lt J G (Knobby) Clark
> Lt G A Garbutt   Lt J R (Johnny) Koensgen
> Lt Staff Shawcross   Lt A G C Richards
> Later in the evening we were joined by RSM Bennett, Sgt Routledge and Sgt Woods (the Transport Sgt).

One officer stood out, head and shoulders above the rest, Hamilton Gault, the Founder of the Regiment. It is difficult to describe the thrill of meeting this great man. From the day I had joined the Patricias he had been my ideal of what an 'officer and a gentleman' should be. Though I had never met him before, I knew from studying his record in the First War and from examining his portrait in the mess, that he was the very embodiment of the great Patricia spirit. With considerable awe I approached his towering figure and immediately felt the warmth of his presence. There was no need to introduce myself; he called me by name and said some kind words about my service. This was a man.

Everyone who met Hammy Gault felt the same way about him:

> *As the Founder, with Cols Farquhar and Buller, he had moulded the Regiment to its original shape. Surviving them, he continued to influence its style and spirit as no other could. If the Patricias have a panache, a lighthearted competence, a sense of dedication, the roots are in him. He was a superb leader and an idealist. He made men believe in the military virtues of duty and honour and the traditions of the Regiment. He gave them confidence in themselves and a standard to emulate.*[2]

Returning to the mess dinner on March 17th, the evening proceeded with toasts to the King, the Colonel-in-Chief, and the Regiment amid much camaraderie and good humour. It was thrilling to know that in other corners of the Empire similar celebrations were being held in honour of our Colonel-in-Chief: in Winnipeg, Shilo and other bases in Canada; in Italy, south of Ortona; in fact any place where two or more Patricias were present to form a quorum.

After the formal part of the dinner, we all adjourned to the ante-room and the party continued in high gear with LCol Bob Lindsay at the piano leading us through the favourite Patricia songs: all ten verses of *The Ric-a-dam-doo, So Clear The Way, The Shiny Two Brigade, Lili Marlene, Waltzing Matilda.* Most popular was the ninth verse of *The Ric-a-dam-doo:*

Old Hammy Gault our first PP
He led this band across the Sea
He'd lose an arm or a leg or two
Before he'd lose The Ric-a-dam-doo

I could easily imagine Sam Potts with the Regiment in Italy organizing some kind of celebration and sing-song in a bombed-out Wop house, ably supported by Andy Mills, Willie Mulherin, Vaughan Allan, Bob Huestis, Cecil Shea and other stalwarts who had taken voice training with me at Shilo. I wondered if I would ever see any of them again.

But this was neither the time nor the place for such negative thoughts. Over in a corner of the mess Maj Paquet was regaling the old veterans with his 'Pokey Joeisms'. At the piano Maj Slug Clark was in good voice teaching a new ditty to some of the new officers, something called *The Winnipeg Swells*. I liked his boisterous humour and hearty chuckle. He paused for a moment to catch his breath and deliver a line that had become a Regimental Password — "Let's have a little drink all around." This popular suggestion was sometimes varied by offering, "Let's have a little kiss all around", depending, of course, on the sex of the company. He would return to Italy to command the Regiment with panache and determination right up to the end of the War.

It was the first time I had met Corky Corkett, though I had met his wife Aileen. Corky, like so many Patricia officers, was deeply dedicated to the Regiment and was a fine leader of men.

Another outstanding officer was my close friend Johnny Koensgen who was about to leave on a draft to Italy. Knowing the martial qualities of my friend, I cautioned him to take care of himself and not win all the medals. He paid no attention whatsoever to my advice and went on to distinguish himself in action and win the Military Cross. Johnny was a born soldier.

Three officers who had recently returned from Italy were Lt Knobby Clark, Lt Richards and Lt Garbutt. All had been badly wounded in the heavy fighting along the Moro River in December. As mentioned, Richards and Garbutt had returned with me on the *Lady Nelson* and were gradually recovering from their wounds. While it was sad to realize that my friends would never return to the Regiment, no one was going to spoil the party on that account and we carried on into the wee hours of the morning.

Like all good celebrations, this one out-lasted many of the players but finally petered out in the cold, cheerless dawn of another day. Final farewells were exchanged and we crept away to our billets, well satisfied that we had done justice to the birthday of our Colonel-in-Chief. March 17th, 1944 was a memorable party that I recall with nostalgia to this day.

I do not have the same vivid recollection of my return to Basingstoke that morning, yet I must have made it: my diary says so. I do, however, remember waking up in a nice, warm, hospital bed and hearing some concerned nursing sisters discussing my condition.

"Oh my heavens, if he's damaged his operation LCol Gordon will do awful things to him."

I instantly remembered LCol Gordon's severe warning of what would happen if I ruined his surgery, and I gingerly checked my face and contraption in my mouth to see if all was in order. Everything seemed to be fine except the wires were a little loose but that was a minor matter and happened after every operation. It could easily be adjusted by the dentist.

My long period of purgatory was slowly coming to an end. LCol Gordon's skilled hands had been so successful that after making a preliminary test, he had high hopes that union of the bones was taking place and he would make a final test in about a week's time. How to occupy myself during this period? The hospital had a fine piano in a hall, well removed from the patients, which I regularly played. Sister Effie Smallwood and Sister Hobson kindly lent me sheet music for some of the popular tunes: *White Cliffs of Dover, Time Goes By, Deep Purple.*

Another diversion was cards. Five old-timers on the ward had formed a very exclusive poker school to which we occasionally admitted novices, if the moon was in the right phase. I had phenomenal luck (skill) that I have never since enjoyed, and salted away a good many quid. On one occasion, immediately after a small preliminary operation, the members of the school gathered around my bed as I was coming out of the anaesthetic. I thought how kind of them to be so concerned about my health. In fact all they wanted was to get me into a quick game of poker while I was still slightly anaesthetized and win back some of their money. The after-effect of pentothol is not at all unpleasant — very similar to a nice 'high' one would get on a mickey of rye. Cards were produced, I played with careless abandon and cleaned them out of a month's pay. It was so ridiculous that in my 'drunken' state it struck me as the funniest thing that had ever happened and I literally nearly died laughing.

On March 24th, LCol Gordon untied the wires binding my jaws, opened my mouth slightly and gently tested the bones for union. The operation had been a complete success! The relief of knowing my troubles would soon be over made this a day to remember, ranking, as far as I was concerned, with the Relief of Khartoum and the Relief of Ladysmith. Life was beautiful again and I couldn't wait to get on with it. At least my diary seems to give that impression.

1944
Mar 24   *My teeth are opened up, making it almost five*
             months that I have been wired together. Can just
             manage to chew a piece of bread.

228

Mar 25   *Asked out to a Mrs Simons, at whose estate the Red Cross girls stay — Miss Lois MacDonald and Mrs. Aileen Corkett. That evening I went out to the Grapes Pub on my own and met two attractive girls, Jean and Peg.*

Mar 27   *Lower splints of my jaw are taken off and behold, there are teeth below them. God, it is a grand feeling to get rid of some of these horrible plates and open my mouth again. It is such a relief that I think I am temporarily unstable.*

Mar 28   *More work done on my teeth. Painful job having cement cut and hacked off. Met Jean in town at 1630 and we had dinner, walked around town and dropped in to the Grapes. Took her home.*

Mar 29   *Upper splints taken off and below lie my upper teeth all sound and OK except a bit discoloured. My appearance has improved 100%. Big day this. My mouth is back to normal and can eat a bit. But occlusion is not good as yet. Met Jean in town at 1530.*

Mar 30   *Out in the afternoon to see Jean but home early after eating huge meal at Venture Restaurant (rabbit stew). I can't seem to get my fill of good food.*

Mar 31   *Dull day. Played Sister Julie Brown tennis and cleaned her clock! Out in the evening for another huge meal at Venture.*

Apr 3   *Best I've felt for a long time. Out to Venture that night for more rabbit stew and Jean.*

Apr 4   *Being fitted for false teeth. In to town at the Red Lion and arranged for a party for Wed night with Jean, Peg and Burgoin.*

Apr 6   *Hugh MacDonald came up at noon on leave. Talked into going down to Aldershot with him. Met Stinchcombe and MacNeill and took over the mess. 'Stinky' in excellent form. At 0200 hrs he decided to go out and get something to eat. I didn't say no. We got a taxi, and rode all over town looking for a restaurant, but too late, so back to barracks and broke into kitchen. Bed 0500 and talked of Italy.*

Apr 7   *Left Aldershot and arrived back at Basingstoke on 1815 bus. Met Sister Quail on bus. She is*

> *married to a Mountie Cpl and gets us up in the*
> *mornings. Several other sisters saw us get off bus*
> *together and we put on a good scandal show since*
> *I was carrying her bag! Like an ass I brought her*
> *home in a cab. Then met Burgoin and away to*
> *town again.*

Such carefree, riotous living, at the expense of His Majesty, could not go on forever. If only I had adopted a lower profile I could probably have remained in hospital for an indefinite period. But I had overplayed my hand and news soon got back to LCol Gordon that one Lt Frost was performing incredible feats of physical stamina and driving the sisters crazy. He gave me a routine physical exam and declared I was in A1 shape. While there was quite a lot of 'cosmetic surgery' to be done, including another bone graft and some dental work, these problems could wait a couple of months, when I would return for a final 'beautifying' job. In the meantime, he would send me to a Convalescent Home at Garnons for a few weeks and then to 1 CIRU at Aldershot until July, when I would return. He ended the interview with, "Are there any questions?"

"That's OK" I replied, "except for the matter of leave to Canada. For the past five and a half months everyone has been telling me I would return to Canada for convalescence and final surgery. Instead of hanging around training centres in England for the next two months, I might just as well do some instruction in Canada."

"No. That's impossible. Every able bodied man is needed here in England."

"Surely I'm entitled to some convalescence and leave. The final operations can be done in Canada and then I'll return to the UK."

"Certainly you'll get some convalescence — at Garnons. As for further operations, the best plastic work is being done right here at Basingstoke, not in Canada. I'm sorry, there's no hope of your returning to Canada."

Actually, LCol Gordon was right. I was quite fit. The finest plastic surgery in the world was being done at Basingstoke and at East Grinstead where Dr Ross Tilley was performing miracles on horribly burned airmen. Anyway, I really didn't require any more surgery to be a fighting soldier again.

Above all, one decisive factor overrode all other considerations — the long awaited Second Front. The whole of southeast England had become an armed camp — British, Americans, Canadians, French, Norwegians, Poles, Dutch, Belgians — all poised to strike a death blow at the Hitler Armies. The tremendous build-up of Allied Forces had impressed me from the moment I had landed from the *Lady Nelson*.

I am sure LCol Gordon had been given instructions to clean out his hospital and discharge every single man who could fight, and not return anyone to

Canada who would be useful for the Second Front. I could not argue with these orders. The only problem was how to tell my parents, whom I had foolishly assured I would be soon returning home. I wrote to father:

> *Now, you are wondering about leave home. I must be quite frank. I have gone into the subject very thoroughly with Col Gordon. His view is that my physical condition has so improved it does not warrant a rest in Canada. Also the best plastic surgeons are over here so I must stay in this country 'til July, when I go on the 'slab' again.*
>
> *Naturally, I would have liked to get home, but Col Gordon cannot see it, so to hell with him, say I, and I will make the best of it. I know you will be disappointed, after my telling you all along that I would be going to Canada — but that was what my previous MOs had assured me. Then, too, you must remember that what little I have learned might be of some use to these fellows, and perhaps I can give them some tips that might give them just that extra bit which makes the difference.*

For once I described my situation as it really was: I told my parents the 'unvarnished, perpendicular' truth. But it was not the whole truth. Perhaps by this time I had become a compulsive liar, or maybe I hadn't the heart to tell them the whole story. The missing fact from my letter was that I had resolved to return to my Regiment in Italy at the first opportunity. In fact I had hinted at this possibility in my letter when I said "to hell with Col Gordon, I will make the best of it." What I meant was that if he considered me as an A1 category, I intended to make the most of it. Any further cosmetic surgery and bone grafts could await the end of the War when surely the operations could be performed in Canada.

If my parental home was being denied me I still had another spiritual home — my Regiment. The thought of wasting time in holding units in England and then more time in hospitals was simply too much. Surely the Regiment needed me and would welcome me back to the fold.

These thoughts, which had doubtless been unconsciously building up during my months in hospital, now surfaced and became a consuming desire. The Regiment came first. All else mattered naught.

The time finally came to say goodbye to hospitals and Basingstoke. As I walked around the ward I realized I had much to be thankful for. If I had been wounded in the First War, only 25 years earlier, there would have been small chance of my surviving, much less being restored to full health and able to lead a normal life. Thanks to modern drugs and the skill of the surgeons I could return to the fray once more.

Many other patients in the ward would never regain their health or lead a normal life. Basingstoke was not only a plastic surgery hospital, but was also a neurological centre for brain and spinal injuries. It was the patients in this division, suffering permanent injury and disability, who desperately needed the loving care and attention of our dedicated nursing sisters:

The saddest cases, recalls a sister who was at Basingstoke, were the paraplegics, young soldiers who did not realize that they would be paralyzed for life. They required intricate and continued nursing care, and in their almost complete dependence upon the sisters the gratitude they showed made the work of helping them deeply rewarding.[3]

The important role played by the Occupational Therapists should never be forgotten. They too are mentioned:

The idea that the object of occupational therapy was to overcome boredom in the patient was no longer valid. Everything he did was designed to contribute to his rehabilitation, physical and psychological. Occasionally the occupational therapist encountered a psychiatric case who deliberately tried to do the opposite to what he had been told. It was a challenge that called for the exercise of much patience and sympathy to win the man over to a co-operative attitude.[4]

Working closely with the doctors, nurses, occupational therapists and staff were the Red Cross Volunteers, who received few of the benefits enjoyed by members of the Forces, but who made a valuable contribution, not only in providing amenities and cheer to the patients, but in driving ambulances and trucks and performing many other services well beyond their normal duties — witness the kindness shown me by Aileen Corkett and Lois MacDonald.

Thus, on April 18th, 1944 I left Basingstoke Neurological and Plastic Surgery Hospital with very mixed thoughts and emotions: happy to be returning to the real world, to be sure; sad to leave behind many dear friends, some of whom would never be whole again; grateful to all the doctors, dentists, sisters, occupational therapists and Red Cross Volunteers who had sustained me through all these months and given me a chance to lead a normal life.

I thought of all the hospitals: 9 Canadian Field Ambulance, 15 Canadian Casualty Clearing Station, 132 Canadian Field Ambulance, 7 Canadian Casualty Clearing Station, 54 British General Hospital (not 45 British General Hospital), 94 British General Hospital, 1 Canadian Hospital Ship (the *Lady Nelson*), 10 Canadian General Hospital, Basingstoke Neurological and Plastic Surgery Hospital.

I remembered, too, the Canadian nursing sisters, my 'angels', so pertly dressed in their blue and white uniforms, with white veils and starched cuffs: Sisters Lindy Carr, Meisner and Bateman on the *Lady Nelson;* Sisters Dee Simpson, Bert Nesbitt, Effie Smallwood, Julie Brown, Eva Wannop, Fertie Finlayson, Irene Millar, Hobson and Margery Quail. I loved them all and would miss their TLC. The names of the nurses in Italy and Algiers had gone from me except old Sister Cleghorn, and I even forgave her .

I thanked my lucky tokens for placing me in the hands of so many skilled surgeons, dentists and anaesthetists who beyond doubt had saved my life in the first critical days, and later had restored my health and appearance. I could not remember the names of the doctors in North Africa but I remembered their devotion, and frustration with the conditions in their hospital. They really had no chance.

Lastly, I personally thanked LCol Stuart Gordon, Maj Hoyle Campbell* and Capt G M McDonald for the miracles they had performed, and said I would be back. Almost two years were to slip by before I saw them again, in Christie Street Hospital, Toronto.

As I climbed into the station wagon bound for the railway station, a captain in the Discharge Office of the hospital handed me a Morning Sick Report form which he suggested I keep on my person at all times:

Age	*21*
Disease	*Bone graft, lower jaw*
Remarks	*This officer was discharged from Basingstoke Neurological and Plastic Surgery Hospital on 18 Apr 44 following bone graft and plastic surgery on lower jaw. At present time he has fairly good function but the scar and bone is tender. He should be excused wearing respirator and refrain from wearing chin strap of helmet under the chin.*

Twelve years later I returned to Hackwood House, drove past the gate-house, up the tree-lined driveway and discretely parked my Mercedes in a remote corner of the courtyard. Advancing on the massive front doors I timidly knocked several times until a butler in formal dress slowly opened the portals.

No, His Lordship was in Town and the butler had never heard of the Basingstoke Neurological and Plastic Surgery Hospital.

I explained how I had been a patient there in 1944 and wondered if I could just have a quick look around the estate.

"By all means, Sir, and by the way, there *is* some kind of a marker on the back lawn, near the swimming pool, that has something to do with the war."

---

* Maj Campbell was another skilled plastic surgeon who operated on me.

I strolled through the main floor of the mansion where the administration offices, store rooms and recreational rooms of the hospital had been located; I checked a wing of the building which had once served as the Operating Room. Not a trace of the old hospital remained: only elegant, richly furnished library, ballroom, music room and dining rooms. Through french-doors opening onto a carefully manicured lawn, I saw the marker the butler had mentioned, and went out to examine it. On the marker were inscribed the following words:

> On this lawn from 1940 to 1945 stood the No I Neurological Hospital erected and maintained by the Royal Canadian Army Medical Corps. The hospital contained 750 beds and was staffed by Canadian Nursing Sisters and Orderlies. 16,500 patients of all nationalities were admitted and cared for. Many owed their lives to the devotion of the surgeons, physicians and nurses of Canada.

All the buildings that had once covered several acres and housed 750 patients at one time had vanished, as had the thousands of patients who had passed through the hospital or died within its walls. All that remained was the plaque — and the neatly cut lawn and the rolling fields and the beautiful trees.

I bowed my head for an instant and stood very still.

THE STATELY HOMES
OF ENGLAND

Garnons, Hereford — Sir Richard Cotterell
Welbeck Abbey — The Duke of Portland
Thoresby Hall — The Earl of Manvers
Lintmill Cottages — Angus McArthur Esq
The Old House, Canonbury — Ronald Carton, Esq

April 18 to August 20, 1944

The stately Homes of England
How beautiful they stand
Amidst their tall ancestral trees
O'er all the pleasant land
            Felicia Hemans, The Stately Homes of England

The train left Basingstoke at 0945 hours, April 18th. I relaxed as best I could in a compartment jammed with a mixed bag of American GIs, Polish airmen, British soldiers and a few civilians. Hereford was only 90 miles away, in a straight line, and I looked forward to a quick trip. But I had forgotten that this was wartime and millions of Allied troops had taken over the country; civilian trains had very low priority. My journey took all day, as I changed trains at Reading, Birmingham and Shrewsbury and arrived at Hereford at 1800 hours. There I was met by a station wagon and driven about seven miles to the Massey Foundation Convalescent Home for Canadian Officers, on the estate of Sir Richard Cotterell, set in the lovely Hereford countryside, near Wales. The estate, known as Garnons, included 24 homes and six parishes and churches — 5600 acres in all; its name came from one Robert De Garnons who had owned the land in 1352. The mansion had been built in 1816 and was much added to over the years. Sir Richard was now away fighting and his Lady and children lived in a small cottage nearby.

The Convalescent Home had been established early in the War by Vincent Massey, the Canadian High Commissioner in London — one of the many generous acts he performed for Canadian troops overseas. The 'Home' accommodated about 40 officers. Butlers served gourmet meals in a candlelit dining room; valets cleaned clothes and shone shoes; maids made up the beds. Breakfast was served in bed if such was your wont. In short, Garnons was probably the most civilized home in the whole of England at that time.

All this background was given me by the driver as the station wagon drove through the peaceful, green, wooded countryside, towards this Shangri-La. It seemed like a just reward for the various discomforts I had endured.

As soon as I arrived, two servants appeared, took my baggage and showed me to my room. "What will Mr Frost be wearing tonight?" purred a valet, as if I had dozens of uniforms in my wardrobe.

Dinner was at 1930 hours, served just as the driver had described. My diary entry that evening was short, but said it all.

> *Slept that night as I haven't for months. Woke up in the morning feeling healthy.*

Next morning I wrote a long letter home describing my new abode. Even today I find it hard to believe.

> *You are now talking with an officer and a gentleman. Here I am, living a perfect life of luxury in a mansion set in one of the finest estates in England!*
>
> *Mrs 'Ma' Reid is the chief hostess, and is helped by three young ladies, Marion Campbell, Elizabeth Walker, Kitty (somebody) — all Canadians — and they are certainly charming creatures. Dinner is at 1930. We dress for that in service dress and the like. The hostesses wear their evening gowns, long dresses, or whatever ladies wear.*
>
> *A normal day's activities might be any combination of the below.*
> *1. Sleep and eat — always high on the list, and only once have I been known to refuse a second helping.*
> *2. Games — croquet, for a warmer up — ping pong, to really smarten up those reflexes — badminton — tennis, my special favourite.*
> *3. Riding — both horse and bike — personally I'll stick to the*

bike, and I've done a good many miles around these parts.

4. *Library and piano — when feeling indisposed.*
5. *The local pub — a couple of hundred yards away and a good idea just before lunch.*
6. *Sunbathing — easiest and laziest of all — children and officers love it.*
7. *Hiking — plenty of interesting places to hike to, and always the chance of meeting up with a nice Land Army Girl. Now don't get me wrong, Mum.*
8. *Discussion — strictly for the Eighth Army fellows here. Consists of handing out sage words for the other fellows who haven't been to Sicily or Italy and thereby making them feel very happy indeed — indeed!*

I get great enjoyment out of being able to lick stamps again!

As if this surfeit of fine living was not enough, a nearby American Base issued regular invitations to attend their dances and even supplied partners — Land Army Girls. By this time I had been thoroughly spoiled, living the life of the nobility, and the dance I attended was somewhat of a let-down.

Only one other discordant note interfered with my otherwise idyllic existence at Garnons. My parents had now received news from me that I would not be coming home on leave despite all the assurances I had given them over so many months. They were not pleased and couldn't understand it. In his despair, father uncharacteristically hinted he might try and 'do something' at his end. I was furious and didn't quite know how to reply. Luckily, there was a surrogate father at the Home, Maj Rusty Gordon, whom I had met at the Colonel-in-Chief's birthday party on March 17th at Aldershot. I told him about my parents and confided that my sole desire was to return to the Regiment as speedily as possible.

Rusty was a veteran of the First War who had joined the Patricias on the outbreak of the present conflict. He came overseas with the Regiment, but because of his age had to return to a training unit. He had a great fund of common sense and acted as a sort of father confessor to the junior officers. He took quite a shine to my classmate Vaughan Allan and gave him much helpful advice and encouragement. Vaughan in turn worshipped Rusty. When Vaughan was killed later that year, Rusty was saddened as if he had lost a son.

It was therefore only natural that I would turn to Rusty with my troubles. We strolled through the lovely gardens of the estate and talked the matter out. He suggested that I shouldn't tell my parents, at this point, of my desire to return immediately to Italy. They had first to accept the fact I would not be coming home. He calmed down my annoyance with father's hints that he wanted to apply some pressure. In the circumstances, Rusty said, he would probably have felt the same way as father; what I hadn't realized was that

father himself was under considerable pressure from mother to do something.
I composed a letter, which Rusty approved whole-heartedly.

> *I can fully realize that you and the family would do anything in your power to get me home, if I were to approve it. LCol Gordon has passed me as A1 and will not consider my going back to Canada for the reasons I've mentioned in my last letters. So be it. His job is to get officers and men back to duty, and my duty lies over here. While I am of any use I must do a job. Thanks just the same, Dad, but I can't approve of any influence over LCol Gordon. Best leave the matter as it is. That is the only way I can have a clear conscience. Please understand, and help Mother to see it that way.*

My pleasant interlude at Garnons came to an end on May 3rd. I would always remember it with much happiness, but I had had enough and wanted to get on with the war. I left Hereford at 1000 hours with my trunk and all my kit, fully rested and eager to come to grips with whatever lay ahead.

Almost immediately I was faced with some dandies. My instructions had been to report to a Reception Centre at Cove to be posted to nearby 1 CIRU (Canadian Infantry Reinforcement Unit) at Aldershot for unspecified duties. I had also been told I was entitled to a further week's convalescence leave, perhaps two, but I would have to make arrangements at the reinforcement unit. Considering myself to be still on leave, I decided to travel in service dress, as did all smart officers who wanted to make the most of their furloughs. In any event my only other uniform was a baggy 'Limey' battledress I had purchased in Algiers, which was a poor imitation of the neat Canadian pattern.

On arriving at Aldershot I found that 1 CIRU was in the process of moving north, destination unknown. No one had the slightest interest in a PPCLI lieutenant, dressed in service dress and encumbered with trunk, suit case and two kit bags. After getting nowhere at several Orderly Rooms, I finally flagged down a passing cab and set off for the railway station with all my excess baggage, hoping to find a friend, or at least catch the next train to 'destination unknown'.

As I stood in the pouring rain, surrounded by my luggage, I wondered why I had left Garnons — for that matter, why I had left Canada. Exactly a year earlier I had been stationed at 1 CIRU while my Regiment went off to Sicily, leaving me behind as a reinforcement. Now I was back again with the paper pushers and draft dodgers, only this time the situation was so chaotic that even poor old Capt Snafu was put to shame — his finest efforts in Sicily were only second class compared to the confusion that now reigned. Green troops, just over from Canada, under equally inexperienced officers, were milling about the railway station trying to board the trains as they arrived. One officer bellowed at the troops to get aboard while another ordered them to get off; more troops arrived in lorries and were pressed into the coaches or told to return to base. No one knew where he was going, or why, or when. One train pulled out just as a vehicle appeared with rations for the departed troops. The truck promptly sped away, but no one seemed to be concerned who would profit from these rations which had now become 'buckshee'.

This extraordinary situation clearly could not be classed as a simple 'snafu'. It required a new word — something that would signify the ultimate foul-up. According to my diary there was such a word: tarfu — 'things are really fouled up'. Only once in my diary does this word appear. Whether it was coined then and there or whether it was stolen from a top secret list of code words, I do not remember. I do, however, vividly recall bulldozing my way onto a train through a motley throng of soldiers in battle order, pretending I was a staff officer in service dress, Sam Browne belt and dress hat, accompanied by two batmen (whom I had coerced into carrying my luggage). The train gave two toots and I was on my way.

Late that night I arrived at Welbeck Abbey, the Estate of the Duke of Portland, set in a park in the middle of Sherwood Forest, about 25 miles north of Nottingham. The park was known as 'The Dukeries' because of the number of ducal seats in the area, including Welbeck, Thoresby, Clumber and Worksop.

After my sojourn in the stately homes of Hackwood House and Garnons I felt it only right and proper that I should now be quartered in one of the largest and richest estates in all of England, comprising some 60,000 acres. The enormous mansion, stables and outbuildings had been erected in the 1860s by the fifth Duke of Portland, an eccentric whose vast fortune in coal mines and London ground rents enabled him to indulge his idiosyncracies by spending many hundred thousands of pounds in creating Welbeck Abbey. One of the oddities on the estate was a vast sunken state banquet room.

The reinforcement unit had pretty well taken over the mansion and surrounding manor houses, lodges, cottages, stables and out buildings, except a wing of the main residence where the Dowager Duchess of Portland lived with her son. The headquarters and staff of 1 CIRU were naturally set up in the mansion, while peons (lieutenants and the like) were quartered in the stables and out buildings. This is not to say that the stables were inadequate accommodation; before the war they had housed some of the finest horse flesh in England, and were more commodious than any of the barracks at Aldershot. It was said that in peacetime the whole establishment employed 2,000 servants.

While the staff settled into their posh quarters and the peasants into theirs, I looked about trying to find someone who would admit I was actually there

239

and on strength of 1 CIRU. It seemed that once again I was the 'disappeared one', and would remain so until I found a friend who could vouch I was Lt C S Frost and set the wheels in motion to get me on strength. That was only the first step. The next thing was to have me posted to the staff, or PE (Permanent Establishment), so I could live in the mansion and not have to muck about in the stables with hundreds of green reinforcement officers, lieutenants and captains just over from Canada.

I realized that until the staff got themselves organized there was no point in asking them to solve my problems, so I found myself a comfortable stall, parked my kit and wandered around the estate. I entered the mansion and strolled through its halls, picture galleries, library, chapel, armorial rooms and heraldic galleries, almost stumbling into the private apartments where the Dowager Duchess resided. Not having my calling cards with me I withdrew in haste, to await a more appropriate occasion to meet Her Grace.

My tour of the grounds of the estate continued without incident until I encountered what appeared to be the entrance to an underground tunnel, so huge that a double-decker bus could drive within its walls. One of the immense doors was ajar so I peeked inside. Through the gloom I could make out a long passageway lined on each side with large wooden boxes marked WD (War Department). This was worth exploring.

The door easily opened and I entered, trying to adjust my eyes to the interior. About one hundred yards down the tunnel a shaft of daylight pierced the gloom, and beyond that further beams of light seemed to occur at regular intervals. I approached the first beam of light and found it came from a vent, covered with steel bars, cut in the roof of the tunnel. From this light I could make out the heavy black printing on wooden boxes — respirators. My Lord, I thought, there must be enough respirators to equip the entire British Army. Remembering, however, the injunction from the Medical Officer at Basingstoke that I was not to wear a respirator, I resisted the temptation to break into the boxes and 'liberate' a few. At the same time I hoped that the Medical Officer had sent a copy of his report to the Germans so they would not be so unkind as to use gas when I was in the front lines.

I headed deeper into the tunnel in search of something useful. At the next vent I checked the labels on the boxes and found 'helmets, steel'. Again I was frustrated by that report from the Medical Officer. It specifically said I was also excused from wearing the chin strap of a steel helmet under the chin. As there was really nowhere else to put a chinstrap, it followed that the steel helmet itself was also on the 'excused' list.

I ventured deeper into the cavernous interior, past a third and fourth vent and stopped. On each side were smaller boxes painted with wide red lines — 'Bombs, mortar 3 inch'. This was a more promising find and I imagined the exciting scheme I could lay on with live ammunition. I started to climb to the top of the pile of boxes when I heard the unmistakable click of a

.303 rifle.

"Don't move. Put up yer 'ands, mate, and come over 'ere, slowly." I obeyed immediately and precisely, and found myself facing a cocked rifle in the hands of a very determined corporal in the Home Guard. "Oh, so yer one of them Canadian officers. Better get t'hell outa 'ere smartly before some'un puts a bullet in yer arse. Come along, *Sir*."

I thanked him for such helpful advice and apologized for trespassing on his bailiwick. I explained that I had served with Gen Montgomery in the 8th Army in Sicily and Italy, been wounded and returned to England where I was now awaiting a draft to return to my Regiment, the PPCLI.

The corporal, who was wearing two rows of ribbons, including the Military Medal from the First War, had heard all he needed to excuse my little peccadillo — Montgomery, 8th Army, wounded, PPCLI — that was enough to establish my credentials. If I had had the nerve, I think I could have made off with half the reserve of mortar bombs for the whole 8th Army.

As we walked together toward the tunnel entrance, he told me something of the history of this immense cavern. Many years past, that same eccentric fifth Duke of Portland, who was also badly deformed, could not bear to show his ugly face in public, particularly to his many servants and tenants, yet he was obliged to visit London frequently to manage his vast estates. The disfigured Duke solved the problem by constructing a tunnel from his estate to the railway station, about a mile and a quarter long. Every hundred yards a vent let in light and air, and additional illumination was supplied by torches in the walls. I thought this was an ingenious solution but wondered why he hadn't simply pulled down the shades in his carriage. Not wanting to embarass my friendly captor with such a silly question, I let the matter pass.

In any event, I could not dispute the fact that there was indeed a large tunnel crammed with bombs and I was in it. I asked the corporal what else was stored in all the boxes along the walls. He nonchalantly replied, "Enough equipment and ammo t'supply t'whole friggin' Second Front." He added that Sherwood Forest was one vast ammunition dump and if ever the Jerries found out, they could blow the "whole bleedin' issue" to kingdom come. I only hoped that the authorities in charge of security were not as prone to divulge all this information as my friendly corporal of the Home Guard.

My satisfaction with this little caper soon gave way to frustration when I realized that I had completely lost sight of the 'aim' since arriving at Welbeck Abbey. What indeed was my aim? It wasn't a very difficult question. My aim was to get myself on strength of this crazy CIRU so I could get more convalescence leave before the war ended, or before I, too, became eccentric, or worse.

I decided to do the rounds of Orderly Rooms and Headquarters once more. This time success. As I entered the Orderly Room of D Company I saw seated behind the company commander's desk an old friend from Sicily days, Capt

G F (Jud) Chapin. I thanked the gods of war that the Patricia network was still functioning. Very quickly I told Jud all my troubles and he put me in the picture regarding 1 CIRU. The unit had been moved out of Aldershot to make room for all the troops and supplies being gathered in the south of England for the invasion. Furthermore the staff expected the Germans to bomb the area heavily as soon as D-Day arrived. It was nonsense (so the staff alleged) to let the enemy blow up all our reinforcements (and, incidentally, the staff), so everyone had been 'evacuated' to the Midlands and northern England. The place was in an awful snafu and was driving Jud crazy too; he could hardly wait to get out of the unit and back to the Regiment. With these sentiments I heartily agreed.

Jud then called in another officer I had served with in Sicily, Capt N M (Norm) Cousens. He had been stricken with malaria and was with me in hospital in Catania before rejoining the Regiment in Italy. It was wonderful to see two old friends again and we promptly adjourned to the mess. There, Jud introduced me to the commander of 1 CIRU, LCol Mothersill, and explained my problems to him.

"Ah, yes, Frost, I just received a letter from Maj Rusty Gordon today saying you would be reporting here shortly. I didn't expect to see you so soon. You will be taken on strength as a member of the Permanent Establishment and posted to Capt Chapin's company."

This was exactly what I desired but I wanted to make one thing very clear to the Colonel (fortified no doubt by several good rounds at the bar). "I hope, Sir, that being on Permanent Establishment will not affect my returning to the Regiment as soon as possible." Immediately I suspected I had gone too far and a kick in the shins from Jud confirmed this.

"Young man, I can't make any promises like that. There's lots of work to do here and we need good men like you."

I had heard that all too many times before. Jud dragged me away before I really put my foot in it and we spent the afternoon discussing matters that had nothing to do with training troops. Very quickly Jud got me proper quarters as a member of the staff, arranged for me to draw new kit and sent me off on seven days' convalescence leave. I was ungrateful enough (and knew his kindly nature well enough) to say that while I appreciated seven days' leave, I had been in hospital six months and thought an extension of, say, another week might be possible — in fact LCol Gordon had so indicated, depending of course on the 'exigencies of the service', which so far had treated me rather badly. Jud said he would see what he could do and wire me if the extension came through.

I was away before the ink was dry on the travel warrant. My destinations will not surprise my reader if he recalls my earlier weekend passes — Neilston (near Barrhead, Scotland) and London. I caught the train at Worksop at noon, passed through Sheffield and arrived at Glasgow at 1900 hours. There

I changed trains for Neilston, arriving at 2200 hours, a long ten-hour journey in crowded compartments. I tumbled off the train onto the platform and was overwhelmed by the McArthur family — Angus (Pop), 'Ma', Betty, Jessie, and many of their relatives and friends. Amid great rejoicing, I was carried away to the nearest pub, where I was fêted and dined like a conquering hero, as if I had single-handedly captured the whole of Sicily.

The celebrations continued over the next ten days with every publican in the village vying for the privilege of opening the bar in my honour, drinks on the house — very embarrassing for one who had seen so little action. If Gen Montgomery had seen the goings-on I would probably have been court martialled for impersonating a hero. Well, I thought, there was nothing I could do about it and I was never one to spoil a good party. I wrote my mother a report of these happy days, omitting, of course, some of the more interesting details that the censors would doubtless have expunged anyway.

> *17 Lintmill Cottages*
> *Neilston, Renfrewshire*
> *Scotland*

This is the home of the McArthurs, of whom I've spoken many times. Angus (the old man) and I have been having one glorious time at the various pubs. The two girls, Betty, whom I go out with, and Jessie have been taking me to all the dances, and Mrs McArthur (I call her 'Mom'), has been attending to my appetite by way of quantities of good home-cooked food. So naturally I am going to reciprocate as best I can, but it would be nice, Mum, if you could help me, by sending the McArthurs a box of chocolates and perhaps a box of cigs to Angus.

The 'Macs' live quite simply, in a little cottage by the mill where they all work. As 'Ma and Pa' were originally born in Scotland, they still retain their customs and accent, but the girls are strictly Canadian types. So I fit into their family parties with great gusto, singing Scottish songs and playing the piano while Angus plays his dulcimer. I am learning to speak with a real brogue and dance all their old fashioned reels.

On Saturday night whole families congregate at the village pub and everyone takes a drink. Just as one reads in the books! Thus I am getting an intimate insight into the life of quite ordinary working class people. It is all a great experience, and of course an education. I think I can say that during my visit to Scotland I have maintained their admiration and respect of Canada and Canadians.

The warmth, kindness and down-to-earth goodness of these wonderful people meant a great deal to me in those days and their memory has given me much happiness since. The stately homes of England where I had been staying had certainly impressed me, but they could not compare with the home of Angus McArthur in Neilston.

My seven days' leave was now up and still no word from Capt Chapin at 1 CIRU about an extension. Should I go by the book and return to the reinforcement unit, or should I gamble that the 'fickle finger of fate' was at last on my side? With the help of the McArthurs and every publican in town, I came to the decision, naturally with some reluctance, to gamble that my friend would come through with an extension. My training in military law gave me some solace, as I knew I could only be charged with AWL, not desertion, because I was not in the face of the enemy (excluding staff-officers) and I had not been warned to proceed on active service.

Two days after my leave had expired a telegram arrived granting the extension. This meant I could have one more day with the McArthurs before finishing off my leave in London.

One final send-off party was accordingly laid on and convened; one last chorus of *I belong to Glasgow* rendered; mutual toasts exchanged, and promises made to meet again. *We'll meet again, don't know where, don't know when. But I know we'll meet again some sunny day.*

I left Neilston at 2000 hours on May 23rd for the long journey to London, including a short stop at Welbeck Abbey to ensure my leave had been duly extended.

If London was crowded three months earlier, there were no words to describe the present congestion. Some wag on the train had suggested that the only reason London was still afloat was because of the barrage balloons. All the hotels were filled to the garret, with three and four people to a room and cots set up in rooms formerly used as cleaning and storage areas. Cabbies were making a fortune, some offering their services to the highest bidder. Luckily, Jane Carton had offered to put me up at their home whenever I was in London and I readily accepted her kindness.

Next day I had the pleasure of taking the Cartons to lunch at their favourite restaurant, the Café Royal, where they had entertained me three months earlier. Their fine tastes were beginning to rub off on me.

After lunch we returned to their country-like house in Canonbury, a fashionable London village. There, in the lovely garden of the Old House (as their house was known), we talked about the War and when the invasion would be launched across the Channel. From the tremendous activity in London, on the railways, on the roads and in the air, it was obvious that the date could not be far off.

Much as I enjoyed the company of the Cartons I could not intrude on their generosity any longer; also Jane's cousin, Jim Harding, my friend from Saint John, was coming to stay with them. We parted and I returned to London to try to find lodging for the night.

I saw the Cartons once more before I left for Italy and on several occasions near the end of the War. After the War Jane Carton visited Canada from time to time in the course of her journalistic career and always gave me a call. On my extensive tour of Western Europe in 1956 my wife and I had a wonderful visit with the Cartons, who were still very active with *The Times*; we also looked up their daughter Polly in Rome. When Ronald passed away in 1960 it was as though I had lost a favourite teacher. London would never be the same; nor would the Old House on Canonbury Place where I had spent so many happy times. For me, it would always remain one of England's stately homes.

My quest for a hotel in crowded London on May 26, 1944 turned out to be an almost impossible task. No hope at my favourite hostelry The Park Lane, nor at the Great Northern at King's Cross where my train would leave for Welbeck Abbey. Finally I found a room of sorts at the Waldorf to be shared with a staff captain from some training headquarters, recently arrived from Canada. Having to share my ablutions with such a low type was a severe test to my sanity and weakened powers of endurance, but it was better than sleeping on the sidewalks of Piccadilly Circus.

Next morning I decided to pay my respects to CMHQ (Canadian Military Headquarters), the supposed nerve centre of the Canadian Forces Overseas. Perhaps I would find a friend or sympathetic ear who would free me from the horrors of a reinforcement unit and get me back to the PPCLI in Italy. It was worth a try, though I suspected the headquarters might have other business they considered more urgent. At any rate I had one simple request that even a corporal could attend to for me. I had heard that CMHQ kept a large library of pictures of the 1st Division in action in Sicily. I wondered if they had copies of the newsreel taken of the guard I had commanded in Militello, and other photographs of the Regiment. Through my bank manager I had got the name of a Col Abel who was supposed to be the Number One Man in Photography.

My venture began auspiciously enough. I was lucky to catch a cab and drove to Cockspur Street where I presented myself to the sergeant of the guard, with the buttons of my service dress sparkling, and my Sam Browne shining like any other officer of the staff. My two pips looked a little skimpy, but there had been cases where smart young officers were given training as staff learners. Once past the guards, I felt I was well launched on my mission. At the next checkpoint I faced a lieutenant whom I easily outflanked until I was stopped by a captain who demanded some identification. I complied and asked to see Col Abel. "That's quite impossible, Mr Frost. You must realize we are working 24 hours a day on . . . . on a forthcoming operation. And Gen Crerar is expected at any minute!"

I thought I might get around this barrier and speak with the major at the next checkpoint but I realized it was hopeless. I sat down and waited to catch a glimpse of Gen Crerar as he hurtled past. Suddenly I noticed an attractive member of the CWAC seated at a desk — Charmian Sansom, daughter of LGen E W Sansom who had recently retired as commander of 2nd Corps and returned to Canada. Charmian had made her point about earning her promotion overseas and was now a full lieutenant in charge of CWAC matters at CMHQ.

At last Old Field Marshal Fate was obviously trying to give me a break and I made the most of it. Copies of the pictures taken at Militello would be no trouble at all, Charmian assured me, and produced several volumes of photographs taken of the 1st Division in Sicily and Italy. Would I join her for dinner in their mess? Of course, I'd be delighted, and could I reciprocate by asking her to 'my Club', The Cocoanut Grove?

These happy arrangements were no sooner made than flashes of photographers' bulbs and a bevy of staff ushered in the General himself. What he thought of a young lieutenant lounging around his headquarters making dates with his staff, on the eve of D-Day, I have no idea. At any rate my presence does not appear to have affected the outcome of the invasion, one way or the other.

Like all good leaves, this one came to an end all too quickly, leaving me broke and exhausted. By judicious use of cabs, English train schedules, and army vehicles, I managed to get back to Welbeck Abbey a few minutes before the 2400 hours deadline only to find that Capt Chapin and his D Company had moved again.

In my absence 1 CIRU had made some progress in unsnarling the tarfu at Welbeck Abbey. Most of the troops and many of the officers had been dispersed to other estates and camps in Sherwood Forest to give them an opportunity to do some field training, which they badly needed.

D Company was now set up in a hutted camp at Norton, near the Duke of Portland's estate, whence I forthwith proceeded, happy to put some distance between me and the stables of the eccentric Duke. My job was to instruct reinforcements but there were precious few to train. Apparently all available reinforcements had been sent to Special Base Reinforcement Depots in the south of England, ready to support the invasion. It was the same old nonsense all over again that I had endured in reinforcement units before Sicily — no men, no work, acres of red tape and constant inspections. After seven months of inactivity I had a very short fuse and paraded before the Commanding Officer, LCol Mothersill, demanding to be posted to another company until the next draft left for Italy. LCol Mothersill was happy to oblige as I had been upsetting his tranquil routine of doing nothing during the day and even less at night — all officers were supposed to go to bed at 2130 hours so they would be thoroughly rested for the next day's inactivity.

To ensure LCol Mothersill's co-operation, I had sung one of my favourite ditties outside his window, quite late at night, on the evening before the parade, hoping he would get the message:

> *Kiss me goodnight Colonel Mothersill*
> *Tuck me in my little wooden bed*
> *We all love you dearest Colonel*
> *Col Mothersill be a mother still to me.*

When I paraded the next day he already had the form made out in sextuplet. For my sins I was 'sentenced' to F Company stationed at Thoresby Hall, commanded by one of the toughest soldiers in the business — Brig Guy Gostling.

Thus ended my tour of the Duke of Portland's estate, and I began my visit to Thoresby Hall, the last of England's stately homes on my long itinerary, prepared for my exclusive use by the Department of National Defence.

This estate, though not as extensive as the Duke of Portland's, boasted a palatial mansion. It had been built for the Earl Manvers in 1864-75 by one of England's greatest architects, Anthony Salvin, and was said to be his grandest house. Stairs led up from the main entrance to an enormous stone-lined great hall, hung with the flags and pennants of past glories. Beyond this lay high-ceilinged reception rooms, libraries, picture galleries and private suites, the whole planned round a central courtyard. This edifice was so magnificent that it was referred to by everyone as 'the castle'.

As was the case at Welbeck Abbey, the brigadier and his staff occupied suites in the castle while the reinforcement officers were quartered in huts and tents on the estate. At first I was required to do penance by living in a tent but eventually I was 'promoted' to a garret in the castle from which I had a fine view of Sherwood Forest. I couldn't resist writing to my young sister, ten years old, about this 'Robin Hood' country.

> *Dear Vivian*
>
> *Do you remember reading stories of Robin Hood? I am living in a castle right in the middle of Sherwood Forest where Robin Hood and his merry men used to play games and rob the rich to help the poor. Not so far away from where I am now writing there is a cave where he used to sleep.*
>
> *In the courtyard of the castle, there is a huge statue of Robin Hood. I can see it now directly out of my window. There's old Robin, with his bow, ready to defend the poor. Wouldn't you love to run around here and explore old caves and ruins!*
>
> *All the country is so peaceful and very beautiful with plenty of trees and green fields and proper hedges around them. This makes the country look like a patchwork quilt. Each tree is cared for like Grandma Frost looks after her cherry tree. Everything*

is so unlike Canada. The fields are small, the houses are small, and even the trains and cars are just tiny little things.

For my parents I had a slightly different version of what Robin Hood country was like.

For the past months I have been most fortunate in having my quarters situated in beautiful estates. This one is the estate of an Earl, in the midst of famous Sherwood Forest. The place just reeks of tales of Robin Hood and his merry men. Almost every other pub round about claims to be a direct descendant of one of Robin's old lairs.

During the days the officers are running about, with me giving them a helping hand. Often I have them do a house-cleaning (not really) on a nearby pub, and so the scheme is off for a period while another Robin and his men make merry and quench their thirst after a hard morning's training. Great institution, these pubs — but I've given you the lowdown on them before.

In the evening everything is so peaceful and quiet that war hardly seems a reality.

Twelve years later, in 1956, I returned to Thoresby Hall and Welbeck Abbey. At Thoresby Hall all traces of the camp and the occupation by Canadian troops had vanished, but the enormous mansion, the castle, seemed more palatial than ever. The rooms were fully furnished and decorated very much as they were in Victorian days. As I approached Welbeck Abbey I had a severe case of déjà vu. The area was crowded with troops. Directly in front of my car, a one hundred man guard of honour was smartly brought up to attention and arms sloped, in obvious readiness for the 'present'. What a splendid reception, I thought, for an old two-legged inmate of the Duke's stables!

A military policeman shattered my fantasies. He jumped in front of my Mercedes and motioned me off the driveway and onto the grass, while a procession of Rolls Royces and Daimlers rolled past and stopped on the parade square. It was the annual inspection of the Welbeck Military Academy. Later I found out that the school offered courses at the High School level for young men who wanted to make a career in the technical branches of the Army. From there the graduates went on to Officer Schools to complete their technical training and gain a commission. Graduates of the school had established a fine name in the army and proudly referred to themselves as 'Welbeckians'.

I was happy that the hundred thousands of pounds spent so lavishly a hundred years earlier had at last been put to an enduring and worthwhile purpose.

Chapter XIX

THE D-DAY DODGERS
1 Canadian Infantry Reinforcement Unit
Hitler's Secret Weapon
May 23 to August 8, 1944

We are the D-Day Dodgers, way out in Italy
We're always tight, we cannot fight
What bloody use are we

May 23, 1944

My story now returns to May 23rd, when I left Scotland bound for London and 1 CIRU at Welbeck Abbey. On that very day, the PPCLI was engaged in one of the heaviest battles of the war — the breaching of the vaunted Hitler Line in the Liri Valley, west of Monte Cassino. My company commander of Sicily days, Maj 'Bucko' Watson, was one of the few who gained the objective, but every man accompanying him had been a casualty, and he himself was wounded twice. He managed, however, to evade capture and finally settled down in a "large and quite comfortable shell hole."[1]

By nightfall the Patricias were down to a fighting strength of 77 all ranks. My friend of Shilo days, who had accompanied me on the draft to Sicily, Cecil Shea, was among the dead. Another member of that draft, Browne-Cleighton, had been badly wounded and taken prisoner. Second Brigade had suffered total casualties of 543 (including 162 killed), a number unequalled in a single day's fighting by any Canadian Brigade during the entire Italian campaign.[2]

Details of this gallant action by the Regiment were not, of course, known

249

to me until some time after the event. All I knew was that the Patricias had been engaged in the bloody battles swirling about Monte Cassino which had barred the Allied advance on Rome for so long. It was frustrating to be so far away from my Regiment and to receive so little news of its exploits. Further frustrations were on the way.

June 4, 1944

Late that evening, news arrived at Welbeck Abbey that the Allies had entered Rome. I imagined the joy and excitement of my friends as the Regiment liberated the Eternal City, and the hysterical reception they would receive from the jubilant citizens. But all my vicarious pleasure was based on fantasy. Gen Alexander, taking advantage of the Germans' determination to retain Rome at any cost, had decided to direct the British 8th Army to pass to the east of Rome, while the US 5th Army was given the honour of taking the city.[3] Thus the Regiment's advance to Rome was halted at Frosinone and the US 5th Army, under Gen Mark Clark, liberated Rome. It was a sad blow for my friends who had fought so long and so bravely for this honour. Field Marshal F F Fate was guiding the hand of even Gen Alexander.

June 6, 1944 — D-Day

"Our landings . . . . have failed . . . . . The troops, the Air and the Navy did all that bravery and devotion to duty could do. If any blame or fault attaches to the attempt, it is mine alone." Gen Eisenhower never issued this message which he had prepared if the invasion of Normandy should end in disaster.

Despite a gale on June 5th, and only a 'gleam of hope' that the weather would clear, Eisenhower boldly gave the momentous order to three million troops assembled in southern England to undertake the greatest seaborne invasion of all time — the assault on Hitler's Atlantic Wall.

For me, languishing in the backwaters of a reinforcement unit, the news of the invasion was almost anti-climactic after learning of the liberation of Rome. For the permanent instructors, content in their bomb-proof jobs, the news was received with something less than wild enthusiasm, as it meant they now might have to risk their necks in action.

Field Marshal Fate had again intervened in the highest councils of the Allies to relegate the occupation of Rome to an incidental footnote in the history of the War, compared to the liberation of France. Thenceforth, the whole Italian campaign would be strictly an expensive sideshow that, but for the support of Churchill, might have ended in a complete withdrawal of most of the forces for the Second Front.

This affected me profoundly, although I had realized long before that Italy would be put in the shade by the invasion of France. I felt like a malingerer twice over. Here I was, stuck in the 'anus of creation', with little prospect of ever returning to Italy; and even if I somehow returned to my Regiment, Italy was now only a second-rate battle. In short, I was a 'D-Day Dodger'. To add to my frustrations, some of the younger reinforcement officers, who had just arrived from Canada, soon left on a draft for Normandy; but not before they had given me a hard time for being an instructor in a holding unit.

Thus it was that I paraded before LCol Mothersill and asked for immediate transfer to another company, if he couldn't get me on a draft to Italy — with the aforementioned result. In defence of my somewhat erratic behaviour, the entries in my diary give an idea why I was so disenchanted with the whole reinforcement set-up in England at that critical time, when every single infantry officer and man should have been engaged in serious, meaningful, combat training.

1944

June 4   *No work at all except a Church Parade that was thoroughly mucked up.*

June 6   Invasion Day. *Feel pretty rotten being here with a bunch of zombies who don't want to fight. Must get out of here. This place has no life, none at all. Everyone in bed at 2130!*

June 21   *No work, no men. Celebrated my 22nd birthday.*

June 23   *Paraded before LCol Mothersill and sentenced to Thoresby Camp.*

June 24   *Drew rifle, web equipment, etc, and left for Thoresby Camp. Well this is about the end. Here I am living as a private with officers who have just come over from Canada or who have been knocking around England in cushy jobs. We queue for meals, make our beds, have inspections, do drill, etc. Saw Lt Abe Pettem and Fred Sims who have returned from Italy. Also saw Gord Sellar, Gordie Grant and Yusher Forbes of my class. They can't understand how I can take the hell around here. Now my mind is more firmly made up than ever. Italy — back I come! Bed at 2300 — lights out.*

June 25   *Cleaned up my web and got ready for tomorrow's inspection.*

June 26   *Same old bull. Drill and elementary lectures. Only reason I am sticking it is to get back in condition.*

June 29   *The camp now consists of some 400 officers. There has been a great mistake committed by staff . . . re reinforcements. Most of these two-pippers know nothing.*

This phase probably marked the lowest point in my army career. Instead of having a platoon of men or perhaps a company that I could train realistically based on my experience in Sicily and Italy, I was back in the ranks, like an ordinary soldier, taking tests of elementary training! The incredible part was that I was not the only veteran from Italy who was being wasted and demoralized in this way. My two seniors from RMC, Abe Pettem and Fred Sims, who had seen a lot of action with the RCR (The Royal Canadian Regiment) in Sicily and Italy were being subjected to the same treatment. Yet, there was hope. Capt George Corkett, whom I had met at that memorable birthday party in honour of the Colonel-in-Chief on March 17th, was now our new company commander. Like us, he had been battling the higher authorities for months to get back to Italy, without any success. He had even reverted from major to captain to convince the staff he meant business. When he found that Pettem, Sims and I were being treated like green officers just over from Canada, he had us paraded before the officer commanding Thoresby Hall, Brig Guy Gostling.

The last time I had met the 'Goose' was at RMC when, as a major in The Royal Regiment of Canada, he had given the cadets an excellent lecture on Iceland. His staff training at RMC had obviously done him some good — from major to brigadier in two and a half years was not so bad. Brig Gostling quickly saw the idiocy of having us do elementary training with inexperienced officers, and 'promoted' us to the staff. This meant we could move from the tent line into the mansion of the Earl of Manvers, where officers were treated as officers and gentlemen and even had an officers' mess. Whether we would now be permitted to give these uneducated 'two-pippers' some realistic battle training was yet to be seen.

Brig Gostling was a tough disciplinarian and tried to rule his 400 ill-trained and poorly motivated reinforcement officers with an iron hand; but even for him it was an almost impossible task. They nearly drove him round the bend.

The brigadier had no use for any officer who disobeyed orders, or attempted to cross him. During the course of one of his lectures on the importance of maintaining discipline, several officers started to talk and one even lit up a cigarette. His well known temper exploded. He grabbed his revolver and started to brandish the weapon in the air, declaring he would not hesitate to shoot any officer or man *in action* who defied his orders. I was relieved he had emphasized the words 'in action', but I was still not certain whether we had another Gen Patton on our hands. My fears were allayed when he calmly replaced the weapon in its holster and quietly asked the chief instructor to take the names of the offending officers. They were never seen again, at least not at Thoresby Hall. Evidently there was another place of banishment more terrible than even Thoresby Hall, where delinquent officers spent their last days.

This little act with the revolver was repeated in slightly different circumstances during another lecture to a different group of officers. I realized then that Brig Gostling was not only a tough officer who would not brook any nonsense from junior officers, but also a showman with a flair for the dramatic. His charges were terrified of him, but sad to relate, their discipline and motivation improved only marginally. They continued their slovenly ways and even made up a very rude coat of arms for the brigadier: a goose flying at great height, crapping on a gaggle of junior officers.

Not all the officers at the camp were so disrespectful of the well-intentioned brigadier. The staff were behind him 100 per cent but for different reasons. One group were very happy with their life in the castle and wanted to maintain their status quo forever; the other group, the veterans from Italy, agreed with maintaining discipline but had no time for the rest of the staff or the 'zombie' reinforcement officers, and only wanted to get out of the place and return to action.

Thus there was conflict not only between the brigadier and the reinforcement officers, but also within the staff itself. Very soon the enemy resolved all these conficts by causing heavy casualties to our forces in France and Italy, and we all went off to war, except, of course, the chair-borne officers, so thoroughly entrenched in the castle.

The reinforcement situation, as it was in summer 1944, was beset with problems.

Firstly, there was the quality of reinforcement officers and men from Canada. The officers came in two categories: those who had recently graduated from OCTU (Officer Cadet Training Unit) and those who had spent some time in the training centres in Canada. In this second category were officers who had sat behind a desk for years performing administrative duties, or who were experts in some specialist subject such as gas, 3 inch mortar or vehicle maintenance; many of these types came over as captains and had the nerve to keep their rank. Of all the frustrations of the war that battle-experienced lieutenants had to bear, the 'made in Canada' captain headed the list. Not only was it manifestly wrong, it was clearly unfair to give these 'three-pippers' command over lieutenants who had seen action, in many cases far more than their share. The damage these inexperienced captains caused in terms of morale and unit efficiency, cannot be measured. How many lives were lost to salve their egos will, fortunately, never be known. In fairness, however, some overcame their handicap and rendered good service, but I can name some who didn't.*

At Thoresby Hall, the majority of reinforcement officers had never commanded a platoon, even in barracks, and none had led men in the field.

---

*"There is no doubt that training can do just so much and no more; there is no umpire and no instructor like a bullet. Other things being equal, in an encounter between an army with battle experience and one without it, the former will win."[4]

Not surprisingly, their man-management and leadership skills were non-existent. Even their ability to look after themselves ('interior economy' they called it) was pitiful to see. One officer had been strolling around for days with a large hole in his battle dress. I asked him where his 'housewife'* was. He thought I was trying to be funny.

Most had never lived out in the open for any extended period and hadn't the faintest idea of basic survival skills — how to make a shelter, keep themselves warm, build a fire in the rain. Even their knowledge of the basic platoon weapons — rifle, bayonet, Bren gun, Sten gun, 2 inch mortar, grenade, revolver — was limited. Grenades were looked upon as some kind of time bomb, ready to blow them up at any minute. Some got what they feared. The basic infantry platoon tactics of fire power and movement were foreign to all, except the very few who had taken the battle drill course at Vernon. Company and battalion tactics and manoeuvres were quite beyond their ken.

Yet these were the junior officers who were soon to fill the depleted ranks in Normandy. Against all odds, most of them probably did quite well, if they were lucky enough to survive their initial blunders. How many were cut down because of inadequate training will never be known, but I would guess they numbered in the hundreds.

Compared to the officers, the men were better trained for their tasks. Most had fired all the platoon weapons and had a fair idea how to handle them in the field. Few, however, had much experience in platoon and company schemes with live ammunition. Yet they seemed more adept at roughing it in the field than the officers.

Another problem was the numbers of officer and other rank reinforcements. During the time I was stationed at Thoresby (June 23rd to August 14th) the camp seldom had less than 400 officers, much too large a body to discipline or train properly for any long period. It was obvious to everyone that an error had been made by the staff. Indeed two miscalculations had been made in planning for reinforcements for the landings on D-Day and the subsequent battles in Normandy. In simple terms, the casualties had been overestimated on the landings and underestimated in the later battles. Happily, the casualties on D-Day were only half of what the planners had expected.[5] As a result, the reinforcement unit at Thoresby was clogged with surplus officers, who were not required at the front. Had this good news been given to us at the time, it might have helped to calm the 'in-house' battles that raged between the reinforcement officers, resentful at being couped up like private soldiers, on the one hand, and the staff, distracted by the insubordinate officers, on the other.

This unsatisfactory state of affairs existed until I escaped from Thoresby on August 14th. By this time the second, more serious error by the staff

*Soldier's name for a sewing kit.

was becoming apparent. The planners had based the expected ratio of wastage in the infantry, in Normandy, on the losses suffered by the British in North Africa. It was a gross miscalculation.[6] The fighting in Normandy turned out to be a more bloody affair for the infantry than the engagements in Africa, where armour had played such a large part. Why the planners had not foreseen this simple fact, I have never been able to fathom. They had only to ask me, or anyone who had fought in Italy, and we would have set them straight. Col Stacey confirms that the percentages of the actual infantry casualties in Normandy were almost identical to those in Italy.[7]

Except at Welbeck Abbey, I had little contact with the men. There, I trained a platoon for a short time until they were sent to Normandy. From my observations at this camp it was very clear there was no surplus of men, as there was with officers, in the initial stages. In fact, I had 'arranged' my transfer from Welbeck Abbey because I was fed up with not having men to train. On many occasions a draft of men would arrive from Canada and be sent to Normandy the next day. There never seemed to be enough men to fill the boiling cauldron in France.

Finally, the so-called training of so-called officers has to be mentioned. The inertia and complete lack of enthusiasm of reinforcement officers and staff was shocking to me, as it was to all the Italian veterans. After wasting much valuable time on elementary training, route marches and inspections, the staff were finally persuaded to get down to some realistic tactical training; on one occasion, even an exercise with live 3 inch mortars. The fact that some inexperienced officers almost led their platoons of fellow officers into the killing zone of the mortar bombs did much to liven up their somnolent attitude. On most schemes things would get so balled-up that the instructors from Italy would have to take over the platoons and do the job for the incompetent platoon commanders.

These were the main problems in the reinforcement units, and with reinforcements generally, as I personally experienced them at that time. I believed then, and still do, that the officers who created the mess should have been court martialled. I would willingly have offered my services as prosecutor, without fee. My opening statement to the court would have been the following. "If the German general who rendered the highest service to the Allied cause was the madman Hitler, the Canadian unit which gave the greatest aid to the German cause was 1 CIRU."

If further evidence is required, my diary tells it 'like it was':

1944

June 30   Spent day touring country in a station wagon with Chief Instructor on a recce for a big scheme they are planning. It'll be good — no doubt. We got in a pub with a paratrooper Lt and all proceeded to get high.

Great recce this! Back to camp at 1700, having gone 90 miles and done nothing.

July 5   *'We Three' (Pettem, Sims and me) have to take over the platoons as the officers just don't give a damn and are botching the scheme right, left and centre.*

July 7   *Administration is completely fouled up. Meals are horrible. Made a dawn attack on BARBAGE ROCKS my pl leading. Fog came down and we couldn't see 10 feet. Rained heavily. Here again I had to take over the pl and went by guess and by God to our position — 3 inch mortar came quite close but we were OK. Scheme balled up because of mists and called off.*

We stood 6 hours in the rain while the DS went to pub and made 'We Three' go back in trucks with the students. So finishes exercise 'Fafu'.

July 13   *Training at camp still a horrible fafu. Begin with 100 officers on parade and by 1000 hrs only 50 are left. They are all completely fed up and so am I.*

July 18   *Did another small scheme and shocked officers re tactics of defence. They are all too book minded. Fifty officers put out in tents and what a howl!*

July 26   *Preparations for night attack. Walked about 8 miles. Saw a VD lecture and film. Everything went very well until Lt McDonald almost burned down a house and set a haystack afire. From now on he is known as 'Haystack'. Night scheme called off to fight the fire.*

My letters home give further evidence, but it must be stressed that they are written in a subdued tone so as not to upset the censors.

It's the same old stuff. All the best men are away fighting and I'm stuck at an Officers Training School with a group of officers just over from Canada. 'Zombies' we call them. Many of them have been brought up on the pamphlet and are all for having everything laid down in black and white — much the same attitude as I had in 1942 when I instructed at Shilo. But this is 1944 and training is supposed to be carried out on much different lines.

The officers are learning a few things I suppose, that is, those who have the ability, but so many of them these days don't know the score, and what is more, aren't fussy whether they learn something or not. It appears that any man with High School education is given a commission. And still 'zombie' captains arrive over here who have been lying around Canada for three and four years. The situation is enough to drive a poor man to drink, and a good man to desperation.

The time was now approaching when I had to come clean with my parents and tell them of my resolve to return to Italy, and 'to hell with LCol Gordon''.

> *A holding unit is not the place for me while I can help it. Bob wanted to know if I would be sent to France to another Regiment, and you are constantly asking me about my next operation, so I had best give you the score.*
>
> *Right now I have an A1 category and am in perfect shape after my convalescence and leave and am just marking time till August, when I am due to have my face made beautiful. However, as the need for reinforcements grows more acute, I am sure that all men will be needed. So I think that I'll just forget about the operation for the present and have it done after the war.*
>
> *LCol Gordon, the plastic surgery bloke, told me that I could do a good job in the field after I had been rested and fattened up. That has been done, so I feel that some time in the next month, if I can, I shall take another trip to Italy. There is no question of my going to France, as I am a Patricia who has served with the Regiment — and so I shall rejoin it.*
>
> *I thought it best to tell you this now. As I am fit and well again and jaw working good as new, you have no idea how awful it is for me to be kept around an inactive place like this.*
>
> *Then again, it might be some time before a draft for Italy is called. I'm just a bit annoyed that the Regiment will be through Italy by the time I reach it — but return to it I must and as quickly as I can.*

My prediction that the PPCLI would be out of Italy by the time I reached it was, like most of Capt Snafu's forecasts, grossly misconceived. Much hard fighting remained for the Regiment in Italy before it departed to rejoin the Canadian Army in Holland.

Following my usual procedure of censoring my own letters (telling the truth but not the whole truth), I didn't mention that I had received an offer to return to the battle drill school at Vernon, Canada, as an instructor, with, of course, a promotion to captain. It unquestionably would have meant the end of the war for me; but I was not by any means ready to call it quits, with the Regiment still in action and desperately in need of reinforcements. I had also received offers from senior officers in other units fighting in Normandy to join their regiments, including my father's regiment, again with an increase in rank. While these offers to get into action, almost immediately, were attractive, I could not bring myself to consider them seriously. As I had written my father: "There is no question of going to France, as I am a Patricia who has served with the Regiment — and so I shall rejoin it." It was that simple.

How serious the reinforcement situation really was in Italy, I did not find out until I arrived at the Regiment in September, during the heavy fighting in the Gothic Line. It was obvious at Thoresby Camp and at Welbeck Abbey that the Italian theatre had become a sideshow. Draft after draft of officers and men left for Normandy but not a trickle for Italy. Finally it was rumoured that a small draft of men and a few officers would be despatched to Italy from another camp. By the time I tracked the rumour down and found it was indeed true, it was too late. The draft had left, including one young officer for the PPCLI, whose family had a long association with the Regiment. I was livid, and so was Corky, that we had not been chosen. I paraded before a LCol Kempton and demanded an explanation. He was most sympathetic and promised an enquiry but I had heard all that before, so I made a trip to 1 CIRU HQ to see my surrogate father, Maj Rusty Gordon. Much to my chagrin he calmly admitted that he had approved the other officer going on this draft as he deserved a chance, and he thought I was not quite ready to return to action. For the first and only time I got mad at Rusty, but at that stage I would probably have given the Colonel-in-Chief herself a hard time. Rusty eventually mollified me with liberal doses of pain killer at the bar and I apologized for such an outburst. He promised to get me on the next draft, but warned it might take some months.

The sequel to this little contretemps was that, as far as I can ascertain, the officer who was sent on the draft never did serve with the Patricias in Italy. As so often happens, the 'exigencies of the service' intervened and he ended up with some other unit.

So it was back to the old routine of workless days and sleepless nights. Yet old Field Marshal Fate had not completely forsaken me. The day after my showdown with Rusty Gordon I received an urgent call to report to the Orderly Room. It couldn't be another draft, so I wondered what new disaster was in store — what regulation had I recently circumvented or, worse, blatantly ignored? I reported to the adjutant, a miserable little man who, for the first time in his existence at the camp, was actually smiling. In unctuous tones he purred: "Ah, Mr Frost, so glad to see you. I have the most incredible news that I am sure will make you happy. I am sorry we have given you such a hard time at the Camp."

Jackass, I thought. Why the hell doesn't he get on with it? Probably he'll give me five chances to guess whatever this incredible news is. But I remained silent.

"Well, you know the pressure we are under, with a war on and so forth. What I wanted to tell you is that you have just received — I mean it's quite unbelievable — you have just received 27 parcels!"

It was indeed incredible news and for a moment I was slightly stunned — 27 parcels! Then I understood the reason for the adjutant's ingratiating voice, which continued:

"Of course you'll need a vehicle to transport all these parcels to your quarters. May I call up a jeep for you?"

"Christ," I mumbled to myself, "the SOB will probably invite himself to dinner." However I accepted his offer and prepared to make a donation to the adjutant, on behalf of the King, of course.

The parcels were duly delivered to my room in the garret of the castle, after 'tipping' the adjutant with a carton of 300 cigarettes and a fruit cake. "There's a good man. Enjoy yourself." I took inventory and found I had the following provisions on hand, enough to supply my pals and me for weeks: 14 food parcels, seven boxes of chocolates and six cartons of cigarettes.

Most of the parcels had been down to Italy and sent back. Several had been in transit for over a year! One well travelled food parcel had 20 addresses on the cover. It had been sent from Toronto in May, 1943 and followed me half-way around the world — Aldershot (1 CIRU), Scotland, Sicily, the Regiment, hospital in Catania (when I had malaria), back to the Regiment, hospitals in Italy, Algiers, England and finally back to 1 CIRU where it had started out more than a year before. I kept the cover and the Customs declaration which is before me as I write:

List of Contents

Lobster	Coffee	Concentrated orange
Chicken	Peaches	Cake
Salmon	Chocolate bars	

Miraculously, everything was in good shape except the cake, which I had so generously given to the adjutant. Not disclosed on the customs declaration was one mickey of rye that was secreted in the cake — and which the adjutant did not receive.

News of this amazing cache of provisions soon spread throughout the camp. For the first time in many weeks I 'got some respect' from staff and officer students. I wondered how my career would have been enhanced if all these goodies had arrived two months earlier.

A letter to my mother was long overdue.

What a day this has been. I was called to the Orderly Room and there were 27 parcels waiting for me.

So now, you wonderful providers (and I just can't thank you in words here), please be sensible and for the next month hold on to your foodstuffs until I have a chance to consume the stock on hand. God, this is wonderful! Just where I can store my provisions, I haven't the slightest idea. Think I'd best stage a mess dinner. Do you realize I now have 4,000 cigs on hand! And they are all quite smokable.

I am intending to send a box to the McArthurs, as I know they would appreciate things like coffee, canned goods (fruit),

> *etc, and I'll still have lots left over. And I'll also send them some*
> *chocolates. I have now about 8 lbs of coffee, with milk and sugar*
> *on hand! Honestly, Mum, you're just too grand, and all the chaps*
> *say so too. I feed them every night!*

The problem of storing all these provisions in my attic room was solved by exchanging quarters with an obliging captain who had a spacious room on the second floor of the castle. I was then allowed the privilege and pleasure of dining in my own quarters and I set quite a table. I even thought of having the old Earl in for tea, but he was liable to ask for sherry and my wine cellar was not quite up to that. However I did seriously think that I might receive an offer from HQ to become the camp quartermaster, with rank to match.

One of the real pleasures was to be able to treat the veterans from Italy — the D-Day Dodgers who had been given such shoddy treatment. Night and day we gorged ourselves to the point at which I could feel a certain easing in our desire to get back to Italy. But if such was the case, it only lasted until the next morning.

Among my dinner guests was a very special friend from Italy who had been my right-hand man in the Scouts and Snipers — LCpl Slimkowich. He had been badly wounded after I had left the battalion and spent many months in hospital. We had some fine feeds together while he was waiting to go home. When he arrived in Toronto he looked up my parents and gave them first-hand news of my wounds and complete recovery. When my parents told me of his visit I wrote them a note about my friend.

> *It was nice to learn that LCpl Slimkowich of the Scouts and*
> *Snipers had a great write-up in the paper. You ask do I know*
> *him? Well, I should think so. It was I who gave him the stripe,*
> *and he was my right-hand man on many of the more difficult*
> *patrols. It was he who helped me get the platoon out of action*
> *when I got it in the face. Yes, he's a veteran of the Spanish wars,*
> *and his experience was a great asset to my outfit.*

Our Field Marshal Fate continued to smile on me. My claim for reimbursement of kit that I had long ago purchased in Algiers was finally approved and I received the handsome sum of 14 quid. It was six quid less than I had expended in re-equipping myself but I was not going to quibble. One week later my old kit was delivered along with more parcels, so I had to refund the 14 quid to the the government. I was just amazed how efficient the staff were when it came to money.

It is only fit and proper that the staff, whom I have consistently maligned in this chapter, and indeed throughout the book, should also get some credit for a fine piece of planning — moving 1 CIRU away from Aldershot. It will be recalled that some weeks before D-Day, the staff had moved the reinforcement unit to Welbeck Abbey to make way for masses of troops being concentrated in southeast England for the invasion. A further reason for the move was that the staff anticipated the area would be heavily bombed by the Germans as soon as the invasion was launched.

For once the staff guessed right. The area was bombed, but probably not by the kind of weapons the staff had expected. On June 13th, Hitler launched the first of his secret terror weapons against London — the V-1 unmanned missile, or flying bomb (or 'doodlebug' or 'buzz bomb', as it came to be called by the hardy Londoners). About 8,000 of these bombs were launched from the Pas de Calais area of France against London, but only 2,400 got through. Nevertheless the bombs did considerable damage and caused numerous casualties.

The target for all the missiles was the London Tower Bridge, but they landed over a wide area from Hampshire in the south to Suffolk in the north and especially in parts of Sussex and Kent which lay along the flight path of the bombs. This area, including Aldershot and my plastic surgery hospital at Basingstoke, was known as 'Bomb Alley'.

Whether any bombs actually fell on or near the former quarters of 1 CIRU at Aldershot I do not know, but the unnerving sight of these little monsters flying at speeds up to 400 miles an hour and packing a ton of explosives was a common occurrence at nearby Basingstoke — so I was told when I visited the hospital after the war. The effect on the nerves of the staff of 1 CIRU, had they stayed in the area, might well have rendered them *hors de combat*.

When the Allies captured the sites of the V-1 bombs in the Pas de Calais area in early September, the Germans unleashed a second terror projectile, the long-range V-2 rocket. This missile weighed about 12 tons with a one ton warhead. Unlike the buzzbomb, which could be seen and made a distinctive noise, the V-2 descended out of the atmosphere in silence and gave no warning to people to take cover. These rockets were more accurate than the V-1 and most of them fell in and around London or in the countryside to the east. Just the same, the threat of a V-2 descending out of the skies on the HQ of 1 CIRU would doubtless have affected the 'offensive' attitude of the staff, had the reinforcement unit remained in Aldershot.

In the final analysis, Hitler had out-foxed the staff and 1 CIRU. By forcing them to move to safe areas, well north of London, he had ensured their continued efforts to confuse and confound the Canadian war effort.

Chapter XX

ITALY REVISITED

Malaria Again
SS Orontes
Naples — Avellino
Rome — Jesi
No 1 Canadian Base Reinforcement Depot
August 8 to September 18, 1944

South of the Sangro, down Echelon way
That's where the Wops and the Quartermasters stay
A quiet night told me, it's better to stay
South of the Sangro, down Echelon way

O n August 8th, I received another summons to report forthwith to the Orderly Room at Thoresby. This time the Adjutant's smile was broader than ever and his words were brief and to the point.

"Mr Frost, you're on the next draft to Italy. You leave within the week."

The sense of relief obviously felt by the Adjutant was nothing compared to my delight at this wonderful news. The long months of waiting and struggling to return to my Regiment were over! I burst out of the Orderly Room to find Corky. As soon as I saw him I knew he had already received the same orders — we would be leaving together.

The next few days were filled with gathering up my kit that I had temporarily stored at Welbeck Abbey, Camp Norton and Thoresby Hall. When I got it all together — my trunk, suitcase and kit bags from Pickford's

Depository, the clothes I had bought in Algiers, the kit that had been returned from Italy, and all the stuff I had acquired in England — I found I had about ten times what I would be allowed to take to Italy. It took some time to sort it all out, sell or give away some of the surplus, and store the rest in the Canadian Kit Storage Depot.

On the financial side, I decided to assign home a further $20 a month from my pay. This left only $80 a month to be deposited in my bank account with Lloyds of London. After six months in England I was broke, but I counted on my good luck at cards to keep me solvent.

It only remained to make the rounds to say goodbye to friends in the area. There was no chance for 'impromptu' leaves to Scotland or London this time. Such exploits were now considered very bad form. I spent a very enjoyable afternoon with Aileen and Corky Corkett at their place in Edwinstowe and thanked her for all her kindness to me in Basingstoke. We talked of RMC, the PPCLI and how much it meant to us to be on our way at last. I learned that Aileen was expecting, wished her well and said something to the effect I would keep an eye out for her husband. I never made such a thoughtless commitment to anyone again. Corky had only another month to live.

While I was making all these last minute preparations I started having headaches and generally feeling pretty rotten. I wasn't particularly concerned. The strains and frustrations of the past months and the high living from the food parcels would have given anyone a king-size migraine, if not a duodenal ulcer.

But about a week before we were due to leave, I woke up one morning with a fever, and later in the day got the chills and started to vomit. I became so weak I could hardly make it back to my room. I collapsed on the bed and yelled at Field Marshal Fate: "No, no, no, you SOB, not now, please not now." When I awoke in a heavy fever a little later I knew I had malaria again.

I tried desperately to pull myself together and form some plan. If news of my condition got around the camp and came to the knowledge of the staff I would immediately be taken off the draft. Furthermore, if I were caught trying to hide my fever, I would be in a lot of trouble. Still I was pretty well packed, and my medicals, fortunately, had been completed. The boat left in only seven days. I would somehow have to hang on until I was safely embarked and the ship sailed, then I could report to the sick bay for treatment. In the meantime I needed help to finish packing and get on the inevitable final parades and inspections. My friends did not disappoint me. They nursed me, packed my kit, practically carried me out to the parade ground and held me up while the group was inspected.

Another thing that helped was that the worst attacks came only every second day. On the 'days off' I was able to get around to the Orderly Room

263

and complete all the forms and red tape required to send a soldier off to war. Still, that week of waiting for my 'dream boat' was absolute hell. I am convinced that despite all the help and encouragement I got from my friends, I would not have made it without my training at RMC.

On August 21st, too sick to carry my kit, I embarked on SS Orontes and went to bed. My 'bed' was actually a hammock; the quarters were so crowded that everyone, officers and men alike, had to sleep in hammocks. My friends had done all they could but in the crowded quarters they couldn't prevent news of my condition from spreading about the decks. A medical officer soon appeared and placed me in the ship's hospital. I was so weak I probably 'confessed' to more than I should have, but I didn't care because I thought the ship had sailed.

The ship had not sailed! The Medical Officer was very annoyed that I had been smuggled aboard in this condition and threatened all sorts of action, including having me removed from the ship forthwith to a hospital on shore. I pleaded, like a man condemned, to have my company commander, Capt Corkett, brought to my bedside, as a final request. The Medical Officer seemed surprised and immediately agreed. Corky was duly summoned. He opened the door, took a quick look at me and grabbed the hand of the Medical Officer. "Harold, great to see you again. Last time was on some exercise in England before I went off to Africa."

"Corky, what are you doing here. I heard you were badly wounded and bound for a soft job on staff."

"Never mind that. What are you trying to do to young Frost? He's only got a mild case of constipation — probably nervous about going into action again. Give him a couple of 222s and he'll be alright."

Corky pressed my hand and left. The moisture around my eyes was not caused by any fever.

SS Orontes, 20,000 tons, of the Orient Line, left Gourich two days later on August 24th at 2100 hours, in a convoy of 14 troop ships, five destroyers and one aircraft carrier. Lt Frost was listed among the passengers but in hospital, taking quinine three times daily. Never had such a vile taste felt so good.

Next morning we were well out to sea, rounding the north coast of Ireland. Soon we turned south, the weather became much warmer and everyone donned KD (Khaki drill) uniform — everyone except me and a few others in hospital. While the troops sweltered in their hammocks, in crowded, steamy quarters below decks, I slept on a soft hospital bed, cooled by a large fan directly overhead. Three days of quinine had broken the fever and I started five days of pamoquin, a much milder medication than the foul-tasting quinine. I was allowed out of bed and to stroll around the deck. Apart from aching muscles, general weakness and loss of weight, I felt pretty good; so good, in fact, that some of my friends who had succoured me and got me on the boat, and who were now crammed below decks, began to wonder if I hadn't been putting on a bit of an act to get 'posh' accommodation. (I did, indeed, have a port view from the hospital bay. Whether I would get a starboard view on my homeward trip remained to be seen).

On September 1st at 0200 hours the convoy crept past Gibraltar. This time I missed the opportunity to go on deck to see the dark hulk of the Rock and get mad again about the lights blazing away in the nearby Spanish town of Algeciras. I was satisfied to remain in my cool room and recall that my father had passed the Rock in a hospital ship some 29 years earlier, going west and home to England. I had now passed Gibraltar twice in hospital, once each way.

Soon after leaving Gibraltar, the *Orontes* slipped away from the convoy and headed for Oran, where we arrived at 1600 hours. The harbour was crowded with Allied ships of all kinds, including the battleship *Arkansas* and two other US battleships. At 2000 hours that evening, we left Oran and joined another convoy, escorted by nine corvettes. Like the approach to Sicily, we hugged the burning sands of the North African coast to avoid any fanatical attack by enemy submarines, but unlike the earlier convoy none came. The U-Boats could no longer penetrate these waters. As we passed Algiers, I thought of 94 General Hospital and wondered how Sister Cleghorn was making out. Perhaps the Wogs had finally overrun the place and carried her off into the hills. I didn't know whom to be sorry for — her or the Arabs.

We passed Cape Bon and turned north toward Naples. The heat was now intense and even crept into the hospital bay, despite the cooling fans. I had forgotten just how enervating the climate in southern Italy could be and wondered how I would cope with the heat when we landed.

In the short time left on board ship, I tried to get back into condition as fast as I could by jogging around the decks and running up and down the gangways. I also ate six meals a day — three in the hospital bay and three more in the officers' dining saloon. Despite the crowded arrangements for sleeping, the meals were close to peacetime standards, though not quite as elaborate as on the *Arundel Castle* that had taken me to Sicily. Food seems to have been my one abiding interest throughout my service. My diary always mentions it — good or bad; my letters home never fail to comment on it; and I faithfully collected menus of every ship I ever sailed on.

September 4, 1944

On September 4th, in the early morning mists, the *Orontes* cautiously approaches the Gulf of Naples, passes the Isle of Capri and other islands sheltering the bay, threads its way through masses of supply ships, warships and sunken vessels and finally docks at 0900 hours. The harbour and its installations are a shambles from Allied and German bombing, but the city rising up from the harbour seems as picturesque and intriguing as I've read about in the guide books. The old castles around the harbour look as formidable as they must have been when Garibaldi entered Naples to unite the south with the rest of Italy.

Like MacArthur, I have returned. Unlike MacArthur my feet are dry, just as they were when I landed on Sicily.

It has been an uneventful and unremarkable voyage of only ten days. In a letter home I describe the entire trip on one page, omitting, of course, irrelevant incidents such as a malarial attack.

> *No 77*   *On board ship*
> *Just over a year ago I was sailing on the very waters I am on now. Conditions are, of course, much different. This time I am in the know re my destination, tasks ahead, etc. It is not as thrilling as my Sicilian trip, but more like the crossing of the Atlantic, in March '43. Nevertheless, there is a certain thrill attached to the fact I am returning to the job I have been after these past four months..*
>
> *My old vim and vigour is just as it was last summer and I am spoiling to get off ship onto Italian soil with the Regiment. The voyage has been perfect — calm seas and warm, balmy weather. In the evenings a glorious moon throws its soft beams on the rippling waters. Ah, for the compan of a lovely girl!*
>
> *Well — the situation is becoming too romantic. Hm-m-m, reminds me of being in good spirits and happy that I'm on my way to the Unit.*
>
> *My Italian lingo is in excellent shape, ready to keep the Wop on the hop. They make excellent slaves!*

June 6, 1956

Twelve years later, another ship enters the Gulf of Naples, in light fog, and carefully steers a course past the outlying islands into the bay, crowded with vessels from many foreign ports. She has been at sea nine days. The voyage has been perfect — calm seas and warm, balmy weather. In the evenings a glorious moon has thrown its soft beams on the rippling waters. One passenger in particular is enjoying the company of a lovely girl as the ship glides into the harbour — Maj C S Frost of The Royal Regiment of Canada; the lovely girl is his wife, and the name of the ship is the *Cristoforo Colombo*, 29,200 tons, flagship of the Italian Line.

Only a dozen years ago I was landing at this very port, ready to do battle with the evil forces of Nazi Germany. The Allies had knocked most of the Italians out of the war, but some were still carrying the fascist banners and fighting alongside the Germans in northern Italy. Apart from the few Italians fighting on our side, as partisans, we considered the Italians as irresponsible, unreliable, beaten people — we called them 'Wops'.

That was in 1944. Now it is 1956. For the past ten days I have entrusted my wife's life and my own not just to an Italian naval captain, but also to a crew of 600 Italians! I have thouroughly enjoyed every minute of the experience. And why not? Three outdoor swimming pools, air-conditioned staterooms, 31 different public rooms, each decorated in murals and panels of rare woods, mirrors and mosaics. But the *Cristoforo Colombo* is not just a floating luxury hotel. She is a ship, one of the largest and fastest in the world, a living testament to the artistry, craftsmanship and industry of the Italian people. She is unique.

As I ponder these things, lounging against the rail of this magnificent ship, I find it hard to rationalize how the Italy of 1944 has become the Italy of 1956. Try as I might, I cannot understand it. It is truly 'a puzzle wrapped in an enigma'.

While the *Cristoforo Colombo* docks, an even more perplexing thought goes through my mind concerning my former hated enemies, the Germans. A mere 12 years earlier I couldn't wait to get at their throats. Now the latest model of one of the finest automobile makers in the world awaits me on the docks at Naples — a Mercedes-Benz from Stuttgart.

What am I doing on an Italian luxury liner, waiting to pick up a German automobile? What was accomplished by all the killing, all the destruction to this beautiful land? There is no answer. There never will be an answer. I look out across the bay, into the hills surrounding the harbour and see the inscrutable face of old Mount Vesuvius. Centuries before it had vented its displeasure with human frailty by engulfing the populace. Perhaps it will do so once again. But please not before I have had a chance to enjoy driving my fine German automobile along the super Italian highways, constructed by the descendants of the great road builders of ancient Rome.

Thankfully, these confused thoughts are brought to an abrupt conclusion by the voice of the ship's purser: "The *Cristoforo Colombo* will dock shortly. Please prepare to disembark."

My wife and I set foot on the dock and shortly after drive south in our Mercedes towards Sicily, the first leg of a memorable 7,000 mile pilgrimage to the battlefields of the PPCLI in Sicily, Italy and Northwest Europe. This long journey will awake many stirring memories but I will never forget my voyage on the *Cristoforo Colombo*.

I must give thanks to a force more powerful than even Mount Vesuvius for bringing me home safely from my pilgrimage in 1956 — none other than old Field Marshal F F Fate himself. The war had been over for some years and he was now quite elderly, but being a field marshal he was not allowed to retire. It was a good rule, because, in his mature years, he at last gave me substantial support. It happened this way.

Early in 1956 I was planning my European trip. After mapping out the general itinerary and time available, the next thing was to reserve a berth on an ocean liner. The main purpose of my tour was to see Italy; the shortest route was from New York to Naples, and was serviced by the Italian Line which had recently commissioned two of the fastest liners afloat, the *Cristoforo Colombo* and the *Andrea Doria,* named after two of Italy's most illustrious sea captains.

It didn't take me long to decide to take the Italian Line. The only question was the dates. I had planned to be away about eight weeks, leaving the end of May and returning about July 24th. It turned out my plans fitted perfectly with the schedules of the Italian Line. The *Cristoforo Colombo* left New York on May 29th for Naples. The *Andrea Doria* left Naples July 19th, arriving at New York on July 26th. If I preferred, I could catch the ship at Cannes, on the French Riviera.

What could be finer! An opportunity to travel on not one, but two of the most modern ships in the world! I made my reservations and paid a deposit.

During the next few weeks I refined my land routes in Sicily, Italy, Switzerland, Germany, Holland and France and found that it would be almost impossible to cover everything in six weeks, allowing 16 days for sea voyages. Furthermore, I could not go all this long distance and not hop across the Channel to see my good friends in England, especially the Cartons and the McArthurs. When I added up this extra time (today I would factor it into the equation and probably never get the answer) I found that I needed about eight weeks instead of six. This would mean a drastic change in plan — cancelling my return voyage on the *Andrea Doria* from Naples or Cannes and booking another liner sailing from England or northern France.

The first liner I thought of was the *Queen Elizabeth* but its date of departure did not fit my new schedule. Then I tried the *Queen Mary* but it was fully booked. However, the Cunard people could offer me accommodation on the *Ivernia* which would suit my itinerary; if space became available on the *Queen Mary* I could switch bookings.

I went back to the Italian Line and told them my new plans. They were 'not amused'. They pointed out, quite rightly, that a return passage on the Italian Line would be cheaper than one-way tickets on two separate lines. Besides, the *Queen Mary* was an old crock, fit for the Italian equivalent of Davey Jones' locker!

At this point I was so far over my head that this extra expense really didn't matter. I cancelled my voyage on the *Andrea Doria* and booked the *Ivernia*. A few weeks later, accommodation became available on the *Queen Mary* and I took it.

The *Queen Mary* sailed from Southampton on August 1st and safely landed my wife and me at New York on August 7th. The *Andrea Doria* left Naples on July 17th, collided with the Swedish ship *Stockholm* on the night of July 25th and sank to the bottom.

Field Marshal F F Fate had finally paid me his debt in full.

On September 4th, 1944, the *Orontes* docked at Naples and within an hour the troops were taken off the ship and embussed in lorries for 2Bn, 1 CBRD (2nd Battalion, No 1 Canadian Base Reinforcement Depot) at Avellino. A more ideal spot for a camp would be hard to imagine. Set in vineyards and olive groves in the high hills of the Campania, the Depot was only 35 miles east of Naples and about 20 miles north of Salerno, the beginning of the breathtaking Amalfi drive to Sorrento. A few miles to the west, Mount Vesuvius dominated the countryside and the towns of Pompeii and Herculaneum it had buried so long ago.

It was indeed a splendid site, and I envied the staff their fine eye for appreciating ground. I also found that for the first time ever, I was an inmate of a reinforcement depot that was well organized: large marquees; ample space to store kit; clean indoor ablutions. A few yards away a real officers' mess served excellent meals at tables, with waiters in white coats.

"We've got to hand it to you base wallahs," I admitted to a member of the staff after enjoying a splendid five-course dinner, "any damn fool can be uncomfortable." My kindly attitude was no doubt influenced by the warm reception the staff had given me and the excellent quality of the wine. But, above all, I was happy to be on the last leg of my long journey home to the PPCLI. I reported to father:

> *Everything down here seems to be going well. The organization is good, so different from the shambles of Sicily. Where I am now quartered has better accommodation, facilities, etc. than in England! I find it hard to reconcile this with the old days when we had to scrounge round the country on our own for food, cook it ourselves, and sleep on the side of a hill. In town there is a swanky officers' club-hotel run jointly by Army and Wops.*
>
> *Gone are the days when one could 'take over' a town and lay down the law, as I did in Ispica. The Wops are pretty well off here, and govern themselves for the greater part. It is so funny to see painted on all the walls 'Viva Stalin, Viva Communismo'. Just a year ago it was 'Viva Democrazia', and a year before that 'Viva Mussolini'. So the Wops are as crazy as ever.*
>
> *It appears that I shall be here in 2Bn, 1CRBD for a while before going up to 4Bn, and a longer wait till I get to the Regiment. My prospects of doing any fighting this time are getting less and less.*

Once again my amateur appreciation of the strategic situation was way off the mark. The PPCLI was in action again and had been having heavy casualties. I would be in the thick of it in less than two weeks.

Late in the evening of September 5th, Corky (Capt George Corkett) and I received a warning order to be ready to move next morning to 4Bn, 1CRBD on the Adriatic coast, near Ancona. We left Avellino at 0900 hours and followed Highway No 6, the ancient road to Rome, also known as the Via Casilina. Soon the massive Monte Cassino loomed ahead, crowned by an enormous pile of rubble that had once been the famed Benedictine Abbey. At the foot of the mountain lay the ruins of the town of Cassino, levelled to the ground as if a giant bulldozer had swept through the area.

We entered the Liri Valley and passed through the remains of the vaunted Hitler Line where the Patricias had suffered so terribly in May. Even though three months had passed since these savage battles, evidence of the fighting was everywhere — burnt out tanks and vehicles, both enemy and our own; shattered pill boxes, Panther turrets, anti-tank guns; blown bridges, road blocks, diversions; fields and woods shorn of all vegetation; temporary graves.

We drove on through all this appalling destruction, past Frosinone, where the Patricias had finally come to rest in May, and reached Rome at 1700 hours. It had taken all day, but this was nothing compared to the months it had taken the fighting troops to break through to the Eternal City. For them it must indeed have seemed like an eternity.

As we drove through the streets of Rome, clogged with traffic, including to my surprise, some civilian vehicles, I tried to identify the sights. Our driver knew his way around, having taken many a draft of reinforcements this way. We entered the Via dei Fori Imperiali and stopped for a moment to admire the most famous of all the monuments of ancient Rome, the Colosseum. Our driver took pains to tell us it was also known as the Flavian Amphitheatre. Passing the Arch of Constantine and the Forum we entered the Piazza Venezia and saw the balcony of the Palazzo Venezia where the deposed Mussolini once stood to harangue his fascist legions. At the other end of the Piazza rose the white marble mass of the Victor Emmanuel II Monument and the Tomb of the Unknown Soldier, dominating the whole area. Our driver told us, however, not to be overly impressed. The proud Romans, so conscious of their ancient glories, deride this 'modern' monstrosity (built 1885-1911) and refer to it as 'the wedding cake'.

By this time the driver was getting a little edgy, having been behind the wheel some nine hours, and wanted to drop us off at our billets for the night and do a little 'sightseeing' on his own. I persuaded him, however, to take us to the Vatican City to admire for a few moments the magnificence of Saint Peter's. The other sights and treasures of ancient Rome would have to await another visit, if someone would ever be good enough to give me leave.

Our billets turned out to be a modern hotel, or at least a modernized old hotel, with the familiar name of 'Chateau Laurier', on the Via Cavour. Its real name was the Hotel Massimo d'Azeglio. I made a mental note of the place for future operations.

Next morning, September 7th, Corky and I were up at the crack of dawn to get an early start on our long journey through the Apennines to the Adriatic coast. Our route lay to the north, through Terni, Spoleto and Foligno to Jesi, about ten miles from the Adriatic and 20 miles from the coastal town of Ancona. Again it was a long, hot drive in heavy traffic; all the bridges had been blown by the retreating Germans and some of the towns were badly damaged, but nothing like the destruction in the Liri Valley.

We arrived at 4Bn, 1CBRD at 1700 hours, in a torrential downpour that momentarily cooled the intense heat. I stood out in the rain and gave my hide and filthy bush uniform a good soaking, their first in Italy. I was surprised how hot it was and how badly I was out of condition. A year ago, I was in the very tip of the Italian 'toe', at Reggio, at least 500 miles south of Jesi, and the heat had not seemed to bother me then. After a moment's reflection, I realized that only a week earlier I had been in hospital on the *Orontes* with malaria. Little wonder I felt exhausted, was bothered with bronchitis and had difficulty adjusting to the heat. As luck would have it, the whole coastal area was suffering a blistering heat wave that was most unusual for this time of year.

By now I was so accustomed to old Field Marshal Fate throwing all sorts of curve balls at me that I was determined not to strike out just when I was on the verge of joining my Regiment again. I was certain that a few more nights' sleep and a steady increase in physical exertion would cure my ills. Once again my training at RMC kept me going.

As soon as we reported to the Orderly Room at 4 battalion and got ourselves organized, Corky and I went looking for Patricias. We soon found them — V S (Vaughan) Allan, my classmate from RMC, who was now a captain; W H J (Bill) Stutt, also a captain; W D L (Bill) Roach, soon to win a DSO; and E A (Ernie) Shone. From them we learned that LCol Ware had left the Regiment on June 29 for extended leave, long overdue, and then for other employment. LCol D H Rosser was now in command, with Maj R P Clark as Second-in-Command. It was sad news for me, as it was for all Patricias, to hear that LCol Ware had gone. He had made me his first Scout and Sniper officer; helped and encouraged me in forming the platoon; appointed me again when I returned after a bout with malaria. During the few weeks that followed he had entrusted me with the task of being his 'eyes and ears'. I would have done anything for him. He had given me a unique opportunity to serve the Regiment, for which I would always be grateful.

His boisterous laugh and sometimes casual manner belied a quiet determination and an intense dedication to his Regiment. The officers and men loved him and he repaid their devotion by his constant concern for their welfare.

The Regimental Historian describes in brief, but moving words the send-off given LCol Ware.

> *He was sped upon his way with roaring cheers but there was a*
> *catch in many throats, for LCol Ware had been the very body*
> *of the Regiment throughout his period of command and his loss*
> *was equivalent to that of an essential member.[1]*

News that LCol David Rosser was now commanding officer came as a surprise. Assuredly he was qualified from a staff point of view to take command, but he had had little battle experience. He had arrived at the Regiment as a major in March, 1944 and became second-in-command in May when Rowan Coleman left to command The Loyal Edmonton Regiment. He had never commanded a Patricia company in action, which to me and all other experienced officers was the litmus test for a prospective Commanding Officer. I had nothing against David Rosser personally, but I had severe reservations about a system that would allow an officer to become a Commanding Officer, or a Second-in-Command, without being given a real test in battle. It was unfair to the officer concerned, it was unfair to the officers who had been fighting with the Regiment for months, and above all it was unfair to the men who deserved the very best leadership available. There was no lack of good, fighting officers in the Regiment, who had landed in Sicily — Slug Clark, Bucko Watson, Colin McDougall, Patty Crofton, Sam Potts, to name a few who had led companies time and time again with distinction.

Indeed, in the Italian campaign, I would rate an experienced company commander miles ahead of a staff-trained Commanding Officer who had not seen his fair share of battle. Without this experience, a Commanding Officer is simply not credible to the men he has to lead. When all the chips are down it is the company commander who will win the battle, and deserves the promotion to Commanding Officer. Eric Linklater understood the worth of a battle experienced company commander:

> *The general who has made a plan for a successful battle will*
> *believe that his plan was the main cause of success, but the*
> *Company Commander and his company who have fought all day*
> *and by their valour and tactical ability have dislodged the enemy*
> *from an important position will remain convinced that it is they*
> *who have tipped the balance toward victory.[2]*

The appointment of Maj 'Slug' Clark as Second-in-Command was quite another matter. He had landed in Sicily in charge of A Company; he had fought both with the Regiment and with The Loyal Edmonton Regiment and was an aggressive and determined company commander. He would go on to become Commanding Officer when LCol Rosser was wounded on September 16th, and lead the Regiment with distinction to the end of the war.

Maj S A Cobbett would succeed Maj Clark when he took over from Rosser. Maj Cobbett was also staff-trained and came up to the Regiment as a major after the Hitler Line. He had seen a little action at the start of the Gothic Line offensive but was soon promoted to Second-in-Command and remained in that position to the end of the war.

I received news of these appointments and promotions with mixed feelings. Whoever was responsible for making such decisions was obviously not interested in my opinions but I wasn't going to lose any sleep over the matter. The important thing was to find out from my friends at 4 Battalion what the Regiment had been doing since I last had news of its battles in the Hitler Line and the Liri Valley in May.

I learned that after passing throught Frosinone on June 1st, the Regiment went into reserve on June 7th in the Piedimonte D'Alife area in the mountains north of Naples, about 30 miles southwest of Frosolone, where I had been wounded the previous October. There, the battalion rested and trained until July 27th when it took part in a gigantic deception plan to create the impression that the Canadians were going to attack in the area of Florence, whereas in fact they would assault the Gothic Line on the Adriatic coast near Rimini. To carry off the plan, 1st Canadian Division would be moved in great secrecy to battle positions on the Arno River, near Florence, and there make their presence known to the enemy.

Unbeknown to anyone at the time, except commanders and staff officers at the highest level, there were in fact two plans for the employment of the Canadians in Italy. The first plan was for 1st Canadian Corps actually to attack the Germans in the Florence area. This required an elaborate scheme to create the impression that the corps was assembling on the Adriatic Coast. This plan was, however, changed while the Canadians were moving into the Florence sector. The new plan called for the Canadians actually to assault the Gothic Line on the Adriatic coast, which in turn required a new deception plan to create the impression the Canadians were going to attack in the Florence area. Whether all these plans and deceptions fooled the Germans is a matter of dispute, but they undoubtedly gave Canadian staff officers a lot of unpaid, overtime work.[3]

On July 27th the Patricias embussed, made their way back to Highway 6, and turned north toward Rome, passing Cassino, and Frosinone. At Rome they took the Flaminian Way north through Orvieto, then left the main highway, followed the west shore of Lake Trasimene and camped near Siena. Finally, on August 6th, the Regiment reached the sector allotted to them in the second cover plan — a position a few hundred yards south of the Arno River, one mile south and two miles west of the centre of Florence, which was held by German paratroopers.

The Regiment, believing they had made the desired impression on the enemy, within a day or two secretly withdrew from the line, embussed, and

273

were borne southward, via Siena, Arezza and the northern shore of Lake Trasimene, to a 'hiding' place near Perugia. There, the Regiment camped and waited while the final preparations for the master plan unfolded.

On August 18th, the Patricias embussed once more for their new (and real) battle ground — the Gothic Line on the Adriatic coast, south of Rimini. Their route took them west along Highway 76 to Jesi, where they turned north and proceeded to a concentration area for their first attack — the crossing of the Metauro River, about 30 miles north of Jesi.

In the evening of August 25th the battalion crossed the river in silence and gained its first objective without encountering any resistance — surprise had been achieved. The 8th Army had moved more quickly than the Germans had expected and had attacked before they were ready. Furthermore the assault had not come where it had been expected.[4]

The Patricias now moved forward to their next objective, Osteria Nuova in the main Gothic Line fortifications, about one mile north of the Foglia River. Fording the stream in the early hours of August 31st, the Regiment ran into a mine field and suffered casualties, including their popular padre Hon Capt K Eaton who was blown up on a schu mine while going to the aid of the wounded in the mine field. Lt E E (Egan) Chambers was awarded the MC for leading his company through the deadly ground.[5]

The Patricias pressed on and gained their objective, after killing the German commander and capturing the remainder of the garrison.

The Regiment was then ordered to assist the West Nova Scotia Regiment on the right who had not made headway because of stubborn enemy resistance at Point 133. Mounting the supporting tanks, the Patricias wheeled to the right and charged the enemy position, killing 20 Germans and capturing 95 prisoners.

By dawn on September 2nd the Regiment had gained its final objective one mile southeast of Gradara. The Gothic Line had been smashed and the enemy beaten; but the tough German paratroopers were not yet finished with the Regiment. They would exact their tribute at the next battleground — San Fortunato in the Rimini Line.

The battalion then went into reserve and was withdrawn to Cattolica, a small seaside town that had been a favourite German resort before the war. The Patricias were still resting at Cattolica on September 7th when Corky and I, having just arrived at 4 Battalion, received all this exciting news of their exploits. We were exhilarated to hear how well the Regiment had done and happy to be at last among our own people. At the same time it was depressing to have missed so much action in the almost eleven months I had been away.

The terrible battles of the Moro River and the Hitler Line I was familiar with, but I had mixed feelings about them. On the one hand I had honestly to admit that I was lucky not to have been involved; on the other, I had a nagging feeling of guilt. To those battles was now added the breaching of the Gothic Line; but perhaps I would yet see action in the final stages of that engagement. I was not to be denied this wish.

News of our arrival at 4 Battalion near Jesi, soon reached the Regiment at Cattolica only 50 miles away. Maj Clark, Capt A M (Andy) Campbell and Capt A S (Snuffy) Ennis-Smith came down to see us and the other reinforcement officers, and give us the 'score'. Casualties had been heavy in the recent engagements and more were expected in the forthcoming operations. We need have no fear that our services would not soon be required.

Andy Campbell and Snuffy Smith took us into nearby Ancona for a further 'briefing and appreciation of the situation'. Our discussions were hardly brief, nor were they appreciated next morning when we crept back to camp. But it was glorious to be so close to home and enjoying the camaraderie of brother officers.

The next few days were taken up with further briefings both serious and for fun. We found that Maj Colin McDougall was down with malaria again at 1 Canadian General Hospital at Jesi. I took off an afternoon and went in to see him. We soon remembered that we had both had malaria a year earlier in Sicily and were in hospital together in Catania. Apparently the bug had surfaced again, as it was known to do, and knocked us out. The attack, fortunately, was not nearly as serious, for either of us, as the earlier one. We wondered if the fever would come back to haunt us next September but we didn't waste much time worrying about that.

The Patricias left Cattolica on September 15th to rejoin the battle. While they had been at rest, other formations had been carrying on the fight to capture Rimini — Greek Brigade, 5th Canadian Armoured Division and other elements of 1st Canadian Infantry Division. The Germans had resisted fiercely and had thrown in five fresh divisions to save Rimini. The Canadians had suffered heavy casualties, particularly the armoured division. Now it was the turn of the Patricias.

Our final objective would be to cross the Marecchia River, to the west of Rimini. But before that river was reached the last line defending the Lombardy Plains had to be broken — the Rimini Line, which included a formidable feature, San Fortunato Ridge.

Those two words, Rimini and San Fortunato will be remembered as long as the Regiment exists — they are emblazoned on its Regimental Colours.

Early on September 19th, I was warned for duty with the PPCLI.

Chapter XXI

SAN FORTUNATO RIDGE MARECCHIA RIVER

September 19 to September 23, 1944

We will debouch into the Valley of the Po
We will deal the Hun a mighty, mighty blow
We will debouch into the Po
This we know, for Corps says so
Onward to Bologna, onward to the Po

September 19, 1944 - 1400 hours

Leaving Jesi with Capt Corkett, Lt W D Roach and a draft of men, I head north toward the Regiment, some 60 miles distant. The last few miles through the recent battlefields of 1st and 5th Canadian Divisions are still littered with the offal of the past week's fighting. The devastation is horrible and reminds me of Cassino and the Liri Valley; but now the feeling of death and destruction is immediate and unsettling.

What were once proud Tiger and Churchill tanks are now blackened, twisted hulks. Whole towns and villages have disappeared, except for ugly piles of rubble. On each side of our dirt track through the vineyards are signs, *Achtung Minen*. To veer off the trail means instant destruction. Fresh graves show where some of the fiercest battles have raged. On some, the only indication of whether the grave is friend or foe is a Canadian or German helmet atop a rifle or rough wooden marker.

Ahead, the sounds of battle grow louder and fiercer. We pass our own medium artillery heavily engaged in a shoot; a little later a battery of 25 pounders shake the ground with their salvos.

276

The mass of San Fortunato looms before us in the failing light. We can go no farther in daylight. The ground ahead is being heavily shelled by everything the Germans have in their arsenal — 105s, 88s, 75s, Moaning Minnies.

We gingerly pull off the road and wait for nightfall to hide our movement. Then a squadron of Churchill tanks grinds past and halts, inviting the enemy to engage in a duel with armour-piercing shells. We quickly leave the vehicle, form up and march along the side of the road, hoping the verges have been cleared of mines. Soon, we see the PPCLI Tac sign-60.*

September 19 — 2100 hours

We move off the track and find rear BHQ in a demolished *casa*. It has taken us seven hours to cover the 60-odd miles from Jesi. The Adjutant, Capt Andy Mills, greets our little band of reinforcements with obvious relief. The Regiment has had a bad time since returning to action on September 16th. On that very day, Tac HQ (Tactical battalion headquarters) received a direct hit and the CO, LCol Rosser, was wounded. Maj Clark immediately took over and is now the Colonel.

The battalion has been under intense shellfire ever since. On September 17th, while advancing to the kick-off position for an attack, Capt L G Burton, OC of Charlie Company, was killed by an enemy shell and Lt H E Dalquist took command; he was soon wounded and command passed to Lt J W MacNeill. On the same day, Dog Company lost 31 men from shellfire, including 14 men in one platoon who were killed or wounded by a single salvo.

Yesterday (September 18th), the battalion was ordered to attack a railway embankment just south of the Ausa River. By 0800 hours half the rifle strength of Baker and Dog companies were casualties; Maj Patty Crofton, OC of Dog Company, was wounded again and Maj Colin McDougall took command of both companies. At 1000 hours Baker and Dog Companies, with only 60 men, dug in near the railway. Total casualties for September 18th were 67. Most of the tanks accompanying the forward companies have been knocked out; their commander has been killed.

This morning (September 19th), the Regiment secured a crossing over the Ausa River and is dug in some 200 yards north of the river. Casualties today have been at least 15.

The enemy is paying dearly for the punishment he has inflicted on us. Scores of his dead litter the battlefield and many prisoners have been taken, including paratroopers. The survivors have withdrawn to their last bastion guarding the northern plains of Italy, the San Fortunato feature, lying about

---

*Every battalion was given a tactical number which the battalion displayed on its vehicles and signs.

two miles to the northwest.

This obstacle and one other, San Martino lying to the right of us, have been the cause of most of our troubles. From these ridges the Germans have had complete observation of every move we have made in the past three days.

At this very moment practically the whole 1st Division is attacking San Fortunato. Our turn comes tomorrow.

Capt Mills tells me to report to Dog Company, Capt Sam Potts, about 2,000 yards ahead. A guide will take me there. Suddenly I realize I have no weapon. When I left 4 Battalion this morning I requested not only a service revolver but also a rifle or a Tommy Gun. No sane platoon commander would try to take on these paratroopers with a single shot revolver. What was needed was stopping power and distance. A submachine gun would be perfect.

4 Battalion had no weapon of any sort to issue and told me I would have to get one at the Regiment. Andy Mills is annoyed that I am not armed. There are no spare weapons here or at Tac HQ. My best chance is to pick one up from a recent casualty. A guide from Dog Company appears out of the darkness. Andy suggests I had better get going. They will need all the bodies they can muster for the attack tomorrow.

Corky and I shake hands. I ask him what he is going to do about a weapon. In typical fashion he flourishes his shooting stick. "No trouble at all. I'll give Jerry a good prod in the backside with this." We say goodbye and I trudge north toward the sound of the guns. I will never see Corky alive again.

September 19 — 2200 hours

I set off with the guide to find Dog Company about 2,000 yards straight ahead. We are not going to bother reporting in at Tac HQ who have their hands full planning tomorrow's battle. Despite what Andy Mills has said, one officer will not make much difference to the outcome of the battle, particularly an officer without a weapon.

We follow the line of attack Baker and Dog companies took yesterday, past the evil San Martino feature on our right, now in friendly hands, and through the remains of vineyards, on the flats leading to the Ausa River. Hulks of Churchill tanks that had supported Baker and Dog companies' death march to the river loom out of the darkness.

Soon we reach the railway embankment where Baker and Dog companies finally arrived with Maj Colin McDougall, Lt MacNeill and 60 men. How anyone survived the enemy fire directed from San Martino behind us and San Fortunato ahead is a miracle. We stumble over empty Patricia slit trenches dug into the embankment, and craters from large enemy shells. Many trenches have received a direct hit and bits of equipment and uniforms are strewn about. I half expect to see corpses of the dead, but the Padre has done his job quickly and well. Some of the trenches have been turned into temporary graves with neat white crosses at the head and shell torn helmets or rifles stuck in the ground at the foot. I am still without a weapon. I am tempted to check the rifles of these fallen Patricias and take the first one that will work. Something holds me back.

We continue along the track, cross the Ausa River on a bridge just completed by the engineers, and move forward another two or three hundred yards. This is where Dog Company is supposed to be dug in, but there is no sign of them or anyone else. Ahead, about 1,500 yards, San Fortunato rises abruptly from the plain. The whole feature is aglow with tracers, bursting shells, Verey lights and parachute flares. Every few minutes a sheet of flame shoots into the air and a tremendous explosion rolls down the slopes. Another tank has 'brewed up' — Tiger or Churchill, I do not know. Other explosions rent the air, as artillery from both sides pound the area. Soon fires are raging all along the ridge and down into the flat ground just ahead. Clouds of smoke from the artillery, and dust from the destruction, overhang the battlefield and are silhouetted by a full moon.

I ask my guide what's going on. All he knows is that our division is trying to take San Fortunato from a panzer grenadier division supported by a parachute battalion and seven other battalions packed along the ridge.

This is war on the grand scale, the likes of which I have never seen before. I am fascinated but apprehensive of the outcome.

I remember joining the Regiment in the middle of a night attack on Monte Seggio in Sicily. Pray God I will not be thrown into the attack tomorrow without any chance of being briefed or of getting my platoon organized. While the guide stumbles around trying to locate Dog Company, I see a shell hole that seems to offer some cover. I decide to have a cigarette. One more small light is not going to bother anyone with so many fires raging across the valley. I shield my lighter and flick the wheel. In an instant six voices from six different directions yell at me from the darkness: "Put out that goddamn light."

I have located Dog Company — if not by the approved method, at least by the quickest one. Immediately a very angry sergeant jumps into my hole, "Sorry, Sir. We have been catching hell from Jerry's artillery the past five days. He seems to have forgotten about us the last two hours and we want to keep it that way."

I understand the sergeant perfectly and apologize. By way of explanation for my sins, I offer that the battlefield is lit up, almost like daylight, by a full moon.

"Full moon? There's no moon, Sir. It's anti-aircraft searchlights from the rear lighting up San Fortunato and demoralizing the enemy, while we advance on the dark low ground ahead."

I have now committed two blunders and the third is on the tip of my tongue, when the sergeant beats me to it.

"And by the way, Sir, where is your weapon?"

I tell him the story of how I have been sent forward unarmed, with instructions to pick up a rifle or Tommy gun on the way. I can feel the sergeant's contempt when he speaks.

"You'll find no rifle or Tommy gun up here that's any good. There's lots of Schmeissers around but I wouldn't recommend them. You're liable to get shot by your own men before you run out of ammo. I suppose you know that German machine guns don't take our 303?"

I have one other question but it, too, will probably explode in my face. I try it anyway. "Where is Capt Potts? I'd like to know which platoon I'll be taking over."

"Capt Potts is away at an 'O' Group for the attack tomorrow. You'll be commanding my platoon. I have a wound in the leg that needs attending to. I'm going back to the RAP as soon as Capt Potts gets here."

"What about the men? They must be pretty beat?"

"They're beat all right and need rest. Better get some yourself. I'll call you when Capt Potts returns. You're okay in this shell hole. It's better than my slit over there about 30 yards."

The sergeant limps off to his trench. I hunker down to the bottom of mine and carefully light up another cigarette.

September 20 — 0600 hours

The first streaks of dawn appear over the Adriatic. We have been standing to for the past half-hour, in drenching rain. The battle of San Fortunato, less than a mile away, has raged all night. Never have I seen or heard such a concentration of artillery fire on one objective. Surely our attackers have prevailed. No enemy, not even paratroopers, can withstand such a hail of high explosives and lead.

Capt Sam Potts appears out of the early morning haze of smoke and mist. "Hi, Syd, what the devil are you doing sliming in that shell hole?"

Sam hasn't changed a bit and is his usual bluff, aggressive self. The best retort I can think of is a line from the First War: "If you know a better hole, go to it, Sam."

With a sound clap on the back he kneels beside me and quickly puts me in the picture. The Eddies (The Loyal Edmonton Regiment) and the Seaforths (The Seaforth Highlanders of Canada) of our 2nd Brigade, along with most of the other units in the 1st Division, assaulted San Fortunato Ridge last night supported by tanks and artillery. They have won the ridge and sent the Hun reeling back into the plain. It has been a bitter hand-to-hand fight with many casualties on both sides; prisoners have been taken and are now coming back through our lines.

The Patricias will move forward this morning, climb San Fortunato and make a dash for the Marecchia River, about 4,000 yards north of the ridge.

Sam is leaving now for a final 'O' Group at Tac HQ. In the meantime, Dog Company will move forward to an assembly area 1,000 yards ahead, under the lee of the ridge.

Dog Company is down to about 60 men. The only officer beside Sam and me is Lt Harrington. I will take command of 18 Platoon.

Sam briefly shows me around my platoon area and departs for his 'O' Group. The sergeant hands me a tattered notebook with a list of the men in 18 Platoon. I count the names. "Only 21 men, sergeant?"

"That's right, Sir, and two of them were slightly wounded yesterday. They want to go in with the platoon this morning but they may have to go back if their wounds start to flare up. One other guy is sick, probably malaria coming on, but he insists on sticking with the platoon."

Time is running out. Soon we must move off for the attack. I ask the sergeant to call the three section commanders together — one corporal, one lance corporal and one private. There is not much I can tell them about the battle. I listen to what they have to say. They have taken a hell of a beating from shellfire directed from those goddam ridges - San Martino and San Fortunato. Where is our artillery? Why can't they silence those Jerry 88s and Moaning Minnies? We'll be slaughtered when we hit the plain and charge for the Marecchia River.

I tell them that San Fortunato is at last in our hands and now we'll be able to direct our artillery from the ridge onto the enemy in the plain. Besides, our air force is standing by ready to beat them up as soon as we attack. (No one has told me this, but from my observation of the activity in the last 48 hours it seems a reasonable assumption.) On top of all this, we'll be supported by tanks to take on the Tigers.

The section commanders return to their men and the sergeant leaves for the RAP. I realize I have not said anything they haven't heard a hundred times before. I feel they have very little confidence in a fresh platoon commander, coming into the middle of a battle. I know they would much rather have their sergeant back. I am angry that I have again been thrown into battle in this way but I realize it can't be helped. Old Field Marshal Fate has had his way once more.

In a few minutes we will have to move. I quickly go round my platoon area and say a few words of encouragement to each man. I have done all I can do.

September 20 — 0830 hours

Orders are received to move immediately to the assembly area, 1,000 yards ahead. I am surprised how small Dog Company looks on the ground as we trudge forward — hardly the strength of two platoons. But if we are short in numbers, we are long on determination. The Patricias have been selected to make the charge to the river; we are going to succeed, despite the casualties and lack of sleep during the past four days. At the assembly area we shake out into battle formation and 'marry up' with the tanks of B Squadron, 48 Royal Tank Regiment that will support us in the assault.

San Fortunato rises only 500 yards ahead. The tank commander is concerned how the tanks will negotiate the steep slopes of the feature now made greasy from the rains during the previous night.

September 20 — 1300 hours

Capt Sam Potts arrives back from the 'O' Group at Tac HQ and gives his platoon commanders the plan of attack. The Patricias will capture crossings over the Marecchi River. The Regiment will first climb the San Fortunato feature, advance to jump-off positions in the Edmonton area, code-named Bovey and Moire (San Lorenzo) then push for the river.

There are two intermediate objectives before the Marecchi is reached: Nylon (Monticello) 1,000 yards past Moire, and Pique a further 1,000 yards past Nylon. At Pique the Regiment will deploy for the crossing, about 1,500 yards ahead.

Baker and Charlie companies will advance to Bovey and then to Moire to secure a firm base for the attack. Then Charlie Company will attack Nylon supported by tanks. As soon as Nylon is 'snug', Baker Company will capture Pique. Finally, Able and Dog companies will establish the bridgehead. Dog Company will move off at 1500 hours.

"Any questions?" asks Capt Potts, knowing there are many doubts in the minds of the platoon commanders, especially in mine. But the platoon commanders also know that doubts don't count as questions; they have already been erased from the mind.

September 20 — 1500 hours

Dog Company crosses the start line and moves forward to climb San Fortunato. The past two hours have been hell. Jerry knows we are preparing to attack and has been blasting the assembly area and FUP (Forming Up Place) with his artillery. We have no cover. Our slit trenches are far behind. There is nothing we can do but stand and take it. At least we are in the lee of San Fortunato and the low trajectory shells can't get us. But Jerry has the answer — deadly air-bursts from his 88s. Now the shells come in like express trains. Casualties begin to mount. Calls for 'stretcher bearer' fill the air. Finally, we are on the move. We start to climb in single file.

An air burst explodes a few yards in front of me. Two men from another platoon fall. The platoon keeps climbing up the slope, leaving the two men face downward on the trail. As I reach them, the column halts for a moment. I take a quick look. Blood is trickling from somewhere underneath their bodies but their backs are unharmed. I roll one over to check if he is still alive. He is not. His face is a mess of pulp. The second one is also dead.

A piece of steel has severed his throat.

The column starts to move again. Now the Germans are sending in their Moaning Minnies. But the column forges ahead. I look back at my boys. Not a man has dropped out of line or gone to ground.

Only 200 more yards to the summit where a large white *casa* might offer temporary shelter. Suddenly a shell crashes into the house, blows away a corner room and sends chunks of masonry over the approaching troops.

The trail is now a sea of mud. Our tanks and anti-tank guns cannot climb the steep, greasy slope. We will have to fight without them.

At last we gain the crest. We huddle in the lee of the white house to get our bearings. Our next firm base is Bovey, hopefully still in the hands of the Edmontons. I look at my map. Bovey is off to the left, about 1,000 yards distant, on the northern slopes of San Fortunato that gradually fall to the plain.

From our position on the summit an incredible sight now unfolds. In the plain directly ahead of us, only 700 yards away, are six Tiger tanks and a party of German Infantry with mortars and Moaning Minnies. Oblivious to our gaze, the mortar crews are loading and firing at us as if on a range practice. Meanwhile the tanks move about the area sending their deadly missiles into what remains of our sheltering white house.

Capt J R Koensgen and his MMG Platoon will not stand for this arrogant display. They charge ahead in their carriers, down the slope and scatter the infantry and gun crews. The Tigers are not intimidated. They respond by knocking out a carrier.

Dog Company prepares to move down the slope to Bovey before descending into the plain. We hear the grinding and clanking of tanks behind us. Three Churchills churn over the crest and head along the trail to Bovey, in full sight of the waiting Tigers. We see the Tigers elevate the barrels of their 88s. In a second we hear the sickening sound of steel through steel and then a tremedous explosion. The rear Churchill blows up. Instantly the lead Churchill meets the same fate. The middle tank is now a sitting duck for the expert German gunners. They calmly dispatch it with one round. Some of the crews escape from their burning tanks, but most do not.

It is all over so quickly that at first I do not realize the consequences of this drama enacted before my very eyes. Slowly the significance of the action becomes clear. Somehow, three of our tanks were able to climb the summit despite the mud and steep incline. Now they are gone and we have to advance into the plain against those Tigers without any tanks of our own.

I gather my platoon together and start for Bovey, still in full view of the Germans on the flats below. They are not interested in my little band. They are keeping their fire for bigger and better prey — tanks and vehicles. Ahead lies a sunken road that will protect us if the Germans change their minds and start machine gunning and mortaring us. We race forward and our way is blocked — blocked by a heap of German dead — 20 or 30 of them. They had taken shelter from the bombardment, in caves dug into the sides of the sunken road. When the barrage lifted, they came out of their holes to take up their battle positions on the crest of the hill. But the Edmontons were too quick for them. They got to the positions first and caught a whole company of the enemy. All were killed, wounded or taken prisoner.

Bodies, parts of bodies, helmets, gory uniforms, shattered weapons fill the roadway. Our blood-soaked boots crunch through this obscene mess of the remains of Hitler's vanquished troops. I feel neither elation nor even satisfaction at this horrible scene — only relief that the corpses are the enemy and not our own.

We emerge from this charnel-house in the sunken roadway and see more German dead in the fields leading down to the plain. They had tried to flee the hail of the Edmontons' fire and were caught in our barrage.

September 20 — 1600 hours

Dog Company arrives at Bovey, in the Edmonton area, still without our tanks or anti-tank guns. From here we will descend into the plain. Miraculously, my platoon has suffered only two casualties from all the shelling during the advance from the start line in front of San Fortunato. We are now down to 19 men, including the two who were slightly wounded the day before and the one with suspected malaria. They are still hanging in and seem none the worse for wear. According to plan, Charlie Company is now to attack Nylon, and Baker Company to take Pique. As soon as these objectives are captured Dog Company is to head for the Marecchia at full speed.

But now information comes in that enemy tanks are in the vicinity of Nylon. Charlie Company, without its Churchills or anti-tank guns, won't have a chance against the Tigers. LCol Clark makes a bold decision.[1] He decides to by-pass Nylon and head straight for Pique. At 2030 hours he sends orders over his 18 wireless set, for Baker and Dog companies to attack Pique, but the orders do not reach them for several hours. Communications have been extremely bad all evening. The enemy jams the air, no matter how many times the wireless operators change the frequencies on their 18 sets. Static also interferes with our messsages.

The enemy now steps up his shelling, knowing that we are forming up for another attack. We dive for the slit trenches abandoned by the Germans earlier that day. Some of the former occupants are still there, clutching their Schmeissers in lifeless hands. We throw the bodies out and ignore the mess, happy to find any cover from the continuous torrent of lead falling on our platoon. But there is no escape from the stench of death.

September 21 — 0200 hours

The message LCol Clark sent at 2030 hours yesterday evening has finally got through to Baker and Dog companies. Capt Sam Potts calls an 'O' Group of his platoon commanders. I am the only other officer. Lt Harrington has just been wounded in the thigh and is being patched up. He refuses to go down the line and will remain at BHQ. Sam tells us the other companies have also suffered heavily from the shelling. Lt J W MacNeill has just been killed by a direct hit from a shell. He had taken over Charlie Company when Capt Burton was killed by shellfire on September 17th. I recall for an instant that Lt MacNeill was one of my students at Shilo and my mind flashes back to those happy days. Capt Corkett has now assumed command of Charlie Company. Total casualties today have been 58.

Sam goes over our route to Pique, on the map. First, Dog Company will advance to Moire and pick up Colin McDougall and his Baker Company. Then both companies will attack Pique. As soon as we have captured Pique, Able Company will push forward to the Marecchia, while Charlie Company sends patrols to Nylon, where the enemy is reported to be in strength with tanks. I feel concerned about Corky being thrown into battle against Tigers, in command of a company that has no tanks. For that matter I feel the same way about myself in charge of 18 Platoon, without tank support or even a personal weapon.

As soon as the 'O' Group disperses I resume my search for a Tommy gun, or anything that will fire. In between salvos of Moaning Minnies I dash from trench to trench looking for a weapon. I wrench a Schmeisser out of the death grasp of a paratrooper and try the action. It works. I search for ammunition. There is none. The paratrooper had fought on until his ammunition ran out. Finally I stumble over a Tommy gun lying beside one of our dead section commanders. I snatch it up and dive into a slit trench. Something is wrong with the action of the gun, but it does not appear to be damaged. I strip the weapon down and reassemble it. Still the action will not move. I curse the bloody thing, but I hold onto it.

There is no more time. Dog Company has started to move.

We pause at Moire to combine forces with Baker Company. I am the only officer platoon commander in both companies. I will lead both companies down the slope into the plains of northern Italy infested with a vengeful enemy supported by tanks. Sam Potts pokes me in the ribs and says what a great favour he is doing me. The PPCLI will be the first battalion of the division to break out of the mountains into the Lombardy Plains for which we have been fighting since we landed in Italy. Indeed, 1st Canadian Division will be the first Allied formation to enter the plains. This makes me the first soldier, of the leading platoon, of the leading company, of the leading battalion, of the leading division, of the whole goddamn Allied Army, to set foot on the Plains of Lombardy.

A shell whistles in and we dive for cover. There is no chance to let Sam know what I think of this special honour, or to tell him there is one other fact that makes the honour even more unique. I will be the first darn fool to do it without a weapon.

As I lead the two companies down the slope I continue to try to fix my Tommy gun. It is no use. In the darkness and constant shelling a trained artificer would have trouble finding the problem. Finally I do a silly thing. I impulsively throw the obstinate weapon into the ditch. Every man in the section behind me knows I have been struggling with a useless weapon for the past hour. Still I should have kept it. Never have I felt so vulnerable. At any moment I expect to hear a guttural voice commanding me to halt. Or will it be the sudden death blast of a Schu mine? Or bullets from a Schmeisser? I try to calm myself by thinking that whether I have a weapon or not will not make the slightest difference if the enemy get off the first burst. But that thought doesn't help. Then I tell myself that not having a weapon adds a nice touch of bravado to this special occasion Sam has provided for me. That's nonsense too. I shouldn't have thrown my weapon away. While my men knew it couldn't fire, it gave them some comfort. Perhaps it would somehow start to work again. I have placed an added burden on my leading section they don't need, as we advance through the night into the Tiger's den.

Suddenly a motor roars into life; then another and another. Tanks! We jump for the ditch and wait. Slowly the clanking fades away into the night. The tanks are withdrawing.

We are back on the road again. Soon we approach the first crossroads, cautiously leave the road, and advance through the fields on each side — crossroads are clear.

The advance continues. A second crossroads is cleared, then a third and a fourth. Here is where we should turn left and head for Pique. I start down the road with the lead section. After 50 yards I hear a familiar voice: "Where the hell do you think you are going? It's the next crossroads we turn." Sam Potts comes up. So does Colin McDougall. We confer. Sam is right. One of the 'crossroads' we had passed was little more than a trail leading off to the right. We have not yet come to the fourth crossroads.

We retrace our steps to the main road, advance another 100 yards to the fourth crossroads and turn left. Pique should be only 400 yards away. Not a sound ahead or on the flanks. Where is Jerry? Has he withdrawn from Pique and Nylon to the other side of the river? We'll soon find out.

September 21 — 0445 hours

My leading section commander taps my shoulder. He has been counting the paces since we turned down this road at the last intersection.

"Sir, I think we're almost there. Yes, there's a white building about 100 yards ahead."

286

The column stops for a moment. My section commanders come forward. I say a few words. Two sections advance on each side of the road. The third section and 2 inch mortar crew are ready to give supporting fire. The forward sections charge the house. The enemy has gone from Pique. The rest of Dog Company and Baker Company move up and occupy the position.

Sam Potts tells his wireless operator to report to Tac HQ that we have just taken Pique. The enemy and static are still interfering with our communications. Finally at 0545 hours a message gets through to LCol Clark that Pique is snug.

We have been very lucky. It's time for breakfast.

September 21 — 1000 hours

Able Company reports it has crossed the Marecchia, having met very little resistance, but is encountering some shellfire. Dog Company is warned to prepare to move across the river and take up positions on Able Company's left flank. Since arriving at Pique I have been busy checking my men in 18 Platoon and sizing them up. They are dead beat, having been in action and under constant shelling since September 16th. I have only been with them since the evening of September 19th and am beginning to feel the effect of that greatest enemy of all — lack of proper sleep. When I tell my men we will soon move off for the river they muster their last reserves and willingly fall in. They are a great bunch of lads.

I am thankful that we have had a couple of hours to rest, eat, check weapons and issue ammunition. I have managed to get my whole platoon inside a strong Itie house that provides some relief from the constant shelling; also we have had a chance to get warm, and dry out from the rain and mud of San Fortunato. Best of all, just before we move off, one of our carriers, that somehow negotiated the mud and greasy slopes, arrives with extra ammunition and weapons. I race to the vehicle as if pursued by the whole Panzer Grenadier Corps, vault into the carrier, and find two Tommy guns and several rifles.

Dog Company marches off. This time I will not have the honour of being 'the first of the first', but I don't care. I have a sturdy weapon and lots of ammunition.

We are now advancing in open order across the broad stony bed of the Marecchia. Incredibly, there is only desultory shelling. I can't understand why the Germans, so expert at laying down defensive fire, do not give us their best shot. A heavy artillery stonk on these flats would tear us to pieces. But I don't waste any time pondering the problem. Ahead, a wooden bridge has been thoughtfully left for our use. We pour over it and reach the far bank, unscathed by the air bursts. We burrow into the hard, rocky soil with a will, scarcely believing our good fortune.

No sooner have we exhausted ourselves digging slit trenches than orders are received to advance and cut the main east-west road from Rimini, the Via Emilia. This, we are told, will be our final objective. Thank God. We are near the end of our physical and mental endurance.

Dog Company pushes forward. Air bursts and Nebelwerfers continue to pour their deadly rain of lead. At last the roadway is in sight. I yell orders to my section commanders to capture a large white house and consolidate around it. The men automatically shake out into attack formation and advance in short rushes, firing from the hip. The leading section is pinned down by small arms fire from the left flank. The 2 inch mortar men quickly lay down a smoke screen. The two rear sections pass through and storm the house. I see three Germans tumble out of the building waving white flags and clasping their hands over their heads. We have taken our final objective.

Dog Company is completely out in the blue. Again, it is the lead company and the Patricias are the spearhead of the division. Able Company is about 500 yards east and south of us. On the west our left flank is wide open. From a group of houses on this flank we are still getting heavy small arms fire — Spandaus and rifle. I send a runner to company HQ to ask for artillery support. In minutes our 25 pounders saturate the area. The hostile fire ceases.

I organize all-round defence, with the house as our strong point. Platoon HQ and one section is in the house and the other sections are dug in behind and on each flank. The position is a strong one except for one thing — no tank support. Our PIATs are well sited but are no match for two or three Tigers. We might get one but the rest would blow us apart. Then I remember the enemy tanks we had by-passed at Nylon, and the tanks we heard last night. Where have they gone? Will they withdraw through our advance position? Or are they now in front of us, or on the exposed left flank?

We have to clear the decks for the expected counter-attack. Disposition of two enemy dead is easy. The three prisoners and two other wounded Germans are a problem. I hate to spare even one man to take them back to company HQ. Just then a salvo of 88s explodes outside. Two men in slit trenches are hit. Their wounds are not serious, but they will have to go back for repairs. They can take the prisoners. My platoon is now down to 17 all ranks.

It is now 1745 hours. Soon it will be last light and prime time for a German counter-attack. Nightfall will be a mixed blessing. We'll be free of the constant sniping and small arms fire from our left flank and I can move about to check my sections outside the house. But the Germans can also infiltrate our thinly held perimeter. It will be another sleepless night.

September 22, — 0530 hours

We stand to. Jerry has not bothered us during the night except for intermittent shelling. Will he make his last effort now? One hour passes, then another. Still no attack, but the shellfire has increased.

Suddenly a sickening crash shakes the house; then another and another. Chunks of stone, wood and plaster fly around the large downstairs room where I have my platoon HQ and one section. A lance corporal who was keeping a lookout upstairs comes tumbling down the stairs, his head covered in blood. "Christ, those were big ones. The front room is a shambles."

While the dust settles I help him dress his wounds. There's a large gash in his forehead, but it is only a flesh wound. He'll be OK when he gets over the shock.

I call for a volunteer to go back upstairs and keep a sharp lookout. A little guy jumps up and mounts the stairs. He barely makes it to the top when another brace of heavies crashes into the upstairs rooms blasting the poor little guy back down the stairs. He picks himself up and starts up the stairs again. I hold him back. I won't let him press his luck any further. A second earlier and he would have joined the bits of plaster, bricks and dust now flying around us.

Outside, the Nebelwerfers are covering every inch of ground. I can't see how any of my men in slits can survive this constant bombardment. I go to the rear door to rush outside and contact my two flanking section commanders. I am almost bowled over by one of them as he hurtles through the doorway.

"God Almighty, the bastards are throwing everything they've got at us. Never seen anything like it." He collapses at my feet.

He has been wounded in the arm. It is broken. He has lost blood, probably a lot. I dress the wound and put the arm in a rough sling.

"Sir, you've got to let those men come into the house. Two other guys in my section are also wounded. If they stay out there much longer, there won't be any left."

I agree. The only problem is to get word to the men and get them in the house between the short breaks in the stonks. I go to the door again and look out. The other section commander is standing in his trench. He sees me. I give him a sign to bring all the men into the house. In minutes they are inside.

I make a quick appreciation of the situation. The 2nd New Zealand Division is supposed to relieve us today. The 5th Canadian Armoured Division is also coming up on our left flank. They can't be far away. Jerry hasn't attacked us yet and won't when he sees the armoured divisions pouring through. All we have to do is survive his awful shelling for another few hours. Our house is our only refuge.

I quickly survey what's left of our *casa*. By now the two upstairs rooms have been shot away, and the 88s are working on the three downstairs rooms. Their high explosives can't penetrate the sturdy walls. What's left of the upstairs gives us a roof of sorts and some protection unless the Germans drop a lucky shot clean through the house.

Do I keep all my platoon in this strong room? Or do I divide the men up into the three downstairs rooms? Immediately my problem is partly solved. A mortar bomb goes right through to the east downstairs room and blows it to pieces. I have two rooms left. Do I split the men up? Or keep them together in this room?

I think of my phenomenal luck at poker. What have I got in my hand? Damn little. Certainly no chance to draw a 'full house'. That's shot to hell. Do I keep my pair or throw one away and draw a straight? I feel like I am on a high induced by sodium pentothol after one of my operations. I'll let the pair go and try for a straight.

A little later the room next to the one we are in receives a direct hit from a 105 and disintegrates. My 'pair' were obviously not good enough; but can I draw a straight and win?

I bend down to speak to one of the wounded. An AP (armour-piercing) shell tears through the wall where I had been standing and exits through the rear. Everyone hits the deck. Another AP screeches through the room. I can't get my body any closer to the ground. Outside the 88s and Moaning Minnies explode near the walls and into what is left of the upstairs. Whole sections of the roof come crashing down but strong beams above our heads give us some protection.

There is no let up. We are lying flat on the earthern floor packed like sardines, with our heads hard against the front wall. Most of us are covered with debris that has fallen through gaping holes in the ceiling. Smoke and dust fill the room and eat at our eyes and throats. How long can we take it?

It's been too long for one man. He sobs hysterically. He digs a bible out of his pack and starts to pray. There is no hope. We are doomed. We must confess our sins to Him before we are all blown straight to hell.

"No one is going to be blown to hell in this platoon." I jump up and shake the man by the shoulders. I hit him lightly with the back of my hand. He calms down. I growl at the rest of the platoon: "Anyone else think he's going to Hell?"

No response, except a whimper from a badly wounded man. I speak to him quietly and give him a shot of morphine. The shelling starts to slacken a bit. I peer out the window. Crash! Another AP screams through the walls that now look like Swiss cheese. Will it never stop?

Then I hear the most dreaded of all sounds to an infantry man — tanks — on the open left flank. The clanking gets louder. I rush to the rear door-way, barely able to suppress my panic. Through a cloud of dust a troop of tanks emerges and comes right at us. I run out into the open and wave and shout — Churchills of the New Zealand Division!

I have just drawn my straight — ace high.

The battle was over. Next day, September 23rd, we were relieved in the line and the Regiment marched back to Cattolica.

Many of us did not return. On September 22nd, at about 1050 hours, while Dog Company was enduring its own hellfire, a Carabinieri station that was serving as Charlie Company HQ was hit. Capt G R Corkett was killed — the third Charlie Company commander to be killed in this battle.[2]

A despatch written at the time by Maurice Western, a Canadian War Correspondent with *Winnipeg Free Press*, vividly describes the fighting and intense shelling experienced during the battle.

PATS UNDERGO INTENSE SHELLING TO FORGE MARECCHIA BRIDGEHEAD
By Maurice Western
Free Press War Correspondent
With the Canadians on the Adriatic Front, Sept 25 (Delayed)
(By Radio and Cable)

The bridgehead across the Marecchia — was established by the Princess Patricia's Canadian Light Infantry. It was the climax of week-long fighting during which the prairie men ran the gauntlet of shelling — the most intense and prolonged ever experienced by this veteran western regiment.

The Pats drove a spearhead deep into enemy territory and clung doggedly to their positions, even when the left flank was completely open. Seldom has a battle imposed greater demands upon courage, endurance and initiative of non-commissioned officers and private soldiers.

A company made the initial crossing, using a wooden bridge which the Germans had left intact. Maj Sam Potts, Saskatoon, then brought D Company across under heavy shellfire, establishing a position in a cement factory. The situation was still extremely confused with the left flank wide open, until C Company moved in to close the gap. As dawn broke, the Germans turned their heavies and Nebelwerfers on the Canadian positions and the Pats, clinging to ditches and slit trenches, endured the worst shelling of the entire campaign.

Lt Syd Frost, Winnipeg, had set up platoon headquarters in a strong five-roomed house. By noon the place was perforated with jagged holes and only a corner of one room remained occupyable.

But in this — the toughest battle of Italy for a Canadian corps — one company of Princess Pats changed commander no less than five times, with three officers killed and one wounded, before the Marecchia crossing was over.[3]

LCol G W L Nicholson describes the losses:

> *Canadian losses were heavier than for any period of equal length, either before or after, during the Italian campaign. From 25 August to 22 September the 1st Division suffered 2511 battle casualties.*[4]

Gen Sir Oliver Leese, the 8th Army commander, sent the following message to LGen Burns, the Canadian corps commander:

> *You have won a great victory. By the bitterest fighting since El Alamein and Cassino you have beaten 11 German Divisions and broken through into the Po Valley. The greater part of the German armies in Italy were massed against us and they have been terribly mauled. I congratulate and thank you all. We must now hit hard day and night and force them back over the Po.*[5]

Gen Leese also sent the PPCLI the following signal:

> *The Regiment may be proud of its part in a great and hard fought victory. Well Done, Canada.*[6]

June 20, 1956

Twelve years later I return to San Fortunato Ridge. Vineyards and orchards now cover the terrible killing grounds around the feature. The large white house that had taken so much punishment from German artillery still stands. Most of the damage has been repaired; the shell holes have been roughly patched up; the masonry has been restored. But evidence of the destruction is clearly visible. Several families now live in the *casa* and dozens of *bambini* romp through gardens that once were so hotly contested by ourselves and the Germans.

The sunken roads, shorn of their dreadful human sacrifice, look much the same. The paratroopers' caves in the sides of the road are still there, blocked off by steel bars. I peer inside and see torn helmets and bits of equipment. I scale crumbling steps, dug into the walls by the German defenders, to examine the positions from which the Edmontons cut down a whole paratroop company. The positions are still there, but so are the mine fields. A weather-beaten German sign says *Achtung Minen*, and underneath the Italians have scribbled *Proibito*.

From the positions I look over the ground the PPCLI advanced 12 years ago. While the renewed vegetation blocks some of the view, I can see for miles in every direction. How anyone survived the intense shellfire directed from the ridge I still do not understand. It will always remain a puzzle known only to old Field Marshal Fate.

I climb into my German automobile and retrace my steps of 1944 along the road to Bovey, past the very spot where three Churchill tanks and their crews perished from the guns of the Tigers firing in the plain. For a moment I relive the horrible scene and hear the crash of the German 88s blowing our tanks apart.

I stop at Bovey where Sam Potts exhorted me to advance by issuing his historic dictum — 'the first of the first of the first'. The *casa* he occupied is empty and in exactly the same condition as it was 12 years ago — shell holes and all. I wonder if perhaps it is being preserved as a historic site!

I return to the house on San Fortunato and drive west in my Mercedes. A few old ladies in their black shawls shake their fists at me and cackle, *"Tedesco, cativo, non buono."*

I am confused and overwhelmed by the irony of it all. My tears, and the anguish in my heart, are for the mothers, wives and lovers of all those soldiers who died at San Fortunato: ours who fought so bravely; theirs who died in vain.

There is one other feature I must visit before the sun goes down — the Republic of San Marino, only four miles west of San Fortunato. It rises abruptly out of the coastal plain to heights of 2,400 feet above sea level and overlooks the plain clear to the Adriatic. This tiny independent state is only 24 miles square, but its significance during the War was out of all proportion to its size.

Throughout the advance of the PPCLI to the Marecchia River in September 1944, the fortress-like height of San Marino, on our left flank, seemed to watch our every move. Whenever we were caught by German shellfire in the open plain, we blamed San Marino, particularly after San Fortunato had fallen. The staff, as always, had a fine legal answer to our paranoia. San Marino, as everyone knew, was a neutral state and the Germans would never occupy a non-belligerent country. I didn't believe it and resolved to find the answer after the war.

As my Mercedes approaches the border, I see a barrier across the road, a small customs house, and two guards smartly dressed in military uniform. They smile broadly and, in German, politely ask for my passport. When I produce a Canadian one they become less enthusiastic, but wave me through, muttering something about the *canadese*. I wonder whose side they were on in the last War.

Negotiating a series of hairpin bends and narrowly missing being killed by busloads of German tourists, I reach the summit of this natural fortress and stop at an open air café clinging to the side of the cliff. What a breathtaking view of the countryside for miles in every direction! The Ausa River, San Martino, San Fortunato, the Marecchia River, Rimini, all lie at my feet. A waiter approaches and I order a small *caraffa* of the local wine. In Italian, I tell him I am a Canadian solider who fought in the plain below in September 1944. The waiter is not impressed. I continue by saying we had a lot of

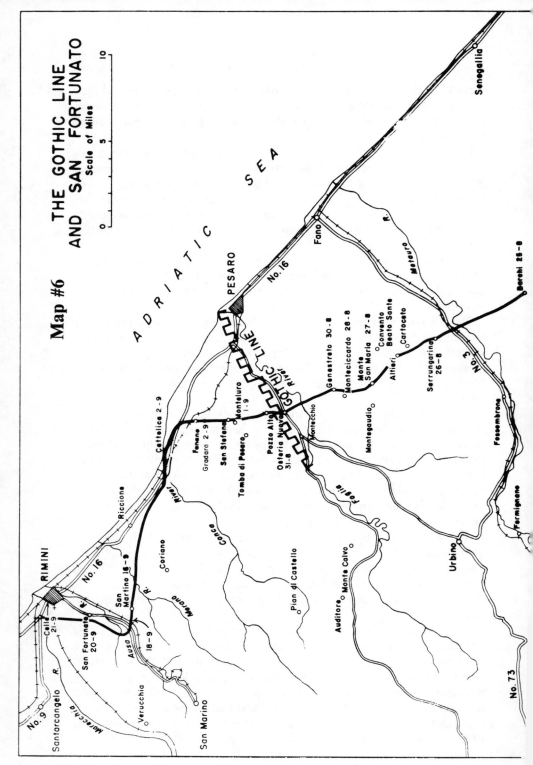

Map #6

THE GOTHIC LINE
AND SAN FORTUNATO
Scale of Miles
0   5   10

ADRIATIC SEA

PESARO

No. 16

Fano

Metauro R.

Borchi 25-8

No. 3

Cattolica 2-9

Genestreto 30-8
Monteciccardo 28-8
Monte San Maria 27-8
Convento Beato Sante
Cartoceto
Altieri

Serrungarina 26-8

Fossombrone

GOTHIC LINE
GOTHIC River

Monteluro 1-9

Montecchio

Montegaudio

Fanano
Gradara 2-9
San Stefano
Tomba di Pesaro
Pozzo Alto
Osteria Nuova 31-8

Riccione

Conca River

Pian di Castello

Foglia R.

Auditore Monte Calvo

Urbino

Termignano

No. 73

RIMINI

No. 16

San Martino 16-9

Coriano

Marano R.

Celle 21-9
San Fortunato 20-9
Ausa 18-9

Santarcangelo
Marecchia R.
No. 9

Verucchia

San Marino

Senegallia

294

trouble with German shellfire and some of us suspected that it was directed by Germans in San Marino. However our staff officers assured us that this could not be the case as, after all, San Marino was neutral and the Germans would respect this.

The waiter nearly falls over the cliff, laughing. He wishes he could have ten lire for every German officer he served at this very *ristorante* during the War. There were hundreds of them. Several of their powerful 'spy glasses' were left behind (stolen by the Ities) and are available for the tourists, for a small fee, of course.

The waiter then realizes that several of his German patrons are giving us dirty looks. He bends down and whispers that when the British came in September, 1944, San Marino cast aside its neutrality and declared war on Germany. All 57 members of the Republic's armed forces volunteered to fight the Nazis. He was one of them.

I thank the *cameriere* for this belated report on our former enemies, and pay 50 lire to follow the route of my advance to the Marecchia, through a fine pair of German binoculars. Field Marshal Kesselring would not have been amused.

In the fading light, as I sip my vino rosso, I think I hear a faint chuckle from Field Marshal Fate.

Chapter XXII

AT EASE
Cattolica
September 23, October 12, 1944

We'll unleash the recce, we will let them go
We know the mighty Maroon Machine is very, very slow
While they are trailing far behind
We'll break right through and smash their line
Onward to Bologna, onward to the Po

As we marched back to Cattolica, weary, dazed and with an immense hunger, we felt proud of ourselves, the Regiment and 1st Canadian Division. We had every right to feel this way. The division had mauled the best the Germans had to offer. The army commander himself had said so. We had broken through the last mountain barrier and descended into the northern Italian plain.

Now, we were told, the armoured divisions would be 'unleashed' and roll across the plains to the Po River and even beyond; perhaps right to Venice. At last the end was in sight.

But alas the end was nowhere in sight. It was not even the beginning of the end. The triple factors of weather, ground and a determined enemy would continue to frustrate the armour, the generals and ourselves for the next five months.

Happily, for the moment, the realities of the situation were hidden from our view and we could enjoy the three luxuries of a soldier — sleep, food and shelter. I had gone only four nights without sleep, the rest of my platoon many more. How they had carried on all this time I could not understand.

296

Obviously, they were in much better fighting shape than I.

The high brass now showered us with favours. The division commander, MGen Vokes, came around to thank us for the fine job we had done. He announced there would be no parades of any kind for the next three days. Loud cheers. Then he really outdid himself. All towns in the area would be 'IN Bounds'.

I couldn't believe my ears. The general had certainly mellowed since the old days in Sicily. But one veteran in my platoon was not impressed.

"They're just gettin' us fattened up for the kill. Wait till y'hear the rest of it."

The general went on. There was still hard fighting ahead. The battalion had a high percentage of new men. The old hands would have to teach them all the tricks. There would be lots of spit and polish, gobs if it.

"I told you so," the old hand muttered under his breath.

But the general was as good as his word. For the next three days the troops relaxed and did SFA. The weather was bright, the Mediterranean deliciously warm, and the beaches crowded with idle soldiers, not yet recovered enough to be unduly licentious. The general knew his men. They would need three days to recover their strength. If they had been given one day more, no Italian signorina within miles would have been safe.

I trust it will not strain my credibility to say that the officers had little time to enjoy this easing of restrictions. Our first responsibility was to compose letters to the next-of-kin. This was always difficult, yet it meant so much to the families of the deceased that I spent many hours talking with the deceased's buddies (if any were left) to get an idea what the man was like and how he had died. I was always relieved to hear that he had died instantly, without apparent pain, for that was what his next-of-kin wanted to hear. The exact manner of his dying was another matter. I couldn't tell his mother he had been blown into small pieces by a 105 gun.

Another task I found depressing was auctioning off a brother officer's kit. The strictly personal effects were usually bundled up and sent home; the uniforms, sweaters, boots, trench coats and the like were sold to the highest bidder. We tried to make light of the matter, knowing that our comrade would have wanted it that way, but we were not always successful. Still, the proceeding made sense. Everyone was short of clothing and equipment and there was no point in shipping it thousands of miles back to Canada where the stuff would serve no purpose except to add further grief to the family.

There was one other duty that bothered me even more — pushing the sale of war bonds. Whenever the troops were at rest, and even in action, the officers were expected to put pressure on the troops to part with their hard-earned $1.50 per diem to help the government buy the weapons and ammunition we needed to kill Germans. No doubt it was a good investment, but that wasn't the point. What annoyed me was the way the men were badgered to buy the bonds as patriotic Canadians, as if offering their hides and their lives was not enough. Many a time a soldier was induced to make a commitment to buy bonds that was frustrated a few days or even hours later by his death.

I used to get quite angry with the way we were ordered to give sales talks to the troops, and I absolutely refused to have anything to do with it. When the number one bond dealer in the Regiment appeared with a fist full of applications, I threw him out of my platoon area. "For God's sake, Jimmie, stop bugging my platoon with your lousy bonds. Send them back to Mackenzie King and burn them. But let the troops die in peace."

Jimmie was our popular paymaster, affectionately known as Jimmie the Pay. He entirely agreed with me, but he had his instructions. I suspect he was also given a quota by brigade which he ignored at his peril.

Still another duty in rest areas was censoring the men's mail. This could be an onerous task if the men in your platoon were great writers, but most were not. Seldom did they breach security regulations, largely because their knowledge of operations was seldom of interest to the other side. The fact that No 9 Section captured a house and took some prisoners was hardly news to Field Marshal Kesselring and his intelligence service. It was happening all the time. Yet, occasionally, a letter would provide a little comic relief. The men knew, of course, that you were censoring the mail, and some liked to pull your leg a bit, or make a point they wouldn't dare say to you in person, such as, "Our platoon commander is Lt Frost — he's hopeless." You could usually ignore this unless of course it was the consensus of the mail of the entire platoon. Then you were in trouble.

On the other hand, a letter might say: "Our platoon commander is a fine officer." Whether this was a prank or an attempt to suckhole, you soon learned to decipher — but it wasn't easy.

The most interesting letters were those discussing the love life of the writer. Some of the men handled this with a frankness that amazed me and I probably learned quite a few points. One letter to a wife confessed: "On my last leave, I went to bed with an Italian girl and she was great. But you are better."

The Padre, always ready to step into the breach, saw the evils of men telling the truth and devised a handy check list for writing letters home, which gave the troops a few chuckles.

MEASURE UP YOUR LETTERS HOME
A *The Cheerful Start*
   1 Circumstances at time of writing
   2 Thanks for gifts (Be specific)
   3 Answers to letters (Have them there)

4 *Greetings-Birthdays-Anniversaries, etc*
B *News*
   · 5 *A word about your pals (no gossip)*
   6 *Wisecracks and jokes (Sterilized)*
   7 *Interesting places you have been on leave*
   8 *Some people you have met*
   9 *Remarks on news from home*
   10 *Your entertainment lately, shows, etc*
   11 *The general war situation*
C *Requests*
   12 *Information wanted of family, business, etc*
   13 *What the next parcel might contain*
D *Plans, Hopes and Ambitions*
   14 *Concerning your duties and rank*
   15 *The next leave*
   16 *When you return home*
E *The Ending*
   17 *Some praise for someone*
   18 *A reference to a lovely memory*
   19 *Love*
   20 *Never end without a 'God Bless You'*
Give Cheer — Tell the Truth — Keep it Clean
Watch Security!

Despite this plethora of administration and red tape I was getting to know my boys and beginning to realize what a great bunch they really were. On September 25th, only two days after arriving in Cattolica, I received a summons to report to the adjutant, Capt Andy Mills, who had been an instructor at Shilo when I was stationed there. Since that time I had seen him just once, and then only briefly, when I reported to the battalion on September 19th, without a weapon. I thought perhaps he was going to congratulate me for being 'the first of the first' to debouch into the Valley of the Po, unarmed, or, depending on his mood, maybe he was going to tick me off again for appearing at the battalion without a weapon. Neither of my guesses was near the mark.

"Syd, glad to see you survived that bit of shelling. There's a vacancy in the MMGs. Johnny Koensgen is taking up other duties and has recommended you to take his place. I believe you had Vickers training at RMC."

Andy had a memory a mile long. "Yes, Sir, but that was two years ago. I'm a little rusty."

"No matter, it'll come back. You'll take over the MMG Platoon October 1."

Andy never minced his words. "In the meantime, I have some court martial cases I want you to defend. You thought were a hot shot on Military Law at Shilo. Now's your chance to prove it. One of our men has been charged with desertion. Here's the Summary of Evidence. The Court convenes tomorrow morning.''

Andy didn't expect a reply. ''Glad you'll take on these jobs. And, by the way, nice to have you back.''

I would have to move quickly to interview my 'client' dig up witnesses and prepare my case. It had been two years since I had taught Military Law at Shilo and I hadn't opened the *Manual of Military Law* or *King's Regulations and Orders* since.

The charge stated that the accused, when on active service, deserted His Majesty's Service, in that on the night of September 21st, during the advance from San Fortunato to the Marecchia River, he absented himself without leave with the intent to avoid such advance.

The charge was brought by a young sergeant in whose platoon the accused served. The sergeant was a tough NCO, who had seen considerable action and kept a pretty tight rein on his platoon. During the advance, enemy shelling was intense and had wounded and killed many of the sergeant's men. When the platoon arrived at Pique, the accused was missing. The man turned up four hours later and the sergeant charged him with desertion.

The accused's story was that during the advance a stonk of enemy mortars landed near his section and everyone took cover in a ditch. The shellfire ceased but two men in front of him did not move. He waited a while and then went forward. He found one man dead and the other dying. The next man was badly wounded and could not move. He gave first aid and went ahead to find his section. In the darkness and shellfire he could not locate them. He did not know what direction they had taken. He waited for the shelling to slacken and then made his way back to the RAP where he reported the casualties. At first light he rejoined his section at Pique.

The story was a pretty good one but it had some holes. Why did he wait so long in the ditch? He must have heard the cries of the wounded and dying men as soon the shells exploded. Further, the route ahead was along a straight road, although there were intersections, one of which I myself had missed. Why didn't he return with the stretcher bearers to the wounded man and at least help evacuate the casualty?

I looked up the man's record. He was only 19. He had fought in both the Hitler and Gothic Lines. He seemed to deserve a break. On the other hand, the position of the platoon sergeant had to be considered. He could not allow men to drop out of a line of march, or stop to tend casualties. His platoon was way under strength; one missing man might make the difference between an attack succeeding or failing. The absence of the accused put all the other members of the weakened platoon in jeopardy.

I realized that the sergeant had a case and wanted to make an example of the accused. Still, my duty was clear. I was bound to give my man the best defence I could muster. A charge of desertion was a very serious matter.

While the Canadian Army no longer shot deserters, my man could get a stiff jail sentence that would remain a blot against his name for the rest of his life.

I scouted around and found out the name of the President of the court martial. It was absolutely forbidden, of course, to speak to him, but I was greatly encouraged when I discovered he was one of the company commanders from another unit who had taken part in the San Fortunato attack, and was known as a fair and understanding officer.

Next, I dug up a lance corporal in the accused's section whom I persuaded to testify on my man's behalf. The lance corporal was naturally loath to get in the bad books of the sergeant, but he gamely agreed to tell his story. He confirmed that a shell had landed on his section and killed or wounded at least four men. He thought my man was one of them. He didn't wait, and quickly pressed on in the dark to find the next section. In the blackness and shellfire he had difficulty locating the rest of the platoon, but he eventually did and reported my man and three others missing, presumed dead or wounded.

I also talked to the RAP Sergeant. He remembered someone reporting the casualties in the accused's section but in the confusion he couldn't remember if it was my man or someone else.

The court martial was duly convened. I had no trouble persuading everyone present that the night in question was as black as the insides of a donkey and that the German shellfire was the worst of the entire campaign. How any of us escaped was a miracle. Even the sergeant had to concede his platoon scattered and other men strayed from the fold for a short time.

In my closing address I reminded the Court that the charge of desertion was one of the most serious ones in the book and that the prosecutor had to prove that the accused had an intention to escape from the advance on Pique. I casually asked the indulgence of the Court to allow me to state, somewhat immodestly, that I had the privilege of leading that advance and could say, as a matter of public record, the enemy had departed before we launched our attack on Pique. Thus, the accused's presence was, fortunately, not missed in that particular action. I also reminded the Court that the burden of proof was on the prosecution to establish beyond reasonable doubt the guilt of the accused.

The Court retired to consider the verdict. Shortly they returned and the President asked if the accused would consent to the lesser and common charge of absent without leave.

I promptly agreed on behalf of my client.

The Court let him off with forfeiture of 30 days' pay, and he rejoined his section a very happy man. Thenceforth he followed the example of his sergeant and served the Regiment faithfully in many engagements until January 1945, when he was badly wounded, evacuated and returned to

Canada. His honour had been fully redeemed. But the sergeant who had taught him courage never knew about his final act of penance. This brave NCO was struck down in the same engagement, at almost the same instant, as the man he had helped redeem. He died instantly. Such are the fortunes of war.

News of my man's lucky break soon spread throughout the battalion and even to the other units. For the next few months, whenever the Regiment was at rest, I was bedevilled with requests to defend men accused of all manner of offences. It became quite a burden as I was busy administering my platoon and had to do a lot of study to regain my alleged 'expertise' in military law. There were no lawyers in the battalion I could turn to for help, so I went around the other units trying to find a real expert. Finally, I met a lawyer in a tank regiment who turned out to be very helpful and gave me much advice. He had made a name for himself by winning an acquittal for a man charged with causing a self-inflicted wound. Apparently the accused was not trying to avoid action, but was thoroughly fed up with the way medals were being handed out to everybody, regardless of whether they had seen any action. The award of these medals had, in fact, become a bit of a joke to the fighting troops, especially the one for service in Canada which was called the 'Spam' medal.

To show his defiance and contempt for the system, the disgruntled man ate the ribbon of his spam medal and even the bar denoting overseas service. Through some technicality my lawyer friend got him off the serious charge of self-inflicted wound and settled for the minor misdemeanour of 'conduct to the prejudice of good order and military discipline in that he attempted to destroy a medal granted to him for faithful service to his country'. Apparently, the ribbon and bar were salvaged and restored to their rightful place on the left breast of the accused.

On September 29th, a distinguised visitor from Canada arrived on our doorstep — Col Ralston, Minister of National Defence. Unlike the Prime Minister, who usually got roundly booed whenever he addressed the troops, Col Ralston was highly respected by the men, and for good reason. In the First War he had been severely wounded, awarded the DSO, and had commanded the Nova Scotia Highlanders, the predecessor unit of The Cape Breton Highlanders who were now fighting beside us in the 5th Armoured Divison.

The venue for the battalion to meet the colonel was the local fish cannery. It was an appropriate choice — we were packed in like sardines. After giving us a short review of the war situation and a few genuine words of praise, he said he appreciated our problems and would try to do something about them. He then encouraged questions from the floor. No encouragement was needed. Much as the men liked this dedicated soldier and public servant, they were not going to pass up such an opportunity. Their questions came faster than machine gun bullets from an MG42.

"What about reinforcements? In every action we go into we're always way below strength. Why are casualties not replaced?"

"I've been overseas for five years and so have a lot of other guys. Why can't we get some leave home ?"

"I've heard there's a new scheme that allows a man to go home when he's been wounded three times. He sure deserves it. But what about me? I landed in Sicily, been wounded twice. I don't think I'll survive another wound."

"When we knock the Germans out of the war, can we go home? Or will we have to fight the Japs first?"

"Why can't we join the rest of the Canadian Army in Europe? Italy is just a sideshow."

The Minister fielded the questions pretty well, but he couldn't give us all the answers we wanted. He did undertake, however, to recommend to the government that the reinforcement situation be given priority and that leave to Canada for the 'old timers' be started in time to get them home by Christmas. At this point, LCol Clark adroitly stepped in and called for three cheers. The Minister probably got the loudest ovation he had received during his tour of the front.

Col Ralston kept his word. Shortly after his visit, the tri-wound scheme was amended to allow soldiers who had been wounded twice, but who had three years' continuous service overseas, a six-month tour duty in Canada or the UK. Moreover, anyone who had five years' continuous service overseas (time in a theatre of operations counted double) was granted a 30 day leave in Canada.[1]

The problem of lack of reinforcements gave Col Ralston deep concern. He got the same story we had given him from everyone else he spoke to, from the lowest private to the officer whose responsibility it was to keep CMHQ in London informed about the theatre's need for reinforcements — Brig E G Weeks. From him, Col Ralston learned that "if the Canadian Corps continued to be actively engaged in operations, by approximately October 10th all general duty infantry reinforcements would be committed and there would be no reserves.[2]

Col Ralston was so concerned about the effect the lack of reinforcements would have on the Canadian Corps that he asked Gen Leese, commanding the 8th Army, what he thought about reducing the 1st Canadian Division by one brigade. Gen Leese declared that "the division was undoubtedly the best in the 8th Army, that it could always be relied upon to take on a tough job successfully, and that any reduction in its infantry would be a mistake".[3]

The seriousness of the reinforcement situation was hardly news to the hard-pressed troops. But it was news to Mackenzie King and the government, or so they pretended. It led to Col Ralston demanding conscription and ultimately being fired by the Prime Minister. It was a tragic end to the career of a Minister who placed the lives of his men ahead of the requirements of the politicians.

Col Ralston had his principles and he stood by them. How different was Mackenzie King's ambivalent stand on all issues — "Conscription if necessary, but not necessarily conscription." Too bad Field Marshal Fate had not intervened to confound the 'knavish tricks' of the Prime Minister.

The problems of the politicians were of no concern to the battle-weary men gathered in a fish factory in a small Italian village on the Adriatic coast, on September 29th, 1944. What they really wanted was to be given the men and the tools to finish the job. It was a forlorn hope.

For those who were left to carry on the fight prospects were not encouraging. Despite Col Ralston's assurances, we had little faith in the politicians' will to enforce conscription, and anyway, who wanted to soldier with 'Zombies'. If necessary, we'd carry on alone, to the very limit of our resources — which is exactly what we did.

The officer reinforcement situation had, for months, been a critical problem for every infantry battalion in the division. That huge surplus of lieutenants languishing in training camps in Welbeck Abbey and Thoresby Hall in England had long since been thrown into the cauldron in France. The staff were desperate to find replacements before they themselves were sent into battle. Luckily, there were still a few sources of keen young officers, spoiling to get into action — lieutenants in the engineers and artillery. These officers had completed their training but had little chance of seeing any fighting because casualties in their arms had been light, and there was no need for reinforcements.

In the artillery holding units, much the same situation existed as I had encountered at Thoresby Hall — hundreds of officers milling about with nothing to do except route marches and tests of elementary training.

The staff soon realized that these surplus officers were the answer to the shortages in infantry reinforcement. No matter that they had no training in infantry. A short course would soon remedy that minor deficiency. A call for volunteers went out to the artillery and engineer holding units. The quota was quickly filled, the officers given a 'quickee course', and despatched to infantry battalions. Many came to fill the depleted ranks in Italy.

One of the first arrivals was Lt W E Harrington of the artillery, already mentioned, who joined the Regiment in September 1944, and was with me in Dog company during the Marecchia River operations. Others arrived in December.

Despite their limited training in infantry and their short time in action, all gave outstanding service to the Regiment. Three won the Military Cross (out of 12 awarded during the entire war).* More will be said of these fine officers in the forthcoming battles in Italy and Holland. After the war, one entered public life and went on to render further distinguished service to his country as Minister of National Defence.** I had the privilege of being his company commander in the last battles of the war.

Still another source of 'buckshee' officers for Italy was a scheme to send out from England, to gain experience, officers from the other divisions that had not seen any action. The idea was that these officers would return to their units after a short tour of duty in Italy.

However, because of the critical reinforcement situation, many of the officers were kept in Italy and never saw their original units again. One such was Lt Egan E Chambers, who arrived at the Patricias in November 1943. The loss of his former regiment was our gain. He remained with the Patricias to the end of the war, was wounded, won the Military Cross at the Foglia River and came home with the Regiment as adjutant.

This experiment was of course discontinued as soon as the Second Front opened up. The plan had mainly benefited the depleted regiments in Italy and not the units in England, contrary to the intention of the staff. For once we had outwitted the higher brass.

Another scheme that backfired on the staff, but was of no benefit to us in Italy or to anyone else in the Canadian Army, was the 'Canloan' scheme. In September 1943, when an invasion of Canada was no longer seriously threatened, the government disbanded two divisions, the 7th and 8th, and part of the 6th that had been guarding Canada's shores.[4] What should be done with thousands of surplus officers from these divisions? The government came up with a plan. They offered to lend a number of these officers to the British Army. In February 1944 'arrangements were made for 2,000 Canadian officers to be attached to the British Army'.[5]

The scheme was nicely underway and the first group of officers despatched to British units in April 1944, when the staff suddenly woke up. Oops! The Canadian Corps in Italy was crying for reinforcements. The government hastily informed the British that the total of infantry officers that could be sent was unlikely to exceed 625.

In the event, a total of 673 Canloan infantry officers were sent to British units.[6] What a difference these officers would have made to the units in Italy if someone on the staff at NDHQ in Ottawa had not forgotten all about the Italian Campaign and the D-Day dodgers.

From the very day I rejoined the Patricias in the bloody plain below the heights of San Fortunato, on September 19th, I had a gut feeling it was not same kind of Regiment I had know in Sicily. But I couldn't understand

---

* Lt W E Harrington, Lt A B McKinnon, Lt E J Berryman
** Maj The Honourable Allan B McKinnon, MC, PC

why. It was only after I had thought about the terrible casualties and reinforcement problems that I realized that the close fraternity and easy camaraderie developed during the years in England had gone. In Sicily, even though I had been with the Regiment in England, had worn Patricia badges for a year, and knew Regimental customs and traditions as well as or better than many of the serving officers, I was still considered a 'new boy' on probation. There was no such thing as an 'instant' Patricia.

I looked over the present roll officers to see how many were left from the time I joined the battalion in Sicily. Out of 39 officers serving at that time, only nine remained. A few would subsequently return, but their influence would not alter the new character of the Regiment.

A consideration of the fate of the 60-odd officers who had served as platoon commanders, from the landing in Sicily (July 10th, 1943) to the Hitler Line (May 23rd, 1944), was even more revealing. Of all these young officers, only two or three were still serving as platoon commanders who had not been wounded. Seven had been killed; 20 or more had been wounded at least once; another 20 had been struck off strength because of sickness or transferred to other units; only six had been promoted and were still serving with the Regiment as captains or majors.

Clearly, this attrition in the ranks of the 'Old Guard' could not help but affect the Regimental spirit as I knew it. Moreover the tradition of 'once a Patricia, always a Patricia' had been eroded by the exigencies of war. When another battalion was cut to pieces a Patricia officer would be sent to fill the gap. And vice-versa. When PPCLI reinforcement officers dried up, replacements from other units came to our rescue. Then there were those attachments from the units in England who came for dinner and stayed the duration. Again, pockets of sappers and gunners had started to infiltrate our brotherhood, with their feelings of inherited seniority in the service.

It was little wonder that officers and men from so many diverse backgrounds and bearing allegiance to so many other units had not yet developed that intense pride of being a Patricia that I felt so strongly.

These new personnel would certainly account for some of the perceptions I had about the change in Regimental spirit. Yet there was something else at work that I could not quite put my finger on. There seemed to be a profound change in attitudes toward the war — cynicism of the grandiose schemes and plans of the generals; contempt for the 'bumph' of the staff from whom all troubles flowed; resentment over the mounting casualties; surliness because of the appalling weather and tortuous terrain; intolerance of the mistakes of others; a feeling of injustice due to the lack of reinforcements and equipment; above all, a weariness of the war.

All this contrasted with the light-hearted dash and devil-may-care attitude I had seen in Sicily and southern Italy. After a moment's reflection I realized the new Patricia's were entitled to feel the way they did. The bloody battles of the past 12 months had exacted their toll — Villa Rogatti, Vino Ridge, the Hitler Line, the Gothic Line, Rimini.

The war had become serious, dirty, never-ending, toe-to-toe slugging it out, with a desperate, ugly foe. It was no longer a free-wheeling, Popski-type pursuit in the open country. It was a battle of attrition. It was a task for which only professional soldiers need apply. The Patricias had become professionals. Killing was their business. In short, the Regiment had matured into an efficient fighting machine.

That the Regiment still had spirit was undeniable. Only it was a different kind of spirit — one of cold resolve to finish off the enemy and the war. The men would soon shake off their lassitude and be ready once more ruthlessly to follow their trade. It would take me some time to adjust to this new war.

But time, as always, refused to wait while I pondered these matters. A chit arrived from the Adjutant telling me to report forthwith to Support Company and take over the MMG Platoon.

Once again I had to say goodbye to D Company after serving with it only a short time. In England I had managed to stay two weeks under Capt Waterman before getting my marching orders. Actually it was called No 3 Company, but it contained many D Company personnel. Next, I had served in D Company under Capt 'Foo' Hunter in southern Italy, but had lasted only four days before being posted to the Scouts and Snipers. Finally, in the recent show I was with Sam Potts for six days. Clearly I was not meant to be a D Company man. But Field Marshal Fate was only playing games with me. He would give me command of D Company for the last operation of the war.

Before moving on to my new home with the MMG Platoon, I feel bound to say a further word about the lot of the infantry platoon commander. It will be realized that the numbers given above cover only the causalties for the period from Sicily to the Hitler Line. During these ten months, 60 lieutenants served as platoon commanders. From the Hitler Line to the end of the war, many, many more young officers would join the Regiment and become casualties. Some would be struck down after serving only a week or two, their names passing from the record without recognition or remembrance.

The obvious conclusion to be drawn from all these figures is that the chances of a platoon commander coming through the war unscathed were practically nil. Even promotion to captain or major increased his chances only marginallly, as company commanders were no more immune to small arms fire and shells than their platoon commanders. Indeed, sometimes the life expectancy of company commanders was less than their subordinates. In at least two cases, a company commander who had served with another unit joined the Regiment one day and was killed the next.

What effect these statistics had on the minds of platooon commanders I do not know. Certainly no one dwelt on them and they were rarely discussed, if at all. Hope springs eternal in the human breast. I met only one officer who really believed he would not come through the war alive — his premonition came true. Everyone else was convinced, at least so they let on, that their number would not come up except for a wound or two, which was taken for granted.

The story is told that before one hazardous patrol behind enemy lines, the leader paraded his ten men and said that if anyone wanted to drop out of the mission, all he had to do was to step forward. No questions would be asked. Not a man moved. The commander then told his section they didn't seem to understand how dangerous the mission was. Chances were that only one man would return. It would be no disgrace for anyone to step forward now. Still not a man moved. Finally, the leader lost his patience. "Look, men, I'm the only one who's coming back. You'd better write your last letters home." The parade was dismissed and the men prepared for their mission. No one wrote a letter home and no one came back.

It is a good thing human nature is made this way. As long as there is hope, even just a glimmer, a man will usually accept the risks, if he is well led. It is only when there is no hope at all that the average man will falter.

Commanders at high levels are very aware of this basic human instinct and therefore strive to paint a rosy picture of forthcoming operations — It will be a piece of cake; our artillery concentration will pulverize the enemy defences; our bombers will obliterate all opposition; the enemy is very weak at this point; his morale is low; prisoners are coming over in droves...

Platoon commanders and company commanders in close contact with the enemy know better. How can they lie to their troops, attack after attack, about how strong we are and how weak and demoralized the enemy is? The fortunes of war partly solve the problem. Few commanders survive more than a couple of actions and new faces arrive, eager and unknowing, ready to continue assuring the troops 'the attack will be over before Jerry knows what hit him'.

I had said this very thing myself, to my troops, time and time again. I wondered how I would be delivered from my dilemma of having to follow orders and yet maintain my credibility with my men. Field Marshal Fate no doubt had an appropriate solution ready for me. Only the time and place of my deliverance remained uncertain.

Chapter XXIII

MACHINE GUNS
IN THE ROMAGNA

October 1 to October 20, 1944

The Lewis guns are always true
To every call of the Ric-a-dam-doo
They're always there with a burst or two
When'ere they see the Ric-a-dam-doo, dam-doo, dam-doo

What was I getting into this time? While I knew the battalion had formed a machine gun platoon which fired the Vickers, I had no idea of the organization of the platoon or of the tactical handling of the gun. I also knew that the Saskatoon Light Infantry was a machine gun battalion that formed part of 1st Canadian Division, and supplied supporting fire to the Regiment whenever it was in action. Where our battalion MMGs fitted in I hadn't a clue. Fortunately, there was one person who could soon put me in the picture — Johnny Koensgen.

From him I learned that, like the Scouts and Snipers, the MMG Platoon was unofficial and carried the brand name 'made in Italy'. Perhaps the infantry battalions in France also had MMGs, but Johnny didn't know for sure.

It was true the SLI supported us in action, but their guns gave us mainly indirect fire at considerable distance from the forward companies. They also covered our flanks and generally fired in enfilade; in other words, the guns covering our front fired from the locality of another battalion. The SLI guns also fired on fixed lines at night.

In the fighting in Sicily and southern Italy it was found we needed something right up in the front lines to neutralize the tremendous fire the

Jerries were pouring at us with their quick-firing MG42s. We also needed more fire power in the forward companies to break up counter-attacks immediately. So the MMG Platoon was formed during the Hitler Line with Johnny as its first commander.

The role of the MMGs could be expressed in one word — morale. Bolster ours and destroy theirs.

I thought of Johnny's sally down the slopes of San Fortunato, in his carrier, to break up a party of enemy mortars and MG42s firing on our forward troops. "I see what you mean. Do you usually go forward in a carrier?"

"Usually, but not always. In the fighting before the Gothic Line I man-packed the guns with the forward companies. It was tough going."

"Okay — something else I don't understand is where the old carrier platoon fits in. It used to have four sections, each of three carriers, 12 in all."

"Well, the old carrier platoon has pretty well disappeared. You'll remember the original carriers were supposed to take men close to the objective, dump them off and let them dash forward to the enemy position? Well, they found this was nonsense, as the armour on the carrier was too thin to stop anything except sling shots; the carriers were getting knocked out at the start line.

"Now carriers are used mainly to carry MMGs and mortars, cart supplies, and transport the CO, adjutant, MO, company commanders and others.

"Your MMG Platoon has two sections of two guns each, and you'll be lucky if you get three of them to fire at any one time. You know they're exactly the same gun used in the First War. I swear our guns were made in 1914."

"Yeah," I laughed, "I believe you. We had some old Vickers guns at RMC that were made *before* the First War."

Johnny continued, "Each section is commanded by a sergeant; each gun is commanded by a corporal and manned by three men plus the driver of the carrier. Your platoon HQ should be seven, including yourself. I guess that makes 29 all ranks.

"As well as being in command of the MMGs, you'll also be in charge of all the carriers in the battalion and their drivers, except the Mortar Platoon — they're a law unto themselves. Your total strength, MMG Platoon and Carrier Section, should be about 45, but you'll never be up to strength.

"Really, your main job is to keep in touch with the CO and advise him on deployment of the machine guns. At the same time, you've got to keep those carriers running, and make sure those who are entitled to carriers are happy with their drivers."

This was all as clear to me as mud. Italian mud. But I thanked Johnny for his exposé on the unofficial MMG Platoon and hurried off to my *ad hoc* command.

My platoon sergeant was Sgt J L Rennie who had joined the Regiment on the outbreak of war and had served with it ever since. It was reassuring to have such an experienced veteran as my right-hand man and I looked forward to going into action with him. It was not to be — he left the Regiment under the new scheme to return long-serving members to Canada. His place was ably filled by Sgt R R (Russ) Mableson, also a veteran, who had joined in 1939 and been wounded in the fighting for Villa Rogatti.

No 1 Section was commanded by Sgt W Goodburn who had been wounded near Ortona and was to suffer a tragic death a year later, to the day. No 2 Section was commanded by Sgt J E Jennings, again a veteran from 1939. He would survive to the end of the war. The Carrier Section was commanded by LSgt F R Adkin, another original who had joined the Regiment on the outbreak of war. I soon found out that many of the men were also veterans who had seen much action and survived one or two wounds.

The carrier drivers were a special breed. They had been dashing about in their beloved chariots for years — on training schemes in England, through the dust of Sicily, back and forth across the Appenines a dozen times, and now into the Po Valley. Most of them could have had promotions years before, but preferred to manoeuvre their beasts over treacherous Italian trails and mined roads and through constant shellfire, to bring supplies and ammunition to the troops in the front lines. They were professionals and they knew it. They were survivors; and they were characters.

The machine gunners were likewise highly competent, but casualties and sickness had taken their toll and I had a difficult time trying to get reinforcements and keep four guns in action. Just as Koensgen had warned, the Vickers had seen a lot of service and often required spare parts which we sometimes had to borrow (steal) from the SLI, if we couldn't get them through legitimate channels.

Speaking of characters, my batman, Pte M A Murdy, was a typical example of the state of the art. A tough little guy, he had joined the battalion in 1942 and had been one of the first to be wounded in Sicily. (He would be badly wounded in January 1945, never to return to the Regiment). He was somewhat older, and had seen much more action than me. In his mind, this allowed him to bully, or 'mother' me to death, depending on his mood. He would sometimes go to great lengths to do some little act he thought would please me. For example, early in the morning, he would wake me up with a cup of tea, which he would place beside my inert form curled up in a bed roll or blanket. It became a ritual that he was determined should continue, even in action, when I needed all the sleep I could get.

I tried to explain to Murdy that while I appreciated his fine service, I needed my sleep more than the tea. Still the brew appeared each morning before dawn. Finally, I had to tell him the tea was cold and not fit for a mule to drink. He was to cease and desist forthwith.

"Sir," smiled Murdy with a sly wink, "you're not supposed to drink the stuff. Just stick your finger in the cup. When it's cold, you know it's time to get up.''

How to cope with characters like these? The answer wasn't easy, but I had some clues. Though I had not nearly the experience in action of my boys and knew nothing about Vickers guns or carriers, I had been handling men in all manner of situations for the past four years. By now, I knew all their tricks as well as their foibles.

I always tried to keep in mind the excellent advice the Earl of Athlone had given our class at RMC:

> *The first duty of a young officer is to gain the confidence, the respect and affection of his men. Once this has been accomplished, the handling of the men becomes quite an easy matter, and they will follow him anywhere.*
>
> *Then I must warn you against the man who tries to play 'the old soldier' on a young officer, which is no rare occurrence. My advice to you is this — just think quickly and turn the joke against the man. You will find the other men will appreciate your adroitness and you will be saved from any further inconvenience on this score.*

I had indeed learned to walk the thin line between exercising reasonable discipline and being 'one of the boys'. What was needed now was to get to know the strengths and weaknesses of these characters, and for them to have a chance to assess me before our next action. At this point, I half suspected that I too had become a bit of a character.

Clearly a platoon smoker was needed to clear the air. It would bring out the best, as well as the worst, in them and in me. Sgt Mableson was placed in charge of vino and any other forms of alcohol he could scrounge; Sgt Goodburn was ordered to liberate a 'live beef' (not one that had been aged on the battlefield); Sgt Jennings was made OC Entertainment; and I detailed myself to acquire a piano. A quick recce around our rest area soon revealed that the prior tenants had destroyed or taken away all cattle, vino and pianos in the town. There was nothing for it but to go up to the front and liberate the stuff from under the very noses of the Germans and our own MPs (Military Policemen). Of the two, the MPs would probably cause the most trouble as all roads were clogged with vehicles of 5th Canadian Armoured Division trying to debouch into the Po Valley. Scrounging parties were strictly forbidden.

I called over Sgt Mableson. ''While 5th Div is busy debouching, why don't we do some 'debauching' in our carriers, in the area of the 56th British Division. They're not nearly as strict as our 5th Div and I'm sure they'd appreciate a carton of Sweet Caps I just received today.''

''Great idea, Sir, but I doubt if they'd let you take back a piano in a carrier. Looks a little . . . . unwarlike. And I doubt if the thing would fit.''

"Good point. See if you can find a 15 cwt with flaps and a large tarp to cover over the piano."

"Yeah, and if they stop us, we're just taking back our dead for a decent burial."

In short order the required vehicle arrived with Sgt Mableson, Sgt Goodburn and three strong men. We set off for the front about 15 miles ahead. I had taken the trouble to get a map from the IO which he had kindly marked up showing the current dispositions of the units of 56th British Division and the Germans. Santarcangelo had just been captured by the 1st British Armoured Division and the 56th Division was pushing through to take the next village, Savignano, about three miles to the north.

It was slow going to Rimini through heavy traffic of the 5th Canadian Division along Highway No 16, known since ancient times as the Via Adriatica. At Rimini, we crossed the famous Ponte di Tiberio, erected in 27 AD, which the Germans had incredibly left standing. The other bridges and nearly all the buildings and monuments had been destroyed by the enemy or our own artillery.

We weaved our way through the terrible destruction and turned west onto another venerable landmark — Highway No 9, known in Caesar's day as the Via Emilia. Ahead lay Santarcangelo, and beyond that, Savignano on the Fiumicino River, said to be the Rubicon that Caesar himself had crossed some 2,000 years before.

I had no wish to duplicate Caesar's feat, which after all was a simple, unopposed crossing. He didn't have to face the whole 76th German Panzer Corps.

On the outskirts of Santarcangelo we were stopped at a crossroads by a British MP, immaculately dressed in summer drill, white belt, red band around the hat. In the midst of all the congestion and shellfire he was cooly directing traffic as if he were in Hyde Park on a Sunday afternoon.

"Can't go any further. The Germans are only two miles ahead and have been shelling the town all day, trying to knock out our OP in the church."

Just then a German 105 crunched into a house a few yards away, filling the intersection with debris and dust. Sgt Goodburn involuntarily stepped on the gas and we shot past the MP who had been knocked to the ground by the blast.

"Christ," cursed one of the men, "we'll be court martialled if they catch us."

"No fear of that. That MP has his hands full straightening out the mess behind us," yelled Sgt Goodburn.

In town, we stopped at the first large house, pulled into the little courtyard and dashed inside. The vehicle would be safe except for a lucky mortar bomb plunging from a high angle. Now the shells came over in salvos and crashed into the houses and streets of the little village. The Germans were really mad about the OP in the church and were giving it a terrible pasting. Several direct hits tore away parts of the steeple and demolished the roof. I was glad I wasn't the unfortunate FOO the Germans were trying to dislodge.

Then I started to think about my own situation, my men and the vehicle. "Jesus," I muttered to myself, "if we get hit there'll be hell to pay all round. We're supposed to be at rest in Cattolica. No one knows we're here in the forward area of a British division. Second Echelon will never find us. It will the "disappeared person' routine all over again. Worse still, if our 15 cwt gets damaged, there'll be a hell of a court of inquiry and I'll have to pay for the bloody thing."

Sgt Mableson eased such depressing thoughts with a gleeful shout "We've hit gold. Come down the cellar. There's gallons, I mean barrels, of vino, whatever you want — rosso, bianco, even marsala, and a few bottles of spumante."

His find spurred me on to complete my mission — one second-hand piano. A quick check of the house left me empty-handed. I ducked into the house next door. There, in the front room stood the object of my search, slightly damaged, but still playable.

Only Sgt Goodburn was disappointed. There were no stray cows in the town, but he had corralled a fat little pig in the courtyard. I assured him this was a fine substitute. Anyway, we couldn't possibly have transported back in our small vehicle one 'live beef', one piano and three barrels of vino.

We waited for a break in the shellfire, jumped into the vehicle and hurtled down the road, the flaps securely tied down, the pig duly throttled. We flashed past the MP still calmly directing his traffic, though the intersection was now a pile of damaged vehicles and fallen masonry.

We eased into our platoon area at dusk. That evening, the MMGs had a memorable barbeque, washed down with quantities of vino, accompanied by voices raised in song, and music by a non-stop piano player. Most popular ditty of the night was: *We have 'debauched' into the Valley of the Po. We have dealt the Hun a mighty fucking blow.*

Next morning Pte Murdy gave me a confidential report, along with his cold cup of tea. The platoon generally agreed that the piano player had shown commendable stamina both at the piano and the bar, in the true Patricia fashion. He had passed the test. I confidentially informed Murdy that the piano player was likewise well satisfied with his boys.

A report to father on my new command was long overdue. I had a lot of news to cover since arriving at the battalion.

> *When we came out into rest where we are now, there were several vacancies for promotions, so I went to command the MG Pl, where I now am. It's not an increase in rank for me, but a specialist's job. My training in Vickers which I had at the*

College will be a great help.

Now I shall work with the Colonel, as I did in the Scouts. It seems to me that you had the Lewis gun Platoon for a time in the last war. Once again, I'm following your footsteps. Although my guns are MMGs, their employment will be somewhat the same. It is an interesting job, and of course, a 'cushy' one.

My hopes of getting a Coy will take some time. Since I've left the Regiment, almost all the officers have changed around, and they have been bringing out tailor-made Captains from England and Canada in my absence. This is a very bitter business for me, and I shall never be able to reconcile myself with the zombie captains. I suppose it was the same in the last war. Chaps who deserved promotion were done out by the 'base wallahs'. However, I now have a responsible job.

No need to worry about getting malaria. I had a recurrence on the boat coming down, so I'm safe for another year. I didn't want to tell you till I had been in action and found out how I was. Well, I was OK — so no worries in that line. This attack was nothing compared to my first one.

It was nice to learn that Capt George (Knobby) Clark is doing well at Christie Street Hospital. I know him well. We had a big reunion last March 17th in England, and as he couldn't talk and I had my jaws wired, we made quite a pair sputtering over our drinks!

Sam (Bob) Potts received his A/Majority this week. He has been very lucky and of course done very well. The snap of you and brother officers standing and lying about a jeep was rather good. Do they supply jeeps to your unit? They are very hard to come by out here, and right now I am putting up a big fight to get one for my MG Pl.

I couldn't resist getting in a dig at father for having a jeep in a Reserve Army Unit. This was the ultimate mode of transportation and I fought long, and finally with success, to get one. But it was the source of my undoing, as will be related.

Following my usual custom, my letter to my mother spoke of the lighter side of my adventures. Among my various duties as a member of Support Company was mess secretary of the Officers' Mess of that company.

I must tell you something of our Officers' Mess. When we go into rest, usually for a couple of weeks, our main thought is to make ourselves as comfortable as possible, and this applies particularly to Support Coy. I am the Mess Secretary for the Coy, with full powers of commandeering things for the mess. I've set up an establishment that is second to none in the Bn. The officers are quartered in a well-to-do Wop Villa with all household facilities in good order — beds, armchairs, lights, tables, chinaware, etc.

Our meals are the envy of all other officers. Today's menu included steak, French fried potatoes, lemon pie, coffee, doughnuts. This is not issue rations, as you can see. But with an eye to the countryside and armed with the Wop lingo, there's nothing in the way of food which is too hard to obtain. Tomorrow I expect to find a nice fat little pig, or maybe a few turkeys or chicken.

Luckily the troops can usually find a house to set up in and thus get cover from the terrific rains we've been having lately. You will remember the downpour we were caught in when the family crossed Death Valley en route to California. Last night's rain reminded me of that.

There's strong rumour of a Regimental party tonight. Expect I'll be the pianist as I've been much in demand this past week at Coy parties, to supply the music.

Our pleasant interlude at Cattolica was coming to an end. The omens were there for all to see. October rains beat against our walls and poured through openings that had once been protected by windows and doors. Strong gales hurled down from the north; heavy seas flooded our villas by the sea. Soon it would be time for us to advance once more into the flooded Romagna plain.

Training in the use of assault boats gave further clues as to forthcoming operations. Crazy rumours flew around that we would now lead the way across the Po River and on to Venice, but even Pte Murdy was skeptical about that one. "How t'hell is the armour going to cross a dozen rivers and push through 100 miles of mud to the Po? They can't do it without our support." Murdy had a keener appreciation of ground and climatic conditions than the corps commander.

The past two weeks had been busy ones for me: learning about Vickers guns and their employment, firing range practices, doing assault boat training, working in the new reinforcements and training new drivers. I was beginning to understand the workings of my new command and to enjoy my new responsibilities.

I now prepared my MMG Platoon for action, deciding whose turn it was to be LOB and allocating carriers and drivers to the CO, adjutant, MO, rifle company commanders and others entitled to such transport. All four Vickers guns were in good shape so the MMG Platoon would have five carriers forward: one for each gun and one as my command post. Six carriers and their drivers under Sgt Adkin would be left behind in X area as LOB to come forward and replace casualties.

Clear signs of pending action now arrived in the person of MGen Vokes, his bushy moustache bristling more fiercely than ever, who gave all the officers a pep talk. He warned us against undue optimism regarding the early end of the war, and said that the last shot was by no means fired. This was hardly news to any officer who had eyes to read a map and ears to hear the steady torrent of rain. Good thing, I thought, that Pte Murdy wasn't present. I could just imagine him yelling, "Who t'hell feels optimistic about this God-forsaken war?"

Then the corps commander himself gave the officers and NCOs a little talk on things to come. He too warned there was much hard fighting ahead — dead silence in the assembly hall. But I could almost hear Pte Murdy, two miles away in his billets, yelling, "So what else is new?"

In an effort to bolster our morale, the general proceeded to tell us that we were not to think that Italy was a secondary theatre of operations. Again silence from the audience, though I imagined an angry "HS" from Pte Murdy.

Then, in a last-ditch attempt to stroke our ego, the corps commander declared that the Allied forces in Italy were opposing as many enemy divisions as were holding the West Wall on the Western Front. This was such patent nonsense that this time I really did hear a muttered "HS" from the audience. Numbers of divisions meant nothing. It was the quality, type and strength of divisions that mattered.

Even a private soldier knew that all the German Divisions were way understrength; many contained a high proportion of foreign, impressed troops. Polish deserters came through our lines in droves. Furthermore, the enemy order of battle included Italian Divisions and even a converted Air Force Division.

Finally, the corps commander delivered his *pièce de résistance*: "The Germans will give up when they realize they are beaten." To which Murdy's retort: "Profound, boss, profound."

All that remained, we thought, to complete this star-studded performance, was a personal appearance from the 8th Army Commander, Gen Leese. But the general had just been called to higher duties and his successor, LGen McCreery, was sensibly spending time poring over the maps of our new killing grounds.

More signs of an imminent return to action continued to appear. The IO passed out a new set of maps and code-names for us to study. These maps were so bad that we were convinced the cost of production had been secretly subsidized by the Germans. Their scale was usually 1/25,000, meaning 1 inch = .395 miles, normally a fairly good scale for military operations. But the maps were based on Italian maps prepared before the turn of the century and updated by various other sources including road maps.

The ancient Italian map makers must have been artists from the impressionist school for they covered their maps with their impressions of what hills, rivers and valleys looked like. The result was a cluttered, undecipherable mess, showing authorities such as "copied from an Italian Map 1894, principal communications revised from Italy Road Map 1938, reproduced by 2nd Polish Corps, August 1944." The reason the Polish Corps got into the act was that they were originally supposed to take over our front on the Adriatic coast and had therefore prepared maps of the area. When LGen McCreery took over command of the 8th Army from Gen Leese on September 29th, he changed these plans and directed the Canadian Corps to remain on the east coast.

As we pored over the colourless, dull grey maps, we found one thing had been made abundantly clear by the 'impressionists': the low-lying plain was one continuous swamp, criss-crossed with rivers and canals.

Field Marshal Alexander was under no illusions as to the morass the troops would have to flounder through in the battlefields ahead:

> *The whole area is nothing but a great reclaimed swamp — and not wholly reclaimed in some parts — formed by the lower courses of numerous rivers flowing down from the Apennines. In addition there are hundreds of smaller streams with canals and irrigation ditches between them. By canalization of the main rivers the primitive swamp had been drained after centuries of patient effort; as the water flowed off so the level of the ground sank. The river beds were left thereafter higher than the surrounding country. As soon as they descend to the plain all these rivers need high banks on each side to keep them in their courses and to guide them against sudden rises of level which heavy rainfall or snow melting in the mountain invariably cause. Even in the best drained areas the soil remembers its marshy origin. When rained on it yields the richest mud known to the Italian Theatre.[1]*

The conditions reminded me of father's stories of the mud and filth of the battlefields of France in the First War. I also remembered the 'gumbo' of Camp Shilo, Manitoba, and before that in Saskatoon. There was no escaping the sticky stuff.

We wondered how the 'Mighty Maroon Machine'* had fared in all this muck since taking over from us on September 23rd near Rimini. We remembered how this cocky Division had boasted they would "unleash their armour" in the plains and roll straight on to the Po River and beyond.

They had failed miserably, albeit through no fault of their own. The rains came, the streams turned into torrents and the enemy fought hard at every obstacle. In five days they advanced only five miles to the Fiumicino River,

---

*5th Canadian Armoured Division, so named because of the maroon patches on their shoulders.

and there they sat, not able to move one inch. We were not unduly distressed with our haughty friends getting their come-uppance after their vain boasts of throwing the Hun back across the Po River. In truth, it gave me some satisfaction. Twenty percent of my class at RMC had joined the 'Recce' because they would be always in the vanguard in armoured vehicles, well ahead of the plodding infantry. One of the most famous recce regiments in the Canadian Army was the PLDGs (Princess Louise Dragoon Guards) the recce regiment of 1st Canadian Division, who had fought in Sicily and southern Italy in their light tanks. However, by July 1944, the staff realized that the rugged Italian terrain was no place for tanks; furthermore, 5th Canadian Armoured Division badly needed another infantry brigade. The upshot of the matter was that a new infantry brigade was formed, named the 12th Infantry Brigade, and the PLDGs, stripped of their armour, joined it as foot sloggers.

While I hoped that the heavy fighting of the 5th Division in the advance to the Fiumicino River had not claimed any of my friends, I shed no tears for the miseries they now had to share in common with the rest of the foot soldiers in our division.

But if the men of the 5th Division were beaten by the weather, you had to admire their superior administration. According to LCol Nicholson, "the arrival of the cold, wet weather was officially recognized in the brigade order of 3 October: Effective immediately, winter underwear, long, as issued, will be taken into wear.[2]

The 5th Division always did things with class, while poor old 1st Division floundered around the mud in their shorts. I recalled with some bitterness how my own mother had given away my long underwear to the bloody Russians. The war was getting out of hand. Now we had to compete for supplies with our own troops, the Russians and misguided mothers.

On October 11th, LCol Clark gave us preliminary orders for the forthcoming operation. The 1st Brigade would begin the advance by leap-frogging out of the bridgehead established by the British 56th Division at Savignano, on the Fiumicino River. The brigade would continue to advance to the Pisciatello River where our brigade (2nd Brigade) would cross the river and exploit to the Savio River.

On October 12th we said goodbye to our billets and friends at Cattolica and moved toward the front, in cool, cloudy weather. The traffic on the coast road was extremely heavy and caused many delays. At Riccione we halted, after an advance of only five miles, and remained there for the next 36 hours while the staff tried to sort out the congestion on the road ahead. I was quite happy to have this unexpected bonus of free time. I relaxed and read a novel I carried in my pack — *One More River to Cross* by John Galsworthy — a particularly apt choice, I thought.

On the morning of October 14th we moved again to another area near

Santarcangelo, where I had performed my 'piano caper' a couple of weeks earlier. The town was now a complete ruin. This somewhat eased my conscience, as the piano and other things I had liberated, and which had served a very useful purpose, would have been wasted had they remained in the town.

My MMG Platoon was suffering no pain. Kenny, our cook, was right up with us and served excellent meals. While the town had been flattened and wasn't even worth exploring, the countryside yielded considerable 'game' (cows, pigs, chickens and the like). Murdy continued his ministrations and even managed to produce a *hot* cup of tea. In my diary I gave him full credit: "Murdy has become *molto buono* batman."

The weather had now improved considerably, which was a lucky break as we were living in the open. But if we were happy, the staff were ecstatic. They figured the bad weather was all behind us and we would be able to renew our charge to the Po. "We will debouch . . . . ."

The Seaforths now received orders to secure a bridgehead over the Pisciatello River at Ponte della Pietra. The PPCLI would then pass through and establish a bridgehead over the Savio River.

While the Seaforths formed up for their attack, we continued to move forward, ready to leap through the moment they crossed the river. On the night of October 17th, the Seaforths launched their attack but ran into trouble from a determined enemy and needed the help of the Edmontons to form the bridgehead.

Late on October 18th, we finally received our orders to enter the battle. We had been standing by on three hours' notice since 1300 hours, October 16th, and the waiting was beginning to test our nerves. The PPCLI would cross the Pisciatello at 0730 hours on October 19th and cut the lateral road, at San Egidio (code-named Three Nuns) and at a crossroads code-named Upperchurch. The MMG Platoon would remain near Tac HQ, ready to move forward on a moment's notice.

I called my boys together and gave them the picture. They were ready for the fray and itching to fire their Vickers which had been silent for almost four weeks.

Sgt Mableson was in a fine fighting mood — "I wish the CO would 'unleash' the whole platoon, and we'd sweep right through to the Savio."

"Oh yeah," said Sgt. Goodburn, "Just like the Mighty Maroon Machine, I suppose!"

At 0500 hours on October 19th, the battalion moved forward, crossed the Pisciatello River, and took their immediate objectives without much trouble, except for mines, which the Pioneer Platoon under Lt Horton promptly removed. But as D Company approached Upperchurch they were pinned down by enemy tank fire and two of our own tanks were knocked out. In the meantime A Company went forward and took San Egidio. Then

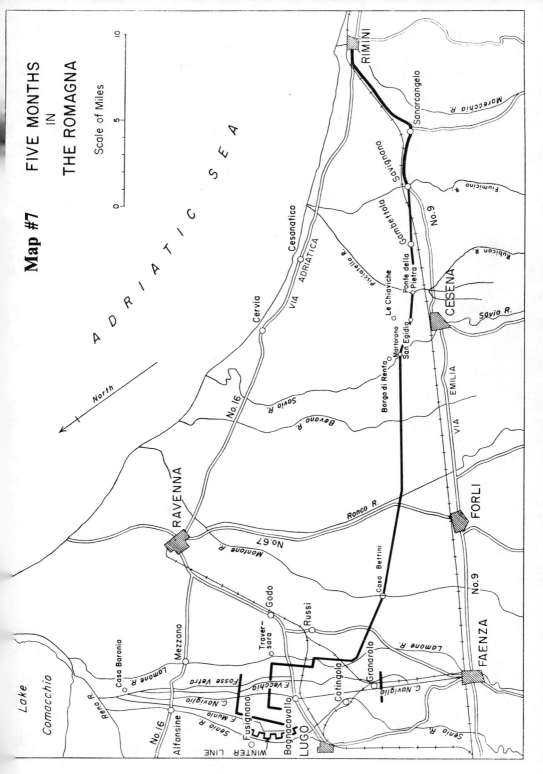

Map #7

FIVE MONTHS
IN
THE ROMAGNA

Scale of Miles

0   5   10

A and D companies put in a pincer attack on Upperchurch and cleared the crossroads.

Early next morning the remainder of the battalion moved forward. B Company was despatched to take the crossroads at Tay, close to the Savio River; C Company was ordered to capture the crossroads at Snake, also near the river, and some 1,000 yards south of Tay.

The two companies reached their objectives and sent forward patrols to the river. The patrols met enemy fire and were not able to cross. They reported that the river had risen with the recent rains and was quite swift. The banks were steep, with little cover. Enemy were seen in the open on the opposite bank with dug-in positions.

Rain had started to fall. The stage was set for the crossing of the Savio.

Chapter XXIV

THE SAVIO RIVER

October 20 to October 23, 1944

4th British Div is trailing in our wake
We occupy the towns that they're supposed to take
They get the houses free of rent
While we are living in our tent
Onward to Bologna, onward to the PO

October 20 — 1300 hours

Col Clark calls an 'O' Group for 1430 hours in San Egidio, to give the plan for establishing a bridgehead over the Savio River, lying some 2,000 yards west of Tac HQ.

The Savio River is not like the Pisciatello nor any of the small streams the Patricias have crossed in the past few days. In the dry season the river is only 50 feet wide; but now, swollen by the storm waters from the mountains and the rain last night and this morning, it is three times its normal size and the current is swift.

In many places the water is too deep to ford; the troops may have to swim. Earthen dykes, 300 feet apart at their crests, keep the swollen waters from overflowing into the low-lying plain where the battalion will form up for the attack. The soft banks of the dykes are steep and have turned into walls of mud.

As if these obstacles are not enough, the Germans have cleared the banks of all trees and vegetation to give their machine gunners unrestricted fields

323

of fire.

This morning the corps commander ordered MGen Vokes to get a bridgehead over the Savio. Despite the obstacles, the adverse weather conditions, the impossibility of tank support, the likelihood of mine fields on the greasy banks of the river and the fact that the initial attack will be made in daylight, despite all these things, MGen Vokes has arranged with the brigade commander that the Patricias will cross today on a two-company front.

October 20 — 1430 hours
The 'O' group assembles in a shell-torn house on the outskirts of San Egidio. There is barely space for all the members in the smoke-filled room: adjutant, intelligence officer, signals officer, medical officer; four company commanders: Maj Ted Cutbill (Able Company), Capt Andy Campbell (Baker Company), Maj Sam Potts (Charlie Company), Capt Robinson (Dog Company); commanders of the battalion support platoons: mortars, anti-tank guns, MMGs and pioneers; representatives from artillery, tanks, engineers and SLI. All are packed together in one room, poring over map boards and studying new code-names just issued by the IO. In an adjoining room the wireless sets screech and whine as the operators adjust frequencies and try to net the sets.

Outside, enemy shells and Moaning Minnies explode around the *casa* and shake the walls. One of the vehicles is hit. The MO slips outside to check for casualties.

LCol Clark enters the room and immediately issues his orders. The crossing will be made by two companies: Able and Dog. Able Company will cross in the vicinity of Charlie Company's position at a road intersection near the river code-named 'Snake'.

Dog company will cross in the vicinity of Baker Company's position, also at an intersection near the river, code-named 'Tay', about 1,000 yards north of Snake. There will be no tank support until the engineers have thrown across a bridge, but there will be strong artillery, mortar and MMG fire.

My Vickers are already in position to support the attack with direct fire; two guns are with Charlie Company at Snake; two guns and my HQ are with Baker Company at Tay.

I ask the CO if he has any special instructions for the MMGs. Yes, he has. As soon as Able and Dog companies have established the bridgehead, I am to take my four guns across the river and set up for the counter-attacks that are bound to develop. I will remain with the CO throughout the initial attack in case something goes wrong that requires my guns to cross the river immediately.

October 20 — 1530 hours

The 'O' Group breaks up and the members hasten to their HQ to prepare for the attack. Zero hour is 1700 hours, only an hour and a half away — hardly enough time to make all the preparations for such a difficult operation. But LCol Clark has received his orders to proceed immediately and this he intends to do.

I want to make a last minute check of my guns at Snake and Tay. Capt Andy Campbell sets out for his company HQ at Tay. I jump in his jeep and we roar off toward the river. Our artillery have been firing all afternoon; now they are making their final corrections for the assault. The Germans are not standing idly by. They are countering with their heavies, 88s and Moaning Minnies. As we race along the road, Andy at the wheel, an enemy stonk laces the crossroads we have just gone through. Jerry has obviously registered all likely targets in the area and knows something is up. Another cluster of bombs explodes 50 yards ahead of us. I have a horrible feeling the enemy gunners are following our jeep from an OP on the dyke, 300 yards ahead; their next salvo will surely land on top of us.

The jeep spurts forward, slews off the road and skids to a stop in the lee of a strong *casa*. Immediately, the house is shaken by the blast of an 88 exploding in the front yard. Andy only smiles and welcomes me to his company HQ. He offers to take me forward to the river in the jeep so I can check the guns of No 1 Section. I know he's only kidding but I'm not going to call his bluff.

I head toward the river at a steady trot. A carload of Moaning Minnies screams overhead and crashes on the road behind me. Only 100 yards more to my gun position in the strong house. My mind flashes back to running races at RMC and the Biferno River. One hundred yards should only take ten seconds. I will do it in eight.

I hurtle into the house. My gun crews are glad to see me; but they are not impressed with my world record. Running scared doesn't count.

The two Vickers of No 1 Section are mounted in an upstairs room and have been zeroing in on targets across the river in preparation for the assault by Able and Dog companies this afternoon. Cpl Kilborn points out German weapon pits and dugouts clearly visible around a large white house on the other side of the river. He tells me that Jerry has been pretty cocky and is not afraid to expose himself as he ducks in and out of the house. I think I see a couple of the enemy and quickly raise my binoculars. Cpl Kilborn restrains me. I am much too close to the window. Jerry also has a couple of snipers waiting to drill anyone who offers them a target. One man in Baker Company bought it this morning when he leaned on the windowsill to take a shot.

I check the fields of fire of the guns though I know they are covering the ground perfectly. My boys are real professionals. Still, I want to tie in this section and my other section in Charlie Company's area at Snake, to ensure the four guns cover the entire battalion front as well as the flanks.

I see that both gun barrels are resting on steel bars supported by stones and that a piece of signal wire is attached to the traversing handle of the guns. I ask Cpl Kilborn, "What kind of contraption is this?"

He gives me a large grin. "You know how we don't have any proper indirect or night firing equipment. Well, I rigged up these iron bars so they will keep the guns on the right elevation for night firing. The signal wire holds the traverse handles on the line of fire."

This is a pretty ingenious way of firing at a target at night. "What about the flash from the guns?" I ask. Cpl Foulis has the answer. "We fire through wet blankets. They conceal the flash at night." I think this is also a great idea, but it's going to deplete the QM's store of blankets in short order. "Don't worry, sir," laughs Cpl Foulis, who can read my mind, "we use liberated Itie blankets."

My No 1 Section is in good hands. I wish them luck and quickly head for No 2 Section at Snake, 1,000 yards south. It is now past 1600 hours and the attack goes in at 1700 hours. If I'm going to check No 2 Section and get back to Tac HQ before Zero hour, I had better get the lead out of my backside. In fact, with constant enemy shelling along my route, there's a good chance I will add a considerable amount of lead to my derrière. Fortunately, the river road connecting Tay and Snake, that Jerry is now blasting, runs through the small village of Martorano and there is an almost unbroken line of houses facing the road. I exit from the back of my section's house at Tay and hop from backyard to backyard in the lee of the houses that are taking the brunt of the German shelling. I have now added the record for the hop-step-and-jump to my other world records.

At Snake, I quickly check out No 2 Section to ensure their fields of fire tie in with No 1 Section at Tay. All that remains is to get back to Tac HQ at San Egidio, some 2,000 yards in rear, before 1700 hours.

I speak to Maj Sam Potts, OC of Charlie Company. I tell him I've just come from Tay and urgently need a carrier to take me to Tac HQ.

Sam hasn't got a carrier or any other vehicle. Just then a message comes over his 18 set. "Sunray* is proceeding to Tay." Sam chuckles and says he has done me two more big favours — saved me from going back a mile or so on foot in heavy shellfire that would probably have blown me apart; saved me from the wrath of LCol Clark who would surely have blasted me if the shellfire hadn't, for not being at his Tac HQ on time.

I head north again, back to Tay. The Germans are now shelling the river road with everything they've got, suspecting we'll use it as a Start Line; so I take the same route through the backyards, over fences, across vineyards,

---

* Sunray is a code-name for Commanding Officer.

narrowly missing cesspools and other barnyard hazards, and arrive at Tac HQ just before Zero hour.

October 20 — 1700 hours, Zero hour

The whole front erupts in one tremendous roar. Shells scream over our heads. Mortars fill the air with their deadly missiles. MMGs spew forth streams of lead. Tons of steel land on the far side of the river and explode in sheets of flame and clouds of smoke and dust.

Able and Dog companies rise from their positions as one man, seemingly guided by some unseen hand, and surge forward to the riverbanks. Our barrage lifts 100 yards. The Germans stream out of their dugouts and run to their weapon pits. Smoke from our 4.2 inch mortars gives our attacking troops little cover. It has pillared into columns instead of spreading out across the front. Enemy MG42s criss-cross the fields like scythes. Our men start to fall. German tanks are seen closing up to the river. The enemy is in unexpected strength. We are faced by the tough 26th Panzer Division.

Dog Company can go no farther in this deadly hail of lead. It is pinned to the ground on our side of the river, 200 yards west of Baker Company at Tay.

Able Company somehow continues. As the leading platoon approaches the riverbanks, it falls upon a minefield. The platoon moves to its left to try to outflank the obstacle, strays too far south and loses contact. The other two platoons push forward through the minefield; more men get lost, but some reach the swollen river, wade or swim across, and gain a foothold on the far bank.

Back at Tac HQ news of these disasters starts to trickle in; but LCol Clark is not a man to accept temporary failure as a final verdict. He calls me over. "Frost, we've got to get some help to Able and Dog Companies right away. I'm going to make another attempt to get Dog Company across the goddamn river. I want you to take the two guns and their crews now at Tay and cross the river with Dog Company. Able Company's 18 set is out so I don't know what's happening over there; as soon as I find out, I'll send over your other two guns at Snake."

It is a tall order and a dangerous one. LCol Clark knows it. I know it. But it has to be done. All the other troops are committed. What is needed now is firepower to stop the counter-attacks that will develop at first light.

I throw on my web equipment, check my Tommy Gun and ammo and head for the door, wondering how my gun crews are going to manhandle the heavy Vickers across the swollen river. The barrel alone weighs 40 pounds, the tripod another 50, and the bloody ammunition weights a ton. I dread the outcome.

327

October 20 — 2312 hours
I open the door and step out into a maelstrom of fire and water. LCol Clark shouts at me to come back. A message has just been received from brigade HQ. "Firm up in present positions. The Eddies and Seaforths will attack tomorrow night."

I feel like a condemned man who has just been given a reprieve on his way to the gallows. But the reprieve is only temporary; a new trial may yet exact the supreme penalty.

"Frost, cancel that order to cross the river tonight. But stand by until we get more news of Able Company. Their 18 set is still dead."

I curl up in a corner of the room and try to catch 40 winks. It's no use. Outside, the shelling and rain continue without pause. I think of my friends in Able and Dog companies, in sodden trenches, fending off the Hun and his Panthers without supporting tanks or anti-tank guns. Damn the generals and high brass for throwing us into this mess in such haste, with so little support, and without considering the enemy, the ground or the lousy weather.

October 21 — 0130 hours
Sgt Sparrow of Able Company arrives at Tac HQ. He is soaked to the skin, filthy dirty and dead beat. But he is one tough soldier. He has bravely bested Jerry and the elements to bring information from Maj Cutbill on the other side of the river.

The story he tells of Able Company's ordeals is one of courage beyond praise. When the leading platoon moved to the left to avoid the minefield, the following platoon, led by LSgt Whitford, continued on, straight ahead, over the deadly ground. In single file, the platoon crossed 600 yards of minefield, struggled through the rising waters, now up the shoulders, and floundered up the greasy riverbank. There they met a hail of fire from MG42s and dug in. Maj Cutbill counted heads — 17 all ranks, including himself. His wireless set was missing — it was with the leading platoon. Maj Cutbill did not hesitate. He sent out a scout to recce the ground ahead. When the scout was killed by a burst from a machine gun, he immediately went forward himself. He found a hedgerow running inland and led his little band along this covered approach. They bumped into a German outpost. In the ensuing fight two Germans were killed and three prisoners taken. The party returned to the riverbank and Sgt Sparrow was dispatched to find Tac HQ and bring back an 18 set.

Sgt Sparrow is of the same breed as Maj Cutbill. Despite the dangers and his fatigue all he wants to do is get back to Able Company with a new wireless set and with the rest of the company who didn't make it across the river. He's confident they can hold the tiny bridgehead. I ask him if he wants to take along a section of the MMGs who have been supporting Able Company from Charlie Company's position at Snake. No, they wouldn't have a chance lugging those heavy guns across the swift current of the river and in the face of enemy machine gun fire. Better to keep our MMGs at Snake where they have been giving excellent supporting fire.

October 21 — 0300 hours
Sgt Sparrow picks up his new 18 set. Once more, he braves enemy fire and the swirling waters and returns to Able Company, picking up a number of stragglers en route. Maj Cutbill again counts heads; he now has 35 men and they are well dug in, though the rain has increased and collapses some of the positions. He is certain he can withstand the enemy counter-attacks that will start at first light. With his 18 set he can now call down immediate artillery, mortar and MMG support.

October 21 — 0900 hours
The indomitable Sgt Sparrow appears again at Tac HQ, cold, wet, hungry, but still full of fight. He is immediately taken to brigade HQ to help them plan the attack by the Eddies and Seaforths tonight. The enemy shelling increases in intensity and covers the whole battalion area. On his way back from brigade HQ, Sgt Sparrow's luck runs out. He is wounded and his place as runner *extraordinaire* is taken over by CSM Woods.*

During the rest of the day, the battalion firms up its position and prepares to support the attack by the Eddies and Seaforths. The rain continues in torrents and makes life miserable for Able Company on the far bank who have enough problems repulsing attack after attack, by an aroused and determined enemy.

From my HQ at Tay I can hear the steady chatter of my Vickers guns in Baker Company area. They will be getting low on ammunition and food. I organize a carrying party and we dash forward to the gun position during the short intervals between enemy stonks. The section has been having a field day, pumping belt after belt of ammo into Jerry positions in front of Dog Company. Their strong *casa* has taken several direct hits and is a shambles. One man has been wounded and will have to be evacuated immediately. I will leave one of the men from my relief party as a replacement.

The guns are in good shape despite the constant firing. Even the contraption rigged up by Cpl Kilborn for night firing is still working and from reports of the forward companies has been right on target.

I return to Tac HQ, pick up more ammo and food and head for Snake where No 2 Section has been supporting the hard-pressed Able Company. It is a long haul and I would like to take a carrier, but the slightest movement

---

* Sgt Sparrow survived and was awarded the Military Medal for his bravery at the Savio River.

329

by vehicle draws intense fire.

No 2 Section is right out of ammo. They have had an exciting time helping to break up the counter-attacks on Able Company. I peer out of a window and see Able Company's positions along the far bank of the river. How they have clung to their bridgehead, I can't understand. In my book they are the bravest of the brave.

I raise my binoculars and observe the Jerry positions. He has taken a hell of a shellacking from our 25 pounders, mediums and mortars. The houses I had seen yesterday have been blasted apart. But I know that Jerry is still there in his deep dugouts waiting to come out and cover the ground with fire. His snipers are still active and I take only a few moments to observe the scene before ducking away from the window.

My boys are in fine spirits now that they have fresh supplies of ammo and food. No one has been hurt though they've been shelled and mortared constantly. Apparently, the Germans have lost the knack of dropping bombs down the chimney as they did at the Marecchia River.

As I start to leave, an MG42 sprays the house with bullets. A few lucky shots go right through the window I had just left and wack against the walls. Jerry has been challenging us to a duel all afternoon, but my boys will not be suckered in. They'll wait until a counter-attack develops or until the Eddie-Seaforth attack tonight. They know their jobs and will continue doing them to the King's taste so long as I keep bringing up the ammo. I wait for a break in the firing and shelling, exit by a rear door and follow my old backyard route to Tay.

The engineers arrive to recce the riverbanks to erect a bridge at Snake, as originally planned. They soon find that the swollen river, swift current and steep, greasy banks make it impossible to build a bridge at the site.

October 21 — 2000 hours
A volcano of our artillery erupts and covers the German positions. The Eddies and Seaforths move through our area in pouring rain, plunge into the swift current and doggedly climb the far bank. Despite increasing enemy resistance, they stubbornly fight their way forward and take their first objectives. The Germans counter-attack with tanks and self-propelled guns. At Pieve Sestina, 1,000 yards from the river, a singular act of high valour takes place. Charlie Company of the Seaforths is attacked by three Panther tanks, two self-propelled guns and about 30 infantry. Pte E A Smith, a member of the tank-hunting platoon, single-handedly takes on this formidable foe; when the smoke clears away one tank has been disabled and the others and their supporting infantry have withdrawn in disarray, leaving the field strewn with dead and wounded Germans.*

---

* Smith was awarded the Victoria Cross.

330

October 22 — 0300 hours

A party carrying supplies across the river to the beleaguered Able Company is fired on. Sgt Nile is killed and four others wounded. The party presses on and finally delivers their precious supply of ammo and food to Able Company, the first in more than 30 hours.

The engineers, working under constant shelling and heavy machine gun fire, get a pontoon ferry into operation at Tay by 0900 hours; further supplies are sent to Able Company, and casualties and POWs evacuated.

October 22 — 1600 hours

An 'O' Group assembles in a battered house 1,000 yards north of San Egidio where LCol Clark issued his first orders for this "lousy" operation two days ago. That I call the operation lousy is no fault of LCol Clark. Despite the reverses, the casualties, the constant shelling, the relentless rain, the lack of sleep, he has kept up the morale of the battalion and is still making plans to deal the Hun a knock-out blow. The fault can be laid clearly at the feet of the staff officers at brigade, division and corps. They have failed miserably to appreciate the problems involved in crossing the river. Even a cursory glance at their precious pamphlets on staff duties in the field should have warned them that the Patricia attack had no chance of success.

As I wait, half asleep, for the 'O' Group to assemble, I try to keep myself awake by thinking of the factors the staff should have considered when they made an appreciation for that ill-fated attack two days ago — if in fact they made any appreciation at all:

1. *Relative strengths of the enemy and our own troops.* We are opposed by the tough 26th Panzer Division who are well dug in with supporting tanks, artillery and mortars. They have clearly shown in past actions they are determined to delay our advance at every obstacle. They have had months to prepare their positions.

2. *Ground.* The ground ahead is made-to-measure for the enemy. Our tanks haven't a hope of climbing the steep, slippery banks and navigating the river. The roads and fields are morasses of mud. Enemy tanks will be right up with the forward troops. The river is a natural obstacle, even in good weather. The rains have made it impassable. The enemy have cut down all trees and vegetation. They have perfect fields of fire and observation. All approaches will doubtless be mined.

What possible hope is there that two rifle companies, even if they are Patricias, can secure a bridgehead?

3. *Time and space.* I remember the hurried preparations for the attack and the pressure from brigade and division to "get a bridgehead over the Savio". There was no time for a proper recce of the river or the approaches. Why the indecent haste? Why a daylight attack? Why not a silent night attack? I doubt if any of these factors were considered.

331

4. *Administration.* Supply of ammo and rations to the bridgehead depends on the engineers quickly erecting a bridge across a river 300 feet from crest to crest. The banks are soft from the heavy rains and the approaches are walls of mud. How will the troops be supplied?

5. *Air situation.* The Desert Air Force have been grounded for days because of the weather. I concede this is not the fault of the staff. They cannot control the weather, but they should damn well take it into consideration. Our overwhelming air superiority will be lost to us.

6. *Climactic considerations.* It has rained most of the night and morning. The river has swollen to three times its usual size. This is a normal condition in the Lombardy Plains at this time of year. Why wasn't it anticipated by the staff? I conclude that lack of appreciation of this factor, more than any other, is the cause of all our misfortunes.

7. *Intercommunication.* Crossing a river obstacle always leads to problems in communications. The wireless sets, at the best of times, are unreliable. Batteries wear out quickly. Enemy jamming and static are to be expected. On top of this, the 18 sets will be useless if they get soaked with water. Runners are more reliable but they are not immune from shellfire. All these problems are compounded in an opposed river crossing in torrential rain. How will communication be maintained?

As I drowsily mull over this appreciation of the situation I would have made two days ago, if anyone had taken the trouble to ask me, I realize that I have worked into it a bit of hindsight and probably a lot of frustration over the way the operation was conceived by the higher authorities. Just the same, one stark fact proves beyond all doubt that the staff erred, and grossly so — they sent one battalion to do the job of two. Even the gallant Eddies and Seaforths' attack was a bitter fight that succeeded only because of incredible heroism.*

And the ordeal is not over yet. We still do not have a bridge across the Savio, but it is rumoured that the sappers have reported a likely bridging site opposite Borgo di Ronta, 2,000 yards north of Tay. No doubt our upcoming 'O' Group will reveal a plan to cross the river at this point.

I look around at the members of the 'O' Group. They are a wet, weary, dirty-looking bunch. The lack of sleep for 48 hours, the constant battle with enemy shells, mortars and machine guns, and the horrible weather shows on every face. Some are a little punchy. Most are going by memory, or on their nerve or both. New faces have replaced many who assembled here two days ago and have since been killed or wounded but even the newcomers look haggard.

---

* The bitter fighting to cross the Savio brought units of the Second Brigade one VC, four DCMs and four Military Medals.

October 22 — 1638 hours

LCol Clark enters the room, the adjutant asks the weary group to "Please pay attention", and the CO briskly issues his orders.

The sappers have indeed confirmed that a crossing place near Borgo di Ronta seems suitable for bridging. The West Novas (The West Nova Scotia Regiment) will secure a crossing over the river at this site.

The West Novas have been placed under command of 2nd Brigade for this operation, but it is understrength so Dog Company of the Patricias will be attached to the West Novas and lead the way across the river to establish the initial bridgehead. Then two companies of the West Novas will cross the river and expand the perimeter. Finally, the sappers will build the bridge they have been trying to get across the river for the past two days. Zero hour is at midnight.

It is a simple plan, but again the staff have ignored all the basic factors that militate against success; or the staff pretend they do not exist. The advantages the enemy had in the last attacks across the river have not changed. In fact, the odds in favour of the enemy have increased. Now he is thoroughly alerted. He knows as well as we do that we can't get tanks and vehicles across the river in the area of the present bridgehead. We will have to make a further attempt at another crossing place. He also knows he has nothing to fear from the Air Force for several days because of the poor visibility: Further, rain has started again, causing the swollen Savio to rise even higher.

On top of it all, the staff, not satisfied with the débâcle they have already caused, are again going to commit the cardinal sin of sending one battalion to do the job of two.

I sense the disbelief among the members of the 'O' Group that higher authority are persisting in their suicidal plans. It is particularly tough on Dog Company who have already had their share of suffering. Once again, they have to lead the way through the ordeals of fire and water and under command of another regiment.

But goddammit, the general wants his lousy bridge and he shall have it even if it takes us all winter!

The 'O' Group disperses. We wish Capt Robinson and his Dog Company luck. They will certainly need all they can muster.

During the evening the rain keeps pelting down without pause and the swift-running river continues to rise. A patrol to the river returns to Dog Company just before Zero hour to report the water is breast-high, the banks are steep, the footing treacherous and the enemy alert.

October 22/23 — Midnight — Zero hour

Dog Company jumps off the Start Line and heads for the river. Right away things start to go wrong. The company bumps into a German patrol on our side of the river which promptly withdraws, alerting the enemy on the far bank. MG42s firing on fixed lines spew lead into the crossing; mortar bombs crash among the advancing troops. Still they press on, flounder across the river, gain the far side and force a shallow bridgehead. Then two companies of the West Novas cross the hail of fire and swirling waters and enlarge the perimeter.

At first light the enemy, itching to teach us another lesson, counter-attack with tanks and cut right through Dog Company, isolating one platoon. Without supporting tanks or anti-tank guns, Dog Company and the West Novas are at the mercy of the enemy. They withdraw to the home bank taking with them a few POWs, but leaving behind the Dog Company platoon that was cut off by the tank attack. It is assumed the platoon are all killed, wounded or taken prisoner.

The attack has failed again and for the very same reasons the earlier attacks failed.

More bad news comes in to Tac HQ. The engineers now report that the crossing site we attempted to secure last night is impossible for bridging because of the caved-in banks. Not only is the attack a failure, it was made in vain.

We lick our wounds, curse the elements, the Hun and our staff, not necessarily in that order, and wait.

October 23 — Noon
LCol Clark calls an 'O' Group. He has just received orders from Brigade that the Patricias will consolidate in their present positions. The battle for the Savio River is over!

My account would not be complete without a final reference to the gallant fight of the Seaforth tank-hunting platoon. Soon after the combined Edmonton-Seaforth attack on the night of October 21st, Baker Company at Tay started providing parties to carry ammo and food across the river to these hard-pressed battalions, and take back casualties and POWs. Several times I had run the gauntlet myself. I was happy to give our friends this help, but frankly I also undertook these exciting missions in the hope of seeing the carnage wrought on the German Panzers by Pte 'Smoky' Smith and his tank-busting platoon. I was not disappointed. On my last mission to the Seaforth position 1,000 yards from the river the evidence I came to see was strewn about the area — three Panther Mark V tanks, a half track, a scout car and two self-propelled guns. What a fantastic achievement for a handful of men! I had only a moment to marvel at the sight before a mortar stonk crashed on the road. I ducked into a ruined house and was met by two old *signore* crying and wringing their hands.

"Che cosa c'e?", I demanded.

"Due soldati sono morti," they wailed, and pointed to a corner of the room where two bodies lay wrapped in blood-soaked sheets surrounded by

flickering candles. I asked the women to unwrap the corpses and found two Germans, one an officer. The *signore* carefully wrapped the bodies again. I told them to keep the remains until a burial party arrived after the action was over. We were much too busy dodging German efforts to have us join their departed comrades, to do anything ourselves.

One happy note, and probably the only one of the entire operation, concerns the lost platoon of Dog Company which was thought to have been annihilated by the enemy. Early in the evening of October 23rd, Lt Ernie Shone staggered into my HQ at Tay, bedraggled, covered in mud, dead beat, but clearly alive, though he looked as if he had been resurrected from the dead; which he figuratively had been. He and his platoon had lain doggo after the Panthers had ground through his position forcing the rest of his company to withdraw. The platoon remained there until last light and then crept back to the river and dashed across at Tay. It was his first real experience in action and one that he doubtless never forgot. He was very lucky and I am happy to say that his luck held out for the rest of the war.

Another footnote to the Savio operation is not so pleasant to recall. After learning of the disasterous attempt by Dog Company and the West Novas to cross the river on October 23rd, the corps commander, LGen Burns, "decided to make a second attempt, using fresh troops, and conveyed this intention to the army commander by telephone."[2]

How LGen Burns arrived at such an incredible decision is difficult to understand. All the factors that were so advantageous to the enemy on October 20th, which I have taken some pains to describe, became even more favourable to him as one miserable day gave way to another. By October 23rd, the odds were so heavily weighted against our troops that only a miracle, akin to the parting of the Red Sea, could have saved us. Generals are neither paid nor qualified to usurp the powers of the Almighty, though some have been accused of assuming such powers.

The soldiers of the 1st Canadian Division can thank the new army commander, LGen McCreery, for casting aside any notion of Divine Right. He rightly appreciated that "the operations of the 5th Corps would soon bring about a further withdrawal by the 76th Panzer Corps", one of whose divisions, the 26th Panzer Division, was facing us. Accordingly he "ruled against committing 1st Canadian Division to another brigade operation."[3]

LGen McCreery was well satisfied with 2nd Brigade's achievement. He wrote to the brigade commander:

> *The way your Brigade secured a big bridgehead, smashed an enemy counter-attack, and surmounted all the difficulties of having no bridge behind was magnificent.*[4]

The part played by the MMG Platoon should not be overstated. While they endured constant shelling and heavy machine gun fire and had casualties, their efforts cannot be compared to the terrible ordeals suffered by the assaulting companies, Able and Dog. Still, the machine gunners performed their tasks with skill and determination and not a little panache.

The Savio will never be forgotten by the men who fought there. The name will endure as long as the Regiment lives. It is one of its proud Battle Honours.

MORE RIVERS TO CROSS
Bevano River — Ronco River
October 23 to November 1, 1944

They never knew where they were at
Till the old Ark bumped on Ararat
One more river — and that's the River of Jordan
One more river
There's one more river to cross

By late afternoon, on October 23rd, it was apparent that the Germans knew the game was up. The shelling of the ferry crossing at Tay eased sufficiently for the engineers to start bridging operations at the site.[1] LCol Clark received orders to move over the river and occupy positions held by The Loyal Edmonton Regiment.

During the evening and early morning the move was completed and a pontoon bridge, that had frustrated the efforts of so many troops for so long, was ready. But the approaches were so bad that a bulldozer had to tow each vehicle up the far bank.

Now the bugles were sounded at corps, division and brigade for a speedy pursuit of the departing Hun. Once again the Patricias would lead the way and throw the enemy back over the next obstacle, the Bevano River. The battalion was organized so that each rifle company was a self-contained force with its own tanks, MMGs, anti-tank guns and mortars.[2]

Each of my four Vickers guns was detached to a company, while I remained with Tac HQ. It was fun to be on the move again, even if the rain and mud slowed our 'pursuit' to a snail's pace.

337

The crossroads on the featureless plains ahead had been given code-names by the staff, which we noted on our maps or on fancy map boards covered in talc, if you had the luxury of a vehicle to carry one. I never bothered with map boards or chinagraph pencils, preferring to mark up the actual map and stuff it in a large pocket in the front of my battledress trousers. The IO and others warned me the map would disintegrate in the rain and I would lose my bearings. Get lost I did, in almost every operation, but not because of soggy maps. More often than not it was the map itself, based on ancient Italian surveys, that got me into trouble.

Most of my maps survived not only the waters and muck of the Italian rivers but the rain as well, and are before me as I write. The code-names, mainly in pencil, are a little blurred, but I can clearly follow my advance on the map, from house to house, from intersection to intersection, and from code-name to code-name — Breen, Cygnet, Dromara, Chaudiere, Ottery, Lonan, Plym, Cherwell, Annaverna, to name a few. How the staff officers dreamt up these peculiar names I never knew for sure. One officer told me the staff simply dug out a map of the British Isles and used the names of small towns in out-of-the-way places. This might account for names like Cherwell and Lonan; but Chaudiere and Snake? I never did find the answer; however, in my second career, after the War, I used this idea of choosing names from a map when I had to find a distinctive name for a new company. My clients were always impressed with the ingenious names I produced, not knowing that some village in Wales was having its name taken in vain.

Returning to our pursuit of the Hun across the Romagna, the ground ahead was exactly what Field Marshal Alexander had said it would be — reclaimed swamp land, crossed by canalized rivers with high banks on each side. The whip was out, but the hounds had been outfoxed by the weather, the nature of the ground and the departing enemy. By 2200 hours on October 24th, the Patricia companies, moving by bounds as self-contained units with their supporting arms, had covered only two miles and the leading company, Able, was at Cygnet.

This was not nearly fast enough for LCol Clark. Despite the fact the Patricias were out in the blue, with no support on either flank, he was determined to push forward to the Bevano River with all possible speed. Perhaps we could get there before the Hun had a chance to dig in. Perhaps the enemy would decamp without a fight. It was worth the risk.

LCol Clark's instinct was right. When the Scout and Sniper Platoon reached Ottery on the Bevano River, at 0850 hours on October 25th, they reported it clear. The enemy had evacuated at 0400 hours, blowing up the bridge behind them. However, the scouts reported the river could be crossed by infantry, and that the engineers should have no trouble constructing a crossing for vehicles.

As soon as LCol Clark heard this good news he ordered Dog Company to cross the Bevano and head for Lonan, 2,000 yards west of the river. Then another report came in from the scouts — "Enemy armour at Lonan". The scouts withdrew a few hundred yards and directed artillery fire on the position. The first salvo by our gunner friends was right on target and the enemy tanks withdrew in haste. Dog Company occupied the position and reported it snug by 1530 hours.

The Scout and Sniper Platoon were having a field day charging around the front in their carriers, over mined roads, bypassing snipers, well in advance of the battalion and on each flank. They were up to their old tricks of being the 'eyes and ears' of the CO. But like all platoons they were understrength and could not be everywhere at once. By the evening of the 25th, the right flank of the battalion was wide open and the companies were on the move and strung out along a 4,000 yard axis. LCol Clark called me over to his jeep.

"Frost, I don't like having my right flank so exposed. Call in all your MMGs that have been attached to the companies and, as a platoon, give me flank protection. I'll have the Anti-tank Platoon join you. By the way, you were once the Scout Officer?"

"Yes, sir, way back in southern Italy."

"Well, until your guns and the Anti-tank Platoon get organized, I have a small scout job for you."

It was the best news I had heard since rejoining the battalion.

"Look at the map. See the crossroads at Tomba and at Bradi on our right flank, about 2,000 yards from here?"

"Yes, Sir, there's quite a cluster of houses and a church."

"Well, I haven't had any reports on that area. A German column could roar down that road and slice my battalion in two. I want Capt Newlands and you, and any men you can find, to get out there right away and report back in two hours."

I soon located 'Bunchy' Newlands and we set off in two carriers with a dozen men. As the carriers skidded along the greasy road in the silent, pitch-black night, toward our objective, I experienced the same feeling of exhilaration I had known so many times with the scouts, so long ago. For a moment I felt young again — until a warning from earlier days burst in my mind. Mines!

Bunchy Newlands, in the lead, had the same premonition and brought his carrier to a stop. We both jumped to the road.

"Syd, I think we've pressed our luck far enough."

"Me, too. I'm too young to get blown up on a mine."

"Better leave the carriers here and do the last 800 yards on foot. Anyway, we'd be crazy to enter the village in a carrier. If Jerry is there, he'll wipe us out with two rounds from his 88s."

The troops dismounted from the carriers and we advanced along the road in two single files, Bunchy and six men on the right; I and five men on the left. As we approached a small bridge, Bunchy halted. I went forward to see what was the trouble.

"Lucky thing we left those carriers behind. Look at those mines near the bridge that the rains have exposed."

"Yea, I had the same feeling you did. I'm glad you stopped."

We pressed on in the silent, heavy night. Soon outlines of houses in the village appeared. The sections left the road, quietly climbed the stone fences on each side, and advanced slowly through the back yards of the first houses. A dog barked. "Curse the Wop bitch," breathed a corporal.

We halted a moment. Then I motioned my section to advance. I took a step and felt the ground give way. My other foot came forward; it too started to sink into the earth. Now both feet were together and my whole body slowly disappeared into the ground. I did not utter a sound but I was going to if I sank much farther. Then my feet hit solid ground. A pleasant warmth embraced my body; an overpowering stench filled my nostrils; sulphur fumes ate my eyes. I was up to my armpits in a farmyard cesspool!

Involuntarily I had raised my Tommy gun over my head and moved forward as I was taught at Vernon Battle School. I looked back and saw my section, one by one, silently follow me into the stinking sump hole.

We ploughed through the sewage in single file and climbed out the far side of the pool, saturated with excrement and gasping for air.

Whether the house was full of Jerries hardly entered our minds. We burst into the place looking for something to wipe away some of the foul mess. An Italian family emerged from a cellar. An old man squeeked, *"Madona, il diavola!"* I felt like the devil and smelt worse.

The village was not occupied by the Germans. They had left a few hours before, after thoroughly mining all the roads. When my section met Bunchy at the far end of the village as planned, he wouldn't let us come within 20 feet. Bunchy thought he should shoot us right there and then and save us, and incidentally his section, any further suffering. He left us standing in the road with orders not to rejoin our carrier until his had departed and was at least 500 yards down the road. We followed, as directed, like a band of outcast lepers.

News of our encounter with the cesspool rapidly spread throughout the battalion and the brigade. LCol Clark immediately moved Tac HQ forward to an unmarked intersection and refused to see me. It was rumoured that the brigade commander wanted to send us forward at once as a secret weapon, straight through the German lines to Bologna. The brigade major vetoed the idea as the enemy might consider it was the start of a gas attack and retaliate. Our gas masks were somewhere back in Sicily.

For the first time in the Italian Campaign, we blessed the rain. After several good soakings, the lethal gas fumes abated somewhat and we were allowed to join the MMG Platoon and the Anti-tanks for our role of protecting the right flank in the pursuit to the Ronco River. For the next three days we performed this task, roaming far and wide over the countryside to the north, the 'leper' section always in the lead. To no one's surprise we never caught up with the enemy, who always seemed to get advance notice (smells) of our coming and decamped just before we arrived.

During the entire advance, the Patricias remained out on a limb, miles ahead of the other units. Charlie and Dog Companies finally reached positions about 400 yards from the Ronco River. Patrols to the river reported it was now about 200 yards wide and six feet deep with a very swift current. Boats could not be launched on the steep riverbanks. The enemy was very active on the other side; snipers had engaged our patrols and armoured cars had been observed. It looked as though the battalion had another river to cross by wading or even swimming. My 'leper' section was probably the only one who accepted the news with stoicism. We would cleanse ourselves or perish in the attempt.

Such drastic action, it turned out, was not needed. On October 28th, the Regiment was relieved by the 12th Royal Lancers and withdrew to a rear area at Cygnet, mid-way between the Bevano and Savio Rivers. Quarters were crowded, but everyone was under a roof and protected from the rain. A Echelon met us as we arrived and we enjoyed our first hot meal in days. And we finally satisfied the most pressing need of all — sleep.

The MMG Platoon liberated a cow; how, whose or whence, I didn't inquire. Neither did I question the appearance of four jugs of SRD (issue rum) and several cases of vino. The ensuing feast and party was billed as an MMG Platoon 'smoker' to camouflage the glorious piss-up that soon developed.

The next day the padre, Hon Capt Ivison, cleansed our souls. The following day, October 30th, the mobile bath cleansed our bodies, five days after my cesspool adventure. I stripped off my rotten clothes and gave my lice-ridden body its first bath in weeks.

For three days, we stood fast in the countryside waiting for the occupants of our billets in Riccione to depart. All sorts of rumours spread throughout the battalion: the Canadian Corps would be withdrawn and join 1st Canadian Army in Northwest Europe; the Corps would be transferred to Burma.[3]

The German Luftwaffe, in one of their rare sallies over our lines, added to our confusion by dropping propaganda leaflets calling attention to their radio broadcasts made for the benefits of the Allies:

JERRY'S FRONT
B E W A R E ! !
JERRY (the guy you are fighting) is putting on the air SEVEN
BROADCASTS DAILY. The American doughboy and Tommy
Atkins are duly warned that such broadcasts are only designed

341

to mislead and trick them under the cover of entertainment. Don't listen to Sally, Grace, Pat, Irene, George, Donald, Percy, Lander, Bill, Fat, Jolly and Stubbs, nor to Bruno and his Swinging Tigers and the rest of them, BUT stick to the BRITISH BUNKING CORPORATION which will always show you the "little things that aren't there" or "My mother didn't raise me to be a soldier", BUT HERE YOU ARE!

TIME	*PROGRAMS*
6:30 to 7:30 am	*For those fellows who like to get up early and enjoy music as a background to reveille.*
7:40 to 7:50 am	*A snappy 10-minutes of news*
2:00 to 3:00 pm	*Your favourite records*
5:00 to 5:30 pm	*A half-hour of really good swing-music by BRUNO and his SWINGING TIGERS*
6:30 to 7:30 pm	*The BIG SHOW, especially dedicated to UNCLE SAM'S boys, featuring BRUNO and his SWINGING TIGERS, SALLY, GRACE, PAT, IRENE, GEORGE, DONALD, PERCY, LANDER, BILL, FAT, JOLLY and STUBBS, not to mention the Ninth Earl of Swakerton, Bowles, the butler, Solly Mendel, and whatever the producer feels like unloading on you.*
10:00 to 10:30 pm	*A special programme for the BRITISH FORCES.*
Midnight sharp to 12:30 am	*JERRY'S NIGHTCLUB. Thirty glamourous minutes chock-full of music and merriment for the nightbirds. You boys who suffer from insomnia(?) will feel better disposed towards the German gunners who keep you awake!*

We felt somewhat piqued that Jerry had lumped us in with the Brits and Yanks and not recognized the Canadians as a separate group requiring a special program. However, this didn't stop our wireless operators from tuning in on the Jerry programs for a little comic relief.

Our pause in the farmhouse of the sodden Romagna gave me an opportunity to catch up on my letters home. I knew that as soon as we arrived in Riccione, Capt Andy Mills would put me to work as a defending officer on those time-consuming court martials.

I'm at ease in a Wop house with my MMG Platoon and all things are under control.

This has been another long silence from me, but as you perhaps guessed, we were in the line for the past couple of weeks and now we are back in rest again. It's quite a routine for me, as my new job calls for a 24-hour day shift most of the time when the Coys are advancing. Of course it's the same for every other officer, with the exception that I have more men and vehicles to get about the country; oftentimes my men are a good distance apart and I must tie in all the gun positions, get the carriers from Coy to Coy, keep the Coy Comds happy — not to mention the CO. So my job is really one of liaison. But I do like it. And there are the comforts of having my Pl HQ set up near BHQ where I can always come back for a few winks before setting out to see how my guns are.

In a way, it's rather good experience watching the battles progressing and getting onto the inside track of just how a Bn or Bde operates. And of course it's what we term 'a bomb-proof job' — most of the time.

And my batman is a very careful fellow who always sets up my bed in a room that has walls about 4 feet thick! So I take over the house and become father not only of my platoon, but also of about 20 Wops whose home we are using on the lend-lease set-up!

Incidentally, issue rum is excellent stuff in this miserable cold and rainy weather and is a real comfort to the inner soul. Only one thing better for that purpose — you've guessed it — a mickey of rye. And just at the crucial time when the Adj and I were discussing the quality of Can rye, your parcel No 40 arrived. So with great ceremony we had a good nip from the mickey which Dad had so thoughtfully sent along. Thanks a million.

Received Dad's grand letter of 15 October with the clippings enclosed. Say, wherever the press got all that nonsense I don't know. If that clipping or any like it was ever published here in Italy the troops would riot. Here a fellow does a job and that's that. The press always love to put on glamour.

Finally, on November 1st, we received word that our quarters in Riccione were vacant. We embussed at 0845 hours and followed our old familiar route south on Highway No 9, through Cesena, Savignano and Santarcangelo to Rimini. Here again, we crossed over the Ponte de Tiberio and took the coastal road, Highway No 16, to Riccione. Immediately the troops in B Echelon and X Area joined us and the battalion was together once more.

Throughout my story, reference is made to the various echelons that supported the fighting troops in action:

F Echelon *contained vehicles required to accompany the troops in action, such as jeeps or carriers for CO, IO, MO, RAP and*

Signals; carriers for Mortar Platoon, Anti-tank Platoon, MMG Platoon and Pioneers; one carrier per rifle company, containing ammunition, mines, stores and stretchers.

A Echelon *contained vehicles ready to support F Echelon, for example one 3 ton truck for the RSM carrying ammunition; water truck; one 15 cwt truck per company carrying ammunition and tools; one 3 ton truck per company carrying rations, cooking equipment and small packs.*

B Echelon *contained most of the remaining vehicles of the battalion, and was usually located in the divisional administrative area: one 3 ton office lorry for BHQ; one winch truck; two 3 ton trucks carrying petrol and oil; one 3 ton truck carrying reserve rations for the battalion (ie compo rations); one 3 ton truck per company carrying large packs, greatcoats, blankets, denims, rubber boots and pup tents.*

X Area *contained the remaining administrative personnel and the LOBs (usually 10% or 11% per company). Also extra blankets, kit bags, leather jerkins and other special clothing and equipment.*

X Area was somewhat of a mystery to me as I was never long enough in action to be entitled to LOB status. I suspect it was another of those 'made in Italy' concepts.

Behind these echelons within the division were two other mysterious echelons, purportedly dedicated to winning the paper war, known as First Echelon and Second Echelon. These bastions of red tape were so far removed from the front lines and were so inundated with their files and records that none of their personnel was ever seen by the troops. Indeed, no one was certain the Echelons were run by real people or by machines. My only contact, or lack of contact with them was after I had been wounded. For weeks, I was on a list "wounded, but disappeared" and was given a new identity — Lt Delues.

Rear echelons, however, were not of the slightest interest to the troops as they debussed from their lorries in Riccione on November 1st. Their only thought was to make the most of the next 30 days while the battalion was at rest.

Chapter XXVI

RICCIONE AND ROME

November 1 to November 18, 1944

Eleventh Brigade is sitting on our right
We really wonder if they're ever going to fight
We have been waiting so goddamn long
I just sat down and wrote this song
Onward to Bologna, onward to the Po

O ur new billets in Riccione were a far cry from our former villas in Cattolica. Practically every building carried the scars of war — *sans* roofs, windows and doors — the floors were covered with a foot of rainwater.

In the words of the War Diary, "During the night and during the morning hours, the rain, driven by a wild seaward gale, literally soaked the Bn area. All the roads and yards were miniature lakes. A goodly amount of this water found its way into the billets and things were a sorry mess."

"Sorry messes" were not allowed by LCol Clark nor his adjutant, Capt Mills. An 'O' Group was promptly convened and the following points emphasized:

1. *Clean billets.*
2. *Closed latrines.*
3. *Sanitary kitchens (with special note to sump holes).*
4. *Dress to be clean serges, and all officers and NCOs to be responsible that a high standard be kept up.*
5. *Signs will be placed outside all Coys.*

6. *A smart picket will be supplied by the duty Coy to be at Bn HQ at all times.*
7. *The Transport Pl will be responsible that there is a Transport Vehicle Park where all the unit rolling stock will be pooled.*
8. *Jeeps to be used for training and for recreational purposes.*
9. *There will be a daily kit lay-out as per Peace Time.*
10. *All ammo to be collected and stored in Pl or Coy stores.*
11. *All maintenance on vehicles will be brought up to date.*
12. *The practice of saluting will be enforced. Disciplinary action will be taken against those who fail to comply with this order.*[1]

This return to peacetime soldiering was readily accepted by the troops who, momentarily, had had their fill of fighting Jerries and the Italian mud. Everyone set to with a will and soon transformed the shattered village into a proper-looking battalion area — not exactly Aldershot, but a reasonable facsimile. Even LCol Clark, 'who never praised for praise's sake, expressed his amazement at the changes that had been wrought.'[2]

The Second-in-Command, Maj Cobbett, not to be outdone by the general smartening up, directed that an Officers' Mess be organized forthwith, and appointed a committee of three to do the work — Maj Cobbett, Capt A M (Alex) MacLeod and Lt C S Frost. It was an appointment I didn't need. I had just been warned to prepare for three more court martials (news of the lucky break I had got for the man charged with desertion had spread like wild-fire).

On top of these extra duties, I was supposed to be training and re-organizing my MMGs and carriers; and I had been told I was due for leave. Once again, Field Marshal Fate was giving me a rather large finger and I was not amused.

Maj Cobbett was sorry he had to hand me this little extra duty, but my performance in Support Company left him with no alternative.

"Performance in Support Company?" I queried, with just a touch of disrespect.

"That's right, I saw the Officers' Mess you set up in Support Company. Best in the battalion — sterling silver, fine china, crystal wine glasses. I won't ask where you got it all but I'd like you to bring it to BHQ for our new Officers' Mess. You also have my permission to gather up, from the other companies, any other dishes, glasses, silverware or furniture you need to make a first-class establishment.

"One other thing — you'll need cooks, kitchen help, waiters and stewards. I am temporarily placing under your command all batmen in the battalion, to help out in the mess. While you're at it, you can smarten them up a bit. Some of them badly need it."

It was the same old army story: do a reasonably good job and you're stuck with it for the duration. Just the same, I was damned if I was going to sacrifice my leave to make my brother officers more comfortable.

"Fine, Sir, but there's the matter of my leave. I haven't had any since I entered RMC in 1940."

"Yes, yes, I understand. We'll probably be here for the next month. Soon as you get the mess in shape, you can go on leave. By the way, I think there are a few plates around BHQ you can add to your inventory."

There was no point in mentioning to the 2IC that my own plate was already filled with courts martial and the MMG Platoon. I didn't want any more plates. What I needed was smaller helpings of work so I could enjoy a little R&R before the war started again.

I jumped on my bike and slithered through the mud, back to my platoon HQ. When I told Murdy he would be working in the Officers' Mess, it was his turn not to be amused. "Washing dishes for 30 officers? What the . . . ."

I cut him off before he had a chance to use his favourite expletive. "Just a minute, I haven't finished. You'll be assistant bar steward and I'll let you put up a stripe while you work behind the bar."

"OK, Sir, but I won't be able to bring you that nice hot cup of tea in the morning."

"I'll manage."

Murdy realized his one stripe was only temporary, without pay, not even a Part I Order entry; but it satisfied him for the moment. Promotions, as Murdy well knew, came in three categories: official, local and temporary. Official promotions were published in Part II Orders, entered on the man's documents and entitled him to an increase in pay. Local promotions were authorized by the Commanding Officer and published in Part I Orders, but did not show on the man's documents and did not affect his pay. Temporary promotions were not published anywhere; nor were they authorized by the CO. In fact, he was very much against these 'ad lib' promotions made by subordinate officers without any authority. However, he could not possibly keep track of every lance corporal in the battalion, a fact I heavily relied on in Murdy's case.

Cajoling the other 31 batmen in the battalion to work in the mess was not so easy, mainly because their bosses wouldn't hand them over. But when I threatened to put the men on parade every morning (something most hadn't done since leaving England), I got enough volunteers to do the job.

Despite the 2IC's exhortation to smarten up the batmen, I shied away from taking any drastic action. They were, after all, a special breed whose services went far beyond the master-servant relationship. Besides looking after and cleaning an officer's kit and equipment, thus freeing him to look after his men, a batman was an invaluable, unofficial link between the officer and the rest of the platoon.

Whenever I was upset about some action, or lack of action by the platoon, and was considering drastic steps to rectify the matter, Murdy would pass the word that 'the lieutenant was going to raise hell if the mess wasn't cleaned up *pronto.*' Likewise, if the platoon had some legitimate beef about me, about something I had done or not done, Murdy would discreetly (and sometimes not so discreetly) suggest that I smarten up. One such occasion concerned a new motor bike I had wrangled from the TO, my good friend John Koensgen. I was very proud of this machine and used it a lot, liaising with the rifle companies, reporting to the CO and 2IC, and on scrounging missions in the countryside. When I returned to the platoon, I would casually leave the bike with the carrier section, expecting them to clean off the mud and do the maintenance. But I had not realized that carrier drivers had their hands full maintaining their own machines, and were most unhappy with my cavalier attitude. It was an unwritten rule that everyone, junior officers included, maintained their own bikes. The moment Murdy mentioned the matter to me I saw the error of my ways and thenceforth learned a good deal about the care and cleaning of motor bikes. Indeed, after skidding around all day through seas of mud, mostly by pushing or being pushed, I began to think that the bike wasn't worth the effort. I resolved to renew my attempts to acquire a jeep.

These underground messages, via Murdy, saved everyone a lot of unnecessary confrontation and grief, and made for a happy platoon. No one considered Murdy to be an 'informer', and he was, in fact, shown a lot of respect by the men.

Another service Murdy rendered was to offer suggestions on how to improve the welfare of the platoon. "We're getting low on cigarettes; haven't had a mobile bath in a month; all the other platoons are going on leave; when's our next smoker?" On the other hand, he also acted as a good sounding board on which to bounce off my own ideas on how to keep the platoon in good humour.

Murdy, however, was not just a service type; he also had an important role in action: carrying and operating the 38 wireless set, and acting as my personal bodyguard. In an emergency, he could also man the Vickers guns and drive a carrier. In actual fact, he wasn't much of a signaller, because he got so little practice. Our 38 sets were always breaking down. In any case, on most operations we were mounted in carriers and used 18 sets which were operated by trained signallers.

This brief digression in praise of batmen has, unfortunately, a sad ending. The high-tech, computerized, modern army has no use for characters like Pte Murdy, or for that matter, for any of the intangible things that help to build morale and *esprit de corps* within a battalion. The honourable company of batmen has been abolished. More's the pity.

Returning to my labours to set up an Officers' Mess in Riccione, it was not long before the mess was organized and functioning to the satisfaction of all concerned. I doubt if the Officers' Mess at corps HQ was more finely furnished and equipped. Perhaps the place settings didn't match one another (coming as they did from so many different sources) but all the chinaware and sterling silver was of the finest quality. What happened to most of this valuable loot I do not know. Some was stored in crates and left back in the mysterious X Area when we returned to action, and as far as I know, was never seen again. Strangely enough, a few pieces of silverware did turn up in one of my kit bags after the war, and were shipped home. There, they were put to good use and are still a prized memento of my happy days in Riccione.

Now that the mess was running smoothly, I could turn my attention to my machine gunners and carriers. In our last action the Vickers had fired thousands of rounds and needed a complete overhaul, as well as new parts — packing, corks, stoppers, tripods, flash eliminators. The casing on one gun had been damaged by shellfire and had to be sent down the line to the workshops for repair. It was never returned, though curiously, I still have in my possession the tag I placed on the gun, marked "Urgently required for action." I have forgotten the circumstances, but probably the tag was returned with a note that the casing was beyond repair. Yet no replacement ever showed up. What was I supposed to do when the CO ordered me to send four guns forward? Tell him I was sorry I only had three guns and a tag from base workshop? Not bloody likely!

Damaged parts were not our only problem. As mentioned, the guns had been made in the First World War (or perhaps even earlier), and were dying from old age. Like an old soldier, they had given good service but were slowly fading away. It would be an exciting race to see which finished first, the war or the guns.

Our only hope was to appeal for help to our old friends in the divisional machine gun battalion, the SLI. With the help of the IO I located their position and sped off on my bike along Highway 6, hugging the Adriatic coast. The weather had finally cleared, and I enjoyed the warm days of the sun as I weaved in and out of the traffic on my powerful machine. At the HQ of the SLI, I pulled into the vehicle park and went looking for the quartermaster, who had been very helpful in the past. This time our luck had run out. The QM had no spare casings for us or, for that matter, for his own guns. He suggested I might try the PLF (The Princess Louise Fusiliers) who provided Vickers guns for the 5th Division.

At the PLF I got the same story. The entire Canadian Corps was out of spare casings. There was nowhere else to turn except, possibly, the German Army. I quickly realized, however, they had long ago discarded their guns from World War I and would probably be greatly amused if they knew we were still using such ancient weapons. When I returned to my platoon HQ in Riccione, I reported the result of my fruitless search to Sgt Mableson. "I guess you'll have to lead a raiding party and snatch a German MG42."

He had a better idea. "Send all our Vickers guns over to Jerry and the whole front will collapse in laughter."

The next problem was a common one throughout the Canadian Corps in Italy — lack of reinforcements. I appealed to the 2IC to let me take some men from the rifle companies and train them as machine gunners. The 2IC quite rightly turned down my request. The companies were 20 to 25 men understrength. Not a man could be spared. Furthermore, no reinforcements were expected from the holding unit.

Actually, lack of men was not my main problem. With one gun out of operation I didn't need any more gunners for the upcoming operation, unless we had heavy casualties. What I was trying to do was build up a reserve for the future. It was a futile task.

Still, compared to an infantry platoon, I was in pretty good shape. My platoon was probably the strongest one in the battalion. I looked over my nominal roll — 25 machine gunners, 15 carrier drivers and 32 batmen — a combined strength of 72. When I added in signallers and mechanics attached from brigade I had more men than an infantry company.

Well, even if we were short of machine gunners and equipment we had some ammunition and we could still train and fire our guns. The nearby beach provided an excellent range. An old pier and several wrecked ships made perfect targets.

One evening, we teamed up with the mortars and anti-tank guns and blew the pier to bits. A rocket from division immediately appeared in the person of a very upset staff captain. We were to cease firing immediately as the bullets were coming too close to their HQ.

With my machine gunners gainfully employed, I could at last turn my attention to the many courts martial that had been piling up while I was engaged on mess matters and training. With Murdy's help I found a secluded office, where no one except him could find me, and went to work on the summaries of evidence and on the tools of my trade as a defending officer — KRCan and the Army Act. I was nicely into my brief and rather enjoying this quiet interlude, when Murdy knocked on the door and marched in. "Sir, sorry to bother you, but there's a big problem with a couple of men who just got leave to go to Rome."

"That's a problem?"

"Well, not exactly a problem. They have no cigarettes."

"No cigarettes? They can get them from the canteen. You mean they need a few lire?"

"No, they need *cigarettes*. At least a carton each. You just got a batch from home. They'll pay you back when their parcels arrive."

The light was beginning to dawn.

"Ah yes, I see what you mean. The men need cigarettes to barter in Rome. Is that it?"

"Yes, Sir. Can't get *anything* without cigarettes."

I handed over my supply of Sweet Caps and returned to my law books.

The first case was a charge of leaving a post as a guard at a road leading to the company position, contrary to the Army Act Section 6(2)(h). This was not as serious a matter as desertion, but the accused could go to prison if convicted.

The evidence of the sergeant who made the charge was as follows:

"At approximately 2300 hours I posted the accused as a sentry at the road leading to our position. About 30 minutes later I went to the sentry post and found the accused absent. I went in search of him and found him in a barn being used as a company billet. I gave the accused a direct order to return to his post and he refused to do so. He said it was raining and he did not see why he had to go out. I then said to the accused — "Do you refuse to return to your post?" He replied, "If you put it that way, I guess I'd better return."

When I interviewed the accused, he admitted leaving his post, and taking shelter from the rain in a nearby barn, from which he could clearly observe the road. His only duty was to stop any RAP jeeps that came along, and direct them to casualties in the barn. No vehicle came along the road while he was on duty.

I felt I had a pretty good case for getting the man off with only a forfeiture of pay. I looked up his record and found he was only 18 years old and this was his first action.

At the trial, the sergeant admitted that the barn where the accused took shelter was only a few yards from the road and that even though it was a dark night and raining heavily, the accused could have observed any vehicles coming down the road, if he was keeping a sharp lookout.

The accused then stood up to tell his story. He was so nervous and shy I was afraid he would collapse on cross-examination. But he didn't. He came through as just a young kid, who had no clues about the duties of a sentry or the consequences of leaving his post on active service.

In my closing address I had to admit he had technically left his post. While ignorance of the provisions of the Army Act was no excuse, there was a distinction between leaving a post in the face of the enemy and leaving a post in a rear area, such as the road, where the accused had been posted. I stated that the accused now understood the duties of a sentry and the consequences of leaving his post, and was sorry for what he had done. He would not make the same mistake again.

The court took only a moment to consider the evidence, reduced the charge to "conduct to the prejudice of . . . .", and let my man off with a token forfeiture of pay.

During the next few days, I defended other men charged with various crimes and misdemeanours; almost everyone had the good luck to have the charge reduced with a light forfeiture of pay, or dismissed. I was on a 'hot roll' and every accused in the battalion demanded my services.

All hope of my ever getting any leave had long since vanished. Then came a case I knew meant trouble. The charge was that the accused had disobeyed a lawful command given by his superior officer contrary to Section 9(2) of the Army Act. The evidence in the Summary was that the accused's section had been ordered to attack a farmhouse. When the section captured the objective the accused was missing. The section leader went back to locate him and found him hiding in a house on the start line.

The accused had little to offer in his defence, except in mitigation of punishment. Again, he was a young soldier, but he had seen a fair amount of action. However, in this attack the shellfire had been intense and one shell had exploded quite near him on the start line. He claimed he was shaken and dazed and could not remember what he did for several hours.

His only hope, I advised him, was to plead guilty and throw himself on the mercy of the court. I knew the President of the court. He was a fair and reasonable man, who had seen a lot of action and understood how a man could become 'shell shocked' in a heavy barrage. The accused accepted my advice.

On the day of the trial, I attended the court half an hour before the appointed hour, as was my custom, to go over my notes. To my surprise, I found a lawyer from the JAG (Judge Advocate General) on hand. In none of the other trials had brigade sent down a member of the JAG's Branch, and I asked him why this time.

"It appears that too many accused have been getting off with light sentences or even scot-free. I've been sent down to make sure the court is properly advised on the conduct of the trial, the interpretation of the evidence and the appropriate sentence."

It was not an auspicious start. I could feel the noose tightening even before the trial commenced. Then came another shock. The members of the court entered, led by a President whom I had never met, but who was known as a very tough officer, who went by the book. The officer who was supposed to be the President was nowhere in sight.

The new President opened the proceedings by explaining that the officer slated to preside had become ill and he was called in at the last minute to take his place. He had not had a chance to study the charges and asked the indulgence of the court while he read through the material. I didn't believe a word of it.

The outcome of the trial is not difficult to imagine. The court 'threw the book' at the accused and he spent the rest of the war far removed from German shells. At least he survived.

My reputation as a defending officer was ruined. No further 'clients' beat their way to my door and I returned to my MMG Platoon feeling not unlike a disbarred lawyer. Murdy, now thoroughly enjoying his new stripe and his duties in a real Officers' Mess, was in a great mood and tried to be helpful. "Never mind, boss, now you may have a chance to go on leave."

Then he edged closer, and with a conspiratorial wink said, "I'll bet you set that guy up so's you wouldn't be bothered with any more of them court martials."

He jumped back out the door before I could lay my hands on him.

That evening, after dinner, I lingered around the bar, trying to decide whether to throttle Murdy or just forget the whole business and take the night off. (My first since arriving in this so-called 'Rest Area'.) Someone slapped me on the back. "Hi, Syd, greetings from Col Mothersill."

It was Jud Chapin who had just returned to the Regiment from England.

"Jud, how did you ever escape that nut-house at Welbeck Abbey?"

"It wasn't easy, I want to tell you. Finally, I reverted back to lieutenant and caught a draft for Italy. Rusty Gordon sends his regards. So does Brig Gostling. I was only kidding about Col Mothersill. He still gets mad when someone sings that favourite ditty of yours. How's it go? Kiss me good night, Col Mothersill. Tuck me . . . ."

"Enough of that, I'll play it later tonight when some of the old gang appear."

Soon the mess started to liven up as Sam Potts, Patty Crofton, Bill Stutt, Johnny Koensgen, Bob Huestis, Vaughan Allan and others dropped in. It was like the good old days at Camp Shilo. Sam was in good form and started the singing with *The Ric-a-dam-doo*, followed by *So Clear The Way, Who Was The Man Who Invented The War, The Shiny Two Brigade, Lili Marlene, Waltzing Matilda* and *Kiss Me Goodnight Colonel Mothersill* (which I played, and sang, with great feeling). I wondered what he would think of this mob, singing rude ditties, draped around an old piano I had liberated under shellfire in Santarcangelo.

During one of the numerous breaks to allow the piano player a breath of fresh air, or whatever else he needed to refresh himself before the next set, Pte Murdy sidled up to me. "Sorry, Sir, for that dumb crack about the court martial and your leave. Truth is that your leave was approved yesterday. I couldn't tell you because you were about to strangle me. You're supposed to leave tomorrow." He dashed back behind the bar where he knew he was pretty safe.

"The little bugger," I mumbled. "I think I'll kill him anyway."

But it was true. A short while later the adjutant, Capt Andy Mills, appeared and called me over. "Syd, what the hell are you doing up at this hour? You'd better get organized to go on leave tomorrow. Transport leaves at 0900. But let's have another verse or two of *The Ric-a-dam-doo* before you go."

Andy could belt out a song as well as anyone in the mess. Three hours later we were still at it.

Shortly before the transport left, I managed, with Murdy's help, to get my kit together and tumbled into the jeep with three other weary, but very happy officers — Snuffy Smith, Bill Stutt and Don MacCulloch. Destination — Rome!

One of us took the wheel — who, I don't remember. But someone must have, because I recall waking up at Jesi about two hours later, hungry and frozen to the seat. How we all didn't die of pneumonia on that long, ten hour trip, in an open jeep, over the Apennine Mountains, in the dead of winter, I will never understand.

Something else I could never fathom was why the Canadian Army in Italy was not issued with closed-in jeeps, like the Americans, who built the vehicles for us. Probably some penny-pinching on the part of Mackenzie King and his cohorts. True, we tried to close in the jeeps ourselves by using the carpentering skills of the Pioneer Platoon and pieces of wood taken from ration boxes; but it was impossible to block out all the icy drafts and snow that came through the cracks as the jeeps zipped along the mountain trails. And of course there was no heat.

The Yankees, as was their wont, had no trouble making themselves comfortable. They knew how to convert their jeeps to cope with the weather. The vehicles were completely closed in, even with a roof, and many had open stoves (a rather dangerous practice that must have given more comfort to the Germans than to the Yanks).

Our route to Rome was the same one, in reverse, that I had taken in September when I left Avellino to join the Regiment — Riccione, Jesi (20 miles east of Ancona), Foligno, Spoleto, Terni, Rome. Two months earlier the heat had been intense and we had prayed for rain (which we got in buckets-full). Now, the weather was bitterly cold and the mountain passes clogged with snow. Every so often, huge traffic jams built up at Check Points along the route. These breaks gave us a chance to get out and beat our limbs back to life, but we had to be careful not to step too close to the unmarked side of the road, and disappear over the edge into the snow-filled valley below. Exactly what the Check Points were checking no one seemed to know. No vehicles were ever turned back — it would have been quite impossible to turn around anyway. There was hardly room for two vehicles to pass. Perhaps the MPs were looking for Germans. If so, I doubt if they ever found any. They were all snug and warm in their deep dugouts along the Lamone River waiting for us to come back from leave.

By now I was thoroughly awake and it was my turn to take the wheel. Normally, I enjoy driving anything that has two or more wheels, but navigating a jeep through narrow mountain passes, in a swirling snow storm, with huge tank transporters grinding and skidding toward you, is not quite as thrilling as it may sound. In some places, the destruction wrought by the Germans in June was still being repaired, and only one way traffic was permitted. How some of the Bailey bridges bore the weight of so many heavy vehicles must have defied all principles of military engineering.

After two and a half hours of battling the snow, hairpin bends and on-coming traffic, I was happy to turn over the wheel to the next volunteer and go back to sleep. Finally, at 1900 hours we entered the Eternal City and made our way to the Massimo d'Azeglio (otherwise known as 'The Chateau Laurier') where Corky and I had stayed in September. As we checked in at the desk, a small bomb went off in my head. "My God, I've forgotten my cartons of cigarettes!"

Rome without cigarettes was like the Vatican without the Pope — just a glorious show place. I naturally placed all the blame on the absent Murdy and even convinced myself he had done it on purpose — whether in the interests of my chastity or for some other purpose I wasn't sure. When I returned from leave I said nothing about the matter to Murdy. In fact, I silently thanked him. From some of the horror tales I heard about the after effects of acquiring merchandise with cigarettes, I was glad someone had been looking after me.

During the next five days, I tried to do what the Romans do, with varying degrees of success. After a solid 18 hour 'ziz', between white sheets, in a warm room, I gorged myself on a combined meal of breakfast, lunch and dinner. Then I luxuriated in a turkish bath, where the remnants of that cesspool were at last expelled from my body.

Next morning, a soothing facial massage completed my sensual pleasures for the moment and I was ready to see the glories of ancient Rome. The city was certainly ready and waiting to see me. Hordes of young boys had been pestering me, ever since my arrival, to avail myself of their services to arrange all kinds of entertainment, from sleeping with their sisters, to a private audience with the Pope. My lack of *sigarette* precluded the former and I was not yet ready for the latter.

I decided to buy a guide book and see the sights on my own time and in my own way. It would be a good test of my Italian vocabulary. But even acquiring a guide book was a challenge. One street urchin pressed me to buy a book he claimed was *numero uno* for every tourist. It was full of dirty pictures. Finally, I bought a small pamphlet for 50 lire (about 50 cents) and headed for the main Railway Station at the top of the *Via Cavour*, quite near my hotel.

The square opposite the station was named the *Piazza dei Cinque Cento* in memory, so the guide book said, of 500 Italian soldiers who were slain by the Ethiopians in 1886. No wonder Mussolini was so keen to avenge this disaster and throw out poor old Emperor Haile Selassie. I remembered, however, that in 1942, Mussolini, in turn, had been ejected from Ethiopia and Haile Selassie had declared war against Italy. "Plus ça change, plus c'est la même chose."

355

I walked across the square and viewed what was left of the immense Baths of Diocletian, which in the days of that great Emperor catered for 3,000 bathers daily. Pity they were not in operation now. There were 3,000 dirty little *ragazzi* following me, who would have benefitted.

Pushing on, or really being propelled forward by these yapping little monsters, I came upon the Quirinal Palace, the residence of the Kings of Italy. I wondered what had become of the diminutive King Victor Emmanuel III who had handed over his powers to his son Crown Prince Umberto. Likely the King still resided in the palace but on a very short lease.

The next point of interest in my perambulation was the Spanish Steps in the *Piazza di Spagna*, but there was no way I could make it with all these kids badgering me with: *Jig-a-jig mia sorella-molto buona. Sigarette per Papa. Cioccolato per me.''*

I ducked into a Trattoria, collapsed in a corner and ordered the specialty of the house — lamb *alla cacciatora* with, naturally, a side order of *fettucine* and a large bottle of vino. The chunks of meat came in different colours and had different tastes, suspiciously similar to bully beef and spam. But it was good and apparently free of the kind of creatures I had encountered in southern Italy.

Refreshed by my light snack, I strolled over to the Spanish Steps, said to be one of the most characteristic places in Rome, and perhaps the most beautiful. I had not yet seen enough of the city to make such an assessment, and to speak the truth I was more interested in seeing the beautiful artists' models that, according to my trusty guide book frequented the place. Alas, these gorgeous *signorine* were nowhere to be found. Their places had been taken by street vendors hawking cheap-looking (though not in price) souvenirs, dirty postcards and trivia of all sorts. I paused at the house where the poet Keats had lived and died in 1821. What would he have thought of the rabble now around his door, I wondered.

Leaving this little English enclave, I wandered down to the *Via del Corso*, the main thoroughfare of Rome, formerly known as *Via Lata* (Broad Street). Its former name aptly described the kind of signorine who now accosted me, but it did not describe its width. It must be one of the narrowest main streets in the world.

There was one building on the Corso I wanted to see — the Pantheon. From school days I had been told it was the most perfect pagan building in the city. But I had a terrible mental block about remembering its name, and always confused it with the Parthenon in Athens. As I gazed at this ancient wonder, my mental block suddenly disappeared — 'Pan' rhymes with 'man' — Ro*man* Pantheon. The solution was a little late for my high school exams, but it still gave me some satisfaction.

I consulted my guide book and found that the Pantheon had been built in 27 BC as a pagan temple. Centuries later it was dedicated to Christian worship. To my surprise, I learned that on its consecration as St Mary-of-the-Martyrs, the Pope caused to be buried there 28 wagon-loads of the bones of martyrs brought from the catacombs. The Pantheon also contained the tombs of the Kings of Italy and the burial place of Raphael.

I reluctantly left this enduring link between the ancient and modern city and proceeded along the Corso. Ahead lay the *Piazza Venezia* and the centre of ancient Rome: the Capitol, the Forum, the Palatine Hill and the Colosseum. The day had gone quickly and I had only touched the fringes of this wondrous city. The War, San Fortunato, the Savio River, Riccione, even the Regiment itself had faded into the background; they all seemed far away and unreal.

It was time to call a temporary halt to my tour and return to the 'Chateau Laurier' where my pals would no doubt bring me back to the twentieth century in short order.

As soon as I entered the bar at the hotel my resurrection was immediate. Friends from other units, whom I had not seen in years, filled the place, particularly pals from Saskatoon and classmates from RMC. After a very happy 'happy hour' the next item of business was to decide where to eat, followed by where to go for an evening's entertainment. The first question was easy. Cuisine at the 'Chateau' had apparently deteriorated since my stay in September. The main dish, in fact the only dish, was bully beef — fried bb for breakfast, bb hash for lunch, bb à la Wellington for dinner. The consensus of the gang was to have dinner at another hotel, the Realto.

Next question, entertainment, was a toss-up between attending an opera (when in Rome, do what the Romans do) or check out one of the various 'legitimate' night clubs — Nervineta Club, Apollo Club, San Georgio Club. To assist our deliberations more rounds of Brandy Alexanders appeared, my first introduction to this seductive drink. In due course all hands floated out the door bound for not one, but all three clubs.

Next day, or more correctly, that afternoon, I returned to my tour of the ancient city. This time I realized I had to have a reliable guide, as I was wasting too much energy wandering about, and time was running out. Again, I cursed not having brought a good supply of cigarettes, but I still had some lire left and I hadn't forgotten how to deal with the natives. I remembered the way I had persuaded a gendarme in Sicily that PPCLI meant Police.

Armed with this crutch, I strolled down to the Forum and was soon beset with types of all sorts, professing to be guides. I sloughed them off by pointing to my shoulder flashes and uttering 'Polizie'. Then I spotted an old man, sitting quietly on an ancient stone in the Forum, who beckoned me to join him. I went over and, in Italian, started to give him my routine about being a policeman and no nonsense about cigarettes for papa or whomever.

He laughed and in English said, "You don't have to kid me. I saw your performance with those boys and you put on quite an act. You also spoke pretty good Italian. I'm a retired Professor of English here in Rome. I'd be pleased to show you some of the wonders of this majestic city."

He immediately set off, with me in tow, and climbed the steps leading to the Capitoline Hill.

"Here, young man," said the out-of-breath Professor, "you are standing on the most famous spot in the world — the Capitoline Hill — the stronghold and the religious centre of the ancient city. It is the smallest, but it is the most famous of the Seven Hills of Rome."

"I understand. Yet there is nothing left of that stronghold."

"Correct, but just the same, the Capitol is the very symbol of ancient Rome. Come, let us see more."

We passed along a narrow street and came out to a small platform overlooking the Forum.

"Before you lies the heart of Ancient Rome — the courts of justice, the market places, the public promenade. Julius Caesar built splendid monuments here, as did all the Emperors. Their triumphal arches are still the wonder of the world."

We returned to the *Via dei Fori Imperiali* and headed for the Colosseum. The Professor deliberately avoided making any reference to the monument to Victor Emmanuel II. I touched his arm and pointed to the monstrosity. "I'm told it's not too well liked by the Romans. They call it the 'Wedding Cake'."

"It's worse than that. It looks like a typewriter."

We were now standing before the Colosseum. I was tempted to show off my knowledge by saying the structure was originally called the Flavian Amphitheatre, but I wisely shut my mouth and listened.

"This vast building was begun in 72 AD and completed in 80 AD. Its seating capacity was around 80,000 people."

Incredible, I thought. The Ball Park in Toronto was only a sideshow compared to this colossus.

The Professor continued. "The main purpose of the Colosseum was of course for gladiatorial combats, man against man, man against beast; but it could also be filled with water for naval combats. It also had a canopy that could be drawn over the top to shade the sun or keep out the rain."

The Professor went on to describe some of the horrors that were perpetrated in the name of entertainment, to satiate the brutal populace that was then Rome. Gladiatorial combats were staged that sometimes continued for 100 days and in which 5,000 animals were slaughtered. Wretched criminals were torn limb from limb by wild animals; naked Christian women were hoisted in nets in front of the spectators and then dropped into the arena to be gored to death by bulls.

Some of these atrocities I had read about, without realizing the depravity of it all. Now, standing on the very ground where tens of thousands had suffered such terrible agonies, I could almost feel the blood-drenched soil give way under my feet.

"It's horrible to think about, Professor. I guess the Germans didn't invent atrocities after all. They only refined some of the methods."

My guide gave a sad smile. "Young man, that's the first intelligent comment you've made all day."

It was getting late and still I had only scratched the surface. If only I had a month to explore these ancient monuments with my informative guide! I made a vow to return again at the first opportunity. Happily, it was a pledge I was able to honour on many occasions.

Before leaving the Professor, I had one last question which I suspected might upset him, yet the subject intrigued me.

"What monuments remain from the Mussolini era? Is there anything worth seeing that the great Duce built?"

My teacher snorted: "Nothing remains that's worth seeing because nothing was erected that had any enduring quality. Oh, there's a mean little Mussolini Forum with horrible imitations of ancient sculpture, and even a fascist church. Can you imagine, a church dedicated to the creed of those pagans, 'Might is Right'. Nobody pays any attention to fascist architecture anymore. *Sic Transit Gloria Mundi*."

I left my friend with real regret. He refused any fee, not even a *mancia*, but the few cigarettes I had with me were gratefully accepted. If only Murdy had packed a few cartons in my kit.

The following day was my last chance to see the sights of Rome. My Catholic friends urged me to accompany them to the Vatican where Pope Pius XII was giving an audience for Allied soldiers. I had already had a glimpse of St Peter's Square and the towering dome of the Basilica and I was not sure I wanted to spend my last day there. My friends insisted and I went with them. I am glad I did.

As we approached the majestic church with the beautiful fountains and colonnades of Bernini on each side, we could not help being deeply impressed. My friends told me, and I believed them, that the Basilica was one of the wonders of the world, perhaps the most stupendous of all. Nowhere else was there anything like it.

We entered a room where the audience was to take place and sat down. Soon the Pope entered, borne aloft in a throne by his faithful Swiss Guards dressed in their medieval uniforms. After delivering a warm greeting, repeated in several languages, to the 300 or so troops assembled, he gave us his blessing. The short but moving ceremony was over and he slowly departed amidst enthusiastic clapping and cheering of the troops. One of his attendants handed each of us a small picture of the Pope with his facsimile signature. I kept mine throughout the war and it is still a treasured memento of the occasion.

A brief reference to the subject of religion on the battlefield might be appropriate at this point. It has been said, with good reason, there are no non-believers on the battlefield. Cases have even been quoted where a soldier promised the Almighty he would become a man of the cloth if only he were spared a particularly dangerous mission. After the war, some kept their vows and became priests or ministers. I personally know a few who did.

The padres who served in action with the troops were a very special breed. Their quiet faith gave much comfort to the sick and dying. But, ironically, their sheer physical courage also inspired many a soldier to persevere and kill more Germans than he might otherwise have done without the example of bravery under fire shown by his chaplain.

The Army tried to resolve this difficult conflict between spiritual and temporal roles of the padre by giving him only an honorary commission, hoping the Almighty would understand that the padre had no responsibility to lead men into battle or encourage them to kill their brothers in the human race. But even this façade was dropped after the war. Padres are now fully commissioned officers and thus are apparently licensed to kill.

Certainly, during the war, the distinction between padres as spiritual leaders and padres as combatant officers was a very fine one. Their bravery was recognized numerous times by awards of the Military Cross, out of all proportion to their small numbers. One even received the Victoria Cross.*

Still another dilemma for the Almighty, and presumably for padres generally, was whose side was entitled to Divine Intervention? All the armies had chaplains, except possibly the Russians. It must have given all concerned a monumental headache trying to justify special consideration for one side over the other.

Fortunately, as a simple soldier of the line, it was not my duty to resolve these theological puzzles. What was of greater concern to me in late November, 1944, was that my leave in Rome was over and the mud, the cold, and the Germans were waiting for me at the next canal. I hoped that if the Almighty was otherwise occupied, old Field Marshal Fate would at least smile on me.

The long journey home, through snow-covered mountain passes, in the dead of winter, in an open jeep, was just as cold and miserable as the one six days earlier; but, thankfully, we made better time and it took only eight and a half hours to reach Riccione.

I was happy to be back with my MMGs even though I had to face the usual administrative fafus, and some not so usual, that had happened while I was away. Someone had taken our 15 cwt truck in A Echelon, without any authority, and smashed it up, necessitating a Court of Inquiry. Kenny, our irreplaceable cook, had been badly burned when his cooker exploded.

---

*Hon Capt J W Foote, Chaplain of The Royal Hamilton Light Infantry, at Dieppe.

While he couldn't be replaced, we had to find someone who was at least willing to learn.

In my absence, sickness had continued to take its toll. Several men had come down with jaundice or fever. And still there were no reinforcements.

I purposely stayed away from the Orderly Room, knowing how quickly I could become enmeshed in their 'bumph'. But I could not avoid more court martial duties. Despite my lack of success in my last case there were still some accused who were willing to put their lives in my hands, and asked for my services. I agreed to help them, but as we were now preparing to return to action, I had their cases adjourned until we were back in rest area again. At least they would get another month's reprieve, in a warm room, safe from Jerry's shellfire, while I was slugging it out in the trenches. The thought that I might not come back never occurred to me. I just naturally assumed I would. It was probably at this point that Field Marshal Fate finally decided it was time to show me he was still in command of my destiny.

Chapter XXVII

ADVANCE TO THE LAMONE RIVER

November 18 to December 13, 1944

On our way to Venice, we had a lovely time
We drove a bus from Rimini right through the German Line
Then to Bologna we did go
We all went swimming in the Po
We are the D-Day Dodgers in sunny Italy

The number of 'O' Groups, demonstrations and administrative conferences now began to increase, giving sure signs that our return to action was not far off. But this time we received a few pleasant surprises we could scarcely believe. New types of equipment, that had long been used in Northwest Europe and that had been denied to us D-Day Dodgers, were at last being issued to our division.

Heading the list was a fine assortment of flamethrowers. Four of these deadly weapons mounted in carriers and called Wasps were attached to my steadily growing MMG Platoon. The battalion was also issued a number of smaller, man-handled flamethrowers called Lifebuoys. The tank regiment that supported us in action, the British 12th Battalion, Royal Tank Regiment, were equipped with flamethrowing tanks known as Crocodiles. After a demonstration of this awesome weapon to our Able Company, the War Diarist recorded that in the opinion of the infantry, "anything in the direct burning zone has, to use the vernacular, had it."

While we were ecstatic finally to receive all this modern equipment, we were under no illusions that our job would be made any easier. If the staff thought that where we had failed, new machines and weapons would succeed, they were in for another rude shock. To be of any use, this new equipment had to close with the enemy and that meant overcoming mud, rain and rivers.

This time, however, the staff had really done their homework. They had acquired from the Americans a small, tracked, lightweight, amphibious carrier called a Weasel. It had been originally designed for operations in snow, but "its light construction and wide tracks particularly suited it for use in swampy ground."[1] Four of these fantastic little 'mud-hens' were attached to my platoon; more were to be added later.

Then to our great relief, a new lightweight, portable foot-bridge called the 'Olafson' bridge was introduced. It has been invented by Capt E A Olafson of the Royal Canadian Electrical and Mechanical Engineers: "Fifteen foot lengths of half-inch pipe were welded into sections 18 inches wide, each weighing 200 pounds; by connecting these together a gap of 45 feet could be spanned."[2]

Finally, our Anti-tank Platoon received a modified 2 pounder anti-tank gun known as a 'Littlejohn'. It has a tapered bore that increased its muzzle velocity.[3] It was also called a 'Squeeze Gun', which accurately described its effect on a round of ammunition — like squeezing toothpaste out of a tube. I was glad this particular weapon wasn't part of my arsenal. As one of my men put it, "what happens to the shell when the squeeze doesn't squeeze it out?" Presumably, the barrel just blew up.

With Wasps, Lifebuoys, Crocodiles, Weasels, Olafsons and Littlejohns on our side, who could be 'agin' us? Plenty — Germans, rivers and the weather.

To confound the enemy further, and to encourage our own troops, two changes were made in the higher commands of the Corps. LGen Burns was replaced by LGen Charles Foulkes; MGen Vokes exchanged command of 1st Canadian Division for command of 4th Canadian Armoured Division in Northwest Europe; MGen H W Foster took command of 1st Canadian Division.

The replacement of LGen Burns came as no surprise: "Although he was an officer of very distinguished abilities, nevertheless there did not exist between Gen Burns and the British senior officers that personal relationship of friendly, mutual understanding which is so important."[4]

The departure of MGen Chris Vokes was another matter. He had been the 1st Division in body and spirit ever since he had assumed command in southern Italy. We all loved his rough, down-to-earth, soldierly approach to battle, even if at times we called him names for kicking us in the tail to fight harder. We figured it was a promotion for him and wished him luck.

Still another event occurred that meant action was close at hand, but which puzzled us somewhat — we were issued respirators and put through a gas chamber. I had not seen a respirator since my days at Camp Shilo in Canada, and I thought our stocks of respirators, if any, were in southern Italy, somewhere near 2nd Echelon. What did it mean? Had Intelligence got wind of some last-ditch gas attack planned by Hitler? Anything was possible from that madman.

The Second-in-Command continued his daily briefings on training and administration for the upcoming operations. After his conferences, I would then call together my over-sized platoon and give them my version of what was important. My notes of a briefing I gave them on November 24th read as follows:

1. New Equipment
   Jeep, Weasels, Wasps, Lifebuoys, Mae Wests, Storm boats, Olafson Bridge and Rafts
2. Ground
   Marshy, wet, rivers and canals
3. Therefore
   Man-pack the guns
   Take 4,000 rounds per gun
   Carry rations and get along as the companies do
4. Reinforcements
   None
   No men from the companies who are 20 - 25 men understrength
5. Gun Crews
   Only 3 forward this time
   2 men LOB
6. Cook
   Pte Webb, RCASC cook, may work for us for a time; give him a chance
7. Training
   Loading and unloading
   Stoppages
   Targets
   Fire tonight at 1800 hours
8. Tactical Use of MMGs
   Close support
   Overhead firing nil because of flat ground
   Counter-attacks
   Morale NB
9. Mobile Bath
   1430 - 1530 hours today
10. Loss of Equipment
    Steel helmets a problem
11. Yellow Smoke Generators
    SOS for dive bombing
    Packed on man

12. RAP
    Must get permission to go down
    Written chit
    Other RAPs not allowed
13. Out by Christmas!
14. Platoon Dinner and Smoker
    1830 hours 25 Nov
    Party of 8 men report to Platoon HQ at 1730 hours to move piano from 5 Field Ambulance to here
    Guests:
      the new cook
      CSM
      CQMS
      paymaster
    Peron: make sandwiches
    Cpl Foulis: rum and vino — 42 bottles; make brew tomorrow

It will be observed that I finally got my jeep, not just for my personal use, but also to haul ammunition and equipment. This was very important in the upcoming operations, where carriers would be unable to navigate through the mud. Jeeps, with their light weight and four-wheel drive, could traverse almost any terrain and, unlike a carrier, could be propelled by manpower as well as horsepower.

As the war dragged on, the platoon smokers became important morale builders and helped relieve the tensions and dreariness of our daily lives. Forty-two bottles may sound a little exuberant, but my platoon and attached personnel, not to mention guests and gate-crashers, had grown to 80 or more. Half a bottle a man was probably a little on the short side for that party — but I don't remember!

Farewell parties in the Officers' Mess were also the order of the day. As a member of the Mess Committee, I organized dances and arranged female participation. But, like my last disastrous court martial case, my luck had run out. I was unable to find any suitable young ladies, and was never again entrusted with such heavy responsibility. The War Diary tells the sad tale:

> *The dance that was to be held in the Officers' Mess fell through because of the lack of feminine partners. But the dinner and other refreshments were put to good use. After a brief O Gp a plan evolved which changed the party from an unsuccessful dance to a highly successful stag.*

On November 26th all the officers of the division gathered in the *Teatro Dante* to hear the acting General Officer Commanding the division, Brig J D B Smith, give a general outline of the forthcoming action, which some idiot on the staff had named Operation Chuckle. As the Regimental Historian so aptly observes, the operation "promised to be no laughing matter".[5] Indeed, the theatre, named after the great author of the Divine Comedy, had probably never witnessed a tragedy of such proportions.

The plan envisaged the two Allied Armies in Italy making a concerted blow to capture Bologna within a fortnight. The 5th Army would have to advance ten miles through the rugged foothills of the Apennines; the 8th Army would have to cover 35 miles in the water-logged Romagna and storm no fewer than three fortified river lines — the Lamone, the Senio and the Santerno. Not only was the plan no laughing matter, "it was audacious to the point of folly".[6]

The 1st Canadian Division would break out from a bridgehead established by the 10th Indian Division over the Montone River at *Casa Bettini*. There would be four phases for the operation: 3rd Brigade would lead the way, capture Russi and force a crossing over the Lamone River; then our Brigade (2nd Brigade) would seize Bagnacavallo and establish a bridgehead over the Senio. Further phases were all carefully laid down, but not even the second phase was ever completed.

If the nature of the ground over which we had to execute these phases gave the staff any concern, there was little evidence of it. They simply assumed we could read a map and understood that the battlefields would be much the same as before — endless rivers and canals with high floodbanks giving the enemy excellent observation and fields of fire; waterlogged fields between the rivers, oozing with sticky mud and confining vehicle movement to the roads; soggy approaches to the rivers, making bridging operations almost impossible.

The planners, God bless them, had foreseen these obstacles this time and had supplied us with all that new equipment — Wasps, Lifebuoys, Crocodiles, Weasels, Littlejohns, Olfasons and all the rest of the menagerie. Besides, we would have overwhelming artillery support including the whole 1st Army Group artillery. To top it off, for the first time, US Thunderbolts would be working with Canadian troops (weather permitting). And we were not to overlook the fact that the enemy (as usual) were poor in gun strength.

The sad thing was not that we didn't believe half of it but that we knew it would make little difference to the outcome.

On December 1st we climbed into our lorries and left Riccione at 2035 hours, following in the wake of the 3rd Brigade who were to break out of the bridgehead on the Montone River, established by the 10th Indian Division. By December 3rd we had reached a concentration area just west of our old friend the Ronco River.

Meanwhile, 3rd Brigade made steady progress from their bridgehead over the Montone. In two days of heavy fighting, they had captured Russi and reached the Lamone River. Now the carefully laid plans started to unravel:

"As the 3rd Brigade had been fighting for more than 48 hours, during which its infantry battalions had suffered 106 casualties, the acting divisional commander now gave Brig Calder (Commander of 1st Brigade) the task of securing the crossing over the Lamone River before the enemy should have an opportunity to settle into his new line."[7]

Why it was decided to throw in the 1st Brigade at the eleventh hour to complete the task originally assigned to 3rd Brigade, without a chance to recce the battlefield and arrange proper artillery support, has been debated ever since the doomed operation was conceived. Why our brigade (2nd Brigade), which was originally supposed to advance through 3rd Brigade, was not chosen, I do not know — but I am thankful to Field Marshal Fate for sparing us the approaching disasters.

On December 4th we moved forward once again, crossed the Montone River at *Casa Bettini* and occupied the area where 3rd Brigade had broken out of their bridgehead two days earlier. Ahead the Lamone beckoned, 4,000 yards distant.

Earlier that day, 1st Brigade had assaulted the Lamone River by trying to throw across the Hastings and Prince Edward Regiment without any prior recce. The battalion never even got to the near bank. A hail of MG42s and Moaning Minnies stopped them cold on the flats leading to the river. It was then decided to use the Hastings and the RCR (The Royal Canadian Regiment) in a combined assault at one o'clock that night (ie, the morning of December 5th).

Back in our cold, wet shelters in shell-torn farmhouses, we awaited news of 1st Brigade's attack. Throughout the night the sounds of battle swelled, faded away, then erupted again as a cheerless first light appeared through the heavy rain and morning fog. By mid-afternoon, rumours started to come in. First Brigade had suffered a disaster; the Hasty Ps had been pushed back; the RCR had been slaughtered; we would be thrown into the breach. Gradually the facts emerged. The rumours were all true — some worse than we had imagined — except that, thankfully, our turn had not yet come.

It is not pleasant to record the failure and slaughter of another fine Regiment. The story may not seem relevant to the tale I have to tell, yet it is so typical of the way troops were thrown into battle, day after day, month after month, with so little thought given to proper recce, or careful, intelligent planning that the disaster on the Lamone deserves at least a passing reference. And, but for the grace of God, our Regiment would have been involved.

Out of a total of 205 all ranks of the RCR who crossed the river that night, three officers and 26 other ranks were killed, three officers and 43 other ranks were wounded and two officers and 29 other ranks were missing. Total casualties 106.

My friend and fellow instructor on the Battle Drill Course at Vernon, BC,

Capt P H A Hertzberg, son of the Commandant of RMC, was among the dead. He and his platoon were caught in a devastating mortar shoot. Only three of his 21 men escaped injury.[8]

The 'Reason Why' this disaster came to pass has been analysed by LCol Stevens in such a frank, soldierly, thought-provoking manner that his words should be enshrined in stone for the benefit of all officers aspiring to higher rank in the Canadian Forces.

> *Why such an unmitigated disaster? It seems plain that the fault lay not in the fighting men but in their management. At the Lamone planning and execution alike could only be described as appalling. Undoubtedly there was too much high level optimism; the new tools of battle, the harassed enemy and the certainty of his defeat had led some echelons of command to forget that the trapped animal often fights to the death. A site for the crossing had been chosen before corps and divisional commanders, who might have been expected to know what they were about, would appear to have provided any information about the size and depth of the river. Nor had anyone apparently deemed a ready-made parapet (in the form of the railway embankment) on the immediate flank of the crossing to be a menace to the operation.*
>
> *Finally, the prime cause of tragedy lay far behind the line, in the very structure of the operation. After Canadian experience on the Pisciatello, the Savio and the Montone, any plan of battle designed to capture three successive floodbanked river lines in a single gallop was ludicrous. It did not make sense in the light of what was known either of the terrain or of the enemy. An operation that lacked such essential determinations could only be described as slapdash and unworthy of Canadian military organization in the fifth year of a World War and after 17 months of field service. The prompt dismissal of three commanders was in the Montgomery tradition of tolerating no failures; but in the minds of many this sorry performance stemmed more from unrealistic planning than from faulty execution.[9]*

LCol Stevens should know what he is talking about. He served in the field in Italy and has written 12 military histories, including the PPCLI, RCR and The Loyal Edmonton Regiment.

The full extent of the RCR agony was, fortunately, not known to us as we huddled in our cold, damp billets surrounded by seas of mud. The Germans had flooded the area, not counting on just the rain to make us miserable, and supplies could reach us only by roads which were under constant shellfire.

For some, the incessant shelling was a severe test for the nerves; for others, it was a kind of game trying to guess where and when the shells would land. The unearthly wail of the Moaning Minnies sent shivers up the spine, but at least they gave you enough warning to hit the dirt in time. The German 88s slammed in so quickly that you had little warning to take cover. The larger 105s gave you a chance to duck, but they exploded with a fearful roar. Armour piercing shells gave you no chance whatsoever; neither did air-bursts. I hated them all.

It is a fact that trained soldiers, by and large, came to accept shellfire as a fact of life, and became skilled at picking up the scream of the shells and guessing where they would land. Still, a prolonged period of intense shelling could temporarily daze and unnerve the best of soldiers, even the tough German paratroopers.

I recall one occasion during this period on the Lamone River when I decided to check one of my forward guns and the only route lay along a road that had been registered by the enemy. Despite the heavy shelling, I got half-way to my post when a stonk almost caught me as I dived for the ditch. I stayed there a good ten minutes before I could force myself to get back on that road and advance through the shellfire. Even if LCol Clark had come along and given me a direct order I don't think I would have budged. But, on second thought . . . .

If the shelling got on our nerves, the waiting and uncertainty of when we would be called on to make another futile assault across the bloody river was almost as bad. Indeed, it has been said that the worst part of a battle is the contemplation of it. I would not go quite that far, as the sights and sounds of men being torn apart is beyond human contemplation. Yet waiting for the order to advance while enemy shellfire blows your comrades to pieces calls for discipline of the highest order.

For five days we remained in our positions in the sodden plain while the weather worsened and the staff made plans and counter-plans. Unbeknown to us, meteorological reports had warned that mountain storms might not only flood the Lamone in front of us, but knock out the bridges over the Montone at our backs. Once again, we can thank the 8th Army Commander, Gen McCreery, for postponing all attacks until the water levels receded to normal levels to give us at least a reasonable chance of success.[10] While we had no knowledge of this sensible and humane decision, we prayed that he would honour a pledge that both he and Field Marshal Alexander had given us earlier — we would not be asked "to fight both weather and the enemy". The general was a man of his word.

Finally, on December 9th, the weather began to clear and we received orders to move right up to the Lamone River in preparation for an attack the next morning. Able and Baker Companies dug in on the near bank. At first light, an enemy patrol tried to get through our lines and was jumped by Able Company. The leader was killed and the rest fled back across the river.

Then new orders arrived: 2nd Brigade's attack was postponed; 3rd Brigade would now establish a bridgehead over the Lamone 2,500 yards north of us in the same area where 1st Brigade had failed so miserably five days earlier. Our turn would come later. We wished them luck and kept our thumbs on the trigger ready to press off a long burst the moment Jerry gave us an excuse to open fire.

That evening, December 10th, 3rd Brigade launched their attack. This time there had been ample opportunity for recce, the artillery had a superior fire plan and three battalions made the assault instead of two, as in the previous attack. Two of the battalions achieved success, but the third ran into an inferno of mortar and machine gun fire, and was momentarily repulsed when its Olafson bridge capsized in the swift current. However, the battalion soon renewed its attack through the bridgeheads of the other two battalions and was ultimately successful. The strength of the German defences in the area was then revealed. The attacking troops "discovered on the reverse side of the embankment numerous weapon-pits near the crest and a series of deep and strongly timbered dug-outs spaced at intervals of 20 feet, impervious to artillery fire, and equipped with every possible device, including electric lights."[11]

The success of 3rd Brigade meant that our 2nd Brigade would not be required to establish another bridgehead across the Lamone. We would now cross the river through the bridgehead of 3rd Brigade. On December 12th, we moved north to the area from which 1st and 3rd Brigades had launched their attacks. The Hun were still mad as hell about losing their strongly fortified and, so they thought, impregnable line to the cheeky Canadians, and were still plastering the area with 88s, 105s and Moaning Minnies. I could easily understand why the enemy were so sore. Their positions should have been impregnable against ordinary troops. The soldiers of 1st and 3rd Brigades were not ordinary troops. They had bested the Germans and earned not only their hatred but the respect of our entire division. We couldn't wait to get into the fight with them.

My MMG Platoon was set up in an enormous structure beside the east bank of the Lamone River. The ancient building had once been a magnificent palace, Palazzo San Giacomo, but now appeared to serve as a convent and a temporary hospital for civilians and soldiers. The Germans gave not a hoot what the building was used for and clearly resented the fact that the place was still standing; they continued to blast it with everything in their arsenal. Occasionally, a shell dropped cleanly through the remains of the roof and exploded with a terrific crash. A large number of civilians from the surrounding countryside had foolishly taken refuge in the convent and could not seem to comprehend why the Germans were trying to destroy it. They milled around, wailing and sobbing, imploring the help of their

Protector, as well as ours. We rounded up these poor farmers, and the nuns who were bravely tending the sick and wounded, and got them into strong rooms forming part of the outside walls. The sad, despairing looks on the faces of the nuns were pitiful to behold.

Some of the rooms still showed evidence of the casualties that 1st, and later 3rd Brigade had suffered in the recent fighting — broken stretchers, bloodied bandages, empty plasma bottles and torn equipment. The smell of death was still there.

Our stay in this house of peace and war was, thankfully, short. Third Brigade had made good progress after breaking out of their bridgehead over the Lamone and had now pushed the enemy back to the Naviglio Canal. Early in the evening of December 12th, we received word that 1st Brigade would attempt to cross the canal that night and 2nd Brigade would be committed to consolidate the bridgehead.

By this time, we had been waiting in the wings for a fortnight, trailing in the wake of 1st and 3rd Brigades. In the words of our favourite ditty, "we had been waiting so goddamn long we really wondered if we were ever going to fight." Furthermore, we had received so many orders, counter-orders, plans, changes in plans, that I had filled two notebooks and had almost ceased taking notes of plans that were changed as soon as they were written down. For some reason, instead of throwing away all this bumph I kept most of it. I am glad I did. The notes are tattered, dog-eared and stained, but they have at last, after all these years, served some purpose, by giving me a feel for the frustration of those days.

First Brigade crossed the Naviglio Canal during the night and in the early morning hours of December 12th/13th. At first, things went well, but soon the Germans recovered and launched their inevitable counter-attacks with tanks. It was touch and go until our tanks arrived to drive off the enemy armour.

Meanwhile, the Patricias crossed the Lamone River by rafts, under intense shellfire, and moved up to Traversara where we paused, ready to enter the battle on one hour's notice.

Chapter XXVIII

NAVIGLIO CANAL FOSSO MUNIO GRANAROLO

Wounded Again

December 14, 1944 to January 5, 1945

When you meet the Wehrmacht over the next canal
That is the time I wish you well old pal
When you go into that attack
Just think of me, I'm ten miles back
For I am LOB, for I am LOB

On December 14th, the Patricias began their advance toward the Naviglio Canal. The weather finally started to clear and there was a promise of sun later in the day. Even the sodden fields had dried out enough to be traversed, at least by foot. The troops, restrained so long in a support role, were eager to get forward and take out their frustrations on the Hun. But the enemy were not about to pack their gear and retreat behind the Alps. They were still annoyed about losing their positions on the Lamone. If they could not, for the moment, bring their MG42s to bear on our troops advancing along the roads and through the fields, they would retaliate with their artillery and mortars.

I called my MMG Platoon together to issue the plan for the advance. The three guns would have to be man-packed forward because the ground was still too soft for carriers. Traffic on the road in our area would be restricted to armour, anti-tank guns, jeeps and a few carriers with ammo and equipment.

In past actions, I had marched with the troops and, if Murdy didn't object, lent a hand with carrying the ammo. This time I had a jeep at my disposal that I had fought long to acquire. I couldn't bear to leave it behind, and besides, it could haul a lot of ammunition and some spare parts. So I elected to drive to war in style.

Murdy, of course, wanted to come aboard, but there was no room. Two other officers in Support Company needed transportation — Lt. Jim Horton of the Pioneers and Lt Al Fairburn of the Anti-tanks — but because of restrictions they could not use their own vehicles. In any event, it was time to let Murdy stay behind on LOB, but still he wanted to come forward.

"Look, Sir, I wish you would leave that damn jeep in B Echelon. You know that Jerry has the road taped and will be clobbering it for all he's worth. You would be safer marching with the troops in the ditches and fields. Besides, I can carry as much ammo as that jeep can."

"Murdy, you are beginning to sound just like the corps commander when you make wild statements like that. There is no way you can carry eight full boxes of ammo; and don't worry about me. Enjoy a rest in LOB while you can. See you when I get back."

I never saw Murdy again. He was badly wounded in the next action and evacuated home to Canada.

The Patricias continued to advance toward the Naviglio Canal, the tanks and some 'thin-skinned' vehicles (including my jeep) keeping to the road, the troops ploughing through the fields on each side, in open order.

Murdy had not been far off the mark when he said that Jerry would be clobbering the road. He was paving it with lead. Up ahead, one of the vehicles had been hit and was holding up the rest of the traffic. I pulled out to get around a troop of tanks, thought bettter of it, turned back and squeezed in between the lead tank and the one following it. I figured that if a shell landed on the road in front of or behind these two tanks I would have some protection.

Crash! A heavy shell slammed into the tank in front, then a pause, and a red sheet of flame shot into the sky.

Someone yelled, "Christ, it's going to brew up." I pressed the accelerator to the floor and shot past the burning tank as the ammunition started to explode inside.

Now shells began to fall on the troops in the fields. Over the roar of our tanks and the firing of our guns, I could not hear the explosions but I could see men hit the ground, quickly get up and continue the advance. No one stopped or hesitated unless he was wounded or killed. The wounded were left for the stretcher bearers who rushed forward and carried their charges to the rear.

"God," I thought, "they are well trained men. Well, no wonder. They're Colin McDougall's boys."

Then Jerry switched back to the road. We were now about 400 yards from the Naviglio Canal where the Germans were trying to dislodge 1st Brigade from the bridgehead.

Al Fairburn shouted something in my ear. I couldn't hear a word. He pointed down the road. About 300 yards ahead, I saw six dirty yellow flashes, as six mortar bombs exploded, one behind the other.

Al yelled again, "The next stonk may get us . . . . watch out . . . . Here comes a . . . . ."

"What's that . . . .?"

The bomb exploded in a blast of heat and dirt. A great rush of air seemed to bear me aloft. I felt I was going out of this world — like the sickening, spinning sensation of going down a long tunnel when given ether before an operation.

I came back to earth (both in my imagination and in fact) as soon as I hit the ditch. I got up a little dazed, but seemingly unhurt. Jim and Al were dusting themselves off. The jeep was a few yards down the road.

"What took you so long to abandon ship?" yelled Jim. "Didn't you hear that salvo of Moaning Minnies grinding up? They come in sixes." Jim was giving me a small dig.

"I was talking to Al and the next thing I knew I'm in this ditch. I must have jumped, but I think I got an assist from the shell that landed beside us."

We climbed up to the road. The vehicle in front of ours had been badly damaged. Two men lay on the road.

"Get a stretcher bearer," someone shouted. I looked back and saw two men with red crosses on their arms come running out of a house only 50 yards away. Stroke of luck — the RAP.

We hastened to the two men on the road. The first one had taken the full impact of a shell and was finished.

I looked down at the shattered body, the limbs askew in grotesque patterns. I couldn't believe that minutes before it had been a man. He seemed so flattened out, so insignificant, lying there in the mud that had already begun to claim his remains.

The other man was still alive, but badly wounded. The stretcher bearers soon got him back to the RAP.

I started back to the jeep and Horton yelled, "What happened to your pants? You've got a hell of a hole in the seat. For God's sake, you've been hit too!"

I put my hand inside my trousers and felt something warm and sticky covering my right buttock. "Christ sake, not again!" Suddenly, I felt very tired.

They helped me back to the RAP and the MO, Capt S A (Steve) Worobetz, had a good 'looksee'.

"Yeah, you've got a slug in there — deep, probably right to the bone, but you're lucky. Anywhere else in the back and you'd be a dead man."

A little voice whispered in my ear, "I'll bet, Sir, you got hit on purpose so's you'd be out of the line for Christmas.''

"Murdy, you ....," but Murdy was way back in B Echelon.

My little contretemps with a Moaning Minnie got me no sympathy at all. In the first place, it was true that I only had a flesh wound that would ensure my being out of the line for Christmas. My guilty conscience, in the form of Murdy's voice, had already told me that. Secondly, my supposed ignorance of the characteristics of a Moaning Minnie had been, so the story went, the sole cause of my misfortune. If I had been smarter and jumped the moment the banshee wail started, like Horton and Fairburn, I would not have been wounded.

The story, of course, improved with each telling. The final version was that Horton or Fairburn had yelled at me that a Moaning Minnie was on the way; to which my reply allegedly was, "A moaning what?"

This version fitted perfectly with a well-known cartoon by the famous Bing Coughlin that had appeared in the Army newspaper, *Maple Leaf*. The cartoon showed soldiers dashing for cover while a new recruit stood in the roadway asking, "Here comes a moanin' what?"

When I returned from hospital, the story of my naiveté about Moaning Minnies was so well entrenched that nobody would believe my version of the facts. So I just went along with the gag and even repeated it myself because it did make a good story.

Many years later, I was pleased to learn that Capt Stephen Worobetz MC had become Lieutenant-Governor of Saskatchewan. I wrote him a note of congratulations and couldn't resist making a humourous reference to the Moaning Minnie incident.

February 19, 1970

In the afternoon of December 14, 1944, I was driving in a jeep with two friends along a track quite close to Regimental Head-quarters when a siren type noise seemed to pervade the battlefield. Before I could make an 'appreciation of the situation' my friends jumped out of the jeep (which was till moving) and into a ditch yelling at me to do likewise, and uttering curses about a 'Moaning something'.

You have no doubt seen the humorous cartoon of the raw recruit standing in a field while his buddies are streaking off in all directions. The recruit says 'A Moaning what?'. I am told that that is exactly what I said.

The answer to my question came in the form of a large hunk of shrapnel which caught me in the behind as I was trying to follow the example of my friends. I was taken to the RAP where I believe you gave me a shot of vino rosso or some other kind of medicine, and I was on my way down the line.

375

This account of my innocence and/or ignorance of the prime German mortar weapon has had a good run — 40 years — and I am glad to put the matter finally to rest!

Capt Worobetz himself was wounded that same day but, in keeping with his fine character, he refused to be evacuated and remained on duty.

To return to the RAP on December 14th, 1944, while Capt Worobetz patched me up shells and mortars continued to blanket the road and fields. Soon, the little stone house that served as an RAP was filled with wounded. Then the RAP itself received a direct hit. Capt Worobetz and his helpers worked calmly through it all and dispatched casualties to the rear in a jeep ambulance in between the mortar bursts.

As soon as I arrived at 4 Advanced Dressing Station, I was made a stretcher case and laid out in an open field to await the journey back to 4 CCS (Casualty Clearing Station). Other casualties soon arrived and joined me in the field. The Germans started up their mortaring again. Some of the bombs landed awfully close to the ADS. Shell splinters screamed over our heads. One of the stretcher bearers was wounded. I could hardly resist the urge to get out of my stretcher and head for the nearest ditch. What a stupid, goddamn way to get killed, I growled to myself — in an open field, just like a sitting duck for those rotten German gunners.

Then a most peculiar feeling seized my body. My breath started to come in quick gasps; my limbs started to tremble. I appealed to an orderly. He took a quick look, "You'll be okay, just a slight case of shock."

I felt confused and ashamed. All about me were casualties much more serious than mine and I was in shock from a scratch in the rear. I thought back to my first wound (probably I had already been thinking about it subconsciously). I had no recollection of being so distraught then. I couldn't understand it. I still do not understand it, but, no doubt the psychiatrists have an answer.

Whatever my problem, it started to ease as soon as I was on my way to 4 CCS at Cesenatico, on the Adriatic coast. There, I had my first operation to remove the hunk of lead in my backside. When I came out of the anaesthetic I found a piece of gauze hanging from my left wrist with an object wrapped inside. I opened the gauze and found an inch-square, steel slug that the doctors had skillfully removed from the wound. Capt Worobetz had been right. The slug had gone right through to the bone and left a hole bigger than a 50 cent piece.

Casualties from the Naviglio Canal battles kept streaming into the already crowded CCS, and it was soon necessary to send to the rear hospitals all slightly wounded cases to make way for the Priority 1 cases who could not be moved. The next hospital in rear was 3 CHG (Canadian General Hospital) at Cattolica, but it, too, was filled with casualties. This meant I would have to be evacuated to Jesi (some 20 miles west of Ancona) by a roundabout route, much of it over dubious roads. Athough it was only 75 road miles distant, it could take as much as eight hours to get there.[1]

By now, the happy glow from the new pentothol anaesthetic had worn off and I had a very sore wound in a very awkward place. But the ward had to be cleared right away. So I was bundled up in a stretcher, my slug still dangling from my wrist, and placed in an ambulance for the long journey to Jesi.

I glanced at my watch. It was now 8:00 pm, December 14th. It had been a very long day. Early that morning I had started out in great spirits in my jeep from Traversera, on the banks of the Lamone River, heading west for the Naviglio Canal. I never quite made it. Four hundred yards from the Canal I was hit. One lousy slug had severed me again from the only home I knew — the Regiment. Now, here I was, bouncing along a rough diversion, in a cold ambulance, headed for Jesi, where I had started out three months earlier to rejoin my Regiment. Despite the fact that the wound was not a serious one, I had the terrible feeling I would never return to the Regiment. If I were sent back to the base at Avellino, near Naples, I might just as well forget all about the damn war. It would be over before I got back to the battalion. A deep anger and resentment overwhelmed me and blocked out the pain.

At 0600 hours, December 15th, the ambulance pulled into 1 CGH at Jesi with six very tired, cold, aching and hungry patients. It had taken ten hours instead of the usual eight. My leg was now quite stiff and hurting like blazes. Quickly we were carried into the hospital and carefully tucked into bed by those gentle angels of mercy who had been so good to me in England — Canadian Nursing Sisters.

After having our dressings changed and a hot meal we slept the sleep that only a soldier can appreciate. Some were so exhausted they fell asleep while their wounds were being dressed.

Later that day, I roused myself enough to ask for a pen and paper and wrote a short note to my parents.

> *Well, it looks like I'll be spending Xmas in a nice warm building with plenty of good food and nice Nursing Sisters. It's a funny thing that I can't seem to put in more than three months with the Regiment. I expect to be out in a month and then go through the old channels back to the Regiment. This time you'll note I kept my head down, but these 6-barrelled Jerry mortars throw an awful lot of metal about.*
> *I don't have much pain, but the wound is in an awful spot!!*

In case the letter was waylaid by the enemy, or suffered some other misfortune, I also spent a postcard, supplied free by the army, called a Canadian Army Priority Casualty Post Card, that saved considerable writing and even thought. All you had to do was check off the appropriate paragraphs. This handy, pro-forma sick report arrived in CMHQ in London on December 30th, but was not received by my parents until two weeks later. My letter, fortunately, arrived home first.

The official telegram was sent by the Director of Records at Ottawa on December 21st and delivered to my home in Toronto on Friday, December 22nd. Father was in Saint John, New Brunswick, having just been transferred there by the Bank. Fortunately, my brother was home from school. In the presence of my mother, he tore the envelope open, saw the words 'slightly wounded' and, I gather, heaved a sigh of relief. It wasn't much of a Christmas present, but a lot better than the year before.

Mother immediately wrote me, and I received her letter on January 12th — having taken only three weeks in transit. Despite a warning in the telegram not to divulge the name of my unit to prevent giving aid to the enemy, mother wrote to 'Support Company, PPCLI' (adding 'in hospital'). The disclosure does not, however, seem to have given much aid or encouragement to our enemies.

In fact, my absence made not the slightest difference to either side. The battles on the Naviglio Canal continued unabated with both sides fighting on to the point of exhaustion. In one 24-hour period (December 14th/15th), all four members of my class at RMC who were fighting with 2nd Brigade became casualties. From the PPCLI, Lt R S (Bob) Huestis came down with fever and had to be evacuated; Lt V S (Vaughan) Allan was killed; I was wounded. From The Loyal Edmonton Regiment, Capt G G (George) Brown was also wounded. My classmate Vaughan Allan met a brave death. The Regimental History gives this account of his last attack on December 15th:

> *When Lt V S Allan and his men approached a group of buildings they were fired upon; whereupon the officer told off two sections to give covering fire while with the remainder of his men he charged the enemy nest. Resistance was too strong; when the platoon withdrew Lt Allan and three of his men were missing. Their graves were found afterwards.*[2]

The bearer of these sad tidings of my friends was George Brown himself. He arrived at No 1 CGH on December 16th and was in the same ward as me.*

Other news of the heavy fighting in the Naviglio Bridgehead continued

---

*George went on to have a distinguished military career. He remained in the Army after the War, as a Patricia, rose to the rank of major general and served as Colonel of the Regiment.

to arrive. On the day I was wounded, Lt W E Harrington knocked out a Panther tank, killed a number of the enemy and brought back 16 prisoners. For this and other sterling acts of leadership, he was awarded the Military Cross.

On December 19th, my senior from RMC, Maj R W (Sam) Potts, in command of C Company, finally ran out of luck. He had landed on the beaches in Sicily as a platoon commander and had served the Regiment with distinction ever since, including a stint as Adjutant. In the evening of December 19th, his company attacked a house which commanded a road junction. On capturing it, Maj Potts entered the house and flicked on his flashlight to scan his map:

> *Apparently one or more enemy tanks or self-propelled guns had crept up to point-blank range; on the flicker of light a series of shells crashed through the building. Its upper floor collapsed; Maj Potts, painfully wounded, was dug out from under the rubble.*
> *Maj Potts comments: "I hit the deck and I recall having one shell go through the wall so close to my head that I saw the gun flash of the next round through the hole, without taking my chin off the floor."*[3]

Command of the company then passed to Lt W D L (Bill) Roach whose platoon had led C Company's attack on the house and silenced the defenders. His subsequent acts of bravery on that day are also recorded:

> *Lt Roach could smell counter-attack in the air. Out of the night groups of Germans dashed to the close, seeking to overwhelm the small garrison. The young officer took charge in magnificent fashion, rushing from post to post to encourage and to direct the defence. Inspired by his example, his men gave no ground and beat off two successive assaults. The enveloping force was estimated at company strength; against it stood no more than a dozen Patricia riflemen.*[4]

For his gallant leadership, Lt Roach was awarded the DSO, a very rare distinction for a junior officer. Indeed, such an honour was considered the next thing to a Victoria Cross. It was usually awarded where a junior officer's valour merited a VC, but the overall nature of the operation was not of sufficient importance (in the opinion of Higher Command, of course) to warrant a VC.

Whatever the Higher Command thought of the battle at the time, the Committee that awarded Battle Honours after the War held a very clear view of the significance of the operation in which Lt Roach won his DSO. The name of the battle, Fosso Munio, is emblazoned on the Regimental Colours of the Regiment.

News of the Regiment's hard fighting continued to trickle down to No 1 CGH at Jesi, where I was one of many recovering from the effects of the battle. I was proud of the gallant actions of my friends, but sad to see so many of them being struck down. The bitter fighting had not been confined just to the PPCLI. In the 20 days of the offensive that began at the Montone River on December 2nd, the Canadian Corps (1st and 5th Divisions) had suffered casualties of 548 officers and men killed, 1,796 wounded, and 212 taken prisoner — a staggering total of 2,646.[5]

These figures do not take into account the large numbers that had been evacuated because of fever, jaundice, hepatitis and other illnesses caused in part by the appalling weather conditions. One brigade had even suffered from trench foot, brought on by long periods in water-soaked slit trenches. Our fine Medical Services quickly introduced measures to counter this dreaded affliction from World War I: "drying and massaging the feet after immersion and changing socks as often as possible . . . Arrangements were made to send clean, dry socks forward with daily rations".[6]

The wards in No 1 CGH were quickly filled to capacity with casualties from the Canadian Corps. Medical officers, nursing sisters and orderlies worked around the clock to save lives and comfort the sick and wounded. From my long internship with my first wound and bouts of malaria, I considered myself to be at least an undergraduate doctor and got along famously with the sisters, many of whom I had met before in other hospitals — Sisters Hopkins, Staples, Smith, MacGillivary, Wright, Ewing, Baxter, to name a few.

They took wonderful care of me, despite the rather embarrassing location of my wound, and, as usual, I fell in love with them all. But, sad to relate, my romantic overtures came to naught, mainly because, I like to think, my tender years put me at a disadvantage in competition with the older, more experienced officers; also, my lowly rank as a lieutenant was no match for the senior officers who out-finessed my every move.

I was not the only one who worshipped Canadian Nursing Sisters. A far more interesting and colourful patient than I had been badly wounded while serving with the Army on the Adriatic coast — my hero, LCol Vladimir Peniakoff, DSO MC, more commonly known as Popski. On December 9th, after a long career dodging German bullets, his luck ran out when his left wrist was shattered by a grenade. He was taken to 5 Canadian Casualty Clearing Station in Ravenna, where his hand was amputated.

"These Canadian girls," he wrote in his autobiography, "were the kindest in the world, and they spoilt me thoroughly."
Besides spoiling him, one nursing sister would appear to have taught their patient a useful lesson. This very busy sister had

380

brought him his breakfast on a tray, and some time later asked
him why he was not eating. Somewhat abashed, he made a
helpless gesture with his left stump and his plastered right hand,
which had also been injured.

She laughed and said, "But you can feed yourself, you know.
Just try. I'll help you if you like, but I'm very busy."

"The lesson, " relates Popski, "was good — I never felt sorry
for myself again." [7]

It was the same lesson I had already learned in Basingstoke.

Another obstacle to any involvement with my 'angels' at 1 CGH at Jesi was, of course, the nature of my wound. Despite their tender care, the wound was still draining and smelled like a sewer. This condition gave the nurses some concern and they reported it to the Head Matron, whom I had known in earlier days. At the inspection next morning, the ward came to attention. The Matron stopped at my bedside where I was stretched out, face down, bare-assed to the sky. She gave me a sweet smile and bent down to have a closer look at the wound. Shielding her mouth to ward off any possible germs, she inquired, "Mr Frost, haven't I seen you somewhere before?"

I don't think the dear woman quite understood the loud guffaws that erupted from the rest of the ward.

Actually, the wound was healing nicely due largely to a new wonder drug. Every three hours for four days, I received a penicillin jab in the hip. A little trying, perhaps, especially at night, but highly effective in my case. On December 19th, my surgeon, Maj Dineen, operated on the wound, tidied it up and put in some stitches. By now, I was quite used to operations and actually enjoyed the after-effects of the new anaesthetic pentothol. It was such a relief not to have the terrible wretching and nausea that I had suffered a year earlier, that I wrote my mother a note on the success of my recent operations:

My wound is healing quickly, due I think to the new penicillin
treatment they have used. This cuts out the worst worry —
infection — and makes for a speedy recovery. I had 34 needles
of it, 8 times a day, which was quite sufficient. That and two
operations are the sum total of my treatments so far. Honestly,
I am continually amazed at the efficiency of our hospitals. Just
think, if I had been treated promptly with penicillin for my face,
I would have been well in less than half the time it took.

Well, operations have no fear for me anymore, due to another
marvelous discovery — pentothol. These two operations were not
like my other ones last year, when I was always sick for days
afterwards. Instead, this is what happens — I am given a painless
injection in the arm and in four seconds I'm off to sleep. Next

thing I know I'm in my ward, feeling top-hole, just as if I had about 6 double Scotch. It's more fun. This time when I came out I evidently put on quite a good show!

As Christmas approached, our ward took on a festive air. The sisters organized a competition to see which ward would have the best decorations: the prize — two bottles of sherry. I was detailed to persuade our young Italian waitress, Teresina, who helped the other orderlies bring in our meals, to go out and acquire reams of old paper for us to make ornaments and bunting; also to bring back some vino to help us do our job. We won the event hands down, or bottoms up, depending on your point of view. The celebration started Christmas Eve and pretty well lasted all Christmas Day, with time out to change dressings and the like. Besides our prize of two bottles of sherry, a variety of other stimulants appeared to keep the party rolling — cognac, whisky, vino and beer. My second Christmas in hospital was a big improvement over the first. Now I was in a heated ward among friends, comrades, Canadian Nursing Sisters and beautiful Italian waitresses, and suffering no pain.

Just recovering from a stupendous turkey dinner, not to mention quantities of candy, nuts, fruit, cake and pudding. Now I'm 'tapering off' on a glass of first-class sherry. This all sounds more like a hotel than a hospital, eh wot?

The Red Cross came through in great style with a Xmas stocking for every patient, containing chocolate, candy, fruit, etc. The hospital gave 100 cigs, a bottle of beer and a bag of candy.

Then there was a male singers' group and an MO bedecked as old Santa himself. Of course he was about three parts gone, which added greatly to old Santa's wit and charm! Altogether a jolly time, with the Nursing Sisters adding their share of the fun.

Here is a point of interest for Vivian. In Italy there is no such thing as Santa Claus. Instead, on 6 January there is a fairy lady who supplies gifts to the children, but for a long time now, due to Fascist propaganda these 'gifts' have always been in the nature of toy weapons of war. So the Wop kids don't enjoy much of a Xmas.

There was a nice snowfall last night, making it a real white Xmas today. Air is so clear that I can see the mountains quite distinctly and I am thankful to be here in a nice ward resting comfortably.

Up front, the newspapers say there is snow 3 ft deep in some places, and temperatures well below freezing. Not very pleasant for my MMGs and their carriers. If they have to man-pack the guns, it will be a difficult task.

I need not have worried about my MMGs. The Patricias had been withdrawn from the line and were enjoying the usual Christmas cheer:

> *In traditional style, the men were served by the officers and sergeants; the menu contained the seasonal delicacies and there were four bottles of beer per man. Each company had its own witches' brew of punch containing many and varied ingredients. Brig Hamilton Gault had supplied cigarettes for all ranks. The Band came forward and serenaded the companies.*[8]

Of course, I had no knowledge of this lucky break of my friends and I drank a silent toast, wishing them good luck, good hunting and safe deliverance from their present and future battles. Neither did I, nor anyone else for that matter, have any knowledge of the future of the Canadian Corps in Italy. The corps had, in fact, fought its last major battle.

While I had been 'frousting' in hospital, major changes had occurred in the Allied Command. Field Marshal Alexander had taken over from Gen Wilson the position of Supreme Allied Commander, Mediterranean. LGen Mark Clark, former Commander of the 5th US Army, had succeeded Field Marshal Alexander as Commander of the Allied Armies in Italy, the 5th and the 8th, which again became known as the 15th Army Group. Gen McCreery remained in command of the 8th Army.

Gen Clark lost no time in telling Gen McCreery to "proceed with current operations with the object of launching an attack to force a crossing of the Senio River in conjunction with 5th Army's attack," which he hoped to deliver against Bologna a few days before Christmas.[9] And on December 20th, Gen Clark warned his two Army Commanders that "the time is rapidly aproaching when I shall give the signal for a combined all-out attack of 5th and 8th Armies."[10]

But Gen Clark had ignored a lot of things he should have taken into account and had failed to allow for the intervention of the highest ranking officer on both sides of the conflict, one Field Marshal Fate. He had ignored the same basic factors so many commanders had ignored throughout the Italian campaign — insufficient men, lack of reinforcements, shortages of ammunition, the abominable weather, the difficult terrain, and, not by any means the least important factor, the unpredictable Germans.

On December 26th, the Germans delivered a sudden attack on the left flank of the 5th Army which was lightly held by a division of coloured US troops. The attack penetrated five miles and if successfully exploited, it might have endangered Leghorn, an important supply base for the army. What gave added significance to this attack was that ten days earlier the Germans had launched their do-or-die Ardennes offensive on the Western Front. Gen Clark could not ignore the possibility that the attack on his left flank might also be a desperate attempt to cut off his supply base.

As a result, Gen Truscott, new Commander of the 5th Army, postponed the opening of the winter offensive on his front. Thus was Gen Clark's plan frustrated by the intervention of unforeseen events.

Gen Clark might be forgiven for not anticipating the German attack, but he should have realized that the serious shortages of men and ammunition precluded any sustained winter offensive. From the capture of Rome in June, 1944, when the Allied Armies in Italy probably reached their maximum effectiveness, the strength of the armies had gone steadily downhill. In August, the 5th Army lost seven divisions that took part in Operation Anvil (the invasion of southern France); in November, the 8th Army lost two and a half divisions that were sent to Greece. Over the period, other formations had been nibbled away until, by December, 1944, the Allies could place only 13 divisions in the front lines with a few in reserve. In the matter of shortage of ammunition, both armies had insufficient reserves for a prolonged attack. The shortages were probably more evident in the 8th Army where the recent heavy fighting had seriously depleted its stocks of ammunition.[11]

> *In these circumstances the poor prospects of reaching Bologna that winter were only too apparent to Field Marshal Alexander. On 30 December he decided to abandon the existing plan and to go on the defensive for the present and to concentrate on making a real success of our spring offensive.*[12]

We can thus thank Field Marshal Alexander for saving the lives of countless Canadian soldiers who would have been sacrificed if Gen Clark had persisted with his plan. On that account alone, Field Marshal Alexander earned his appointment as our Governor General after the War.

So much, then, for the factors that Gen Clark should have taken into account. There remained, however, one other factor he could not have foreseen when drawing up his plans for a winter offensive. The Canadian Corps would be withdrawn in February to be reunited with 1st Canadian Army in Northwest Europe. Such a possibility was only a cherished hope of the Canadian government and the soldiers involved in December, 1944.

All these considerations of high strategy were hardly matters that I was privy to as I lay between clean, white sheets in a warm ward on December 31st, 1944. More important to me was how to get out of bed and make my way back to the Regiment. The blasted wound was taking its time to heal despite expert care. There was still a nasty hole the size of a 50 cent piece and long sutures on each side. Apart from a desire to rejoin my Regiment, I felt an even more compelling urge — a visit to the bathroom. I remembered the 'lost stool' episode in the hospital in Bari the previous year, and I didn't want to be faced with (or assed with) the *Queen Mary*, as my friend had been.

One evening, late at night, I sneaked out of bed and made my way to the bathroom. After a prodigious effort I passed not only the *Queen Mary* but the whole of His Majesty's Atlantic Squadron — painful, but what a relief!

New Year came and went very quietly. Apparently we had shot our bolt at Christmas time. My diary records simply, "only one patient got drunk last night."

On January 3rd, 1945, I had my third operation and the final stitches were put in. Again, I had a marvellous jag from the pentothol and apparently put on a great show for my fans, including our waitress Teresina with whom I carried on a romantic conversation in perfect Italian for half an hour. My continuing study of that beautiful language seems to have made me quite fluent, though the pentothol may have helped. I suspect, too, that the doctors gave me an extra shot of this fine anaesthetic to ensure I put on a sparkling performance.

More casualties from the fierce December fighting on the Naviglio and Fosso Munio continued to arrive, including my friend Sam Potts, who had been badly wounded. Because of the seriousness of his wounds, he was sent back to base hospital to recover and did not rejoin the Regiment until near the end of the War in Holland.

A short time later, Capt A G Robinson MC also came through. From him I learned that the Patricias had been in action again on the bloody Naviglio Canal. In spite of Field Marshal Alexander's directive to go on the defensive, there was still a pocket of enemy in and around Granarolo, on the east side of the Senio River which had to be cleared up before the troops could establish a winter line along the river. The task fell to 2nd Brigade.

On January 3rd, the Patricias assaulted across the canal, half a mile south of Granarolo, under a heavy artillery and mortar barrage, and quickly gained their objectives, taking 60 prisoners and capturing intact a self-propelled gun and a fancy staff car. The Germans counter-attacked with SP guns and infantry and were driven off, but only after we had suffered the inevitable casualties, including Lt W A Groomes (who had been with the Regiment less than a month) killed and Lt G D M Nicholson wounded.

Two officers in particular distinguished themselves in the battle and contributed greatly to its success. At the point where the Patricias had crossed the canal there was no bridge, but there was a built-up road leading to the canal through the marshy fields — the only possible route for tanks and support weapons. It was vital to clear this road of mines and build a bridge as soon as the battalion crossed the canal so our armour and anti-tank guns could be pushed across to meet the inevitable counter-attack. The building of that bridge is the story of the coolness under fire of Lt J H Horton, the Pioneer Officer.

As soon as the attack opened, Lt J H Horton, Pioneer Officer, hurried to inspect the road which had been allotted to the Patricias. It was under fire; in addition the enemy before withdrawal had cratered it. An armoured bulldozer and an Ark bridge were sent forward, but before these heavy pieces could be moved the road had to be swept for mines. A number of Teller mines were discovered so firmly embedded in the surface of the roadway that all attempts to remove them by hand failed. A tow was attached to individual mines; the tow-bar bent, the mines did not give.

Lt Horton set charges to explode them but only one mine obliged. Heavier charges were prepared, and the mines blew up with a resounding blast. The bulldozer and the Ark bridge lumbered forward. The Naviglio was of no great width or depth but its dykes rose about six feet above ground level; they were impassable to tracks or wheels. Lt Horton brought up more charges, blew the dykes inward and used the rubble as filling for his crossing. All this was done at great speed, working against time and under fire.[13]

The building of the bridge, however, was only one of many feats of daring that saved the day and brought distinction to the Regiment. Unless immediate anti-tank support could be sent forward, the bridge would be of no avail; by the time it was completed and ready for tanks, the enemy counter-attacks might throw the battalion back to the canal. Into the breach stepped Lt A B McKinnon of D Company.

It was not enough to stand by and wait for the road to be opened, as it was known that the Germans had tanks in close support of their outpost lines. Lt A B McKinnon of D Company was given a taper bore two-pounder and was told to use his native wits in getting it forward. He and his men manhandled the piece for 1,000 yards across the fields, surmounting en route three drainage ditches and a railway embankment. Shortly after midnight they reached the canal. In two hours they built their own crossing; they were constantly under fire. Having dragged the weapon to the far bank they were given the location of the forward companies and were told that the available road was mined. By this time the extempore gun crew had had enough of cross-country routes. Lt McKinnon walked ahead and tested the road; the gun followed in tow of a jeep. At 0845 hours it was delivered to B Company.

Lt McKinnon's day was not yet over. As he and his men retraced their steps a British fighter plane crashed in a nearby field and burst into flames. Ordering his men to stand back because of exploding ammunition the officer climbed into the cockpit and dragged out the badly burned pilot.14

For his spirited leadership and determination to succeed, despite the odds, Lt McKinnon was awarded a well-earned Military Cross.

Once again, the Regiment had added another name to its long list of Battle Honours — Granarolo.

This was to be the last major offensive action of the Regiment in Italy. During the next six weeks they would hold a series of defensive positions along the Senio, and to the east of that barrier, until they and their comrades in the 1st Canadian Corps were called back to join the fold of 1st Canadian Army in Northwest Europe. None of this of course, was known to anyone except the Higher Command.

Chapter XXIX

SENIO RIVER
WINTER LINE

January 6 to February 20, 1945

I love to hear the music of the Shiny Two Brigade
I love to hear the music of the Mills hand grenade
I love to hear the music of the old whizz bang
A bursting on the parapet of the dirty old Allemagne
I love to hear the music of the nine point two
That puts Jackie Johnston in the shade
But the best damn music in the whole wide world
Is the music of the Shiny Two Brigade
Trench Mortars, whizz, bang, boom

While the Regiment was enduring its last ordeal by fire, in Italy, one Lt C S Frost continued to lie on his backside and fiddle — but unlike Nero, he was not amused.

The pesky wound had still not closed and I was in a foul mood. The earliest the doctors said I could leave hospital would probably be mid-February, a month away. In the meantime, as beds were urgently needed for fresh casualties from the Granarolo operations, I would be sent even farther back to another hospital at Perugia, 14 CGH, high in the midst of the snow-covered Apennines. When I was finally discharged from there I would be returned to a holding unit, probably at Avellino where the staff and the echelons played.

While I had no knowledge of the future operations of the Canadian corps, or their plan to move to Northwest Europe, I knew very well the War was in its final stages and the Germans were on their last legs. The Russians had overrun East Prussia and were pressing into Germany itself. Likewise, the armies of the Second Front were on the German frontier. Even if the enemy had temporarily stopped us at the Senio River, it made little difference to the outcome of the War. It would all be over before I could get back to my Regiment.

Ever since joining the Patricias I had harboured three ambitions — to go into action with the Regiment, to command a company (as my father had done in the First War) and to be with the Regiment at the end. Through no fault of my own, I had missed being one of the first into action. Now, with the War almost over, and me still a lieutenant, my hopes and plans were in ruins.

Then came the final straw. I got word that on January 16th, because of the heavy casualties, three lieutenants had been promoted to captain. Not that they were not deserving. All had given outstanding service to the Regiment; two had been captains in England and had gamely reverted to get into action. One had won the Military Cross. But only one had served with me in Sicily, and southern Italy. They were all friends and I was happy for them that they had survived long enough to receive their promotions.

All the same, I was damn mad and disillusioned, and almost ready to call it quits. It seemed clear that Field Marshal Fate had made his final pronouncement — a lieutenant I was born, a lieutenant I would die. But I wouldn't even be allowed to die gracefully if I didn't get back into action soon.

These depressing and nonsensical thoughts rode with me in a stretcher, as the ambulance laboured, hour by freezing hour, through the snow of the Apennines carrying me farther from my Regiment and my home. It took seven hours to reach Perugia. But my journey had not been wasted. I had overcome my anger. I was going to get back to the Regiment if I had to crawl there and defy old Field Marshal Fate to do his worst.

Perhaps the bitterly cold weather had something to do with it. Thoughts drifted back to RMC — standing in the snow on a square on a cold November day, without gloves — Jake Wyatt bellowing at me "get moving, get moving, left, right, left."

Maybe it was a favourite expression of Sam Potts, "when the going gets tough, the tough get going."

It could have been Corky and his fierce determination to return to the Regiment and fight right to the very end.

It was in fact a decision born of all the people I had known and the training I had received since August, 1940.

There was no time to lose. I would have to wrangle an almost immediate discharge from hospital, deep in the Italian mountains. I knew so many of the doctors and nurses that this should be no problem. Then, I would have to by-pass the holding units and go straight to the Regiment. The adjutant, Capt Andy Mills, would pretend he was unhappy about my 'freelance' work, but he would sort out the paper. God only knew where my kit was — probably back at Avellino (that's exactly where it was!).

Just planning another escapade was a big boost to my morale as was seeing friends in the hospital who understood my problem and gave me extra moral support. One friend, who was very helpful and encouraging, was Maj Colin McDougall, who was being invalided home. His constant bouts with malaria, jaundice and other maladies had taken their toll. We had been together in hospital in Catania when we had our first attack of malaria. He never took time to properly convalesce after these attacks because he couldn't bear to be away from his beloved B Company. I don't believe he ever went LOB. He felt it was his duty to be with his men at all times. I had the greatest respect for Colin McDougall and was sorry to see him go. There would be precious few left of the Old Guard.

Colin McDougall was awarded the DSO for his outstanding leadership in action as well as an MID. After the War, he became Registrar of McGill University and wrote a book about Canadian soldiers in Italy under the name *Execution*. While it was supposed to be a fictional account of their experiences, some of the episodes, I thought, were very similar to those we had encountered together.

I left 14 CGH at Perugia on January 30th, with orders to report to a Transit Camp to be posted to a holding unit for convalescence. Nothing was said about my ultimate return to my Regiment. With the help of some of the sisters I smuggled out a supply of penicillin and bandages as the wound was still open and had a slight discharge.

At the door I was greeted by a driver to take me to the Transit Camp. I told him there must be some mistake, as I was just going out for a stroll. I gave him permission to "carry on, please".

I limped away until I was out of sight of the hospital and the driver, and then hurried to the nearest hotel. There I met some Seaforth officers who were on their way back to Riccione. I bummed a lift and was on my way. I felt as if I had engineered an escape from Alcatraz.

Late that night, we arrived at Riccione and checked in at 3 CGH, where I had briefly rested six weeks earlier. My 'angels' were happy to put us up in one of the wards as the hospital was now pretty well clear of patients. My wound was given a friendly examination and dressed without charge.

We left next morning, January 31st, and headed north toward the Senio River where our battalions were supposed to be dug in. The Seaforth officers dropped me off at X area of the PPCLI outside Ravenna, and then went looking for their own headquarters.

I stood in the snow and stretched. The weather was cold, but bright. It was good to be home again. I was ready to give the Hun another crack.

The Second-in-Command was somewhat surprised to see me back and didn't quite know what to do with me. He called over Capt E D 'Oop' McPhail who was acting as Adjutant while Andy Mills was away on course.

"What do we do with Frost, Oop? He's just arrived back from Perugia with no documents or kit."

"Yes, Sir, I know about his kit. We shipped it down to Avellino when he was wounded. Never thought we'd see him... for some time."

"Well, for heaven's sake, don't let him near the front line. He'll probably get hit again and brigade will raise hell because he's not on strength."

"That's right, Sir," replied Oop, looking very serious, but giving me a wink and a nudge. "Can't get killed unless you're on strength."

What a clever way, I thought, to avoid getting shot. Just keep your name off the battalion nominal roll! I was about to make that 'smart-ass' suggestion when Maj Cobbett gave a chuckle.

"I wish that were true, Oop. We'd have won the war a long time ago. Keep Frost here in X area until you figure out a way to get him on strength again and his kit has come back from Avellino.

"In the meantime, Syd, get some rest and get fattened up. You look like you need it. When LCol Clark returns from leave, we'll decide what to do with you."

Maj Cobbett was a gentleman and I appreciated his kindness. For the next few days, I hung around Main BHQ and enjoyed the comforts of living in a fine house — heat, lights, hot and cold running water. My desire to go forward steadily waned; Maj Cobbett's injunction to stay away from the front lines hardly seemed necessary.

Anyway, there was enough excitement around BHQ to remind me that a state of war still existed between the opposing armies, even though we had settled into a so-called Winter Line along the Senio. Enemy guns and mortars searched the area from time to time, but caused little damage except to some of the strong houses we occupied as tenants. We left the repairs to the landlords as our short-term leases provided we were not responsible for damages caused by acts of God, or the King's enemies.

The forward companies of the battalion had recently taken over a deserted, cheerless sector north of Mezzano on the coastal highway, about 800 yards east of the Fosso Vecchio. The Germans still held the area between the Fosso Vecchio and the Senio River, including a strong point, Casa Baroni, on the banks of the Vecchio. While the Patricias were making plans to raid this strong point, an Italian formation holding the line on our right, the Gruppo Combattimento Cremona, was fiercely attacked by the Germans and lost part of their front line. All companies were warned and told to be ready for a 100 per cent stand-to. Meanwhile, reinforcements from another battalion were rushed to the area and the situation restored.

The Patricias could now proceed with their planned raid on Casa Baroni, which someone, with a misplaced sense of humour, had code-named X-Lax. If the staff officer who perpetrated this inappropriate moniker had taken part in the raid, he would not have required Ex-lax for many a day. The code-name for success was just as objectionable — Cheese.

In the early hours of February 3rd, C Company, under Maj J M D Jones, put in the attack, heavily supported by artillery, 3 inch mortars, 4.2 inch mortars and our MMG Platoon. When the leading section of 14 Platoon, commanded by Lt N J Lewis (who had only recently joined the battalion) entered the first house, a prepared charge was set off by the Germans that brought down the building on the heads of the attacking section. The rest of the platoon tried to dig them out, but they in turn were caught in a mortar stonk that caused many casualties. After first light, a party under the flag of the Red Cross went out and gathered up the bodies. The casualties had been heavy. Lt Lewis and an officer of the Jewish Brigade (who was attached to the Regiment) had been wounded, six other ranks killed and 26 wounded. One man was missing.[1]

So ended the last attack of any size by the battalion in Italy.

On February 3rd, the Regiment moved back to a rest area in Russi, where I waited for LCol Clark to return from leave and decide my fate. Though my official status within the battalion was still in doubt, it did not deter the Adjutant from giving me plenty of jobs to keep me from getting bored. The defunct Mess Committee was reborn, I was restored to my former estate as a member in charge of organizing another mess dinner for the purpose of inculcating a little of the Patricia spirit into the many new officers. If I was perplexed and unhappy about the camaraderie and *esprit de corps* in the Regiment when I joined it in September, I had good reason to be even more concerned with the present state of the Regimental spirit. In the past two months, no fewer than 15 new platoon commanders had joined the Regiment (including seven from the artillery and the engineers), and 16 officers had been struck off strength. Of the 38 officers who had embarked for Sicily in June, 1943, only seven remained, five of whom had actually assaulted the beaches at Pachino. One other officer had also embarked for Sicily in June, 1943 and landed on those beaches three days after the assault troops. Ever since he had made a career (albeit, not much of a one) of trying to catch up to the Regiment.

If the Old Guard were shy in numbers at the Mess Dinner on February 8th, there was no evidence that they had lost any of their stamina to old age; neither was there any indication that the New Boys were slow in learning some of the rudiments of what it meant to be a Patricia. For many, it was the first time they had heard of any of the Regimental songs — *The Rick-a-dam-doo, So Clear the Way, Who was the Man, Shiny Two Brigade, Has*

Anyone Seen the Colonel and all the rest. If they wanted an occasional artillery or sapper ditty thrown in, the non-stop piano player was happy to oblige as long as they sang the words with gusto. A new generation of Patricias was being born and would carry the Regiment through to the end of the War.

LCol Clark had now returned from leave and called me into his office. "I hear you have been up to your old tricks of by-passing authority and not going by the book. I don't know what I'm going to do with you. I can't put you back with the MMGs. Capt Stutt has taken them over and is doing a good job. But there's a vacancy for a Second-in-Command of D Company. Do you know anyone there?"

"Yes, Sir, Maj Smith is the OC, but I only met the platoon commanders last night."

"Well, I'm going to post you to D Company for the moment. I suppose that means I should make you a captain."

Not a breath from me, in or out.

"First, I have got to get approval from brigade. Maybe there's a captain coming up the line or some senior lieutenant who's entitled to promotion ahead of you. I'll let you know in a few days. If I were you, I wouldn't tell anyone about it until the promotion is authorized. In the meantime, report to Maj Smith."

LCol Clark wasn't shilly-shallying when he mentioned the possibility of other captains or senior lieutenants coming back to the battalion. It was always a toss-up whether they or the Germans would stand in the way of your promotion. The only difference was that German interference was sometimes final.

It took me some time to come down to earth. It took me more time to savour the possibility of finally putting up that damned elusive third pip. Was there really a chance that my second ambition might come true — command a company in action? I would have to wait until the CO gave the final verdict. In the meantime, I had lots to do.

On February 10th, I reported to Maj 'Snuffy' Smith and met his platoon commanders — Lt A B Allan McKinnon MC, Lt W W (Bert) Bolton, and Lt H E (Harvey) Beardmore. Both McKinnon and Beardmore had been gunners; Bolton a sapper. Al McKinnon had already proved his mettle by winning the Military Cross in the Granarolo operation. The other two seemed keen enough, but they would have to show me they meant business.

In the early evening of February 10th, the battalion moved forward to the Senio River and occupied the same position northwest of Bagnacavallo that it had held three weeks earlier after the Granarolo operation. D Company was on the right, with company HQ and three platoons in fortified houses in the flats just below the high, flood banks of the river. The two forward platoons were no farther than 20 yards from these dykes.

393

The Germans occupied the near bank of the river which rose 35 feet above the plain and gave the enemy a commanding view of our position. Movement was pretty well restricted to night time when supplies, food and ammunition were brought forward, along carefully marked lines, through the heavily mined and booby-trapped positions.

It was exhilarating to be so close to the foe that when they were hit by our fire I could hear their shouts and screams. Our lives were also enlivened by a platoon of Italians attached to our company. These irregular Partigiani loved to wander around the front at night and pick up the odd prisoner from the other side. How they wheedled these troops out of their safe slit trenches, and coaxed them through the mine fields, barbed wire and booby-traps to our side, I only found out many years after the War. Some prisoners, of course, were Polish deserters and presumably assumed the risks, not because they didn't fear death, but because they loved liberty more.

One night, the Partisans brought in three Polish deserters to my company HQ. They were a scared, bedraggled, filthy-looking lot and were willing to give me all the information they knew. As conversation in German, Polish or English was impossible, they 'talked' in broken Italian and gave me some interesting news — their division was being relieved that evening. This intelligence was immediately despatched to BHQ and a solid artillery and mortar stonk fell on the Poles' departing comrades to help them on their way.

German snipers were very active, but apparently not too well trained in their deadly art. Few of our troops were felled by these supposed sharp-shooters, though we gave them not a few fleeting opportunities in an effort to locate their positions. One of our favourite games was to dash along a road connecting company HQ with one of the platoons, know as Sniper Alley. The unit which had held this position before us had hung camouflage nets along the route, in trees and on stakes, to give us some protection from enemy observation. As I recall, only two or three of our men were hit along this route. Personally, I didn't care much for this game and confined my visits to the platoons to the evening hours.

Of more concern were the MG42s firing on fixed lines. One corner of my *casa* was a favourite target for these machine gunners; each night it was hotter than the action in Piccadilly Circus on a Saturday evening.

Another favourite pastime of the Germans was to roll Teller mines down the river embankment into our heavily sandbagged houses. Usually the mines became ensnarled in obstacles placed in front of our strongholds, or the mines simply didn't explode on contact. But when they did, they gave our *casas* a severe test.

On February 12th, LCol Clark himself appeared after last light. His coming had been billed as an inspection of our positions, but I hadn't the slightest doubt he had also received from above the verdict on my promotion. I could scarcely contain my excitement as he checked over our defensive layout on the ground and on the map. I half-hoped Jerry would send in a patrol so we could kill or capture the bunch and show the CO how well prepared we were to repulse the foe.

LCol Clark expressed satisfaction with our layout, asked a few questions and prepared to depart. Not one damm word to me about my promotion. Obviously, it hadn't been approved. Well, he had done his best. As he stepped out into the inky blackness, I thought that the least I could do to show my appreciation was to warn him about that MG42 firing on fixed lines at the corner of the house. He thanked me and then put out his hand. "By the way, Frost, you can put up that third pip."

I can't think of anything before or since that has given me such a feeling of satisfaction. Instantly, I knew that I would survive the War. If LCol Clark had ordered me to assualt the dykes single-handedly, I would probably have complied. I realized, of course, that I was only an acting captain. At the end of three months, I could be recommended for confirmed rank, provided I behaved myself and no other senior captain showed up. I was not too much concerned about the first proviso, and if another captain appeared he would have to contend with me personally as well as with the German Army.

Another Lieutenant for the Princess had run the course.

I could hardly wait to tell my father I had, at last, attained the rank he had reached in the First War.

> *Here I am, back with the Regiment in another capacity, as 2IC of 'D' Coy, along with three pips. Of course my new rank is just an acting one, and should a senior captain come along I would have to step down, but in the meantime I'm earning the pay of a captain and doing his job. After 2 1/2 years as a lieutenant, I guess it's about time.*
>
> *There is a great step between Pl Comd and 2IC or Coy Comd. Luckily, my Coy Comd is an ex-cadet of the College and is very helpful to me. My previous experience as MG Pl Comd has also been a great help. As it was an independent Pl I had many of the problems of a Coy Comd. Also, I was always in liaison with the CO and Coy Comds, and working in close conjunction with them during battle.*

On the day following my promotion, an announcement was made that many people seemed to think was even more important than my new rank — Gen Marshall, Chief of the United States General Staff, was going to visit brigade HQ. It seemed only fitting that my promotion should be marked by the attendance of such a distinguished officer. When I mentioned this to Snuffy Smith, he was kind enough to observe, "Sure, the general is probably bringing you congratulations from the President of the United States."

In the event, the great man did not appear and we had to be satisfied with an inspection by LGen Sansom, now the Inspector General of the Canadian Army. With my new rank, I would probably have had enough nerve to ask him how his daughter, Charmian, was doing, but something intervened and I didn't have a chance to meet him.

My good mood was cut short by a tragic accident. Sgt Goodburn, of the MMG Platoon, and five other men were wounded when several of our 3 inch mortar bombs fell short. Sgt Goodburn died the next day. The fault lay not with our expert mortar crew, but with the ammunition which was defective. This was a sad blow to me. Sgt Goodburn and I had been through good times and bad and had always got along well together. He was undoubtedly one of the mainstays of the MMG Platoon and was much liked and admired for his ready wit and soldierly qualities. I tried to see him before he died, but I was too late. I was told that even in his extremity he was able to cast a parting shaft of wit at the Mortar Platoon: "First time they've ever been on target."

Accidents continued to plague the battalion. When a party from D Company went forward to lay wire near the house the Partisans occupied, they tripped one of our booby-trapped grenades and eight of our men were wounded — casualties we could ill afford in our understrength company. Our records had given no indication there were booby-traps in that area.

Incorrect traces of mines and booby-traps that had been prepared by other battalions were something that always bothered me, right from my first days in England when I used to go on beach patrols through our heavily mined obstacles. There wasn't much that could be done about it, but I always wondered how the Partisans avoided destruction on both ours and the German booby-traps.

Despite these cruel fortunes of war we maintained constant pressure on the Hun and like all Canadian soldiers kept our sense of humour. Much time and thought was spent in devising fiendish new ways to best the enemy. PIATs, that had been designed to knock out tanks at point blank range, were fired over the dykes at high angle and proved to be devastating aerial torpedoes that could demolish a house with a tremendous roar.

The Germas retaliated by digging 'mole holes' through the dykes and used these openings like portholes in a ship to fire heavy weapons at us. We secretly brought up a medium gun, and when the first streaks of dawn appeared, blasted the German 88s and 105s to bits.

Other means of terrorizing the enemy were more prosaic, but also more lethal, such as loading up a truck with bombs and mines and sending it careening down a road to greet the Germans, *sans* driver of course.

Still another secret weapon was the 'Dagwood', said to have been invented by the Lanark and Renfrew Scottish Regiment, in the 5th Division. This creation rivalled the best in Hitler's secret arsenals. A 36 grenade was sandwiched between two Hawkins 75 grenades in a sandbag and sent over the dykes. The 36 went off first and detonated the other two. The result on a platoon of the enemy was, according to one observer, "most horrid — all blood and no forehead."

Probably the most ingenious weapon in our arsenal was a super sling-shot that rivalled the one David used to knock out Goliath. A soldier in Lt Bolton's 16 Platoon, one Cpl L L Cosford, liberated a rubber inner tube from one of our trucks and cut it to form a gigantic rubber band. He then attached each end of the tube to a fork in a tree and declared he was going to use the device to catapult hand grenades into the German positions on the other side of the dyke. Lt Bolton, an engineer by trade, had severe doubts whether the contraption would work without blowing up half of 16 Platoon. But, with true Patricia panache, he let Cosford try a large rock in his infernal machine.

Eureka! It tossed the missile clear over the river bank. Then Bolton allowed the Corporal to try a few grenades *without* fuses. Again, success.

No one will ever know what the Germans thought about this antediluvian method of hurling projectiles. No doubt, they thought it was all a huge joke. If so, it was probably their last laugh. As they were examining the rocks and dud grenades, a salvo of live grenades suddenly landed in their midst. Their howls of glee quickly turned into cries of pain and anger.

Cpl Cosford was thereafter known as 'Bing' (the man with the sling). After surviving the War, he decided to remain in the Army where he figured that his talents with unguided missiles would be appreciated. But in 1947, his career was abruptly cut short when he was badly injured in an accident at Wainwright. He has been a quadriplegic ever since.

On February 20th, I was called to BHQ and told that Maj Patty Crofton, Capt R J (Bob) Prince (a new officer attached from the Black Watch) and I would be proceeding as an advance party to 'destination unknown' to set up a training and rest area for the battalion. It seemed odd that only three of us were on the advance party when normally there would be a dozen or so. And why were we not told where we were going? It couldn't be very far away. None of our prior rest areas had been more than 10 or 15 miles behind the lines so that we could always be brought back on a few hours' notice. Whether Patty Crofton knew our ultimate destination, I do not know to the present day. It all seemed a little strange.

ARRIVEDERCI ITALIA
San Benedetto — Pisa — Leghorn
February 21 to March 13, 1944

Arrivederci, italia
My ship's far out to sea
Farewell to Lombardy's Plain
Rivers, dykes and mud and rain
Will I 'ere come back again?
Who can foresee

Arrivederci, italiani
My heart goes out to thee
Goodbye sturdy peasant folk
Who suffered under Fascist yoke
For you we cleft a mighty stroke
And set you free

We left the battalion area before first light on February 21st, and drove south in a small brigade convoy along Highway 16, the Via Adriatica, which I and so many other Canadian troops had travelled so many times before. Soon the sun rose over the Adriatic and shed its warm rays on our cold, aching bodies half asleep in the open jeep. Many times I had experienced the relief of going back to a rest area after weeks of soggy trenches and cramped quarters. Yet this time it seemed different. There was a devil-may-care attitude among the troops.

We continued south and passed through towns we had liberated and rested in during our long drive north — Cesenatico, Rimini, Riccione, Cattolica. Not only did we sense there was something different about this trip; there

398

were concrete signs that something was amiss. Vehicles from 5th Division were neither in the towns nor on the roads. The division was supposed to be in reserve in this very area, yet not one of its men was to be seen.

We carried on in the bright sunshine, seemingly getting warmer as we went farther south. Pesaro and Fano were soon behind us and we were approaching Ancona. About ten miles north of Ancona a road branched off to the west, leading to Jesi, where I had been hospitalized in 1 CGH in December, and where I had spent a short time at 4 Battalion CBRD before joining the Regiment in September. I expected we would take this road and camp in the same area. Much to my surprise, our convoy carried right on to Ancona where we stopped for a break. Now things were definitely not kosher, and I asked Patty: "What's the score? We must have gone 150 miles this morning and we're still heading south. Do you think brigade know where they're going?"

Patty gave me that wonderful enigmatic smile of his. "You know as much as I do. I'm hungry. Let's find some roasto-toasto."

Patty was a great guy, but he slaughtered the Italian language! He was very impressed with my supposed command of Italian and how I kept the "Wop on the hop". On a prior occasion, we had been kept waiting for a meal in an *Osteria,* perhaps for half an hour, and we had to get back to the front lines. Time was of the essence, something the Italians could never seem to understand. We had ordered roast lamb (goat). Finally I bellowed at the waiter, *"Arrosto tosto"* (bring the roast immediately). The reaction was immediate and the meal appeared pronto.

Patty was so taken with the phrase that from then on, no matter what was on the bill of fare, he demanded 'roasto-toasto'. When nothing happened I would step in and help him out, but not until he was quite red in the face trying to make the waiter understand. He felt the words were particularly apt for ordering toast at breakfast time; "roasto-toasto," he would shout at the waiter.

"What's that supposed to mean?" I would ask him.

"Hot buttered toast, of course," came the indignant reply.

Ah, the fun and games we used to have!

We found a *ristorante* in Ancona and settled for a simple meal of spaghetti washed down with vino roso. Then we were on our way again, heading south through villages I had never seen before. Late in the afternoon, we stopped at a lovely resort town on the coast, San Benedetto del Tronto, 50 miles south of Ancona. Immediately I knew I would have trouble with Patty trying to pronounce the last name so I beat him to it. "Thanks for dropping me off at my home town."

Patty's deep laugh was probably heard clear back to Toronto.

Our orders were to find billets for the battalion and we had carte blanche authority to commandeer anything that took our fancy. I believe I was given responsibility for getting quarters for C Company and my own D Company. I tried to be fair and get equal accommodation for both. I remember earmarking the annex of the Hotel Progresso for D Company; what I secured for C Company I do not recall.

As a charter member of the Mess Committee, I was also in charge of locating the Officers' Mess. I reserved the Hotel itself, facing the sea, for the Officers' Quarters and set aside the adjoining restaurant for the Mess. Such comfort most of us hadn't seen since England, or even Canada. Every officer had a bed, pillows, sheets and towels. Maid servants and waiters did all the work. I was not too sure poor old Murdy would have approved. Nor was I sure who was supposed to foot the bill. It is little wonder the government is still wrestling to pay a monumental national deficit!

The battalion was not expected for a week so we settled down to a life of ease; a fitting reward, we thought, for having lived in the slums for so long. In fairness to whoever was going to pay the bill, we thought we had better pay for our own food and drink, wines and liqueurs. My bill for the seven days came to $45.00, but as I was now a captain my pay had jumped from $5.00 to $6.50 per diem. I was eating and drinking exactly what I was earning — something I was never able to achieve thereafter. My only regret was that my promotion had come so late in the War.

The only other troops in the neighbourhood were negroes from a transport company of the US Army. They constantly broke into our Mess and demanded service. This upset me, but sent Patty into fits of laughter as I unceremoniously showed them the gate.

An intrusion of another nature was more happily received. One day, a charming *Signora* appeared at my doorstep bearing a note on embossed letterhead. The note explained that the lady's husband had been a colonel in the Italian Tank Corps and had been sent to the Russian front to help out the Germans. He had not been heard from for almost two years and the lady was desperate to have news of him. She suggested I attend her home for dinner when her mother would also be present and help to translate.

I accepted the invitation and implied that perhaps it would not be necessary for her mother to be present as I could get along fairly well in Italian.

Selfishly, I did not mention this invitation to Patty Crofton and that evening I set off alone to find the *Signora*. Her villa seemed a little run down from the outside and had obviously seen better times, but it had a wonderful location on a promontory overlooking the Adriatic. I knocked at the door and was greeted by a maid. In Italian, I introduced myself and was surprised when the maid replied that the Contessa and her mother would be down in a moment. Would I mind waiting in the ante room. Now I wished I had brought Patty along as I really had no experience in dealing with countesses. For that matter, nor had he, but I figured he could have at least looked after the Contessa's mother.

They soon appeared, extravagantly dressed, in long gowns and looking every inch members of the nobility. I felt a little out of place but I reminded myself that, after all, we had conquered their country and beaten their army. Furthermore, I wasn't entirely certain of the status of contessas under the Mussolini regime. I thought they had been pretty well abolished except for a few henchmen like Mussolini's son-in-law, Count Ciano. However, I greeted her with what I hoped was a cavalier approach by kissing her extended hand. Her mother discreetly remained in the background.

The Contessa spoke rather good English. She apologized for the state of disrepair of the villa, but I would understand that the war had caused her great inconvenience — this, in fact, was only a little summer retreat by the sea; her main estates were some miles inland.

I was led into the library or study which obviously had been the domain of her husband. The bookshelves were filled with military books, particularly about tanks, and on the walls were many pictures and drawings of armoured vehicles of the former Royal Italian Army. The Contessa opened a drawer and brought out a whole series of photographs of her husband and high brass of the Italian Army inspecting a tank regiment. Other pictures showed her husband on training exercises and taking part in tests of new Italian tanks. The pictures were quite old, probably from the early 1930s. The Contessa wanted to turn over all this material to me as she was sure it would be of great interest and probably help the Allies to win the War. I had to demur; Italian tanks were really no match for the German Panthers and Tiger tanks. Actually, the tanks were not much of an improvement on the tanks of World War I that I had seen at Camp Borden in 1941. So I simply stated that we were so busy fighting the German forces that I would not have time to take the papers to higher command. However, I would let them know, and no doubt they would be in touch with her. My new rank of captain was obviously giving me wisdom I had not formerly possessed as lieutenant.

At dinner, we got down to discussing the war situation and the chances of the colonel being alive somewhere in Russia. I had to tell her, quite frankly, that the chances were not too good as everywhere the Russian armies had overwhelmed the German and Italian troops, and were now on the very borders of Germany itself. I really couldn't give her much hope, but I undertook to pass on her request for information to "higher authorities".

The dinner went very well and I was feeling in a very pleasant and expansive mood. The Contessa also seemed relaxed and casually enquired why the brave Canadian soldiers weren't fighting in the Front Lines. Suddenly a little voice reminded me that I had not the slightest clue who this lady was; after all, her husband had been my late enemy. Perhaps I was dealing with a modern-day Mata Hari. (Indeed the Contessa's mother looked as though she might have been an associate of this famous German spy in the First War.) I finished my espresso and brandy and politely excused myself, as I had other duties to perform that evening.

When I returned to my hotel and told Patty of my dinner with a Contessa, he naturally wouldn't believe a word of it, but he did agree to send a message to division about the missing Italian colonel. With a sly wink, he added, "Well, I hope you had a good roasto-toasto," which of course could have meant almost anything. I had no desire to disabuse Patty of his suspicions. I was satisfied I had at least honoured my undertaking to the Contessa to pass on her request for information to a "higher authority", ie Maj Patty Crofton.

I hope the Contessa, or whoever she was, finally found her husband. If perchance he did return, I give full credit to Patty for arranging such a miracle.

The battalion arrived on February 27th, having left their positions on the Senio River on the 25th. All ranks were supremely happy with the billets that Patty, Bob Prince and I had selected for them and quickly settled in to their posh quarters.

The CO then called an 'O' Group and said we would be here for a while, resting and training for our next operation. Why we had come so far south to rest and train was still the question in everyone's mind, but there were no answers. The puzzle was rapidly becoming an enigma. I even began to suspect that Bob Prince, who had just been attached to us from brigade, for "training", knew a lot more than he was telling; but even stupendous sessions at the bar revealed absolutely nothing.

Seldom before had the battalion found itself quartered in more agreeable surroundings. The Second-in-Command rightly appreciated that it was the ideal venue to hold another mess dinner, and put me to work organizing the affair. His timing was exceptional, as a perfect reason for holding a mess dinner now occurred (not that we really needed any excuse). News had just been officially received that LCol Clark had been awarded the DSO for his services at the Naviglio Canal operations. We were all happy that his leadership had at last been recognized and proud of the distinction it brought the Regiment. "His officers and men knew that it had been amply earned on a dozen occasions."[1]

No efforts were spared to make the dinner memorable. The menu was carefully discussed with the hotel chef and a six course meal arranged that would have been a credit to an officers' mess in peacetime. The actual menu, printed on embossed PPCLI letterhead, has survived:

PRINCESS PARTICIA'S CANADIAN
LIGHT INFANTRY
MESS DINNER

Ricco Antipasto	*Sherry*
Consume	*Vino Rosso*

Spaghetti
Fritto di pesce assertito
Pollo arrosto

Vino Bianco
Champagne

— Insalata verde
— Patate al forno
Frutta
Caffe

Porto
Acquavite

2 Marzo 1945

San Benedetto del
Tronto

Even the War Diarist, not known for extravagant language, was moved to record the event for the benefit of future mess committees:

The Officers of PPCLI this evening held a Regimental Mess Dinner. Retreat was sounded at the Mess at 1800 followed by cocktails at 1900 and dinner at 2000 hrs. It was a very successful affair and the various Carusos, Nelson Eddys and Frank Sinatras could be heard warbling far far into the night.[2]

There were, of course, a number of other frolics that were not enshrined in Regimental records. After brandy and cigars, some of the officers engaged in a little indoor wrestling. Across the street from the restaurant, the waters of the Adriatic beckoned to cool down the participants. They madly dashed out the door, crossed the road and made beautiful swan dives over the high seawall. At the last instant, they realized the tide was out. Such was their athletic ability that they converted the dive into a harmless headroll and tumbled down to the water's edge, thus saving the Regiment countless hours practising the slow march with muffled drums. Indeed, so impressed was the War Diarist with the stamina of the officers that he made another entry next day: "The usual training as per syllabus. Heads were counted this morning and no serious casualties appeared to have resulted among the officers after last night's party."[3]

What the Italian waiters and waitresses thought of these shenanigans I have no idea, but the new officers were certainly impressed. I believe that that evening marked the beginning of a new camaraderie and Regimental spirit that continued to grow right up to the end of the War.

The only criticism I received was from one junior officer who barely survived the six course meal with six different wines and did not participate in or even see the post-prandial activities. "Next time," he pleaded, "please cut down on the drinks until after dinner." It was the one and only time in my service that I received such a request. The young man obviously needed more training.

Patty Crofton was delighted. "That was some roasto-toasto you had last night." Patty's Italian was improving. The menu had actually included roast chicken, *pollo arrosto.*

Early next morning, to atone for my sins the previous evening, I was again sent ahead with Patty and Bob Prince to recce a new "training ground" (so the orders read) at Foligno in the heart of the Apennines, where the battalion had paused before its trek to the Gothic line in August. Here, our quarters were an old Italian barracks, quite adequate, but hardly up to the standards we now expected.

The troops could no longer be hood-winked that they were training for the next river crossing. Something big was clearly in the air. But what? Once again, the 'latrine-o-grams' started to spread — we were going to Yugoslavia, or to Greece, or even to France. I was still eyeing Bob Prince pretty carefully, but he seemed as clueless as the rest of us.

The battalion arrived at Foligno on March 5th and our little advance party was off again to a new area. Our route took us north through the centre of the mountains, past Perugia (where I had been in hospital only five weeks earlier) and along the east side of Lake Trasimene, to Arezza. This was the route the Regiment had taken in August, but going in the opposite direction to a new battlefield. The weather now turned cold and we ran into a snow storm. Our mission began to take on all the appearances of another of those wild deception schemes to fool the Hun, even as we confused ourselves. We were now in the middle of Italy, heading north, straight for the front line of the 5th Army south of Bologna. That night we halted in a place called Pontesieve, about 15 miles east of Florence. Here, we were quartered in tents in a bleak, muddy camp and spent a cold, miserable night under canvas. It was a situation normal. They were preparing us for those soggy Romagna plains again.

In the morning, we were away before daybreak on another advance recce while the battalion followed at a more leisurely pace. To our great surprise and relief, instead of heading north, we were going due west! As we left the mountains and came down to the Tuscany plains, the sun came out and warmed our bodies and spirits. In the distance, I spotted the outline of the most famous tilted tower in the world — Pisa. On the outskirts of the city we were directed to an encampment, Harrod's Camp No 2, located in a beautiful pine forest. The leaning tower was clearly visible from our tent line.

While under canvas we suffered no hardship. The camp was run by Americans from the 5th Army and they knew how to look after the troops. On our first night an American canteen opened up, offering hamburgers and coke. The waiters ran out of supplies after the first ten minutes and were themselves nearly eaten in the crush. We had heard tall tales of the fantastic Yankee rations — doughnut-making machines in A Echelon; floating coke factories at the Anzio beachhead — now we believed them.

Our brigade commander, Brig M P Bogert, could not keep the troops in suspense any longer. On March 9th he called the battalion together and gave us the big secret — we were headed for France and then Germany. Loud cheers. One of the men expressed what was in the minds of many; "We'll show 'em that the D-Day Dodgers know how to fight."

The brigadier had the opening he had been waiting for. He warned us against bragging about our actions in Sicily and Italy — 1st Division would prove itself by deeds rather than words. It was sage advice from our soldierly, gentlemanly brigadier. I could understand why some officers became brigadiers while others... well, I still had a lot to learn.

Our pleasant stay at Harrod's Camp lasted six days. The weather remained bright and warm and the troops were engaged largely in doing SFA — euphemistically called 'Interior Economy'. Even in those days the horrors of modern-day gobbledygook were at work.

Short visits, under the strict control of officers, were allowed, to see Pisa, the leaning tower, and the other architectural wonders of this ancient city on the Arno River. Security still remained tight. Any man who held a secret desire to have one last fling was sadly disappointed. His quest for forbidden fruits would have to await his arrival in a new and different land.

On March 12th, D Company and the rest of the battalion, except BHQ and part of Support Company, left camp and, after a short drive, arrived at Leghorn where we immediately embarked on LSTs (Landing Ships Tank). These amazing ships had been designed to transport tanks and armoured vehicles, but could be used to carry men and all kinds of material, equipment and supplies. A, C and D companies, numbering about 300 all ranks, were loaded into LST 692 and waited for the convoy to assemble. We slept wherever space was available — under trucks or on the open deck. I was made OC Kitchen (Chief Cook) to organize meals for the entire group. It seemed an inglorious way to leave the Italian battlefields and a demeaning task for someone who had spent almost five years trying to be a fighting soldier. Just the same, it could have been worse. The rations were typical Yankee gourmet food, the night was warm, and tomorrow was the start of another adventure.

At 0600 hours on March 13th, our LST 692 pulled out of Leghorn. I was on deck even earlier to say goodbye to this beautiful, strange land of so many contrasts that had been my adopted home for so many months. What sights I had seen; what people I had known; what challenges I had met. The long months seemed like years. Already the names of the places, the faces of the people were beginning to fade away. I cast my thoughts back to July 13, 1943.

Sicily: that hard, rugged land of antiquity; blistering sands, parched river beds, dirty hill-top villages, stony, barren fields.

Pachino: landing on the beaches in a DUKW; liberating the stone *casa* of a poor Sicilian peasant while he offered me his last bottle of vino; uttering my first Italian words from an Army phrasebook.

Ispica: perched on a high cliff; a nervous major who tried to billet my troops in a filthy Italian barracks; the lovely Signorina Fratele, who gave me the good luck charm still hanging around my neck; the sly Baron Modica who loved to hunt rabbits; the grateful priest whose church I opened. Those were exciting, happy times.

Monte Seggio: the Regiment at last; the eerie midnight advance through the wild Salso Valley on the backs of our tanks; burning houses lighting the hills on each side; Mt Etna's volcanic mass dominating the battlefield.

Militello: at rest amid the vineyards and orange groves; changing of the Guard; the intense heat; the torment of flies and mosquitoes unlimited; the stench of the town; the friendliness of the people; the incessant braying of donkeys dragging their creaking Sicilian carts; forbidden ice cream and watermelons.

Formation of the Scouts and Snipers: the most irregular band of fighters in the army; scrounging missions for horses; receipts signed on behalf of Mackenzie King; confrontation with a Police Chief — "no horses, no marshal".

Then disaster: malaria; hospital in Catania; air raids in the harbour; nursing sisters struck down by shellfire; escapades in Catania; learning to speak Italian; playing Ben Hur in a borrowed buggy; impersonating a policeman; confounding the carabinieri.

Messina: camping on the beaches; Taormina, the lovely hillside resort of the founder of the Regiment; passage of the Strait to the Italian mainland; worms in the rice at Reggio.

Off into the blue: up the toe of Italy to find the Regiment; 500 miles through the rugged mountains of Calabria, across deep chasms and makeshift bridges; encounters with other trucks, a donkey cart, the Italian Army, a polite *capitano* and a blown bridge; saved by Joe, our carefree Italian driver; succoured by the kind dwellers of the mountain tops.

Back with the Regiment: Scouts and Snipers again; Popski; Greg Clark; the castle at Lagopesole, where I slept in the bedroom of a prince; the massacre of 17 civilians at Rionero.

Then the rains: mud, sleet and cold; patrols through mountain mists and icy rivers; no sleep for days; troops going sick with malaria and yellow jaundice; summer uniforms that couldn't keep out the cold; margarine that wouldn't melt.

More patrols up greasy slopes: Casteluccio, Basilice, Point 750; Decorata, where the Hun had ransacked the village; Cercemajore; La Rocca where we chased the enemy off the mountain top, *sans* dinner; the Biferno River where I ran races for the Germans.

The kindness of the Italian peasants; their joy of liberation; their willingness to share their food and shelter; their eagerness to help us drive away the hated *tedeschi*.

Wounded at Frosolone; then a blank; a British hospital in Bari; the long flight to Algiers.

And that's only the start of it all. England, plastic surgery and back to the Regiment. How long was I away? It seems like only a few weeks, but that can't be possible. I was wounded on October 26th and returned during the Gothic Line on September 19th — almost 11 months!

Malaria again; carried on board the SS *Orontes;* confined to hospital; landing at Naples under the glowering stare of Mt Vesuvius; beautiful Avellino; the journey to the front past devastated Cassino and the Liri Valley; Rome for a night; across the Apennines in blistering heat; Jesi on the Adriatic coast.

Return to action before the bloody heights of San Fortunato; the awful shelling; piles of German dead; debouching into the Po Valley without a weapon; crossing the Marecchia River; lofty San Marino observing our every move; my strong *casa* blown to bits.

The war has become serious, dirty, never-ending; the enemy, desperate, ugly and defiant; the Regiment has changed.

Cattolica: at rest beside the sea; pleasant villas, warm water, sandy beaches; a new command, the MMG Platoon; a piano caper; Santarcangelo; Caesar's Rubicon.

Five more months in the Romagna plains: continuous swamp crossed by rivers and canals; the richest mud in the Italian theatre, if not in the world.

Then rain in torrents; rivers swollen to the tops of their floodbanks; attack, attack, attack.

How many rivers? What were their names? Makes no difference, they were all the same — high dykes manned by a determined foe; ice cold waters, greasy slopes, rain, mud, rain.

Pisciatello, Savio, Bevano, Ronco: always one more river to cross, one more cesspool to navigate; baptism of the 'Leper' section.

Riccione: flooded billets, chill winds from the north; harsh gales from the sea; preparations for the next attack.

Rome: my first leave in the Army; journey through the snow-covered Apennines; the Forum, Colosseum, Pantheon, St Peters, an audience with the Pope. What was the name of that Professor?

Then the Lamone: brave nuns in a shattered convent; stoic farmers in their ruined *casas*; the Naviglio Canal. What happened there? Oh yes — Moaning Minnie; wounded again; more hospitals; cheerful Italian orderlies, Teresina; back to the Regiment; winter on the Senio; Partisans; thank God for the strong Italian houses.

San Benedetto; Hotel Progresso; fun and games on the beach; an Italian Contessa; roasto-toasto; another long journey over the Apennines; Pisa; the leaning tower; Leghorn; LST 692.

Will I remember half of it, a quarter, a tenth of it; 10 years from now; 20 years; 40 years from now? There is so much to tell.

And I haven't even thought about all the casualties or about my friends who are not leaving Italy with me this morning.

My reverie was broken as the early morning sun peeked over the Apennines and played in the wake of LST 692. The shores of Italy slowly dipped below the horizon. Suddenly I felt overcome by a wave of sadness and regret that surprised me. Was this any way to say goodbye to the land so many Canadians had fought so hard to set free? No ceremonies, no special orders of the day, nothing to mark the passing of the most important period in my life.

And *what about* the casualties? All that Canadian blood that had been shed and would forever remain in the mountains, valleys and plains. I had left a little myself. Would these sacrifices ever be recognized, or appreciated, or remembered? Whether they would be or not, I knew what I had to do. I entered into a convenant with myself to return to the battlefields of my Regiment and the graves of my comrades at the earliest opportunity. I realized too, it was not just the battlefields and the casualties that were pulling me back. Despite all the dirt, blistering heat, bitter cold, rain, mud, rugged mountains and treacherous torrents I knew I loved this land and its people.

Eleven years later I honoured my pledge in a 7,000 mile personal tour of Italy and Northwest Europe. Then in 1975, I visited the cemeteries as part of a Pilgrimage by Canadian veterans of the Italian campaign. Again, in 1985, I made another personal tour of the battlefields and cemeteries. It is beyond the scope of this chapter to describe these emotional visits. Perhaps it is enough to say I shall never tire of returning to the land where I suffered so much pain and misery, and yet gained knowledge and experience that stood me in good stead for the rest of my life; where I matured from youth to man and learned to appreciate and enjoy the culture and traditions of another people. *Viva Italia.*

Not everyone in the 1st Canadian Corps shared my feelings about returning to Italy. For the vast majority, there was manifest relief to be rid at last of the mud, filth, rain and cold that had been our lot for so many months. Then too, the Italian farmers in the Romagna were not the same as the friendly peasants we had known in the south. The northern Italian was prone to be obstinate, even sullen at times, and did not seem overly enthusiastic about being liberated by the Allies. It should be remembered, of course, that the Romagna was the birthplace of Fascism.[4]*

It is beyond doubt that every soldier in the 1st Canadian Corps was proud to be reunited at last with with Canadian Army. For months this had been the hope, not only of the soldiers, but also of the generals and politicians back home. Indeed, "it had become a matter of national policy that the enforced separation of the Canadian Forces should be ended as soon as a reunion could be justified on military grounds."5

Finally, at the Malta Conference in January, 1945, it was decided to repatriate the 1st Canadian Corps to its alma mater.

Just the same, many officers and men, including myself, would not have been disappointed to have been left in Italy to finish the job we had been sent to do in July, 1943. After all, it was abundantly clear in March, 1945, that the end was near. One more push over the Senio River and we would be in Venice. Also, almost everyone was sorry to leave the famous 8th Army that had defeated Rommel in North Africa and won further honours in the Sicilian and Italian campaigns. Then, too, we were proud of our ability to improvise and make do when supplies and equipment were denied us. We also enjoyed our freedom from some of the rigid procedures followed by 1st Canadian Army, although Lord knows, we had our own brand of red tape. Last, but not least, our deliberate contravention of dress regulations was a cherished part of belonging to the 8th Army. Field Marshal Montgomery himself had fashioned the style and we slavishly followed his suit!

The end in Italy came quickly and with a vengeance. On April 9th, our old comrades in arms, the British 5th Corps, and the 2nd Polish Corps stormed across the Senio River. Let LCol G R Stevens finish the story:

> *Six weeks and a day after the Patricias left the river lines the kill came. Behind the greatest artillery bombardment ever fired in Italy, British, Indian and New Zealand divisions stormed the Senio and Santerno defences. Fifth Army attacked in Tuscany; the Poles broke through on 8th Army's left and raced for Bologna; a British commando brigade took to Lake Commacchio in amphibious craft and cut the enemy line of retreat behind the Argenta Gap. Under an avalanche of blows the German armies in Italy staggered; within a week they were dying. With victory in the air 8th Army took the Po in its stride and drove on to Venice and Trieste. "Guerra e finita", screamed the Italian crowds in the streets as long columns of infantry and guns surged into the north to utter victory.*
>
> *On April 22nd, 230,000 Germans in Italy laid down their arms. Six days later an Indian armoured car returned to report that far up on the wall of the Alps, on a rocky hillside under snowy peaks, a German formation had dug in and was prepared to fight*

---

* When I returned in 1956, and again in 1975 and 1985 I found that many of the houses I had occupied during the war were plastered with the hammer and sickle instead of the old fascist signs. The people had merely exchanged one symbol of totalitarianism for another.

to the death. Or, at least, it would not surrender to anyone less than a divisional commander. A general was found and hurried forward; on the mountainside all that remained of the Canadians' greatest antagonist, 1st Parachute Division, formed up, laid down its arms and marched into captivity.[6]

My account of the Italian campaign would not be complete without a reference to the casualties suffered by the Canadian troops:

Of the 92,757 Canadians of all ranks who served in the Italian theatre (the figure includes 1178 members of the 1st Special Service Battalion) more than a quarter became casualties. The killed numbered 408 officers and 4,991 men; the wounded 1,218 and 18,268 respectively; and 62 officers and 942 men were taken prisoner. The addition of 365 who died from causes other than enemy action brings the total Canadian casualties to 26,254. Approximately 60 per cent of these were suffered in the five major operations in which the Canadians were engaged, for, as we have seen, the men who wore on their shoulders the name of Canada were identified with the costliest struggles of the entire campaign.

Total Canadian battle casualties in these operations were: Sicily, 2,227; the Moro River and Ortona, 2,605; the Liri Valley, 3,713; the Gothic Line and the Battle of the Rimini Line, 4,511; and the advance from the Montone to the Senio, 2,581.[7]

These bare figures do not, of course, tell the whole story of the casualties suffered by the Canadians. The 1st Division bore the brunt of these casualties, if only because it was in action many months before the 5th Division arrived on the scene. In fact, 5th Division did not see any action until January 17th, 1944 when its 11th Brigade made an abortive attack north of Ortona, on the Adriatic coast.

Furthermore, the total casualties of 26,254 given above do not include the large numbers who were evacuated because of sickness — malaria, jaundice, dysentery and the like. I have no idea what these numbers were, but my guess would be at least equal to the total number of battle casualties.

Finally, this number does not indicate the group who suffered the majority of the casualties — the infantry soldiers. First Canadian Corps comprised basically two divisions, 1st and 5th; in addition, a Canadian Independent Armoured Brigade fought in Italy. There was also a host of support troops, rear echelons, holding units, base hospitals and many other similar units.

A division had an official establishment of roughly 20,000 men; an independent brigade, roughly 5,000. In theory, therefore, the total number of soldiers of 1st Corps in the field at any one time was about 45,000.

Of these 45,000, less than one-third were at the 'sharp end' — in actual contact with the enemy (meaning soldiers who were within range of small arms fire and medium mortars). In World War II the effective range of a German medium mortar was about 2,000 yards (small arms were much less). This would place at the 'sharp end' the infantry battalions, the MMG battalions, the recce regiments, the tank regiments and the anti-tank regiments. Brigade, divisional and corps headquarters would be excluded (has anyone ever heard of a brigadier or general being killed in Italy in World War II?).

Thus, the total number of troops at the 'sharp end' may be determined as follows (using official establishments):

First Division		
9 infantry battalions at 1,000	9,000	
MMG battalion	500	
Armoured car regiment	1,000	
Anti-tank regiment	800	
Total		11,300
Fifth Armoured Division (in Italy)		
6 infantry battalions at 1,000	6,000	
3 tank regiments at 800	2,400	
Armoured recce regiment	1,000	
Anti-tank regiment	800	
2 MMG companies at 200	400	
Total		10,600
Independent Armoured Brigade		
3 tank regiments at 800		2,400
Total		24,000

However, several factors reduced this total figure sharply. All units were at least 25% below their official establishments. Thus 75% of 24,000 is 18,000. Furthermore, in each unit about 30% of its personnel were in various echelons well behind the front line. Thus 70% of 18,000 is 12,600. And finally, in each action, 10% of the fighting strength was LOB to provide a quick reserve for the next action. Therefore 90% of 12,600 is 11,340 fighting soldiers at the 'sharp end'.

However, in each division and in the armoured brigade there were engineers, artillery and signallers in the front lines, as well as elements from the various services. I would estimate the number of these 'sharp end' supporting troops in each division to be 700, and in the armoured brigade to be 400.

The total of these supporting troops was therefore 1,800, comprised as follows:

Infantry Division	*700*
Armoured Division	*700*
Armoured Brigade	*400*
Total	*1,800*

Adding these 1,800 supporting troops to the 11,340 fighting troops gives a total of 13,140, or say 13,000 soldiers in actual contact with the enemy. So of the total of 45,000 soldiers, in theory, serving with the two divisions and one independent armoured brigade, only 13,000 were actually fighting at the 'sharp end' where the 26,254 casualties mainly took place.

The significance of this figure of 26,254 casualties thus becomes apparent. To make good these casualties meant replacing the entire fighting strength of two divisions and one armoured brigade at least twice during the campaign.

I personally believe that the figure I have estimated for 'sharp end' fighters of 13,000 is too high. Perhaps 9,000 would be nearer the mark.

The gallant record of the Canadians in Italy speaks for itself. It is enshrined in a host of Battle Honours of the Regiments who fought there. This is a good thing, for otherwise their deeds would soon be forgotten — unremembered by all except the D-Day Dodgers. They will never forget.

Chapter XXXI

OPERATION GOLDFLAKE
France — Belgium — Germany
March 13 to April 7, 1945

In every outpost of our Empire
There flies a flag that makes us free
As we go marching ever onward
Side by side in unity
Oh we're the lads who fought for freedom
In every land from sea to sea
We're all for one and one for all
Marching along to Victory

LST 692 continued its voyage across the clear blue waters of the Ligurian Sea, toward its destination, Marseilles. The weather became quite hot, we stripped off our worn, dirty battledress, impregnated with the mud of a hundred rivers, and lazed about the deck. The combination of sunny skies and excellent meals reminded me of another pleasant cruise I had taken on the Mediterranean, almost two years earlier, aboard the SS *Arundel Castle*. But my illusions of a peacetime voyage were soon shattered by the sights and sounds of our destroyer escort as they relentlessly scoured the seas for mines, enemy U-Boats and surface craft.

I almost resented this intrusion of our warlike naval friends, who became even more aggressive as we approached the northern tip of the island of Corsica. It never occurred to me that the Germans still held the Italian coast from north of Pisa to the French border, including large naval bases at Spezia and Genoa. The enemy were quite capable of attacking our convoy at any time. Indeed, four nights later, three German destroyers sailed from Genoa to lay mines off the northwestern tip of Corsica, in the very area our convoy had passed through on March 13th. The enemy craft were intercepted by the Royal Navy and two German destroyers were sunk. Thereafter, convoys to Marseilles took a more southerly route between Corsica and Sardinia.[1]

If he were alive today, old Field Marshal Fate (in his dual capacity as Admiral of the Fleet and Field Marshal) would doubtless take credit for protecting my convoy and the many other convoys of Canadian troops that landed safely in Marseilles. While he probably had a hand in the matter, the proximate reason there was so little interference from the enemy with the transfer of the Canadian Corps and the Independent Armoured Brigade to Northwest Europe was the effectiveness of the security measures for the operation. These included a cover plan to disguise the moves as no more than a mere regrouping in rear areas.[2]

The immense task of transporting approximately 60,000 officers and men and their equipment, code-named 'Goldflake', began in mid-February and was completed by the end of March. During the whole of that time the enemy had not a clue as to the whereabouts of the Canadians. The Germans, however, were not the only ones bewildered by the movements of our troops. I had no idea where we were going until March 9th, when Brig Bogert told us at Leghorn we were bound for France, then Germany; and even that was not the whole story — we would actually fight our last battles in Holland. But perhaps even the brigadier was not privy to this information at that time.

5th Canadian Armoured Division, which seemed to have vanished into thin air when I passed by their area on February 21st, had in fact left for Leghorn on February 10th and was in action in Holland by the end of the month — at which time I was arranging a six course mess dinner at San Benedetto, blissfully unaware that my armoured friends were getting their heads shot off in Northwest Europe.

So completely were the Germans taken in by the clever deception plan and security measures for 'Goldflake' that it was not until April 19th that their maps showed the Italian theatre free of all Canadian formations.[3]

The staff had again hood-winked the Hun, just as they had done in the invasion of Sicily. The master bluffer had been beaten at his own game. He should have thrown away the Duce two years earlier.

Early in the morning of March 14th, LST 692 entered the port of Marseilles, threaded its way through the busy harbour and tied up at the quay at 1000 hours. The voyage from Leghorn had taken only 28 hours. I was surprised to find the harbour had not been too badly knocked about, then realized that perhaps the damage had been quickly repaired by the efficient Americans who ran the place. Within half an hour of landing we were loaded into lorries waiting on the dock, and whisked away, heavily laden

414

with 'buckshee' US rations I had scrounged from our friendly Yankee skipper.

The more I saw of American soldiers, sailors and airmen, the more I liked them and appreciated their immense talents for conducting war on the grand scale, with super efficiency, but shorn of much of the red tape and 'pickiness' that bedevilled our own war effort. To use their vernacular, they had 'come a long way, baby' since their baptism by fire along the shores of North Africa.

As our TCVs wound their way through the streets of Marseilles, we marvelled at the clean, orderly boulevards and modern homes, and gawked at the well-dressed, friendly people. My new batman, one Pte Norton, cast in much the same mould as Pte Murdy, never called a spade a shovel. "Great to be back with the human race again," he declared. "Just look at those French signorinas, — I mean — madames — hell, no, I mean dames."

Whatever the new species of female sex was called, they certainly looked attractive in their colourful short skirts, as they gaily pedaled their bikes through the city traffic. I had to admit that my sadness at leaving Italy was slowly giving way to the excitement of meeting a new and different kind of people.

Our lorries soon left the city and climbed the sandy hills to the north. Fifteen miles from the outskirts we were deposited in a dusty, tented camp that reminded me of the barren Sicilian landscape. Our contact with civilization had been short-lived.

While we waited for the rest of the battalion to catch up with us, we were given more details of Operation 'Goldflake'. 1st Division would be transported by TCVs to a rest area in Belgium, north of Brussels. The journey would take six days and would follow a route north through the Rhone Valley, past Lyon, Macon, Dijon, Compiègne and Cambrai to a rest area at Boisschot, mid-way between Moliner and Antwerp — a total distance of more than 800 miles from Marseilles.* Five Staging Areas would accommodate us each night of our long journey — St Rambert, Macon, Les Laumes, Sens and Cambrai. After a week of rest and training at Boisschot, we would join 1st Canadian Army in driving the Germans out of Holland.

Strict security measures would continue to be enforced, as the enemy still believed we were sitting in our strong *casas* along the Senio River in northern Italy.

The staff went to incredible lengths to preserve the security measures they had taken such trouble to devise. I received an order a few days later:

TOP SECRET   *TO BE DESTROYED BY*
                                FIRE WHEN NOTIFIED

---

*My father's regiment, the Royal Newfoundlanders, had taken this same route through France in March, 1916, after the disasterous Gallipoli Campaign, on their way to the battles of the Somme.

19 Mar 45
All Officers D (203/BS/89)

1. To avoid any breach of security the following points are again brought to your attention and all tps under your comd will be informed.

2. Exercise 'GOLDFLAKE' does not *terminate upon the arrival of this serial at destination, and security will be maintained until written instructions are given.*

3. Mail will be *unit censored — no 'on my honour' airletters* will be forwarded.

4. All documentation that indicates this serial has arrived from ITALY will be destroyed.

5. Italian money will be confiscated by the officer or NCO making the discovery, and disciplinary action will be taken.

6. Personnel are confined and will be confined to all camps, staging areas or billets until further orders (written).

7. No contact will be made with civilians under any pretense.

8. Greater care must be exercised with reference to cigarette boxes, chocolate bar wrappers or any literature that may indicate that this serial is CANADIAN. The practice of using addressed envelopes and airletters as toilet paper is forbidden.

9. Wireless silence will be maintained throughout.

10. Local leave to towns or cities will not be permitted.

11. Personnel whose duties entail leaving any area will only do so after consulting adjutant.

12. All personnel who become detached from unit or leave for medical care will only identify themselves by '21 Army Group'.

13. It is anticipated that our serial may be separated in small groups in an area where it is very difficult to segregate tps from civilians. In such cases sub-units will ensure that no buildings or houses are entered and bounds are defined and maintained in that camp.

14. Bartering for eggs, vegetables, etc, will NOT be permitted.

15. It is appreciated that some civilians think they know who we are. The only confirmation they will receive is from you. It is your job to see that their thoughts remain unconfirmed.

NB: THIS IS TO BE READ TO ALL TPS INCL HQ COY, BN HQ AND ALL DVRS BEFORE OCCUPANCY IN NEW NO 5 STAGING AREA.

(R P CLARK) Lt Col
CO, PPCLI

As far as I can recollect, I have not, to this date, received an order to destroy this Top Secret document by fire. Chances are that after 40 years, the perpetrators of the order have themselves been destroyed by fire, or by some other means — which only confirms the viewpoint of an earlier writer to the effect that "the bumph that staff officers spew lives after them; the good is oft interred with their bones."

To be fair, most of the points in the order made sense and I made a conscientious effort to abide by them. However, ordering the destruction of documents was too much for me — I could not bear to part with my diaries, operation orders, messages and the like that I had so carefully preserved in Italy. Likewise, confiscation of money meant handing over a hoard of Italian lire I had been accumulating for almost two years, for my old age. As it turned out, it made no difference to my financial status whether I kept the lire or burnt them. But they made interesting play money for my children.

Point 8 probably caused the greatest concern of all, particularly the prohibition against using envelopes and air letters as toilet paper. What was a poor fellow supposed to do when nature called and the two pieces per man, per diem of issue toilet paper, marked 'Government Property' had not in fact arrived? I suspect that a good many copies of the order itself were destroyed in this way, rather than waiting for a further order to destroy them by fire. Pte Norton was incensed that he could be 'crimed' for putting his old airmail letters to some worthwhile purpose. He insisted that if he were convicted on such a "bum wrap", I would appeal his sentence.

Lastly, prohibiting barter struck at the very existence of the men of the 1st Division. Without bartering and other forms of acquiring buckshee food, the division would have starved long ago. We could only hope that the extra rations I had acquired would see us through.

The remainder of the battalion arrived at our camp, north of Marseilles, on March 15th. Next morning, at 4:30 am the entire Regiment climbed into TCVs and headed north up the Rhone Valley on the first leg of our long journey to Belgium. Almost immediately we were presented with compelling evidence that we had joined the big leagues in the game of war. Mile after mile, the wreckage of the German 19th Army was piled up on each side of the highway, forming a tunnel of twisted steel rising high above our heads — tanks, armoured cars, vehicles, guns, horse-drawn carts of all kinds, field kitchens, Red Cross Ambulances, and every other conceivable piece of enemy equipment. It looked as though the German 19th Army had been caught in a devastating air attack and annihilated as it tried to retreat before the American 7th Army that had landed on the south coast of France on August 15th. I could not understand how any army could survive such apparent slaughter. Yet the next day, and the day after that, the same scene was repeated until it seemed that the entire German Wehrmacht had been destroyed. And still we were told that the German 19th Army had withdrawn in comparatively good order up the Rhone Valley.[4]

If this was an example of the enormous forces engaged on the Western

Front, what difference would our 1st Division make to the outcome? We hoped the Supreme Commander could find a slot for us in the front lines before it was all over.

Once past the carnage of the German 19th Army, the lovely, fertile valley opened up before us, dotted with fine old towns and clean farm villages. The driver of my TCV was a farm boy from Ontario and couldn't take his eyes from the pastoral scene. I was so afraid we would end up in the ditch or in one of the farmhouses beside the road that I asked him to let me take a turn at the wheel. This was contrary to orders, of course, as these lorries belonged to the Service Corps and only their trained drivers were allowed to operate them. The love of the land, however, proved too much for the man and he reluctantly let me take over while he relaxed and enjoyed the scenery.

For the remainder of the journey that day I drove the heavy lorry in a tight convoy, as it rolled along the country roads and through the narrow streets of the villages and towns. While I loved driving, and had driven just about every vehicle in the army, this lorry was a new type, and I had very little experience of driving in a convoy. I found it difficult trying to keep the exact distance between vehicles using only the gears instead of the brakes. By the end of the day I was thankful to return the wheel to the driver for the rest of the long trek to Belgium.

As had happened so often in my service, the experience taught me a new respect for another branch of the army — The Royal Canadian Army Service Corps. Though they were not front line fighters, and were sometimes incapable of putting one foot in front of the other on a parade ground, these drivers were a hardy, dedicated breed who pushed themselves and their vehicles to the limit, to bring troops and supplies to the front lines.

Another group that impressed me were the DRs (Despatch Riders). In action they were absolutely fearless and would deliver their messages regardless of mines, shells, bullets or terrain that would have stopped lesser men. In convoy work, they roared up and down the long line of vehicles, goading drivers to speed up, slow down, or just wake up, hour after hour, in all sorts of weather.

The hazards of convoy duty were just as great as those from contact with the enemy. A slippery road, a treacherous turn, a deep hole, all meant possible injury and often death. Such was the case during our journey from Marseilles. On the first day, one of our DRs was killed in an accident when he collided with a vehicle coming the other way.

Another hazard of riding a motor bike was the damage caused to the kidneys from bouncing up and down all day over the bumpy roads and trails, with no support for the back. Later in the war, DRs were issued 'kidney belts' which were supposed to give some support.

Even if a DR survived all these hazards, and others I have not mentioned, there was still no respite from his duties. The blasted bike had to be maintained, repaired and cleaned. I had learned something of these duties when I had a bike for a short time with the MMG Platoon. It was great fun to charge along a dry road, in and out of traffic, on a sunny day. But when the rains came and the roads turned to mud, I couldn't wait to turn in my bike for a jeep.

Our convoy arrived at the First Staging Area at St Rambert, some 30 miles south of Lyon, at 3:00 pm. It had been a pleasant journey of 152 miles, and the troops were in a holiday mood: "Everyone is delighted with their first impressions of this new part of Europe. It's a real treat to be in a 'civilized' country again, and to see clean, happy people. The genuine friendliness of the inhabitants is very evident."[5]

Next day, March 17th, was a very special day for the PPCLI — the birthday of Lady Patricia, its Colonel-in-Chief. For most of the officers, it was the first time they had been with the Regiment on this important day. It will be recalled that on the previous March 17th I was in hospital in England, but managed to get an overnight pass to attend a memorable dinner at the Officers' Club in Aldershot, where Brig Gault and 40 other officers celebrated Lady Patricia's birthday in fine style. The question on March 17th, 1945, was how properly to honour the occasion while in the midst of an 800 mile journey. Clearly there was no possibility of setting up a mess dinner in the style of San Benedetto — even if a convenient sea wall could be found. But help was at hand from an unexpected quarter.

Once again we had underestimated the savvy of the staff. Weeks before, when they were setting out the timings and distances for the route through France, someone had the foresight to reduce the journey on March 17th to a mere 73 miles, about half what we had to cover the previous day. Thus, on March 17th, the PPCLI arrived at Macon at 1:00 pm leaving ample time to celebrate the occasion, if only someone had the wherewithal. Into the breach stepped LCol Clark. With a commendable appreciation of the situation, he sent around 'a touch of the whip' so that the officers could at least toast the health of Lady Patricia on her birthday. It was indeed a fine touch by the Commanding Officer and demonstrated to the new officers that the traditions of the Regiment were never forgotten, not even during operations.

Next morning, we got under way at the ungodly hour of 5:00 am and arrived at our Third Staging Area, Les Laumes, at 2:00 pm having covered 122 miles. It had been another warm, pleasant journey through scenic, wooded country: "The country we have passed through so far has been very lovely and not unlike parts of England. After the filth and squalor of Italy, the clean towns and villages, with their up to date shops and modern homes, were a wonder to behold."[6]

March 19th brought the battalion to its Fourth Staging Area, mid-way between Sens and Rozay-en-Brie, after a journey of 112 miles.

On March 20th, I left camp at 6:30 am as part of an advance party, whilst the battalion followed at a more leisurely pace. We skirted Paris to the east, passed through Compiègne, Ham and Peronne, and arrived at Cambrai at 2:00 pm, a journey of 143 miles. The names of the towns and villages were familiar to me through father's stories of the First War and from reading the history of the PPCLI. Now, 27 years later, I was passing over these same battlefields, that bore brutal evidence of the present confict — miles of road lined with smashed and burned out German tanks and vehicles. I thought how fitting it was that this evidence of the death throes of the Hun was not far from Compiègne, where the Germans had surrendered in the First War.

After making a recce of the Cambrai Staging Area for the battalion, which would soon arrive and remain there that night, we set off again at 3:00 pm for our final destination. Crossing into Belgium, we passed through the northern outskirts of Brussels and arrived at Boisschot at 6:00 pm on March 20th, exactly one month since leaving our *casas* on the Senio River, and after a journey of more than 1,500 miles. Not a bad effort for a bunch of foot sloggers and D-Day Dodgers who had advanced only 50 miles in the previous five months. Perhaps the accommodation and meals were not always first class, but the price had been right. I had even been compensated $6.50 per diem for any inconvenience I had suffered during my journey!

The *Burgomeister* and half the townsfolk of Boisschot turned out to welcome us, and a great competition developed as to who would have the honour of billeting us for the night. We were so tired that we gladly accepted the first or any offer. I submitted to being dragged off to a nearby pub where I was invited to occupy the owner's main bedroom. Again I offered no resistance. A home-cooked meal and copious draughts of warm beer satisfied all my desires for the moment and I tumbled into a huge feather bed with bolster and clean, white sheets. That night I slept the sleep of the gods.

Next morning, after breakfast in bed and a monumental exercise of willpower, I pulled myself together and got on with the job I had been sent to do — arrange accommodation for D Company. I knew they would be arriving early in the afternoon so I really had to get moving. A quick 'O' Group and recce with the other members of the advance party revealed that there were not enough billets in the town to accommodate the whole battalion; one of the companies would have to occupy a nearby village, Hulshout. I quickly offered to locate D Company there — the farther from BHQ the better.

D Company arrived at 1:00 pm while I was frantically trying to arrange the accommodation I should have sorted out the night before. But it didn't matter. There was plenty of room for every man in the company to have his own feather bed, pillow, sheets and whatever else he could reasonably expect to make himself comfortable during our short stay in the village.

A letter to my parents was long overdue.

25 March 1945

I guess this has been my longest letter silence for a long time.
When I tell you why, you will understand. I am now in Belgium*!!*
Don't tell me you already knew from the papers!! This is the
first time I have been allowed to write.

I am billeted in a private home, or rather in the home of a
'Pub' keeper. I can remember Dad speaking of the lovely homes
in Belgium, and now I see how true it is. Everything is spotlessly
clean and tidy, and the people are wonderful. Never have I seen
such hospitality, and how the troops enjoy it. We are all like a
bunch of school boys. Oh yes — I have a grand *piano to play,*
right here in the house.

At present, I am sitting in the kitchen beside a roaring fire,
with the family around. It would make quite a picture. Most of
the natives speak French, and it isn't taking me long to pick it
up again. The 'pub' helps a lot! Soon I can add Belgian and
Flemish to my list, and a bit of German!

PS The beer is good, but not very alcoholic.

The wonderful hospitality of these fine people was almost overwhelming
and certainly embarrassing. We tried to reciprocate in any way we could.
We shared our rations with the good burghers; we helped them with many
of their daily chores. With the help of the Transport Officer, Lt Don Munro,
I arranged for two truckloads of coal to be delivered to the village. One task
I could not force myself to undertake was assisting the local 'honey man'
to clean out the storage tank on the premises of my landlady. Besides, my
brother officers, who knew about my 'cesspool caper' in Italy, were fearful
I would fall in again, and would not allow me near the tank.

The local school teacher, Mathilde Van Baelen, and her mother, in whose
house we set up our company Officers' Mess, treated us as sons and brothers
and insisted on our sharing their meagre supply of vegetables, and cooking
and serving our meals. We tried to repay their kindness by giving them sacks
of flour, sugar, tea, canned goods and other items they had not seen for years.

Lt W E (Larry) Harrington, who had been attached to our company as
a kind of 3IC, while I was away on advance parties during the move to
Belgium, came up with a brilliant idea how to show our appreciation to the
townsfolk. He organized a party for all the children in the village. Five
hundred came. After seeing a Popeye and Mickey Mouse show, each child
received a chocolate bar and chewing gum supplied by the Auxiliary Services
(Salvation Army). The spontaneous laughter and sheer joy of our little guests
was wonderful to behold and gave us a tremendous lift after so many years
of witnessing the carnage of war. Several tough old veterans, who had been
through some of the bloodiest fighting, unashamedly wiped away tears, or
pretended to blow their noses with much wiping of faces with dirty khaki

421

handkerchiefs. If Larry Harrington had volunteered to run for *Burgomeister* of Hulshout he would have been elected for life.

On March 25th, Palm Sunday, our padre, Honorary Capt Ivison, held a voluntary Protestant church service which was well attended but ran into competition from the local Catholic church: "During the day a surprising number of Catholic and non-Catholic soldiers were seen attending Palm Sunday Services with their landladies."[7]

Our two weeks in Boisschot and Hulshout (from March 21st to April 3rd) will long be remembered. Indeed, I formed a lasting friendship with the school teacher Mathilde and her mother. One of the subjects Mathilde taught was English. (Belgian children start learning other languages at an early age when their active minds are like little sponges — something our Canadian school systems are only now beginning to understand). For someone who had never conversed in English before, she had an amazing command of the language, especially the grammar. Still, I was able to help her out with some of our strange idioms, and in turn Mathilde helped me polish up my French and tried to teach me some German, and a bit of Flemish. She was fluent in those languages, as well as in Dutch. I'm afraid I was not a good student. At this stage of the War, I could see very little chance of becoming proficient in German, Flemish or Dutch, with their difficult syntax and guttural sounds.

After the War, I corresponded with Mathilde and her mother for many years. During my long overseas trip in 1956 I went many miles out of my way to visit them. I'm glad I did. The wonderful memories of 1945 flooded back and gave us all much happiness. The school children had, of course, grown up — some were married, and all were overjoyed to see 'the captain' again and meet his wife. They thanked me a hundred times for the party and the little gifts we had given them. Mathilde, I suspect, had a hand in refreshing their memories before I arrived. She admitted that each year, in March, she told the new generation of children about the wonderful soldiers of the PPCLI who lighted up their dreary lives and gave them hope during the dark days of 1945. Canadians will not soon be forgotten in Hulshout.

My reader must not assume that the Regiment turned itself into an Auxiliary Service Unit and played games with the children during the whole of our two weeks' stay in Belgium. Training was carried out each day, "as per company syllabus", and preparations made for our forthcoming operations. Though D Company was detached from the rest of the battalion and pretty much on its own, it was not entirely immune from the flow of 'bumph' from BHQ and the daily conferences convened by the CO, 2IC and adjutant on training, administration and future operations.

The War, it was obvious to all, was in its final stages. In probably the greatest river crossing of all time, 2nd British Army and 9th US Army, of Field Marshal Montgomery's 21st Army Group, had crossed the Rhine River on March 23rd. Even though 1st Canadian Army (of which we were now a part) was not directly involved in the assault, a copy of the message of the field marshal arrived at D Company headquarters on March 23rd with instructions that it be read to all troops. I do not recall actually digging out every last member of the company from his warm billet to hear the stirring words of our C-in-C, but I must at least have briefed the troops on one of our morning parades.

Old 'Blood and Guts' had certainly polished up his style since the days in the 8th Army in Sicily, when he was very fond of using the word 'magnificent'. But many of the phrases in his message were all too familiar to us and we indulged in a few chuckles at some of the exhortations. Of course we had no intention of being disrespectful. After all, we were old comrades. He had practised his act on us when he was a mere general.

By April 1st the encirclement of the Ruhr was complete and the armies of the field marshal were poised to "crack about in the plains of northern Germany, chasing the enemy from pillar to post", as he had ordained. It was now the turn of Canadian Army to enter the fray. Its first priority would be to operate northwards to clear northeast Holland, then eastwards to clear the coastal belt up to the line of the Weser. The second priority would be to operate westwards to drive the Germans out of western Holland.[8]

The role of our 1st Division was not yet clear and many of us were sure the War would be over before there was time to commit us to action — "The Allied Armies in the west continue their spectacular dashes into Germany. Even the most pessimistic are beginning to think in terms of tailor-made suits, and collars and ties."[9]

We need not have worried — there was still one last river to cross.

Finally, the usual tell-tale signs of impending action appeared. We were allowed to put up our PPCLI shoulder flashes, but not our beloved 'red patch' denoting our 1st Division. Capt Bob Prince (who had been with Patty Crofton and me on that advance party in Italy) left on a recce party to 2nd Canadian Corps. This was a strange one, as we were part of 1st Corps. Who were the staff tying to fool now?

Then another party left to recce a concentration area in the Reichswald Forest in Germany. It returned two days later with little information except that there were no houses or billets, and it was a cold, miserable place. The troops reacted by digging into their feather beds and comforters as if to extract the last ounce of luxury from their warm billets.

Yet we were ready and anxious to rejoin our old comrades in the Canadian Army and show them how to fight. This may seem strange to someone who has not served with the fighting troops, but it is a fact. It is the eternal dilemma of a soldier — he is never completely happy for long. After a short rest he becomes bored and itches to get back into the fight. But when he has been in action for a prolonged period, gone days without proper sleep, food or shelter, endured constant shelling, narrowly escaped death or injury a hundred times and seen his comrades blown to bits - after these and other discomforts, he can't wait to get back to the rest area. As Pte Norton succinctly put it: "Why the hell did I ever join this goddamn army in the first place!"

And so the strange life of a soldier continues — up a few weeks, back a few weeks, until finally his luck runs out — a fascinating game, not unlike Russian roulette.

Many former Regimental officers who were serving in other formations now appeared to wish us luck in the forthcoming operations: Capt W H (Willie) Mulherin, ADC to MGen Volkes (now commanding 4th Armoured Division), who had won the George Medal for saving an airman from a burning plane; Maj E W (Ted) Cutbill, DSO, Brigade Major of 3rd Brigade, whose gallant stand on the Senio River would long be remembered; Capt R S (Stu) Graham, GIII of the same brigade, who was adjutant when I was wounded with the Scouts and Snipers in October, 1943; Capt W S (Walter) Dewar, GIII of 1st Brigade, who was the IO at that time. I hoped that the appearance of these two gentlemen did not portend another present for me from the Wehrmacht.

Another visitor who was always welcome at the Regiment was LCol R C (Rowan) Coleman DSO, MC, now commanding The Lincoln and Welland Regiment in the 4th Armoured Division. Rowan was, beyond doubt, one of the most liked and respected officers in 2nd Brigade. He had been adjutant and a company commander of the PPCLI in England and was one of the chosen few sent to North Africa to gain experience with the British Army; he returned to England and led C Company in Sicily where he won the Military Cross at Leonforte. When LCol Ware assumed command at the end of the Sicilian campaign Rowan Coleman became 2IC of the battalion. Shortly before the Hitler Line he took command of The Loyal Edmonton Regiment and was wounded in that engagement. Later he was given command of The Lincoln and Welland Regiment, where he won the DSO.

Armed with only his pipe, he was completely unflappable, and always exuded a quiet confidence, no matter how desperate the situation. I was fortunate to have served in his company in England, if only for a short time. He was one of the few officers who went out of his way to show me the ropes and give me a little encouragement when I badly needed some help. Yet, he would not suffer gladly junior officers who didn't measure up, or who groused about their problems. I remember one occasion in southern Italy. I had just returned from a day-long patrol behind enemy lines and was ordered by brigade to take out a night patrol immediately. I was tired, wet and hungry, and stomped back to my Scouts and Snipers muttering fearful oaths about staff officers and their mothers. Out of the darkness appeared Maj Coleman, pipe at the ready: "Mr Frost," he said in a cold, steely voice

424

that cut the evening mists, "what seems to be the trouble?"

I was speechless and had the horrible feeling that I had just uttered my last words as a Patricia Officer. But my training at RMC finally surfaced and I was able to reply with the only acceptable excuse in the circumstances, which was really no excuse. "I'm sorry, Sir, that you had to hear that. I have no excuse. It won't happen again."

Rowan Coleman came up to me. "I understand. I would have felt the same way myself. But you probably didn't realize that some of your men heard you. You can't expect to win their loyalty if you question the orders of your superiors in their presence."

From then on I tried to keep my opinion of the competence of staff officers and others to my diary.

One of Roman's many qualities was his ability to size up men. When he needed a new 21C for The Lincoln and Welland Regiment, he came to the Patricias and carried off Maj W de N Watson DSO, MC. He could not have found a finer officer. But the gain of the 'Links & Winks' was a severe loss for the Patricias.

'Bucko' Watson was of the same mould as Rowan Coleman — cool, steady, determined, cheerful under fire. Except for three periods in hospital as a result of wounds, he had served the Regiment continuously since he joined it in 1942. He was adjutant for the landing in Sicily and took over command of A Company toward the end of that campaign. He commanded that company with distinction throughout the advance up southern Italy and in the fierce battles of Villa Rogatti and Vino Ridge in December, 1943 when he was wounded twice. In February, 1944 he returned from hospital, resumed command of his A Company and led it until the Hitler Line when his company and the Regiment itself were almost annihilated. He was the only officer and probably the only member of the battalion who reached the objective. Wounded in one arm and with a piece of his helmet and a Schmeisser bullet in his forehead, he evaded capture by moving from shell hole to shell hole until he was finally located by our own troops the morning following the attack. It was an epic performance that gained for him a special niche in the annals of the Regiment's deeds of valour.

With Maj Watson gone, the ranks of the officers who had landed in the assault wave in Sicily and had remained with the Regiment ever since, except for periods in hospital, were reduced to two hardy veterans — Maj P D (Patty) Crofton and Capt A M (Andy) Campbell.

Thus the Regiment, its name, its spirit and all that it embodied, had passed to a new generation. Thanks, however, to the example of steadfastness, fortitude and gallantry that had been set by those who had gone before, and that had been embraced by those who followed, the future of the Regiment was in safe hands.

On April 3rd, at 0600 hours, the Regiment embussed for the Reichswald

Forest. Sad were our farewells to the good people of Boisschot and Hulshout as our vehicles carried us away to our last battleground. "In spite of the early hour, the people of the village were on hand to wish us goodbye and not a few tears were shed. Never have we been more welcome or experienced more genuine hospitality than during our short stay in Belgium."[10]

Our convoy, heading northeast, soon left Belgium, crossed the southeastern tip of Holland, entered Germany, and arrived at our bivouac in the Reichswald Forest at 3:30 pm. Our camp was about 15 miles southeast of the Dutch city of Nijmegen and just a few miles south of the German city of Cleve.

The great forest had been heavily shelled by both sides and was a jungle of shattered trees and uprooted trunks, as though a crazed army of lumber-jacks had gone through the area, carrying away all the fine trees and desecrating the remainder. Just as we arrived, a cold, heavy rain soaked the ground and added to the sense of doom and gloom about the place. We cleared away the debris as quickly as we could and pitched our pup tents on the soggy ground; some fashioned bivouacs from the fallen trees and boughs. It reminded me of those wild schemes in England with the rein-forcement officers. I wondered how many had survived the rigours of the elements and the shells of the Hun.

In no time we were snug in our shelters — not quite like Hulshout, but better than the mud and water-filled trenches of the Italian plains.

No sooner were we settled than we were warned to expect a visit the next day (April 4th) from the very top brass — no less a personage than the Army Commander himself, Gen Crerar. We had heard tales about the rigid, formal way things were done in the Canadian Army and I wondered what sort of a reception we would receive from our reserved looking GOC-in-C. I was pleasantly surprised. He seemed more like your friendly banker than a general who commanded half a million men. In a very informal, relaxed manner he poked about our area, said a few friendly words and genuinely made us feel welcome to the Canadian Army. I thought of the last time I had seen him at CMHQ in London just before the invasion, when I was the relaxed one, as I dated a female officer on his staff.

A little later a former Patricia NCO dropped in to welcome us to our new battleground: Lt R B (Buzz) Mainprize, now serving with the KOYLI of the British Army. He had been a CSM in England, returned to Canada to take his commission, then joined the Canloan scheme whereby the Canadian Government 'lent' junior officers to the British Army.

As soon as the general departed, Capt Koensgen, the field, or battle adjutant, came over to speak to me.

"Syd, I've got some good news for you."

"Don't tell me the general wants me to be a staff officer," I smirked.

"Hardly. You'll be taking command of D Company in the next show.

'Snuffy' Smith is going on leave.''

It was the best news I had received since my promotion to captain. At last, after all the frustrations, I would have the chance to lead a company in action.

Later that day the CO held an 'O' Group to give us the background for the upcoming battles. 2nd Canadian Corps, under LGen Simonds, were advancing rapidly north from the Rhine River into northeast Holland, east of the Ijssel River. They had just crossed the Twente Canal and were still making good progress. 3rd Division was preparing to capture Zutphen and Deventer on the east side of the Ijssel River. As soon as these two towns had been cleared, our 1st Division would assault across the Ijssel River, midway between them. The codename for the operation was 'Cannonshot'. We would be temporarily under command of LGen Simonds, as we would be fighting in the sector allotted to his 2nd Corps. As soon as the crossing had been made, 1st Division would revert to LGen Foulkes' 1st Corps whose remaining divisions (5th Canadian Armoured Division and the British 49th(WR) Division) would capture Arnhem and join us in throwing the Germans out of western Holland.

The IO, Lt J V (Vic) Spurr, then issued us a flock of air photos, maps and codenames to study. Vic had joined the Regiment after the Sicilian campaign, had been wounded in the Hitler Line and was a solid, worthy soldier. He was also a first-rate IO with a sense of humour. After handing out the maps he asked the usual, "Any questions?" I had only a moment to glance at the sheets, and to my complete astonishment saw they were of the southeast coast of England. "My God," I thought aloud, "the staff have finally gone round the bend; they want us to attack England!"

Vic laughed. "That's right, but it's only a diversionary attack. The main effort will still be in Holland!"

Now I thought Vic had gone crazy too, or had gone to a lot of effort to pull a weak joke. I took a closer look at the maps and saw German words in the margins, opposite the English words describing the conventional signs. The maps had been made in 1940 by the Germans from captured English maps, and were for the great invasion of England that never came.

Vic Spurr then suggested that we turn the sheets over and look at the backs. We did so and found beautifully lithographed maps of the Ijssel River, Zutphen, Deventer and the whole area of our upcoming operations, all to a scale of 1/25,000. They made our impressionistic Italian maps look like the amateur efforts they were.

The next two days were busy ones for me. I had never dreamed I would be given the chance to lead our company in our first attack in Northwest Europe and I had a lot to learn in a short time. My first concern was how well did I know my officers and men. I had only joined the company on February 7th when it took over static positions in the Senio River Winter

Line. As each platoon was isolated, there was little chance to get to know anyone, except to meet the three platoon commanders, platoon sergeants, company sergeant major and company quartermaster sergeant.

Then on February 21st, I had left on advance parties for Leghorn, followed by the long road trek to Belgium. Finally, in Hulshout, I had had two weeks to size up most of the key personnel and form an idea of their strengths and weaknesses, even though we were only in a rest area and not in action. However, I was lucky to have had even this short period, as many, many times in Italy, company and platoon commanders had been thrown into action without even a chance to meet their platoon or section commanders, a fact to which I could personally attest. Now, at least, I knew their names and something about their background.

My three platoon commanders were: Lt W W (Bert) Bolton (16 Platoon) who had transferred from the engineers and joined the Regiment on December 29th, 1944; Lt A B (Allan) McKinnon, MC (17 Platoon) who had transferred from the gunners and joined the Regiment on December 6th, 1944 — in his very first action he had shown outstanding leadership and won the MC; and Lt H E (Harvey) Beardmore (18 Platoon) who had transferred from the gunners and joined the Regiment on December 19th, 1944. One further officer would be attached to my company in charge of a pioneer detachment who would clear mines and help to demolish obstacles — Lt H F (Herb) Pragnell, a classmate from RMC who had transferred from the sappers and joined the Regiment on February 19th, 1945.

With two engineer officers and two artillery officers under my command I felt more like a brigadier surrounded by supporting arms advisors than a mere captain of infantry. In fact, I felt somewhat intimidated by all this talent from the senior services. But the fact remained that, except for McKinnon, none had seen much action or even commanded a platoon for any length of time. Their apparent lack of experience, however, need not have concerned me. They were 'quick learners' and led their men with dash and determination. If the War had gone on longer they would have gained further honours and promotions. The company sergeant major was CSM Milko, M, who had joined the Regiment early in the War and had worked his way up through the ranks to CSM.

The three platoon sergeants were Sgt Coderre, A (16 Platoon) who had joined the Regiment on January 25th, 1944 and been wounded on December 20th, 1944; Sgt Berry C H (17 Platoon) who had joined the Regiment on December 22, 1943 (and would be wounded in the upcoming operation); and Cpt Whyte, D (18 Platoon) who had also joined the Regiment on December 22nd, 1943 and had been wounded on December 29th, 1943 and again on December 22nd, 1944.

Another key figure in the forthcoming action was LSgt Hanbury, T of 17 Platoon, who had joined the Regiment on August 17th, 1943 in Sicily and served with it ever since. Another man who would play a notable part in the battle was one Pte Sykes, RE in charge of the Piat in 18 Platoon. He had joined the Regiment on December 11th, 1943 and been injured in action on January 4th, 1944. Still another man who would render a vital service was my 18 set operator, Pte Favel, H. He had joined the Regiment on July 25th, 1943 in Sicily, and been wounded on September 17th, 1944.

Thus I had a solid base of proven veteran NCOs whom I could count on to back up my platoon commanders if they became casualties; also the long promised reinforcements had finally arrived. For the first time since the landing in Sicily, the battalion was pretty well up to strength. In fact I had surplus officers in my company. Lt Harrington, as already mentioned, acted as a kind of 3IC in Belgium, helping with training and administering the company. Lt C M (Corky) Pyne had joined the Regiment just before we left Italy and was a supernumerary platoon commander.

Consequently, D Company had seven officers on strength when we arrived in Belgium — an unheard of and unbelievable number. The fact can be easily proved, however. A picture taken at Leghorn shows the seven of us gathered about the D Company Tac sign. Years after the War, I sent a copy of the photo to Allan McKinnon (who appeared in the picture as one of the platoon commanders), and reminded him how delighted we then were to have surplus officers. Allan McKinnon wrote back (tongue very much in cheek) that his reaction now was that we were 'overstaffed'. Of course, he was no longer Lt A B McKinnon, MC of D Company. He was speaking as Minister of National Defence in charge of an Army that was smaller than the 1st Canadian Corps had been in Italy.

Now on with the War and the crossing of the Ijssel River. On April 7th, we embussed in our TCVs and moved off to a concentration area in Holland. En route, we passed through what had once been the ancient city of Cleve, now completely flattened by the allied bombing and shellfire. A few sullen civilians crawled out of their holes and half looked at us, with dull, expressionless eyes. The same scene of utter devastation was repeated at Emmerich, where we crossed the Rhine on a long pontoon bridge. The horror of seeing these dead cities and cities of the dead is hard to describe. Forty years later, it is impossible to believe.

How, I wondered, could the Germans go on fighting us when their homeland had practically ceased to exist. I must confess I felt no mercy or pity toward them at all.

It was a relief to leave this depressing country that had sown so much evil and was now reaping such dreadful retribution. We crossed into Holland and came to rest at Baak, four miles south of Zutphen on the Ijssel River, in a pleasant wooded area.

Chapter XXXII

THE IJSSEL RIVER HOLLAND

No More Rivers to Cross
April 7 to May 5, 1945

The Ric-a-dam-doo, pray what is that?
'Twas made at home by the Princess Pat
It's Red and Gold and Royal Blue
That's what we call our Ric-a-dam-doo
dam-doo, dam-doo

While the companies settled into their new areas, the commanding officer led a recce party (consisting of the five company commanders, Intelligence Officer, Signals Officer, Field Adjutant, representatives from Mortar, Anti-tank and Pioneer Platoons and the artillery) to the site where the battalion would cross the Ijssel. We had no trouble getting forward to a covered spot, in a wood, from which we could carefully survey the area. With my glasses, I easily picked out my company objective, a group of houses about 1,000 yards from the crossing place, but they were sheltered by a dyke that could mean real trouble. The river itself seemed about 100 yards wide, muddy and sluggish. From our vantage point to the near bank of the dyke, the area was as flat as a billiard table and no cover was available.

I turned to Maj Jones, whose C Company would be on the left of my

D Company in the assault. "Does this remind you of anything we've seen before?"

"Christ, it's the Italian plains all over again."

"Yeah, but maybe this will be our last river."

"It sure as hell will be, if we don't have lots of smoke and reach those dykes *molto pronto*."

I then formed some tentative plans on how to tackle D Company's objective. I had to agree with Maj Jones that our best chance was to go like hell for the dyke with two platoons, while the third gave covering fire. With any luck we'd get there before the Germans had recovered from our artillery and mortar bombardment.

Later that day, I returned to the OP with my three platoon commanders and worked out a firm plan. Having all this time to recce our objective and make plans was a new experience for us and we made the most of it. It was such a sensible way to go to war compared to the Italian campaign, where we had been thrown into river crossings so many times with no chance for any recce or planning. The more I saw of the orderly, deliberate way the Canadian Army went about its tasks, the more I liked doing business with them.

There was one feature, however, from the Italian campaign, that I missed — the strong, shell-proof *casas* of the peasant farmers. So far, in Holland, we had received only intermittent shelling from the other side of the river, but I noted with some apprehenision that when a lucky shot hit a Dutch house, it completely disintegrated into a pile of red bricks.

Something else we left behind in Italy was our trusty Thompson sub-machine guns. They had proven themselves just as effective shooting Germans as they had cutting down mobsters in the United States before the war. On our arrival in the Reichswald Forest we had been issued with another deadly weapon — the Sten gun — deadly, that is, for both the firer and firee. This mass-produced submachine gun looked more like a plumber's tool than a gun. It was composed of a steel pipe (the barrel) welded to another piece of steel pipe bent to form a butt. A long magazine stuck out the left side of the barrel and served as a grip. Not a piece of wood appeared on the machine. Its costs of manufacture were said to be about $3.50 compared to, say, $25.00 for the finely-tooled Thompson submachine gun. The Sten may have saved the government a lot of dollars, but it also cost a number of casualties. The gun was so poorly made that the slightest jar to the weapon was liable to set off a stream of bullets. If, for example, the weapon was dropped on the ground, the ensuing burst of fire could wipe out a section. We had been issued a few of these monsters in Italy and quickly 'traded' them for Thompsons, acquired in various ways.

With our recces all made and our plans firmed up, there was nothing more to do but wait — and wait, and wait. This test of the nerves would never

431

change, no matter where the battle was fought. What we were waiting for was for the 3rd Division to capture Zutphen and Deventer on the east bank of the Ijssel, so we could launch our attack across the river, mid-way between the two cities.

On April 8th, the Army Commander, Gen Crerar, paid a flying visit to HQ of 1st Division, presumably to give MGen Foster the latest information and advise him on how to fight this new kind of war. At the conclusion of the conference, Gen Crerar's plane took off from a field a few hundred yards from our BHQ and 'buzzed' us at an altitude of only 150 feet. The General was not only a fine soldier, he was a good sport.

By April 9th, 3rd Division, after a tough fight, had cleared Zutphen and was in the process of capturing Deventer. We climbed into our lorries and headed for our last Assembly Area, in a wood, two miles directly east of the point where we would cross the Ijssel. On arrival, the CO reminded us we were well within range of enemy guns and mortars. The troops could take a hint and dug in with a will; some excellent field works appeared in record time.

In our Assembly Area we 'married up' with the crews of the 'Buffaloes' of the 4th Royal Tank Regiment that would ferry us across the river. Here was another animal to add to our menagerie. In Italy we had run into Crocodiles, Weasels and Wasps, not to mention Lifebuoys, Olafsons and Littlejohns. Our new beast of burden was unique: it was tracked, armoured, and could swim. Unlike the DUKWs on the Sicily beaches, it gave its passengers some protection against small arms fire and shell splinters. The task of the Buffaloes was to transport us from our Assembly Area to the river, swim across, and deposit us safe and dry on the other side. It seemed too good to be true, but the friendly crewmen assured us it was no trouble. "Piece of cake, old chap."

Each craft could take 30 men and their equipment. Four Buffaloes would be sufficient to transport the whole of D Company.

I reviewed the nominal roll of my company and found that I would be going into action with almost a full-sized company. The authorized strength for a platoon was 32 all ranks, comprising three sections of eight men each, and a platoon HQ of eight. Thus a company of three platoons had a strength of 96 all ranks plus company headquarters, whose numbers varied in each operation but were normally about 14. So a full-sized company had an authorized strength of about 110 all ranks. In this operation omitting ten attached pioneers, I had a strength of exactly 100 — quite a luxury for a D-Day Dodger who was brought up on companies with a strength of 60 or 70 all ranks.

1945 April 10 — 0800 hours
LCol Clark is called to brigade HQ to receive final orders for Operation 'Cannonshot', the crossing of the Ijssel River.

1945 April 10 — 0900 hours

LCol Clark returns and immediately calls his 'O' Group for the attack. We gather eagerly at BHQ, quartered in a fine Dutch country home, in a wooded estate. We are happy and relieved to receive orders at last for our first action in Northwest Europe.

The enemy on the other side of the river has been very quiet this morning. Usually, he sends over a few salvos into the woods every day to smarten us up in the morning, break up our afternoon siesta (inherited from our days in Italy) and keep us awake at night. Even the main road running north from Zutphen to Deventer, in places only 2,000 yards from the river and under enemy observation, has not received its usual attention from the German gunners. They know, of course, that the main attack of the Canadian Army has been northwards toward Zwolle and Groningen. Perhaps they are content to sit, undisturbed, in their dugouts on the west side of the river, while their comrades in the north take a licking.

Whatever the reason for Jerry's silence, it is conducive to a relaxed 'O' Group. We have had days to prepare and make our plans and now we are keen to get on with it. LCol Clark senses our mood and keeps his orders short, omitting the standard 'boiler plate' about the demoralized enemy, the tremendous artillery bombardment and other items we already know and have heard a hundred times. One point about the artillery is, however, vital — for 20 minutes the area will be thoroughly smoked by all the resources available. Without this cover we would be sitting ducks.

The assault across the river will be made by two companies, Dog Company right, Charlie Company left. Dog Company's objective is the group of houses behind the dyke, code-named Ness. Charlie Company's objective is the house and orchard, code-named Winnipeg.

On success of Charlie and Dog Companies, Able and Baker will cross the river; Able to Dog Company area, Baker to Charlie Company area. Able Company will then pass through Dog Company and occupy crossroads, code-named Watrous. Baker Company will then pass through Charlie Company and capture a group of houses at road junction, code-named Byron.

On Baker Company reporting 'Snug', Dog Company will pass through Byron and capture a group of houses on the outskirts of the village of Wilp, code-named Winchester. On success of Dog Company, Baker Company will move forward and occupy the village, code-named Champlain.

Further advances will be ordered after the bridgehead is secure. H-Hour is 1630 hours.

The 'O' Group breaks up and we return to our companies to give them our final orders. Everyone is ready and itching to go.

April 10 — 1215 hours
Brig Bogert, the brigade commander, visits LCol Clark and tells him the attack is off. We accept the news with stoicism, but hope the postponement is only temporary and not a cancellation of the crossing. Not much sleep tonight, waiting for news.

April 11 — 1000 hours
Cannonshot is on! All companies report to their Buffaloes at 1430 hours. Smoke will begin at 1600 hours for 20 minutes. High explosive fire will start at 1620 hours, right up to H-Hour. H-Hour is 1630 hours.

April 11 — 1430 hours
Dog Company quickly loads on the Buffaloes. We've practised this so many times we can do it blindfolded. I speak briefly to the platoon commanders and wish them luck. No words of exhortation are needed or expected. They know what has to be done and are keen to do it. I say a few words to CSM Milko. He's pleased with the mood of the men. They'll blast the Jerries back into the Zuyder Zee.

The Buffaloes roar into life and fill the woods with their heavy fumes. I run back to my vehicle and hop on the ramp just as it is pulled up. Herb Pragnell has checked off the loading table for No 4 Craft. All are present and raring to go. I look at my lifeline to BHQ, the 18 set wireless operators. They give me a big grin and raise their thumbs. Their sets are netted and ready to transmit and receive as soon as wireless silence is broken.

The great beasts snort and lurch forward to the river. God, it feels good to be leading my company into action at last!

I look at my watch — 1530 hours. In 30 minutes the smoke screen will start. It's a fine day for smoke, just a light breeze. We meet Charlie Company Buffaloes. I wave at Maj Jones. I have bet him I'll be on my objective while he's still climbing out of his craft. We exchange V signs but I am not sure whether his gesture is Churchillian or rude.

Ten minutes to smoke — five minutes. We emerge from the woods. The artillery opens up. Shells whine over our heads and land on the far bank of the river. Smoke drifts across the whole front, completely shielding us from enemy observation. McKinnon and Beardmore were right. The artillery have delivered the goods.

Now we are churning along the flats. The river is about 1,000 yards away. The artillery starts to fire HE. We can't see the targets, but the tremendous explosions tell us Jerry is getting a pasting.

April 11 — 1630 hours
My Buffalo hits the water and dives in without missing a stroke. The nose dips down and then bobs up again. The thing actually floats! More important,

it also swims.

In minutes we are across the river. The craft has trouble negotiating the bank. I indicate to the driver to stay in the water. We can jump to the bank. He is happy. The lower the Buffalo, the smaller the target.

The enemy has hardly reacted to our attack. Only a few scattered shells fall. Once again, he's been faked right out of his drawers. He has assumed that the entire 2nd Corps has by-passed him and is headed for Groningen and northeast Germany. The enemy's assumption is partly correct. Second Corps, as constituted before the arrival of 1st Division, has in fact by-passed the enemy west of the Ijssel. But 1st Division has been secretly attached to 2nd Corps to cross the Ijssel and break into western Holland.

Tomorrow the enemy will receive another rude shock. 5th Armoured Division will cross the Rhine near Arnhem and roll north behind the Germans facing us on the Ijssel River. It's a clever, well-thought-out plan. Whatever harsh words I've had for generals and the staff in the past, I've got to admit they occasionally come up with some brilliant ideas.

These thoughts flash by as the Buffalo nudges into the far bank. We rush over the nose of the vehicle, fan out, and hit the ground. Now the smoke starts to thin out. We have to get our tails up. CSM Milko charges over from his Buffalo and urges the men forward. They don't really need any urging as now we are getting small arms fire from Ness. But sergeant majors are supposed to give men hell — "Come on, Dog Company, move it, move it!" he yells. "Now's the time you earn your King's shilling."

Lt McKinnon and his 17 Platoon are in fact earning their King's shilling and several months' pay besides. The dyke I was so concerned about is not occupied, but the houses at Ness are full of Jerries and they are supported by a tank. They pour fire on 17 Platoon. What happens next is best told by the Regimental Historian.

> *D Company on the right encountered a dyke which fortunately was unmanned; as it crossed this ramp fire opened from a group of houses 150 yards ahead. A German tank was spotted; the 17 Platoon PIAT missed with its first three bombs. Further ammunition was being brought forward when LSgt T Hanberry discovered another bomb in hand. He crept forward, boldly stepped into the open for his shot and scored a bullseye.* Thereafter the advance continued without opposition and at 1720 hours Capt C S Frost reported his situation as 'Snug', although his men were under harassing fire from the right flank.[1]*

---

* For his brave action that allowed the advance to continue, LSgt Hanberry was awarded a well-deserved Military Medal.

April 11 — 1720 hours

I turn to Pte Favel on the 18 Set. "What's happening to Charlie Company? Are they snug yet?

"Oh yes, Sir, they reported success at 1643 hours."

"Damn it, Favel, are you sure? I bet Maj Jones my next EFI issue that I'd be on my objective while his feet where still in the water."

"I guess you're out one bottle of whiskey."

April 11 — 2100 hours

Pte Favel has more messages for me. Able Company have reported they are firm on their objective, Watrous. Baker Company are snug on Byron, and the CO wonders why I am sitting on my derrière. He wants me to start moving immediately to Winchester, via Baker Company. We can't expect any tank or anti-tank support tonight. The Germans have finally wakened up and are shelling the hell out of the crossing where the sappers are trying to build a bridge.

I hold a quick 'O' Group with my platoon commanders. "The attack has gone well. All the objectives in the second phase are secure. It is now vital to the whole operation that we reach the third and final objective, Winchester, before the enemy has a chance to organize a new defensive position.

"We'll move out immediately — to Baker Company's area. To save time, and because it's dark, we'll move together as a company, in single file, with scouts ahead. The woods and lake directly in front of us are a damn nuisance. We'll skirt them on the left flank.

"Make sure the platoons keep well closed up."

April 11 — 2330 hours

It takes us longer than I had planned to go around the lake and reach Baker Company at Byron. Capt Egan Chambers reports no recent enemy activity in his area, but is concerned that Jerry will soon move into Wilp if we don't get there first. I agree. We pore over our maps and discuss routes to our objectives.

I decide to send Lt Beardmore and his 18 Platoon immediately to Winchester, about 1,000 yards ahead. With any luck, if they move quickly, they can occupy the place before the enemy has brought in reinforcements.

As soon as the platoon are snug they are to send back a runner and the rest of the company will join them. If they run into any trouble, I'll bring up the other two Platoons pronto and form a plan of attack. If for any reason I don't hear from the platoon within 40 minutes I'll assume they have occupied Winchester and I'll bring up the company.

In the meantime 16 and 17 Platoons will form a firm base to the right of Baker Company and block any counter-attacks. Two points are essential to the operation — speed and silence.

April 12 — 0100 hours
Not a word has come back from 18 Platoon, nor has there been any sound of firing up ahead. The runner has probably got lost. The night is as dark as the insides of that dead cow we passed on the way here. Egan Chambers is fretting to get moving and dig in before first light. So am I.

Still no runner appears. We'll have to get going and take a chance that 18 Platoon is safely on the objective and has not strayed.

I move off across the fields and immediately realize it would not be difficult for a runner to get lost. While the map shows the country to be flat, there are innumerable streams, hedges and orchards to negotiate and I am glad I have a compass. We continue our silent approach along the ditches and through hedges. Any moment I expect a challenge or the burst of a Schmeisser. Our single file, tightly closed up to maintain contact, would be cut to pieces by a well sited MG42. Can't do a damn thing about it. We've got to get there before the Germans do. Where is 18 Platoon?

Sooner than I had expected, I see the outlines of a barn and a small house. Whether this is Winchester, I am not at all certain. Still not a sound, except the crickets and a dog way in the distance. Lt Bolton goes forward to investigate. In minutes two figures appear out of the darkness. One is Bolton and the other has to be Beardmore. I can tell by his relaxed, rolling gait. He comes up close to me so that I can see his grin and a finger at his lips. "We sneaked right into those buildings without any trouble," he whispers, "but I can't believe there aren't Jerries in the village. Just a few moments ago we heard rumbles coming from that direction. Sounded to me like tanks. Could be an attack going in against Seaforth on our left, or they could be heading for the village."

I hurriedly give orders to the platoon commanders to take up positions in all-around defence. Beardmore has already occupied a good position north of the buildings covering the road in front. McKinnon digs in covering the approach from the northeast and Bolton locates his platoon in an orchard covering the area to the southwest. Company headquarters is set up in a house facing the road.

I get off a signal to BHQ that we are snug at Winchester. But for how long, only time will tell. Sounds of tracked vehicles on our left are getting louder and closer. It is now 0200 hours.

April 12 — 0300 hours
Beardmore reports that tanks are definitely entering the village. He has two good PIAT men ready to greet them if they come along the road in front of our position.

I try to send off a signal to BHQ that a counter-attack is coming in with tanks and probably infantry — how many we don't yet know. I make an urgent appeal for anti-tank guns. As usual the lousy 18 set is acting up, despite the efforts of my best signaller. He can't get any response to the message. He keeps trying.

Then all hell breaks loose in the village. Thuds and explosions of guns are mingled with rapid bursts of Schmeissers and the steady beat of our Bren guns. Good old Baker must have got into the village and is intercepting the Jerry tanks.

I keep huddled over the 18 set trying desperately to get through to BHQ to send anti-tank guns. Still no response to our messages. Then a small chill goes down my spine. I suddenly remember the earlier message from the CO — "the crossing is being heavily shelled. The sappers are having trouble erecting a bridge. No anti-tank guns can be expected before first light.

Everything now depends on our PIAT gunners with Harvey Beardmore's 18 Platoon on the road in front.

A runner from 18 Platoon bursts into the house. "Three tanks are coming down the road in front with a bunch of German infantry. They're travelling fast and seem to be heading for Able Company's area, 600 yards to our right. They haven't yet spotted 18 Platoon."

Clang — swoosh — crash! A shell hits the lean-to outside. It disintegrates. Then another explodes in the front yard. I wish I were back in a strong *casa* in Italy.

Then a PIAT bomb explodes outside. Bren guns open up. A shell crashes into the front of the house. A look-out at the window yells: "They're coming at us." I jump up from the 18 set and pull out my pistol.

Norton is at my side. Favel the signaller grabs his Sten gun and heads for the door. He doesn't quite make it. The door bursts open and four or five Germans rush in. Favel lets off a deadly burst, then another. I lift my pistol to fire and then lower the weapon. Favel has cut down the entire party. Five Germans are writhing on the floor in agony.

The RAP man comes up to help the wounded. Favel goes outside. The tanks and infantry have passed our position and are heading for Able Company. The battle is not yet over.

I look briefly at the Germans. All are wounded quite badly. I ask if anyone speaks English. One says he can. I tell him I want to know how many infantry are with those three tanks. He says a company — about 120.

I rush back to the 18 set. The other signaller has stayed with the set trying to establish contact. He finally gets a message through — we are being counter-attacked by three tanks and a company of infantry. There is no point in asking for anti-tank guns. The need is obvious. Anyway, they can't get across the river.

438

I go outside to check the platoons. They have had a hot time of it beating off the tanks and infantry. McKinnon comes up. "I don't think we're finished with them yet. Able Company will give them a warm reception. Then they'll turn tail, and head back. We're ready for them."

McKinnon is right; flares go up in Able Company's area. The night explodes in a fearful roar of shells, PIAT bombs, Schmeissers, mortars, Brens and Stens. I can't tell who's getting the best of it, but I'm putting my money on 'Bunchy' Newlands and his Able Company.

McKinnon returns to his platoon and I hurry over to Beardmore. "We'll get the SOB this time, Sir. Pte Sykes is ready and waiting."

I hasten to Bolton's platoon. He's fine, but a little annoyed that the tanks have escaped without his fine PIAT section having a chance to deliver a few well-aimed shots.

A shell whistles overhead. The tanks are returning and firing wildly in all directions. I tell Bolton he may yet get his chance and hurry back to my headquarters. As I reach the door a great explosion rents the night air and red flames shoot into the sky in front of Beardmore's platoon. Pte Sykes has got his tank!*

The two remaining tanks turn about and head back again to Able Company. In minutes, they too go up in flames, destroyed by PIAT bombs from 'Bunchy' Newland's company. The counter-attack is over. The bridgehead is secure.

Later that day (April 12th) the 48th Highlanders of Canada of 1st Brigade pushed through our position to expand the bridgehead westward to Apeldoorn. In the course of the fighting, they lost their fine, young commanding officer, LCol D A Mackenzie, who was killed by a shell.

At 10:30 pm the CO called an 'O' Group to outline a plan to launch another attack a little farther south, to make the bridgehead more secure. The battalion would move to a concentration area early next morning, about three miles south of our present position, and seize the villages of Busloo and Gietelo, on the eastern fringes of the Appensche Veld, a dense woodland mid-way between Zutphen and Apeldoorn and lying on each side of the highway connecting those two cities. The Patricias would then clear the northern portion of the wood. A and C companies would lead the way in this attack, while B and D were in reserve.

When the CO said "early next morning" he meant it. After only a few hours' sleep, we roused ourselves at 0300 hours and marched to our new

---

* Pte Sykes received a Military Medal for his determination and skill in helping to break up the German counter-attacks, the second MM earned by Dog Company in the river crossing.

concentration area, arriving at 0500 hours, dead tired and hungry, but ready to chase the Hun once more.

A and C companies married up with their tanks, pushed off behind a solid artillery bombardment, and easily gained their preliminary objectives. Jerry had departed. The CO, always ready to take advantage of the enemy's apparent collapse, ordered the leading companies to carry on to the final objectives without the usual 'leapfrog' system of bringing up reserve companies to take over the running. As usual, the CO's battle sense was right and the final objectives, Busloo and Gietelo, were occupied with little resistance.

Ahead lay the dense woods of the Appensche Veld where, the Scouts and Snipers reported, at least 100 enemy lurked. How to flush out these itinerant forest dwellers? The answer was a classic wood-clearing operation, tailor-made for Support Company — flamethrowers, carriers and MMGs with an assist from the rifle companies if serious opposition threatened.

These support troops were quickly divided into three battle groups and sent out to their objectives — code-named Alice, Blue, Gown. Why such prissy code-names for such a deadly force? Maybe the staff were running out of good, macho names, like Husky, Overlord, Totalize. No matter. The sequence of names for the present operation was at least easy to remember.

The three battle groups worked perfectly and soon prisoners were streaming into BHQ. If the Germans tried to flee from the flamethrowers they were cut down in the open by the Vickers guns. I felt very envious of Capt Bill Stutt as he charged down the road with his MMGs blazing and his flamethrowers spewing liquid death.

As each Battle Group reached its objective, a rifle company hurried forward to firm up the position. Group Three ran into some stout opposition in a wide stretch of forest they could not handle, and D Company were called forward to assist. At last I had a chance to try out the wood-clearing technique that I had learned at Vernon Battle School two years earlier, and which I had never had occasion to use.

My three platoons were organized into two long lines that stretched from one end of the wood to the other. The first line (the beaters) poked about the under brush with much shouting and firing of ammunition and flushed out any enemy lying in covert. The second line looked for enemy in the trees and were ready to come to the support of the beaters if they were pinned to the ground. It sounded great in theory, but I soon found the battle was very difficult to control when bullets were flying about. But the men loved it and shot off, so it seemed, more 303 rounds than they had used in some of the big battles in the Italian campaign. In the face of this barrage, the Wehrmacht either gave up or dashed for the open where Bill Stutt was waiting with his flamethrowers and MMGs. Altogether it was a lot of fun and thankfully no one got shot by his own men.

By 1600 hours the wood was thoroughly cleared of all life, and we consolidated on the edge of the forest, about 400 yards from a railway embankment. Our POW score had been augmented by 20 more beaten and dejected Jerries.

And what was left of the enemy forces would still not acknowledge that the game was up. From the railway embankment, a roving SP gun poured shells into our positions on the edge of the forest, and snipers made movement difficult until after last light. My platoon commanders were getting very tired of these cheeky Krauts, and wanted me to attack the embankment and rid us of this pestilence. I was inclined to agree, but the War was just about over, whether the Germans agreed or not, and I didn't want to sacrifice even one man needlessly.

Then a more compelling request arrived from one of the platoons, the like of which I had never encountered in my entire army career. The message form simply said 'Woman in labour; pains every 20 minutes; help.'

The MO was back at BHQ. I looked helplessly at the company HQ personnel but no one volunteered to act as mid-wife. Finally, Norton mumbled something about hot water and blankets and volunteered to go with me. I really hadn't yet decided to volunteer myself, but realized everyone expected me to do my duty.

Norton and I made it to the house, despite the efforts of the SP and snipers to stop our mission of mercy. We were ten minutes late. But, as so often happens, the platoon sergeant had risen to the occasion and mother and baby girl were doing just fine. Only much later I wondered what name the baby was given. I could have suggested an appropriate one that would have indicated the Regimental connection.

D Company remained in this position the next two days covering the brigade front, while the remainder of 2nd Brigade swung south to mop up any enemy still lurking between the west bank of the Ijssel River and the Apeldoorn Canal, and to join hands at Dieren with the 49th British Division coming north from Arnhem.

On April 15th the battalion (less D Company) set off in TCVs for Rotting and Tonden, two miles west of Zutphen. There, the troops debussed and formed up to attack while the carriers were sent forward to feel out the objective. They soon reported back that the enemy had left for parts unknown. Again LCol Clark sensed that the front was on the verge of collapse. He 'unleashed' the carriers and gave them a free hand to patrol the entire area allotted to the battalion by brigade. Capt Stutt took off into the southwest and soon reached Voorstonden, which he reported clear. Then he pushed on to the Apeldoorn Canal and contacted the 49th British Division near Eerbeek. Meanwhile, A, B and C companies were doing their own 'swanning' over the area without encountering any opposition, but gathering in large numbers of prisoners (who surrendered without even a show of resistance) and acquiring much loot from the beaten Hun. "The front was disintegrating and the Patricia advance was neither an attack nor even a chase. It was an occupation."[2]

The War Diarist of The Loyal Edmonton Regiment could not restrain his envy of the staff cars, vehicles, household wares, food and other loot left by the Germans for the Patricias:

> --- *the PPCLI --- had been busy on our right, capturing hundreds of wandering enemy with so much loot that most of the Patricias were offering to resign their position as privates and go home to live in a manner befitting their status as millionaires.*[3]

While A, B and C companies were thus enjoying the spoils of war, D Company was cooling its heels back in the Appensche Veld forest, supposedly covering the brigade front. It was too much for McKinnon. On April 15th, he patrolled forward to the railway line from where the SP gun and snipers had been pestering us the day before, and found the enemy gone. Later in the day a whole platoon of Germans marched in to surrender and after a thorough inspection were hustled off to the rear. Then a girl in the Dutch Underground brought in an SS trooper, shorn of all his former arrogance, who had shamefully cast off his uniform. Everywhere the Dutch Underground were very active and were of great assistance in rounding up their hated oppressors.

Our task now seemed superfluous and I reported the information (and my opinion) to the 2IC, Maj Cobbett, at Rear Tac HQ which had also been left with D Company as a firm base. He had no authority to move ahead, but passed the information to brigade. Whether he also gave them my appreciation of the futility of our task, I have never discovered. In any event, on April 16th we received the welcome news to rejoin the battalion who were now concentrating in the area of Klarenbeek, five miles southeast of Apeldoorn. Now it was our turn to do a little swanning and we set out in fine style using any mode of transportation we could lay our hands on. My three enterprising Platoon commanders quickly 'liberated' scores of bicycles and wheeled off into the blue hunting the Hun. Soon Beardmore and Bolton were locked in a fierce competition to be the first to link up with the 49th British Division. This honour, according to Bolton, belongs to him. But the Regimental Historian gives the prize to Beardmore:

> *A D Company patrol under Lt H E Beardmore, wearying of footslogging, borrowed bicycles from the Dutch Resistance and rode in carefree fashion into the south. Out of the ditch beside the road a balaclavaed head rose and in broad East Anglican shouted "CLOSE". As one man the Patricias replied "SHAVE".*

*It was the joint codeword and the gap between 1st Canadian and
49th British Division had been closed.4*

As soon as we rejoined the battalion we were off again on a night march
through dense woods to a new concentration area five miles south of
Apeldoorn. In the morning, April 17th, the rapid advance continued without
pause, first in TCVs, then a few miles on foot, and then on the backs of
M10 tanks to a village called Harskamp where we made contact with 5th
Armoured Division coming up from the south.

Prisoners continued to surrender in droves; loot continued to pile up; the
Dutch Underground continued to round up their chastened overseers, and
the civilians welcomed us with open arms and tears in their eyes. Infantry
regiments became intermingled with tank regiments, artillery regiments and
units from 5th Armoured Division. And the whole, happy, confused array
madly pursued the scattered remnants of the retreating Hun. It was an
exciting, glorious time to be with the Regiment and I silently thanked old
Field Marshal Fate.

Yet, he still had one final card to play before the game was over. Cpl
Weir, my company clerk, sent me a message that Maj Smith had returned
from leave and would take over command next day. I was to report back
to B Echelon as soon as he arrived, and proceed on leave to the UK.

On April 18th the battalion moved to Barneveld, which 5th Armoured
Division had just cleared, and settled down in their new positions for their
first rest in many days. In the morning, Maj 'Snuffy' Smith appeared and
took over the company. With mixed feelings I left my first real command
and reported back to B Echelon, tired and dirty, but well content with the
job D Company had done.

Next day I caught a ride to Nijmegen, a journey of two hours; then a
long train trip brought me to Calais. (It took 14 hours to cover the 250 miles.)
I was surprised the trains were running at all after the terrible damage inflicted
by both the Germans and ourselves. Leaving Nijmegen, I received another
surprise — the nervy Germans tried to shell our train with long range guns
from across the river! I could hardly believe it. I had just left the front where
the Germans were in a state of disintegration and now the SOBs were trying
one last, cheap shot at me. Some of the heavy shells landed very close,
smashing windows and shaking the old-fashioned coaches. It was much safer
hunting Germans in the forests of Holland and I wished I were back.

Then a big one landed on the track ahead. The train lurched to a stop.
A work party soon appeared to make repairs, and the train shunted onto
another track. The British conducting officer showed not the slightest concern
or even annoyance. I asked him, "Does this happen often?"

"Oh yes, all the time, but their gun barrels are worn out and their range
is not what it used to be."

443

An officers' hotel in Calais put me up for the night and next morning I caught the boat to Folkestone, arriving at 10:00 am; then a speedy train trip, and I was back in London town once again. It seemed like years since I had reported in at CMHQ to see how Gen Crerar was making out with his plans for the Second Front and had dated the daughter of one of his former corps commanders. It had been only 11 months.

Finding lodging in London was just as hopeless a task as ever. I decided to head for Scotland where I knew billets were always available. London could wait until the last day or two of my leave. I fired off a warning telegram to the McArthurs and caught the next train to Barrhead and Neilston.

It is not my intention to reveal any details of the glorious nine days' leave that I spent with friends I had not seen for months. My reader, I am sure, can imagine the happiness they gave me. Following two days with the McArthurs, I headed south again and visited, of all places, Worksop, Welbeck Abbey and Thoresby Hall, the scene of my servitude with CIRU a year earlier. The purpose of my visit was not, however, to call on LCol Mothersill. I had made numerous friends in the area with whom I had deposited my service dress and other kit which I now required for my operations in London.

Next stop was Basingstoke and the Neurological and Plastic Surgery Hospital where I had an outstanding date, some ten months overdue, for a 'face-lifting job'. I apologized for standing them all up all these months and promised to return as soon as the War was over. Unfortunately circumstances again forced me to break this further engagement.

The sequence of these events after the War is involved; in the end, they led to my resigning from the Army and leaving my beloved PPCLI. Briefly, what happened was that when the War was over, the government offered the soldiers of the Canadian Army three choices: volunteer for the Pacific Force to beat the Japs and return to Canada (CFEF); remain overseas in the Army of Occupation (CAOF); or return home with the Regiment in September. I had momentarily had my fill of fighting and decided to opt for the Occupational Forces. But the plastic surgery operations were long overdue. So I got in touch with Basingstoke to make arrangements to have the work done immediately; then I would return to Germany in the Army of Occupation. I found that LCol Gordon, who had done the original surgery, had now returned to Canada and set up a plastic unit in Christie Street Hospital, Toronto, my home town.

Plastic surgery was then a highly developed speciality and I was advised that LCol Gordon should complete the job, as he was the only one who was familiar with my case. It made good medical sense to me and it was also a nice 'perk' to have the hospital near my home. Besides, while I was in Canada, I would still be on strength of my battalion in Germany. After the surgery I would return and resume my duties.

Another consideration was that it was important to me to be posted immediately to one of the Occupational Battalions, get in on the ground floor, so to speak, and probably receive an increase in rank. In fact LCol Clark, who was slated to command one of these battalions, had made me an offer I couldn't refuse. Besides the increase in pay, it would mean a lot to my career, as at that point I fully intended to stay in the Army.

The only way to accomplish these objectives — immediate posting to the Occupational Force, plastic surgery in Toronto, return to Germany — was to get authority from 'High Authority' and I mean really 'High', like 21st Army Group, and CMHQ, for a compassionate return (or leave) to Canada. As I had been fighting Italians and Germans ever since I became of age, I was confident I would not have any trouble with paper soldiers. How wrong I was!

With Patty Crofton's help (he was now the CO of the Patricias and I was 2IC), we secured written approval for my scheme (including some unsolicited laudatory remarks about my service) from commander 2nd Brigade, GOC 1st Canadian Division, GOC 1st Canadian Corps, Head of Medical Services at 1st Echelon at 21st Army Group, and the Senior Officer of 1st Echelon (MGen Burns).

At the very summit, CMHQ, my application was refused. For some unstated reason it did not come within the terms of Overseas Routine Order 3525 and therefore compassionate return could not be recommended. In a fine fit of pique and showing the intemperance of youth (I was still 22), I told all and sundry where they could file Regulation 3525. I decided not to join the Occupational Forces and I remained with the Regiment until it returned to Canada in October.

By that time my surgery could not be put off any longer. After seeing my family for the first time in three years I entered Christie Street Hospital. The operations and convalescence took much longer than I had expected. When I was ready to return to duty I found I had lost the high degree of keenness that is absolutely essential for the professional infantry officer. I retired from the Regiment that I had loved with a consuming passion, and started another career.

Basingstoke, April, 1945

After making arrangements at Basingstoke to return to the hospital after the War, I looked around the place to find the sisters who had been so good to me a year earlier. Most had left for duties in Italy and Northwest Europe. However, as a former inmate, I was able to scrounge 'bed and breakfast' and spent a happy evening telling the new nurses what a model patient I had been.

My leave would not have been complete without a visit to Aldershot, where I knew Col Ware was now commanding a reinforcement group, as a full Colonel. It was a real tonic to see him again and we reminisced about Sicily, southern Italy and the Scouts and Snipers, the most irregular bunch of desperadoes in the Canadian Army (his words).

Finally, London and a wild three days' culmination to my leave — three different hotels because accommodation was so difficult (Strand Palace, Berner's and Park Lane); tea with Charmian Sansom; dinner with the Cartons (at the Café Royal); late nights at the Cocoanut Grove (to keep my membership in good standing); visits to my friendly banker to pay the damage.

London, on April 27th, was on the verge of a monumental blow-out. Everyone acted as though the War was over. Rumours abounded: the Russians were in Berlin; Hitler was dead; Mussolini was dead; Russians and Yanks had linked up.

America had already had one fake celebration. On April 28th my leave was up. I made the mistake of taking my date for dinner to the Strand Palace Hotel, a favourite watering place of the Regiment. No sooner had we sat down at our table than three wild horsemen from the PPCLI galloped in — Maj Sam Potts, Capt Johnny Koensgen and Lt Jack Rachlis (our popular Signals Officer), together with assorted officers from the Seaforths, Eddies and SLI — end of dinner, end of girlfriend, end of leave and almost end of me. I just made the last train at Victoria Station for Folkestone. Even the elements gave me a rude send-off. It actually snowed in London on April 28th!

Early next morning I caught the boat for Calais where I tumbled aboard the train to Nijmegen, weary beyond belief, but anxious to get back to the Regiment. This time the long, cold trip took 19 hours, with numerous delays and detours, but at least we were not shelled. At Nijmegen things were in a considerable state of excitement. As in London, rumours flew about: the War was over (slightly exaggerated); Mussolini was dead (true); Hitler was dead (slightly premature — he shot himself next day). I was frantic to get up to the Regiment but no transport was available. Luckily, I bumped into Capt 'Oop' McPhail, who was also returning from leave and was trying to find a vehicle. 'Oop' was a professional scrounger (compared to my amateur status) and soon produced a jeep. We tore off and landed at the Regiment at 1230 hours, May 1st. Immediately I went forward to D Company located in the little village of Achterveld, about five miles east of Amersfoort.

The situation was absurd. While the enemy were only a few hundred yards in front of us and the company was well dug in around the village, the area was filled with the highest brass imaginable — major generals, brigadiers, full colonels, with their attendant retinue and staff cars — all wandering about in the open, as if D Company were CMHQ.

I saw Snuffy Smith. "Hey, what's going on? I guess the rumours are true. The War is over?"

"Not yet. A truce has been called to supply food to the Dutch who are starving to death. As soon as the supplies get through we're back to war, business as usual."

"What's been happening since I left on April 19th? How's the company?"

"Just great. Not much action but we've had a little excitement. After you left, we moved forward from Barneveld and occupied this village. Then a heavy stonk came over and we had some casualties. I'm afraid two men were killed."

"Sorry to hear that. I hope our gunners gave the Krauts a good pasting."

"They sure as hell did. See that church tower? We have a FOO (artillery forward observation officer) there and he's laid on some pretty good shoots. Interesting story about that tower. Jerry, of course, also used it for an OP. When we arrived, the Germans had gone, but they had left a little surprise for us. A Dutch civilian brought in about 25 pounds of dynamite and several feet of fuse he found in the church."

"Lucky break for you and the FOO. You should give that Dutchman a bronze medal with oak leaves, or better still, a box of rations."

"Don't worry, we already have."

"Any other excitement?"

"Yeah. We've been pestered with Jerry patrols. The silly buggers keep coming in and getting ambushed and killed. The survivors are put in the bag. We've done some patrolling ourselves and netted quite a few prisoners. Harvey Beardmore brought in a batch the other night.

"Then on April 28th, this truce came into effect to get food to the Dutch who are in really bad shape. That afternoon our brigade commander went forward between the lines and met some high-ranking German officers. They were blindfolded and brought back to D Company area to work out how the food would be delivered.

"See that schoolhouse across the street? We set up the place for the conference."

"Incredible! I wish I'd never gone on leave."

"Well, it was unbelievable alright. We had to make all the arrangements: guards and pickets around the school; food and refreshments for the officers; 'Fairfax', our MO, got into the act and let them copy the agreement on his typewriter.

"The place was crawling with VIPs from the Brits, Yanks and Dutch — even a Russian colonel. According to reports he drank the rest of them under the table. After putting away four quick rums he refused a fifth, saying he never drank before dinner!

"Prince Bernhard was there too. So was MGen Freddy de Guingand, Monty's Chief of Staff, and LGen Foulkes.

"The head German was the Judge Advocate of German forces in Holland. Forget his name, but he had a huge nose — probably too much schnapps. We called him Big Nose. Turned out he had no authority to act so Freddy

447

or someone else booted him out and told him to come back in two days with a responsible representative who had authority."

"Cheeky Krauts. They should have their asses kicked. Who the hell do they think won the war?" I interrupted with considerable feeling.

"Well, the conference yesterday, April 30th, was even more impressive, as you can see from the staff cars and red tabs still wandering around. This time, Seyss-Inquart attended on behalf of the Germans. Heard of him?"

"Sure have, the obnoxious bastard. He's the Head Hun in Holland and has given the Dutch a fearful time — flooded their country and cut off food, coal and supplies, not to mention sending thousands to labour camps and worse. It's a wonder some Dutchman didn't shoot him as he limped along the road."*

"You're right, but its too bad you weren't here yesterday. Prince Bernhard did a number on him — parked his Mercedes, that used to belong to Seyss-Inquart, right in front of him, so he had to hobble around it."

"Great. Who else was there?"

"LGen Bedell Smith represented Eisenhower, and all sorts of other high Allied Generals, Air Marshalls and Admirals were present. This time the Allies wouldn't take any more nonsense from the Germans and I believe an agreement was signed. The Dutch will get their food, the Germans won't flood any more land and we sit here on our butts until the relief operation is completed and the truce is over.

As a result of this conference, food and supplies immediately started to flow into stricken Holland by road, rail and barges, in accordance with plans previously made to deal with the emergency. 1st Canadian Army was ready to move 1,600 tons daily into the distressed area. In addition, food packages were dropped by RAF Bomber Command and the US 8th Air Force. This relief continued on a rising scale and, during the period ending on May 8th, over 11 million British and American rations were dropped.[5]

Many accounts have been written of this vast relief operation to save the Dutch from starvation. One of the best was an on-the-scene dispatch sent by John Redfern on Wednesday, May 2nd. It vividly describes the events that happened right in my company area.

FIRST FULL STORY OF THE
HOLLAND FOOD TRUCE
ALLIES MET GERMAN
GOC IN SCHOOLROOM

Food to save three and a half million Dutch citizens from

---

* My revulsion with Seyss-Inquart was shared by the Court that tried him after the War for crimes against the Dutch people. He was hanged.

*starvation is lumbering into Holland this morning on 100 Army
lorries, along roads which, only 24 hours ago, were crammed
with mines or roadblocks, right under the noses of the German
front line troops who are doing nothing about it.*

*More food is to be dropped from the sky for 'first aid' feeding
until the supplies by lorry and barge are distributed. Other food
is to come in by sea.*

*All this is possible because of a 'cease fire' order which now
operates in the Grebbe Line, the front 25 miles south of the
Zuyder Zee...*

*Then a rendezvous was fixed at Achterveld, a front-line village
with a modest school building that deserves to go down in history
as the place where, when the free world was quivering over
Buchenwald and Belsen, Britons, Dutch and Germans discussed
the chances of giving humanity a break.*

*Here the Germans came to meet Gen de Guingand, chief of
staff, 21st Army Group, Gen Galloway, Brig Williams, Prince
Bernhard of the Netherlands, Air Cdre Geddes of the 2nd Tactical
Air Force, Capt Jeffreys, RN and Col Zenkovitch of the Red
Army.*

*For four hours they discussed the Dutchman's stomach, with
an interval in which the visitors wolfed the food served them in
one of the schoolrooms.*[6]

After the War it was found "that there were between 100,000 and 150,000
cases of starvation oedema, with a death rate of 10 per cent in the larger
cities."[7]

It was clear that a major disaster had been narrowly averted. Queen
Wilhelmina herself had foreseen the mounting crisis some months earlier and
had written to King George, Roosevelt and Churchill. She declared
"conditions .... have at present become so desperate that it is abundantly
clear that, if a major catastrophe, the like of which has not been seen in
Western Europe since the Middle Ages, is to be avoided in Holland,
something drastic has to be done now, that is to say before and not after
the liberation of the rest of the country."[8]

It has always been a source of immense pride to me that the negotiations
which led to the relief of the starving Dutch people were held right in my
company area, and that the PPCLI played a part, albeit a small one, in making
the arrangements. As John Redfern said in his article, the "modest school
building .... deserves to go down in history."

After the War, during my journey in 1956 through the battlefields in
Holland, I stopped off at Achterveld to show my wife the schoolhouse where
these conferences had taken place in April 1945. We were happy to find a
bronze plaque on which were recorded the momentous events of those days.

449

When I returned to D Company on May 1st, 1945, I found that Field Marshal Fate had not forgotten me. In Part II Orders appeared an entry that my captaincy had been confirmed, effective January 28th, 1945. I also saw another entry that gave me considerable pride and satisfaction. My RMC senior, Sam Potts, who had inspired me to join the PPCLI and who had served the Regiment continuously since the landing in Sicily, in many capacities, always with gallantry and determination, until he was seriously wounded in December 1944, had been confirmed as a major.*

No wonder, I thought, that he was in such fine form when he, Johnny Koensgen and Jack Rachlis had barged in on my date at the Strand Palace in London.

It was a fact that promotion in the Regiment, in the field, was seldom automatic or given just on the basis of seniority, despite my fears of some senior lieutenant coming back and taking away my third pip. Only if all other things were equal was seniority a factor.

No one could argue with the principle of promotion on merit in the field. What rankled, however, was that a few officers who had seen little action, or none at all, were promoted in Canada, England and other non-operational areas and then appeared at the Regiment as confirmed captains and majors. The effect on morale has already been described; suffice it to say that to advance from a junior lieutenant to a confirmed major in the PPCLI, in the field, was recognized as a considerable achievement, Germans and 'base' majors to the contrary, notwithstanding.

As I continued to glance through the Part II Orders issued while I had been on leave (something every conscientious officer was supposed to do if time and the Hun permitted), I found another entry that saddened me. Capt A M (Andy) Campbell had gone down the line and been struck off strength. He, like Sam Potts, had landed in Sicily and had served continuously ever since. Wounded in March 1944, he remained on duty and went on to command a company in the fierce Hitler Line battle. "By the end of the day Capt A M Campbell, who led B Company courageously and well, was the only officer of the rifle companies on his feet."[9]

I admired Andy's cheerful attitude and apparent unconcern when the enemy was doing his best to terminate his record of continuous service with the Regiment. To me, he was a real professional soldier. His departure meant that until Sam Potts returned, only one combatant officer was left who had climbed ashore in Sicily on that far off day in July 1943 and had served continuously ever since, except for wounds — Maj Patty Crofton.

The immense contribution, largely unrecognized, made by this gallant officer to the proud record of the Regiment has been referred to all too briefly.

---

* He also received the DSO for his outstanding leadership.

Patty was a tower of strength in the Regiment and a very popular officer. One indication of his qualities is that he was entrusted with command of the Regiment from June 7th until the Regiment's final parade in Winnipeg in October (except for a few days in June when LCol A H Fraser had temporary command). This period included the difficult tasks of disarming the Germans and concentrating them for removal to Germany, maintaining the morale and efficiency of the Regiment during the long months of inactivity in Holland, and finally bringing the Regiment home. In these demanding duties he was ably assisted by Capt Eagan Chambers, MC as adjutant; but without Patty Crofton's common sense, steady hand and constant good humour, I doubt if the Regiment would have survived. Through some incredible blundering or plain stupidity on the part of the staff, Patty remained a major and was not given his rightful rank of lieutenant colonel. Not once did Patty ever complain, but it annoyed me then and still does.

Before I return to Achterveld and the few remaining days of the War, it is proper, and indeed imperative, that I refer to the service of one other officer whose name has appeared in these pages — Capt J A McLeod (Jimmie the Pay), our popular paymaster. He joined the Regiment on January 27th, 1942 and served continuously until September 25th, 1945, without any break whatsoever — surely a unique record. Jimmie was a banker by trade and certainly understood figures, but he also took an interest in the men of the Regiment and was often an unofficial observer on schemes and operations. He knew more about tactics and handling of men than many officers. His familiar 'Geez' — followed by some criticism of the operation in question, or its execution, was often more to the point than the remarks of the umpires. As he strutted about in the field, he could easily have been mistaken for the corps commander if he had had a couple of red tabs. He was also a mean saxophone player.

I never agreed with his sales pitch for Victory Bonds and almost came to blows with him on that account. But he always disarmed me with his, "Geez, I gotta do it." I am happy to say that, according to my records, the long and faithful service of Jimmie was recognized by the award of an MID. (If, perchance, this is not the case, it should be.)

I make no apology for interrupting my story to say these few words about some of the Regimental personalities, as I knew them. After all, the very essence of a Regiment is the individual officer; it is he who breathes life and character into the Regiment and by his heroism and selfless devotion sets the standards by which it is judged.

The last days of the War in Holland may be quickly told. On May 2nd, our D Company wireless picked up a news broadcast that the German forces in Italy had surrendered. I was happy that our old comrades in the 8th Army had at last "debouched into the Po and dealt the Hun a mightly blow."

451

Yet I was not sure how I felt about not being with them in their great moment of victory. It all seemed so far away and so long ago.

On May 3rd at 5:30 pm, I received a message from BHQ that the truce was over and that the Germans would start offensive action at 0500 hours next morning. "My God," I thought, "those crazy Krauts will not be satisfied until we've killed or captured the whole Wehrmacht in Holland." Now I definitely wished I were back in Italy.

At 0500 hours D Company stood to, ready to repulse a last German charge to Valhalla.

Not a shot was fired. We peered out of our trenches and saw Jerry digging away as if he was building the Siegfried Line all over again. We just let him keep on digging.

Then at 8:30 pm Pte Favel, our signaller, whose prompt, brave action at the Ijssel River had accounted for five Germans and, incidentally, saved my life, picked up this message: "German forces in Northwest Germany, Denmark and Holland have surrendered to Field Marshal Mongomery's forces. All hostilities will cease at 0800 hours next morning (May 5th)."

Official word came through at 11:00 pm — "CEASE FIRE tomorrow, May 5th, at 0800 hours."

The normally stolid Dutch villagers went absolutely berserk, rushed out of their homes and overwhelmed us and each other with their long pent-up emotions. But the War was not over until 8:00 am next morning. I feared that the Germans, having disappointed us after the truce, would now make a final insane attack to avenge their dead Führer. We quietly manned our defences and waited for the time to run out.

The drama of those last few hours has been captured in many writings. My diary simply notes that I was sceptical; no one, except the villagers went mad with excitement, and business carried on 'as per usual'.

A letter written in the evening is more demonstrative:

2300 hours
4 May, 1945
D Coy, PPCLI

Dear Mother
This might be a letter worth saving. Certainly it is one I shall re-read in after years when World War II has been largely forgotten.

This evening, at 2030 hours, my wireless picked up a BBC broadcast: "German forces in NW Germany, Denmark, and Holland, have surrendered to Field Marshal Montgomery's forces." I was in my Coy HQ, in a quaint Dutch house in a village in the front lines. Hardly was the news out than the streets were alive with 'flying Dutchmen', flying not from the Hun but to the town square, where they shouted, cried and embraced. This was the end of almost five years' oppression, and they had a right to be happy.

The troops were different. Many times before we had seen wild celebrations and passed by the cheering crowds, as we carried on to bat the Hun once more across another river. And so we were sceptical, suspicious. Surely this was not the end. Then later, at 2300 hours, official word came down through Army channels. Cease fire tomorrow, May 5th, at 0800 hours.

Then the sky was lit with fireworks, not from us in the forward companies, but from the 'base wallahs'. For us, our job continues 'till tomorrow at 0800 hours. Our thoughts are only — what happens tomorrow at 0800? Will Jerry put in a final suicide attack tonight? So we are not celebrating. But each one of us feels in his heart, firstly, I am a lucky devil; secondly, well, it's a job well done.

The War Diary, laconic to the end, records that "All companies were warned and the news was very quietly received by the troops, who, with no display, remained at their post and carried out their normal frontline duties."[10]

According to my records, the Nominal roll of the Patricia Officers at the time of the Cease Fire was as follows:

COMMANDING OFFICER *LCol R P Clark DSO; SECOND-IN-COMMAND Maj S A Cobbett; ADJUTANT Capt A M Mills; BATTLE ADJUTANT Capt J R Koensgen MC; MEDICAL OFFICER Maj G C Fairfield; CHAPLAIN Hon Capt G A Meiklejohn; PAYMASTER Capt J A McLeod; QUARTERMASTER Capt J H Horton; CARRIER PLATOON Capt W H J Stutt; ANTI-TANK PLATOON Capt E D McPhail; TRANSPORT OFFICER W E Harrington MC; SIGNALS OFFICER Lt J Rachlis; INTELLIGENCE OFFICER Lt J V Spurr; SCOUT AND SNIPER PLATOON Lt J A Shirkie; PIONEER PLATOON Lt H F Pragnell; MORTAR PLATOON Lt E A Shone.*

RIFLE COMPANIES *Maj P D Crofton, Maj J M D Jones, Maj R W Potts DSO, Maj A S Ennis-Smith; Capt J C Newlands, Capt E E Chambers MC, Capt G F Chapin, Capt C S Frost, Lt D Munro, Lt A D Fairburn, Lt H E Dahlquist, Lt A F Tucker, Lt G W Grant, Lt J E Schmitz, Lt E J Berryman, Lt J M Millar, Lt D A Armstrong, Lt C M Pyne, Lt W D L Roach DSO, Lt E R Sharpe, Lt H E Beardmore, Lt R S Huestis, Lt W W Bolton, Lt A M McKinnon MC.*

At 0800 hours, May 5th, Maj 'Snuffy' Smith and I quietly clasped hands.

No words passed between us. We knew, without saying, what each of us had endured on that long, hard road to victory. We were thankful to have survived.

In the same quiet way, I shared this moment with the members of company headquarters — CSM Milko, still the typical, tough sergeant major, Pte Norton, my faithful batman, Pte Favel, the signaller, and all the others. Soon the platoon commanders appeared — McKinnon, Beardmore and Bolton — and things began to liven up.

Then an explosion rocked our house. "Christ," growled CSM Milko, "the lousy Krauts are starting the war all over again." We rushed outside. Down the road lay the remnants of a jeep and two staff officers. A sentry came running toward us. "I tried to stop them, but they wouldn't listen. They wheeled around the road block, tore down the road and were blown up on a mine."

I was stunned — but thankful that the bodies were not those of my men. A few months earlier the untimely end of two staff officers would not have bothered me greatly. It was different now. The War was over. Not even bumbling staff officers deserved this fate. As I gazed at the torn remains I felt pity for the dead officers and their next of kin. Field Marshal Fate had exacted a dreadful atonement for all the blunders the staff had perpetrated on the fighting soldiers.

Later that day, my classmate, Lt R S (Bob) Huestis, called around to say goodbye. He was leaving to become ADC to the corps commander. I was glad that his long, faithful service had at last been recognized in some way. He had joined the Regiment on May 25th, 1944 just after the Hitler Line and had seen his share of action in the bloody battles that followed. It will be remembered that Bob was at least a year younger than I and had to wait that extra year in Canada, until he was 20. He looked much younger than his age and it must have been difficult for him to control hard-bitten, old veterans twice his years. But that he did and earned the respect and affection of all who knew him.

Messages of congratulations poured in from all quarters — Gen Eisenhower, Field Marshal Montgomery, Gen Crerar, The Queen of the Netherlands, The Prime Minister of Canada, and many others.

The most warming and welcome of all came from the original Patricia himself, Brig Hamilton Gault: "You have magnificently maintained the traditions of your Regiment on the battlefields of Sicily, Italy and Germany and have added proud laurels to your Colours. God bless you all."[11]

Our War was over. But our duties were far from finished.

454

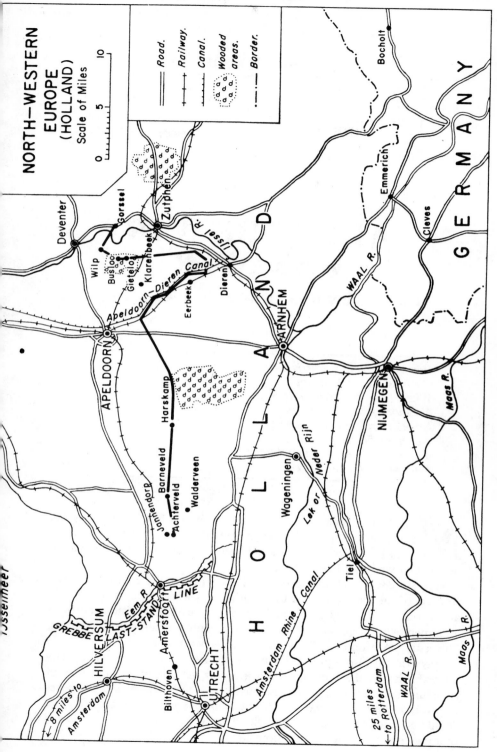

Map #8

NORTH—WESTERN
EUROPE
(HOLLAND)
Scale of Miles

Road.
Railway.
Canal.
Wooded areas.
Border.

IJsselmeer

Deventer

Gorssel

Zutphen

Wilp

Buslo

Gietelo

Klarenbeek

IJssel R.

APELDOORN

Apeldoorn—Dieren Canal

Eerbeek

Dieren

Harskamp

ARNHEM

Jannendorp

Barneveld

Achterveld

Walderveen

Wageningen

Lek or Neder Rijn

NIJMEGEN

GREBBE

HILVERSUM

Eem R.

LAST-STAND LINE

Amersfoort

Bilthoven

UTRECHT

8 miles to Amsterdam

Amsterdam Rhine Canal

Tiel

25 miles to Rotterdam

WAAL R.

Maas R.

Maas R.

WAAL R.

Emmerich

Cleves

Bocholt

GERMANY

H   O   L   L   A   N   D

455

Chapter XXXIII

WHEN THE WAR WAS OVER

May 6 to October 5, 1945

When this bloody war is over
Oh how happy I will be
When I put my civie clothes on
No more soldiering for me
No more rising at reveille
No more filling out a pass
You can tell the Sergeant Major
I am going home first class

May 6th was Sunday and a quiet service was held at BHQ by our Chaplain, Capt G A Meiklejohn, who gave a moving sermon — we who had survived should feel humble when we thought of better men who had been killed.

May 8th dawned clear and bright. In contrast to the cool breezes and showers of the past few days, the weather was warm, almost hot. It was an auspicious start to an unforgettable day in the lives of the Patricia officers and men who were about to enter the Dutch cities of Amersfoort, Hilversum, Amsterdam, Haarlem and Bloemendaal.

May 8th was also a proud day in the history of the Regiment. Exactly 30 years earlier, the Patricias had withstood the poison gas and fury of the Hun at Frezenberg, at tremendous cost — ten officers and 392 other ranks. How befitting it was that on the anniversary of this sacred day, we should be entering the last stronghold of the Hun to disarm him and send him packing to his devastated homeland.

May 8th was also the official date of the end of the German War on every front (VE Day). That day and May 9th had been declared public holidays.

In a little red schoolhouse at Rheims, France, the headquarters of Gen Eisenhower, the German Chief of Staff, Col Gen Gustav Jodl, had signed the capitulation of all German armed forces at 2:41 pm on Monday, May 7th.

Germany had announced the news first. The German foreign minister, Count von Krosigk, had broadcast over the Flensburg Radio:

> *As leading minister of the Reich government whom the admiral of the fleet has appointed for dealing with war tasks, I turn at this tragic moment of our history to the German nation. After a heroic fight of almost six years of incomparable hardness, Germany has succumbed to the overwhelming power of her enemies.*
>
> *To continue the war would only mean senseless bloodshed and futile disintegration. The government, which has a feeling of responsibility for the future of its nation, was compelled to act on the collapse of all physical and material forces and to demand of the enemy the cessation of hostilities.[1]*

The Count was a little mixed up as to who was demanding what. The Germans were not in a position to demand anything: the Allies had imposed unconditional surrender on them. However, later in his speech, the foreign minister abandoned his rather heroic, strident tones, and got down to reality:

> *No one must be under illusions about the severity of the terms to be imposed on the German people by our enemies. We must face our fate squarely and unquestioningly. Nobody can be in any doubt that the future will be difficult for each one of us and will exact sacrifices from us in every sphere of life.*
>
> *We must accept this burden and stand loyally by the obligations we have undertaken. But we must not despair and fall into mute resignation. Once again we must let ourselves stride along the path through the dark future. From the collapse of the past let us preserve and save one thing, unity.*
>
> *In our nation, justice shall be the supreme law and the guiding principle. We must recognize law as a basis of all relations between nations. We must recognize it and respect it from the inner conviction. Respect for treaties will be as sacred as the aim of our nation to belong to the European family of nations, as a member of which we want to mobilize all human, moral and material forces in order to heal the dreadful wounds which war has caused.*
>
> *Then we may hope that the atmosphere of hatred which today surrounds Germany all over the world will give place to a spirit*

457

of reconciliation among nations, without which the world cannot recover.

When we read the translation of this broadcast in the *Maple Leaf*, we were not impressed with the pious hopes of the foreign minister about reconciliation. As Norton said, "They've dug their own grave. Now they'd better hop into it."

Looking back over a span of 40 years, the last few words of Count von Krosigk were prophetic beyond even his wildest dreams. Too bad for Germany that he had not replaced the itinerant wine salesman, Von Ribbentrop, sooner.

In London, Lord Vansittart stated in the House of Lords that he wanted January 30th, the anniversary of Hitler's accession to power, to be observed in Germany as a day of national repentance and atonement.

In Lisbon, Portugal, memorial services for Hitler were held in both the Catholic and Lutheran churches for the German community. The chaplain had the people in tears as he spoke about their fallen Führer who had perished in a knightly fashion against the advancing flood of Bolshevism. "Today," he said, "is a bitter Sunday. If the Germans pray hard enough, the tide will one day be driven back and the great deeds of the Führer and the people of this generation will be matched by those who come after them."[2]

While Churchill prepared to make his historic broadcast on May 8th, the Patricias were on their way through the German lines to help liberate western Holland.

At 0700 hours LCol Clark with the IO, Lt Spurr, an interpreter and DRs from each company set off as an advance party to recce the area the battalion would occupy. The companies followed at 0800 hours.

In subsequent years, a friendly controversy would develop between the PPCLI and the Seaforths as to who was the first to enter Amsterdam. LCol Clark always claimed that honour for the Patricias. Let him describe the occasion in his own words:

> *I started off about dawn on May 8th to contact the German commanders in Western Holland. The enemy, fully-armed and still manning the Grebbe Line, seemed to be extremely surprised to see an Allied vehicle passing through their fortifications.*
>
> *Upon arriving at Amsterdam early in the morning the city appeared to be deserted but continuing down the main street the people suddenly recognized an Allied vehicle. There were a few shouts, then heads began to pop out of windows. Before we got to the end of this long main street it seemed as though the whole population of the city was blocking our path. It took us considerable time to push through to meet the German commanders in the Haarlem area.*

From all appearances no Allied soldiers had been along this main road from the south until my small party arrived. I only mention this to back up the claim that the Regiment was the first Allied force to enter Amsterdam.[3]

The triumphal entry into western Holland on that glorious day in May, 1945 is best described by an officer, who wrote:

Every village, street and house was bedecked with the red, white and blue Dutch flags and orange streamers, which in the brilliant sunlight made a gay scene. The Dutch people lined the roads and streets in thousands to give us a great welcome. Wherever the convoy had to slow up for a road block or a bridge, hundreds of people waved, shouted and even fondled the vehicles. When the convoy reached the outskirts of Amsterdam it lost all semblance of a military column. A vehicle would be unable to move because of civilians surrounding it, climbing on it, throwing flowers, bestowing handshakes, hugs and kisses. One could not see the vehicle or trailer for legs, arms, heads and bodies draped all over it. The enthusiasm of the crowd seemed even to have infected German soldiers, for in many cases they, moving in the opposite direction in wagons or on foot, waved and grinned. Boy scouts as well as civilian police and resistance fighters had turned out in large numbers to attempt to control the crowds and to guide the vehicles to their destinations.

The Dutch people whom we saw looked healthier than we expected to find them but most of them had sunken eyes betraying months of insufficient food. It was said that there were many thousands in Amsterdam not out to welcome us because they were too feeble from hunger to move into the streets.[4]

As we pushed our way through the crowds of delirious Dutch citizens, we threw them our packets of Sweet Caporal cigarettes, chocolate bars and all the rations we carried in our vehicles. They responded by throwing into our vehicles flowers and leaflets proclaiming their joy of Freedom.

The hardships we had endured on the long road to victory were suddenly given meaning. The reason we had gone to war suddenly became clear. It had all been worthwhile.

On our arrival at Haarlem, the Burgemeester received the CO at the Town Hall, and the battalion moved into comfortable billets in Bloemendaal, on the northern outskirts of the city.

D Company officers were quartered in a fine private home that had been occupied by German paratroopers. The night before our arrival they had staged a wild, drunken party and torn the inside apart, smashing furniture, slashing beautiful paintings, firing bullets into the ceiling. When the owners,

459

Mr and Mrs Dekker, appeared they broke down and wept. Their beautiful home was a shambles. We cleaned up the mess as best we could and helped them move in again.

That night we had a small party of our own and learned from the Dekkers about some of the atrocities of the German occupation. We soon understood why many of the Dutch people, particularly the Underground, wanted to take revenge on the German troops who had occupied their homes, stolen their cars and bicycles (almost a sacred item of the Dutch), denied them food, coal and medical supplies.

Next day we set about our enormous task of gathering up a division of Germans, disarming them, and locating and itemizing enemy dumps of food, supplies and equipment of all kinds. For their own protection against the Dutch, we allowed the Germans to keep their arms until we could put them 'in the cooler' at Ijmuiden and send them marching on their flat feet over the causeway across the Ijsselmeer, into northern Germany.

While this process was going on, Germans walked about the town in full battle gear, armed to the teeth — Schmeissers, Lugers, P38s, potato mashers (grenades) and belts of ammunition draped around their shoulders. Needless to say, not all of these fine weapons were properly inventoried and stored in official dumps for the next war. Some found their way into the Regimental museum while others ended up in unofficial depositories.

How to deal with these beaten members of the once arrogant master race presented quite a problem. Few of us had any experience dealing with Germans except as targets on the battlefield. Obviously this approach was a little too severe (although not a few thought it was just the treatment they deserved). On the other hand, any show of leniency would be taken as weakness on our part. Once again the staff showed it was equal to the challenge and produced an excellent memorandum, the introduction to which is reproduced below:

All Officers
First Cdn Army
ATTITUDE TOWARDS GERMANS
IN OFFICIAL CONTACTS
1.   The war in Europe is over but the German has not changed overnight. To adopt a lenient or familiar attitude toward him now is to betray the sacrifice of our dead. Such an attitude will be regarded by the Germans with secret contempt and as a sign of weakness. Their punishment must be severe and will not be affected by personal feelings of sympathy or pity. Few officers will have had any previous experience in dealing with Germans and the following instructions defining the attitude to be adopted and the methods to be employed are therefore given to assist them.

2. It is extremely important that the contacts between Allied officers and Germans should leave no doubt in the German mind that the controlling authorities mean business.

3. In some cases these contacts may take the form of interrogation, interviews with, or issuing orders to German officers by Allied officers. When these contacts take place, it is essential that they impress upon the Germans the efficiency of Allied staffs and the iron determination of the occupying powers to make control complete and inescapable. This can only be achieved if the Allied officer concerned establishes a complete mastery over the person with whom he is dealing.

Another problem was how to cope with the starving Dutch population who surrounded our kitchens, begging for food. We gave them all we could spare, but it was not nearly enough. Finally, we actually had to wire in the company area to protect ourselves and our rations.

Civilians and German soldiers streamed in and out of company head-quarters at all hours of the day and night, telling us their problems and seeking instructions: "Never have so many people, in such a short time, asked so many stupid questions."[5]

On May 11th, D Company left its fine accommodation in Bloemendaal and moved to Noordwijkerhout to gather in a Luftwaffe battalion that had been converted to coastal artillery. In their blue airforce uniforms, they looked a little incongruous as they emerged from deep dug-outs and pill boxes strung along the sea coast. They were, however, quite friendly and joked about how their fat Reichsmarschall had banished them to such demeaning duties for not stopping the RAF. The Oberst in charge gave me a smart military salute and said: "Compliments of 409 Coastal Defence Regiment. Ready to receive your orders, Sir." I ignored the salute (as directed by our Orders), went down to his bunker and received a nominal roll of his regiment and a list of stores in the area. As I turned to leave he coughed and said, "May I ask the captain's indulgence. When do we join forces and fight the Russians?"

I ticked him off for being so disrespectful of our gallant Russian Allies. How could I foresee that the Oberst had a point? But, contrary to orders (I will now admit), I shared a cognac with my former enemy. After a drink or two he relaxed and turned out to be quite a decent type. He was strictly an air force officer and was mortified when Hitler made him transfer to coastal defence. He never wanted to fight the British — only the Bolsheviks.

Another German unit we took over in this area was a Field Hospital, complete with nurses, located in a former Insane Asylum. Acting in typical fashion, the Germans had simply opened the gates when they took over the institution in 1940, and had let the inmates run loose in the countryside. When we arrived, a Dutch doctor, de Witt Hamer, who was formerly in charge

461

of the institution, was trying to round up his patients. He was beside himself. He wanted us to lock up the entire German medical personnel, including nurses, for the rest of their days and let them feed on nothing but bread and water, partly to atone for their sins. In his view the Germans were more deranged than his former inmates.

The good doctor insisted that I stay in his home and meet his three lovely daughters. It was an offer I did not deny myself the pleasure of accepting.

In common with so many Dutch families, the de Witt Hamers had sheltered Allied airmen and escaped prisoners of war in their home, under the very noses of the Germans. They offered me a bottle of champagne if I could locate the hiding place. A thorough search from *"der winkle to der calder"* did not reveal a clue and finally I gave up. The doctor took me to a bedroom, pushed a panel, and a small stairway appeared leading to a fair-sized room, fully furnished with bed, tables and even electric lights. As well as being used by Allied escapees, the room was sometimes occupied by his son Jim, whose ostensible occupation was a doctor, but who spent most of his time as head of the Dutch Underground in the area. While I hadn't won the champagne, it was opened just the same to celebrate the liberation.

And so the days passed by — gathering in Germans and restoring the Dutch to their rightful possessions. Other towns were 'liberated' — Noordwijk-on-the-Sea, Zandvoort, Lisse and Sassenheim. At each place we were welcomed profusely by the Burgemeester in the presence of the entire populace and afterwards attended receptions, parties, dinners and dances. In Sassenheim, I met an exceptional family, the Boots. The father, Phil, had been a prosperous bulb grower, had travelled extensively in Canada and had established a company in the States. Like the de Witt Hamers, he had hidden Allied airmen, and his son was active in the Underground. He also had two beautiful daughters.

The friendships I formed with these fine Dutch families, the Dekkers in Bloemendaal, the de Witt Hamers in Noordwijkerout and the Boots in Sassenheim, were to last a lifetime. During my tour of Europe in 1956, I had the great pleasure and satisfaction of seeing them restored to their former positions and estates, if not entirely to good health. While they would never admit it, the deprivations caused by the Germans had left their mark.

During the emotional 'Return of the Liberators' to Amsterdam, in 1980, I was happy to visit the children and meet their children. Dear old Mrs Boot was still alive and clearly remembered those exciting days of long ago. She gave me a shiny guilder coin that I will always treasure.

Again, in 1985, during my Pilgrimage to Apeldoorn, I called on Mimi de Witt Hamer and spent a pleasant afternoon with her sharing fond memories.

By 1st June, 1945 our job of concentrating Germans was pretty well finished. But now a great change was about to overtake the Regiment. What the Germans had failed to do, the requirements of peace would quickly accomplish. The Regiment began to break up.

LCol Clark was transferred to command the RWR (The Royal Winnipeg Rifles) in the Canadian Army of Occupation. It was a sad day when we gathered to say goodbye to our respected CO. "Thus passed from Regimental service the officer who, together with LCol Ware, had been the outstanding Patricia battle commander of the Second World War. His service had been almost continuous and whenever he had led the battalion in battle he showed the firm, sure touch of a born soldier."[6]

Toward the end of June, other officers followed LCol Clark to the RWR, including Maj A S Ennis-Smith, Capt E D McPhail and Capt W H J Stutt. Meanwhile, officers for the Far East Force started to leave — Maj R W Potts DSO, Capt J R Koensgen MC, Capt A M Mills and Capt G F Chapin. Others left for new employment: Capt A G Robinson MC, Capt J H Horton, Lt W D L Roach DSO, Lt J V Sprurr, Lt A D Fairburn.

As mentioned, Maj P D Crofton took command of the battlion on June 7th and Capt E E Chambers MC was appointed adjutant. Lt W W Bolton became IO. I was pleased to see him get this appointment as he was an efficient, conscientious officer who had served me well on the Ijssel River. Then on June 26th I became acting Second-in-Command of the battalion, which position I held until July 28th when Maj G S Lynch, who had recently returned to the battalion after a long absence, took over.

By the end of June, the exodus of the Old Guard was complete. It was a tremendous blow to me to see all my friends except Patty and Egan depart. Nevertheless, like them, I soldiered on with the remnants of the old battalion and the newcomers, patiently waiting for the Regiment's return to Canada.

In the meantime, the battalion had moved from Bloemendaal to Bilthoven, mid-way between Amersfoort and Utrecht. It was destined to remain there from June 20th to September 4th, when it moved to a transit camp at Nijmegen. During this period I had an opportunity to write a precis on the History of the Regiment which was printed and circulated to all ranks. The purpose of the work was given in the Introduction as follows:

> *This precis is an unofficial recording of the PPCLI's battle experiences. Dates, names and figures are as correct as possible. Now that Victory in Europe has been achieved, the Regiment will presently be proceeding home. Many old members have already left. This precis is therefore a refresher for the older members and a source of information for the newer ones. All ranks will be familiar with the fine Battle Record of the Regiment.*

Whether my injunction to all ranks was duly observed I have no idea. No doubt some of the copies suffered the same fate that befell the Top Secret document covering security measures for the move from Italy to Holland. Actually it was not a bad effort, given the time and information then available, but I am glad I included a disclaimer as to the correctness of some of the dates and names. Hopefully those errors have now been rectified.

In August, I took two parties to see what was left of the Ruhr Valley. The visit began at Hilden, where my father had been stationed after the First War as part of the Occupation Forces. From there we visited Bonn (site of a University and Beethoven's home) and Cologne where the only building left standing was the famous cathedral. Apparently God had a presence on both sides of the conflict.

Our tour continued through the industrial cities of Dusseldorf, Essen, Duisberg, Wesel, Emmerich and Cleve, but there was very little to see. The whole area was nothing but a pile of rubble, twisted steel and cratered roads, clogged with an army of lost souls. My diary records the scene:

> The atmosphere of death, desperation and destruction is fatiguing. I've seen enough. The roads are choked with Germans wandering aimlessly about, carrying tattered briefcases and pushing prams containing their entire belongings — a beaten-looking mob, a nation of tramps.

In August, I also took a trip back to Hulshout, Belgium, to visit Mathilde Van Baelen and her mother. I was given a warm welcome by the entire village and left them with some much needed supplies.

On August 15th, we learned that Japan had quit after the devastation of the atomic bomb. We didn't quite appreciate the fearful power of this new weapon, but neither did a great many other people. Our main reaction was: The Far East Force have had a lucky break. Maybe we'll get home sooner now! The day is hardly mentioned in the War Diary: "Today is the long awaited VJ Day. In celebration, today and tomorrow are holidays for the battalion."[7]

We didn't need any more holidays. It had been one long, three months' holiday, and we wanted to go home.

On August 29th, the 1st Division held its last parade and marched past MGen H W Foster CBE, DSO, our divisional commander. The mighty 'Red Patch Devils' had passed into history.

Finally, on September 4th, our fondest desire was fulfilled. On that date the battalion began its long journey home and moved by TCV to a transit camp at Nijmegen. There we remained for a week getting the men documented and preparing them for their eventual return to civie life.

On September 10th, we left by train for Ostend; then across the Channel to Dover aboard the *Princess Irene* and finally to a repatriation camp between Esher and Cobham.

Five days of embarkation leave allowed only enough time to say goodbye to the Cartons in London, and see some of my old haunts — Cocoanut Grove, Park Lane Hotel, Strand Palace, Café Royal, Fischer's Restaurant.

On returning to the battalion, I found it was busily preparing for an inspection by Lady Patricia, our much beloved Colonel-in-Chief. But the Regiment was now the Patricias in name only. All the officers who had served in Sicily and southern Italy had gone except Patty Crofton and me. The ranks were now filled with westerners from other units, even engineers and artillery, some of whom had the nerve to go around in their distinctive head gear and flashes.[8] Thanks to RSM Gardner, who had joined the Regiment in Holland, these newcomers were 'persuaded' to put up PPCLI flashes and badges for the parade.

On September 19th the battalion was drawn up on a parade ground in Esher, every man wearing the insignia of the PPCLI. The Regiment marched past its Colonel-in-Chief in fine style and advanced in review order. Afterwards she met the officers in the mess. It was my one and only meeting with this wonderful Lady in whose name the Regiment had fought a hundred battles in two World Wars. I was proud to be a Patricia and happy at last that I had decided to return home with the Regiment.

On September 26th, at 0200 hours, we embarked at Southampton on the *Isle de France*, a large ship of 43,800 tons, carrying 10,000 troops — the equivalent of half a division. The accommodation was crowded, with only two meals a day, but no one complained. Canada was practically in sight.

The ship left Southampton at 1500 hours and arrived at Halifax at 1600 hours, October 1st, after a fast crossing of only five days. As we entered the harbour, every ship in port greeted us with long blasts on their whistles, and fire boats threw columns of water high into the air. The troops, all 10,000 of us rushed to the side of the ship closest to the docks to get a better look at the town. Suddenly the boat started to list heavily to port. Someone yelled, "We're going to capsize."

Then a firm voice came over the loudspeakers. "Pay attention. Please go to your boat stations and remain there until further orders."

A short while later the boat anchored in the harbour, where the city was visible from all sides, and the troops were allowed to resume their activities.

Then another announcement: "It has come to the attention of the Captain that many of the troops have contraband in their kit — pistols, bayonets, grenades, machine guns and other weapons. Anyone possessing such items will immediately throw them into the harbour."

The order was greeted with howls of derision. No one was going to part with a P38 he had risked his neck to acquire in some bloody battle in Italy. One lance corporal, however, finally weakened. He solemnly marched to

465

the side of the ship and tossed a grenade into the harbour. Fortunately, it did not explode, otherwise it might have compromised the importation of tons of enemy weapons and equipment that now rest in many private museums across the country.

We were then told that we would remain in the harbour, on board ship, until the next day, when we would come alongside and be loaded into trains bound for our final destination. No one was to leave the ship and only VIPs were allowed aboard.

My home was now in Saint John. Unknown to me, my family had come to Halifax to see me before I was whisked out west to Winnipeg for the final dispersal of the battalion. Had I wanted to stay in Saint John I would have had to join an eastern Regiment, which was quite unthinkable.

As we were stuck on board until next morning, a small party seemed in order to celebrate our safe deliverance to a Canadian port. The party was nicely under way when a firm hand clasped my shoulder. I would have known that grip anywhere — it was my father!

The full story of how he had finagled his way aboard, I only found out much later, under pain of death not to reveal the secret until criminal prosecution was statute barred.

The story was that when he learned he could not get aboard and I could not leave the ship, his old infantry training with The Royal Newfoundlanders came quickly to the fore — use camouflage and put up a smoke screen. Through his banking connections, he met the Harbour Master, an old soldier from the First War. Father explained the trouble he had taken to come to Halifax and see me. Now some silly regulation threatened the entire operation. Could not the Harbour Master make an exception and let him aboard, or get me off?

No, he could not allow father, as such, aboard the ship, but father could temporarily become the Harbour Master (without pay) if he had the Harbour Master's Identity Card.

The switch of identity was quickly made and father, alias the Harbour Master, marched down to the docks, with his fedora well pulled down and his coat up around his ears. Flashing the pass at the operator of the Harbour launch, he was quickly taken to the *Isle de France*, presumably on an inspection.

Patty Crofton was so impressed with this fine tactical move that he gave me permission (without prejudice to having me arrested if caught) to see if I could smuggle myself off the boat for the evening.

With father's disguise working perfectly, he hauled me into the launch as if I were some spy about to be incarcerated in the Halifax gaol. In minutes, I was in the embrace of my family in the Hotel Lord Nelson, after an absence of three years. It was the only occasion in my service when I was tempted to go AWL. But I didn't. Father smuggled me back on the ship and I left for Winnipeg the next day.

On October 5th, the trains bearing the PPCLI pulled into the railway station at Winnipeg where an immense crowd had assembled. In the presence of the Founder of the Regiment, Brig Hamilton Gault, Brig Colquhoun (who had helped me get overseas) and other distinguished Patricias, the Regiment tried to form up for the final parade.

The last words of my story belong, as they should, to the adjutant of that parade: "The Battalion simply melted away into the arms of its welcomers."9

GOODBYE WONDERFUL HOLLAND

By C.S. Frost, May 1985

Score and words for 'Goodbye Wonderful Holland' composed by the author and sung at final gathering of Veterans – 1985.

469

PREFACE
TO
THE PILGRIMAGES

The War had a profound effect on the lives of those who survived, particularly those who saw combat action. Many a soldier, trapped in a burning tank, assaulting an enemy pill box, caught in a savage barrage, lying horribly wounded in an open field, called fervently on his Maker to save him from imminent death or dismemberment. In desperation, some even offered to make a deal with the Almighty, if only they would be spared — I promise to become a priest; I pledge never again to touch drink; I vow to lead a pure life, and so on. Some actually honoured these promises. At least I know a few who did.

My vow was a little different. Not being entirely sold on the efficacy of prayer, I simply vowed that if I survived the War, I would return to the battlefields and the graves of my comrades, at the first opportunity. It gives me no little pride to say I have honoured my covenant several times over; the story is told in the forthcoming chapters. But first, a word of explanation.

I made four pilgrimages in all.

The first, in 1956, was a very personal tour when, accompanied by my wife, I touched all the battlefields of my Regiment from Pachino in the tip of Sicily, to the Ijssel River and Wilp in Holland. When I say 'touched' I mean just that. Time permitted only a quick visit. It was more like a recce patrol than a set-piece attack. My purpose was to set the stage for subsequent visits and also, of course, to impress my wife with my wartime experiences.

This tour covered not only Italy and Holland, but all the countries of Europe in between: Switzerland, Germany, France and Belgium; also England, Scotland and the Isle of Jersey (to check out my wife's relations — the Cabeldu connection).

The journey covered some 7,000 miles by car and took 56 days, not to mention two ocean voyages across the broad Atlantic (as it was then described), and a rough overnight passage from Southampton to Jersey. The chapter describing this long first pilgrimage is only a few pages, however. The reason is simply that most of my experiences, thoughts and ponderings connected with the trip, so far as they relate to Italy and Holland, have already been described in the foregoing chapters.

Perhaps I should have left it at that. I thought, however, that a short chapter would clarify the chronology of my various trips and round out my story. Moreover, it gave me a chance to add several anecdotes I had forgotten about when writing the earlier chapters.

The second pilgrimage took place in 1975. This was a proper pilgrimage in the sense that it commemorated the 30th Anniversary of the end of the War in Italy and was sponsored by the Canadian government. It was known as The First Canadian Corps Pilgrimage, 1975, and was composed of two groups: the First or Official Group, comprising four or five representatives from each regiment or unit that had participated in the Italian campaign (their way was entirely paid for by the government of Canada); and the Second Group, of which I was a member, following much the same itinerary as the Official Group, but paying our own way.

This pilgrimage, quite properly, was devoted mainly to official parades of the veterans, and ceremonies at all the major War Cemeteries in Italy and Sicily, and allowed me little free time. Frankly, some of the ceremonies dragged on far too long because someone in Ottawa had decreed that the whole program be carried out in both English and French, as well as in Italian. I don't know what my fallen comrades would have thought about such political bilingualism. In 1st Canadian Corps nearly everyone spoke English. The vast majority of us couldn't understand a word of French.

In the short time available, I made a side trip to recce the battlefields and places that interested me — Frosolone, near Campobasso (where I had been wounded), Moro River, Ortona, San Fortunato, Rimini, Savio River, Naviglio Canal (wounded again) and the Senio River.

The third pilgrimage, to Holland in 1980, was centered on Amsterdam. The generous people of that city paid the way for 350 Canadian veterans and their wives, and lodged them in their homes. The kindness and warmth of the Amsterdamers overwhelmed us. What it cost them I have no idea, but the bill must have been enormous. I expect they are still paying for it.

Again, the week-long ceremonies left little free time, but I stole away and visited, briefly, my battlefields at the Ijssel River and Wilp and the towns of Barneveld and Achterveld where the Regiment ended the War. I also found time to visit my dear friends from 1945 — the de Witt Hamers and the Boots.

The fourth pilgrimage, to Holland and Italy in 1985, is really the only one where I had time to examine the battlefields and other sites in detail, and reflect. I also had the advantage of having studied my old battle maps and written my book, so I was well prepared to make my recces, correct any errors in my manuscript and fill in any gaps. I am happy to say that, with minor exceptions, the facts and events described in the book, as written, turned out to be accurate and true. What more can I say?

FIRST PILGRIMAGE

June 6 to August 1, 1956

ITALY and HOLLAND

Part I — Italy

In 1956, Europe was still recovering from the ravages of war. In Italy, the country was in the throes of a reconstruction binge — new hotels strung along the Adriatic coast; super highways cut straight through the Apennines (the Strada del Sole, for example, from the toe of Italy to the northern plains). Whole new towns and villages suddenly appeared in the valleys, their inhabitants having forsaken their ancient hill-top abodes.

It was thus very difficult to find old battlefields, places and trails that I had known during the War.

My First Pilgrimage began at New York, where my wife and I embarked on the luxury Italian ship, *Cristoforo Colombo*. Eight days later we landed at Naples where my sleek, new Mercedes-Benz automobile awaited me on the dock. Next morning I was behind the wheel heading south through the heart of the Apennines to Cosenza at the foot of the Sila mountains in Calabria — a long, difficult drive of 240 miles.

The following day, tracing in reverse the wartime route I had taken on my famous (infamous, according to the adjutant) dash into the blue to find the Regiment in September, 1943, I passed through Soveria and Catanzaro to Marina di Catanzaro on the Ioanian Coast. From there, I followed, again in reverse, the route of the Regiment to Locri; then inland to Cittanova and south through the centre of the Calabrian peninsula to Delianuova, high in the Aspromonte range. Finally, I descended to the coastal plain at Reggio di Calabria on the Strait of Messina. Thirty miles to the west, the coastline of Sicily was barely visible. I remembered the thrill of crossing the Strait, from Sicily, in 1943, and landing on the shores of continental Europe.

That night, I rested in the beautiful hillside resort of Taormina, on the Sicilian coast, one of the favourite holiday haunts of Hammy Gault, the Founder of the Regiment. The balcony of my room overhung the pale blue waters of the Mediterranean Sea, some 300 feet below, where a meandering coastline faded into the distance. Bougainvillea, palms and cypress trees crowded into the picture. A few miles to the west, the snow-tipped peak of Mount Etna thrust into the clear blue sky. Nestled into the side of a hill, an ancient amphitheatre, built by the Greeks and remodelled by the Romans, overlooked the scene. I instantly renewed my covenant to return one day to this beautiful place.

The following day I drove south along the coastal road to the little town of Pachino, in the south tip of the island, not far from the beaches where I had come ashore on July 13th, 1943. The scene had changed and yet it was the same — the same poor, sandy soil where peasants still tried to eke out a living; the same shimmering heat, about 110°. But no makeshift harbour filled with ships and landing craft — no enormous piles of equipment, rations and supplies. It took me a long time to accept the fact that it was here that my DUKW had deposited me and my platoon 13 years earlier.

Eight miles inland lay Ispica, hanging on a cliff. This was the town which I had occupied as Town Major. Would any of my friends still be there to greet me — the Baron, the Mayor, the Chief of Police, Dr Lentini, Father Pietro, Signor Salvatore, Signorina Franzo, Signorina Fratele?

I entered Ispica shortly after high noon. Déjà vu. The place was as deserted as it has been in 1943. Then I remembered the reason — siesta time. I wished I could find some cool place myself, to relax and get out of the boiling sun; but I could not afford to waste that kind of time. I looked around and located my old command post, the former fascist headquarters, which was now the town hall. I roused a sleepy official and showed him a list of the people I wanted to see. Did he know them? Where were they?

The official slowly dragged out his records and went down my list. Not one of my friends was still living in Ispica. Some had died, some had mysteriously disappeared right after the War, some had married and gone away; one he had no record of at all — Signorina Fratele.

I fished in my pocket and pulled out the good luck charm given to me by Signorina Fratele so long ago. Would the clerk please be good enough to check his list once more?

He did, after a few moments he snapped the book shut and shrugged his shoulders. "Sorry Signor, she died last year — you are too late."

I hurried out the door and drove away. I will not return.

The heat was now so intense. I began to wonder if I should stop and give both man and beast (my Mercedes) a rest in the shade. Not only could an egg be fried on the hood of the car — a thick steak could be broiled in minutes. Out of the past I could hear Jake Wyatt bellowing at me, "If the Regiment could stand this heat, and fight as well, you should be able to take it now in your fancy automobile."

I drove on, past Modica, Ragusa, Piazza Armerina and Valguarnera. Ahead loomed the hill-top town of Leonforte. Only one, narrow, switchback road led up to the summit. In 1943, a flying column of Patricias with tanks had raced up that road and overwhelmed the German outposts.

About eight miles east of Leonforte, another hill-top town, Agira, was the scene of a sharp encounter with the enemy. Now a beautifully-kept cemetery lies atop a nearby hill. Its terraced slopes contain the bodies of 491 Canadians killed in Sicily. The cemetery is the only one in World War II that is exclusively Canadian.

I located the caretaker and asked him to help me find the graves of my comrades as well as a cousin of my wife, LCol Ralph Crowe of the RCR. I was then asked to sign the visitors' register. Opening the book, I was surprised to see only a handful of names. I was glad I had made the effort to come all the way to this cemetery, so far removed from the homes of those who rest here.

The sun at last was beginning to set. I returned to my car and drove eastward through the wastelands of the Salso River valley — still a "wild and topsy-turvy country much cut by ravines and abounding in cones and pinnacles."[1] It was through this valley that I had advanced on the night I joined the Regiment. On the hills around, fires had flared from burning houses, haystacks and exploding ammunition dumps. No wonder, I thought, that the tanks we were riding on got lost. It would be difficult to keep one's bearings in daylight.

On my left rose Mount Seggio, which I had scaled the morning after our advance through the valley. I was glad I didn't have to climb it now.

In the growing darkness, I pushed on to Catania, skirting the base of Mount Etna, and arrived at my hotel about 9:00 pm, parched, hungry and tired. I headed for the dining room. A sign on the door declared, 'Chiuso'. How could this be? Surely I wasn't too late for dinner. The Italians are late diners. I asked the porter why the room was closed. He seemed surprised at my question. "Signor, no one in Catania eats before 10:30." Sicilians really are late diners!

The following day I paid a quick visit to the hospital, on a high hill overlooking the city, where I had recovered from malaria. It still served as a hospital and looked exactly the same. I went out on the roof where 12 nursing sisters had been wounded when an anti-aircraft shell had prematurely exploded in their midst. I wondered if they had all recovered and how they spent the rest of War. I remembered, too, the cheeky German pilot zipping past the hospital in his Messerschmidt and waving at us. Did he survive the war? I doubted it.

Next day, I returned to Messina at the Strait and crossed over to the mainland. Sicily slowly faded away in the distance and in my memory.

My next objective was Campobasso and Frosolone lying in the middle of the Apennines about 400 miles to the north, a tough two days' drive. Having taken a route along the mountainous spine of Italy on my way south, I decided to follow the coastal road on the west coast, on my way north. At Paola, a small coastal town, I picked up the trail I had followed on my dash into the blue in September, 1943. At Sapri, this trail turned inland to Potenza, but I had my fill of mountains, so I continued along the coast to Salerno where the British and Americans had made an assault landing from the sea. Here, I had no alternative but to enter the Apennines to reach Campobasso.

My visit to nearby Frosolone, where I had been wounded, has been described elsewhere. Suffice it to say that returning to the scene for the first time, with my wife, was quite an emotional experience.

My next objective, or really rest area, was Rome, 200 miles away. En route I stopped at Cassino. The War Cemetery was still being constructed and the place looked pretty barren and forlorn against the sombre backdrop of the mountain and its enormous abbey. (Nineteen years later I would have a much different opinion.)

In Rome, I checked in at the hotel, where I had stayed during the War — the Massimo d'Azeglio. All traces of its former name, Chateau Laurier, had long since been removed. Several members of the hotel staff had been there during the War, so they alleged. One old barman even said he remembered me; probably for a very good reason — how could he forget those five wild nights I spent on leave at this hotel. Thankfully no chambermaids claimed an intimate acquaintance.

I spent several days enjoying the wonder that is Rome; but I missed not having my old professor with me to describe the sights in his knowledgeable and witty way. I hoped that the War and the Canadians had not been too hard on him.

I made an interesting purchase in Rome — a Canadian flag. In Sicily and southern Italy I had been getting a lot of black looks from the people as I drove by in my Mercedes. I wondered why. Then I realized that they thought I was German. For the rest of the trip I prominently displayed the Canadian flag and had no trouble except in northern Italy, where I had the feeling that the hammer and sickle would have been more to the point.

Rimini, 350 miles away, was my next stop. This was a very long drive in 1956, before the new super highways had been completed. But I made it in one day, including stops along the way at Ortona and the cemeteries at the Moro River and Ancona.

I had hoped, but I should have realized it was futile, that I would find in and around Rimini some of the German defences. When we entered the city in 1944, hardly a building remained except the Ponte di Tiberio. In 1956, a brand new city had risen from the rubble. Hundreds, maybe a thousand, new hotels had sprouted up along the coast. They were all filled with Germans.

At San Fortunato Ridge it was a different story. Many of the German bunkers and fortifications remained just as they were when we threw their occupants out. Several areas were fenced off, but in a rather haphazard way. Weather-beaten signs in German and Italian warned there were mines.

I was told that young boys often crawled into these fields and prodded around for old shells and bombs, which they then sold to junk dealers. The boys made quite a lot of money this way; but I don't think many of them lived to a ripe old age.

My last objective in Italy was the Winter Line, along the Senio River. En route, I passed over the endless rivers that had given us so much trouble in 1944 — Marecchia, Savio, Ronco, Montone, Lamone, Fosso Munio and the Naviglio Canal. At every stop, scores of people claimed to remember me. Their hospitality was overwhelming and, I am sure, I accounted for at least half the extra weight I acquired during my journey. Thus, on a rather fulfilling note, my tour of Italy ended.

Part II — Holland

The three days that my itinerary allowed for Holland were not nearly enough to explore fully the battle sites at the Ijssel River, Wilp and Achterveld, and visit my Dutch friends.

Unlike Italy, I had no trouble finding my battlefields. They had hardly changed at all since 1945. At Achterveld, where the Regiment ended the War, I found a plaque on a schoolhouse declaring that this was the place where high-ranking Allied and German officers had come to arrange a truce so that food could be sent to the starving Dutch.

In Sassenheim, Leiden and Noordwijkerhout I spent an enjoyable evening or two with the Boots and de Witt Hamers, remembering the exciting times at the end of the War when we liberated them and sent the Germans packing.

At Bloemendaal, I called on the Dekkers in their lovely home that German paratroopers had almost ruined in a drunken orgy on the last day of the War. The rigours of those harsh days had left their mark on the Dekkers, if not on their home. But their spirit was as great as ever and we had a happy reunion.

Twenty-four years were to slip by before I returned to Holland. In the meantime, I kept in touch with my friends. When they passed on I continued to correspond with their children — and still do.

SECOND PILGRIMAGE

April 20 to May 4, 1975

ITALY

The official representatives from the PPCLI were the following: Wilfred Reilly MM, George Upton MM, Alvin Reilly, Howard Weldon and John Klassen. I tagged along as a member of the 'unofficial' party.

The itinerary for both groups was much the same. The ceremonies began at the Victor Emmanuel Monument in Rome where a flame is kept burning in memory of fallen Italian soldiers. In addition to guards of honour from both the Italian and Canadian Armed Forces, the Carabiniere were present in their colourful uniforms.

Then followed nine days of ceremonies at the following War Cemeteries (figures shown are the number of Canadian dead buried in each cemetery): Agira (Sicily) 490, Cassino 855, Moro River 1375, Ancona 161, Montecchio 289, Gradara 369, Coriano 427, Cesena 307, Villanova 206, Ravenna 438, Argenta Gap 75, Florence 50. At the Cassino War Cemetery, a Memorial gives the names of a further 192 Canadians who have no known grave.

The following cemeteries were not visited officially, but were attended by some of the veterans who had relatives or friends buried there: Bari 210, Sangro River 2, Caserta 98, Beach Head (Anzio) 68, Rome 22.

Altogether, almost 6,000 Canadian dead are buried or commemorated in these cemeteries.

Lest We Forget — Lest We Forget

THIRD PILGRIMAGE

May 2 to May 25, 1980

Dutch Treat

At 1030 hours, May 5th, an 80 vehicle convoy enters the outskirts of Amsterdam with scout cars in the lead, followed by jeeps, Bren Carriers, amphibious vehicles, 15 cwt trucks and TCVs, all crammed with Canadians. The streets are crowded with more than 250,000 wildly cheering people throwing garlands of tulips at their liberators, who respond by tossing packages of Sweet Caporal cigarettes and chocolate bars.

The crowds are so thick that they break through a cordon of members of the Dutch Underground, and climb onto the vehicles, bringing the convoy to a halt. Shouts of "God Bless You — Thank you Canada — We will never forget you" fill the air.

This is not the triumphal entry of Canadian troops into Amsterdam in 1945, though many of the members of the convoy just described had taken part in that entry 35 years earlier. It is the Return of the Canadian Liberators to Amsterdam on May 5th, 1980.

As the 35th anniversary of the end of the hostilities in Holland approached, the Dutch people resolved to mark the occasion by showing their appreciation to the Canadians who had liberated them in 1945. All over Holland ceremonies were planned to honour the event and several thousand Canadian veterans were invited to join in the celebrations.

In Amsterdam, the citizens decided to do something very special to thank the members of the 1st Division who had liberated the city on May 8th, 1945. They invited 350 veterans and their wives to a week-long celebration, paid their return airfares, and housed and fed them for the whole period. Each veteran was presented a medal and received a special tie to mark the occasion.

481

The contingent representing the PPCLI comprised the following veterans (ranks given are those at the end of the War): Capt R B Mainprize, Capt C S Frost, Lt W E Harrington MC, Lt D G MacCulloch, Lt W W Bolton, CSM A C Green, Cpl J Klassen, LCpl J H Moore, Pte B A J Fraser, Pte W Kuzyk, Pte G J Home and Pte L V Rains.

Capt 'Buzz' Mainprize, it will be recalled, had been a Patricia and had served with the KOYLI in Holland as a Canloan officer. The other members of the contingent had all served in Holland with the Regiment. Lt Harrington and Lt Bolton were members of D Company. CSM 'Smokey' Green was a much respected WOII, who had joined the Regiment in 1939 and served with it right through to the end of the War.

I had not seen any of these veterans, except Cpl Klassen, for 35 years. He had been with me on the Pilgrimage to Italy in 1975. The thrill of seeing these hardy veterans, all in apparently good health, after so many years, can easily be imagined. But we had little time to reminisce, as the good burghers had organized seven strenuous days of ceremonies that would have taxed our energies 35 years earlier: dinners, boat trips, concerts, church services, parades, tattooes, visits to cemeteries and the Royal Palace, tours of tulip fields and unveiling of memorials. As one exhausted veteran was heard to exclaim, "the Dutch are doing their best to do what the Germans didn't — kill the survivors!"

Of the many impressive events, two or three deserve special mention, such as the re-enactment of the entry of the Canadian troops in Amsterdam. The 80 odd vehicles were not replicas, but actual vintage specimens of those we drove in 1945 — the Liberation Committee had borrowed the vehicles from museums and car clubs all over the country. The reception of the crowds was truly overwhelming, much larger and noisier than in 1945. Amsterdam was, of course, a much larger city than it had been 35 years earlier. It must be remembered too, that in 1945 the Germans had shot a number of civilians the day before LCol Clark and the battalion arrived in the city. The people were still suffering from the shock of that massacre as well as from starvation.

Another significant difference in the two welcomes was the number and enthusiasm of the children. Most Canadians do not realize the tremendous respect and goodwill the people of Holland still have for our country. These feelings are not confined just to the war generation but are passed down, as part of the Dutch heritage, to each new generation.

The cigarettes we threw to the people in 1980 were replicas of our wartime Sweet Caps, which the tobacco company had supplied without charge for the occasion.

Following the parade, we were received at the Royal Palace by HRH Princess Juliana and Prince Bernhard.

On May 7th we joined another group of 1,500 veterans from Nijmegen in a ceremony at the Groesbeek Canadian War Cemetery to honour the more than 7,000 Canadians who had died in Belgium and Holland and lie buried in nine cemeteries throughout this area. Queen Beatrix, in one of her first official acts following her coronation six days earlier, laid the first wreath. The Honourable Donald MacDonald, the Minister of Veterans Affairs, represented the Canadian government. After the official wreaths were placed, individuals from the crowd of thousands came forward to honour the dead.

Maj Mainprize, escorted by his comrades, slowly approaches the towering stone cross, pauses a moment, and lays a wreath on behalf of the PPCLI.

As the last mournful notes of the Lament fade into the distance, the solemn party turns and slowly marches away, their sad duty over and done.

The Regiment has remembered. It will never forget.

> *The tumult and the shouting dies*
> *The Captains and the Kings depart*
> *Still stands Thine ancient sacrifice*
> *An humble and a contrite heart*
> *Lord God of Hosts, be with us yet*
> *Lest we forget — lest we forget!*
>
> *Kipling's Recessional*

FOURTH PILGRIMAGE

May 2 to May 24, 1985

HOLLAND and ITALY

Part I — Holland

From a vantage point in a wood just west of Gorssel, on the east bank of the Ijssel River, I carefully survey the approaches to the river and the objective on the other side — a group of houses partly hidden by a dyke that shelter a German tank and infantry.

Smoke from our artillery drifts across the front. Our Buffaloes charge over the flats and dive into the river. High explosive shells whine over our heads and erupt on the enemy positions. The scene is so real I can almost hear the sounds and smell the smoke and cordite.

I have returned to this place to honour the men of the PPCLI who fought and died on that far-off day — April 11th, 1945 — when the Patricias crossed the Ijssel River and liberated Wilp. That day marked the beginning of the drive of the Canadian Army into western Holland to help liberate the starving Dutch and end the War.

"To honour the dead." Reason enough for me to return to the banks of this river on May 8th, 1985 — 40 years to the day since the official end of the Second World War. Yet I have another special reason for making this pilgrimage.

The story began January, 1985, when I heard that ceremonies were being planned by the Dutch to mark the 40th Anniversary of their liberation in May, 1945. The arrangements were in the hands of two committees, one in Holland, the Liberation '45 Committee, and the other in Toronto, the We Do Remember Committee.

Having participated in the exciting, but exhausting 1980 Return to

Amsterdam, I felt I did not have the stamina to make a repeat performance. Furthermore, I thought that the wonderful people of Holland deserved more than five years of peace before another contingent of Canadian veterans invaded their country once again. Yet, something moved me to make enquiries about the trip. At a Dutch travel agency in Toronto I found that this time the ceremonies would not be held in Amsterdam but in a number of smaller towns including Apeldoorn, where the Dutch citizens had offered to billet the veterans for a week to ten days.

I told the travel agent this was an offer I found difficult to refuse as I had always wanted to return to the nearby village of Wilp which the PPCLI had liberated on April 11th, 1945, after crossing the Ijssel River.

"PPCLI?" enquired the Dutch travel agent. "Who are they?"

"Princess Patricia's Canadian Light Infantry," I declared, with more than a hint of annoyance and disbelief. "It so happens that I commanded D Company of the PPCLI *in that battle.*"

"Well, I don't understand that. Have you ever heard of the 48th Highlanders?"

"The 48th Highlanders? What have they got to do with that battle?"

"Well they are the ones who attacked across the Ijssel River and liberated Wilp. Their Commanding Officer was killed there. In 1982 a group of their veterans returned and the citizens of Wilp held a great celebration to honour them. Prince Bernhard and a number of other dignitaries were present. A plaque was unveiled in honour of their CO and a street was named after him.

"By the way, what did you say PPCLI stands for?"

"Peanuts, popcorn, candy, lemonade and icecream! And please put my name on your list for billets in Apeldoorn. This is one pilgrimage I don't want to miss."

A few days later a representative of the Liberation '45 Committee from Holland appeared in Toronto to make final arrangements for the visit. The travel agent was kind enough to suggest that I should meet him and tell my story about the PPCLI at the Ijssel River and Wilp.

Armed with extracts from the PPCLI Regimental History, the War Diary and my personal diaries, I had lunch with the Dutch representative. He patiently heard me out and then responded by handing me materials the 48th Highlanders had distributed to the citizens of Wilp in 1982. He added words to the effect that Wilp belongs to the 48th Highlanders and I would have one hell of a time convincing the Dutch that the PPCLI had anything to do with it.

It was a challenge I could not resist. My casual enquiry about a return visit to Holland had exploded into a burning mission to fight once again the crossing of the Ijssel and the liberation of Wilp; and to restore the names of these battles to their rightful owners — the Patricias.

How could such an incredible mistake have been made? Who was responsible? How could the error be rectified? To find the answers to these and other questions I boarded KLM flight 692 at Toronto on May 2nd, 1985.

With its more than 50,000 acres of woodlands, moors, brooks and shifting sands, Apeldoorn is one of the loveliest cities in the Netherlands. Vast expanses of forest border the city; beautiful parks abound; royal forestries shelter a large wild animal population of red deer, moufflons and wild boars. Apeldoorn is indeed a royal city, in many ways. Here it was that William III, King of England, Prince of Orange-Nassau built a hunting seat which became the famous Het Loo Palace, inhabited by the Dutch Royal family until 1975. The palace and its gardens have recently been restored to their original grandeur and magnificence.

To this city of natural beauty I came on May 3rd, 1985, with a very large chip on my shoulder, determined to set the record straight. But my mission was temporarily, and happily, thwarted by the very people we had fought so hard to liberate in May, 1945. At the Schiphol airport in Amsterdam we were given a warm welcome by the members of the Dutch Liberation Committee; then placed in buses, gaily decorated with bunting and flags, and driven away to Apeldoorn through the scenic Dutch countryside. All along the route friendly people waved to us and shouted "Welcome Canada — We Do Remember." Each town had its distinctive arch of flowers, verdant boughs, and neat lawns with tulips arranged in messages of welcome.

At Apeldoorn, our tired but happy group was taken to a club built especially as a centre or rendezvous for the veterans and named the Canadian Club. There, we 'married up' with our hosts and were whisked away to their homes.

It was my good fortune to be billeted with a retired dentist and his wife, two of the most charming and delightful people I have ever known. They gave me the run of their lovely home, pampered me with gourmet meals, drove me around the battlefields that I so desperately wanted to see, and put up with my late nights caused by overindulgence in the Canadian Club.

In the course of a late evening's discussion following my first night in the club, I learned that my hosts were Jewish and had lived in Apeldoorn before the War. When the Germans came in May, 1940, they had narrowly missed becoming inmates of a concentration camp by taking refuge in the embassy of a friendly Central American country. There, they were given new passports and escaped to Spain. After many dangers and delays they finally made their way to England where the doctor took a commission with the British Navy as a Dental Officer. After the War they returned to Apeldoorn to rebuild their lives and his career. Nearly all their relatives and friends had perished in the holocaust.

That same night, I told the doctor a little bit about myself and explained my real reason for returning to Holland — to rectify the calumny perpetrated by persons unknown on the PPCLI's battle record. My host was most sympathetic and eager to help me in my good work, but there were other duties and engagements more pressing.

"It's very late," he said, tapping his watch, "and we have a heavy day coming up, as well as a very busy week of parades, receptions, parties and so forth. As soon as these functions are over we'll take my car and visit the Ijssel River and Wilp and straighten out the terrible wrong that has been done to your Regiment."

I couldn't ask for more.

For the next five days the wonderful people of Apeldoorn opened up their hearts to their Canadian liberators. The ceremonies began with a moving address of welcome by the Burgemeester of Apeldoorn, Mr Beelaerts van Blokland. Urbane, knowledgeable and kind, he presided over the festivities with great wit and charm, ably assisted by various committees of local citizens.

At the welcoming ceremonies each veteran was presented with a medallion bearing the likeness of Erasmus, the famous fifteenth century Dutch philosopher who played a major role in the development of the concept of freedom as a right. He is considered the father of intellectual resistance and hence the father of all resistance against oppression. On the reverse side of the medal is engraved one of his well known sayings: *Non est caustantia semper eadem loqui; sed semper eodem pertenderer.**

One of the most poignant ceremonies was the Silent March which followed a Remembrance Service held in the Grote Kerk. Canadian veterans and their Dutch hosts silently, sadly and slowly proceeded from the church to the beautiful Oranjepark. Not a word was spoken, not a sound was heard, as the long column made its way through streets, darkened by a threatening sky. Even little children sensed the reverence of the occasion and quietly followed their parents.

At the Oranjepark, a short service to Commemorate the Dead was followed by an emotional singing of the beautiful Dutch National Hymn, *Wilhelmus.* Then, as if on cue, to signal the end of the ceremony, thunder rolled across the park and the dark rain clouds spilled their burden over the assembly as they sadly walked away.

Another memorable event was the Veterans' Parade. More than 2,000 veterans formed up in the grounds of the Het Loo Palace and tried to march through the streets of Apeldoorn. We moved off from the Palace in good order, every veteran in step, heads high, arms swinging up to waist, bands blaring. It couldn't last. As we swung into the street we could not believe our eyes or our ears. Most of the 140,000 inhabitants of the city lined the street, some standing 20 ranks deep and waving more maple leaf flags than could be seen at any parade in Canada. As we approached the crowd they

---

* Constantcy is not always to say the same thing, but always to persist in the same thing.

broke through our ranks, hugging us, kissing us, pressing flowers into our hands, crying, shouting, cheering us in one continuous roar. Our fine parade melted away into the arms of our admirers.

We tried to reform and march to the saluting base where Princess Margriet, The Honourable George Hees, our Veterans Affairs Minister and other officials awaited our column. Overcome with emotion and almost buried in tulips, we somehow pressed on through the throng, in single file, toward the saluting base. Several of us made our way forward by passing our tulips to the thousands of little children lining the route. Finally, we made it to the saluting base, in twos and threes, in small disorganized bunches, some all by themselves.

Later, George Hees, in typical fashion, expressed our feelings to Princess Margriet. "This is really a love story. The Dutch people make us feel like delivering angels." The Princess replied, "The Canadians have brought Apeldoorn alive. People are talking to each other who never met before. The feeling is like it must have been at liberation."

The Princess, who had been born in Canada, in 1943, could not have personally experienced the emotion of the liberation in 1945, but she was very close to the mark. In some ways, and for many reasons, the feelings of her people shown us in 1985 surpassed anything we had experienced in 1945. But, on the other hand, the feeling of being free again after five years of Nazi tyranny, must have been an experience that could happen only once in a lifetime. The Princess's remark is perhaps a happy blend of the two thoughts. In any case, as a tiny Princess, in Canada, she captured our hearts in those far off days. And she still does.

Our final parade was at the Groesbeek Canadian War Cemetery where more than 2,300 Canadians have lain buried these past 40 years. The cemetery, on a hill overlooking the Dutch countryside, gives the impression of a beautiful garden with green grass and foliage and flowers. Only the white headstones in neat lines, each decorated with splashes of bright daffodils and red and yellow tulips, remind the visitor that this is not just a place of beauty, but the hallowed resting place of Canada's dead.

I have visited the cemetery many times over the years. Each time I come away angry and perplexed, a little older and a little sadder than when I entered. It is as though on each visit I leave a small bit of myself to lie with my comrades who were not as lucky as I.

This time the same feelings welled up inside me, only stronger, despite the beauty of the place and the atmosphere of peace and serenity. I vowed then I would never return. My covenant had been fulfilled.

I cast up my eyes to the Cross of Sacrifice and saw these words: *Pro amicis mortui amicis vivimus* — We live in the hearts of friends for whom we died. What a beautiful thought! Suddenly my tensions eased, my mind was at rest. As I strolled away through the beckoning headstones, I took my comrades with me. I felt whole again.

We were now nearing the end of the official celebrations and not a moment too soon! In addition to the events already described, our evenings were taken up with parties, receptions and dances at The Canadian Club and elsewhere throughout the city. It was fun but it was exhausting.

For some it was quite startling. One veteran, for example, received a big surprise — a 40 year old son he never knew he had.

While these official and extra curricular activities were going on, I was laying plans to set the record straight about the PPCLI and the crossing of the Ijssel. With the help of a member of the Liberation Committee I obtained an appointment to visit the Mayor of Voorst, in whose municipality the Ijssel River and Wilp are situated.

My host, the dentist, was all geared up to provide a naval escort for the venture. He suggested we recce the area in his destroyer (car) before we attended the Mayor of Voorst.

On a fine morning in May, we set off together; my host armed with a set of high-powered naval binoculars, camera, rations (both dry and wet); I, with my old maps from the War still bearing the exact routes taken by the PPCLI during the battles. Like two young officers, we scouted the area east of the Ijssel River and soon found the assembly area where the Patricias had formed up for the attack. From there, we followed the route the Buffaloes had taken to the river. As we approached the eastern bank, my escort, the dentist, pointed out that the high dykes ahead would certainly bar our way in the car.

"How did the Buffaloes manage to navigate those obstacles?" he demanded.

"Wait and see, Henk. At the end of this trail, make a left incline and you'll find a nice fat opening in the dykes you can drive a tank or your car through."

"I don't believe it."

But in a moment Henk became a believer. The crossing site had not changed and there was the promised gap in the dyke.

"Fantastic," yelled a relieved Henk, "What a memory."

"Yeah, but also a damn good map."

We drove through the gap, stopped the car and got out to survey the situation. Now it was my turn to be the unbeliever. Nothing had changed in 40 years — ahead, the barren flats, and beyond them the river, about 100 yards wide. On the other side more mud flats and dykes and the top of a house hidden behind one of them.

"This is incredible, Henk. Let's leave the car here and go back to that wooded area near the river and plan our attack. It was in that wood that I made my final recce on April 11th, 1945."

After making our recce in the wood, Henk and I returned to his car at the dyke. As I checked the area to the right I saw, 50 yards distant, what looked like a cairn, surrounded by flags and fresh flowers.

"What the devil's that, Henk?"

"I don't know. We'd better investigate."

The object was indeed a memorial cairn erected by Municipalities of Gorssel and Voorst to honour the Canadian troops who had crossed the Ijssel River at this place on April 11th, 1945. Henk suggested I put on my PPCLI beret and medals and he would take a snap of me standing beside the cairn flanked by the flags of Canada and the Netherlands. He had no sooner taken the picture than a dozen or more people suddenly appeared and excitedly gathered around us at the cairn. In moments they were joined by about 50 others on bicycles. They all pressed in on me, touching me, hugging me, kissing me. One fine looking lady tore an orange pin off her blouse and placed it on my blazer. A child of only ten or eleven came up to me, shook my hand and said in perfect English, "Thank you Canada for giving us back our freedom."

Several family groups asked Henk and me to come to their homes and have lunch and stay for dinner. All the while, the crowd continued to grow and I was beginning to wonder how we would ever be able to leave without offending these wonderful people.

Then a reporter and cameraman from a local newspaper appeared and asked me to describe the events of April, 1945 when the gallant Canadians stormed across the Ijssel River and captured Wilp. What a splendid opportunity to place on the record that it was the PPCLI and not the 48th Highlanders who did the job!

To an incredulous reporter, I described how the Patricias, conveyed by the ubiquitous Buffaloes, launched the attack across the Ijssel River at 4:30 pm on April 11th, 1945 and occupied Wilp by 1 am on April 12th. The 48th didn't arrive in their Assembly Area on the east bank of the Ijssel until noon on April 12th. By that time B Company and my D Company had been in Wilp at least ten hours and had repulsed a strong enemy counter-attack by 120 German infantry, three tanks, an SP gun and supporting vehicles. The 48th Highlanders had a strictly break-out role in the operation once the PPCLI had won the bridgehead. The 48th did not assault across the river; they were simply ferried across in the afternoon of April 12th.

It was true that the 48th Commanding Officer, LCol D A MacKenzie, was killed by shellfire late in the afternoon of that day, about 1,200 yards north of my position in Wilp. I remembered him coming through my position and getting briefed on the situation. The 48th rifle companies actually by-passed Wilp and headed for another town, Twello, to the northwest of Wilp. In short, the 48th Highlanders had nothing whatsoever to do with the crossing of the Ijssel or the capture of Wilp.

At the end of the interview the reporter asked me why I wasn't present at the cairn earlier that day.

"What happened?" I queried.

"Well, the Municipalities of Gorssel and Voorst dedicated this cairn in the presence of the 48th Highlanders, its band and other dignitaries. No PPCLI veterans were present."

I was stunned and could barely reply. "The PPCLI were not asked and knew nothing about the ceremony."

"That's too bad. There was also a re-enactment of the crossing of the river. Representatives from Gorssel, Voorst, Wilp and the 48th Highlanders were ferried across the river in a pilot boat and another cairn was dedicated on the far side of the river."

Now I was speechless. I looked at Henk. He put a finger to his lips, indicating I should remain in that state.

When the smoke (from my nostrils) cleared, and my power of speech returned, I asked the reporter if there were any other ceremonies involving the 48th.

"Oh yes, their pipes and drums are putting on a tattoo in the village of Busloo."

"That figures."

"Beg your pardon?"

"I'm not surprised — the PPCLI captured Busloo shortly after taking Wilp."

This time Henk was speechless too. He pointed to the car and we slowly made our way through the throng who had been listening to my remarks with some astonishment, but also, I sensed, with some concern about the way my Regiment had been ignored. With much hugging and kissing and promises to return the next day, we finally said goodbye and drove away.

Henk was the first to speak. "You certainly have a job of work ahead of you to put the PPCLI back on the map."

"Never fear. We'll put the record straight tomorrow when we call on the Mayor of Voorst."

But Henk was right, there was a lot of work to do and very little time to do it before our meeting with the mayor. First, I had to get in touch with any PPCLI members who had returned to Holland for the Anniversary celebrations. None were billeted in Apeldoorn, but I found two who had chosen to stay in a nearby village — Barneveld. They were Lt Bert Bolton who had commanded No 16 Platoon in my D Company in the battles just described, and Cpl John Moore, a member of the Mortar Platoon. I got in touch with them and they enthusiastically agreed to join me in the town hall at Twello, the seat of the municipality of Voorst.

The next problem was to arrange for some kind of memento, or gift, on behalf of the PPCLI, to present to the Municipality. Fortunately, prior to leaving Toronto, I had placed in my luggage a PPCLI bronze plaque, or shield, in case some occasion such as this arose. Of course it was not possible to have the plaque suitably engraved before I left.

I showed the shield to Henk and told him I wanted to present it to the municipality, but it seemed pointless as there was no inscription and no time to have it engraved.

"Leave it to me," beamed Henk, "I have a friend in town who'll do it for us in a couple of hours."

Next day, armed with the plaque and accompanied by Lt Bolton, Cpl Moore, Henk and his wife, I attended Dr J H J van Blommestein, the Burgemeester of Voorst, wondering how he would receive my little band and how he would react to my plea to give the PPCLI their due.

I need not have worried. Dr van Blommestein was cast in much the same mould as the Mayor of Apeldoorn — a kind, gracious man and a professional, who was very much aware of the responsibilities of his office. He had also done his homework.

With genuine warmth he welcomed our delegation and ushered us into his chambers to meet some members of his Council including his Chief of Protocol, Mr J van de Visch and his Chief Engineer, LCol Ritse R Reitsma. After a few words over coffee and cakes, I realized that Dr Blommestein had been made very much aware of the reason for my visit. He could not have been more understanding and sympathetic. I brought out my old battle maps and traced the route taken by the Patricias before and during the battle for Wilp.

"Yes", he said, "we always knew the PPCLI had taken some part in the action but, regretably, I was not informed that there were any representatives from the PPCLI in Holland. Otherwise, of course, they would have been included in all the ceremonies connected with this important Anniversary. We are so happy that we can at last give the PPCLI its proper recognition."

Whereupon, he glanced at his protocol officer who produced a Scroll under the seal of the Municipality of Voorst acknowledging their gratitude to our deputation on the occasion of our visit to the town hall. The mayor then handed me a detailed map of Voorst and presented each member of our group with appropriate gifts, including a tin of cookies made in Wilp in honour of the 40th Anniversary of their liberation and a bottle of fine liqueur.

Then it was my turn to reciprocate his kindness. I thanked my lucky hunch in Toronto that I would need a PPCLI plaque for such an occasion and I blessed Henk for having it inscribed. With a few words of appreciation to the mayor and his council, I presented the plaque. It was inscribed as follows:

Presented to the Municipality of Voorst by Colonel C S Frost
to commemorate the 40th Anniversary of the Liberation of Wilp
on April 12th, 1945, by Princess Patricia's Canadian Light

Infantry.

May 8th, 1985

But the occasion demanded some further token of our appreciation to the mayor himself. I dug into my pocket and produced a PPCLI cap badge which I presented to him personally. At the same time I filed with the clerk extracts from the PPCLI Regimental History giving the correct account of the battles.

Meantime, Henk had been taking pictures of these presentations, and Bert Bolton and John Moore had been ably supporting me in expressing our appreciation to the mayor and council.

The mayor suggested we all attend the cairn erected on the west bank of the Ijssel, and honour the men of the PPCLI who fought and fell in the battle. It was a gracious gesture and I happily agreed.

And so it was that 40 years to the day after the end of the War, three old comrades, Bolton, Moore and Frost, quietly stood, proud and erect, beside a cairn on the bank of the river they had assaulted so long ago. In the presence of the Burgemeester of Voorst and other members of his council a minute's silence was observed in honour of the PPCLI. My mission had been completed.

It was now time to return to Apeldoorn for other ceremonies. The chief engineer of the municipality insisted, however, that we adjourn to the best pub in Wilp and exchange mutual toasts in honour of the occasion. On the way we could follow the route my D Company had taken from the river to the first objective, a group of houses behind a dyke code-named Ness; then we could carry on to the second objective, a farmhouse in Wilp, code-named Winchester, where we had been counter-attacked by German tanks and infantry.

We quickly piled in our cars and in minutes we had 'captured' the first objective, Ness. But instead of 40 year old buildings, a handsome new farmhouse was in the final stages of construction. A workman approached our party.

Through our naval escort and interpreter, Henk, I explained that we were looking for some old farm buildings that we had captured from the Germans in 1945. Possibly we were in the wrong place.

"No, you're not," declared the workman. "This is where several farm buildings stood in 1945. But after your artillery and infantry had finished with them, and with the Germans inside, there wasn't much of anything left. The place was abandoned until recently when this new house was erected."

I looked at Bolton and Moore, not having a clue what to say, but feeling we should never have come here and stirred up old memories. The workman instantly surmised what was going through my head. "Please don't feel like that. The loss of a farmhouse and barn was a small price to pay for our

493

freedom. Thank you, thank you Canada." He ran forward and put his arms around me.

At the second and final objective, the farmhouse code-named Winchester, on the outskirts of Wilp, more surprises awaited us. The farmhouse looked pretty much the same as it did in 1945, although a number of fine buildings had been added to it. The farmer who had occupied the place in 1945 had, however, left many years ago and moved into town. But the Protocol Officer of Voorst, accompanying us, had done his research and took us to the farmer's present home. There, we had a joyful reunion with him, now retired and in his eighties, his wife and his daughter, who was only 15 when we fought off the German counter-attacks against her home.

At least we didn't destroy her home, I thought, with some relief, as I waited for her reaction to our visit.

"There were about 17 of us," she began. "We were so afraid that terrible night, when the Germans came back with their tanks. We thought we would all be killed."

"17 of you?" I queried.

"Yes, we were all in the basement of the house, but didn't dare come out until a day or two after the attack, as we thought the Germans had driven you back. By that time, of course, you had moved on. We are so thankful to you for saving us. Words cannot express our gratitude."

Then the old man perked up. "You know, I lost two horses and 35 cattle that night."

Unfortunately we had to leave or we would be late for the ceremonies in Apeldoorn. Henk took pictures and we stepped out into the street.

News of our presence had spread and a crowd had gathered including people we had met on our recce of the east bank of the river, the day before. The lady who had given me her orange pin was there; also the family who wanted us to come for lunch and dinner. They now insisted we join them. So did half a dozen others.

Again I was overwhelmed. What to do? The chief engineer pushed through the crowd. "Let's make a graceful retreat to the pub down the street, opposite the church. It's our only chance."

As we moved down the street toward the church, a German 88 suddenly exploded — in my mind. This was the very route those tanks and Germans had taken as they churned along the road to my company position.

We were nearly at the pub. "My God," I exclaimed, "This is the place where Egan Chambers and his B Company opened fire on the German column and mowed down half a company of them."

Bolton laughed, "Trust good old B Company to find the only pub in town."

Our 'happy hour' in the pub had to be cut short because of the other events in Apeldoorn. There was time, however, for mutual toasts and expressions of our deep friendship for one another. Finally, the chief engineer (who was a retired Dutch Army colonel) got up on a chair, smiled at me and said, "Colonel, there is one final act we must do to express the close ties that exist between your Regiment and Wilp. We shall exchange our Regimental ties." In a moment the deed was done, amid much cheering and laughter.

My mission had not only been accomplished, it had been done with panache, in the best Patricia tradition.

On the way back to Apeldoorn, with Henk at the wheel of his 'destroyer', neither of us said a word for several miles. Finally, Henk broke the awkward silence. "Syd, you're being awfully quiet. But I think I know the trouble. It bothers me too. You really haven't completed your so-called mission. You swore to find out how such an incredible mistake about the Patricias could have happened. And you vowed to find out who was responsible. What about it?"

"You're right. But the most important part of my mission has been achieved. There's not a person in Wilp, or the whole Municipality of Voorst, for that matter, who doesn't know all about the PPCLI."

"Yes, I suppose you're right. What are you going to do about how the error was made and by whom?"

"Nothing. It doesn't matter any more. Whoever was responsible can worry about it, not me. The 48th may never speak to me again; but I really don't think that will happen. Perhaps some of the blame lies with my own Regiment. After all, they haven't shown much interest in this Anniversary."

"Why's that?"

"Well, as battles go, it wasn't by any means the biggest, and certainly not the bloodiest when you think of the terrible slaughter in Italy."

"Yet it had a great significance; both for you and the Dutch. It was really your last battle and it helped save the starving Dutch."

"I appreciate your saying that, Henk."

When we arrived home a message was waiting for me from the Mayor of Apeldoorn. Would I be kind enough to join him and the City Council for dinner that evening? How Mr Beelaerts van Blokland found out about the PPCLI and what I had been up to, I never did ascertain. But it didn't surprise me. At dinner that evening, I had the honour of sitting beside him and enjoying his wit and charm. There was no need for me to elaborate on the PPCLI — he knew all about the Patricias. He was only sorry the full story had not been known by him earlier. After dinner I presented him with my Patricia blazer crest and my cap badge, as well as extracts from our Regimental History.

An interesting sequel to these events occurred when I returned to Toronto and was invited to attend the change of command of the Commanding Officer of the 48th Highlanders. I was pleased to accept. I have known the 48th since the War. Their officers are gentlemen and I count many friends among them. Still, I wondered what kind of a hornet's nest I was getting into.

I need not have worried. I was seated in the front row for the parade and shown the greatest respect. Indeed the officers could not have been friendlier — all except one ex-officer who came up and quietly suggested I read the history of The Royal Canadian Regiment as it agreed with his version of the crossing of the Ijssel River and the capture of Wilp.

Well, one unbeliever out of thousands is not so bad.

For the Farewell Dinner in Apeldoorn, over 1,500 veterans and their hosts sat down to a sumptuous meal at the Canadian Club and an adjoining café. This occasion was our last chance to thank our wonderful hosts, and was paid for by the Veterans themselves. We ate. We sang. We danced into the small hours, or until we collapsed, whichever event first occurred. The friendship, warmth and goodwill that flowed that evening will long be remembered. Indeed, the theme of the celebration had been 'We Do Remember', meaning of course that the Dutch people remembered it was the Canadians who had given them their freedom.

Toward the end of the evening, the band leader announced that a special song had been written by a Canadian soldier to honour the Dutch people. Song sheets were distributed, the band struck up, and we sang this song:

> *Goodbye wonderful Holland*
> *We do remember you too*
> *Your friendship, warmth and your kindness*
> *Make this a tearful adieu*
>
> *Oh, keep your home fires burning*
> *In polder, town and farms*
> *We'll soon return to see you again*
> *And hold you in our arms**

The celebrations in Apeldoorn were over. The memories would always remain.

Before I could return to Toronto, a few pleasant duties remained. The first was a visit to the small village of Achterveld to see once again the little school house with its plaque commemorating the great events that had occurred there in 1945.

I found the school without any trouble, but the building had drastically changed since 1945 and my visit in 1956. The front portion of the school

---

* Words and music by Col C S Frost

bearing the plaque had been torn down, and the remainder of the building converted to a students' recreation centre. A new school building at another location now housed the student body.

As I entered the old building, wearing my medals and Patricia beret, I was greeted by the strident tones of a 'ghetto blaster'. The youth tending the bar had no knowledge of the historical significance of the place but he was very pleasant and offered me a beer. I wondered what Seyss-Inquart, the No 1 German in Holland, who had attended this very building on April 30th, 1945, would have thought if he had been resurrected from the grave in which the Allies had laid him, after hanging him for war crimes against the Dutch.

Chagrined and perplexed, I quickly left the former school room and went out into the sunlight. I headed toward my former company headquarters, in a house a few yards down the road. Perhaps it had not suffered the same unkind fate that had befallen my school house. I knocked at the door. No answer. I knocked again. The door opened and an attractive young girl gaped at my medals and beret. In halting English she asked what I wanted.

In halting English I briefly explained I was a Canadian soldier who had once lived in her home. Could I speak to her father.

Her father was not at home but she would find him. Would I please come in.

A few minutes later her father, Mr J M Schouten, appeared. When I explained why I had knocked on his door he bounded over and embraced me. Of course he knew all about the PPCLI. Why, a whole company of them had visited Actherveld in 1967. He had several volumes of photographs and material of the visit.

"The PPCLI were here in 1967?" I queried in disbelief. "Don't you mean 1945?"

"Oh no. The PPCLI captured Achterveld in April, 1945, of course, and I have all sorts of photos, clippings and papers about those days. But a company from the PPCLI in Germany visited us in August 1967.

"By the way, I am the official Archivist of Achterveld. I have at least 25 volumes on the War, the truce negotiations with old Seyss-Inquart in the school house, our liberation and the wonderful PPCLI soldiers."

I was incredulous. I had stumbled upon a valuable mine of information and history about this village that had so much significance for me and the Patricias.

First, I wanted to hear all about the visit of a PPCLI company in 1967. I had been out of touch with the Regiment for years and knew nothing of this operation. From Mr Schouten I learned that in July and August, 1967, B Company of 2 PPCLI, then stationed in Germany, had followed the war-time route of the Regiment through Belgium, Germany and Holland. The project was undertaken to commemorate Canada's Centennial Year.

He then showed me extracts from a journal kept by the PPCLI officer in command of the project. I skimmed through the entries. It was too incredible to be true. B Company had indeed faithfully retraced every step the Regiment had taken in 1945. The names of the villages, features and code-names jumped off the pages at me — Zutphen, Ijssel River, Wilp, Ness, Alice Blue Gown, Klarenbeek, Harskamp, Barneveld, Achterveld.

If only I had known about the journal five months earlier when that Dutch representative had asked me, "Who are the PPCLI — what did they do at the Ijssel River and Wilp?" And what a crushing dénouement to the wild stories about what the 48th Highlanders had done!

The journal is such a key part of my tale that it deserves to be reproduced. Here are the relevant entries:

Wednesday, 2 August 1967
A reconnaissance of the river crossing area was made and the actual pillboxes which the Patricias assaulted on the far side of the river were observed with interest.

On returning the OC gave orders for the next day's operation: the crossing of the Ijssel River. The same code-names used on the crossing in 1945 were assigned.

Thursday, 3 August 1967
In 1945, the Regiment crossed on 11th April and took 5 days to reach the Apeldoornsch Canal. We planned to do it one day in four phases.

Phase 1 — River crossing and advance through Wilp. 4 Platoon under 2 Lt Gieser crossed first in two boats with Support Sections in position to give covering fire. The river is 150 yards wide and quite fast but they made good time across and seized the two bunkers. The other platoons then passed through.

On 'Ness', where D Company had been opposed by a tank and two enemy sections, they were greeted by an old man who said, "Welcome Canadians. There are no Jerries here this time." We advanced through Wilp where the Regiment had beaten back a strong enemy counter-attack.

Phase 2 — Advance from Wilp to 'Alice Blue Gown'. Platoons were sent out on two axes to the east edge of a large wood, then moved through. It was there on 13th April 1945 that the Regiment inflicted 100 casualties and captured many more.

My visit with Mr Schouten was, as usual, cut short by the demands of a tight schedule. Had I known about his archives earlier, I would have made arrangements to spend a day or two with him. We parted with mutual promises to keep in touch and exchange material which, I am happy to say, has been honoured by both of us. I only hope that the Regiment will also take an interest in Mr Schouten and his valuable records.

Before returning home I wanted to visit the town of Bloemendaal, a few miles west of Haarlem, where the Patricias had spent a few days just after the War ended rounding up the defeated Germans. I was particularly interested to see whether the magnificent home of Mr and Mrs Dekker was still standing after its desecration by the German paratroopers. It took me a little scouting to locate the place, and when I finally found it I wished I hadn't. Alas, the beautiful old house had been torn down and a modern bungalow now stood in its place. Progress had finally done what the Germans had tried to do 40 years earlier.

My next stop was another town the Regiment had liberated on May 8th, 1945 — Overveen. Here, the grateful citizens had presented us with a charter expressing their thanks and declaring that every door would be wide open to any Patricia who ever paid them a visit.

In the main street of the town, I stopped and knocked on the door of a rather modest house. As on other formal occasions of this nature, I was dressed in blazer, beret and medals. Suddenly I had a funny feeling that perhaps this time my probing into the past had gone too far. The door opened. A beautiful young lady in a very flimsy negligée stood before me. Her mouth opened but no words came forth. I hastily produced the charter and waited. No reaction, except a cold stare.

Then shouts behind me. A young man rushed up and stood between me and the girl. I pointed to the Charter still in the hands of the young lady. He grabbed it and read. "Thank God," I murmured, "he understands English."

Slowly his face brightened, a grin appeared and then a hearty laugh.

"Welcome, Canada, to Overveen. Of course our doors are always open wide. Please come in and share lunch with my fiancée!"

I noticed that he emphasized the word 'lunch'; he was not prepared to share his fiancée. I settled for a little Bols gin and a beer chaser.

My time in Holland was running out but I could not return home without trying to locate the Boots and the de Witt Hamers. Since my visit in 1980 I had lost contact with them, though my recent letters to their last addresses had not been returned. Once again my scouting instincts served me well and I found Mimi de Witt Hamer in Noordwijkerhout. From her I learned that Jean Boot and her husband were in Greece where they now spent most of their time. (When I returned home there was a long letter from Jean).

On the way to see Mimi at Noordwijkerhout, I passed through the lovely tulip country around Sassenheim, where Jean once lived, and stopped for a few moments at the Keukenhof Gardens. Though I have visited these gardens many times their beauty never ceases to enthral me. Bed upon bed of tulips of every kind and hue — soft, pastel shades; bright, vivid colours; the whole set amid forest greenery and winding brooks. Truly an unforgetable sight.

At Noordwijk, a small village near Noordwijkerhout, I stopped again to see if I could find the fine home of Mimi's father, Dr de Witt Hamer. At the end of the War my D Company had taken over his hospital in Noordwijk from the Germans and sent them packing to their homeland. Dr de Witt Hamer had passed away some years earlier and I felt somewhat diffident about calling on his successor who lived in his home on the grounds of the hospital. But I did. Again I was formally dressed for the occasion.

Mr van der Zanden and his charming wife gave me a warm welcome just as though I were a long lost friend. As on so many other occasions, their friendliness and hospitality were overwhelming — almost embarrassing. I imagined for a moment what my reaction would have been if a complete stranger had appeared at my door in Toronto.

But the van der Zandens took it all in their stride, invited me in, offered drinks and showed me around the house I had known so well 40 years earlier. As we ascended the wide staircase I mentioned that there used to be a secret room on the second floor, at the head of the stairs, where Dr de Witt Hamer's son, Jim, and escaped Allied airmen hid during the War. Mr van der Zanden was delighted.

"You know more about this house than we do. We heard about a secret room but have never been able to find it."

We spent the next few minutes pressing wooden panels and poking around the stairwell, but no magic door popped open.

"Perhaps I'm mistaken about the location of the hide-away," I feebly offered.

"No, I don't think so. There is a lot of dead space on the second floor and under these stairs. We'll have to get a carpenter in here some day to help us."

"If you ever locate it, please let me know. You might find a well-aged bottle of champagne!"

When I saw Mimi I told her about my visit to her old home and not being able to find the secret room.

"Well, you were partly right," she said. "There were actually two rooms — one leading off the bedroom at the head of stairs, the other adjoining a small bedroom down the hall.

"Now where would you like to go for lunch? There are dozens of nice restaurants along the seacoast, especially at Noordwijk-on-the-Sea."

I delved into my briefcase and pulled forth three heavy silverplated spoons. "Look at the name on the back of the spoons."

"The Grand Hotel?"

"Yes. I thought we might go there for lunch."

I reminded Mimi that the Officers' Mess of a German Coast Defence Unit was stationed in the Grand Hotel in 1945. They had naturally appropriated all the silverware and furnishings for their own use, and when we threw them out we just as naturally took over the silverware. The spoons had been part of the loot I had taken home and put to good use for the past 40 years. I had thought it was about time to return them.

"That was a nice thought," consoled Mimi, "but I'm afraid you're 15 years too late — the hotel was pulled down in 1970. Let's visit my favourite restaurant on the sea."

After lunch we wandered along the beach, reminiscing about the War and the Liberation. Suddenly I stopped. "Mimi, what's that in the dunes, over there, about 200 yards? It looks like an old German bunker."

"Sure, there's still lots of them in the dunes around Noordwijk-on-the-Sea, and at Zandvoort."

"Do you think I could find the ones near Zandvoort where I took over the German 409th Coastal Defence Regiment?"

"Let's try. Shouldn't by any trouble."

Like two 22 year old kids (which we were 40 years earlier), we set off across the dunes and soon came upon a whole nest of concrete bunkers, dug into the reverse slopes of a long ridge. Their guns had been removed but the bunkers were still ugly and menacing; some wore their camouflage paint.

Sitting on blankets beside one of the bunkers, a family group was enjoying a picnic. Little children ran in and out of the fortifications, playing some kind of game. I wanted to yell at them to stop their frolicking and leave this obscene symbol of Nazi tyranny and oppression. Then the skies blackened and rain began to fall. The family quickly gathered up its baskets and left.

Slowly, I climbed a rusty iron ladder to the top of the command bunker and peered out to sea. Heavy breakers now beat against the beach and lashed at the sand dunes. Storm winds whipped up the sand and seared my face. Soon they would be gale force.

I heard a voice in the bunker below "Herr Oberst, there'll be no invasion tonight. Will the English never come? We've been guarding these God-forsaken dunes four years now."

Another voice replied, "They'll be here soon enough. But not from the sea. The bloody Canadians are attacking the Ijssel River. Our guns are pointing the wrong way. It's all finished for us, Leutnant. It's all finished."

I clambered down the ladder and found Mimi huddled in the lee of the bunker. "I'm going home," I said. "The War is over."

Part II — Italy

The second part of my mission in May, 1985, was to visit once again the battlefields in Italy and pay my respects at the cemeteries where so many

501

of my friends lay buried. It would be my third pilgrimage to Italy; the first in 1956, the second in 1975.

This time I decided to take the train from Amsterdam to Bologna instead of driving by car. This would allow me to relax as I travelled through Germany, along the Rhine and into Switzerland (past Dusseldorf, Stuttgart and Munich, once devasted by our Allied bombers, but now proud cities). As the train entered the Alps and stopped at the Brenner Pass, I remembered that this was the place where Hitler and Mussolini met and plotted the downfall of the Allies. Then into Italy, past Bolzano and Verona, to Bologna. There I took a car to Rimini, which would be my headquarters for visiting the battlefields and cemeteries in northern Italy.

I had rejoined the Regiment in northern Italy on September 19th, 1944, just after it had occupied positions a few hundred yards north of the Ausa River, after crossing a railway line south of the river. It took a good bit of scouting to find the place where the Patricias had crossed the Ausa, which was now just a narrow stream hidden by thick underbrush and tall trees. It seemed impossible that in September, 1944, this was a tank obstacle that could not be traversed without a Bailey bridge. My search was not helped by the fact that the railway line had long since been torn up, but I was lucky to meet a farmer who remembered those events of 1944 and guided me to the crossing place.

To the north, about a mile distant, the towering mass of San Fortunato dominated the ground ahead. I began to advance toward the feature through fields of lush vineyards. Instantly the hellish screams of German 88s and Moaning Minnies filled the air. My stomach tightened. The fear of 40 years ago was still in me.

I pressed on and climbed the steep slope of San Fortunato, where so many men in my company had been cut down by deadly German air bursts. Finally I made it to the top of the ridge and rested beside the same white house my company had briefly occupied in 1944. For a moment it all came back again — four shuddering blasts from German 88s shook the house and hurled hunks of masonry on the troops struggling up the hill.

San Fortunato was the last barrier to our advance to the north Italian plains. Our armour was to sweep ahead and 'debouch' into the Valley of the Po. But they never made it. Rains came and the tanks and infantry got bogged down in the mud and rivers of the Romagna.

From the heights of San Fortunato I surveyed the reverse slopes that gradually fell to the plains and the bed of the Marecchia River. I remembered — with such clarity that it frightened me — how three German Tiger tanks on the lower slopes had savaged our own tanks as they came over the crest of the ridge. I remembered, too, the advance to our next objective, a farmhouse, code-named Bovey, along a sunken road clogged with the bloody remains of German paratroopers. From this position I had led the entire

Division down the slope into the plain, without a weapon.

With excited steps, I set off along the same sunken road to find the farmhouse. I recalled that on my previous visits in 1956 and 1975 the building was in the same condition as it was in 1944 — abandoned and heavily damaged by shellfire.

As I approached Bovey I could hardly believe what appeared before my eyes — a large, modern home surrounded by a high stone wall with an imposing entrance and two immense wrought-iron gates. I wondered what Sam Potts, who had been my company commander, would have thought if he were alive today.

Feeling somewhat overawed at finding this edifice when I had expected to see only the abandoned remains of a farmer's cottage, I slowly advanced on the iron gates, as though they guarded a German stronghold. My fears were not entirely unfounded. A large, black, German shepherd bounded out the door of the house, its fangs and snarls showing it meant business, and raced for the gates. I was glad they were shut tight.

Closely following this fierce guardian of his domain, came the owner, uttering Italian curses: *"Silenzio, silenzio, male cane, va via!"* In a moment he had the dog under control and turned his attention to me.

"Scusate, Signor, che cosa vuole?"

I quickly explained my mission and my surprise at finding his lovely home instead of the deserted, bombed-out *casa* I had seen here in 1944, 1956 and 1975. His eyes widened in amazement. Would I please come in and tell him all about the battle for San Fortunato Ridge.

Over several glasses of vino rosso I described the fearful slaughter both sides suffered in the battle and the subsequent advance to the Marecchia River. He slowly nodded his head in agreement. In Italian he said, "Yes, I know something about those battles. You see, I was a boy of 13 when the Canadians attacked San Fortunato. My home was not here, but further north in the valley. I was badly wounded in the head when a shell exploded in our house, killing my mother and maiming my brother. My left eye is only a piece of coloured glass. May I offer you some spumante?"

This was certainly not the story I had expected to hear and I felt annoyed with myself for once again evoking bitter memories of the War. I rose to leave.

"Oh no, Signor, I want to tell you about this house. I bought the property five years ago. As you say, the *casa* was an abandoned ruin. But the site offers such a lovely view of the surrounding countryside I fell in love with the place and decided to build a fine new home. It's taken me four years, but what do you think of it?"

"It's magnificent. You did all the work yourself?"

"Yes, most of it. I am a builder by trade. Would you like to look around?"

Accompanied by his wife and young son I was given a grand tour. No wonder, I thought, the Italians make such successful immigrants. This man, almost single-handedly, had, by his native wits and hard labour, built a castle for himself and his family.

"One last thing, Signor, would you care to see the *grotto*?"

This was a curious word for my host to use and I wasn't sure what the word meant in English. I assumed it was 'basement'. He led me to a small door that appeared to be part of the original building and, pointing to his head, motioned to me to crouch and follow him. Down we went on a spiral staircase into the bowels of the earth. At the bottom he switched on a flashlight. In the gloom an enormous cavern opened up around us.

"Signor, you are surprised?"

"I certainly am. What is this?"

My host was happy to explain. In the spring of 1944, when the Germans started to fortify San Fortunato, the owner of the property and many of his neighbours decided to build secretly their own 'bunker' — a deep cavern in the side of the hill. The idea was that as soon as the bombs started to fall, all the Italians in the neighbourhood would hide in their 'grotto', bringing with them food, vino and supplies to last several weeks.

The plan worked perfectly. When the Allied guns opened up, all the Italians in the area mysteriously disappeared. Down in the depths they patiently waited while the Germans and the Allies killed and maimed each other overhead.

Only once was their hiding place almost compromised. A huge shell or bomb, German or Canadian my host couldn't say, penetrated almost to the cavern. Part of the roof fell in and two children were buried alive. The damage was soon repaired and the cave dwellers continued to live in their grotto, undetected by either side. When the Allies finally passed on the Italians resurrected themselves and went back to their shattered homes.

"Incredible." I broke in. "Do you mean to say all these people were in this cave when my platoon occupied the house overhead?"

"That's true, Signor."

"How many were there?"

"Two or three hundred!"

I wished Sam Potts could have heard this fantastic tale. I could almost hear him shout at me, "Why the hell didn't you discover that grotto? We could have used it too, with all that German crap blasting our *casa* to bits."

I climbed the spiral staircase and entered the living room. He reached for the mantel-piece, over an elaborate fireplace, and brought down a highly polished shell casing from one of our 25 pounder guns.

"Here, take this as a souvenir of the occasion."

"I'd love to have it, but I can't possibly carry it in my luggage. There's no room."

"I understand. Then please take this piece of one of your shells that I dug out of the garden not so long ago."

With mixed feelings, I accepted this memento of one of the bloodiest battles of the Italian campaign.

We then went outside and stood for a moment admiring the view. In the bright sunlight I could see the Marecchia River as it meandered through the plain to Rimini. Beyond that the vineyards and fields stretched endlessly to the horizon. I thought of the Canadian soldiers who had gazed at that same panorama 40 years earlier. For many it was their last view of the land they had fought so hard to liberate.

I said goodbye to my host and sadly returned to the white house on the summit of San Fortunato, that had taken so much punishment from the German guns. This was my third visit to this place since the War. In 1956, the house had been occupied by several Italian families and still bore many of the scars of battle. In 1975, it had been fixed up and converted to a discotheque. Now the place was a first class restaurant with beautiful gardens, terraces and fountains.

A large wedding reception was in progress. The joyous laughter of the wedding party and their guests filled the restaurant and flowed down the slopes to the valley below. It made me happy too. The horrors of San Fortunato slowly faded away.

I climbed into my car and headed north to the Marecchia River, following the very route I had taken on that black stormy night when I had led the battalion down to the plain and into the tiger's den.

In minutes I was across the river. A few hundred yards ahead, at right angles to my advance, lay the Emilian Way, the ancient roadway running west from Rimini. Somewhere along that highway there should be a dwelling where my platoon had endured the terrible German bombardment that had reduced the place to one battered room. I realized that the chances of the house still being there were remote, but it shouldn't be hard to find the site. It hugged the south side of the highway, about 100 yards east of a large brick works that hardly could have disappeared.

I drove west along the highway, tingling with anticipation as I kept a sharp lookout. Suddenly, there it was. It had been too easy. A combination of maps, diary and memory had done the trick. I turned into the yard and stopped. A large, ferocious dog kept me in the car until a farmer appeared and drove the beast away.

In Italian, I quickly stated my business to the startled farmer.

"Moma, Moma", he cried out to his wife, standing in the doorway. *"Canadese soldato. Vene qua, vene qua."*

She bustled over, grabbed both my hands and kissed them. Pointing to her house and murmuring *"a casa, a casa,"* she pulled me along, while her husband went looking for the children. Once again, I was given the kind of hospitality I had almost come to expect. When the wife insisted I stay for lunch I did not object. For once, I had time to enjoy the generosity of these plain, friendly people.

In between mouthfuls of the best spaghetti I had tasted in years, washed down with *vino di casa* of considerable authority, I told my hosts about my short, but terrifying stay in their house 40 years earlier. I marvelled at how they had not simply repaired, but reconstructed the place, so that hardly a mark remained of the devastation caused by the German shellfire. The farmer modestly explained that after all, Rome wasn't built in a day and neither was the house. It took him many months, in fact years, before the dwelling was restored to his satisfaction.

What an utterly fantastic scene! Here I was enjoying a fine meal in what had once been the only room of the house left intact. Here, my platoon had been prostrate on the dirt floor, clawing into the clay before another shell tore them to pieces. I looked over at one corner of the room, where a comfortable chair beckoned. I hesitated. How could I relax there? In that corner, one of my men had broken under the shelling and sobbed hysterically, "We'll all be blown straight to hell."

How many of those men, I wondered, are alive today? Do they still dream of the hell we endured in this very room?

The farmer leaned over and gave me a friendly nudge. "Are you alright, Signor? Perhaps my vino is a little strong?"

"No, no. Not at all. In fact I'd like another glass. I'm sorry if I looked a little strange. Nothing that a strong drink won't cure. By the way, may I inspect the brick factory down the road? It looks much like it did in 1944."

Escorted by the whole family and several dogs I toured the factory in style. It was indeed much the same except for a couple of new sheds. When I looked closer at the main building, I could not restrain an involuntary "Oh no."

"What's wrong, Signor? Are you sure you're not feeling ill?"

I brushed off his concern and furtively peeked at five weather-beaten, but still legible words: *Credere, Obbedire, Combattere. Viva Mussolini.* The ghost of *Il Duce* still haunted this place. It was time for me to move on.

In my hotel room in Rimini that evening, I spread out my old battle maps on the floor and planned my next operation. My objective would be the infamous Savio River that had caused the Regiment so much grief in October 1944. From Rimini, the Savio is only about 30 miles. In 1944, it had taken us almost two weeks to advance that distance and fight our way across the river. I planned to do it in an afternoon, albeit under slightly more favourable conditions — no rain, no mud, no Germans and no staff officers.

Next day, in brilliant sunshine, I crossed the ancient Ponte di Tiberio, erected by that worthy Roman Emperor and still in service. I noted with regret however, that while the famous bridge still spanned the bed of the Marecchia River, water no longer flows under its venerable arches. The river has been diverted.

Urging my little Fiat to give its best effort, I sped along the Via Emilia, past Santarcangelo, over the Uso River, through Savignano and across Caesar's Rubicon. Here, I took to the sideroads to follow the route the Patricias had taken in October 1944. Crossing one of the innumerable streams, I was amazed to find an old Bailey bridge from the War still doing good service after 40 years — not quite as durable as the Tiberius bridge, but what modern things are built to last for ever!

At Ponte della Pietra, I crossed over the Pisciatello River. Here the Patricias had gone forward to meet their destiny at the Savio River, four miles distant. Now my pace quickened. What would I find at the Savio River? Would the houses in the little village of Martorano, that had sheltered my Machine Gun Platoon from the fury of the battle, still be there? For that matter, would I be able to locate the place where A and D companies had so valiantly fought to cross the river? And would I . . . . .

I slammed on the brakes. I had nearly gone through a stop sign, at the intersection of the trail I was following and the river road running at right angles to my advance. I turned left on to the river road and gave a gasp of relief. There was Martorano; there were the houses where I had set up my machine guns.

Then I turned to look at the river. It should be only 100 yards, maybe 200 yards, straight ahead, winding in and out across the front; but only freshly ploughed fields met my gaze. The river had vanished!

I glanced to the right to get my bearings. My view was blocked by a high, modern bridge and a new four-lane highway! Incredible!

I ran forward, over the ground where A and D companies had lost so many men from mines, shellfire and German machine guns. Soon I came upon what had been the bed of the meandering river. Bulldozers were at work filling it in. A hundred yards further on, a new channel for the river had been cut through fields that once had hidden German bunkers.

No point in shedding tears for the past or decrying progress, I heard myself muttering. Take advantage of the fine view of the battlefield from the high bridge.

Heeding my own good advice, I hastened to the bridge. From this vantage point the battlefield lay before me, as on a sandtable. From Martorano, the ground fell away to the old river's edge. It was still cleared of all trees, as it had been in 1944. The west, or enemy side of the river, was still higher than our side, giving the Germans excellent fields of fire. What a classic killing ground, I thought. But that had been only the first ordeal. If the troops survived this test they still had to face mud, rain, mines and German tanks. It was a miracle that anyone had survived. And Dog Company had tried it not once, but twice.

One further battlefield in this area held considerable interest for me — the place where Pte 'Smoky' Smith of The Seaforth Highlanders had performed acts of supreme courage. Near Pieve Sestina, a few hundred yards from the river, he had taken on three Panther tanks and a platoon of infantry single-handedly, and won the Victoria Cross. I stood only a moment on this field of honour. It belonged to Pte Smith and his regiment.

That night I pondered where my steps should take me on the morrow. Only one day remained to cover the Romagna, where the Patricias had fought and died for five months. Nine cemeteries, containing the bodies of 2,322 Canadians who fell in northern Italy, are located at Florence and at towns and villages along the Adriatic coast, from Ancona in the south to Argenta in the north. It was obvious I could not visit all or even half of them in one day.

In past pilgrimages, I had paid my respects at all these cemeteries, some more than once. But the sorrow and anger, the bitterness and resentment at seeing the names of my friends had always overwhelmed me. This time I decided to visit only one cemetery — Coriano Ridge, near Rimini and San Fortunato, where so many Patricias had fallen. Like all Commonwealth cemeteries, this one had been laid out with great care by an eminent architect, to give an impression of a beautiful garden of peace and serenity. Set on a high hill, amid green foliage and scented flowers, it is indeed a place of great beauty. But for me it will never be a place of peace. No longer do I read the names on the white, granite headstones marking the graves of 427 Canadian soldiers. It is too painful.

I climbed in my car and slowly drove away. But as I said goodbye to my friends I was happy they would be remembered in perpetuity by this fine memorial.

Returning to the Via Emilia, I drove northwest along this ancient roadway, and soon arrived back at Martorano and the Savio River. About 12 miles ahead lay the Ronco River, where the Patricias, in October 1944, had temporarily come to rest after their advance from the Savio River. I recalled with some amusement (not felt at the time) how I had fallen into a farmyard cesspool and was promptly ordered into the vanguard to asphyxiate the Germans.

My next and final objective was the Senio River, where the Regiment's long advance from the tip of Italy, begun on September 2nd, 1943, had finally ended in the last days of December, 1944. Here, the entire 8th Army halted and took up defensive positions for the remainder of the winter.

From the Ronca to the Senio River is only 12 miles, a 20 minute drive in 1985 along a new super highway, the A14. Forty years earlier, the same distance had taken the 1st Canadian Division one month of dirty fighting and hard slogging, through mud and across rivers and canals more numerous than in Venice.

I decided to forgo the 20 minute dash along the A14 and follow the route I had taken in December 1944. From the Ronca River, I pushed forward to the Montone River, which I crossed at the little village of Casa Bettini.

Three miles ahead the Lamone River flowed to the sea, its unpredictable waters restrained by high flood banks. By the grace of God, the Patricias were not involved in the crossing of this obstacle — this tragic task had fallen to The Royal Canadian Regiment.

During the War, I had never had time to visit the ground and study the operation. In any event, I was not aware of the full extent of the tragedy until well after the War. Now, armed with LCol Stevens' excellent *History of the RCR*, I visited the battleground on a bright, warm day in May, 1985. From the west flood bank, or enemy side of the river, I surveyed the crossing site. The river itself was an obstacle even at this time of year — what it was like in December 1944, after steady torrents of rain, I could only imagine.

Once the troops had navigated the river, they had to climb the high flood bank on the other side. If they miraculously survived these two obstacles, they then had to advance over mud flats to their final objective. And if they got that far, a high, sinister railway embankment on their left flank provided a covered approach for the enemy to counter-attack, while their comrades raked the area with fire from the embankment. It would be like shooting fish in a barrel.

And that, in essence, is what the enemy did. The RCR, after valiantly crossing the river and the high flood bank and suffering heavy casualties, were decimated in the mud flats. It will be recalled that my friend, Peter Hertzberg, the son of the Commandant of RMC, and practically his entire platoon were killed or wounded trying to cross the river on the railway bridge.

From my observation post on the west or enemy side of the river, I turned my attention to the other side. About 400 yards to the south, close to the flood banks, rose an enormous building. Though it was standing in the flats some 30 feet below the dykes, the upper part of the structure was clearly visible. This undoubtedly was what I had thought to be a convent in December 1944, when my Machine Gun Platoon had occupied it briefly.

I had to investigate. Sliding down the steep floodbank, I got in my car, crossed the Lamone and drove up to the building. At the portals I met an old man whom I assumed to be the caretaker. I told him why I had come and asked if the place was still a convent.

No, it was not. But it had a long history and I was partly correct. The place was known as the Palazzo San Giacomo and was at least 400 years old. After serving as the palace of a local Prince and his descendants for several centuries, it became a monastery and gradually fell into disrepair. During the War, when it served as a shelter for local farmers as well as a temporary convent, it had suffered quite heavy damage and was eventually abandoned. In recent years the Italian Government had started to repair the damage but soon discovered that due to the low-lying land and constant flooding, the foundations had started to give way. It would cost millions, if not billions of lire to restore. In the meantime, to help defray some of the costs, the government was renting out rooms in the palace to anyone who was crazy enough to risk having the whole structure collapse on them at any moment. My informant patted his chest and told me he was one of these brave tenants. To help him, in turn, to defray the cost, he had converted part of the palace into a junk yard.

After receiving dire warnings about the perilous state of the foundation, I was allowed inside and prowled around some of the rooms I had occupied in 1944. It was not a pretty sight. Beautiful old frescoes, balustrades, altars, statues, leaded panes of glass, all lay in pieces on the once beautifully tiled floors. Gaping holes in the roof, that went through six or seven stories to the basement, caused by German and Canadian bombs, let in the elements. Rats scurried among piles of refuse and debris.

I was glad to get out into the fresh air and be on my way. As I drove through what had once been an imposing entrance to a beautiful courtyard, but was now filled with junk, I spied a strange object clinging to a gate — an ancient bed pan. It described, better than any words, what was inside.

I recrossed the Lamone River at Transversera, where my Machine Gun Platoon had been rafted over the obstacle on December 13th, 1944, on its way to take part in the attack on the Naviglio Canal. I never quite made it to the canal. About 300 yards short, a Moaning Minnie had landed beside my jeep and a large hunk had lodged in my backside as I dove for the ditch.

Without any difficulty, I located the spot on the road where I had been hit. The quiet, pastoral scene had not changed in 40 years. The small house that had served as an RAP looked much the same; so did the ditch that I didn't make in time; so did the open fields on each side where Colin McDougall and his men took a pasting from the same Moaning Minnies that got me. Altogether, it was a quite unremarkable spot. As I drove away I confess I was not impressed with the place I had chosen to be wounded for the second time.

My final objective, the winter line along the Senio River, north of Bagnacavallo, was only minutes away. This should prove more interesting. The Patricias had spent the better part of January and February 1945 holding this line, in houses that were only a few yards from the Germans. Surely some of the dwellings and people would still be there.

The Senio River, like the Lamone, has high floodbanks that dominate the flats on each side of the river. A hundred yards from the east bank, astride a country road, lies a small farmer's village. Some of the houses nestle right beside the bank. This was the position my D Company occupied in early 1945, right under the very noses of the Germans dug into the same bank.

As I entered the village, I gave a gasp of delight. The house that had been my company headquarters was still there, precisely where it should be! And in the same condition as when I had left it — pockmarked with shell holes and abandoned.

I parked my car on the road and approached a small *osteria*, hoping to meet some of the villagers. A warning from long ago flashed through my mind: "Don't leave your car on the open road, you fool. Park it in the lee of the house where it will have some protection from German shellfire." I laughed at my inner voice and entered the restaurant.

In English, and then in Italian, I ordered a *carafa di vino* and spaghetti bolognese. (Bologna was only a few miles away. Spaghetti Milanese would not have been a wise choice.)

"Voi siete inglese?" asked the waiter.

"No, canadese — soldato canadese. In janario 1945, ho stato qui, nella quella casa," I said, pointing to the house across the street. Immediately, everyone in the restaurant gathered around and excitedly started talking. Would I stay a few days? Where was my home? Did I know their brother in Toronto? Where was my wife?

It was wonderful! In a moment I was transported back to January 1945. While the guns roared outside, I was in my *casa* enjoying a fine dinner with an Italian friend, by candlelight, hoping my CO would not catch me engaged in such un unmilitary activity.

Before leaving these friendly, generous people, I told them I would like to look over my platoon positions and those of the *partigani* who were attached to my company.

"Of course," beamed a short, craggy-faced farmer. "I would be honoured to show you around. I was one of those *partigani*."

We climbed the flood bank of the river, where the Germans had their deep dugouts, and surveyed my company positions on the flats 30 feet below. "My God," I murmured. "My headquarters is hardly a No 9 iron shot from here."

My three platoon positions were even nearer. One was in a house so close to the bank that I could smell the kitchen odours and hear the people talk-ing — why the Germans hadn't blown us all to bits was a mystery. Then I remembered the little games we used to play on them — rolling trucks filled with high explosives down the road into their positions; sending over aerial torpedoes in the form of anti-tank bombs; throwing land mines over the banks with huge sling shots. I allowed myself a large smile of satisfaction. The bloody Germans were more afraid of us than we were of them. We kept them so occupied with our patrols and fiendish schemes, they had no time or inclination to really get us mad.

My guide grabbed me by the arm and said he wanted to show me the positions occupied by his *partigani*. I remembered exactly where their head-quarters used to be — in a nearby cemetery — but I let him lead me there. Like most Italian cemeteries, this one was surrounded by a high wall. Inside, magnificent tombs, almost like mausoleums, housed the dead, in sharp contrast to the modest dwellings in the village. In wartime, such monuments were also highly prized shelters for the living.

I asked my guide how his *partigani* wheedled so many Germans out of their safe dugouts in the river bank and brought them through the mines and barbed wire to our positions.

"Very simple," he replied. "Most of them were Poles. You know how they love to eat! Every night we used to cook up minestrone soup, pasta and bread. The cemetery is so close to the Poles that the smell of the food must have driven them mad. Sometimes we left pots of the stuff near their bunkers. When they came out to get the food, we grabbed them. Often they came through the lines themselves."

The mystery of 40 years had finally been solved. I could write a book
. . . . .

Thus ended my tour of the plains of northern Italy. The Apennines in southern Italy beckoned.

Next day I drove south on the A14, along the Adriatic coast, toward my next staging area, Campobasso, the main town of the mountainous Molise District. It would be a long journey, over 350 miles, the last 60 miles or so through mountains. On the way, I would pass by Ortona and the other battlefields where the Patricias had fought some of their bloodiest engagements of the war — the Moro River, Villa Rogatti, Vino Ridge. Unfortunately, time was again my enemy. It would not permit me to visit any of these battlefields. I thought how true was the famous dictum of Napoleon: "Ask of me anything but time." I vowed to return and study these battles which, fortunately, I had missed because of wounds received near Campobasso a month before the engagements.

At noon, I stopped for lunch at San Benedetto del Tronto, and went looking for the hotel and restaurant where the Regiment had rested a few days en route to Pisa, Leghorn, Marseilles and Northwest Europe.

San Benedetto is a very popular seaside resort and there are hundreds of modern hotels strung out for miles along the coast. The chances of my hotel still being in operation, or of finding it, were remote. I asked a pedestrian if he knew the whereabouts of the Hotel Progresso. He had never heard of it. I told him I had stayed there during the War. He laughed. "All those old hotels were torn down years ago."

I was ready to give up the search when I spied a carabinieri. *"Conoscete Albergo Progresso, per favore?"* I pleaded.

"Si. C'e un 'albergo vecchio — rosso colore."

Of course the policeman knew where it was. But the season had not yet begun. It was probably closed. I followed the directions given me and soon arrived at the Hotel Progresso — old, but still elegant, among the shoddy high rise apartments. I crossed the closed in verandah and tried to open one of the heavy glass doors draped in lace — locked. I rang the bell — no response. I peered inside. In the gloom I saw the figure of a very large man lumbering toward me, waving his hands and shouting, *"Chiuso, chiuso. L'albergo non è aperto."*

"Cognosco, cognosco," I yelled through the door. *"Sono un soldato canadese."*

Again I had uttered the magic words. The door opened and a large hand clasped mine and dragged me into the lobby.

I told him I once stayed in his hotel during the War. I was now on my way to Campobasso, but I couldn't pass through without calling on him.

"What was your Regiment?" he asked, in Italian.

"The PPCLI — I'm Captain Frost who arranged a mess dinner in your restaurant. I saved the menu. Here it is."

His eyes sparkled. "Of course, I remember it now. What an evening that was!"

I wanted to believe him but I couldn't remember his face. In the course of my trip so many people claimed to have remembered me that I felt I was the most popular person in Italy. Perhaps I should run for President.

I decided to test him. "You remember that evening?"

"Certainly, Signor. The tables were arranged so — " He described a U shape. "The colonel sat at the head with his senior officers on each side. You were there too as the . . . . chairman?"

"No, the Mess President."

"Yes, that's it. The Mess President. You proposed so many toasts that I believe we ran out of wine. Then you started on the liqueurs. Same thing happened."

"What then?" I asked, innocently.

"Well, a most incredible thing happened. Those officers who could still walk decided they should go for a swim, in their uniforms. So they staggered out the door, crossed the road and dove over the sea wall."

"Yes?"

"Signor, there was no sea on the other side of the wall. The tide was out. But by the Grace of the Virgin Mary, no one was seriously hurt. A few sore heads maybe, but that could have been from the wine."

"Bravo!" I shouted. "What a memory. You were there. It was you I arranged the dinner with."

"No doubt about it. Now let's have lunch and a drink in my private quarters. The hotel doesn't open for another week."

"I'd love to. And I promise not to drink up all your supplies."

After lunch, my host gave me directions how to get back on the A14, and made me promise I would stay at his hotel if I ever came back. I might just do that — but only in season.

As I drove along the seafront, past the garish modern hotels and restaurants, I suddenly saw a very familiar name on one of them. "Hotel

Sydney" the sign declared. My mind shot back 40 years to the Hotel Progresso. What else happened on that memorable evening? I decided I had nothing to worry about. But I didn't stop at the Sydney to check.

At Termoli, I turned inland and immediately entered the foothills of the Apennines. My little Fiat twisted and turned, almost as it if knew the way, and before long we arrived at Campobasso quite late in the evening. I checked in at the same hotel where I had stayed in 1956. Then, it was part of a chain, known as the Jolly hotels, but the experience had been anything but amusing. Now, the hotel had been completely renovated and given a new name — Roxy — with new (much higher) prices. But, after a hard day's drive it was worth it.

I had chosen Campobasso as my base for the next phase of my operations for several reasons. For years I had longed to follow the route my Scouts and Snipers had taken in October 1943, through the heart of the Apennines, from Troia in the south to the northern limit of our advance, Frosolone, where I was wounded. After studying my maps, however, I realized it would take several days to cover this distance properly, so I decided to begin my quest at Cercemaggiore and leave the route south of that town to another time. Campobasso was a community located in the centre of the area I had chosen to explore.

Another reason for choosing Campobasso was strictly emotional. Before I had left on my last patrol, I was told that the division was about to withdraw to an area around Campobasso for a month's rest. The Hun intervened and I only saw Campobasso briefly on a stretcher.

Actually, my hope of 'resting' in Campobasso was once again defeated by the 'exigencies of the service'. This time the service in question was not the army but Canadian Pacific Airlines, in particular flight 207 leaving Rome three days hence. It was thus imperative that I get on with my mission *subito*.

After only a few hours' sleep, I was off into the blue behind the wheel of my faithful scout car (the Fiat). It was exhilarating to be on the move at such an early hour, even though morning mists tried to obscure the twists and turns in the mountain roads. I easily imagined I was back with my Scouts and Snipers blazing a trail for the battalion to follow.

At Cercemaggiore, I turned north toward La Rocca. This feature, over 3,000 feet high, commands the countryside for miles around. In October 1944, my Scout and Sniper Platoon had been ordered to explore La Rocca before the battalion put in an attack to capture it. After a long, hard climb we had gained the summit where we surprised the occupants of an observation post and chased them down the other side of the mountain. They kindly left us a hot meal which, unfortunately, we had no time to consume, as we had to report back to battalion headquarters some five or six miles in rear. We did, however, spot German tanks in harbour on the reverse slopes of the mountain, as well as heavy mortars. This information was duly passed to the artillery who promptly dealt with the tanks and mortars in their accustomed fashion.

One thing had always puzzled me about those tanks. How did they climb the feature, almost to the top? The slopes on our side were strictly made for man or mule. There must be a trail or a mountain track leading up the mountain. But where? I spent an hour or two circling La Rocca trying to find the elusive trail, but finally gave up. There was no way I was going to climb that mountain again *alla piede*. Frustrated, I drove west to the crossroads at Vinchiaturo hoping to find a nice ristorante for lunch.

By a stroke of good luck (how lucky I only realized later) I found an excellent restaurant in the Hotel Le Cupolette and took out my frustration by demolishing a steaming heap of spaghetti with a delicious meat sauce. I showed my appreciation to the *cameriere* in the usual fashion. He politely asked if I were registered in the hotel. I told him I was staying in Campobasso but I was exploring La Rocca trying to find a trail up the mountain. Then I gave him my punch line. *"Sono soldato canadese — Capitano Frost."*

The waiter bowed and said how pleased he was to serve a Canadian officer. Could he fetch the proprietor, who might know something about La Rocca? In a moment Signor Biagio Fazzino appeared and shook my hand. In perfect English he said, "I would be honoured to show you the route up La Rocca. Just last week a Canadian major in the artillery asked me to take him to the top of the mountain. He told me that during the War the Germans had an observation post there from which they directed fire on his guns. Some of his men were killed. When we reached the summit he couldn't believe the view."

"I know, I was there in the War," I interjected. "The Germans would have had no trouble pin-pointing his gun positions."

"That's exactly what he said to me. Then he broke down and cried."

Too bad, I thought, that my patrol had not been sent out a day or two earlier. We might have saved a few more lives.

We hopped into Signor Fazzino's car. He deftly negotiated a maze of tracks and trails and quickly reached the summit. We got out of the car and walked forward to the eastern edge.

What an incredible sight! I could easily understand the feeling of the artillery major. Far below, on the other side of a valley, about six miles distant, was the roadway from Cercemaggiore that I had driven along a few hours earlier. It was from that road that my Scouts and Snipers had set off on foot to climb this mountain. Except for a few copses, the mountainside was still as open as it had been in October 1943. How could the German OP not have seen us? They must have been asleep or not at their post. Whatever the reason, Lady Luck had been on my side that day. Then I remembered that at the very peak of the summit there had been a large cross by which we kept our bearings as we climbed to the top. I turned to Signor

Fazzino. "Is there still a cross somewhere on this mountain?"

"Oh yes, capitano, there certainly is. It stands on top of a large pile of rocks about 100 yards in that direction. You can't see it from here because of the trees. Would you like to walk there?"

We soon found the rock pile and the cross. I suggested that we climb to the top to get an even more spectacular view of the countryside.

"No, no," cautioned my friend. "Those rocks are very sharp and dangerous. There are no foot holds. Some of the rocks are loose. But I can show you another place where you can get an even better view."

We walked through the woods and in a few moments came to a clearing. There stood an ancient looking church with a high tower.

"I don't remember seeing this church when we climbed the mountain in 1943."

"Your memory is correct. For some crazy reason the Germans destroyed it. After the War it was rebuilt, a tower was added and it is now regularly used each week. It is also very popular for weddings. Can you imagine a more romantic and fitting place to be married — on top of the world?"

It was a beautiful thought and I said so.

Signor Fazzino nodded his appreciation and said, "There's an old caretaker around somewhere. Let's find him."

We found the old man peacefully asleep in the grass. He let us into the church and led us up steep, circular stairs to the top of the tower. The view was indeed more breathtaking than before.

"I don't know the name of this church," I said, "but I would call it the Chapel in the Clouds."

"That's pretty good, I'll have to mention it to the priest who comes here each week."

He then told me a fascinating tale. Part of the church was very, very old, perhaps four or five hundred years. It was originally a monastery. The monks were skilled stone cutters and occupied their days carving beautiful statues and other works of art from the rocks strewn about the mountain top. They built their monastery and erected an enormous cairn and cross where the rock pile now stood.

Then something happened. The monastery disappeared, as did the monks. All that was left was the rubble scattered about us — bits of tablets, monuments, statues — and some foundation stones used in rebuilding the church.

Signor Fazzino shrugged his shoulders and spread his hands. "It's all a sad mystery. But there's no doubt about the name. The mountain and abbey have been known for centuries as La Rocca."

Signor Fazzino drove me back in his car, and I said goodbye to another kind, generous host. How would I ever repay all these wonderful people?

Later that day I returned to La Rocca by myself. The place fascinated me and I was tempted to take away a small bit of stone sculpted long ago by the monks. But I didn't. Instead, I walked through the woods to the rough pile of rocks that had once been a beautiful cairn. Carefully, ever so carefully, I slowly climbed to the top, testing each rock before I put my full weight on it. At the summit, I clutched the cross and inched myself up to take a spectacular picture of the lush valley below.

But the valley had vanished. During my climb, a thick mist had, like magic, carpeted the countryside and would soon hide the cross itself.

That evening, in my Hotel Roxy in Campobasso, I met a visiting architect who was working on a project in town. In view of his profession, I thought he would be interested in my experiences at La Rocca and the amazing monks who had fashioned such beautiful works and then disappeared. I told him too, about my bad luck in not being able to get a picture from the cairn because of the mist.

"Bad luck?" he repeated. "Maybe, but have you thought how those monks must have felt about you climbing their cairn and clutching their sacred cross? Some people say they still watch over La Rocca."

Only one day remained to complete my long pilgrimage, begun in Amsterdam three weeks earlier. It would be another exhausting journey. Rising again at the crack of dawn, I drove toward Frosolone and Spinete. On the way, I couldn't resist taking a small detour to have one last peek at the mysterious La Rocca. At a crossroads, west of the mountain, I stopped and looked up. There it stood, proud, magnificent, master of all it surveyed. A circle of mist shrouded the top, but at the very pinnacle the cairn and cross broke through the clouds, triumphant and supreme.

I studied my old maps, notes, sketches. The crossroads I was standing on were supposed to be the centre of a small village, Monte Verde. Not a trace of any dwelling or building was to be seen. I looked at my up-to-date roadmaps. No such village was shown at the intersection, or anywhere in the vicinity. But a hamlet, Montevecchio, was shown about two miles south of the interesection. Then by chance I saw on the map the name Monteverde, a small village about eight miles west of my position, just north of Boiano.

How could such a mistake have been made by the staff and planners at brigade and division? I was glad I had not been ordered to patrol to the crossroads at Monteverde, deep in German territory. I would surely have spent the rest of the War in a prison camp, if I had survived the long patrol into the heart of the enemy's defences.

But was it a mistake? Perhaps there were buildings here in 1943, and the place was called 'Mone Verde'. I thought again about those strange monks. Had they pulled another 'disappearing' act? I laughed at my idle musings as I jumped in my car and quickly drove away.

Frosolone is just another small village in the foothills of the Matese Mountains. In the whole 1st Canadian Division, only one officer still has any interest in the place — Lt C S Frost, PPCLI. It was here I was wounded on October 26th, 1943 while on patrol. The 1st Canadian Division was about to be relieved after a long, tortuous drive up southern Italy (it was in fact relieved the next day, October 27th) but, before we withdrew, the brigadier thought we should 'tidy up' our front so all would be neat and tidy for the 5th British Division who were taking over our positions. Toward this end I was despatched with my Scouts and Snipers to "see how matters stood" at Frosolone. The patrol set off from the village of Spinete about noon on October 26th, 1943, and returned at 10:00 pm that evening.

This would be my third visit to Frosolone since the end of the War. In 1956 I had explored the creek, on the fringes of the town, where I had been wounded. At that time, only eleven years after the War, the approaches to Frosolone had looked much the same as they did in 1943. I had hoped to find the fancy Beretta pistol an Italian major had given me, and which I had lost in the creek. But no such luck.

From the creek I had looked up at the road behind, about 30 feet above. Why the Germans hadn't shot me and my two men as we clambered down the steep slope I couldn't understand. Perhaps they thought we were foolish enough to expose the whole platoon at once, as we attacked their position. If such was their hope, they must have got a rude shock when my supporting sections, in good cover, opened up and killed a good number of them.

Gazing at the roadway high above, I had wondered, too, how I had struggled up the slope, after I had been wounded, while trying to hold my face together with my hands. Then I remembered how my brave men, Knox and Menaar, had stayed with me in the creek and had pulled and shoved me back to the road and had helped me return to home base.

In 1956 I had also walked forward to where the Germans had dug their positions on the outskirts of town, and I had looked back over the route my scouts had taken after passing through Sant' Elena. It was still open all the way. I could just imagine the German gunmen smirking at the crazy Canadians who would soon be dead ducks.

I had then stood where a German soldier had foolishly exposed himself and shot me in the face from a distance of 50 yards — foolish because he was immediately cut down by my own men.

In 1970, during the 30th Anniversary Pilgrimage of the Canadian Corps, I made another visit to "see how matters stood" at Frosolone. The countryside after Sant' Elena was still open, but small trees and thick undergrowth now provided good cover from the road down the slope to the creek and from the creek up to the former German positions. The slope did not seem nearly as steep or as difficult as it had on my earlier visit. My attack had been 27 years too soon! Again I poked around the woods and creek for my Beretta, and again the same result.

Now it was May 1985, and I was once more standing in the creek. Fifteen years of forest growth had pretty well hidden it and covered the approaches. Once more, for sentimental reasons, I started to look for my long lost pistol. Then I realized it had become a silly obsession. I turned back to the road and headed for Spinete.

On the way back, I passed by the foot of the Pesco La Messa mountain with its cross on the summit. This had been a rendezvous for Allied prisoners who had escaped and made their way south. My patrol had picked up some of them and guided them back to our lines.

There was one last thing about Frosolone I wanted to check. After being wounded, I had managed, with the help of my men, to walk all the way from Frosolone to Spinete. I had been told it was a distance of eight miles but I couldn't believe it. In my state, how could anyone cover that distance at night, over fields, around blown bridges, in a drenching rain.

I carefully checked the odometer reading on my Fiat before I left Frosolone and headed for Spinete. As the mountain trail twisted and turned I kept my eyes glued to the gauge. (It was kilometers, but I quickly converted). Four miles, five miles, still we had not arrived at Spinete. Finally, we were there. I looked at the gauge. My God, exactly eight miles! How did I do it? PT, PT and more PT at RMC, rigorous training in the army, the support and encouragement of my men, and above all, the will to survive.

Rome beckoned. Like a weary pilgrim of earlier times I set off for the Eternal City. Only two shrines would impede my progress — Cassino War Cemetery and the Hitler Line, where the Regiment was all but decimated.

The Cassino War Cemetery lies in the Liri Valley, not far from the foot of Monte Cassino and the famed Abbey of the same name. This cemetery is the largest Second World War Cemetery in Italy. Of the 4,200 headstones, 855 are Canadians who died during the battles of the Hitler Line and the advance toward Rome. The cemetery also has a Memorial which commemorates the 4,054 Commonwealth men who died in the Sicilian and Italian campaigns and have no known grave. Among the names on the green marble panels are those of 192 Canadians.

Like all large Commonwealth War Cemeteries, a stone Cross of Sacrifice, bearing on its shaft a crusader's sword of bronze, watches over the marble headstones. A reflecting pool, bordered with mosaic tiles set in attractive patterns, repeats the image of the Cross. In the background, the mass of Monte Cassino and its Abbey shelters the cemetery and gives an added impression of permanence and grandeur.

I have seen the Cassino War Cemetery many times and I am always moved by its setting and stark beauty. But it is the 8,254 names of the fallen that move me most of all. The dead soldiers and airmen commemorated here could have populated a city about the size of Fredericton, New Brunswick in 1944.

I drove away along Highway 6, through the town at the base of Monte Cassino. On the outskirts, I saw a freshly painted sign, *Cimitero Tedesco*, and an arrow pointing toward a hill north of the town. Though I had little time to spare, I felt irresistibly drawn to the graves of my former enemies. I left my car and climbed the hill toward a large, rugged, stone cross at the top. There, I gazed down at the headstones — thousands upon thousands of them in neat circles around the hill, descending into the valley below. In contrast to German cemeteries I had visited on earlier trips, this one was immaculately cared for and adorned with green foliage, hedges and beautiful flowers. Large sprinklers cast their waters over the thick verdant grass. I walked down to the first row of headstones, expecting to find the names of senior German officers who had fallen at Cassino. At the first marker, in bold letters, I read three names, one underneath the other:

Ein Deutsche Soldaten
Ein Deutsche Soldaten
Ein Deutsche Soldaten

I looked at the back of the marker. The same three names appeared. I checked the next marker and the next and the next. All had the same inscription — one German soldier. Near the end of the first row, I found a few names, some with ranks and units but most with just a surname. My Lord, I thought, each tombstone marks the remains of six soldiers. There must be tens of thousands of German dead here. And most are nameless.

To my complete surprise I wept. Within me a voice whispered: Oh the futility, the waste, the utter stupidity of it all. In the valley 8,000 Allied soldiers are buried or commemorated. On this hill lie many, many more German fallen. All died for a cause. They lost, we won.

But where are the spoils of victory? None are evident here. Only the tragic cost.

What differences now separate the men who lie at rest? None at all, except that ours lie victorious in the valley; theirs lie vanquished, on a high hill overlooking their victors.

The Hitler Line. For a Patricia officer this battle represents all that the Regiment stands for — steadiness, tenacity, discipline, duty, courage, gallantry. The attack went in at 6 am, May 23rd, 1944. At the end of the day only 77 Patricias answered the roll call. Later that night a further 50 reported back. They had been cut off or pinned down in the attack. Total casualties for the day had been 246.

I was in England in May, 1944, recuperating from wounds, and thus missed the Hitler Line. But I had read about the battle and was awed by the enormous strength of the German fortifications.[1]

Its northern extremity was anchored into the slopes of Monte Cairo whence it descended the mountainside near Piedimonte, crossed the Liri valley nine miles behind the Gustav Line and climbed into the Aurunci range at Sant' Oliva. It had been built by the Todt organization and contained the latest refinements of military engineering. An historian thus described it:

"It was in the Hitler Line that the defences were the most elaborate. There were evidences that the Germans intended to make it their enduring frontier. Its outposts were semi-mobile pill boxes to hold two men and a light machine gun. Behind these there was a system of concrete gun emplacements covered by weapon pits and connected by tunnels and communication trenches, with Tiger or Panther turrets on concrete foundations, with underground living quarters as key points to the system. Each of these turrets, which had all-round traverse, was covered by two or three mobile anti-tank guns on each flank. Passive protection was provided by deep shelters with thick concrete roofs that sometimes were covered by as much as 20 feet of earth".[2]

The approaches to the Hitler Line were guarded by thick aprons of wire and the ground had been heavily sown with mines. There were long Italian 'N' mines like lengths of rail; paratroop anti-tank mines like over-sized finger bowls; heavy Tellermines which might be buried singly or in sets; shrapnel or 'S' mines whose inner cases filled with ball-bearings sprang breast-high before exploding; limpet mines shaped like Chianti bottles; small 'schu' mines in plastic and wooden cases, unresponsive to detectors; delayed-action mines designed to crater roads or tracks after a certain number of vehicles had passed over them.

The sector of the Hitler Line which the 1st Division assaulted was the northern part between Aquino in the north and Pontecorvo in the south. Here, the German fortifications ran a few hundred yards east of the road connecting these towns. The section of the line I most wanted to explore was, of course, where the Patricias attacked, south of Aquino. For two and a half hours I slowly travelled the Aquino-Pontecorvo road (only four miles long); I traversed the fields; I talked to farmers. But not one trace did I find of the old German fortifications. Not even a concrete gun emplacement. However, in Aquino I met an old man who told me that there were many pill boxes and gun emplacements, even tank turrets, in the area until about ten years ago. Then every trace of the fortification was removed, done, I gathered, as a matter of national pride.

On this unsatisfactory and frustrating note, my tour of the Patricia battlefields came to an end. I was upset that I had not made an effort on other tours to explore the Hitler Line and at least get an idea of what the Regiment had faced on that fateful day in May, 1944. Now nothing remained

— only the peaceful earth, vineyards, grain fields, woodlands and pastures.

Only the peaceful earth? What more could I ask for. Wasn't that why we went to War in the first place?

I wearily drove the last 80 miles to Rome and turned in my faithful Fiat. It had served me well. If I needed transportation in Rome I would take a taxi. No one in his right mind would attempt to drive a car in Rome.

It was very late and I was very tired. I had no difficulty in eschewing the pleasures of 'doing what the Romans do'. But there was one place I still wanted to visit — The Mussolini Forum.

During the War I had been on leave in Rome where, together with my guide, an English professor, I explored all the wonders of the ancient city. I had asked him if the deposed and despised Mussolini had erected any interesting buildings. Nothing of any architectural value, he had said. There was a mean, vile, Mussolini Forum, but it was not worth seeing. Even when pressed, he refused to take me to it. Naturally, my interest was aroused and I vowed to see it some day.

My plane was due to leave at 11:00 am the following day. It was too late to visit the Forum that night. I would have to get up bright and early.

Next morning, dispensing with breakfast, I ran out to the street in front of my hotel and hailed a cab.

"Dove?" asked the driver.

"Mussolini Forum."

"No, no". he shouted. *"Mussolini male, cativo, morte — nome giusto è Stadio dei Marmi."*

"OK, whatever you say."

I almost said step on it, but I remembered the crazy drivers in Rome and remained silent.

My driver soon deposited me at the Stadio dei Marmi, the renamed Mussolini Forum. I passed through a pretentious gate and entered the Stadium. Even though it was still early morning, a number of athletes were working out on the track and in the field.

My first reaction was just as the professor had first described the place — mean. It was open-aired, of course, and designed in the form of an oval — probably patterned after the ancient Roman circuses for chariot races. Plain, concrete bleachers rose around the circumference of the Stadium to a height of only eight or nine tiers. The seating capacity could not have been more than three or four thousand, if that.

Then I saw the 'vile' part of the professor's description. All around the circumference of the Stadium were grotesque sculptures of Roman athletes, in exaggerated athletic poses — boxers, fencers, discus throwers, jumpers, runners, soccer players, javelin throwers. I didn't see any tennis players, basketball players, swimmers, skiers or curlers; or any female athletes. This, I thought, was strange in view of Mussolini's supposed addiction to women.

The statues were stark naked except for a prissy fig-leaf. But some of these ridiculous adornments had apparently fallen off and huge genitals were exposed for all to see; and to admire, or to revile, depending on their point of view.

As I was taking some pictures of the figures, both with and without fig leaves, a man sidled up and whispered, "Mister, you want to see some real dirty pictures?"

"No, not this morning. Too early. I haven't had any breakfast. But tell me about the fig leaves? They don't seem to be very securely attached."

The seedy vendor gave a thin laugh. "In Mussolini's time there were no 'fig-leaves', as you call them. After the War, some people wanted to pull down the whole place, including the 'dirty' statues. Eventually the authorities compromised and covered over the private parts of the athletes. Now the young kids come here at night and tear off the coverings." He paused, then continued with a sleezy smile, "Now, don't you want some filthy . . . . ."

"Va via, subito, sporco, vecchio uomo."

He scurried away to his hole.

I hurried back to my hotel, happy to leave the shoddy statues to their fate. As I sped along the Via Flaminia I heard the voice of my professor friend from long ago.

"No monuments from the Mussolini era are worth seeing because nothing was erected that had any enduring quality. *Sic Transit Gloria Mundi.*"

FINAL
WORD

When I laid aside my pen on Christmas Eve, 1985, having just completed my account of the Fourth Pilgrimage, I was certain that my long story had finally been told. From September, 1939, when my tale begins, to May, 1985, when my last Pilgrimage ends, is a span of 46 years. Enough is quite enough.

Still, there was one unresolved matter arising out of my last visit to Holland that bothered me — the missing secret room or rooms in the home of the van der Zandens. While they had said they would continue the search and let me know the result, I had the nagging feeling that the hiding places would never be found.

Then, in January, 1986, I had the opportunity, whilst in Europe, to visit Holland briefly and found myself at the Schiphol Airport in Amsterdam on January 31st, 1986. Immediately, I phoned Mr van der Zanden in Noorwijk. Before I had a chance to inquire about the secret room, he burst out with the good news.

"I think we found it. Just last week, an old man who used to work in the house during the War came around and showed us where the room was located. But the entrance is all bricked up and plastered over, so we haven't really seen it."

I felt like the seeker of King Tut's tomb when he finally discovered the entrance.

Mr van der Zanden kindly asked me to stay at his home for a few days. I had to decline as there were a number of people I wanted to visit during my short stay, but I would be very happy to see where the secret room actually was. I suggested I get in touch with Mimi de Witt Hamer and bring her along to confirm the location.

Later that day, I picked up Mimi and drove her to the van der Zanden's fine home, where she had lived as a young girl. She had not been in the house for years — perhaps only once or twice since she had moved away after the War — and soon discovered that many of the rooms had altered over the years. But she quickly found her bearings and led us upstairs to the secret room (she had asked the van der Zandens not to give her any clues as to its whereabouts).

At the top of the stairs, she turned left and went down a hallway to a small bedroom that was unoccupied, entered the room and went straight to the west wall.

"This is where the entrance was. There used to be a bookcase against this wall that could be quickly raised and lowered. Behind the bookcase was a spiral staircase leading to the attic. The room was actually in a corner of the attic, but it was too obvious to have the entrance in the attic — the Germans would have found it."

The van der Zandens were delighted. Their workman had described the hideaway exactly as Mimi had said.

But I was skeptical. "Why didn't the Germans climb into the attic through the trap door in the ceiling of the hallway?"

Mimi nodded. "Sure the Germans went into the attic, but it looked just like every other attic. In all the large, old Dutch homes there is a brick wall, four or five feet high, running around the attic, between the slanting roof and the floor — to help insulate the attic and keep it dry. The hiding place was in the triangular space between the roof and the floor."

I was still not convinced, so Mr van der Zanden produced a ladder and we all climbed into the attic. Just as Mimi had said, there was the brick wall all around the attic. I could see how difficult it would have been to make a hidden entrance in the wall without showing evidence of the work.

We carefully clambered down the ladder and returned to the bedroom where the entrance had been located. Immediately, we all started to pound the wall and feel for any cracks. But it was as solid as a Dutch dyke. I am certain everyone had the same thought — bash in the wall and expose the blasted entrance, spiral staircase and room that have been driving us all crazy since I brought up the subject last May.

Mrs van der Zanden sensed what was on everyone's mind: "I would love to break down that wall, but I had the bedroom redecorated last spring. Let's leave it for the moment. Didn't Mimi say there was another secret room?"

"That's right. Just follow me." We followed Mimi as she headed for another larger bedroom near the head of the stairs, through this, and then into a smaller dressing room adjoining the larger room. "Here is the other secret room," she declared. "See this doorway between the two rooms? It's not a normal doorway. First, there is no door and, second, look how wide the walls of the doorframe are. And see the horizontal strips of wood along each wall of the doorframe, about a foot between each one? Well, that doorway used to be a built-in bookcase that was part of the main bedroom. Removable shelves were laid on the wooden strips and a large sheet of wood, that could easily be removed, formed the back of the bookcase. It was painted to look like the walls on each side. When the shelves were filled with books, it looked exactly like the usual built-in bookcase. But in fact it was the entrance to secret room number two."

It was a clever arrangement, but I couldn't imagine it fooling the German Gestapo who were past masters at ferreting out hiding places. I asked Mimi if the Germans ever discovered the room.

"No, they never did, incredible as it may seem. We were so sure they would find it that we only used the room when we had too many airmen or Underground workers to hide in the other room. As you know, my brother, Jim, kept his printing press for the Underground newspaper in the other room.

"This room we are in was an emergency hideaway, but it also helped to protect the other room. If the Germans discovered this second room, they would probably have stopped searching for any other hiding place."

"Oh yeah?" I queried. "What if they had found half a dozen airmen in the room at the time?"

"Well in that case," Mimi nonchalantly replied, "we had no more worries, had we?"

I had no answer for that one — only admiration for a very cool, determined, brave lady. I had not the slightest doubt that if the Germans had found the room, even if it was unoccupied, she and her family would have been deported. If the room had just sheltered one Allied airman, the whole family would have been taken out in the street and shot.

During dinner that evening, Mimi told us more about the horrors of the German occupation, as well as a few amusing incidents perpetrated by the generally humourless German soldiers. On one occasion, the Gestapo burst into their home looking for a military bike that had been stolen by someone in the Underground. It had, in fact, been taken by Jim for his clandestine operations. As the Germans were grilling the family, a motor suddenly started up outside. The Germans rushed out only to see their motorbike, with its sidecar, rapidly disappearing down the road. The Underground had added another bike to their fleet of captured German vehicles.

On another occasion, the Germans rushed into the house looking for a radio that an informer had told them was hidden there. They poked around the walls and shoved their bayonets into the upholstery of a beautiful armchair, narrowly missing the buttocks of the person who was calmly sitting there 'reading' a Dutch newspaper upside down. Frustrated in their search, the Germans finally left uttering terrible threats if they ever found a radio on the premises.

The occupant of the armchair was an Allied airman who had momentarily come out of his hiding place to answer the call of nature and had almost caused a tragedy. However, he had had enough presence of mind to grab a newspaper and adopt a casual air, though his whole insides must have been on the point of explosion.

A similar incident happened in wintertime, when another airman was on his way to the bathroom on the main floor. Fortunately, this time, the intruder was a German officer who politely knocked at the door, giving the airman a few precious moments to disappear. But where? No chance to rush upstairs. He quickly looked around and saw a solid rack in the hallway piled high with long winter coats. He dashed into the middle of the pile and became an instant coat rack himself. When the German officer entered, the airman hoisted himself up in the trees of the coat rack so that his feet would not show.

The officer stopped at the rack, casually deposited his own greatcoat on the pile and marched into the living room. It was the local Commandant, who was actually quite a decent fellow and was only paying a social call. After a short while he departed, taking his coat with him, and the airman came down from his tree, nursing a monumental ache in his armpits.

Mimi was never sure whether the German officer realized what was going on and overlooked this little prank for the sake of establishing peaceful relations with the local Dutch people. Unfortunately, he was soon posted away and a tough SS Commandant took his place.

At this stage of the War, January, 1945, the Germans were desperate to find reinforcements to replace their dwindling troops in the front lines. All the German soldiers in the neighbourhood of Noordwijk were sent away to fight.

The places of the departing troops were taken by a battalion or two of Ukrainians who had been captured and pressed into service in the German Army. They moved into the mental hospital which Mimi's father had headed until the Germans had occupied the place in 1940 and let the inmates go free.

Shortly after their arrival the SS Commandant appeared at the de Witt Hamer residence accompanied by armed guards. "We require your house for officers' quarters," snapped the Commandant. "You have exactly two hours to get out."

The de Witt Hamers, with their three young girls, had no place to go and nowhere to store their beautiful furnishings, paintings and silverware, even if they could have found transportation — their son's motorcycle brigade would hardly have been appropriate.

Then they thought of secret room number two. In desperation, they moved as many of their valuable possessions as time and space would allow into this room, then replaced the phony built-in bookcase and hoped for the best.

Their plan worked perfectly. The Germans never discovered this cache

528

of fine furnishings, although they must have wondered why the house was so bare.

While the de Witt Hamers hated to leave their home and contents to the mercy of the Germans, they were relieved to get away from the Ukrainian soldiers. They were a ragged, ill-disciplined, dirty bunch — peasants from the great plains that bear their name. Mimi and the girls were terrified of them.

When the PPCLI arrived on the scene, shortly after the end of the War, the Ukrainians had departed, but there were still a number of Germans around, including a medical battalion. We gathered them all up and sent them to their devastated homeland. The hospital buildings and the de Witt Hamer house were a mess, but a least the officers had not deliberately shot up the home and burned all the furnishings like the paratroopers had done in Bloemendaal. The only serious damage to the house was in the basement which was flooded and smelled like a sewer. I asked Mimi what had happened.

"Apparently the toilets became plugged, so the officers called in some German engineers to clean out the drains. The sergeant in charge went down to the basement to try to find the trouble. When he couldn't clear the drains, he simply tossed in a couple of grenades and blew the watermains and sewers all to bits. That's German efficiency for you!"

On that shattering note, my saga about *De Wra,* the House of de Witt Hamer, ends. May the mansion live on to a ripe old age, its secret room in the attic remaining inviolable to the very end.

De Wra, not I, shall have the final word.

Appendix A

POSTSCRIPT
TO
CHAPTER VIII

Late in 1985 I learned that the autobiography of MGen Chris Vokes CB, CBE, DSO, CD had just been published.[1] I was delighted. 'Uncle Chris', as some of us called him behind his back, was undoubedly the 'fightin'est' Canadian general in World War II. He was also a very great character.

When I joined the Regiment in England in early 1943 to gain some experience, he was in command of 2nd Brigade. My first meeting with him was typical. Knowing he was an RMC man, I blurted out that I had graduated in 1942.

"Good," he growled. "Then you know how to box. All officers in my brigade box. I'll see that you get a chance to show your stuff in the brigade championships." Luckily for me, the War intervened. All the more experienced officers were called back to the Regiment and I was returned to a reinforcement battalion.

The next time I met Brig Vokes was just after the end of the fighting in Sicily when he inspected our battalion.

As mentioned in Chapter VIII, many stories circulated about the brigadier, including the one about the melons fertilized with human excreta. It was a good tale, but I had heard it only after much retelling by others, so I was interested to see whether the anecdote would be mentioned in the general's memoirs. I bought the book and settled down to a nice evening's read about one of my favourite soldiers.

I wish I had never read the thing. I wish the book had never been published.

General Vokes told the story about the melons. I was happy to see that while my version was not exactly the same, it was close enough. But that was about the only thing that pleased me in the entire volume, except for

531

a lot of other funny stories from the day he was five years old until his retirement from the army. One expects more than funny stories from Canada's most experienced leader in World War II. One also expects that his early sex life will not be bared (for lack of a better word) for all to see. He proclaims that he lost his virginity to a young married woman in Halifax, when he was 22. From her he developed a great fondness for women. He spent nights "appreciating" the flesh pots of Halifax. He got a cut-rate price at a Montreal whorehouse from a girl who had been "done wrong" by an RMC professor; in fact, on her days off, she used to come and visit him for free. Then he got a monumental dose of crabs, even in his bushy eyebrows.

To be fair, when War breaks out and he goes overseas, no more is said of the personal sex life of the lieutenant colonel, as he then was. But he can't resist telling more outrageous stories about his licentious troops, such as his abortive attempt to set up a brothel in Sicily. He takes seven pages to describe how to set up a brothel (his expertise gained, one assumes, by his own earlier experiences).

Another story he tells about his lusty men concerns a soldier in his battalion who had an erection on parade and was ordered by LCol Vokes to go on leave to London. On the next inspection, the same man was on parade in the same condition. Vokes glared at the RSM and asked what was wrong with the man. The RSM replied that perhaps he had fallen in love with the colonel. Vokes claims he fired the RSM on the spot.

A funny story to some, perhaps, but not to me, nor to many veterans of my Regiment. The man with the alleged problem and his RSM were, according to Vokes, members of the PPCLI. The whole foolish episode is pure fantasy. It simply did not happen while Vokes was Commanding Officer of the PPCLI, and Vokes did not fire the RSM.

Why, then, does he attribute the story to the PPCLI?
The answer is pretty obvious when you read his parting comments on the alleged incident.

> My housecleaning of the regiment had begun. *And the word about me began, I am sure, to spread. If I had stayed as the Patricias' commanding officer for another three months I'd have cleaned it entirely.*
> *The price to be paid for the regiment not being cleaned out would be substantial.* The reckoning would come in Sicily.[2]

Clearly Vokes is using this story (and several others) to justify the removal of LCol Lindsay at the end of the Sicilian Campaign. LCol Vokes commanded the PPCLI for only five weeks in late 1941 while LCol Lindsay was away on course. Vokes barely knew Lindsay and Lindsay was not at the Regiment when Vokes arrived or departed.

The purpose of his brief tour of duty was not to smarten up the Patricias, as Vokes seemed to think, but to give him some experience in commanding a battalion. At that stage in the War the Canadian Army had been sitting in England almost two years. The troops, eager to get into battle, had been buggered about on endless exercises and concentrations all over the south coast of England. For the troops, all these great exercises meant only marching and more marching. By Vokes' own admission there was a huge discipline problem throughout the Canadian Army. The troops were browned off and some went AWL to vent their frustrations.

The Patricias no doubt experienced the same problems as all the other units. As soon as Vokes arrived he determined to cure absenteeism by holding parades on Saturdays. The soldiers were billeted all over Surrey. Vokes claims that on the first Saturday only 400 were on parade out of about 800. He does not, however, take into account that at any given time in a battalion, large numbers of men are on legitimate leave, sick in hospital, away on courses, detached for other duties at brigade and elsewhere. Given the circumstances, Vokes was lucky that 400 men appeared on a Saturday that was usually a free day, particularly after a gruelling exercise.

On the next Saturday parade, according to Vokes, attendance had improved but there were only about 500 bodies turned out. He was still not satisfied. As he puts it: "Again I raised hell. I wanted EVERYBODY out."[3]

He was reaching for the moon, and he knew it. But he had at least accomplished his main objective — word about him had certainly started to spread, not only throughout the ranks, but more important to Vokes, among his superior officers.

The next story Vokes tells concerns a sniping incident in Sicily. Vokes is now a brigadier in command of 2nd Brigade. He claims he received a report from LCol Lindsay that three civilians had been captured sniping at his troops. No soldier had been killed or wounded. The CO asked Brig Vokes what to do with the civilians. Vokes told him to "use his bloody head." The CO pressed for a clear order. Vokes told him to send back the civilians to his brigade headquarters and he would cope with them. His idea of "coping" was to shoot them on the spot. Luckily for the civilians and for Vokes along came MGen Simonds who vetoed any shooting. Vokes then put the three Italians in a ring of soldiers and had a big, tough sergeant give them a sound thrashing. Vokes' final comment on the incident: "I was not pleased with Lindsay."[4]

That's crazy in my opinion. As I read Vokes' book, I could not believe (a) half the stories he told, and (b) that he or anyone else would put all this trash into print. He had been such a great leader, so highly respected by all the fighting men in his brigade and division. Perhaps they might have forgiven him for some of his peccadillos, but I would think most of them would have been disappointed, if not annoyed, by all the revelations. Personally, I was shocked and saddened.

In the hands of his co-author, one John P Maclean, Vokes comes through as a strange man who could be vindictive, vicious, impulsive, impetuous; uncaring about casualties unless they were prohibitively heavy; unconcerned about a man's intellectual characteristics. Any civilian, not knowing Vokes, would come to the conclusion that the man and the soldiers he led were a bunch of brutal, licentious, hired assassins (to use one of his favourite expressions). The book is a cruel defamation not only of Vokes' character but of the character of the fine soldiers he led. There was so much that was good about the man and so little of this comes out. Witness this assessment of Vokes by one of his battalion commanders in Italy:

If you stood up to him, he would trust you implicitly, support you to the end and be a considerate, even a compassionate commander who engendered your loyalty and confidence. How could he lose it all?" [in his memoirs].

I do not blame MGen Vokes for publishing the volume. In my opinion it is his co-author, Mr Maclean, who bears the responsibility. From him one learns that Vokes simply sat down and dictated his memoirs into an audio cassette. Maclean and Vokes spent many an evening together going over the cassettes. Sometimes, they got into the sauce late at night (a fact the quality of the book readily confirms).

Inadvertently, the tapes were water-soaked and frozen but were refurbished. Then Maclean more or less reproduced the tapes on paper, taking out most of the "jesuses", "bastards" and "aw shits". It is a great pity he didn't delete the rest of the vulgarities. The cassettes should have been left in their soaked and frozen condition, never to see printer's ink. Though Vokes claims he does not intend to hurt anyone, he has done just that. I feel sorry for his family and his friends. He deserved a better memorial.

I also feel sorry for Bob Lindsay who got such a raw deal. The great irony of the book is that while it denigrates Canada's great general, it confirms beyond any doubt that LCol Lindsay was unjustly blamed and fired for postponing the attack on Mount Seggio. It is important to the memory of Bob Lindsay that the record, with the help of MGen Vokes, now be put straight.

In Chapter VIII, written a year before Vokes' memoirs were published, I gave the main reason why the attack was postponed — the tanks carrying the two forward companies had got lost in the inky blackness and were bogged down on the edge of a ditch.

I was in command of a platoon in one of these companies and I can attest that the tanks did get lost. It was not the last time that our troops lost their bearings in Sicily and Italy. I did on most operations. Our inaccurate maps practicallly guaranteed it.

Despite the darkness and the impossible maps, the two companies made their way forward to their jumping off position. It was then decided by the two company commanders to postpone the attack until morning when the artillery could give us some support.

I did not know at the time of writing that account whether Lindsay had actually agreed with the postponement. In any case, in my opinion it didn't matter who made the decision. It was an inevitable, sensible decision.

In his memoirs, Vokes now admits that he was never able to confirm whether Lindsay condoned the decision. He then goes on to make the incredible statement that "Lindsay never referred the matter to him *as he should have had he known of the delay.*"[5] Nonetheless, on the basis of this hypothetical, specious reasoning he fired Lindsay on the spot and sent him back to England.

It is obvious that this impulsive decision must have bothered Vokes in his later years. Thus, in his memoirs, and with a liberal dose of hindsight, he gives us a series of "incidents" which he hopes will help to justify his action in finally removing Lindsay at Mount Seggio. Fortunately for Lindsay, the whole case against him, as now revealed by Vokes, simply does not wash.

If further evidence is needed to clear Bob Lindsay's name, a senior officer who was with the Regiment at the time, has recently written:

> *I have just had a long session, regarding the removal of Bob Lindsay, with two other officers who were at Mount Seggio. We all agree that the decision to postpone the attack to daylight was made by the two company commanders. The decision was neither known to nor condoned by Lindsay. In fact the two company commanders were completely out of communication with him and acted in accordance with their own judgment.*

But the damage done by Vokes to the Regiment, after Mount Seggio, is not confined to Lindsay. Another aftermath of the affair, as now revealed in the memoirs, is his so-called "housecleaning" of the Regiment:

> *Now I ordered the Patricias to attack Montesseggio and the Edmontons to press their attack on Monte Revisotto.*
>
> *To my amazement, neither advance got off until daylight of the 6th. Then, both battalions occupied their mountain objective without any opposition because the enemy had gone.*
>
> *I was extremely annoyed when I learned about the delay. I called Lindsay back immediately and found out he had given the task to two rifle companies, but that the two company commanders decided between themselves to postpone their advance*

until daylight!

I was never able to confirm whether Lindsay condoned their decision or not. In any event, Lindsay never referred the matter to me as he should have had he known of the delay.

True enough, the advance would have taken place over ground that the attacking troops had had no opportunity to examine in daylight. It certainly would have been difficult. But it would not have been the first time infantry had been called upon to move forward in the dark without previous reconnaissance against a badly shaken and retreating enemy.

There was some excuse for the delay by the Edmontons. They were faced with a more rugged ascent, and their experience in assaulting Revisotto on the afternoon of the 5th led them to believe that it would require observed artillery support. Besides, the Edmontons had just completed several days of heavy fighting and they were very tired.

But there was no excuse for the Patricias. They were fresh and had seen no action in contact with the enemy during the operations in the Salso Valley. I felt they had missed an opportunity to deal the enemy a telling blow.

There was no point in blaming the soldiers of the PPCLI. There were none better in the 2nd Brigade.

I blamed Lindsay, as commanding officer, and the two company commanders for the cancellation of the operation without my permission and I made up my mind really to houseclean the regiment's officers when the battle cooled. And I did.

* *Three days later, the Patricias' War Diary shows, nine officers were shuffled: Colonel Lindsay to 4 Bn CBRD, with Captains J L Wiswell, T H Knight, R G Woodward-Jewsberry, Major R P Clarke to 49 Edmonton Regiment: Captains L G Beamish and C M McDougall to HQ 2nd Cdn Inf Bde, along with Lt R D Browne-Clayton; Signal Corps Lt R S Graham, aide-de-camp to General Simonds, was promoted acting captain and appointed Patricias' adjutant, in effect a "new broom" office manager.[6]*

Vokes was not content with getting rid of the Regiment's CO. He claims that he also "shuffled" eight other officers in his housecleaning operation. Such a claim is a terrible calumny, if not an actual libel, on the officers concerned. It is true that three officers were sent to 4 Battalion, Canadian Base Reinforcement Depot. But all the other Regimental officers remained with 2nd Canadian Infantry Brigade (commanded by Brig Vokes himself) and later gave outstanding service to the Regiment.

Maj R P Clark temporarily went to the Edmonton Regiment to help them out; he subsequently returned to the Patricias where he gave distinguished service, commanded the Regiment from September 12, 1944 to June 4th,

1945 and won the DSO.

Acting Capt L G Beamish, who had been the Transport Officer of the Regiment, was confirmed as a captain and made Transport Officer at Brig Vokes' headquarters.

Capt C M McDougall also went to 2nd Brigade HQ and temporarily became a staff officer there. He soon returned to the Regiment and saw much severe fighting. He never went LOB. He became a major, won the DSO and was mentioned in despatches.

Lt R D Browne-Clayton, who had landed with me in Sicily as part of the reinforcement group, also went to 2nd Brigade HQ as a staff officer. He subsequently returned to the Regiment and took part in many actions, including the Hitler Line, where he was seriously wounded and was invalided home due to the severe nature of his wounds.

The "Signal Corps" mentioned in Vokes' book refers to the Signal Officer, who was not a Regimental officer.

So much for the so-called "housecleaning". The fact that three of the officers joined Vokes' own staff indicates that he did some housecleaning of his own headquarters in order to make room for the three Patricia officers. If so, he made at least one intelligent move.

This dreary ballad of the postponement of the attack on Mount Seggio has some further sour notes. Vokes says he blamed Lindsay and the two company commanders for cancellation of the operation. In fact, the operation was not cancelled, but only postponed until morning, for the reasons already given. The important point, however, is that the two company commanders who actually made the decision were not fired, as was Lindsay, and sent away with the "housecleaned" officers. Vokes' actions make no sense, but are understandable. He took advantage of the situation to get rid of Lindsay.

But why Vokes now claims he also banished the four officers Clark, Beamish, McDougall and Browne-Clayton, who had nothing to do with the postponement, defies any understanding. The most charitable view is that the passage of 40 years has taken its toll. Such an excuse is not, however, available to co-author Maclean. In his Writer's Note to the book he states that the general delegated matters of accuracy to him. Any mistakes, he admits, are his fault. Unfortunately that admission does not cure the damage he has done.

The last stanza in this sorry tale has to be told. When Vokes didn't fire the two company commanders, who had postponed the attack, little did he know that his decision, while inconsistent, was fortunate for him and the Regiment. For some reason, neither he nor Maclean mentions the names of the commanders, although the reason is probably the result of hindsight on their part. I will mention their names, because they too have been unfairly castigated by Vokes for making the only sensible decision that was available to them at the time. They are Capt W de N (Bucko) Watson in command of A Company (in which I was a platoon commander at the time), and Capt D Brain in command of B Company.

Both these outstanding officers were soon promoted to major and continued to serve the Regiment with distinction. Maj Brain's luck finally ran out on December 10th, 1943. During an enemy shoot on San Leonardo, LCol Ware, Maj Brain and Maj Watson were in consultation in the lee of a tank. A shell struck the vehicle; Maj Brain was killed instantly and Maj Watson was wounded for the second time in four days.

Maj Watson served continuously with the Regiment throughout the Italian campaign, except for periods in hospital due to wounds. He was officially wounded three times, but that does not count the innumerable times he was wounded and remained on duty. He was one of the heroes of the Hitler Line, being the only officer who reached the objective. After the action he was found in a shell hole suffering from a wound in one arm and a piece of his helmet and a Schmeisser bullet in his forehead. Bucko Watson won the DSO and the MC.

On this happy note my review of MGen Vokes' book comes to an end. I am grateful at least that the volume has given me this opportunity finally to clear the good names of so many fine officers. But I am saddened that in so doing I have had to add further evidence of the serious flaws of a great soldier that are revealed in this book.

I am unhappy, too, about the damage Mr Maclean has done to MGen Vokes, his family, the Canadian Army, its soldiers, and the place where he received his military education, The Royal Military College. I cannot see how the damage can ever be repaired. Yet, I hope that someone will take up the challenge and produce a balanced view of MGen Chris Vokes, as a great battlefield commander and leader of men, without all the claptrap that has ruined Mr Maclean's work.

May you rest in peace, Uncle Chris.

Appendix B

PRINCESS PATRICIA

HRH Princess Patricia of Connaught was a granddaughter of Queen Victoria. Her father was HRH the Duke of Connaught, Governor General of Canada, 1911-1916. During the illness of the Duchess of Connaught, Princess Patricia acted as hostess at Rideau Hall, Ottawa. She endeared herself to Canadians by her simple, natural manners, her lack of stiff etiquette and her love of Canadian games and outdoor sports. The Princess won all hearts by her great beauty and charm.

On August 3rd, 1914, A Hamilton Gault of Montreal, who had served in the South African campaign offered, in the event of a declaration of war, to raise and equip, at his own expense, a military unit to serve in the British Army. He proposed that HRH Princess Patricia be asked to lend her name to the Regiment.

War was declared on August 5th. The Governor General, the Canadian Government and the British Government promptly accepted Hamilton Gault's offer and recruiting for the Patricias commenced. On August 23rd Princess Patricia presented her newly-recruited Regiment with a Camp Colour which she had designed and worked herself during the fortnight of mobilization. The Colour incorporated her personal cipher including the initials VP in gold upon a blue centre against a crimson background.

On February 22nd, 1918, Princess Patricia was appointed Colonel-in-Chief of the Regiment.

Princess Patricia married Commander the Hon Alexander Ramsay, DSO, of the Royal Navy on February 27th, 1919. At her request, she relinquished her title and became the Lady Patricia Ramsay.

Lady Patricia died in 1974 and was succeeded as Colonel-in-Chief of the PPCLI by her goddaughter and cousin, Lady Patricia Brabourne, the elder daughter of Admiral of the Fleet, The Earl Mountbatten of Burma. Upon his death in 1979 she became Countess Mountbatten of Burma.

Appendix C

THE RIC-A-DAM-DOO

The Camp Colour which Princess Patricia designed and presented to the Regiment on August 23rd, 1914, is known affectionately throughout the Regiment as Ric-a-dam-doo. The name also refers to the song of the Patricias composed in World War I and sung with great enthusiasm to the present day. Many of the verses appear in my book.

The origin of the name has never been clearly established, but it seems very likely it was inspired by the words of a British Army song before World War I.

The original Camp Colour, though not an official Regimental Colour, was carried into every battle in which the Regiment fought in the First World War — the only colour carried into action by a British unit in World War I.

On January 28th, 1919, in Belgium, the Camp Colour was consecrated and officially became the first Regimental Colour; and at a farewell parade in England, on February 21st, 1919, Princess Patricia attached to the Colour a wreath of laurel in silver gilt.

In 1922, the Original Colour, tattered, torn and shot through by shell and bullet, was encased and retired as the Regiment's most prized possession. It rests now in the Regimental Museum.

ABBREVIATIONS
General

ADS	Advanced Dressing Station
AMGOT	Allied Military Government of Occupied Territories
AP	armour-piercing
ASC	Army Service Corps
AWL	absent without leave
Bn	battalion
BHQ	battalion headquarters
BMA	British Military Authority
CBRD	Canadian Base Reinforcement Depot
CCS	Casualty Clearing Station
CGH	Canadian General Hospital
CIRU	Canadian Infantry Reinforcement Unit
CITC	Canadian Infantry Training Centre
CMHQ	Canadian Military Headquarters
CO	Commanding Officer
Coy	company
CWACs	Canadian Women's Army Corps
D-Day	day for landing — Sicily, Italy, Normandy
Div	division
DR	despatch rider
DSO	Distinguished Service Order
DUKW	amphibious truck
Eddies	The Loyal Edmonton Regiment
EFI	Expeditionary Forces Institute
FDS	Field Dressing Station
FOO	forward observation officer
48th	The 48th Highlanders of Canada
FUP	forming up place
GIs	American soldiers
GOC-in-C	General Officer Commanding-in-Chief
GPO	gun position officer
Hastings Hasty Ps	The Hastings and Prince Edward Regiment
HE	high explosive
H-Hour	time for attack (used after Dec. '44. See Zero hour)
HQ	headquarters
IO	Intelligence Officer

Ities	Italians
JAG	Judge Advocate General
KR & O	Kings Regulations and Orders
KR Can	for the Canadian Militia
LCI	Landing Craft, Infantry
LCT	Landing Craft, Tank
LER	The Loyal Edmonton Regiment
LMG	light machine gun
LOB	left out of battle
LSI	Landing Ship, Infantry
LST	Landing Ship, Tank
MC	Military Cross
MID	Mentioned in Despatches
MM	Military Medal
MMG	medium machine gun
MO	Medical Officer
MP	Military Police
NAAFI	Navy, Army and Air Force Institute
NCO	non commissioned officer
NDHQ	National Defence Headquarters
OP	observation post
OC	officer commanding
'O' Group	orders group
PIAT	Projectile, Infantry, Anti-tank
PL	platoon
PLDG	Princess Louise Dragoon Guards
PLF	The Princess Louise Fusiliers
POW	Prisoner-of-War
PPA	Popski's Private Army
QM	Quartermaster
RAP	Regimental Aid Post
RCA	Royal Canadian Artillery
RCAC	Royal Canadian Armoured Corps
RCAF	Royal Canadian Airforce
RCAMC	Royal Canadian Army Medical Corps
RCASC	Royal Canadian Army Service Corps
RCE	Royal Canadian Engineers
RCR	The Royal Canadian Regiment
recce	reconnaissance
R & R	rest and recreation
RV	rendezvous
RWR	The Royal Winnipeg Rifles
Seaforths	The Seaforth Highlanders of Canada
2IC	Second-in-Command
Sec	section
SLI	The Saskatoon Light Infantry
SOS	struck off strength

SRD	service rum, demerara
SP	self-propelled
TCV	troop-carrying vehicle
Tac HQ	tactical (battalion) headquarters
TEWT	tactical exercise without troops
TO	Transport Officer
Ts OET	tests of elementary training
TSMG	Thompson submachine gun
VE Day	Victory in Europe
VIP	very important person
VJ Day	Victory in Japan
West Novas WNSR	The West Nova Scotia Regiment
Zero hour	time for attack (used up to Dec. '44. See H-Hour)

Army Ranks

Field Marshal	not abbreviated
General	Gen
Lieutenant General	LGen
Major General	MGen
Brigadier	Brig
Colonel	Col
Lieutenant Colonel	LCol
Major	Maj
Captain	Capt
Lieutenant	Lt
Second Lieutenant	2Lt
Temporary Second Lieutenant	Temp 2Lt
Regimental Sergeant Major	RSM
Battalion Sergeant Major	BSM
Company Sergeant Major	CSM
Company Quartermaster Sergeant	CQMS
Lance Sergeant	LSgt
Sergeant	Sgt
Lance Corporal	LCpl
Private	Pte

CHAPTER NOTES

Author's Preface
1. John Grigg, *Nancy Astor, Portrait of a Pioneer* (London: Sidgwick & Jackson), 167.

Chapter I — The RMC
1. Joseph Schull and J Douglas Gibson, *The Scotiabank Story, A History of The Bank of Nova Scotia, 1832-1982* (Toronto: Macmillan of Canada, a division of Gage Publishing Limited, 1982) 197.
2. Richard Arthur Preston, *Canada's RMC, A History of The Royal Military College* (University of Toronto Press, 1969), 287.
3. *Royal Military College of Canada Review and Log of HMS Stone Frigate,* No 51, Vol XXVIII 1947, 39.
4. *RMC Review,* No 45, Vol XXIII June, 1942, 57.
5. *RMC Review,* No 46, Vol XXIII December, 1942, 35.
6. *RMC Review* No 44, Vol XXII December, 1941, 35.

Chapter II — The RMC
1. *RMC Review,* No 43, Vol XXII June, 1941, 46.
2. Ibid, 16
3. *RMC Review,* No 47, Vol XXIV 1943, 50.
4. *RMC Review,* No 44, Vol XXII December, 1941, 37, for much of the detail of the conducted tour.
5. *RMC Review,* No 46, Vol XXIII December, 1942, 37.
6. Richard S Malone, *A Portrait of War 1939-1943* (Toronto: Collins Publishers, 1983), 93.
7. *RMC Review,* No 46, Vol XXIII December, 1942, 19.

8. Address to the Ex-Cadets at the Annual Dinner: June 5th, 1943, *RMC Review,* No 47, Vol XXIV 1943, 51.

Chapter III — Canada
1. Jeffery Williams, *Princess Patricia's Canadian Light Infantry* (London: Leo Cooper Ltd., 1972), 3,4.
2. Ralph Hodder-Williams, *Princess Patricia's Canadian Light Infantry, 1914-1919:* Second Edition (Edmonton, Alberta: The Executive Committee of the Regiment, 1968), Appendix IV, 66.
3. *Taunton Daily Gazette,* March 18, 1943.

Chapter VIII — The Regiment
1. G R Stevens, *Princess Patricia's Canadian Light Infantry:* Volume Three (Griesbach, Alberta: The Historical Committee of the Regiment, 1958), 90.
2. LCol G W L Nicholson, *The Canadians in Italy, 1943-1945:* Volume II (Ottawa: Queen's Printer, 1956), 164.
3. War Diary, PPCLI, 19 August, 1943.
4. Ibid.
5. J A M Cook, 'Pats Running Sicilian Ranch with True Western Flavour', *Winnipeg Free Press,* September 9, 1943.

Chapter IX — Malaria
1. LCol G W L Nicholson, *The Canadians in Italy, 1943-1945:* Volume II (Ottawa: Queen's Printer, 1956), 176.
2. Ibid, 190.

Chapter XI — Scouts and Snipers
1. LCol G W L Nicholson, *The Canadians in Italy, 1943-1945:* Volume II (Ottawa: Queen's Printer, 1956), 258.
2. Ibid, 236.
3. Ibid, 245.

Chapter XII — The Last Patrol
1. LCol G W L Nicholson, *The Canadians in Italy, 1943-1945:* Volume II (Ottawa: Queen's Printer, 1956), 249.
2. War Diary, PPCLI, 13 October, 1943.
3. Nicholson, *The Canadians in Italy,* 249.
4. Nicholson, *The Canadians in Italy,* 267.
5. War Diary, PPCLI, 23 October, 1943.
6. Nicholson, *The Canadians in Italy,* 261.
7. War Diary, PPCLI, 26 October, 1943.

Chapter XIII — Wounded
1. War Diary, PPCLI, 26 October, 1943.
2. G R Stevens, *Princess Patricia's Canadian Light Infantry:* Volume Three (Griesbach, Alberta: The Historical Committee of the Regiment, 1958), 116.

Chapter XV — Algiers
1. LCol W R Feasby, *Official History of the Canadian Medical Services 1939-1945:* Volume II (Ottawa: Queen's Printer, 1953), 186.
2. Ibid, Volume I, 128.

Chapter XVI — England Again
1. G W L Nicholson, *Canada's Nursing Sisters* (Toronto: Samuel Stevens, Hakkert, 1975), 196.
2. Ibid, 205.

Chapter XVII — Plastic Surgery
1. LCol G W L Nicholson, *Canada's Nursing Sisters* (Toronto: Samuel Stevens, Hakkert, 1975), 122, 123.
2. Jeffery Williams, *Princess Patricia's Canadian Light Infantry* (London: Leo Cooper Ltd, 1972), 100, 101.
3. Nicholson, *Canada's Nursing Sisters,* 122.
4. Ibid, 205.

Chapter XIX — The D-Day Dodgers
1. G R Stevens, *Princess Patricia's Canadian Light Infantry:* Volume Three (Griesbach, Alberta: The Historical Committee of the Regiment, 1958), 161.
2. LCol G W L Nicholson, *The Canadians in Italy, 1943-1945:* Volume II (Ottawa: Queen's Printer, 1956), 423.
3. Ibid, 442.
4. Col C P Stacey, *Six Years of War, The Army in Canada, Britain and the Pacific:* Volume I (Ottawa: Queen's Printer, 1955), 253.
5. Col C P Stacey, *The Victory Campaign, The Operations in North-West Europe 1944-1945:* Volume III (Ottawa: Queen's Printer, 1960), 119.
6. Ibid, 284.
7. Ibid, 284.

Chapter XX — Italy Revisited
1. G R Stevens, *Princess Patricia's Canadian Light Infantry:* Volume Three (Griesbach, Alberta: The Historical Committee of the Regiment, 1958), 171.
2. Eric Linklater, *The Campaign in Italy,* reproduced with the permission

of the Controller of HMSO.

3. LCol G W L Nicholson, *The Canadians in Italy, 1943-1945:* Volume II (Ottawa: Queen's Printer, 1956), 482.

4. Stevens, *Princess Patricia's Canadian Light Infantry,* 181.

5. Ibid, 185.

Chapter XXI — San Fortunato Ridge, Marecchia River

1. G R Stevens, *Princess Patricia's Canadian Light Infantry:* Volume Three (Griesbach, Alberta: The Historical Committee of the Regiment, 1958), 194.

2. Ibid, 195.

3. *Winnipeg Free Press,* September, 1944.

4. LCol G W L Nicholson, *The Canadians in Italy, 1943-1945:* Volume II (Ottawa: Queen's Printer, 1956), 562.

5. Nicholson, *The Canadians in Italy,* 563.

6. Stevens, *Princess Patricia's Canadian Light Infantry,* 196.

Chapter XXII — At Ease

1. LCol G W L Nicholson, *The Canadians in Italy,* 1943-1945: Volume II (Ottawa: Queen's Printer, 1956), 608.

2. Ibid, 574.

3. Ibid, 574.

4. Col C P Stacey, *Six Years of War, The Army in Canada, Britain and the Pacific:* Volume I (Ottawa: Queen's Printer, 1955), 184.

5. Col C P Stacey, *The Victory Campaign, The Operations in North-West Europe 1944-1945:* Volume III (Ottawa: Queen's Printer, 1960), 634.

6. Ibid, 634.

Chapter XXIII — Machine Guns in the Romagna

1. G R Stevens, *Princess Patricia's Canadian Light Infantry:* Volume Three (Griesbach, Alberta: The Historical Committee of the Regiment, 1958), 197, 198.

2. LCol G W L Nicholson, *The Canadians in Italy, 1943-1945:* Volume II (Ottawa: Queen's Printer, 1956), 575.

Chapter XXIV — The Savio River

1. LCol G W L Nicholson, *The Canadians in Italy, 1943-1945:* Volume II (Ottawa: Queen's Printer, 1956), 587, Note.

2. Ibid, 590.

3. Ibid, 590.

4. Ibid, 590.

Chapter XXV — More Rivers to Cross
1. LCol G W L Nicholson, *The Canadians in Italy, 1943-1945:* Volume II (Ottawa: Queen's Printer, 1956), 592.
2. G R Stevens, *Princess Patricia's Canadian Light Infantry:* Volume Three (Griesbach, Alberta: The Historical Committee of the Regiment, 1958), 206.
3. Nicholson, *The Canadians in Italy,* 606.

Chapter XXVI — Riccione and Rome
1. War Diary, PPCLI, 2 November, 1944.
2. G R Stevens, *Princess Patricia's Canadian Light Infantry:* Volume Three (Griesbach, Alberta: The Historical Committee of the Regiment, 1958), 209.

Chapter XXVII — Advance to the Lamone River
1. LCol G W L Nicholson, *The Canadians in Italy, 1943-1945:* Volume II (Ottawa: Queen's Printer, 1956), 607 Note.
2. Ibid, 607
3. Ibid, 592 Note
4. Ibid, 606
5. G R Stevens, *Princess Patricia's Canadian Light Infantry:* Volume Three (Griesbach, Alberta: The Historical Committee of the Regiment, 1958), 211.
6. G R Stevens, *The Royal Canadian Regiment:* Volume Two (London Printing & Lithographing Co, Limited, 1967), 171.
7. Nicholson, *The Canadians in Italy,* 616.
8. Stevens, *The Royal Canadian Regiment,* 172.
9. Ibid, 174, 175.
10. Nicholson, *The Canadians in Italy,* 623.
11. Ibid, 625.

Chapter XXVIII — Naviglio Canal — Fosso Munio — Granarolo
1. Col G W L Nicholson, CD, *Seventy Years of Service, A History of the Royal Canadian Army Medical Corps* (Ottawa: Borealis Press, 1977), 197.
2. G R Stevens, *Princess Patricia's Canadian Light Infantry:* Volume Three (Griesbach, Alberta: The Historical Committee of the Regiment, 1958), 214.
3. Ibid, 216.
4. Ibid, 216.
5. LCol G W L Nicholson, *The Canadians in Italy,* 1943-1945: Volume II (Ottawa: Queen's Printer, 1956), 640.
6. Nicholson, *Seventy Years of Service,* 198.
7. Ibid, 195.

8. Stevens, *PPCLI,* 219.

9. Nicholson, *The Canadians in Italy,* 633.

10. Ibid, 641.

11. Ibid, 641.

12. Ibid, 643.

13. Stevens, *PPCLI,* 222.

14. Ibid, 222, 223.

Chapter XXIX — The Senio River — Winter Line

1. G R Stevens, *Princess Patricia's Canadian Light Infantry:* Volume Three (Griesbach, Alberta: The Historical Committee of the Regiment, 1958), 226.

Chapter XXX — Arrivederci Italia

1. G R Stevens, *Princess Patricia's Canadian Light Infantry:* Volume Three (Griesbach, Alberta: The Historical Committee of the Regiment, 1958), 229.

2. War Diary, PPCLI, 2 March, 1945.

3. Ibid, 3 March, 1945.

4. Stevens, *PPCLI,* 230.

5. LCol G W L Nicholson, *The Canadians in Italy, 1943-1945:* Volume II (Ottawa: Queen's Printer, 1956), 657.

6. Stevens, *PPCLI,* 228.

7. Nicholson, *The Canadians in Italy,* 681.

Chapter XXXI — Operation Goldflake

1. LCol G W L Nicholson, *The Canadians in Italy, 1943-1945:* Volume II (Ottawa: Queen's Printer, 1956), 665.

2. Ibid, 664.

3. Ibid, 665.

4. Col C P Stacey, *The Victory Campaign, The Operations in North-West Europe 1944-1945:* Volume III (Ottawa: Queen's Printer, 1960), 269.

5. War Diary, PPCLI, 16 March, 1945.

6. Ibid, 18 March, 1945.

7. Ibid, 25 March, 1945.

8. Stacey, *The Victory Campaign,* 548.

9. War Diary, PPCLI, 29 March, 1945.

10. Ibid, 3 April, 1945.

Chapter XXXII — The Ijssel River — Holland

1. G R Stevens, *Princess Patricia's Canadian Light Infantry:* Volume Three (Griesbach, Alberta: The Historical Committee of the Regiment, 1958), 236.

2. Ibid, 240.

3. *Ibid*, 240.

4. *Ibid*, 240.

5. Col C P Stacey, *The Victory Campaign, The Operations in North-West Europe 1944-1945:* Volume III (Ottawa: Queen's Printer, 1960), 608, 609.

6. John Redfern, 'First Full Story of the Holland Food Truce'

7. Stacey. *The Victory Campaign,* 609.

8. Ibid, 583.

9. Stevens, *PPCLI,* 162.

10. War Diary, PPCLI, 4 May, 1945.

11. Stevens, *PPCLI,* 245.

Chapter XXXIII — When The War Was Over

1. *The Maple Leaf,* May, 1945.

2. Ibid.

3. G R Stevens, *Princess Patricia's Canadian Light Infantry:* Volume Three (Griesbach, Alberta: The Historical Committee of the Regiment, 1958), 246.

4. Ibid.

5. War Diary, PPCLI, 11 May, 1945.

6. Stevens, *PPCLI,* 248.

7. War Diary, PPCLI, 15 August, 1945.

8. Stevens, *PPCLI,* 252.

9. Ibid.

The First Pilgrimage — Italy and Holland

1. G R Stevens, *Princess Patricia's Canadian Light Infantry:* Volume Three (Griesbach, Alberta: The Historical Committee of the Regiment, 1958), 88.

The Fourth Pilgrimage — Holland and Italy

1. G R Stevens, *Princess Patricia's Canadian Light Infantry:* Volume Three (Griesbach, Alberta: The Historical Committee of the Regiment, 1958), 150.

2. Eric Linklater, *The Campaign in Italy*, reproduced with the permission of the Controller of HMSO.

Postscript to Chapter VIII

1. Maj Gen Chris Vokes, CB, CBE, DSO, CD, with John P MacLean, *Vokes My Story* (Ottawa: Gallery Books, 1985).

2. Ibid, 69 (the italics are the author's).

3. Ibid, 69.

4. Ibid, 97.

5. Ibid, 119.

6. Ibid, 119/120.

PHOTO CREDITS

PPCLI Museum - **1, 20, 23**
Unknown - **2, 3**
Ken Bell - **4,** inside jacket
DND - **5** - PA 72123
MGen G G Brown, OStJ, CD - **6, 10, 55**
BGen W W Turner, CD - **7**
BGen G H Sellar, CD - **8**
R S Huestis - **9**
G M Bourke - **11**
H F Pragnell - **12**
Col C Sydney Frost - **13, 14, 15, 17, 18, 19, 28, 38, 39, 40, 45, 46, 50,
56, 57, 58, 59, 60, 61, 62**
Yousuf Karsh - **16**
Mrs. G G Simonds - **21**
Canadian Army Photo - **22**-22030 R
Frederick G Whitcombe/DND/National Archives of Canada - **24**-PA
163661 - **25**PA 112259
Sir Charles Mander - **26**
Aileen (Corkett) Howes - **27, 34**
Canadian Military HQ London - **29, 48**-56887, **54**-57406
Alexander Mackenzie Stirton/DND/National Archives of Canada -
30-PA 162145
Jack Smith/DND/National Archives of Canada - **31** -PA162141
Dwight E Dolan/DND/National Archives of Canada - **32** PA162140
Dr R D Appleford - Canadian Military HQ, London, **33**-42831, **35**
Dr H H Campbell - **36, 37**

Edith (Potts) Shuter - **41, 51**
Col W de N Watson, DSO, MC - **42, 43, 44**
C E Nye/DND/National Archives of Canada - **47**-PA 163657
G Barry Gilroy/DND/National Archives of Canada - **49** PA133333
R J Frost - **52**
D A Armstrong - **53**

INDEX
GENERAL

NOTE: *Ranks given are generally the highest rank attained during World War II, except for RMC ex-cadets of the author's class, whose ranks in some cases are those held at the College.*

Lewis, Lt NJ 392
Lewis, Lt JWD 226
Lifebuoys 362, 366
Ligurian Sea 413
Lindsay, LCol RA 85, 124, 125, 221,
 225, 226, 532 - 537
Liri Valley 270, 407
Lisse 462
Littlejohns 363, 366
Liverpool 84
Lombardy Plains 285
Lonan (Code-Name) 338
London 89 - 91, 217, 244, 444, 446
Long Branch 39
Lynch, Maj GS 221, 223, 226, 463
Lyon 415, 419
Mableson, Sgt RR 311 - 313, 320
MacCulloch, Lt D 354, 482
MacDonald, Hon Donald 483
MacDonald, Lois 229
MacDonald, Lt GH 73, 229
MacGillivary, Sister 380
MacKenzie, LCol DA 439, 490
MacLeod, Capt AM 346
MacNeill, Lt JW 226, 277, 278, 285
Macon 415
Mainprize, Capt RB 426, 482, 483
Malone, Brig RS 51
Malta Conference 409
Mander, Lt Marcus (Sir Charles) 202,
 203
Manvers, Earl of 247, 252
Marecchia River 275, 282, 287, 291,
 293, 295, 407, 479, 505
Margriet, Princess 488
Marseilles 414, 415, 417
Marshall, Gen GC 395
Martello Towers 22
Martorano 507
Massey Convalescent Home 235 - 238
Massey, Vincent 91, 236
Massimo d'Azeglio — see Chateau
 Laurier
Matese Mountains 174
Matthews, The Hon Albert 35
Mayfair Hotel 89
McArthur, Angus 93, 243, 244
McArthur, Betty 93, 243, 444
McCreery, Gen Sir Richard 317, 318,
 335, 369, 383
McCullouch, LCol K 63
McDonald, Capt GM 221, 233
McDougall, Maj CM 133 - 139, 146,
 272 - 275, 277, 278, 285, 286, 373,
 510, 537
McGill, Capt WLC 160, 180
McKinnon, Maj the Hon AB 305, 386,
 387, 393, 428, 429, 435, 437, 439,
 442, 453
McLeod, Capt JA 298, 451

McNaughton, Gen AGL 53, 128, 135
McPhail, Capt ED 391, 446, 453, 463
Meiklejohn, Hon Capt GA 453, 456
Meisner, Sister 213, 233
Melfi 151
Menaar, Pte WL 168, 176 - 178, 518
Mepacrine 100, 133
Mezzano 391
Messina, Strait of 134, 137, 406, 475
Metauro River 274
Middleton, Cpl RC 180
Mighty Maroon Machine — see 5th
 Division
Military Law, Manual of 70, 300
Militello 126, 127, 129, 406
Milko, CSM M 428, 434, 435, 454
Millar, Lt JM 453
Millar, Sister Irene 233
Miller, CSMI GE 25
Mills, Capt AM 63, 277, 278, 299,
 342, 345, 353, 390, 453, 463
Minto Armouries 73
Mitchell, LCol RH 53, 60, 62 - 65, 73,
 74, 79
Moaning Minnie 374 - 376
Modica 109, 477
Moire (Code-Name) 282, 285
Molise 174
Monasterace Marina 139
Monte Seggio 121 - 123, 125, 406, 477,
 534 - 537
Montecchio Cemetery 480
Montefalcone 158
Montevecchio 517
Monteverde 166, 517
Montgomery, Field Marshal 97, 128,
 137, 243, 409, 422, 423, 452, 454
Monticello — see Nylon
Montone River 366, 479, 508
Moore, LCpl JH 482, 491 - 494
Moro River 208, 472
Moro River Cemetery 478, 480
Mothersill, LCol 242, 246, 247, 251,
 353, 444
Mount Etna 121, 125, 137, 406, 476
Mount San Marco 160
Mount Seggio — see Monte Seggio
Mount Vesuvius 267, 269, 407
Mountbatten, Countess 539, 540
Mountbatten, Earl 540
Mowat, Farley 60
Mulherin, Capt WH 60, 62, 63, 69,
 136 - 139, 227, 424
Munro, Capt HG 225
Munro, Lt D 147, 421, 453
Murdy, ,Pte MA 311, 314, 316, 317,
 320, 347, 348, 350, 353, 354, 359,
 372, 373, 415
Mussolini 98, 118, 270, 355, 359, 414,
 446, 502, 506

INDEX

Formations, Units & Corps

Hospitals, Casualty Clearing Stations, Field Ambulances
Canadian General Hospitals (CGH)
1 CGH (Jesi) 275, 377, 380
3 CGH (Cattolica) 376, 390
5 CGH (Catania) 133
10 CGH (Watford) 216, 232
14 CGH (Perugia) 388, 390

Basingstoke Neurological and Plastic Surgery Hospital 219 - 234, 444, 445

Christie Street Hospital 225, 233, 445

No 1 Canadian Hospital Ship (Lady Nelson) 212 - 215, 232

Casualty Clearing Stations (CCS)
4 CCS (Cesenatico) 376
5 CCS (Ravenna) 380
7 CCS (Foggia) 180, 232
15 CCS (Campobasso) 180, 232

Field Ambulances
9 (Campobasso) 180, 232
132 (Campobasso) 180, 232

BRITISH

Armies
2nd Army 422
8th Army 97, 250, 274, 303, 366, 383, 384, 409, 451

Corps
5th Corps 335, 409
13th Corps 145
30th Corps 97

Divisions
1st Armoured Div 313
4th Div 323
5th Div 135, 142, 145
49th (WR) Div 427, 441, 442
51st Highland Div 97, 108
56th Div 313, 319
78th Div 125, 154

Regiments
4th Bn Royal Tank Regiment 432
12th Bn Royal Lancers 341
12th Bn Royal Tank Regiment 362
48th Bn Royal Tank Regiment 282

Hospitals
54 (Foggia) 181, 185, 187, 232
94 (Algiers) 193 - 211, 232
95 (Algiers) 208
98 (Bari) 181, 184, 232

No 1 Maxillo - Facial Team
Advanced Section (Foggia) 180
Main Section (Bari) 185

FORMATIONS, UNITS AND CORPS INDEX